Dawn Orlowski

Business Law

About the Authors

The late **R. Robert Rosenberg** was a leading author of books on business and consumer law and business and consumer mathematics, which are known to thousands of teachers throughout the fifty states and in many foreign countries. He wrote or coauthored over twenty-nine books, including such titles as *Business and the Law, Outline of College Business Law, Essentials of Business Law, Business Law/30,* and *Understanding Business and Consumer Law,* all published by McGraw-Hill. Dr. Rosenberg taught at all educational levels, including high school, junior college, business school, and university. In addition, he held administrative positions on the elementary, secondary, and collegiate levels and was president of Jersey City Junior College.

William G. Ott has served as president, vice president, and director of law at Goldey Beacom College. He is the coauthor of *Business and the Law* and *Outline of College Business Law.* In addition, Mr. Ott has written articles on law, credit, and school management for publications such as *Credit World, EBTA Journal, Business School Executive,* and *Creative Service.* His qualifications as an author and educator include a varied and practical background in retailing, business management, advertising, and journalism. One of the largest student law associations in the eastern United States, the William G. Ott Association, is named in his honor.

Edward E. Byers has served as editorial director and is currently editor in chief of business management and supervision publications in the Gregg Division of the McGraw-Hill Book Company. In these positions he has influenced the development of many publications in the areas of general business, supervisory management, office education, and business law. He is also an author of general and specialized secretarial procedures programs as well as medical secretarial reference works. Dr. Byers has taught in both high school and college. At the business college level, he has served as an academic dean. He is also a speaker for teacher groups and contributes to professional magazines on methods of instruction and curriculum development.

Gordon W. Brown has served as chairman of the Business Division at North Shore Commmunity College and is currently a professor at that school, teaching business law, accounting, legal secretarial studies, and other business subjects. He is the coauthor of *Understanding Business and Consumer Law* and has contributed articles on the law to *Business Education World.* In addition, he has been a speaker at workshops and conferences concerning methods of law instruction. A practicing attorney with over fifteen years of experience, Mr. Brown enjoys a reputation for an in-depth knowledge of the Uniform Commercial Code and is recognized for his ability to translate the Code's complex legal concepts clearly and accurately into terms the layperson can readily understand.

Business Law

Sixth Edition

With UCC Applications

R. Robert Rosenberg, Ed.D., C.P.A.
Late President of Jersey City Junior College

William G. Ott, A.B., LL.B.
Former Director of Law and President
Goldey Beacom College

Edward E. Byers, Ed.D.
Editor in Chief, Business Management and Supervision Publications
Gregg Division
McGraw-Hill Book Company

Gordon W. Brown, J.D.
Member of the Massachusetts Bar
Professor of Business Law
North Shore Community College

Gregg Division/McGraw Hill Book Company
New York Atlanta Dallas St. Louis San Francisco
Auckland Bogotá Guatemala Hamburg Lisbon
London Madrid Mexico Montreal New Delhi Panama Paris
San Juan São Paulo Singapore Sydney Tokyo Toronto

Sponsoring Editor: Lawrence H. Wexler
Editing Supervisor: S. Goldfarb
Production Supervisor: Laurence Charnow
Design and Art Supervisor: Karen Tureck

Cover Designer: David R. Thurston

Library of Congress Cataloging in Publication Data

Main entry under title:

Business law: with UCC applications.

    Rev. ed. of: College business law / R. Robert
Rosenberg. 5th ed. c1978.
    Includes index.
    1. Commercial law—United States.   I. Rosenberg,
R. Robert (Reuben Robert), date.   II. Rosenberg,
R. Robert (Reuben Robert), date. College business
law.   III. Title.
KF889.3.B84   1983   346.73'07   82-13001
ISBN 0-07-053901-4   347.3067

Business Law: With UCC Applications, Sixth Edition

Previously published under the title *College Business Law*, Fifth Edition.

0   DOCDOC   8 9 8

ISBN 0-07-053901-4

Preface

This sixth edition of *Business Law: With UCC Applications* represents a thorough review of the basic framework of commercial law and administrative law. The topics covered will concern those who plan to work in the business environment, including C.P.A. candidates. The law relating to contracts, agency, business torts and crimes (including computer crime), and business organization is covered extensively. Also fully presented are the federal laws dealing with employee health and safety, discrimination, product safety and liability, warranties, and enforcement of antitrust regulations.

Expanded treatment has been accorded to such topics as business taxation, Subchapter S corporations, limited partnerships, franchises, and securities regulation. New chapters are devoted to checks and bank collections, security devices, and defective agreement in contracts. The substantive and procedural changes introduced by the Federal Bankruptcy Reform Act of 1978, as they influence individuals and business reorganization, are carefully reviewed.

Relevance

The information about legislation, case law, and uniform law that relates to the subject matter of the text has been fully updated. There is coverage of the broad legal effects of the Magnuson-Moss Warranty Act of 1975, the Electronic Funds Transfer Act of 1979, and the Copyright Software Act of 1980, among other laws.

Cited cases, mainly of recent derivation, are provided at the end of each chapter. These cases, which call upon students to apply the legal concepts learned through their study of the text, were chosen for their relevance, realism, and interesting fact patterns. Within the text, over a thousand cases are used to illustrate the major principles of law discussed. These case illustrations, which present either hypothetical or actual situations, are based upon well-founded court decisions. New expanded case studies called "Case Briefs" are located at the end of each of ten parts of the text. Their case method format enables students to explore in greater depth the way in which the courts interpret and apply the law in the course of the judicial process.

Uniform Statutes, Model Acts, and Restatements

Emphasis has been placed on the Uniform Commercial Code (UCC). Throughout the chapters on contracts, the UCC is discussed whenever it applies. The UCC has also been cited in the chapters on sales, commercial paper, and secured transactions to reflect changes brought about by the Code.

Appropriately positioned in the text are discussions of the legal ramifications of the Model Business Corporation Act, the Uniform Partnership Act, the Uniform Probate Act, the Uniform Arbitration Act, and the *Restatement (Second) of Agency,* among others.

Teaching/Learning Resources

Correlated with the text is a separate Study Guide. In addition to student performance goals, it contains student activities to encourage mastery of legal vocabulary and legal concepts, as well as practice in solving case problems by applying legal principles and using reasoning and judgment. Students can score and diagnose their own progress by completing the self-check activities that are provided.

A booklet of performance test masters is available to adopters of the Sixth Edition for evaluation purposes. Each of the eleven tests contains objective questions and case problems that measure student comprehension of topics covered in the text chapters. Additional case problems for testing purposes may be taken from the end-of-chapter materials provided in the text and in the Study Guide.

Helping to meld these teaching/learning resources into a coherent and effective instructional system is the Instructor's Manual and Key. It has general suggestions for law course management; suggested schedules for courses of varying length; chapter outlines, which can serve as a framework for lecture presentation; and keys to review and discussion questions and cases in the text as well as to the case problems in the Study Guide.

Acknowledgments

The extensive revision of this edition has been influenced by the expressed preferences of hundreds of law instructors who were surveyed. Their expertise and direction influenced the extent of the revision and the retention of a conversational and nontechnical writing style to help simplify complex legal concepts. The quality of this business law program was also improved by the professional knowledge and expertise of Donald W. Evans, J.D., and Michael Katz, J.D. Donald Evans is a member of the Connecticut Bar and a legal research specialist. Michael Katz is a professor of law at Goldey Beacom College, Delaware, and a member of the Bar, both in Delaware and Pennsylvania. Each conducted extensive research in finding the end-of-chapter cases and "Case Briefs" presented in this edition. This revision also benefited from the constructive criticism of David S. Cook, J.D., of the Attorney General's Office of New York State; Clark Wheeler, J.D., a law teacher at Santa Fe Community College, Florida; Era Boone Ferguson, law teacher at the Sullivan Junior College of Business, Kentucky; Carl Settle, President of Hamilton College, North Carolina; Wilson Sanders, Chairperson, Business Division, Florence-Darlington Technical College, South Carolina; and Dr. Charlotte Mastellar, Chairperson of the Business Department and law professor at Butler County Community College, Pennsylvania.

William G. Ott
Edward E. Byers
Gordon W. Brown

Contents

Table of Cases

The principal adjudicated cases illustrating key points of law within chapters are in roman type. (Numerous additional hypothetical cases, extracted from actual cases, illustrate rules of law throughout the text.

These cases are not listed in the table below.) Cases cited at the end of chapters or those briefed at the end of each part of the text are in italic type. All *p.* or *pp.* references are to pages in this text.

Business Law

Part I — Law and the Judicial System

Chapter 1 — Nature and Sources of Business Law

In a world whose population included only one person, there would be a state of complete harmony. There would be no difference of opinion about any problem or issue. And there would be no public or private injury to another's health, welfare, property, or reputation. But if the population were to increase, even by only one, there would immediately be a different situation, with potential conflicts and disagreements as to each person's individual rights. Eventually there would have to be some agreement on rules to be observed.

Without a body of rules and principles, individuals would act to suit their own wishes or objectives. You might choose to drive your car in a manner and at a speed that endangered others, just because you enjoyed doing so. You might give in to the urge to shout "Fire!" in a crowded theater. In doing business with others, you might be inclined to be your own judge in determining your duties and in deciding whether to honor your oral or written agreements. Thus, without an accepted body of rules that state what is right and forbid what is wrong, community living would soon be reduced to a level of chaos.

1-1. Justice and the Law

Rules which society adopts and enforces in order to operate in an orderly way are called *laws*. And their ultimate goal is *justice*—the determination of a person's rights according to the rules of law or on the basis of fairness and good conscience. The basic purpose of justice in a democratic society is fourfold:

○ Recognition of each person's human dignity and freedom and right to life, security, property, privacy, family, home, movement, beliefs, and reputation.
○ Recognition that all persons have an equal right to be given the greatest possible opportunity to develop their potential.
○ Observance of responsibility so that all persons may enjoy the benefits of common purpose, interests, or pleasure in an evenhanded manner.
○ The impartial adjustment of conflicting claims by individuals or groups or the assignment of merited rewards or punishments.

Laws conform to social trends; laws do not determine them. As the patterns and conditions of people living together and doing business together change, laws are adapted to fit these changes. It would be impossible to achieve justice for today's citizens if we were obligated to live according to laws written fifty years ago. Similarly, laws of the late 1970s and the 1980s would not provide justice for the larger population projected by the year 2000.

● Stannus drove the family car through a town in rural Pennsylvania. She was stopped by a deputy sheriff and issued a traffic ticket for violating a local ordinance by traveling at 20 miles an hour in a 15-mile-an-hour zone. As long as the law remains unchanged, it is legally enforceable, even though current traffic control practices might suggest that this law is socially unjust.

It should be recognized that the terms *law* and *justice* are not necessarily synonymous; nor is the law an exact science. Law is created by the agents of society, such as legislatures and the courts, but each individual has a personal view of what is right or wrong. Nevertheless, in the struggle for justice, differences are generally resolved by applying the law rather than our personal views, even when we ourselves disagree with the law. Thus it is safe to say that we remain basically a law-centered rather than a justice-centered society.

1-2. Sources of Law

The sources of present-day law include *federal and state constitutions, federal and state statutes* (laws passed by legislatures), *court decisions,* and *administrative regulations.*

A. Constitutional Law

The Constitution of the United States is the basic and supreme law of the land. All other laws not in agreement with it have no legal force. The Constitution provides the organization for government, dividing it into executive, legislative, and judicial branches. The powers and functions of the branches operate as checks and balances on each and establish the doctrine of separation of powers. This doctrine holds that the branches of government operate independently of one another in order to prevent the arbitrary exercise of power.

1. **Federal and State Constitutions.** The U.S. Constitution is a delegation of authority from the states. All powers not delegated to the federal government in its seven articles and twenty-six amendments are retained by the states, unless denied them by their own constitutions. As a result, the laws passed by the several states differ in many respects. Actions enforceable by law or subject to remedy in a court in one state may not be in another. Although the distinction between federal authority and states' rights is established, legal problems often arise in connection with the boundary line separating the two.

2. **Articles of the U.S. Constitution.** Article I establishes the legislative branch of government (the lawmaking authority). Its sections define Congress's functions, powers, and manner of conducting business. Section 8 grants Congress a number of powers that directly affect business enterprise. For example, Congress is given the power to lay and collect taxes and to regulate commerce with

foreign nations and among the several states. Congress is also granted the power to establish uniform bankruptcy laws and to establish courts that are inferior to the Supreme Court. Section 9 prohibits the taxing of goods exported from any state and the giving of preference to one state over another by any regulation of commerce. It also prohibits states (but not the federal government) from passing any laws impairing the obligations of contracts.

Article II gives the executive power and responsibility for enforcing laws to the President. It outlines the President's term of office, the qualifications for office, and the manner of election. The President is identified as Commander in Chief of the Armed Forces. Exclusive power to make treaties, by and with the advice and consent of the Senate, is also given the President. And it is from Article II that the President derives authority to make executive agreements with foreign governments that are not subject to advice and consent by the Senate. Similar to the power to make treaties, the authority to make executive agreements with foreign nations is inferred from the broad powers granted the President under the authority of the United States, the Constitution of the United States or the laws of any state notwithstanding. This complete power to enter into executive agreements is illustrated by the Iranian hostage release agreement, in which the President authorized the transfer of frozen Iranian bank deposits out of the United States. Central to this power is the President's capacity to speak and act for the United States in the conduct of its foreign relations.

Article III establishes the judicial branch of government with power to interpret laws and adjudicate legal claims and disputes. It creates the Supreme Court of the United States and authorizes the establishment of other federal courts. A trial by jury for all crimes (except impeachment proceedings) is provided for. Treason against the United States is defined.

Article IV contains provisions relating to relationships between states. The *full faith and credit* clause generally obligates each state to recognize the public acts and proceedings of other states. Section 2 deals with the *extradition* of those accused of crimes in other states. This is the act of the governor of one state turning over a prisoner to the governor of another state. It occurs when an arrest is made in a state other than the one in which the crime is committed.

Article V outlines the method for amending the Constitution.

Article VI establishes the Constitution and federal laws and treaties as the supreme law of the land. Judges in every state are bound thereby, anything in the constitution or laws of any state to the contrary notwithstanding. All federal and state officials are bound by oath to support the Constitution of the United States.

Article VII provides for the original ratification (approval) of the Constitution by the states.

3. Constitutional Amendments. The first ten amendments to the Constitution are known as the Bill of Rights. They deal with the freedoms of speech, press, religion, and assembly and with such matters as search warrants and the validity of searches related to an arrest.

The Fifth Amendment provides protection against compulsory self-incrimination. For instance, a court would not accept a defendant's confession of guilt obtained after a beating by jail personnel. The Fifth Amendment also requires indictment by a grand jury for capital offenses, requires compensation in emi-

Chapter 1:
Nature
and
Sources of
Business
Law

3

nent domain proceedings, and prohibits double jeopardy—the trying of a person twice by the same authority for the same offense. The *due process of law* provision gives individuals a right and a process that aims at fundamental fairness in actions used by the government to enforce and take away rights—particularly the rights of life, liberty, or property. A statute violates the requirements of due process when the courts hold it to be arbitrary rather than reasonable. Setting the standards as well as applying them, the Supreme Court may set aside for undue harshness not only the statutes of Congress but acts of state legislatures and ordinances of local municipal councils as well.

The Sixth Amendment gives everyone in criminal cases the right to a speedy and public trial by jury, to be informed of charges, to be confronted by an accuser, to subpoena witnesses, and to have the assistance of an attorney. The Seventh Amendment provides for a trial by jury in civil cases involving more than $20. Subsequent Bill of Rights amendments provide protection against excessive bail in criminal cases and recognize the limited powers given the federal government by the states and the people.

The Fourteenth Amendment makes all constitutional guarantees of the Bill of Rights applicable to the states: "No State shall make or enforce any law which shall abridge the privileges or immunities of citizens of the United States; nor shall any State deprive any person of life, liberty or property, without due process of law, nor deny to any person within its jurisdiction the equal protection of the laws." In due process cases, the issue is whether the law is fair, reasonable, and appropriate use of police power of the state or an unnecessary and arbitrary interference with the right of the individual. Other amendments authorized the income tax, gave women the right to vote, and gave eighteen-year-olds the right to vote.

Proposed constitutional amendments are pending. Facing near certain defeat at the time of this writing is the equal rights amendment, which would guarantee equal rights for women. The proposed amendment states: "Equality of rights under the law shall not be denied or abridged by the United States or by any state on account of sex."

4. Supremacy of Laws. The basic principle of constitutional law is the supremacy of federal over state law. While a few areas of regulation are reserved to the states, the Constitution of the United States has been interpreted to allow the federal government to act in most areas, if it chooses to do so. Once the federal government acts, its action takes priority over any inconsistent state laws or regulations, unless the federal action is unconstitutional. If Congress expresses its wishes as to whether or not the state law stands, its wishes will be followed. If Congress is silent, the following analysis is employed by the court:

○ Is the law or regulation in an area which the Constitution permits the federal government to regulate? (If it is, federal law usually prevails.)
○ Does the federal law violate a specific constitutional right reserved to the people against *any* government action? For example, does it violate the First Amendment's guarantee concerning freedom of speech?
○ Is there a state law or regulation touching the same subject matter? If there is and the federal and state laws are inconsistent, then the federal law or regulation takes precedence over that of the state.

● Congress enacts a law setting an air pollution standard which manufacturers must abide by. A state passes a similar statute but allows the manufacturer to pollute the air to a greater extent than the Congress did. The federal law would take priority over the state law.

Federal and state laws may touch the same subject matter without any inconsistencies. This generally means that the state law may stand concurrent (alongside federal law) if it does not conflict with, is not contrary to, or does not interfere with the similar federal law.

All state officials, courts, and administrative agencies are bound to obey all valid federal laws and regulations. Therefore, a state governor may not ignore a valid order of a federal district court.

5. Ranking of Laws. When a law is passed that is in conflict with any other law, its validity is decided according to the following order of precedence and rules:

1. The Constitution of the United States is the highest law of the land.
2. Acts of the Congress of the United States and federal treaties take precedence over all other laws, except the provisions of the Constitution.
3. State constitutions have precedence over all other state laws but may not conflict with federal laws.
4. Acts of a state legislature must conform to the constitution of that state and must not conflict with the U.S. Constitution, federal treaties, or acts of Congress.
5. Town, city, or township ordinances must conform to the state laws and the federal laws.
6. If there is no written law applying to a particular case, then court decisions, handed down by other courts in similar cases, become the law on which the case is judged. Such court decisions make up the body of law derived from usage and precedents that is known as the *common law*.

B. Legislated or Statutory Law

As stated previously, the laws passed by legislatures are known as *statutes*. At the federal level, these are the laws passed by Congress and signed by the President. They include among others the tax laws, labor laws, security laws, product safety laws, and civil rights laws. The term *statute* may be applied broadly to include orders and proclamations by the President and state governors. And broadly interpreted, the term usually includes the ordinances and resolutions of subdivisions of the states, such as cities, towns, and villages. These are enactments by appropriate local officials to regulate activities such as the construction of buildings and to protect the community from hazards and nuisances.

C. Court Decisions or Case Law

A court can review and rule on the validity of any statute or regulation and hold it invalid when it is inconsistent with the Constitution. This principle of *judicial review* is one of the focal points that provide for the doctrine of separation of powers. Through the process of review, the courts can check and balance the power of the executive and legislative branches of government. And through this process as well, any citizen may appeal to the courts to have a law declared

Chapter 1:
Nature
and
Sources of
Business
Law

5

invalid and unenforceable should it violate a particular freedom or in some way interfere with a constitutional right.

Courts also interpret legislation by deciding the meaning of and filling in the gaps in the statutes. The courts' interpretations, expressed in decisions, are then considered to be law; the process is known as judicial or court decision, and the resulting law is called *case law.*

● A local union filed a refusal-to-bargain charge with the National Labor Relations Board (NLRB) against Airco Construction. Hearings were set, and Airco Construction asked the NLRB for permission to inspect and copy all written statements in the Board's case file. The request was denied, and Airco asked the federal district court to order the NLRB to produce the records and to suspend proceedings until the NLRB had done so. The court held that information in unfair-labor-practice cases and the sources from which it was obtained were subject to disclosure under the Freedom of Information Act. The court also held that the agency must suspend its proceedings until Airco (the employer) had a chance to obtain and study the Board's case file.

This was the first judicial interpretation of the then newly enacted Freedom of Information Act. The NLRB's claim of privacy had to be balanced against Airco's equally strong claim that disclosure was required by the act. To be sure, the court took into account the intent of Congress in passing the new law. It examined the legislative record to this end. However, the court had no judicial precedents or case law to guide it in determining how much and what type of disclosure was required under the particular circumstances presented. The court, therefore, had to "jump into the breach," so to speak, and make new law in this area by defining just how much disclosure was required. Its verdict will then serve as precedent in other similar cases presented to it or to other courts, unless the decision is subsequently overturned by a higher court.

1. Common Law. Common law is a system of uncodified law that courts have developed and followed for a period of time based on *precedent* (decisions in previous similar cases). In the main, it consists of the rules that have resulted from custom and usage and that have been enforced by the courts. It is usually applied by courts when legislatures have not enacted written law dealing with the issues in dispute.

● Regulations affecting the rights and duties of automobile drivers on state highways were enacted into law by a state legislature. Since the statute did not specify penalties for violation of the law, courts would refer to and apply common law rules.

Early common law developed in England and other European countries and was eventually embodied in the *law merchant.* This was the commercial law developed by merchants who needed a set of rules to govern their business transactions. Much of our present business law dealing with such matters as commercial paper, credit, and partnerships developed in the early mercantile courts that administered the law merchant.

In addition to the areas of *crimes* (wrongs committed against society) and *contracts* (rights created by agreement and consent of parties), common law developed in *torts* (wrongs committed against another's person or property). Common law was applied to such personal torts as acts that cause fear of bodily harm, the infliction of actual bodily harm on another, and the printing of false statements that damage another's reputation, and to such property torts as acts that cause damage to another's business or its products.

2. *Stare Decisis*. The principle of *stare decisis* (to stand by the decision) allows a court to rely upon the rules of law applied in previous decisions when deciding a similar case before it. *Stare decisis* serves as an instrument of stability in the legal system. It helps to assure each person equal and uniform treatment by its reliance on long-accepted legal principles and well-established rules. It remains a flexible principle, however, in that a court may decide that a prior decision has lost its usefulness or is in error or that there are conflicting precedents.

Courts are subject to changing social forces and conditions and are free to express new rules of law. Neither the U.S. Supreme Court nor the lower federal and state courts hold themselves totally bound by their own prior decisions. In a similar fashion, state courts are not totally bound by the decisions and precedents handed down by the federal courts on matters relating to federal issues. State courts are free to weigh conditions and circumstances peculiar to their own geographical locale and make decisions that depart from federal court decisions on similar or related legal issues. Supreme Court decisions are binding, of course, on all federal and state courts.

3. Suits in Equity. The idea of justice due to natural right, or *equity*, was introduced into the United States because of the failure of the courts of law to give adequate and proper remedies in certain cases. In most states, procedural differences have been eliminated between courts of equity and courts of law. In federal proceedings, federal rules of civil procedure have been adopted for actions of law and suits in equity.

Actions of law and suits in equity do differ in the method used to resolve issues. For example, disputes are settled in actions at law by applying existing statutes and prior decisions. Suits in equity, by contrast, are guided by equitable principles and by *maxims*. These are truths or rules that need no proof or argument. They are based on moral rights and natural justice. An example of such a maxim is: "He who comes into equity must do so with clean hands." In other words, a person who is guilty of misconduct in a case is prohibited from receiving the aid of the court. Other similar maxims are:

○ Equity aids the vigilant, not those who sleep on their rights.
○ Equity will not suffer a wrong to be without a remedy.
○ Equity considers that done which ought to be done.
○ Equity assists ignorance, but not carelessness.

In civil actions at law the remedy is usually money. Judgments are awarded in the form of a process known as *execution*. With this process, a writ is obtained from the clerk of court. It authorizes the seizure of the defendant's property and its sale to satisfy the judgment.

In equity, however, decisions are called *decrees*. They are directed to the defendant, who is ordered to do or not to do something. The remedy may be in the form of a temporary or permanent *injunction*. This is an order to refrain from doing something which would result in a loss or harm that cannot be remedied.

Chapter 1:
Nature
and
Sources of
Business
Law

7

For example, an injunction might be issued to stop one person from harassing another. *Specific performance* can be ordered where money damages are inadequate to compensate the complaining party. For example, this might be the remedy when a party to a contract fails to deliver something promised, such as a deed to property. Failure to abide by a decree is punishable by a fine or a jail sentence.

In suits in equity, there is no right to a jury trial. An equity judge considers the facts and determines what is reasonable. In contrast, almost all criminal actions at law are guaranteed a trial by jury by the Constitution of the United States.

4. Doctrine of Laches. The *doctrine of laches* is related to the maxim "Equity aids the vigilant, not those who sleep on their rights." According to this equitable doctrine, persons bringing a suit in equity must do so within a reasonable period of time, which is decided by the facts of the case. The objective is to discourage a delay in bringing suit if that delay would operate as an injustice to the defendant. If those bringing suit were aware of their rights and yet failed to assert them, they could be found guilty of laches.

● Cotter gave over all of her property to pay three of five creditors. If the creditors excluded from this assignment made no inquiry regarding the transaction for a period of five years, they would most likely be guilty of laches and barred from recovery.

5. Resolving Conflict of Laws. Inasmuch as each state has the power to legislate its own law, within the limits imposed by the Constitution, important statute differences exist between states. This lack of uniformity or agreement in state law does not present a problem when the parties to a dispute live in the same state. Often, however, people have interstate business interests and relationships. It is not unusual for a person to live in one state, work in another, and own property in still another. A body of laws known as *conflict of laws* deals with the jurisdiction of cases involving persons with interstate conflicts. In a typical situation, a court sitting in one state but dealing with an injury or wrong that occurred in another state will generally follow its own *procedural law* (rules that deal with matters of evidence, procedure, and appeals used in court) but will generally use the other state's *substantive law* (law which regulates the rights, duties, privileges, and immunities of the parties to an action). For example, suppose X and Y sign a contract in New York to build a condominium in Florida. If a conflict over the terms of the contract arose, the suit would be heard in New York, where the defendant lived. Thus, New York's procedural law would be used in determining matters of evidence and court procedure. However Florida's substantive law as to contracts would be applied by the New York court in determining the rights of the parties. In so doing, the court recognizes Florida as the state with the most "real" contact and interest in the subject matter of the contract, namely the business transactions pertaining to the construction of the condominium.

● Bounty, doing business as Able Construction and engaged in home construction, was located in Pittsburgh, Pennsylvania. All of Bounty's sales and customers were in Pennsylvania. He ordered 20,000 ad inserts at $100 per thousand from an Illinois printer, to be shipped f.o.b. Chicago, for insertion in a local Pittsburgh newspaper. Bounty received and returned sample copy with corrections. Subsequently the printing was done in Illinois and the inserts were shipped as directed by Bounty. When Bounty did not pay for them, the printer started suit in Illinois. Bounty argued that he could not be sued in Illinois since all he had done was phone in an order and return the sample copy. The Illinois court disagreed, holding that the acceptance of the contracts, the printing, and the f.o.b. shipment were all "transactions of business" within Illinois.

A state's jurisdiction over the parties of a case and the power to hear a case are further established by *long-arm statutes,* which provide for the service of process by mail on out-of-state defendants. This is the means by which a defendant is notified of the beginning of a legal action. But service of process to out-of-state defendants cannot be arbitrary. Due process requires that the defendant must have had sufficient contact with the plaintiff (the person who brings the action in court) who is a resident of the state in which suit is brought.

● Cruz was employed by a Puerto Rican drug company, wholly owned by a Connecticut corporation. He suffered a loss of his reproductive capacity, a condition he felt resulted from products he worked with at the drug company. He started a lawsuit, making use of a Puerto Rican long-arm statute giving the local court jurisdiction over parties or their agents outside its borders when a claim arises from business transactions within its borders. The parent corporation and its directors and officers were served with a copy of the negligence complaint and an order of the court (summons) directing the defendants to appear in the Puerto Rican court within a specified period of time.

D. Administrative Law

The courts have held that administrative agencies may be set up with delegated power to regulate or supervise complicated areas of our economy. These departments, boards, and commissions administer statutes enacted by the Congress in specific areas, including interstate commerce, communications, securities, social security, and labor relations. Similar bodies have been designated by the states to supervise and regulate insurance, banking, workers' compensation, and public utilities. These bodies formulate rules, regulate and supervise, and render decisions which have the force of law. Their decrees and legal decisions —the whole body of law that they generate—are known collectively as *administrative law.*

The power of administrative agencies to adjudicate decisions is subject to review by the courts. Problems arise since those who administer these agencies make the rules and then serve as both prosecutor and judge. In an effort to remedy this problem, Congress passed the Federal Administration Procedure Act. Similarly, most states adopted a uniform law known as the Model State Administration Procedure Act.

Under the provisions of these acts, courts may conduct a judicial review of an administrative agency decision in order to determine the law. Specifically, courts may change, reverse, or remand (send back to another court or the agency) an agency decision when it violates a constitutional provision, exceeds the authority of the agency, or is based upon unlawful procedure. Courts may also reject an agency decision when it incorporates errors of law, is arbitrary and

Chapter 1:
Nature
and
Sources of
Business
Law

9

capricious, or lacks substantial evidence in view of the entire record. It is important to note that the substantial evidence rule requires courts to accept agency decisions that are based on the case presented by all parties to the dispute. In this manner, courts are prevented from substituting their conclusions of fact for those based on the facts found by the agency.

E. Uniform Law

To reduce the variation in statute law and its interpretation from state to state, uniform acts and restatements of common law have been adopted. The first was the Uniform Negotiable Instruments Act in 1896. Since then, a number of other uniform statutes have been adopted, including the Uniform Partnership Act, the Limited Partnership Act, the Uniform Commercial Code, and the Uniform Consumer Credit Code.

1. Uniform Commercial Code. The latest edition of the Uniform Commercial Code (UCC) is known as the 1978 Official Text. The UCC is a unified set of statutes designed to govern almost all commercial transactions. It superseded a number of prior unified acts, including the Sales Act, the Negotiable Instruments Act, and the Bills of Lading Act. It should be understood, however, that the exact meanings of the UCC are not found in the UCC itself, but rather in court decisions interpreting the UCC.

The basic principles of commercial law were not drastically changed by the UCC provisions. Merchants are held to a high standard of performance by its definition of what good faith means in a commercial setting. Under UCC 2-103(1), *good faith* is defined as honesty in fact and the observance of reasonable commercial standards of fair dealings in the trade. By defining and clarifying often misunderstood business and legal terms, the UCC helps the parties to construct their contracts and aids the courts in interpreting and enforcing them. It declares that contract terms which are clearly unfair and unreasonable (unconscionable) may be unenforceable. It provides rules that state what business people may or may not do. For example, shippers of goods may not contractually exempt themselves from liability for inaccurately counting packages received for shipment; and a warehouse may not write a contract so as to limit its own liability for illegally taking the goods of others for its own use.

Except in Louisiana, all the states and the District of Columbia and the Virgin Islands have now adopted the UCC making minor changes in it to reflect state laws and needs. Louisiana has adopted some but not all of the UCC Articles since its civil law is based on European civil law rather than on English common law.* For all practical purposes, however, the rules governing commercial transactions are the same throughout all the states because of the UCC. A decision in one state's court involving a UCC issue has persuasive value in the courts of other states.

The UCC contains eleven articles. Article 1, *General Provisions,* presents the purposes and policies of the UCC. These are: (*a*) to simplify, clarify, and modernize the law governing commercial transactions; (*b*) to permit the continued expansion of commercial practice through custom, usage, and agreement of

---

* At the time of this writing, Louisiana had adopted Articles 1, 3, 4, and 5 of the UCC.

the parties; and (*c*) to make uniform the law among the various jurisdictions. Article 2, *Sales*, supersedes the Uniform Sales Act. It unifies the rules governing transactions in the sale of personal property and goods. However, it does not damage or renounce any law regulating sales to consumers or farmers. Neither does it recind contracts to sell, such as agreements to buy at a later date where ownership is not transferred and possession is not usually transferred. Article 3, *Commercial Paper*, is a revision of the Uniform Negotiable Instruments Law. It deals with the form and interpretation of negotiable instruments such as checks and drafts. Article 4, *Bank Deposits and Collections*, classifies many of the rules of the American Bankers Association Code. As its title suggests, this article deals primarily with the rules and liabilities relating to bank deposits and collections. Article 5, *Letters of Credit*, is a codification of decided cases. It applies to credit issued by a bank or a person other than a bank. Article 6, *Bulk Transfers*, is a uniform consolidation of bulk sales statutes enacted by the several states. It deals with the rules governing the transfer of a major part of a business's inventory of materials or merchandise not in the ordinary course of business. Article 7, *Documents of Title*, is mainly a consolidation and revision of the Uniform Bills of Lading Act and the Warehouse Receipts Act. It sets forth the rules governing the negotiation of documents of title. Article 8, *Investment Securities*, incorporating some amendments adopted in 1978, represents a revision of the Uniform Negotiable Instruments Law and the Uniform Stock Transfer Act. It presents the rules affecting the issue/issuer of, purchase, and registration of securities. Article 9, *Secured Transactions*, codifies various statutes dealing with security interest in personal property. Articles 10 and 11 present the effective date of the UCC and a list of statutes that are inconsistent with its provisions.

2. Restatements of Common Law. The American Law Institute, incorporated in 1923, promotes the clarification and simplification of law. From time to time, it prepares and prints *restatements* of common law. Among the restatements published are those pertaining to the law of contracts and the law of agency. They are scholarly efforts to prepare statements of legal rules and principles for the benefit of both lawyers and judges. Restatements are not official statements of law, since they have not been adopted by state legislatures. Once courts include portions of a restatement in official opinions, however, they in effect become decisional law.

Understanding Legal Terms

Define, identify, or explain the following terms:

administrative law	due process of law	law	statute
case law	equity	maxim	substantive law
common law	full faith and credit	precedent	Uniform
conflict of laws	injunction	procedural law	Commercial Code
constitution	judicial review	restatements	(UCC)
doctrine of laches	justice	specific performance	

Questions for Review and Discussion

1. Explain the relationship between the terms *laws* and *justice* and why they are not necessarily synonymous.

2. Explain what is meant by the statement that the Constitution of the United States is the supreme law of the land.

3. Discuss the supremacy-of-laws principle with respect to the authority of law at the federal, state, and local levels.

4. Explain how judicial review serves as a check and balance to the powers of the executive and legislative branches of government.

5. Distinguish common law from statutory law.

6. What is the meaning of *stare decisis?*

7. Identify the differences that exist between actions at law and suits in equity in respect to resolutions of legal disputes.

8. Explain the concept of conflict of laws and its application to procedural and substantive law.

9. Discuss the circumstances under which courts may change, reverse, or remand an administrative agency's decision.

10. What is the purpose of the UCC?

Analyzing Cases

1. Congress in 1940 passed the Smith Act, which prohibited individuals from supporting the overthrow of the United States by force and violence. The Commonwealth of Pennsylvania also passed an act called the Pennsylvania Sedition Act which prohibited the same activities. Nelson has convicted of violating the Pennsylvania Sedition Act and appealed. What argument does Nelson have that this conviction was unconstitutional? Should Nelson win? Why? ● *Commonwealth of Pennsylvania v. Nelson,* 350 U.S. 497 (1956)

2. Lovett and two others had been employed for several years by the federal government. The agencies which employed them were fully satisfied with the quality of their work and wished to keep them employed on their jobs. Congressional representative Martin Dies accused them of being, among other things, "affiliates of communist front organizations." He proposed to pass legislation requiring their discharge and barring them from further federal employment. After some debate, it was instead decided to give the accused individuals their day in court. This was done by having the Appropriations Committee hold hearings, investigate the charges, and determine the guilt or innocence of the accused. Those charged with subversive beliefs and subversive associations were permitted to testify, but lawyers, including those representing the agencies by which the accused were employed, were not permitted to be present. The committee found the three guilty, and Congress subsequently passed a law which in its effect discharged them from their jobs and barred them from being hired by other government agencies. What fundamental defect existed in the procedure that led to the punishment of Lovett and the others? Judgment in favor of whom? Why? ● *United States v. Lovett,* 328 U.S. 303 (1946)

3. Thompson was arrested in Louisville, Kentucky, on separate charges of loitering and disorderly conduct. The charges against Thompson were totally without supporting evidence. The Police Court of Louisville convicted Thompson of both offenses, and a fine of $10 was imposed for each charge. Since police court fines of less than $20 on a single charge are not appealable or reviewable in any other Kentucky court, Thompson applied to the United States Supreme Court to review his conviction. What major consti-

tutional claim can Thompson raise that would prompt the Supreme Court to grant a review of the police court's judgments? Explain. ● *Thompson v. City of Louisville,* 362 U.S. 199 (1960)

4. The Supreme Court ruled in 1954 that enforced racial segregation in the public schools of a state is a denial of the equal protection of the laws prohibited by the Fourteenth Amendment. This ruling was interpreted to require an end to racial segregation "with all deliberate speed." The state of Arkansas adopted a policy of frustrating the order of the Supreme Court. An amendment of the state constitution was adopted commanding the Arkansas General Assembly to oppose the supposedly unconsitutional desegregation decision. Laws were also passed relieving school children from compulsory attendance at racially mixed schools and establishing a State Sovereignty Commission.

While the state government attempted to thwart the constitutional rights of blacks, the School Board of Little Rock, Arkansas, attempted to formulate a desegregation plan. A plan was adopted and approved by the federal courts, but attempts to implement it led to violent confrontations between blacks and whites at some schools. The governor of Arkansas dispatched units of the national guard to place the school designated for desegregation "off limits" to black students. Explain why the governor of a state cannot (*a*) use the state national guard to prevent the implementation of a federal court order and (*b*) use state police to remove black children from the school because the state is having difficulty controlling a large and hostile crowd gathered at the school. ● *Cooper v. Aaron,* 358 U.S. 1 (1958)

5. The National Housing Act allows the secretary of Housing and Urban Development (HUD) to make expenditures to correct defects in dwellings approved for mortgage insurance. The act further provides that decisions of the secretary in these matters shall be final, and not subject to judicial review. A group of homeowners with federally insured residential mortgages brought action against HUD and the Federal Housing Administration (FHA), attacking the secretary's failure to review and decide their claims and asking for judicial relief. Should the district court decide whether the appellants' claims were valid? Why? ● *Graham v. Caston,* 568 F.2d 1092 (5th Cir. 1978)

6. Section 2-306 of the UCC, as adopted in New Jersey, was used by the court in deciding a sales contract dispute between a utility and a fuel oil supplier. It reads to the effect that contractors are permitted to be indefinite as to exact quantities to be supplied to the purchaser. This means that guarantees (i.e., quantity assurances or promises) must be arrived at in good faith. Additionally, there must be stated estimates or, in their absence, prior comparable requirements.

The sales contract called for the supply of fuel oil by the supplier to the utility at a specified price for a period of years. Estimates in the contract stated how much oil the utility might require. For a particular year the utility's demand for oil was more than double the estimated amount, largely because it had greatly increased its sales of power to other utilities. The price of fuel oil had increased rapidly, rising to more than double the price set forth in the contract. The supplier delivered the amount of the contract estimate for the year, plus an additional 10 percent. The utility sued for breach of contract. How should the court rule? Why? ● *Orange & Rockland, etc., v. Amerada Hess Corp.,* 397 N.Y.S. 2d 814 (1977)

A *tort* is a private (civil) wrong, one that results in injury to another's person, property, or reputation, for which the courts provide damages to the injured person. It is a violation of rights not established by contract. A *crime* is a public wrong, one that affects society as a whole, and is motivated by some kind of intention. It is a violation of a law and is defined by statute or common law.

Tort law differs from contract law only in that the duties imposed by the latter are determined by contract rather than by law. Tort law and contract law are, to a certain extent, "judge-made." That is because common-law rules, in some measure, govern tort and contract cases. Crimes, too, originally were defined by the common law, and for purposes of this chapter, the common-law definitions of various crimes generally will be employed. It should be understood, however, that what constitutes the elements of individual crimes must be determined by referring to the statutes of the particular jurisdiction in which the crime took place.

When the wrong is a tort, the injured party must sue to recover compensation for damages suffered. An exception to this is a *class action,* in which one or more persons sue on behalf of themselves and all other similarly affected persons. When a crime is committed, public authorities bring the legal action to enforce punishment. One act may be both a crime and a tort when both society and the victim are wronged.

● With reckless disregard for the safety of others, Peddicord intentionally drove through a stoplight at a high speed and seriously injured Rudnick following an argument at a local bar. Peddicord's wrongful act (assault and battery) is both a wrong against society (a crime) and a wrong against Rudnick (a tort). Society can punish Peddicord, and Rudnick can sue him for injuries.

2-1. Nature and Classes of Torts

Torts result when there is a conflict between rights to protection of person or property of one person and right to freedom of action of another. The wrong may be inflicted intentionally, negligently, or by unreasonable interference with another's personal or real property. Intentional torts are violations of the law that rely on *intent* (the determination with which one acts) in establishing liability. Liability in negligence torts, on the other hand, relies on *fault* (degree of failure of duty).

A. Negligence

Negligence is failure to exercise the degree of care required by law. It is the theory of fault upon which most claims for personal injury are based. Suits for negligence typically involve the failure on the part of one person to exercise due care when there is a foreseeable risk of harm to others. Four factors must be present in order to establish negligence liability.

1. Existence of Legal Duty. A determination that a legal duty exists between the parties must be made in order to establish liability through negligence. This is solely a question of whether the defendant should have reasonably foreseen a risk of harm to the plaintiff.

2. Lack of Due Care. The judge or jury must determine whether the person charged with negligence failed to exercise due care. To do so, the court uses a standard-of-conduct model. It compares the actions of the defendant with those of a hypothetical ordinary, reasonable, and prudent person under similar circumstances.

● Fire swept Mirenda's warehouse, gutting the interior and destroying furniture stored for pickup and delivery to dealers. A fire investigation indicated that the fire started near the fuse boxes. The dealers sued Mirenda, stressing that the building's electrical wiring was old and faulty and that this represented careless handling of their goods. Mirenda argued that reasonable care had been used and that this is the extent of the duty owed by a warehouse owner to customers. Mirenda pointed out that the cause of the fire could not be conclusively determined. There were manual fire extinguishers, and no smoking was allowed in the warehouse area. The court must decide whether the care exercised by Mirenda in handling the dealers' goods was or was not similar to that displayed by any other ordinary, reasonable, and prudent person in a similar situation.

In applying the *reasonable person* standard to a defendant's actions, the courts generally assume a minimum level of intelligence. Except in the case of the blind, deaf, or physically disabled, all persons are expected to know the extent of their own strength and the normal reactions of other human beings. The degree of care required of a person is not necessarily that which would have prevented harm from occurring. It is more often the degree of diligence, care, and skill that can reasonably be expected under the circumstances.

3. Actual Harm. The plaintiff in an action for negligence must show that actual harm was suffered. In most cases, the harm suffered is a physical injury and is visible. Harm suffered due to fright or humiliation is difficult to demonstrate. Courts often deny awards for such harms unless they result from or precede actual physical injury.

4. Proximate Cause of Resulting Harm. In every court suit for negligence, a *proximate cause* must be determined; that is, a connection must be shown between the negligent conduct and the resulting harm in order to establish the extent of the liability of the defendant. In determining the proximate cause, the court looks for an act or a failure to act, in the absence of which the harm would not have resulted. For example, the court might find that the failure of the defendant to remove an extension ladder was the cause of a child reaching and falling off the roof of the defendant's house. Another measure of proximate cause is the existence of an *intervening cause.* This is some event that occurs after the defendant's negligence and alters the consequences of the defendant's conduct. If fire in the defendant's vacant and unsecured property, set by a stranger, destroys the plaintiff's garage and car, this event is an intervening cause of the damage sustained. Generally, a defendant is liable only if the intervening event is reasonably foreseeable.

B. Negligence Defenses

Defenses to the charge of negligence are usually complicated by the fact that each party is claiming the other is at fault. The major defenses to negligence torts are described in the following paragraphs.

1. Contributory Negligence. The defense of *contributory negligence* involves the failure of plaintiffs to use sufficient due care to ensure their own safety. Such failure can be considered by the court as a contributing cause of the injury.

In some court jurisdictions, contributory negligence is a complete bar to recovery by the plaintiff. In other jurisdictions, it may be used to offset the plaintiff's claim; that is, the plaintiff's award for damages is reduced by an appropriate amount.

● While crossing the street, Bussey was struck by a car driven by Budwig. Bussey proved that Budwig was not exercising reasonable care at the time of the accident. Budwig's lawyer produced a witness who testified that Bussey was glancing at a newspaper and crossing the street against the traffic signal when he was struck. Being partly to blame for the accident, Bussey might not recover all of the damages that would otherwise be awarded.

Last clear chance is a plaintiff's defense to a charge of contributory negligence. Under this doctrine, defendants may be held liable if it can be shown that they had the last chance to avoid injury, even though the plaintiffs were negligent.

2. Assumption of the Risk. Another defense to negligence is any voluntary exposure by the plaintiff to a known risk. The plaintiff's awareness of the extent of the danger is the court's primary consideration in awarding or denying damages. The owner of a hockey arena might present this defense against the negligence charge of a spectator injured by a flying hockey puck. The charge of inadequate protection might not hold if it can be shown that the plaintiff was aware of the risks of spectator injury that are associated with the sport.

3. Comparative Negligence. In recent years a number of states have adopted *comparative negligence* statutes that require courts to assign damages according to the degree of fault of each party. Rather than deny all recovery, the court weighs the relative degree of wrongdoing in awarding damages. If the defendant was 80 percent negligent and the plaintiff only 20 percent negligent, the injured party may be allowed to recover for about 80 percent of the losses suffered.

4. Strict Liability Without Fault. There are instances in which courts may judge a person strictly liable for harm to another without reference to negligence or fault. Activities for which *strict liability* is imposed generally are those representing a danger of serious harm to others or to property that cannot be avoided even when using due care. In most states, the owner of animals that may roam and harm the person or property of another is liable without fault for such damages. Most states, for example, have statutes that hold a dog owner liable for dog bites, with or without prior warning.

State workers' compensation laws impose liability without fault on employers for injuries to employees arising out of their employment. These laws are discussed in Chapter 30, "Law of Employment."

Liability without fault is generally found by the courts when harm to a person or another's property results from a very dangerous activity in an area unsuitable for that activity, for example, storing toxic pollutants or explosives in a populated area.

A number of hazardous activities, including flying an airplane and laying public gas or electric lines, are not subject to liability without fault unless negligence is proved. In the main, these are activities that the courts recognize as essential to the economic health and welfare of the public.

C. Malpractice

A special area of tort liability is *malpractice,* or professional negligence. It involves the failure of individuals with superior education or training to maintain standards of performance set or followed by professional groups. The courts hold lawyers, doctors, accountants, and other professionals to a higher standard of conduct than other members of the community. Actions that fall short of expected skill or knowledge constitute probable evidence of malpractice liability. The accountant who disregards the established rules of audit or the doctor who through ignorance or carelessness subjects a patient to unnecessary suffering would be held liable in a malpractice suit.

● Pizor entered the hospital for treatment of an infection in his arm. The doctor gave the arm a hasty examination and cleansed the wound with an antiseptic solution, assuring Pizor that no other treatment would be required. Later, Pizor was hospitalized and almost lost the use of the arm. The doctor had failed to discover that blood poisoning had set in, a conclusion that could have been reached had Pizor been given a thorough examination. The doctor would no doubt be subject to a malpractice suit.

The standard of conduct principle is a flexible one. It recognizes that a reasonable person, including a reasonable professional, can make a mistake. For example, a physician may prescribe the wrong medicine, since no one can be expected to be correct 100 percent of the time. At a certain point, however, a mistake becomes so bad it becomes a negligent mistake.

D. Personal Harm Torts

Civil wrongs that interfere with personal rights, including assault and battery, mental suffering, false imprisonment or arrest, and defamation, make up an important class of torts.

1. Assault. An intentional threat to harm or to strike another person, with the apparent ability or power to carry out the threat, is considered an *assault.* The touching of another person is not necessary. The harm is the causing of another person to be aware of the threat and fearful of physical harm. A defendant may avoid liability by proving that the act was in self-defense.

Siegel, in a fit of rage, threw a rock at Valenta but missed. Valenta was frightened by the act and developed a facial twitch after the incident. This attempt to inflict physical harm upon Valenta, even though it was not completed, remains an assault for which Siegel may be prosecuted. Valenta may recover money damages in a civil lawsuit.

2. Battery. The intentional touching, without consent or lawful reason, of another person, the person's clothing, or anything attached to the person is defined as *battery*. The tort can take place when the person is touched without being aware of it, for example while asleep or unconscious. Thus, surgery performed unlawfully without the patient's consent may constitute battery. Spitting in the face or on a person is also a battery, as is hitting someone with a rock or throwing acid on the clothing or skin of a person.

3. Mental Suffering. Inflicting mental stress on another by the use of obscene, profane, or abusive language or conduct is sufficient grounds for a tort action. Although courts are not inclined to encourage lawsuits for ordinary insults or vulgar language, they would hold debt collectors liable to consumer-debtors for abusive tactics while trying to collect a debt. Also subject to tort suits are threats of violence that could harm the person, property, or reputation of the debtor. More complete coverage of debt collection torts is provided in Chapter 6, "Consumer Protection and Bankruptcy Relief."

4. False Imprisonment or Arrest. Depriving individuals of their freedom and liberty when one does not have the right to do so can be viewed by the court as *false imprisonment* or *false arrest*. Any form of detention which prevents persons from going about their business constitutes imprisonment. An officer of the law making an arrest without reasonable grounds or suspicion is liable for any loss, injury, or anguish caused the arrested party. In fact, any action or threat of force that compels persons to remain where they do not wish to remain or to go where they do not wish to go is an imprisonment. Anyone who takes away another's liberty may be sued for this tort.

Spano was shopping when a store security officer arrested her as a shoplifter as she was leaving the store. The officer did not see Spano taking merchandise; nor did anyone else. An examination of her shopping bag revealed that she had paid for its contents. Spano may sue the officer for money damages. The court would probably rule that the arrest was made without reasonable cause. In cases of this kind, the employer of the officer is often a codefendant in the suit for damages.

5. Defamation. Any false statement communicated to others that harms a person's good name or reputation may constitute the tort of *defamation*. To be defamatory, the statement must hold the person up to ridicule, contempt, or hatred. Defamation in a temporary form such as speech is *slander;* in a permanent form, such as writing, it is *libel*.

Slander may be expressed person to person, by radio, or by television. Generally, there are grounds for a lawsuit if the complaining person proves that the statements caused financial loss.

Libel includes any unprivileged, false, and malicious publication which tends to expose a person to public scorn, hatred, contempt, or ridicule. It is a ground to sue even when the victim does not suffer financial loss. Such statements may be published as newspaper or magazine articles. They may also appear in motion pictures, dictated letters or memos, signs, or cartoons. Libelous statements must clearly refer to the defamed person either expressly or by implication.

The U.S. Supreme Court has ruled that, to win a libel suit, a public official has to prove that the statement was published either with knowledge that it was malicious or in reckless disregard of the truth. Later decisions have expanded that protection to include other public figures, such as radio, TV, or movie celebrities. In recent cases, the courts have ruled that persons suing for libel damages need not be "public" figures as such in all their actions. This suggests that there may be areas of a celebrity's life that newspapers and magazines may not publicize in print without being subject to a libel charge.

● A California jury ruled that the *National Enquirer* libeled Carol Burnett and awarded her $1.6 million in damages. The subject of dispute was an item published in the *Enquirer* under the headline "Carol Burnett and Henry K, in Row." It went on to say, "At a Washington restaurant, a boisterous Carol Burnett had a loud argument with another diner, Henry Kissinger. She traipsed around the place offering everyone a bite of her dessert. But Carol really raised eyebrows when she accidentally knocked a glass of wine over one diner and started giggling instead of apologizing. The guy wasn't amused and 'accidentally' spilled a glass of water over Carol's dress."

The principal issue contested was whether the *Enquirer* had shown actual malice toward Carol Burnett, that is, whether it published the article about her while knowing that it was false or in reckless disregard of the truth. The writer whose byline appeared over the disputed article indicated that he had not trusted the source of the information and that the article had been written by a senior editor of the *Enquirer*. Another reporter testified that he was asked to check the item's accuracy about one hour before its publication deadline, but had been unable to do so. The *Enquirer* based much of its defense on the First Amendment issue, or the press's constitutional right to report news without restraint. The jury concluded in its deliberations that the publication had not proved that its staff had done enough to check the truthfulness of the item.

A defendant may sometimes show unintentional defamation by apologizing or publishing a suitable correction or retraction. In the above case in which California statutes applied, magazines, but not newspapers, are subject to damages in libel cases even if a timely retraction is published. And in the interests of First Amendment rights to report the news without restraint, some opinions published on matters of public concern may be defended when they represent "fair comment" and are made in good faith.

6. **Invasion of Privacy.** Most states have statutes that protect individuals from invasions of privacy. This tort occurs when one person unreasonably denies another person the right to be left alone or intrudes into another's private affairs. Illegal wiretapping and unauthorized checking into one's investments or bank account are examples. Invasion of privacy can also occur when a person's face or name is used for advertising or publicity purposes without the person's consent.

● Muir, an attractive young woman, discovered that her picture had been used on the box cover design for Purity Flour without her prior knowledge and consent. A photographer who had taken pictures of her had sold one to the flour manufacturer for commercial purposes. Muir sued for $30,000 in damages, claiming humiliation, annoyance, and embarrassment as the result of the public exposure. The court would hold that the unauthorized use of another's name or picture for commercial purposes was a cause of action for invasion of the rights of privacy.

The invasion of privacy concept has been extended to information contained in data banks. This includes information in computers and in manual files, including company personnel files. The courts have also held the use of lie-detector tests by employers to be an invasion of privacy.

● Drug Fair experienced considerable losses from theft and requested that its employees take lie-detector tests. After taking the test, several employees were terminated on the basis of the test results. Each had signed a consent form indicating Drug Fair had not required the test as a condition of continued employment. The court found that an employee's right to privacy takes priority over an employer's right to run a business when it comes to lie-detector tests.

The Privacy Act of 1974 requires all federal agencies to adopt procedures to assure that the information collected on people is kept secret. An individual's mailing address may not be sold or rented by a federal agency, unless such action is approved by law. Agencies are forbidden to disclose information in an individual's record without that individual's consent. The collection and retention of information on people by a federal agency are limited to what bears upon and is necessary to administer the agency properly. When gathering data, an agency must make it known under what authority the data are sought and how they are to be used. An individual has the right to see personal records and to demand correction of inaccurate information. A statement of disagreement may be included in the individual's record if the federal agency refuses to make a requested correction.

E. Property Harm Torts

Wrongs affecting the things people own are *property harm torts.* The harm may be injury to the property or hampering the owner's use of property. The injured person may seek money damages in a civil action.

1. Trespass to Real Property. Entry upon private property without the owner's consent constitutes a tort of *trespass to real property.* Real property includes the land surface and things attached to it, such as trees, minerals, and buildings. Examples of trespass include the entry of animals on private property, the dumping of anything on another's land, and using another's land as an unauthorized shortcut. One can commit this tort by allowing fumes or water to escape from one's property to that of another. Trespass also results when a person causes a wall or any other structure to enter or project over the land of another.

A sales representative has the implied right to go onto land or to enter a business establishment in the hope of selling without committing trespass, but must depart if asked to do so. Police officers have specific powers of entry, as do public health and fire inspectors.

2. Trespass to Personal Property. The tort of *trespass to personal property* is the unlawful interference by one person with the control and possession of any portable property of another. It arises when a possession is taken without permission, even when there is no intention to deprive the owner permanently of the property. For example, borrowing a lawn mower without the owner's permission would make the trespasser liable to the owner for harm to the property or loss of possession.

3. Private and Public Nuisance. Interference with a person's use or enjoyment of land is indirect trespass and may be classified as *private nuisance*. The person(s) whose rights have been disturbed may bring suit. Creating a noise that disturbs another person is an example. Blocking a right of way or taking away a right of light may also be viewed by the court as a private nuisance.

Public nuisances (common nuisances) are annoyances which offend, interfere with, or damage the rights common to all. Public nuisances include offenses to public morals, interference with the use by the public of a public place, or endangerment or injury to property, health, safety, or comfort of a number of persons. The legal means to obtain relief from public nuisances are provided for under state statutes and city ordinances.

Although individuals cannot begin an action for public nuisance as such, they may maintain an action when special damage from a public nuisance is suffered. Generally, only public authorities may begin an action for public nuisance.

● A large cement plant gave off dirt, smoke, and vibration which damaged the neighboring land. Private property owners sought relief and damages. The question facing the court is whether to settle the issue as a private nuisance or channel it to a government body for resolution as a public concern. The court ruled that the cement plant is subject to liability for a private nuisance. Its conduct, which was an invasion of the private use and enjoyment of land, was unreasonable, negligent, and created abnormally dangerous conditions.

4. Conversion. *Conversion* is the unauthorized and unlawful assumption of ownership of personal property known to belong to another. Common forms of conversion involve the unlawful taking or possession of another's property by force, theft, or fraud. Conversion also occurs when possession of personal property is transferred to the wrong person. For example, borrowing a friend's motorbike and without the owner's permission giving it to another party would be held as conversion of the owner's property for one's own use. Another form of conversion is the unlawful destruction or alteration of property owned by another.

● Pendexter has 140 linear feet of cedar rails and 15 posts in his garage. He plans to erect a two-rail fence. While he is away, an unfriendly neighbor enters the garage and cuts the rails and posts into smaller lengths suitable for burning as firewood. This alteration of the identity of Pendexter's property renders the neighbor liable for the wrongful conversion of the fence rails and posts.

In a tort action for conversion, the owner recovers full value of the property at the time and place of conversion. The person committing the conversion becomes the owner of the property, regardless of its condition.

Questions of ownership may arise when employees perfect an invention during the course of their employment by using the employer's materials. In such cases, the employer has a *shop right*. This is a nonexclusive right to use the invention. When an employee invents something unrelated to the employer's operations, using personal time, work space, and materials, the employer has no shop right in the invention.

2-2. Nature and Classes of Crimes

Crimes are acts that legislatures interpret as harmful to the public interest. They are defined by statutes passed by the various legislatures. Although criminal statutes of the states generally resemble each other, the penalties imposed may differ. The exact charge may also differ; that is, grand theft in one state might be petty theft in another state. Since a criminal act or the failure to perform a duty required by statutory law is a violation of public law, action is always taken in the name of the state or federal government.

In common law, crimes are dealt with in the order of their seriousness—treason, felonies, and misdemeanors. Most states divide offenses into only felonies and misdemeanors. Some list *infractions* (i.e., minor traffic and local ordinance violations) as a third category of crime.

Under federal and most state laws, a *felony* is a crime punishable by death or by imprisonment in a federal or state prison for a term exceeding one year. A *misdemeanor* is a less serious crime that is generally punishable by a jail sentence for not more than one year. Included in this category of lesser crimes against society are offenses such as disorderly conduct, drunken driving, exceeding speed limits, and simple assault.

A. Crimes Against the Government

Crimes against the state and public order include treason and espionage. Usually the performance of acts against the state establishes the crime, and there is no need to prove wrongful intent (i.e., a predetermination to commit the act, without legal excuse.

In Article III, Section 3, of the U.S. Constitution, *treason* is defined as the levying of war against the United States or giving aid and comfort to the nation's enemies. Therefore, any citizen who starts a rebellion or aids and abets alien enemies would be subject to the charge of treason. For conviction, a confession in open court or the testimony of two witnesses to the same overt act is required.

Federal statutes define *espionage* as the gathering or transmitting of information pertaining to the national defense of the United States for the political or military use of any foreign nation.

B. Crimes Against the Person

Crimes against the person most often referred to as felonies include homicides, maiming, and kidnapping.

1. Homicide. Any killing of one human being by another may be defined as *homicide*. Criminal homicide is either murder or manslaughter. When the unlawful killing is done with a deliberate purpose or determination formed in the mind before commission of the act (i.e., with *malice aforethought*), the crime is defined as *murder*. In contrast to murder, *manslaughter* is an unlawful killing without malice aforethought. When an unintended killing of another results from an absence of proper caution, the homicide becomes *involuntary manslaughter*. A killing that results when a person acts in a state of extreme fright, terror, anger, or blind rage that destroys reason is known as *voluntary manslaughter*.

● Santoro arrived home to find his wife in the arms of another man. In a state of extreme emotion, Santoro killed the man. The court most likely would find the killing to be voluntary manslaughter. Santoro's act of killing, although intentional, was committed under the influence of blind rage produced by reasonable provocation.

Homicide is justifiable when a person kills another in the performance of a legal duty, by unavoidable necessity, or to prevent a terrible crime. Excusable homicide occurs when the killing is without criminal intent and is done by accident or mistake, or in self-defense. Neither justifiable nor excusable homicide involves any legal guilt or punishment.

2. Maiming and Kidnapping. Maiming and kidnapping are among the most serious crimes committed against the person. *Maiming* includes acts done with the intent to injure or disfigure the victim's person—for example, cutting off part of the body or inflicting a wound that breaks the skin, whether by some kind of instrument or by corrosive acid.

Kidnapping is the unlawful abduction of an individual against that person's will. It constitutes false imprisonment, with the additional element of removal of the victim to another place. Most state laws distinguish between simple kidnapping and the more serious offense involving demands for ransom or child stealing.

C. Crimes Against Property

Burglary, arson, robbery, larceny, and extortion are crimes against property.

1. Burglary. *Burglary* consists of a break-in of a dwelling or building for the purpose of carrying out a felony or theft. The slightest forced entry, such as turning a doorknob, qualifies as a break-in. Inserting a stick through a window while remaining outside constitutes entry. Entry through an open door or window does not alone establish the act of burglary, but once the person is inside, the opening of an interior door would constitute a break-in.

2. Arson. At common law, *arson* is the willful and malicious act of causing or procuring the burning of another's property. In some states arson includes the burning of a house by its owner. The willful burning is often motivated by the intent to defraud or prejudice an insurer of the property.

● Stanke, believing that he had been defrauded by Cogswell in a business deal, set fire to Cogswell's garage. The fire was quickly extinguished, and only a small amount of burn damage resulted. Stanke was guilty of the crime of arson even though the garage was not seriously damaged or destroyed.

3. Robbery. The act of taking personal property in the possession of another against that person's will and under threat to do great bodily harm or damage is *robbery*. When force is not used, robbery is committed when the victim is subjected to extreme fear.

● Threatening bodily harm, Breuner determined where DeLucca kept her jewelry. He left her bound in one room while he took possession of the property in another room. The court would hold that Breuner's actions constituted robbery.

4. Larceny. A person who takes and carries away the personal property of another without the right to do so is guilty of *larceny*. The value of the property taken—$50 in many states, as high as $200 in others—determines whether the theft is grand larceny and a felony or petty larceny and a misdeameanor.

● Basso removed a leisure suit from a department store display rack, put it on, and left the store without paying for it. He obviously had no intention of either returning the suit or paying for it later. Basso would be found guilty of the crime of larceny.

5. Extortion. *Extortion* is the taking of another's property with consent when that consent is influenced by a threat to injure the victim's person, property, or reputation. Public officials commit this crime when they corruptly demand and receive a payment or a privilege, pretending they are entitled to it.

D. Business Torts and Crimes

Nonviolent in nature, business torts and crimes are those carried out by a business or individual in the course of doing business to obtain a business-related advantage. Covering a wide range of illegal practices, business torts and crimes are directed against another business, the government, or the public.

1. Unfair Competition. A business is entitled to compete free from untrue statements made to influence the public not to buy its goods or services. Any such interference with commerce and trade is a business tort. The injured business is entitled to relief in damages or in the form of an injunction prohibiting the wrongful act.

● Cole accepted an offer by Nor-West Auto to sell a three-year-old Toyota and made a $20 deposit. On the way home Cole stopped at New Hope Motors. Cole told Dorfman, the New Hope salesperson, that he had agreed to purchase a car from Nor-West. Dorfman actively persuaded Cole that Nor-West "laundered" the odometers of their cars so that they appeared to be less used and more valuable. Cole confronted Nor-West with the accusation made by the New Hope salesperson and announced his decision not to purchase the Toyota. Dorfman's unproved charge of fraud was a deliberate inducement for Cole to break his contract with Nor-West. It constitutes an unfair method of competition and would entitle Nor-West to an injunction against a repetition of such statements and an action for damages.

Various other unfair trade practices make up a large group of business torts. For example, fraud or *deceit* (injurious misrepresentation) is a tort that may be prohibited by court injunction.

2. Embezzlement. Individuals who wrongfully take property entrusted to their care have committed the crime of *embezzlement*. In contrast with the crime of larceny, in which the offender comes into possession of property unlawfully, the embezzler comes into possession of the property or the money by legitimate means in the ordinary course of business.

● Du Bois, the cashier for Haig Jewelers, removed $500 from the store safe after entering a false credit to the account of a customer. When an audit uncovered the illegal transaction, Du Bois would be convicted of criminal embezzlement in most states even though she might have intended to borrow the money for a short time.

When a person embezzles property to acquire other property, the rightful owner is entitled to that property. The rightful owner is also entitled to any increase in value or profit realized by the wrongdoer. This *constructive trust* rule means that the culprit who steals another's property becomes a trustee of the fruits of the wrongdoing for the benefit of the victim.

3. Bribery. The crime of *bribery* involves a corrupt agreement induced by an offer of reward. Central to the offense is the offering, giving, receiving, or soliciting of something of value to influence official action or the discharge of legal or public duty. Whether the recipient knows that a bribe is being offered, or whether the recipient accepts or rejects it, does not void the offense. Bribery taints a wide range of official conduct. It has been used to obtain political preference in appointments to public office. Company executives have used corporate funds to affect action on pending legislation or to block the calling of a strike. A city works commissioner who awarded a waste-removal contract to a hauling firm without competitive bidding, after receiving a $5,000 cash payment, would be guilty of bribe acceptance.

4. Computer Crimes. Computers have been used for fraudulent purposes. Financial transactions, inventory data, and negotiable instruments such as checks are stored, updated, and printed by computers that are programmed by individuals with specialized skills. Dishonest computer personnel can use a computer to take money from a company. Printouts of confidential company reports can be obtained and then sold to competitors.

Computer crime is a relatively new occurrence. The application of criminal law to it is still developing. The tendency is to treat computer manipulations for personal gain as a theft of a *trade secret*—guarded information that gives a business an economic advantage.

Understanding Legal Terms

Define, identify, or explain the following terms:

assault	crime	infraction	negligence
battery	defamation	larceny	robbery
bribery	embezzlement	libel	shop right
burglary	felony	manslaughter	tort
class action	homicide	misdemeanor	trade secret
conversion			

Questions for Review and Discussion

1. Explain the differences between torts and crimes.

2. Discuss the four factors that must be present to establish liability on the grounds of negligence.

3. Compare the methods of assigning damages under contributory negligence and comparative negligence.

4. What is the nature and degree of liability protection provided individuals when harm results even though the intent to harm is absent?

5. Describe the scope and nature of the torts that interfere with personal rights.

6. Identify the torts that injure or hamper property rights.

7. Distinguish between a felony, a misdemeanor, and an infraction in terms of seriousness as crimes.

8. Compare and contrast crimes (*a*) against persons, (*b*) against property, and (*c*) against the government.

9. Distinguish between public nuisance and a private nuisance.

10. Explain how business crimes differ from other crimes such as robbery.

Analyzing Cases

1. Chena Hot Springs Road is a two-lane public highway near the city of Fairbanks, Alaska.

Guinn, an airline operations agent, used the road regularly to and from the airport. Early one morning, Guinn was found dead on the road in the wreckage of his automobile. He had collided with a truck that had been abandoned approximately eight feet into the traveled portion of the road. The state had also plowed snow around the truck. The administrator of Guinn's estate brought suit, charging that Guinn's death was caused by the negligence of McGee, the owner of the truck, and the negligence of the state of Alaska. McGee was allegedly negligent in parking his truck where he did and leaving it there; the state of Alaska (with comparative negligence statutes) was allegedly negligent in failing to remove the truck and for maintaining the highway in a negligent manner.

How should the Supreme Court of Alaska dispose of this case? ● *State of Alaska v. Guinn*, 555 P.2d 530 (Alaska 1976)

2. Knavel noticed that the brakes of his car were not operating properly. He visited Allison's Service Station, where, at Knavel's request, Allison made a temporary repair by plugging the hydraulic brake line leading to the left rear wheel. Allison instructed Knavel to return the car the next day for permanent repairs.

Despite this warning, Knavel continued to drive the car. He suddenly noticed that the accelerator pedal of his car was stuck in the halfway position and that the brakes were not working at all. Knavel's car glanced off a light pole before colliding with the front of a slow-moving locomotive and then crashing through a phone booth in which Robert Noon was standing. The booth was so located that an automobile could easily strike the booth, which was not protected by steel bumper posts. Noon lost both of his legs. He sued Knavel, Allison's Service Station, the train company, and the telephone company. Noon claimed that these parties were negligent. The trial court awarded a judgment of $216,761 against Knavel and the phone company. Although Knavel did not appeal, the phone company did. It claimed that the injury was not caused by the location of the booth but by Knavel's wrongful conduct.

Should the phone company's argument be accepted? Why? ● *Noon v. Knavel* 339 A.2d 545 (Pa. Super. 1975)

3. This is an action in negligence by a builder against a public utility for damages sustained as a result of a termination of electricity at an unoccupied house that had been constructed. Consolidated Edison had installed electric service to the Pompeii Estates, Inc., property and then disconnected it in midwinter because of two unpaid bills amounting to $25.11. The lack of electricity caused the heating unit to go off, which resulted in burst water pipes. This caused $1,030 in damage to the unoccupied house.

The utility's computer processed a notice to the builder that service to the house would be discontinued. It was mailed to the address of the unoccupied house. The utility's field representative, who had numerous conversations with the builder of the house, had not been consulted when the decision to discontinue service was made. An expert witness from the post office testified that the notice could not have been received as it was not the practice of the post office to deliver mail to unoccupied buildings. The utility's file contained a letter with Pompeii Estates, Inc.'s, correct mailing address. Pompeii Estates sued for damages, claiming negligence. Consolidated Edison contended it followed the mailing requirements set by law for anyone refusing or neglecting to pay for electric service provided. How should the trial court rule? Why? ● *Pompeii Estates v. Consolidated Edison Co.*, 397 N.Y.S.2d 577 (1977)

4. Robert Welch, Inc., was the publisher of *American Opinion,* a national magazine. Nuccio, a Chicago police officer, shot and killed a youth and was tried and convicted of second-degree murder. The family of the youth retained Gertz, a reputable attorney, to represent them for the purpose of suing the officer for damages.

American Opinion published an article titled "Frame-Up: Richard Nuccio and the War on Police." Notwithstanding the fact that Gertz had no part in the criminal conviction of Nuccio, the newspaper portrayed him as an architect of the "frame-up." The article also stated that Gertz was a "Leninist" and a "Communist-fronter" and had been an official of a Communist-front organization known as the "Marxist League for Industrial Democracy." All these charges were untrue.

Gertz brought an action, claiming that the falsehoods published injured his reputation as a lawyer and a citizen. How should the U.S. Supreme Court rule on the magazine's claim that it is privileged under the First Amendment against liability for defamation of a private citizen? Why? ● *Gertz v. Robert Welch, Inc.*, 418 U.S. 323 (1974)

5. Dewey was a welder for American Stair Glide Corp. Stair Glide manufactured elevator chairs designed to operate on rails and used by those who cannot climb stairs. A manufacturing defect caused the chairs at times to fail, resulting in injury to the user.

Dewey learned of the problem through shop talk. Subsequently an idea occurred to him for a safety device and he commenced work on a solution during company time. Told by his supervisor not to engage in such activity on company time, Dewey returned to his regular duties. During lunch breaks and at home, Dewey completed work on his idea. He used the company welder and cutting torch as well as parts from the scrap barrel.

Dewey presented Stair Glide with his idea and a model of the safety device. When it was clear the device was of value, Dewey asked his employer for compensation. When the request was refused, Dewey brought suit. Stair Glide defended, employing the shop right doctrine. Did Stair Glide have a right to use Dewey's idea? How should the court rule? Why? ● *Dewey v. American Stair Glide Corp.*, 557 S.W.2d 643 (Mo. App. 1977)

6. Earnest was alleged to have asked Munoz, a 15-year-old boy, to burn down his house so that insurance proceeds could be collected. It was decided Munoz would receive $100 for the burning. Munoz died in the fire, and Earnest was charged with the crimes of murder and arson.

Martinez, a former neighbor and friend of Munoz, testified to five conversations she had had with Munoz prior to his death. Munoz had told her of his intention to set fire to Earnest's house within the next two weeks when no one would be at home.

The fire department found Munoz's charred body and a partially filled gasoline can in the house. The physical evidence suggested that the boy had spread an inflammable liquid in two areas of the house.

Although the act of Munoz accidentally killing himself did not constitute an unlawful killing, what other crime might Earnest be convicted of? Why? ● *People v. Earnest*, 126 Cal Rptr. 107 (1975)

7. Alberico was a captain serving as a post administrator of the Rocky Mountain Arsenal in Colorado. He had unchecked access to the arsenal's facilities. Alberico attempted to enrich himself by selling government property. While some of the property taken were things of real value (plastic explosives), three of the items taken were checks. They were made out to the Rocky Mountain Arsenal for sums of $13,932, $29,538, and $30,096. They bore the signature of an Air Force disbursing officer and were not indorsed. Alberico was tried and convicted on several counts, including one which makes it a felony to steal property from the government in excess of $100 and a misdeameanor to steal any "things of value." The government did not lose the fair value of the checks since payment on them had been stopped. Alberico contended that because he could not cash the checks and because the government was actually "out" nothing, the checks were not things of value and certainly did not possess value exceeding $100. How should the court of appeals dispose of this argument? Why? ● *United States V. Alberico*, 604 F.2d 1315 (10th Cir. 1979) *cert. denied*, 444 U.S. 992 (1979)

8. Niederberger was employed by the Internal Revenue Service as a large case manager. In this position, Niederberger supervised a group of revenue agents engaged in the task of auditing the corporate income tax returns filed by Gulf Oil Company. Niederberger's responsibilities included making all final decisions regarding areas to be reviewed during the audit.

Over a period of years, Niederberger received a series of vacation trips paid for by Gulf Oil Company. Expert testimony by an IRS security inspector placed the value of these trips at $7,000. Niederberger was at times accompanied by major personnel for Gulf Oil. For example, he spent four days at the Doral Country Club in Miami Beach, accompanied by the manager of federal tax compliance for Gulf Oil.

Niederberger was indicted on charges of accepting illegal gratuities (i.e., something voluntarily given in return for a favor or service, hence a bribe). He was tried, convicted, and sentenced to a six-month prison term, a five-year period of probation, and a fine of $5,000. On appeal, Niederberger argued, among other things, that his conviction should be reversed because there was no *quid pro quo*. That is, he had never promised to do anything in return for receiving the trips. Assuming this argument to be true, how should the court of appeals deal with it? Why? ● *United States v. Niederberger*, 580 F.2d 63 (3d Cir. 1978)

9. Dare To Be Great, Inc., was a Florida corporation qualified to do business in Kentucky. Turner was the parent corporation of Dare To Be Great, Inc.

Dare To Be Great was engaged in the sale of a series of tapes for the sum of $1,000. It alleged that the tapes were prepared by leading authorities and were capable of enabling purchasers to better understand themselves and their relationship to others and of providing inspiration and motivation to achieve greater success. The purchaser was given an opportunity to put into practice and demonstrate the newly discovered magnetism by assisting in the sale of the program to others, for which a commission of $400 would be received on each such sale after the first two. In addition, a commission would be paid on the first two sales made by all of those initiated into the program by the purchaser.

The attorney general of Kentucky brought suit charging pyramid selling and requesting an injunction forbidding Dare To Be Great, Inc., Glenn W. Turner Enterprises, Inc., and Glenn W. Turner from engaging in these fraudulent trade practices. Money damages were also sought. If fraud is established, may the injunction be granted? Why? ● *Dare To Be Great, Inc., v. Commonwealth ex rel. Hancock*, 511 S.W.2d 224 (Ky. App. 1974)

10. Four thieves broke into a storage magazine containing 80,000 pounds of explosives in Anchorage, Alaska. In an effort to conceal the fact that they had stolen explosives from the site, they set a prepared charge and fled. The resulting blast, which registered 1.8 on the Richter scale 30 miles away, damaged dwellings and other buildings within a two-mile radius of the magazine. The owners of the damaged building brought suit against Yukon Equipment, Inc., the operator of the storage magazine, to recover for the damages to their property. Yukon argued that the setting of the charge by the thieves was the cause of the damages; therefore, it was not responsible. How would you decide? ● *Yukon Equipment, Inc., v. Fireman's Fund Ins. Co.*, 585 P.2d 1206 (Alaska 1978)

Chapter 3   The Judicial Process

Law is a system of rules and precedent that members of a society establish as a standard of conduct so that they can live together peacefully. It attempts to regulate the relations of individuals to the government, those of the government to the individual, and those among individuals. If there is a conflict in these relations, the law also provides a court system through which individuals or the government or both may seek relief in the form of a decision. The court may give the injured person or government relief, or it may not. In either case a decision is made.

3-1. The Court System

The laws of our government are interpreted and enforced by a system of courts established by legislated authority. *Courts* are judicial tribunals that meet in a regular place and apply laws in an attempt to settle disputes fairly. Each of these official bodies is a forum for a plaintiff who presents a complaint, the defendant against whom relief or recovery is sought, and the judge and/or jury who weighs facts and settles the dispute.

A. Officers of the Court

The court system operates principally through the work of lawyers, judges, and juries.

1. Lawyers. A *lawyer*, synonymous with attorney, is a trained person who is licensed to practice law. In this role, lawyers serve as advocates by rendering legal advice and aid and pleading the cause of clients before a court. Lawyers also serve as negotiators in seeking compromises and mutually acceptable alternatives to a *lawsuit* (i.e., an action between two or more parties in a court of law). Lawyers play an important role in the disposition of criminal charges by agreement between the prosecutor and the accused, referred to as *plea bargaining*. These negotiations involve the defendant's pleading guilty to a lesser offense or to only one or some of the charges in an indictment on several counts submitted to a grand jury by the public prosecuting attorney. In return, the defendant seeks to obtain concessions as to the type and length of sentence or a reduction in the number of charges in the indictment.

2. Code of Professional Responsibility. The American Bar Association's *Code of Professional Responsibility* outlines the standards of conduct expected of lawyers in their relationships with the public and the legal system. Some of the key standards are as follows: Lawyers should assist the legal profession in carrying out its duty to make legal counsel available. They should preserve the confidences and secrets of a client. In representing clients, lawyers should exercise independent judgment competently and zealously within the bounds of the law. A lawyer should refuse employment if there are financial, personal, or property interests that could cause a conflict of interest in representing a client. Fees should be reasonable so as not to deter the public from seeking professional help. And lawyers have a right to advertise truthfully the availability and terms of routine legal services.

3. Need for Legal Counsel. Day-to-day business transactions do not generally require the services of a lawyer. But in the course of dealing with others, individuals do encounter situations where the legal training of a lawyer is needed to avoid or conduct *litigation*—a legal contest in a court of law. For example, it is wise to consult a lawyer when confronted with the following situations:

- Organizing a business
- Purchasing or selling land and buildings
- Making long-term business arrangements
- Engaging in transactions where the other party has legal advice or insists on unusual arrangements
- Submitting complex tax returns
- Conducting transactions involving large sums of money

4. Judges and Juries. Public officials who preside over a court and administer the law are known as *judges*. They control the proceedings required in bringing cases before the court. Included in this process are all the steps in a lawsuit, from its commencement to the rendering of a *judgment*—the final decision of a case. State judges are often elected or appointed for a long term in office. Federal judges are chosen by the President and according to the U.S. Constitution have life tenure and may not have their salary reduced while in office.

In all criminal prosecutions, the U.S. Constitution establishes the right of the accused to a public trial by an impartial jury in the state and district in which the crime was committed. In federal courts, a trial by jury is required in civil suits where the value disputed is more than $20. In state courts, the parties in civil suits are usually permitted to request a trial by jury when the charges involve judgments of facts or requests for money. If no jury demand is made, or if the case involves the equity judgment of the court (such as a suit for an injunction), or if complex issues are involved, the judge decides the case without a jury.

B. Court Jurisdiction

The authority of a court to hear and decide cases involving a person or subject matter is called its *jurisdiction*. It is fixed by law and is limited as to territory and type of case. A court of *original jurisdiction* has authority to hear a case when it is first brought to court. Courts having power to review a case for errors are courts of *appellate jurisdiction*. Only *courts of record* (those that keep official journals of their proceedings) impose fines or imprison people. Normally, appeals can be taken only from decisions of a court of record. Courts that have the power to hear any type of case are said to exercise *general jurisdiction*. Those with power to decide only certain kinds of cases have *special jurisdiction*. For example, a criminal court hears cases involving wrongful acts committed by individuals against the public. Examples of civil courts with special jurisdiction are probate courts, juvenile courts, and bankruptcy courts.

C. Federal Courts

The federal court system is authorized by the U.S. Constitution. Article III states, "The Judicial Power of the United States, shall be vested in one supreme Court, and in such inferior Courts as the Congress may from time to time ordain and establish." The present system of federal courts includes the Supreme Court of the United States, eleven courts of appeals, U.S. district courts, and several other special-interest courts and administrative tribunals. Figure 3-1 outlines the federal court system, including the specialized courts and administrative tribunals.*

1. U.S. District Courts. Each state and territory has at least one federal district court of record. These trial courts have original jurisdiction over cases involving a federal law or treaty or the U.S. Constitution and cases involving *diversity of citizenship*, that is, cases where the suit is between persons from different states, or between a state or the citizens thereof and a foreign country, if the amount involved is over $10,000.

● An agent of the FBI was wounded by a fugitive who was attempting to avoid arrest. The *perpetrator* (one who commits an offense or crime) was arrested by the state police and jailed to await arraignment and trial. Procedural law would be used to decide whether the federal or state courts would be given jurisdiction. A federal district court would probably be designated, since the offense was committed against an employee of a federal agency.

2. U.S. Courts of Appeals. The eleven U.S. courts of appeals hear appeals on questions of law in cases originating in federal trial courts. Cases brought before a court of appeals are heard by a panel of three judges. These courts cannot review, retry, or correct judicial errors of a state court. State cases must be appealed to the U.S. Supreme Court when they come within the federal jurisdiction.

3. Supreme Court of the United States. Established by the Constitution, the U.S. Supreme Court is the court of final jurisdiction in all cases appealed from federal district courts and in cases sent by state supreme courts. It has original jurisdiction in cases affecting ambassadors or other public ministers and consuls, and in cases in which a state is a party.

The Supreme Court is composed of a chief justice and eight associate justices. They are appointed by the President of the United States with the advice and consent of the Senate and hold office during good behavior. Justices hear appeals made by other courts and indicate by *certiorari* (an appellate proceeding for reexamination of an inferior court's action) which cases will be reviewed. A decision is handed down by a majority opinion of the justices.

* Not shown are the United States bankruptcy courts that are to be established under the Bankruptcy Reform Act of 1978 but whose expanded jurisdiction was ruled unconstitutional by the U.S. Supreme Court. (See *Northern Pipeline v. Marathon Pipe Line*, No. 81–150 __U.S.__ 1982.)

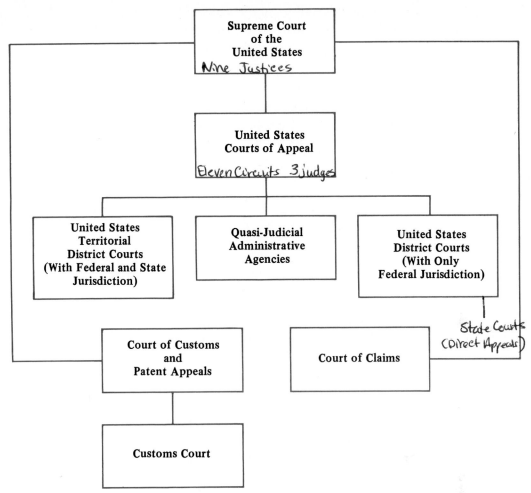

Figure 3-1. Federal court system.

4. Special-Interest Courts and Administrative Tribunals. Congress has established special-interest courts with limited subject jurisdiction. The U.S. Customs Court hears cases involving import duties. The U.S. Court of Customs and Patent Appeals hears appeals of cases involving import duties from the U.S. Customs Court and appeals of cases involving patents from various agencies. The U.S. Court of Claims settles suits against the United States government.

A number of administrative agencies, including the Tax Court of the United States, also function as special courts or administrative tribunals. Appeals from these bodies are first heard by the appropriate U.S. court of appeals and then, if necessary, by the U.S. Supreme Court. Judicial responsibility is generally limited to maintaining consistency with statutes, determining that a fair hearing was provided during an administrative hearing, and ensuring that constitutional rights were not violated.

D. State Courts

The courts of each state are organized according to the provisions of its state constitution and jurisdictional needs. Despite differences from state to state, such as the names for similar types of courts, there are basic similarities. For instance, each state has an arrangement of inferior, or lower, courts which serve as limited-jurisdiction trial courts. Higher-level trial courts with broader jurisdiction are also provided. In addition, each state has appellate courts to which questions of law (not questions of fact) may be appealed. Figure 3-2 outlines a typical arrangement for a state court system.

1. State Trial Courts. State inferior courts are the lowest level of state trial court. They have limited jurisdiction to hear and decide cases and do not hear cases outside their jurisdiction. For instance, family courts decide domestic re-

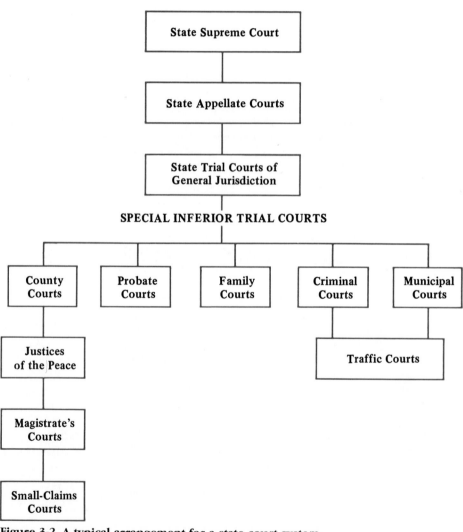

Figure 3-2. A typical arrangement for a state court system.

lations cases, probate courts deal with the estates of the deceased, magistrate's courts decide petty criminal offenses, and justices of the peace handle local matters. Small-claims courts, more fully discussed below, offer a simple way to settle minor civil disputes and place a dollar limit on the amount the plaintiff can ask for.

State courts of general jurisdiction hear all kinds of cases properly brought before them. Often referred to as *circuit courts* or *courts of common pleas*, they represent the highest trial court in the state. The unsatisfactory decisions of an inferior state court may be appealed or heard again in the state's general jurisdiction court.

In most state trial courts, whether the case is in equity or in law is determined by the remedy desired. When the action is equitable rather than legal, there is no right to a jury trial. The judge passes upon questions of both law and fact. The decision rendered by the court in an equity action is called a decree. In contrast to a judgment in a court of law, which is measured in money damages, a decree in a court of equity is directed to the defendant. It may be a remedy in the form of specific performance and include money damages. It may also be an injunction.

● Klaas, an expert in art restoration, sold his business to Bieder and agreed not to open a similar business in the community for three years. In less than one year, Klaas violated the agreement by starting a competitive business six blocks from Bieder's shop. Bieder can begin a lawsuit in a state trial court seeking injunctive relief. By order, the judge could require Klaas to honor the agreement with Bieder. Thus, Bieder's losses from Klaas's competitive business could be halted promptly.

2. State Appellate Courts. The state court system provides for an appeal to appellate courts on questions of law that arise during trial court proceedings. A panel of judges examines the records of proceedings before the trial court, and the lawyers file arguments and make their statements orally before the judges. If the appellate court disagrees on the meaning of the points of law raised, it may set aside or modify the action of the trial court. It may enter such judgment as it concludes the trial court should have taken, or it may send the case back to the trial court for a new trial.

Difficult questions of law may be appealed to the supreme court of the state. Although a person is entitled to one trial and one appeal, another review may be obtained if the supreme court of appeals agrees by certiorari to review the case. A panel of five to nine judges generally hears the lawyers address themselves to the points of law in question. The decision of the state's supreme court of appeals is final unless a federal issue or constitutional right is involved.

● Jordan was arrested by a police officer, who entered her home without a warrant. She was tried and convicted on a criminal charge. Jordan then appealed her case through the state courts, claiming that the initial arrest had been illegal and the conviction secured without regard to her constitutional rights. Should the state courts refuse to accept her arguments relating to the arrest, she would be permitted to petition for certiorari to the federal courts on the grounds that her constitutional rights were violated.

In the preceding example, Jordan may also apply to a federal court for a *writ of habeas corpus*. Under federal *habeas corpus* laws, federal courts have the right to release persons who are imprisoned by state court judgment when their right of personal liberty has been violated. There is, however, a limited choice on the part of the federal judge to deny relief under certain circumstances. For example, the judge may deny *habeas corpus* relief to an applicant who has deliberately bypassed the orderly procedure of the state courts and in so doing lost the legal means to prevent the violation of a constitutional right.

3. Small-Claims Courts. An action in a small-claims court is an alternative to the formal court lawsuit. It represents a simple and inexpensive way to have a complaint fairly judged by an impartial third party. Such courts are usually divisions of general, county, or city courts, and the procedure is an *adversary proceeding*. That is, the plaintiff and the defendant are each required to present the appropriate facts and arguments to a judge. The procedure is so simple that neither party have need to hire a lawyer.

The judge interrogates both parties to learn the facts. In a few courts, some or all of the cases are heard by *arbitrators*—lawyers, for the most part, who have been trained to assume the judge's role. Most judges follow the *preponderance of evidence* rule; that is, in order to win, the plaintiff must present heavier evidence. The cost of taking a case to small-claims court is usually $50 or less.

In a typical case, the judge identifies the plaintiff and the defendant and summarizes the complaint. Both parties are sworn to tell the truth. The judge then hears the plaintiff's side of the dispute and examines any evidence the plaintiff offers. Next the judge hears the defendant's side, examining documents and witnesses as necessary. Finally, both parties have a chance to ask questions or challenge the other's testimony. If the defendant does not appear in court, the judge is likely to award a *default judgment*. This is a judgment entered upon the failure of a party to appear or plead in court at the appointed time.

Although plaintiffs have a good chance of winning a suit in a small-claims court, collecting the award is sometimes difficult. If the defendant is a business, an indication that the matter of the unpaid judgment is being called to the attention of the business license bureau with the request that the license be voided generally results in a prompt settlement. If the defendant is an individual, more formal procedures may be required—for example, asking the sheriff or marshal to arrange to have periodic payments deducted from the defendant's paycheck.

E. Nonjudicial Alternatives to Litigation

Parties to civil disputes may avoid a contest in court by using a nonjudicial method of settling their differences.

1. Compromise. A compromise solution to simple civil disputes is often a more logical course of action than a costly and time-consuming lawsuit. *Compromise* is the settlement of differences or the adjustment of matters in dispute by mutual concessions; that is, each disputing party yields to some extent to the other's claim or demand.

2. Arbitration. Another alternative to litigation is *arbitration*. This is the process of submitting disputes for determination to usually private, unofficial persons selected by law or agreement. The procedures governing arbitration are not so clearly defined as are formal legal procedures. The rules followed are either set by law or agreed upon in an arbitration agreement. The hearing may be informal, with the arbitrator(s) receiving testimony from the disputing parties. The considerations are weighted and a decision is rendered without the reason for it necessarily given. In other instances, the arbitrators may conduct very formal hearings and require formal pleadings and strict rules of evidence.

Arbitration has several advantages over litigation: (*a*) It is a rapid way of dealing with disputes. (*b*) Since lawyers are not required to argue the disputed issues, the cost of settlement is moderate. (*c*) Settlement is usually accomplished without undue hostility. (*d*) Complex, technical areas in dispute can be decided by arbitrators who are experts with desired qualifications and experience.

Various approaches to arbitration have been taken by the states. In a few states, the principles of common law apply. At common law, at any time prior to the rendering of a final award, either or both parties may cancel the agreement to arbitrate, since the continued consent of the parties is required. Other states have laws which cover only the enforcement of arbitrated awards. In these states, the agreement to arbitrate may also be canceled prior to the final award, but once the award is handed down, quick and effective means for enforcing it are available. Most states, however, have adopted arbitration statutes that cover all phases of referring an issue for arbitration, the award, and its enforcement. In states which recognize the statutory method exclusively, the arbitration agreement may not be canceled, and awards are enforceable. In states which recognize both the common-law and statutory method, the agreement may be canceled if common-law arbitration is used, but not if the statutory method is utilized. The Uniform Arbitration Act of 1955 has been adopted by most states.

3. Mediation. *Mediation* is another alternative to litigation. It is the intervention of a third party, the mediator, between two contending parties with the objective of persuading them to adjust or settle their dispute. In contrast with the decision of an arbitrator, the mediator's decision is nonbinding on the disputing parties.

3-2. Litigation Procedure

Although the statutes governing trial procedures differ in detail from state to state, the following examination of common elements to all court proceedings can simplify the task of analyzing the cases presented in this text.

A. Parties to the Lawsuit

The principal parties to a lawsuit are the *plaintiff* and the *defendant*. The plaintiff is the person who begins a legal suit by filing required documents in a trial court of original jurisdiction. The defendant is the person against whom relief or recovery is desired in an action or lawsuit.

B. Filing a Complaint

The plaintiff must notify both the court and the defendant about the intention to begin a lawsuit. This is done by preparing a *complaint* which sets forth the names of the parties to the case, the cause of the action, and in a civil suit the request for relief in the form of money, an injunction, or specified performance. The complaint is presented to the appropriate court officer together with a *summons*. This document names the court of jurisdiction, describes the nature of the action, and demands that the defendant answer the complaint within a given period of time.

A copy of the summons and the complaint is generally served personally on the defendant by a sheriff or federal marshal at the defendant's last known address. Notice by registered mail or by publication is also used when the address of the defendant is unknown, when the defendant is a nonresident of the state, or when the defendant hides to avoid personal serving of the court documents.

C. Pleadings

The parties in a lawsuit define the points about which there is disagreement by a process known as *pleading*. In a pleading, each party makes charges of fact and the other party either admits or denies them. After receiving the summons and complaint, the defendant usually files an answer to the charges raised. This is normally done by the lawyer hired by the defendant. In criminal cases, the court will appoint a lawyer to protect the rights of defendants who cannot afford counsel. In civil actions, the defendant's answer may include *counterclaims,* that is, claims against the plaintiff. If the defendant fails to file an answer to the plaintiff's complaint, or if the plaintiff fails to file a reply to the defendant's counterclaims, the court may enter a default judgement against the offender.

D. Discovery Procedures

After the defendant files an answer to the plaintiff's complaint, the litigation enters a pretrial *discovery* stage. This procedure is designed to allow parties to a civil action to discover all relevant information. The objective is to simplify the issues and to avoid unnecessary arguments and surprises in the subsequent trial. Discovery procedures include requests for depositions, interrogatories, and the ordering of documents and other items of evidence for inspection or copying. *Depositions* are written statements made under oath by witnesses or parties to the action in response to questions from the opposing lawyers. *Interrogatories* are written questions to be answered under oath by the opposite party. The court may also order either party to a civil suit to produce papers, accounts, correspondence, photographs, or other tangible things which are considered to be relevant evidence.

E. Pretrial Conference

Most courts require cases to go to a pretrial conference after the pleadings are completed. At this meeting, the judge and the lawyers attempt to get the parties to settle their dispute without a formal trial or to clarify the pleadings and narrow the issues. If a settlement is not forthcoming, a date for the trial is set.

F. Motion for Judgment on the Pleadings or Summary Judgment

The federal judicial system provides procedural devices which permit a judge to dispose of a civil case without holding a full trial. The state court systems have developed similar devices, although they sometimes differ in name and in the manner of applying them. The Federal Rules of Civil Procedure (FRCP) allow any party in a suit to move for *judgment on the pleadings* for failure of the pleading to state a claim upon which relief can be granted.

● National Bank sues Wilcox, alleging in its complaint that Wilcox failed to donate $10,000 to it. Wilcox hires a lawyer to answer the complaint. Wilcox's lawyer files a motion for judgment on the pleadings. The motion would be accompanied by a *brief* (summary statement of legal point being made) raising the defense that the National Bank failed to state a claim upon which relief can be granted. The brief would present the argument that there is no legal requirement for Wilcox to donate money to the National Bank.

The FRCP also provides for *summary judgment.* The pleading party must show that there is "no genuine issue as to any material fact." Affidavits (sworn written statements of fact) may be used by either party to establish that the matter in controversy does or does not involve a genuine issue as to a material fact.

● Assume in the previous example that the National Bank alleged that Wilcox failed to make a $10,000 installment payment due on a note (signed promise to pay a sum of money to a named person at a specified time). The bank states in its complaint that payment was never received. Wilcox's lawyer files an answer alleging that the payment was in fact made. Attached to the lawyer's answer are the cancelled check, a receipt from the bank for the payment, and a sworn affidavit from Wilcox stating the payment was made. National Bank does not challenge the genuineness of the receipt or cancelled check or offer any other reasons or affidavits supporting its position. A motion for judgment on the pleadings is not proper, since if what the bank alleged were true it would be entitled to relief. However, since no genuine issue as to a material fact exists, Wilcox's lawyer may file a motion for summary judgment. Thus, an expensive and time-consuming trial could be avoided.

A summary judgment is a device for avoiding frivolous trials. The motion is not a substitute for a trial merely because one side's case appears stronger than the other side's case. Also, these procedural rules apply only in civil trials. Defendants in criminal trials are entitled to a jury trial (a day in court) no matter how frivolous their defense may be.

G. Jury Selection

Once it is decided that the judgment of facts and the damages for the wrong are to be determined by a jury, the process of *voire dire* (to speak the truth) begins. In this process, the lawyers for both parties question prospective jurors to determine whether they will be allowed to sit on the jury. Prospective jurors may be rejected if it is found that they are unable to render an impartial judgment owing to prejudice or that they have a relationship of some kind with the disputants or their witnesses. Each party to the dispute is usually given three *peremptory challenges*, that is, challenges for which no cause need be stated. Unlimited *challenges for cause* are allowed each party for reasons affecting the prospective juror's qualifications or fitness to perform.

H. Trial

Upon completion of the pleadings and pretrial conference, the case is ready for trial. A trial by jury is an adversary proceeding in which the judge's role is secondary to that of the jury. Competition between lawyers permits the jury to try and sort out the truth and arrive at a just solution of the dispute.

1. Direct Examination and Cross-Examination. The trial begins when each lawyer makes an opening statement outlining the case and the evidence to be introduced. In this manner, lawyers alert the jury or judge to the testimony to be presented. Evidence and witnesses are then presented to try and prove each of the disputed issues of fact. The examination of witnesses by the lawyers who call them is called *direct examination*. Opposing lawyers have the right to challenge the truthfulness of each piece of evidence presented. In this process of *cross-examination*, the witnesses answer the cross-questions of the opposing lawyer. After each side completes its presentation of evidence and the cross-examination, each lawyer makes a closing statement. In this statement the lawyers emphasize aspects of the testimony and other evidence they believe most meaningful to their arguments.

After all direct examinations and cross-examinations have been completed, either lawyer may make a motion for a *directed verdict*. The lawyer making the motion contends that the facts are so clear that reasonable people could not differ as to the outcome of the case. In directing the verdict, the judge takes the case away from the jury and enters a judgment for the party who made the motion.

2. Charge to Jury. Except when the verdict is directed, the judge instructs the jury as to the rules of law which the jurors are to apply to the facts they have determined. An abbreviated jury instruction is given below. It applies in a case in which negligence resulted in injury and the party injured is seeking to recover money to pay medical expenses.

● "The court instructs the jury that the plaintiff has alleged that she was injured because of the negligence of the defendant and that she, the plaintiff, exercised due care and caution for her own safety. If you find from the evidence that the plaintiff was guilty of contributory negligence which caused the injury, then your verdict will be for the defendant. On the other hand, if you find that the plaintiff was not negligent, your verdict will be for the plaintiff in this case."

3. Verdict and Judgment. After receiving the judge's charge, the members of the jury retire to a private room, where they apply the rules stated by the judge to the facts presented by the witnesses, lawyers, and other evidence. They eventually reach a *verdict* (a finding of fact) as to liability or guilt and damages or penalty. In criminal cases, the accused's guilt must be established "beyond a reasonable doubt"; that is, a doubt that would cause a reasonable person to pause and hesitate to decide on the truth of the matter charged. In civil cases, a preponderance of evidence or clear and convincing evidence is sufficient when weighing contested facts. After the jury announces its verdict, the judge pronounces judgment and awards appropriate remedies to the winning party.

After the verdict has been announced, the aggrieved party may introduce a motion for *judgment notwithstanding the verdict*. This motion requires the judge to rule on whether the jury ignored instructions in reaching its verdict, or having heard the evidence, could not have reasonably reached the verdict it did.

I. Appeal Rights

Either party in a lawsuit may appeal a judgment if it is believed an error was made during the trial that unfavorably influenced the verdict. It must be shown that some material error (not an error in fact-finding) occurred. For example, the aggrieved party may claim that the verdict was excessive or inadequate or not supported by evidence, that evidence that should have been admitted was rejected, that the judge refused to instruct the jury as requested and as it should have been instructed, or that the judge instructed the jury in an incorrect or inappropriate manner.

The party requesting the appeal is called the *appellant,* or petitioner. The party answering the appeal is the *appellee,* or respondent.

Appellate procedures differ from those governing trial courts. A panel of judges examines only the legal issues from the trial, using the transcribed version of what occurred in the trial and the briefs of both sides, which contain their legal arguments. Lawyers for both parties are usually allowed to appear to answer questions asked by the appellate court judges and to argue the merits of the issues presented. All presentations to the appellate court are made without documents, witnesses, or other evidence. The judges listen to the arguments, review the trial records, conduct legal research, vote, and reach a decision. They support their decision with reasons for the ruling. If either party is dissatisfied with the ruling, a final appeal can be made to the court of last appeal, the supreme court of the state or federal system.

J. Enforcement Procedures

In civil cases, a judgment may result in a lien on the loser's property. If the judgment is not paid, the court will order the loser's property to be sold by the sheriff to satisfy the judgment. This order by the court is known as a *writ of execution.* Any excess from the sale must be returned to the loser. Execution may also be issued against any income due the loser, such as wages, salaries, or dividends. This is known as *execution against income,* or *garnishment,* and the proceedings are known as *garnishee proceedings.* By federal law, only a limited percentage of wages or salaries, usually up to 25 percent of a worker's disposable earnings, may be garnished. Checking accounts in a bank are also subject to garnishment.

If the verdict is in favor of the defendant, the court issues a judgment dismissing the complaint.

In criminal courts, the convicted person is given a judgment and sentence by the court according to the law prohibiting the crime. The most common punishments imposed are those related to the principles of correction, rehabilitation, deterrence, and incapacitation. The object of correction and rehabilitation is to encourage prisoners to live normal, useful lives. The object of deterrence and incapacitation, on the other hand, is to discourage persons from attempting to engage in crime or to separate criminals from society and thereby remove the opportunity to commit more crimes.

Understanding Legal Terms

Define, identify, or explain the following terms:

adversary proceedings	circuit courts	directed verdict	plaintiff
appellant	complaint	interrogatory	pleadings
appellee	compromise	jurisdiction	summons
arbitration	counterclaims	litigation	writ of execution
certiorari	default judgment	mediation	*voire dire*
	deposition		

Questions for Review and Discussion

1. What are the key standards of conduct expected of lawyers in their relationships with the public and the legal system?

2. Discuss the circumstances under which an individual is entitled to a trial by jury in federal and state courts.

3. Compare the basic design of state courts with that of federal courts with respect to jurisdiction.

4. Explain the proceedings followed in a small-claims court.

5. Contrast a compromise and the processes of arbitration and mediation in resolving disputes outside of court.

6. Identify the advantages of arbitration as a substitute for litigation.

7. Distinguish between pleadings in a lawsuit and pretrial discovery procedures.

8. What is the purpose of a summary judgment?

9. Contrast the objectives of opening and closing statements in a lawsuit.

10. Explain the function of the appeals process.

Analyzing Cases

1. In Kentucky, landlords are required in certain situations to give tenants 30 days written notice prior to eviction. It appears that in approximately 75 to 79 percent of eviction cases brought before Kentucky magistrates, the tenant defaults; that is, neither the tenant nor an attorney show up. The regular practice of Kentucky magistrates in such cases had been to enter default judgments for the landlords without making any inquiry as to whether the 30-day written notice had actually been given. This meant that since no inquiry would be made as to whether the required 30-day notice had been given, landlords could effectively evict a tenant *without* actually giving it. A group of tenants brought suit arguing that the routine failure of the magistrates to inform tenants that a 30-day written notice was required violated their constitutional rights. Should they win? Why? ● *Branham v. Malone*, 367 F.Supp. 370 (Ky. 1973), *aff'd*. 497 F.2d 923 (6th Cir. 1974)

2. Laufman and his wife applied to the Oakley Building & Loan Co. for a mortgage to purchase a home in a racially integrated area of Cincinnati, Ohio. Oakley denied the mortgage, claiming such factors as the uncertain income of the Laufmans to be the reason. The Laufmans brought suit in district court under Title VIII of the Civil Rights Act of 1968. They alleged that the defendants were "redlining," that is, refusing to lend money or requiring stricter terms because of the racial makeup of the neighbor-

hood in which the home was located. The Laufmans also claimed that the reasons given by Oakley were a sham.

After filing the complaint (but before the trial), the attorney for the plaintiff demanded that Oakley provide computer printouts of data pertaining to its prior history in granting or denying loans. The data requested would show what loans had been applied for, the qualifications of the borrowers, and whether the loans had been granted or denied. When Oakley refused to provide the requested data, the Laufmans asked the court to order it to do so. How should the court rule? If the lawsuit were in a state court, would the ruling necessarily be the same? Why? ● *Laufman v. Oakley Bldg. & Loan Co.*, 72 F.R.D. 116 (S.D. Ohio 1976)

3. Murphy sued Lichtenberg-Robbins Buick in small-claims court in New York for damages done to her automobile. The small-claims court found that the defendant was liable to the plaintiff for damages. On the issue as to how much damage should be found, Murphy introduced an estimate of the cost of repair. The small-claims court allowed it. The defendant claimed that an estimate was not sufficiently reliable as evidence and should not have been allowed to have been introduced. After losing in small-claims court, what further action was available to the defendant? Should the small-claims court have allowed the introduction of the estimate into evidence? Why? ● *Murphy v. Lichtenberg-Robbins Buick*, 424 N.Y.S.2d 809 (1978)

4. Maldonado brought a judicial proceeding in the New York state courts to challenge the action of the New York State Parole Board. He made a motion to have Dana, an inmate law clerk, appointed as his spokesperson or advocate in place of the attorney who had been appointed to represent him. While it was not clear exactly how qualified Dana was, it appeared that his duties were comparable to those of a librarian who assisted individuals in their research while using the prison law library. Should Maldonado's request to replace this court-appointed attorney with Dana be granted? Why? ● *Maldonado v. New York State Bd. of Parole*, 424 N.Y.S.2d 589 (1979)

5. Ross was tried in Massachusetts for the crimes of armed robbery, assault and battery by means of a dangerous weapon, and assault and battery with intent to murder. Ross was a black, whereas the victim was a white uniformed security guard. At the trial Ross requested the judge to ask prospective jurors whether they had racial prejudices that could affect the results. The judge refused to ask any specific questions concerning racial prejudice but did ask questions about impartiality in general. These general questions consisted of inquiries such as whether the prospective jurors believed they could "render a fair and impartial verdict on the evidence in this case." The trial judge explained that he felt no purpose would be accomplished by asking more specific questions. The procedure employed led to the successful challenging of 18 prospective jurors for cause on grounds of prejudice, including one who admitted racial bias. Ross was convicted of all counts, but his challenge to the conviction was eventually heard by the U.S. Supreme Court. Should the Supreme Court uphold Ross's challenge that his constitutional rights were violated by the denial of his request that prospective jurors be questioned specifically about racial prejudice? Why? ● *Ristaino v. Ross*, 424 U.S. 589 (1976)

6. Miller, a former copilot for Eastern Airlines, was insured under a National Fidelity Life Insurance Company disability policy. The policy contained a provision stating that any dispute as to permanent disability must be submitted to medical referees for arbitration. The provision prohibited the beginning of legal proceedings until 60 days after this requirement was met.

Miller, claiming permanent disability under the policy, filed suit in advance of a determination by the arbitrators. He contended that the policy's arbitration clause was so vague, contradictory, and burdensome that he should not be required to arbitrate. An examination of the Georgia statutes regulating business practices in the insurance industry revealed that it had no provision concerning arbitration clauses. Should the federal district court require enforcement of the arbitration clause? Why? ● *Miller v. National Fidelity Life Ins. Co.*, 588 F.2d 185 (5th Cir. 1979)

7. Noia was convicted of murder in the state courts of New York. He was sentenced to life imprisonment, although the judge indicated a strong temptation to impose the death penalty. The conviction rested solely upon a confession which Noia contended was coerced. However, Noia did not at the time appeal the conviction.

Years later, after the allowed time for a direct appeal to a state appellate court had lapsed, Noia was able to convince the courts that his confession should not have been allowed since it was obtained by questionable police conduct. Nevertheless, the New York state courts refused to upset Noia's conviction. The court reasoned that Noia forfeited his state court remedies when he bypassed the appeal procedures that were available at the time he was convicted. Does Noia have any other legal remedies? Explain. ● *Fay v. Noia*, 372 U.S. 391 (1963)

8. Powell was convicted of murder by a California state court. He contended that his conviction was based on an unconstitutional search and seizure. The conviction was affirmed by a California court of appeals, where the unconstitutional search and seizure claim was considered and denied. The Supreme Court of California denied Powell's petition for *habeas corpus* relief. The court found it unnecessary to pass upon the legality of the arrest and search because it con-

cluded that the error, if any, did not affect the reliability of the verdict. Keeping in mind the resolution of the previous *Fay v. Noia* case, does Powell have a federal forum in which to petition for *habeas corpus* relief? Why? ● *Stone v. Powell*, 428 U.S. 465 (1976)

9. The Atomic Energy Commission (AEC) entered into a contract with Peter Kiewit Sons' Company concerning construction of a gaseous diffusion plant. Some of the work was subcontracted to Dressler Gas & Appliance Company.

In the course of performance of the subcontract, a dispute arose as to whether Dressler was required to furnish ductwork for exhaust air in certain lounge rooms. Dressler furnished the disputed ductwork and filed a claim with Kiewit for extra payment.

The subcontract contained a dispute clause which stated that any disputes under the subcontract should be settled, if possible, by negotiation and mutual agreement of the parties and that in the event of their inability to agree, the contractor's authorized representative should reduce the findings to writing and furnish a copy to the subcontractor. According to the dispute clause, the subcontractor was given the right to appeal the finding within 30 days by registered mail addressed to the AEC's manager of Oak Ridge operations, whose decision would be final.

When Kiewit's general manager disallowed the claim, Dressler chose not to appeal to the agreed-upon AEC arbitrator. Instead, Dressler brought suit in common pleas court, which held that the right to petition the court for a redress of wrongs was an inalienable right which cannot be bargained away. Thus the arbitration requirement was found unenforceable.

On appeal to the court of appeals, how should the court rule? Why? ● *Dressler v. Peter Kiewit Sons' Co.*, 144 N.E.2d 269 (Ohio 1957)

Part I

Case Briefs

Youngstown Sheet & Tube Co., et al. v. Sawyer,

343 U.S. 579 (1952)

During the Korean War, the nation's steel companies were unable to reach agreement with their employees concerning the terms and conditions of a new collective bargaining agreement. Efforts by responsible federal authorities to mediate the dispute failed to produce a settlement. Finally the union gave notice of an intent to strike. A few hours before the strike was to begin, the President of the United States issued an executive order authorizing the secretary of commerce to take control of the nation's steel mills. The secretary did so, and issued orders including a directive that the presidents of the seized steel mills serve as managers of the mills for the United States. The steel companies brought suit in federal district court requesting that the seizure be declared invalid. They also requested that preliminary and permanent injunctions be issued restraining enforcement of the executive order. The district court issued the requested preliminary injunction, but its order was stayed by the court of appeals. The U.S. Supreme Court granted a writ of *certiorari* while the case was still pending before the court of appeals.

Petitioner's Position: There was no statutory provision authorizing the President to seize the steel mills. If Congress had wanted the President to have had authority to seize the mills, it could have given such authority to him. The Constitution grants legislative power to Congress, not the President. The action by the President in seizing the mills constituted a violation of the principle of separation of powers and an attempt by the President to exercise legislative, not executive authority.

Respondent's Position: The seizure of the mills was necessary in order to prevent catastrophic consequences during a time when the nation was at war. A strike disrupting steel production for even a brief period would so endanger the nation that the President had "inherent power" to seize the mills. Additionally, presidential power to seize the mills can be implied from the aggregate of the provisions granting presidential power in the Constitution. These include provisions that "the executive Power shall be vested in a President," that "he shall take care that the laws be faithfully executed," and that he "shall be Commander in Chief of the Army and Navy of the United States." If the steel companies suffered injury or damages, the proper procedure for them would be to seek compensation in the Court of Claims.

Legal Issues: (1) Did the President's actions in seizing the steel mills constitute a violation of the doctrine of separation of powers established by the Constitution? (2) Was an equitable remedy (the use of an injunction) proper in this case?

Court Decision: The Supreme Court affirmed the decision of the district court to issue an injunction restraining the President from seizing the mills. The seizure was held to constitute an illegal exercise of Presidential power.

Court Reasoning: (1) Congress had the power to authorize seizure of the steel mills and could have done so if it had wanted to do so. Without a congressional grant of authority, the President's action was an attempt to exercise lawmaking power, which the Constitution vests in Congress alone. (2) An equitable remedy was proper because the companies did not have an adequate remedy at law. There was some doubt as to their legal right to recover damages in the Court of Claims. Moreover, seizure and governmental operation of the steel mills was bound to result in many damages of such a nature as to be difficult, if not incapable, of measurement.

Ex Parte Quirin v. Cox, 317 U.S. 1 (1942)

In 1942, German saboteurs traveled from Germany to the United States in a submarine. They carried large sums of currency and quantities of explosives. The saboteurs had instructions to blow up military and production facilities. They landed and entered the United States wearing civilian clothing, but were apprehended by the Federal Bureau of Investigation. The President established a special military commission to try the agents and set the punishment. He issued an order establishing procedures for review of the commission's determination and provided further that the foreign agents be denied access to the civilian courts. By direction of the attorney general, the FBI turned the captured agents over to the military for trial. While the special military commission was proceeding to dispose of the case, the agents sought review first in federal district court, and then in the U.S. Supreme Court. Oral arguments before the Supreme Court took place in a special summer term called specifically to decide the case.

Petitioner's Position: Congress did not authorize the President to establish special military tribunals to try the accused. Their trial should be before the regular courts. If Congress did authorize the trial before the special military commission, such authorization was unconstitutional as a violation of the constitutional right of the defendants to be tried before the regular civilian courts.

Respondent's Position: The trial before the special military commission was authorized by Congress. Additionally, the President had the right to order such a trial under his powers as Commander in Chief of the Armed Forces. The constitutional right to trial by the civilian courts does not extend to trial for war crimes of this type.

Legal Issue: Was the presidential order establishing a special military commission authorized by Congress or otherwise within the President's powers? Was such action constitutional? Could the foreign agents be denied trial by the regular civilian courts?

Court Decision: The Supreme Court immediately upheld the authority of the special military commission to continue with the trial of the foreign agents and to set the punishment.

Court Reasoning: The Constitution invests the President with the role of Commander in Chief of the nation's armed forces. This means he has the power to wage war which Congress has declared and to carry into effect all laws defining and punishing war crimes. By the Articles of War, the Congress has recognized "military commissions" appointed by military authorities as appropriate tribunals for the trial and punishment of war crimes not tried by ordinary court-martial. Belligerents acting without uniform under the direction of the armed forces of an enemy nation for the purpose of sabotaging the nation's property are guilty of war crimes and, therefore, are within the jurisdiction of special military tribunals. Constitutional guarantees to jury trial and the like do not apply to trial of war crimes of enemy agents.

United States v. Brewster,
408 U.S. 501 (1972)

Brewster, a former Senator, was indicted on charges of soliciting and accepting bribes. The speech or debate clause of the U.S. Constitution states that "For any Speech or Debate in either House [of Congress], they [Senators or Representatives] shall not be questioned in any other Place." The clause was inserted in the Constitution to ensure members of Congress uninhibited debate of vital issues before Congress, free from fear of possible retribution or harassment. The district court granted a pretrial motion to dismiss the indictment against Brewster on the ground that the speech or debate clause shielded him from any prosecution for bribery. That is, the court found the bribery statute unconstitutional as applied to members of Congress. The government appealed to the U.S. Supreme Court.

Petitioner's Position: The government argued that there were no valid constitutional objections to allowing the bribery statute to be applied to members of Congress. To rule otherwise would extend too wide an immunity to members of Congress, immunity beyond what would be needed to prevent harassment.

Defendant's Position: Brewster argued that immunity from prosecution was necessary to prevent possible harassment of members of Congress and to preserve legislative independence. Moreover, misconduct of members of Congress would not necessarily go unpunished because Congress is empowered to discipline and even expel its members.

Legal Issues: Is *any* prosecution of a member or former member of Congress for accepting a bribe unconstitutional as a violation of the speech or debate clause?

Court Decision: The Supreme Court held that the speech or debate clause of the Constitution did not prohibit prosecution of Brewster for bribery.

Court Reasoning: The Court explained that the speech or debate clause must be narrowly interpreted to prohibit only prosecution for actual speech or debate. In this case, Brewster was charged with accepting a bribe, something he did outside of the Congress.

Part 2

Regulation and Consumer Protection

Chapter 4

Lawmaking by Regulatory Agencies

The Constitution of the United States limits the possible abuse of power by government by separating the functions of its three branches. The legislature is appointed the maker of laws, the executive branch the enforcer of laws, and the judiciary the interpreter of laws. The powers given to one cannot be exercised by another. In carrying out its lawmaking mandate, however, the legislature has seen fit to transfer some of its powers to regulate business and personal activity to separate administrative agencies and commissions. These regulatory bodies exercise broad decision-making power and issue *regulations,* rules which interpret and implement the statutes the regulatory bodies are in charge of administering.

4-1. Reason for Regulation

The function of government regulation is basically twofold. Its primary purpose is to correct for market failures such as unfair business practices and *monopoly* (exclusive control of a market by a business). Regulation also has general welfare objectives. In this pursuit, it cuts across industry lines to protect the health and safety of people as workers or as consumers. Examples of regulatory agencies that carry out welfare objectives are the Occupational Safety and Health Administration (OSHA), the Environmental Protection Agency (EPA), and the Consumer Product Safety Commission (CPSC). Government agencies administer welfare and economic regulations by making rules and setting rates; licensing; establishing safety, product, and environmental standards; and requiring information reporting.

The strongest reason for the existence of regulatory agencies is the inability of either legislatures or the courts to act with sufficient speed or expertise on certain problems that private ownership and enterprise create. Regulatory agencies, on the other hand, can usually conduct informal proceedings and enforce their own orders before injury to the public takes place, and they have or can hire technical experts who understand the operations and the problems of a regulated industry. Unlike legislators or court officers, regulators can spend a great deal of their time investigating and remedying problems of one or a few companies. Agencies can also apply national policy to meet local or regional conditions or needs. For instance, while Congress legislates national policy designating unions as the bargaining agents for employees, a regulatory agency can determine when a particular union is the legal representative of employees at a local plant.

4-2. Regulatory Authority

Government has broad authority to regulate particular segments of business and industry and aspects of the individual's general welfare.

A. Federal Regulatory Authority

The federal government's authority to regulate business and industry is contained in the *commerce clause* of the U.S. Constitution. "Congress shall have Power . . . to regulate Commerce with foreign Nations, and among the several States. . . ." In defining this power, the U.S. Supreme Court said that it is a grant of *plenary power* (complete authority) to Congress. The Court added, "It is the power to regulate; that is, to prescribe the rule by which commerce is to be governed."

1. Commerce With Foreign Nations. The power of Congress to regulate commerce with foreign nations is exclusive. It is effective within states in which commerce of the United States with foreign nations is conducted. This federal jurisdiction over imported goods remains in effect until goods are delivered into the possession of local retailers. Any effort on the part of state or local government to regulate foreign commerce would be invalid.

● San Francisco lawmakers passed a city ordinance requiring that all goods sold at retail that had not been produced in the United States or by a Common Market nation be so labeled. This law would be unconstitutional. A state or local law may not distinguish between goods from different sources in such a way as to deny some of the goods equal consideration.

2. Interstate Commerce. The federal power to regulate business activity extends to *interstate commerce,* that is, commerce among the states. In defining this power, the U.S. Supreme Court has ruled that purely *intrastate commerce* (commerce within a state) may be regulated by Congress where the activity, combined with like conduct by others similarly situated, affects commerce among the states or with foreign nations.

● Filburn, who owned a farm in Ohio, raised winter wheat primarily to feed his livestock and poultry, for making flour for home use, and to keep for the next seeding. Under the provisions of the federal Agricultural Adjustment Act, Filburn was given notice of a wheat acreage and yield allotment. The purpose of the act was to control the amount of wheat moving in interstate and foreign commerce in order to avoid surpluses and shortages and consequent high or low wheat prices. Filburn sowed acreage and harvested wheat, however, in excess of his allotment. In a court action, Filburn argued that the secretary of agriculture's marketing quotas amounted to a regulation of production and consumption of wheat. Such activities are, he argued, beyond the reach of congressional authority under the commerce clause, since they are local and their effects upon interstate commerce are at most indirect. The secretary argued that if the act did go beyond the regulation of marketing, it was proper and necessary use of the power of Congress over interstate commerce. The U.S. Supreme Court held that the federal power to regulate under the commerce clause included the power to regulate the prices at which commodities are sold and the practices affecting such prices. Even though Filburn's wheat was not marketed, it supplied a need which would ultimately be reflected by purchases in the open market. Thus wheat grown for home use competes with wheat in commerce. The Court concluded that allowing wheat grown for home use to be unregulated would defeat the act's purpose to stimulate trade at increased prices.

The U.S. Supreme Court has held that there are limits upon the power of Congress to override state sovereignty, even when exercising its otherwise plenary powers to tax or to regulate commerce. For example, Congress may not displace state policies regarding the manner in which they structure the delivery of government services which their citizens require. To do so would hurt the states' ability to function effectively within the federal system. It would interfere with state and local governments' discharge of their dual functions of administering the public law and furnishing public services. To this extent, states as states stand on a quite different footing from an individual or a corporation in respect to the exercise of Congress's power to regulate commerce.

B. State and Local Authority

State and local government authority to regulate stems from their *police powers*. These are inherent powers to regulate where needed for the common good which are recognized by the U.S. Constitution but not delegated.

As defined by the U.S. Supreme Court, the police power is the broad authority of each state to protect the public's health, safety, property, and welfare. It consists of those powers vested in the states through their state constitutions, except those delegated to the United States or reserved by the people. Under these powers, the state governments regulate the conduct of their citizens and the manner in which each uses private property when such regulation is necessary for the public good.

In *Munn v. Illinois,* the U.S. Supreme Court ruled on the question of whether the Illinois assembly had the power, under limitations of state legislative power imposed by the U.S. Constitution, to fix by law the maximum charges for the storage of grain in Chicago and other places in the state. Warehouse owners argued that the state statute requiring a license and fixing the maximum rates violated Congress's constitutional power "to regulate commerce . . . among the several states." They further contended that such state regulation interferred with their right as citizens to pursue a lawful trade or calling as their judgment might dictate. The Court ruled that the warehouses were used as instruments by those engaged in state commerce as well as those engaged in interstate commerce. They were connected incidentally with interstate commerce, but not necessarily so, and hence their regulation was a domestic concern. Until Congress acts in reference to their interstate relations, Illinois may exercise all the powers of government over them, even though in so doing it may indirectly operate upon commerce outside its immediate jurisdiction. Therefore, the state statute in question is not opposed to the Constitution of the United States.

State and federal regulations governing the same areas of commerce may be permitted when compliance with both is reasonably possible. Such dual state or local and federal laws would be held void by the courts under the commerce clause or the supremacy clause, however, if they imposed an undue burden on interstate commerce.

● Arizona passed a law limiting the length of passenger and freight trains entering or leaving that state, as a safety measure. The railroad challenged the constitutionality of the law. The courts would rule that the Arizona law imposed an undue burden on interstate commerce conducted by the railroad. It interfered with the movement of trains through the state as well as with the adequate, economical, and efficient operation of the trains. The need for such a regulation, if any, must be outlined by appropriate federal jurisdiction.

Activities of individuals, even when religiously based, are often subject to regulation by the states in the exercise of their undoubted power to promote health, safety, and general welfare. However, there are fundamental rights and interests, such as the free exercise of religion specifically protected by the First Amendment, that are beyond the power of the government—local, state, or federal—to control.

4-3. Powers of Regulatory Bodies

There is little limitation to the power exercised by federal, state, or local regulatory agencies or commissions, within the areas they administer. Their powers are outlined in the laws that establish them. In most cases, they function as legislator (i.e., they make rules), judge and jury (i.e., they determine guilt or innocence of alleged rule violators), and executive (i.e., they enforce orders).

A. Legislative Power

Although a legislative body cannot delegate its lawmaking powers, it can and does transfer some of its rule-making powers to regulatory agencies. In doing so, legislatures give agencies and commissions the authority to make regulations and rules and to set rates that have the force and effect of law. In order to protect public and private rights, however, the regulations issued by regulatory bodies must comply with policy guidelines issued by the transferring legislature.

B. Judicial Power

Regulatory agencies have the authority to investigate to obtain information needed to make rules and to set rates. They can also carry on investigations to determine if their orders have been carried out. Agencies have the authority to subpoena witnesses, that is, to require witnesses to appear during an investigation, and to require a business to produce records pertaining to an inquiry. Failure to cooperate with an agency investigation can result in criminal penalties. Regulated industries or businesses can also be required to record needed data and to present it in a preferred form at a specified time.

In addition to their fact-finding role, regulatory agencies generally function as both judge and jury in deciding if charges of rule violations filed against a business or person are justified.

C. Executive Power

Most regulatory agencies have the authority to issue *cease and desist orders* (orders to refrain from an unlawful practice) or to seek injunctions from courts to end violations of their orders. Failure to comply is punishable under a contempt of court order by fine, imprisonment, or both. Some agencies are authorized to take immediate action to eliminate a threat to public health or safety. They can seize or require repairs to any property causing a threat. For instance, contaminated food can be taken off the market before an agency hearing or court appeal takes place.

● The commissioner of the Food and Drug Administration published a regulation limiting the presence of toxic chemicals known as PCBs in paper used to package human and animal foods. Natick Paperboard Corp filed objections to the new regulation. The commissioner then announced that until a final decision on the objections was reached, there would be a seizure of any paper food-packaging materials shipped in interstate commerce. The appellants brought action seeking injunctive relief against the announced seizures. The court held that if the Food and Drug Administration has determined there is a threat to public health caused by PCBs in food-packaging materials, it is authorized by statute to seize the materials immediately. Such seizures may not be interrupted by the courts, at least until such time as a district court may decide that the materials are beyond the Food and Drug Administration's jurisdiction.

4-4. Regulatory Personnel

Some *independent federal regulatory agencies* (those that make, interpret, and implement regulations independently) are headed by a single administrator. The administrator is appointed by the President and serves at the President's pleasure. Other regulatory agencies, bureaus, and commissions are multimembered. Their chairpersons and members are presidentially appointed and serve for staggered intervals. These appointees can be removed by the President only for reasons of inefficiency, neglect of duty, or wrong conduct (malfeasance of office). The presidential appointment of the top people in these independent agencies is accomplished with the advice and consent of the Senate. Generally, nominations to federal regulatory commissions must be acceptable to the major industries involved with the agency. The heads of *dependent federal regulatory agencies* (those that are part of one of the three branches of government) are appointed by the President, by Congress, or by the Supreme Court. The top personnel and key staff are appointed or hired for their technical expertise in the area of an agency's authority. Their expertise usually comes through education and experience working in the industry being regulated. Most state and local regulators are appointed by the governor or mayor. A few, such as zoning board members, may be elected by voters.

The supporting staff of each regulatory agency is generally hired through the civil service system, which guarantees lifetime tenure. Included in this category are secretaries, clerks, and many of the technical experts who conduct investigations and advise the top personnel on agency actions. Attorneys are hired to conduct case-related research and to process lawsuits. Law judges, who are experts in the area to be administered, are hired to conduct agency hearings.

4-5. Regulatory Oversight

In establishing independent regulatory agencies, Congress has generally attempted to insulate them from presidential control. However, both Congress and the President—as well as the Justice Department and the courts—have considerable influence over the powers, makeup, and operations of independent regulatory agencies.

A. Congressional Influence

Congress exercises control over regulatory agencies by spelling out the agencies' powers and limitations when they are established. Although some agencies, such as the Interstate Commerce Commission (ICC) and the EPA, have permanent authorization, others, including the Federal Trade Commission (FTC) and Securities and Exchange Commission (SEC), must receive periodic reauthorization. Once an agency has been established, Congress has the responsibility to see that it performs according to the objectives of the statute under which it was created. This includes a review of agency practices in respect to cost and benefit effectiveness, abuses, and possible reforms. Proposed agency budgets are also reviewed and approved by congressional committees. In this process, the purposes for which funds are to be spent are specified.

B. Presidential Influence

The President has some control over independent regulatory agencies through power to nominate and remove agency heads. Approximately sixty agencies, including the EPA and OSHA, are within the executive branch of government. Under the presidential power to appoint and dismiss Cabinet officers, the President has implicit authority and responsibility to direct the actions of these agencies.

C. Public Influence

Regulatory agencies are expected to be responsive to public interest. Several laws give the public access to agency materials and make agency meetings public.

1. Freedom of Information Act. The Freedom of Information Act and its 1974 amendments were designed to provide the public access to agency documents and proceedings upon request. Only a few sensitive categories of records, such as those containing secret national security or foreign policy information, trade secrets, confidential or financial information, and personnel or medical files, are exempt. However, federal district courts are empowered to order agencies to produce properly classified information.

2. Privacy Act. The 1974 Privacy Act was designed to give individuals an opportunity to find out what files the government has concerning them and to challenge, correct, or amend the material. To protect individual privacy, unauthorized persons are prevented from looking at records involving another individual. Exempted from the disclosure provisions are records of the Central Intelligence Agency, those maintained by law enforcement agencies, Secret Service records, and names of persons providing material used for determining the qualifications of persons applying for federal government service.

3. Government in the Sunshine Act. The 1976 Government in the Sunshine Act required that all multiheaded federal agencies conduct their business regularly in public session. The open-door requirements affect regulatory agencies, advisory committees, independent offices, the Postal Service, and most executive branch agencies (except Cabinet departments). Meetings are defined as any gatherings, formal or informal, of agency members, including conference telephone calls. The only exception to openness is for discussion of specific kinds of matters such as court proceedings or personnel problems. District court enforcement and review of the open-meeting requirements are also provided for in the act.

4-6. Regulatory Procedures

All federal agencies follow the procedural rules contained in the 1946 Administrative Procedures Act (APA) which enlarged and amended the Federal Register Act of 1935. This statute is the "bill of rights" for those whose affairs are controlled or regulated by federal agencies. In addition to creating a uniform system for agency procedures. the APA also guarantees due process when settling disputes between parties. That is, the orders, rules, regulations, or rates issued must not be arbitrary, unreasonable, discriminatory, or unrelated to matters properly transferred. The APA does not apply to state or local agencies. Their procedures are outlined in the Model State Administrative Procedures Act of 1944 or in state and local laws.

Federal regulatory agencies can conduct either investigative or adjudicative hearings. When making rules or setting rates, agencies hold *investigative hearings* where interested parties can present evidence. When settling disputes between parties, they hold *adjudicative hearings* in which evidence is obtained to make an informed decision. When an agency holds adjudicative hearings, it acts like a court. Disputing parties present evidence to prove a complaint and answer charges. Investigative hearings do not affect the substantive legal rights of any parties. Such proceedings are more informal than those of a court. See Table 4-1.

A. Investigative Hearings

A quasi-legislative function of federal regulatory agencies involves rate setting and *rule making*. Rules are statements which implement, interpret, or prescribe law or policy or which describe the organization, procedure, or practice requirements of an agency.

The APA requires that rule making by an agency be preceded by general notice of proposed rule making in the *Federal Register*. This is a daily government newspaper containing agency rulings, proposed rules, meeting, and adjudicatory proceedings. Notice must be given at least thirty days before the effective date of the proposed rule. The agency is also required to give interested persons an opportunity to participate in the rule making through written or oral presentation of data, views, or arguments.

The agency decides whether to hold public investigative hearings. A public hearing is not held if the agency determines it is unnecessary or contrary to public interest. Interested parties may submit written data, but not oral evidence

Table 4-1. Agency Proceedings Versus Court Proceedings

Agency Proceedings	Court Proceedings
1. No criminal charges are filed.	1. Criminal or civil charges are filed with appropriate court.
2. General notice of purpose and scope of investigation or hearing is given.	2. Specific notice of reasons for arrest or a complaint is given.
3. Person is not informed of any right before the agency.	3. Accused is informed of all rights.
4. Private counsel may advise but not participate in investigative hearings; private counsel may advise and participate in adjudicative hearings.	4. Accused has right to legal counsel who participates in trial.
5. Evidence obtained in hearings may be used in criminal or civil court proceedings.	5. Unreasonable searches and seizures of evidence are not permitted.
6. There is a limited protection against self-incrimination.	6. Accused has all due process rights.
7. Hearing is before an examiner who is an expert in field being regulated; no jury.	7. Trial is before a judge, with or without a jury.
8. Person has no right to confrontation and cross-examination in investigative hearings; person has right to both in adjudicative hearings.	8. Accused has right to both confrontation and cross-examination.
9. Findings of fact and decisions may be made prior to a hearing.	9. Decisions by court follow the court trial and the determination of guilt or innocence.
10. Agency remedies must be exhausted before a court will hear a case.	10. Trial court decisions may be appealed immediately to a higher court.
11. Penalties other than jail sentences (i.e., cease and desist orders, fines, seizure of property, and loss of license) may be imposed in adjudicative hearings; no punishment other than adverse public opinion is imposed in investigative hearings.	11. Jail sentences, fines, and injunctions may be imposed as criminal and/or civil penalties.

unless the agency permits it. Formal hearings (with trial-type procedure) are not necessary, and cross-examination does not exist. After considering the relevant facts presented by the interested parties, the agency usually issues its rules and states the purpose and legal basis supporting them. The final rule is then published in the *Federal Register*, along with comments received and responses to them. Under the Federal Register Act, a regulation is not enforceable or binding until publication in the *Federal Register* occurs.

B. Adjudicative Hearings

Most federal regulatory agencies have the quasi-judicial power to hear and adjudicate controversies. *Adjudication* is the process of determining an order or final handling of any matter of an agency (other than rule making), including licensing.

1. Complaint. The adjudicative procedure begins with a *complaint*—a statement of the cause of action. The complaint may be filed by the agency, the attorney general of the United States, or a person damaged by an alleged violation. The complaint states the accusations being made, the laws allegedly violated, the legal authority for the investigation, and the time and place of the hearing. Both the complaint and a subpoena are sent to the accused. Upon receiving the complaint, the accused must reply. In the reply, reasons for the alleged violation or defenses are frequently given.

2. Preliminary Investigation. After the accused answers the complaint, the agency investigates the facts of the complaint. Agency experts interview the parties involved in the controversy. When appropriate, on-site inspection of relevant conditions may be conducted. When the preliminary investigation reveals that there are insufficient grounds for the complaint, it is dismissed. When there appears to be a basis for the complaint, a hearing is usually ordered.

3. Hearing. Although agency hearings are similar to court trials, they follow different rules. An *administrative law judge* (ALJ), appointed by the agency, presides over the hearing. The parties involved may submit oral or written evidence, present a defense and rebuttal, and cross-examine witnesses. A jury is not present, since the ALJ is an expert in the matter being regulated by the agency. Evidence normally excluded in ordinary lawsuits may be received in agency hearings. Protection against self-incrimination is also limited. It cannot be employed, for instance, in respect to records which by law must be kept by the parties subject to the investigation.

● National Oil sold gasoline retail in its own service stations, as well as to independently owned service stations. In selling gasoline to its independently owned stations, National Oil gave price-cutting permission in return for a tie-in sales agreement covering other petroleum products. National Oil was prosecuted for making illegal tie-in sales and for unfair methods of competition under the provisions of the Clayton Act. The evidence on which the case was based was obtained from information found in the business records that National Oil had been required to produce. National Oil claimed immunity from prosecution for any matter arising out of its business records on the grounds that the constitutional guarantee against unreasonable search and seizure had been violated. The protection provided against self-incrimination does not apply when an agency obtains information by compulsion and when the records by law must be kept by the person subject to investigation.

The transcript of what is usually a lengthy proceeding, along with all documented evidence filed, constitutes the exclusive record for decision. When the hearing is concluded, the ALJ makes a recommendation with reasons for upholding the complaint and granting remedies requested or dismissing it. Either party may seek an agency appeal. If it is granted, the members of the agency will review the entire hearing proceeding and will make a decision to affirm, modify, or reverse the ALJ's recommendations. Although the time between the conclusion of hearings and the ultimate agency decision may be substantial, any lapse in time does not require that the record be reopened and fact-finding begin anew.

4. Voluntary Settlement. At any point in the hearing proceedings, the agency may accept a compromise settlement in the case and issue a *consent decree*. This is a settlement agreement binding all parties involved in the case. All such consent agreements are for settlement purposes only and do not represent an admission by the alleged offender that they have violated the law.

When issued by the administrative agency on a final basis, however, a consent order carries the force of law with respect to future actions, subject to judicial review. A violation of such an order may result in a fine of up to $10,000 per violation.

C. Judicial Review

Parties dissatisfied with the decision of a regulatory agency can appeal to the courts. Appeals go the federal court of appeals for the circuit in which the agency is located or where the business is headquartered. Only final actions by an agency are subject to review. Preliminary orders and recommendations by an ALJ may not be appealed to the courts, since the agency itself may still modify or revoke them.

Agency members who make the findings are experts in the field being regulated, and court judges usually do not have sufficient special knowledge to reverse them. For these reasons, findings of fact generally are not reviewable unless they conflict with the *substantial evidence rule*. Under this rule, substantial evidence is held to be the complete testimony that a reasonable mind might accept as sufficient to support the conclusion. The courts repeatedly have ruled, however, that well-reasoned expert testimony, based on observation or experience, may in and of itself be substantial evidence when first-hand evidence on the question is unavailable. Legitimate appeal considerations include whether the agency acted outside its scope of authority or acted arbitrarily, capriciously, or otherwise violated the law.

The substantial evidence rule requires courts to accept agency findings and prevents appellate courts from conducting new trials. Consequently, agency decisions are seldom reversed merely because the court itself would have reached a different conclusion based on the facts considered by the agency. Although judicial opinions do not spell out court policy considerations, an analysis of cases does reveal a few additional review generalizations. Where the agency is discharging a regulatory function involving the operation of government, such as the collection of taxes, judicial review is minimal. Where the agency determination involves a technical subject or is primarily legislative in character, the courts are not likely to upset action taken by an agency. And where the legislature expressly intends to make agency findings final, the courts will respect that intention as long as the expression is not an invasion of its lawful authority.

The U.S. Supreme Court has consistently distinguished between regulations that impair civil rights and liberties guaranteed by the U.S. Constitution and regulations that merely regulate business and the economy. Thus the federal courts will rarely strike down a regulation as unconstitutional if the regulation is economic in nature. End-of-chapter case *New Orleans v. Dukes* (item 6 under "Analyzing Cases") illustrates this judicial pattern. It should also be noted that rulings in cases heard in judicial review in a regular court become part of the body of regulatory law and part of case law or precedent used to decide other similar cases in that field.

Understanding Legal Terms

Define, identify, or explain the following terms:

adjudication	commerce clause	intrastate commerce	Privacy Act
adjudicative hearings	complaint	investigative hearing	regulation
Administrative Procedures Act	consent decree	plenary power	rule making
cease and desist order	*Federal Register*	police powers	substantial evidence
	interstate commerce		subpoena

Questions for Review and Discussion

1. Discuss three reasons why regulation is relied upon to deal with some problems that private ownership and enterprise create.

2. Explain the conditions under which intrastate activity may be regulated by Congress under the commerce clause of the U.S. Constitution.

3. Contrast the source of state and local government authority to regulate with the source of federal authority to regulate.

4. What factor limits the power exercised by federal, state, and local regulatory bodies?

5. How does the U.S. Supreme Court hold with respect to government regulation of business when state and federal regulations govern the same areas of commerce?

6. Contrast the separation of powers between branches of state and federal governments with the consolidation of powers within the major regulatory agencies.

7. Explain the provisions and requirements of (*a*) the Freedom of Information Act, (*b*) the Privacy Act, and (*c*) the Government in the Sunshine Act.

8. Differentiate between investigative and adjudicative hearings conducted by federal regulatory agencies.

9. How does a legal proceeding conducted by a federal regulatory agency differ from one conducted in a court of law?

10. How does the substantial evidence rule affect court review of agency cases?

Analyzing Cases

1. The Federal Power Act grants the Federal Power Commission (FPC) jurisdiction over the transmission of energy if the energy is "transmitted from a state and consumed at any point outside thereof." The FPC deter-mined that the Florida Power & Light Co. (FP&L) generated energy transmitted in a manner that would subject that company to its jurisdiction.

None of the FP&L lines directly connect

with those of out-of-state companies. FP&L is, however, connected with other Florida utilities, which in turn are connected with out-of-state utilities. The FPC found numerous instances in which transfers of power between FP&L and another Florida utility coincided with transfers of power between other Florida utilities and the state of Georgia.

The FPC concluded that when FP&L supplied power to another Florida utility which in turn supplied power to Georgia, the power from various sources was commingled (combined) and at least some of FP&L's power went to Georgia. This conclusion rested on testimony before the FPC of expert witnesses and upon the technical judgment of the FPC members.

Claiming that its energy transmissions were entirely intrastate, the FP&L filed suit asking the court to deny the FPC jurisdiction over the company. The matter was appealed to the U.S. Supreme Court. Given the fact that the FPC's claim of jurisdiction was supported by expert testimony, how is the U.S. Supreme court likely to resolve the issue? Why? ● *Federal Power Comm'n v. Florida Power & Light Co.*, 404 U.S. 453 (1972)

2. Perales filed a claim for disability benefits under the Social Security Act after suffering an injury to his back. A hearing was held before the Bureau of Disability Insurance of the Social Security Adminstration (SSA) to determine whether Perales was entitled to receive benefits. At the hearing both Perales and a physician testified that he was disabled. Other evidence was also introduced to support this conclusion. The SSA introduced written reports from four physicians who had examined Perales on its behalf. These physicians were not called to testify. Additional testimony was received from a fifth physician, paid by the government, who had never examined Perales. This doctor reviewed the evidence and offered an evaluation.

Perales' attorney objected to the introduction of the written reports of the SSA physicians because there was no opportunity to cross-examine. The attorney also objected to the testimony of the fifth physician because the physician had not examined Perales personally. His testimony was hearsay.

Should the U.S. Supreme Court hold the hearsay evidence admissible? If so, does the evidence represent substantial evidence in support of the SSA's decision to deny Perales' claim? Why? ● *Richardson v. Perales*, 402 U.S. 389 (1971)

3. The Fair Labor Standards Act (FLSA) requires certain employers, among other things, to pay their nonmanagerial and nonprofessional employees a specified minimum hourly wage. It also requires them to pay such employees at $1\frac{1}{2}$ times their regular hourly rate for hours worked in excess of forty hours during a work week. The provisions of the original act excluded states and their political subdivisions from coverage. Subsequent amendments extended the minimum wage provisions and provisions regarding overtime pay to almost all public employees employed by the states and their subdivisions. Exemptions were for the most part restricted to executive, administrative, and professional personnel. A limited exemption was inserted regarding high government officials, such as elected officials.

How should the U.S. Supreme Court hold on Congress's authority to broaden the coverage of the FLSA to apply directly to the states and subdivisions of states as employers? Why? ● *National League of Cities v. Usery*, 426 U.S. 833 (1976)

4. Ruenkamol had been employed in the Stifel household as a live-in domestic servant for a period of three years. During that time, Ruenkamol received less than the minimum wage required by the 1974 FLSA amendments. Ruenkamol brought suit against the employer, seeking the unpaid required amount as well as damages for violation of the act. The Stifels defended on the ground that the 1974 amendments, which extended

the minimum wage and hour provisions of the FLSA to household domestic employees, exceeded Congress's power to legislative under the commerce clause. They argued that their activity in employing a domestic servant was an intrastate or local activity and that domestic employees have no "substantial effect" upon interstate commerce. Is the question of whether the employment of Ruenkamol had a substantial effect on interstate commerce relevant? How should the court dispose of this case? Why? ● *Ruenkamol v. Stifel*, 463 F.Supp. 649 (D.N.J. 1978)

5. Wisconsin's compulsory-attendance law requires parents to send their children to public or private school until they are sixteen years of age. Yoder and Miller are members of the Amish Church. Their children aged fourteen and fifteen were not enrolled in any public or private school. On complaint of the school district administrator for the public schools, the parents were charged, tried, and convicted and fined.

The parents challenged the constitutionality of the compulsory-attendance law. They argued that it violated their rights to the free exercise of religion as guaranteed by the First and Fourteenth Amendments. The state of Wisconsin argued that the compulsory-attendance law was within the police power of the state.

Should the U.S. Supreme Court find the application of the compulsory-attendance law to the Amish to be within the police power of the state of Wisconsin? Why? ● *Wisconsin v. Yoder*, 406 U.S. 205 (1972)

6. New Orleans passed a municipal ordinance which forbade vendors from selling foodstuff from pushcarts in the Vieux Carré (French Quarter of the city). The ordinance contained a "grandfather clause" which allowed vendors who had operated for eight years or more prior to passage of the ordinance to continue in operation. In practice,

there were two vendors who qualified under this exception, having operated in the area for twenty or more years.

Dukes had conducted business in the Vieux Carré for only two years when the ordinance was passed and was barred from continuing her pushcart business there. She argued that the action of the grandfather clause in granting exceptions to some vendors and not others was a denial of the Fourteenth Amendment's guarantee of equal protection under the law. On an appeal to the U.S. Supreme Court, should Dukes' argument be accepted? Is there a fundamental difference between this case and *Wisconsin v. Yoder?* Why? ● *New Orleans v. Dukes*, 427 U.S. 297 (1976)

7. In 1972 the Atomic Energy Commission (AEC) initiated rule-making proceedings for the specific purpose of deciding what consideration in general would be given to the toxic waste disposal problem in future licensing proceedings. Hearings were scheduled and held. Interested persons were given the opportunity to testify or submit written statements. Certain private parties, who were opponents of the proposed rules, were not given an opportunity to cross-examine the witnesses who testified at the hearings. Rules were adopted which mandated application of a specific cost-benefit analysis to deal with the problem of nuclear wastes in future licensing proceedings.

In adopting the rules, the AEC fully complied with all relevant provisions of the Administrative Procedure Act. However, certain parties argued that the denial of the right to cross-examine witnesses deprived them of the right to participate meaningfully in the hearings. They argued that their right to due process of law as guaranteed by the U.S. Constitution was violated. Having granted an appeal, how should the U.S. Supreme Court hold? ● *Vt. Yankee Nuclear Power v. Natural Resources Defense Council, Inc.*, 435 U.S. 519 (1978)

Chapter 5   Regulation of Business and the Economy

As discussed in Chapter 4, government at the local, state, and federal levels relies upon administrative agencies to regulate major segments of business and the economy. Local administrative agencies regulate such key activities as zoning, enforcement of health and safety ordinances, and consumer protection within a local area. State agencies typically regulate or supervise motor vehicle registration, public utilities, insurance companies, and worker's compensation —that is, the money paid to injured workers. However, in the past decades, it has been at the federal level where administrative regulation of business has increased the greatest and become the most pronounced, despite some recent measures aimed at deregulation. In fact, in the past decade seven new federal agencies, including the EPA, CPSC, and OSHA, were authorized by legislation. At this writing there were over ninety different administrative agencies at the federal level alone. This chapter discusses the activities of certain major federal agencies in regulating the key areas of commerce, communications, taxation, securities and finance, restraint of trade, energy, and environmental protection. Although their authority varies widely, these agencies typify the role played by the federal government in regulating many facets of business and the economy today.

5-1. Commerce Regulation

Subject to the commerce clause of the U.S. Constitution, transportation regulations and taxes are imposed by government on those who benefit from interstate commerce.

A. Interstate Commerce Commission

The Interstate Commerce Commission has administrative authority over the Interstate Commerce Act, as frequently amended and codified by Congress. The primary function of this independent regulatory body is to regulate surface and water transportation. Under the ICC's jurisdiction are interstate railroads, motor carriers, and freight forwarders.

1. Authority. Carriers are required to file a list of rates and charges for specific services with the ICC. Although the commission does not set the rates a carrier may charge, it can order them canceled following an investigation and hearing, if they are challenged. Before entering an interstate transportation business, a carrier must obtain operating authority from the ICC. Before granting such authority, the ICC considers the need for the new service, the carrier's ability to perform adequately and to make a profit, and the operations of other carriers providing the same services. In the case of trucking, an application must be supported by one or more shippers who state that the new service is needed and that they will use it. Either temporary or permanent authority may be granted. Carriers must demonstrate a compelling reason for dropping service before ICC permission to do so is given. A railroad must issue a notice of intent to the public before it files a rail line abandonment application with the ICC. If significant opposition to the abandonment attempt develops, formal proceedings are conducted, following which the ICC may deny the abandonment or issue an initial decision permitting it. Before an effective date of abandonment is set, however, time is provided to allow a community or state agency or group of business interests to make an offer to subsidize or purchase the line.

2. Proceedings and Enforcement. Disputes are processed by the ICC either informally or formally with a hearing and oral arguments before an administrative law judge. Upon completion of formal hearings and arguments, the law judge may issue a report which becomes the final order of the ICC if objections or exceptions are not filed by the disputing parties. Decisions may be appealed to the full commission and through the federal courts, starting with the U.S. court of appeals. The courts may enforce the ICC's order, return it to the commission for further consideration, make changes in the order, or set it aside entirely. Either side may appeal the court's decision to the U.S. Supreme Court. Failure to comply with an ICC order usually results in a court order enforcing it. Further failure to comply may result in a fine or jail sentence.

B. Regulation Through Taxation

Taxation is another form of regulation. Congress can influence business operations by putting high taxes on some activities and low taxes on others. For example, Congress puts a lower tax on profits made from oil exploration than on the profits of manufacturers in order to encourage investors to put money into oil exploration. The taxing power is also used to regulate other activities, such as the public's use of gasoline, tobacco, and alcohol.

1. Federal Taxing Authority. Constitutional provisions pertaining to federal taxing power are found in Article I, Section 7: "All bills for raising Revenue shall originate in the House of Representatives . . ." and in Section 8: "The Congress shall have the Power to lay and collect Taxes, Duties, Imposts and Excises, to pay the Debts . . . and general Welfare of the United States; but all . . . shall be uniform throughout the United States."

Much of the federal revenue results from the income tax on individuals and corporations. The power to levy this tax is found in the Sixteenth Amendment to the Constitution: "The Congress shall have power to lay and collect taxes on incomes, from whatever source derived, without apportionment among the several states, and without regard to any census or enumeration." The laws governing the federal income tax are found in the Internal Revenue Code, which is enforced by the Internal Revenue Service, a division of the Treasury Department. Taxpayers' returns are subject to three levels of review and appeal: the initial audit is made by a revenue agent; the findings of the agent may be reviewed by the IRS District Conference, Appellate Division; and those findings may be appealed in a federal district court.

2. State and Local Taxing Limitations. State and local governments lay taxes to the extent permitted by the U.S. Constitution and by state constitutions. Some state taxing power stems from the Tenth Amendment: "The powers not delegated to the United States by the Constitution, nor prohibited by it to the States, are reserved to the States respectively, or to the people." Article I, Section 10, however, limits state taxing power: "No state shall, without the consent of Congress, lay any Imposts or Duties on Imports or Exports, except what may be absolutely necessary for executing its inspection laws. . . . " In addition, property, sales, or income taxes levied by state and local government are limited by the commerce clause. For example, a state may not tax a person passing through or remaining there temporarily, and it may not tax a person for the privilege of engaging in interstate commerce. Moreover, states may not levy a tax which subjects interstate commerce to multiple taxation or which discriminates against interstate commerce in favor of local interests.

● Several states, joined by the Federal Energy Regulation Commission, challenged a Louisiana tax on the "first use" of gas brought into Louisiana which was not previously subjected to taxation by another state or the United States. The tax was imposed on pipeline companies for natural gas taken from the outer continental shelf, which for the most part was eventually sold to out-of-state customers. The statute provided exemptions from and credits for the tax so that Louisiana consumers were not burdened by the tax, but it applied to gas moving out of the state. The stated purpose of the tax was to reimburse Louisiana for damages to the state's coastal areas resulting from the piping of the gas to processing plants in Louisiana. Costs were also incurred by the state in protecting these resources. The states affected by the tax argued that it was unconstitutional under the commerce clause. They sought injunctive relief as well as a refund of taxes already collected.

The U.S. Supreme Court held that the Louisiana first-use tax violated the supremacy clause and that it is unconstitutional under the commerce clause. The Court explained that no state, consistent with the commerce clause, may impose a tax which discriminates against interstate commerce by providing a direct commercial advantage to local business.

Case law has established that a state tax is not *per se* (in or by itself) invalid because it burdens interstate commerce, since interstate commerce may constitutionally be made to pay its way. The state's right to tax interstate is limited, however, as indicated in the above example. Moreover, no state tax may be sustained unless it can be shown that the business taxed directly benefits from some local activities, such as fire and police protection and facilities such as roads. This linkage with the taxing state is known as *nexus*.

● Coast Industries, Inc., a South Carolina company, produces modular office panel systems for use in new and remodeled office areas. It sells and ships to customers in Ohio but does not maintain an office or regular sales force in the state. Ohio residents sell the panels, and they are paid commissions on the sales. Coast Industries objects to the Ohio requirement that a tax be paid on the modular panels purchased in Ohio. The state of Ohio argues that the tax revenue is used to build and to maintain roads which Coast Industries' carriers use. The court should rule that nexus exists, since Coast Industries derives benefit from Ohio's roads. Thus, a levy of a fair tax on panel systems purchased in Ohio would be permitted.

Another limiting factor in a state's right to tax businesses engaged in interstate commerce is *apportionment*. This is the practice of dividing and distributing the tax burden of an interstate business among states entitled to tax it. In this manner, a business operating in two or more states is not subject to the burdens of multiple taxation. Apportionment formulas are used to avoid violations of the commerce clause. Furthermore, a tax on interstate commerce must be fairly related to the services provided by the state. For example, in the case of Louisiana's first-use tax on gas, 75 percent of the proceeds of the tax were used to service the state's general debt, while only 25 percent was directed to alleviate the alleged environmental damage caused by the pipeline activity.

5-2. Communications Regulation

The Federal Communications Commission exercises its regulatory authority under the Communications Act of 1934 and its amendments and the Communications Satellite Act of 1962. The latter created the Communications Satellite Corp. The FCC regulates national and international communications by radio, television, wire, cable, and satellite. The commission licenses all broadcasters and exercises control over telephone and telegraph rates and charges. It also exercises control over citizen band and amateur (ham) radio equipment and practices, police and fire department communications, and cable and pay television.

A. Radio and Television Broadcasting

All privately owned as well as public and educational broadcasting stations are licensed by the FCC and subject to its regulation. Licenses are issued for three-year periods. When a license renewal is sought, the FCC reviews the applicant station's performance. The station must have operated in the public interest and in accord with the provisions of the regulatory statutes. Misconduct or serious public complaints against a station may result in a fine, short-term license renewal, or a revoked license.

● RKO General held broadcast licenses for its stations in Boston, New York, and Los Angeles. RKO's owner, General Tire, had pressured some companies that wanted to do business with it to advertise on RKO stations. The matter was settled in a consent decree with the Justice Department. Later there was a matter of some questionable payments by General Tire both overseas and at home. Again General Tire reached a settlement, this time with the Securities and Exchange Commission. The Federal Communications Commission decided by a vote of four to three that RKO General no longer qualified to hold its broadcast licenses. The FCC ruled that the nature and scope of its misconduct were so extensive and serious that RKO no longer served the public interest.

To avoid concentration of control, the FCC limits any individual or company to ownership of no more than seven AM radio, seven FM radio, and seven television stations. No one company or owner may operate two commercial stations of the same type covering the same service area.

● The *Inquirer,* a regional newspaper, applied for a federal license to build a radio broadcasting station. The request was opposed by a licensed station that had operated in the area for several years. The licensed station showed that it had operated at a loss and that an additional station would only add to its economic injury. The FCC would rule that economic injury to a competitor is not sufficient ground for refusing a broadcasting license. In short, the *Inquirer* would be granted a federal license if there was an available frequency over which it could broadcast without interference with others and if it could demonstrate competency, adequacy of equipment, and financial ability to make good use of the assigned frequency.

B. Cable Television

Cable system operators are required to obtain a *certificate of compliance* from the FCC. This is an indication that the operator is in accord with commission rules, and it lists the broadcast signals the system is permitted to carry. Cable systems are not allowed to carry sports broadcasts from distant stations if these broadcasts are blacked out for local, noncable stations. In a recent federal appeals court ruling, however, restrictions on the use of distant signals and syndicated programs were removed. Under the court's deregulation move, cable systems are permitted to carry more distant-signal programs and to show syndicated programs that local, noncable stations had exclusive rights to broadcast in the past.

The FCC shares the regulation of cable systems with state and local agencies. For the most part, the FCC regulates signal carriage, pay cable, and technical quality. Local agencies generally regulate franchising, subscriber rates, theft of service, taxation, and pole attachments.

C. Low-Power Television

In a major 1982 ruling, the FCC authorized the licensing of 3,000 to 4,000 new low-power television stations that have a broadcasting range of 10 to 15 miles but are relatively inexpensive to establish. As a result of the affordable cost, thousands of minority firms, nonprofit organizations, small businesses, religious groups, and even individuals are expected to apply for licenses to operate these stations. These low-power stations can be linked by satellite, and therefore can create competition for major networks and for programming sold to cable television stations. Thus it may be possible for these stations to attract national advertising. To further encourage ownership of these stations, it is expected that low-power television will be subject to fewer governmental restrictions and regulations than other broadcasting stations.

5-3. Securities and Finance Regulation

Congress enacted the Securities Exchange Act of 1934 and created the Security Exchange Commission to prevent unfair practices and to ensure fairness in securities transactions. The Federal Reserve System was established under authority of the Federal Reserve Act of 1913 as amended.

A. Securities and Exchange Commission

The SEC regulates all aspects of the sale of securities and the operation of securities exchanges. It requires a registration statement of facts concerning a business and the securities it proposes to sell and list on national security exchanges. These statements include a description of the registrant's properties and business, a description of the securities to be offered for sale, and financial statements certified by independent public accountants.

● The SEC censured Arthur Anderson & Co. for failing to detect major irregularities in the financial statements of Mattel, Inc., which had significantly overstated earnings and understated losses. Although the SEC did not seek sanctions against any of the accounting firm's personnel or mandate any payments or reimbursements as part of its ruling, several top Mattel officials were convicted of criminal charges.

Companies whose securities are registered with the SEC must also file an annual report and other periodic reports. The data in these reports is available to the public at the offices of the SEC and the exchanges. There are penalties for filing false reports as well as provisions for recovery by investors who suffer losses in the purchase or sale of registered securities due to incorrect information in the reports. Another reporting provision governs proxy requests from holders of registered securities. A *proxy* is a written permission from a shareholder in a company allowing another person to vote the shareholder's stock in the election of directors or for the transaction of any company business.

All national securities exchanges and stockbrokers must register with the SEC and agree to comply with governmental regulations and adopt rules to protect investors and to ensure fair dealing. Both brokers and exchanges are subject to a number of trading rules established by the SEC, including rule 10(b)(5). This broad rule prohibits any manipulative or deceptive act in violation of any rule the SEC may establish. The publication of misleading information about a company to encourage investors to buy its stock and buying stock without stating that the purpose of the purchase was for company control are examples of rule 10(b)(5) violations. The SEC also supervises the activities of mutual funds and other investment companies and advises federal courts in corporate reorganization proceedings under Chapter 11 of the Bankruptcy Reform Act of 1978.

SEC investigations are essentially fact-finding inquiries to determine whether there is *prima facie* evidence of a law violation (i.e., evidence that is legally sufficient to establish a case unless disproved) and whether an action should be commenced. If the facts show possible fraud or other law violation, the SEC may seek a civil injunction from an appropriate U.S. district court. It may also refer the facts to the Department of Justice with the recommendation for criminal prosecution of the offender(s). The commission may suspend or expel members from exchanges, deny or revoke registrations of broker-dealers, and censure or bar individuals from employment with a registered firm for misconduct.

B. Federal Reserve System

The Federal Reserve System (Fed) is the nation's central bank. It is charged with making and administering policy for the nation's credit and monetary affairs. It regulates banking in general, including state-chartered banks that are members of the system. Its authority is established by the Federal Reserve Act and Banking Acts as amended.

The Fed's board of governors, known as the Federal Reserve Board (FRB), has authority to examine the activities of the twelve federal reserve banks in the system. It controls the amount of currency in circulation. Also controlled by the board are the issuance and distribution of federal reserve notes (paper money and coin) and the rate of interest charged for borrowing that federal reserve banks charge member banks. Other responsibilities of the FRB include:

○ Setting interest ceilings on member banks' time and savings deposits to influence the level of economic activity.
○ Regulating the issuance of credit cards by state member banks.
○ Authorizing the removal from office of bank officers and directors who violate the law, engage in unsafe and unsound practices, or conduct insider loans and arrangements.

The FRB also has enforcement responsibilities for consumer legislation. Legislation in this category, such as the Equal Credit Opportunity Act, the Fair Credit Billing Act, and the Truth-in-Lending Act, is discussed in Chapter 6.

5-4. Restraint of Trade Regulation

Both the federal government and the states have antitrust laws to preserve the values of competition and to discourage *monopoly*—the exclusive control of a market by a business enterprise. At the federal level, both the Antitrust Division of the Justice Department (ADJD) and the Federal Trade Commission administer the antitrust statutes. The Justice Department is the law enforcement arm of the executive branch, and the FTC is an independent regulatory commission, but their antitrust roles are quite similar.

The ADJD is responsible for enforcing the Sherman Antitrust Act and the Clayton Act, two of the principal antitrust statutes. It has exclusive power to bring criminal prosecutions. It also acts to prohibit anticompetitive mergers and collusive practices. The FTC's power springs from the Federal Trade Commission Act and the Wheeler-Lea Act. These statutes prohibit "unfair methods of competition in commerce, and unfair or deceptive acts or practices in commerce." The courts have interpreted Section 5 of the Federal Trade Commission Act to include all offenses proscribed by the other antitrust laws, giving the FTC equal civil jurisdiction with the ADJD.

The agency to first propose a particular investigation is usually given jurisdiction, provided there is no conflict with the other's ongoing work. While the ADJD must proceed on a case-by-case basis, the FTC has the power to issue trade regulations with the force of law. In effect, the commission proclaims codes of commercial conduct. On request, the FTC issues *advisory opinions* (advice as to legality of a specific course of action) that apply to a practice that a business is considering. It also prepares *industry guides* that explain provisions of laws administered by the FTC. The bulk of the FTC's regulatory activities, however, are adjudicative proceedings to resolve complaints that allege a business is engaging in anticompetitive or anticonsumer activities.

A. Sherman Antitrust Act

Referred to as the Sherman Act, this antitrust law prohibits contracts, combinations, and conspiracies in restraint of trade. It also prohibits monopolization, attempts to monopolize, and combinations or conspiracies to monopolize any part of the trade or commerce among the states or with foreign nations.

Violations of the Sherman Act must involve at least two persons acting together. The restraint involved must affect interstate trade or commerce. And, only those trade restraints which are unreasonable are prohibited. To be unreasonable, the restraint must be a per se violation or outweigh the legitimate commercial purpose of the restraint.

1. Rule-of-Reason Analysis. The common-law *rule-of-reason* approach is a process by which the court determines whether a restraint of trade agreement merely regulates and perhaps promotes competition or suppresses and even destroys competition. To determine that question, the court considers such facts as the history of the restraint, the harm believed to exist, the reason for adopting the agreement, and the purpose to be attained.

● Westman Commission Company hoped to become a one-stop shopping center for institutional and restaurant customers in the Denver area. To accomplish its goal, it was necessary to obtain a formal dealer sales arrangement with Hobart Corporation, the leading manufacturer of commercial kitchen equipment. Hobart sold nationwide through some 540 independent dealers. The process of becoming a Hobart dealer began with a recommendation by the district manager, whose approval was essential. Nobel was another one-stop shopping center for restaurant equipment and supplies and a Hobart dealer. At one point, an executive of Nobel suggested to the Hobart district manager that it might be "smart" for Hobart to do business with only a select group of dealers in the Denver area. The manager gave assurance that Hobart would not appoint Westman as a dealer and subsequently recommended to Hobart management that the Westman request for a formal dealership be rejected. Westman sued Hobart for restraint of trade, arguing that the refusal to deal was unreasonable and therefore illegal. The federal court found that Hobart had conspired with Nobel to keep Westman from competing. Westman was entitled to triple the damages it could show to have resulted from Hobart's refusal to deal with it.

2. Per Se Violations. Any agreement is a per se violation when by its very nature it is so contrary to antitrust policy that harm is presumed. Reasonable or not, high or low, price fixing is inherently unreasonable and a per se violation. *Group boycotts* are held by the courts to be per se anticompetitive activity. They are agreements among competitors to refrain from competition in prices, territories, customers, or products. *Secondary boycotts* may also give rise to a per se violation. This form of unfair labor practice is often linked to an agreement by which a union and company agree that union members will not handle goods which are not made by union members. Other per se violations include resale price maintenance, reciprocal dealing, and dropping a discounting customer at the request of other customers.

The courts have ruled that it is just as illegal to fix the price of professional or repair services as it is to fix the price of goods in trade or commerce. It is unlawful per se for a manufacturer to limit its wholesalers' rights to sell goods purchased from the manufacturer. And all territorial allocations among distributors are unlawful, even if they might foster competition against others. As a result, territorial restriction problems often arise when manufacturers attempt to improve their channels of distribution by licensing distributors of their products in exclusive areas. Similar problems arise when manufacturers are tempted to control the resale price at which their products are sold in retail outlets. Such schemes are *vertical restraints* when the arrangements are between one company and another in its production, supply, or marketing chain. They are known as *horizontal restraints* when the supplier artificially restricts output and imposes noncompetitive prices on independent owners whose prices otherwise might be competitive.

● Ten manufacturers of bathroom fixtures (in control of about 80 percent of the manufacture and distribution of these products in the United States) entered into an agreement to fix and maintain uniform prices—just low enough to discourage competition. Thus, consumers paid more than they would have paid had prices been fixed by competition. The manufacturers argued that they did not have a complete monopoly and that their prices were reasonable. Their agreement would be held a horizontal restraint under the Sherman Antitrust Act.

3. Punishment and Remedies. Persons or companies found guilty of violating the antitrust provisions of the Sherman Act are liable to heavy fines, up to one year of imprisonment, or both. The statute also provides for an injunction to end unlawful practices, termination of offending company operations, and the shedding of assets acquired through illegal practices. Anyone injured by a violation can begin a private suit. Courtroom success is rewarded with triple money damages plus attorney's fees. The U.S. Supreme Court has also approved changes in the procedural rules governing class actions. The ruling makes it easier for large classes of people or groups to pool common claims and seek relief through coordinated efforts of their attorneys.

B. Post–Sherman Antitrust Legislation

Three principal antitrust statutes made the Sherman Act more specific and effective. The Clayton Act of 1914, the Federal Trade Commission Act of 1914, and the Robinson-Patman Act of 1936 sought to prevent practices that tended to reduce competition or that favored the creation of monopolites.

1. Clayton Act. Congress passed the Clayton Act to police business practices and methods of competition closely. The statute made *tying agreements* unlawful per se. These are any arrangements whereby one party refuses to sell a given product except on condition that the buyer also purchase a different (or tied) product. The appropriate issue in a tie-in case is the effect of the tie-in on the competitors of the seller.

● A radio and television tube manufacturer distributed tubes throughout the country and licensed other manufacturers to use its patented circuits, but specified that the latter must buy their tubes exclusively. If the patented circuits would not operate with tubes furnished by other competitors, the restriction would be lawful. If, on the other hand, tubes furnished by other competitors could be used, the restriction would be ruled an unlawful tying agreement and a violation of the Clayton Act.

Section 7 of the Clayton Act governs mergers that eliminate substantial potential competition in any section of the country or in any line of commerce. The term *merger* means the acquisition of one company by another by any means, including the purchase of that company's stock or assets.

2. Federal Trade Commission Act. In addition to establishing the Federal Trade Commission, the Federal Trade Commission Act as amended declared, "Unfair methods of competition in or affecting commerce, and unfair or deceptive acts or practices in or affecting commerce are hereby declared unlawful." The act did not define an unfair method of competition; instead, it allowed the courts to determine unfair practices on an individual basis. The act was amended by the Wheeler-Lea Act and amendments in 1938 and 1975. This legislation authorizes the FTC to act against unfair or deceptive acts without first proving the existence of anticompetitive behavior. Authority was gained to challenge false advertising of food, drugs, and cosmetics, whether the advertiser knows or does not know an advertisement is false.

3. Robinson-Patman Act. The Robinson-Patman Act deals with product pricing and advertising and promotional allowances. It specifically prohibits a seller from charging different prices to different customers for the same product, where such differential might injure competition. Nothing in the law is intended to prevent price differentials due to cost of manufacture, sale, delivery, or bulk purchases. Persons engaged in selling are not prevented from selecting their own customers in bona fide transactions which are not in restraint of trade. Also permitted are price changes in response to changing conditions affecting the market or the marketability of goods. For example, price changes are allowed to reflect the deterioration of perishable goods and the obsolescence of seasonal goods. The courts have held, however, that for price discrimination to exist, there have to be two separate sales at different prices.

● Security Tire & Rubber Company bought tires from Gates Rubber Company under a supply contract which provided that Security was to purchase 80 percent of its tire requirements from Gates. Gates also transferred tires to National Tires, Inc., a wholly owned subsidiary, at prices lower than those it charged to Security. Security considered National a competitor and eventually sued Gates for price discrimination under the Robinson-Patman Act. A federal district court awarded Security treble damages but the court of appeals reversed the finding. The court explained that a transfer from a parent corporation to its wholly owned subsidiary corporation can never be considered a separate sale in a Robinson-Patman suit. Such transfers between parent and subsidiary are transactions within the same economic unit, i.e., intracompany transfers of goods rather than discriminatory sales to a favored customer.

5-5. Energy Regulation

The Federal Energy Regulatory Commission is an independent agency created by the Department of Energy Organization Act of 1977. It operates within, but separate from, the Department of Energy (DOE). The DOE secretary may recommend issues for the commission's consideration, but exercises no control over FERC decisions.

A. Federal Energy Regulatory Commission

The FERC is responsible for regulating the transportation and the wholesale price of natural gas and electricity sold for use in interstate commerce. State utility commissioners regulate interstate prices. Rates are calculated to allow companies a specific rate of return on investment (earnings ÷ total assets), which they may not exceed. When utilities are confronted with increased costs due to higher fuel prices, they can apply to the commission for permission to pass them on to customers through fuel adjustment charges. A utility that makes more than its allowed rate of return or receives fuel adjustment charges that exceed increased fuel costs may be ordered to rebate the overcharges to customers. Rates for the transportation of electric power, natural gas, and oil through pipelines also fall under FERC's jurisdiction.

The FERC reviews decisions made by the Department of Energy's Economic Regulatory Administration (ERA) concerning the pricing of petroleum products and their allocation. The commission also assists the Environmental Protection Agency with the administration of the clean air and water pollution control acts.

The FERC enforces compliance with its rules, orders, and regulations by either administrative or judicial action. Compliance orders may be appealed to the commission. Failure to comply may result in proceedings in U.S. district court. FERC decisions may be appealed to the U.S. court of appeals.

B. Nuclear Regulatory Commission

Mandated by the Energy Reorganization Act, the Nuclear Regulatory Commission is responsible for the licensing, construction, and operation of nuclear reactors. It is also responsible for regulating the possession, use, transportation, handling, and disposal of nuclear material. The NRC develops and implements rules and regulations governing licensed nuclear activities.

The Office of Inspection and Enforcement inspects nuclear facilities to determine whether they are constructed and operated in accord with NRC regulations. The office investigates accidents, incidents, and charges of improper actions that may adversely affect the production of nuclear materials, the facilities, the environment, or the health and safety of the public.

5-6. Environmental Protection Regulation

The Environmental Protection Agency was established as an independent agency in the executive branch of the federal government. It was created to carry out the provisions of the National Environmental Policy Act and other major environmental laws and executive orders dealing with air, water, solid waste, toxic substance, and noise pollution. See Table 5-1.

A. National Environmental Policy Act

The purpose of the 1969 National Environmental Policy Act is to declare national policy that establishes productive and enjoyable harmony between individuals and their environment. The legislation encourages efforts that prevent or eliminate damage to the environment and that stimulate the health and welfare of the public. The act requires a detailed statement of environmental consequences in every recommendation or proposal for legislation and other major federal actions significantly affecting the quality of the human environment. These *environmental impact statements* describe in detail the expected adverse environmental consequences of a proposed action. The alternatives to the ac-

Table 5-1. Environmental Legislation

Statute	Major Provisions
National Environmental Policy Act (1965)	Established Council on Environmental Quality (CEQ).
	Required a national policy on the environment.
Water Quality Improvement Act (1970)	Established liability for oil spills.
	Increased restrictions on thermal pollution from nuclear power plants.
Clean Air Act Amendments (1970 and 1977)	Set initial deadlines for auto emission standards.
	Gave public right to sue alleged polluters.
	Extended set deadlines for air quality standards and auto emissions.
Federal Environmental Pesticide Control Act (1972)	Required registration of pesticides.
	Gave EPA authority to ban use of hazardous pesticides.
Federal Water Pollution Control Act Amendments (1972)	Established grants to states for construction of sewage treatment plants.
	Established municipal pollutant discharge permit programs.
Marine Protection, Research and Sanctuaries Act (1972)	Outlawed dumping of waste in oceans without EPA permits.
Noise Control Act (1972)	Gave EPA authority to set national noise standards for commercial products.
	Required EPA assistance to FAA in developing noise regulations for airports and aircraft.
Safe Drinking Water Act (1974)	Set standards for allowable levels of pollutants and chemicals in public drinking water systems.
Toxic Substances Control Act (1976)	Banned manufacture and use of PCBs.
	Required testing of chemical substances that may injure health and the environment.
Clean Water Act (1977)	Created "best conventional technology" standard for water quality by 1984.
	Raised liability limit on oil spill cleanup costs.
Comprehensive Environmental Response, Compensation, and Liability Act of 1980	Established a $1.6 billion federal "superfund" to clean up chemical dumps and toxic waste.
	Authorized the EPA to sue those responsible for toxic spills to recover government cleanup expenses.

tion and any unavoidable adverse environmental effects which would result if the alternatives were carried out are also described. Mere contemplation of certain actions does not necessitate an impact statement. The courts rely on a four-part test for determining when an agency must begin an impact statement. The factors to be considered are (1) the likelihood and imminence of the action occurring, (2) the extent to which information is available on the effects of implementing the expected program and its alternatives, (3) the extent to which commitments are being made, and (4) the severity of the expected environmental effects.

Environmental impact statements are made available to the public. Suits may be instituted to have impact statements reviewed to determine whether they take everything necessary into account. The federal laws set minimal requirements, but state and local governments are authorized to establish more demanding requirements.

B. Environmental Protection Agency

All major antipollution programs dealing with air, noise, solid wastes, toxic substances, and pesticides were placed under the administrative control of the EPA in 1970. The EPA's primary responsibilities are to conduct research on all aspects of pollution, set and enforce pollution control standards, monitor programs to determine whether pollution abatement standards are being met, and administer grants to assist states in controlling pollution.

The EPA has the power to enforce the standards and programs it initiates. It encourages voluntary compliance by industry and communities and supports state and local governments' efforts to conduct enforcement actions of their own. When such efforts fail, the EPA gathers and prepares evidence and conducts enforcement proceedings. Alleged polluters are notified of a violation and ordered to stop. An informal meeting is usually conducted to negotiate a satisfactory settlement. If the matter remains unsettled, the charge is argued in an open hearing. Without going to court, the EPA may revoke or suspend licenses and permits. For example, registrations of pesticides may be canceled and pesticides may be seized. When all else fails, the EPA can start civil proceedings to force compliance in a U.S. district court.

Understanding Legal Terms

Define, identify, or explain the following terms:

advisory opinion	group boycott	nexus	rule of reason
apportionment	horizontal restraint	per se	tying agreement
certificate of compliance	industry guide	prima facie	vertical restraint
environmental impact statement	monopoly	proxy	

Questions for Review and Discussion

1. What kinds of activities are regulated at the federal, state, and local levels?

2. Discuss the primary function of the Interstate Commerce Commission.

3. Explain the response of the U.S. Supreme Court to the argument that a levy is not a lawful tax when the legislative purpose is to regulate rather than to tax.

4. Discuss apportionment as a limiting factor in a state's right to tax businesses engaged in interstate commerce.

5. Identify the major responsibilities of the Securities and Exchange Commission.

6. Describe the functions of the Federal Reserve Board in regulating the nation's monetary policy.

7. Explain the dual roles of the Antitrust Division of the Justice Department and the Federal Trade Commission in the enforcement of antitrust laws.

8. Identify the elements that must be present in order for the courts to find a restraint-of-trade agreement in violation of the Sherman Act.

9. Discuss the powers and authority of the Federal Energy Regulatory Commission and the control exercised by the Department of Energy over FERC decisions.

10. What was the purpose of Congress in legislating the National Environmental Policy Act?

Analyzing Cases

1. The Trade Expansion Act of 1962 authorizes the President to "take such action, and for such time, as he deems necessary to adjust the imports . . ." when it is found that imports threaten to impair the national security.

The President invoked this authority to impose a small license fee on oil imports. When the program did not wholly fulfill its objectives, the President promptly imposed a somewhat higher but still relatively small license fee on oil imports.

Eight states and a number of utilities challenged the license fees. Suits were filed in which the plaintiffs argued that although the law did authorize the imposition of quotas on oil imports, it did not authorize license fees. It was further argued that if the law was interpreted to authorize license fees, the delegation of power to the President by Congress would be unconstitutional. How should the Supreme Court dispose of the case? Why? ● *Federal Energy Admin. v. Algonquin Sng., Inc.*, 426 U.S. 548 (1976)

2. Chicago and North Western Transportation Company is an interstate railroad subject to the jurisdiction of the ICC. The Kalo Brick & Tile Company operated a brick manufacturing plant in Iowa that used the railroad's cars and branch line to transport its products into interstate commerce.

A series of mud slides, which damaged the tracks of the branch line, forced the railroad to discontinue service. Kalo, with no alternate means of shipping its goods economically, was thus forced out of business.

The railroad filed an application with the ICC for a certificate permitting it to abandon the branch line. Kalo did not properly oppose the request at the ICC hearing, and the commission ruled that the railroad had abandoned the line due to conditions beyond its control and granted a certificate.

Kalo filed an action for damages against the railroad in the state courts of Iowa. Kalo alleged that the discontinuance of service violated Iowa's statutory and common law. The company sought damages in tort, alleging negligence on the part of the railroad in maintaining the roadbed. The state court of appeals ruled in Kalo's favor.

Having agreed to review the decision, how would the U.S. Supreme Court decide as to whether federal law (i.e., the Interstate Commerce Act) allowing the railroad to abandon service under ICC authority preempts the Iowa state law under which Kalo had won its suit? Why? ● *Chicago & N.W. Trans. v. Kalo Brick & Tile Co.,* 67 L. Ed.2d 258 (1981)

3. P.A.K. Transport, Inc., is a common carrier licensed by the ICC to haul scrap from and to points in New England and New Jersey. An issue arose as to whether certain wood chips which P.A.K. hauled qualified as scrap under its license. An ICC investigation resulted. Although an administrative law judge ruled that the chips were scrap, a three-member panel of the ICC reversed the decision. The panel ruled that wood chips were not scrap, but invited P.A.K. to apply for a permanent license which would allow it to carry the materials. P.A.K. did not appeal the adverse ruling, but filed the application.

The ICC granted the application in part, restricting P.A.K. to service of four wood chip shippers who had supported the application. On a petition for reconsideration, the ICC endorsed the restriction without stating precisely what evidence it reviewed or what law it applied. In reaching its decision, the commission had restricted P.A.K. in part to protect a protesting competitor carrier against possible loss of business.

P.A.K. appealed the ICC ruling to the U.S. court of appeals. It argued that the commission failed to apply legal standards and balance properly the evidence of the competing interest in respect to the P.A.K. application. How should the court rule on this issue that the ICC failed to follow statutory standards and consider all relevant factors? ● *P.A.K. Transport, Inc. v. United States,* 613 F.2d 351 (1st Cir. 1980)

4. The comptroller of the currency in the Department of the Treasury made an allegation charging that the First National Bank of Eden had engaged in unsafe and unsound banking practices.

During the hearing, the testimony of three national bank examiners confirmed that the facts set out in support of the charges against the bank were true and constituted unsafe and unsound banking practices. The administrative law judge concluded that the charges had been substantiated and recommended that a cease and desist order be issued. The comptroller of the currency issued the order requiring the bank to discontinue its investment in criticized assets, correct other violations, and limit the amount of salaries and bonuses paid to executive officers. The order also required the bank president and vice-president to reimburse the bank for bonuses paid the prior year.

The bank challenged the validity of the order, arguing that the evidence produced at the hearing did not support the administrative law judge's findings. On what determination would the court base its review decision? Specifically, under what conditions can the decision to require reimbursement to the bank of excess compensation be disturbed? ● *First Nat'l Bank of Eden v. Department of the Treasury,* 568 F.2d 610 (8th Cir. 1978)

5. Topco Associates, Inc., is a cooperative association of small and medium-sized regional supermarket chains. Each of its member chains operates independently. There is no pooling of earnings, profits, capital, management, or advertising resources. The various chains operate stores in some thirty-three states. Topco's basic function is to allow its members to sell "generic" or "store brand" products and thus to compete with similar products sold by the larger food chains.

Each member chain is required to operate under "exclusive territorial licenses" issued by Topco. These provide that member firms will sell Topco-controlled brands only within the marketing territory allocated to them.

The government filed suit in federal district court. It maintained that this scheme of dividing markets violates the Sherman Act because it operates to prohibit competition in Topco-brand products among grocery chains engaged in retail operations. Topco defended by arguing that it needed territorial divisions to compete with larger chains, that the association could not exist if the territorial divisions were anything but exclusive, and that the association actually increased competition by enabling its members to compete successfully with large regional and national chains.

Would the district court's finding in Topco's favor be upheld by the U.S. Supreme Court? Why? • *United States v. Topco Assocs., Inc.*, 405 U.S. 596 (1972)

6. The National Association for the Advancement of Colored People (NAACP) and other organizations petitioned the Federal Power Commission (FPC) to adopt a rule requiring equal employment opportunity and nondiscrimination in the employment practices of those it regulates. The rule would have given persons who believed they had been subjected to employment discrimination by a regulated employer the right to file a complaint with the FPC. The NAACP argued that the statutory duty of the FPC to establish "just and reasonable" rates contained in the Federal Power Act and the Natural Gas Act, as well as the statutory duty of the commission to advance the "public interest" provided authority for the rule it sought.

The FPC refused to adopt the proposed rule. It held that it had no jurisdiction to do so, explaining that the Federal Power and Natural Gas acts were economic regulations and that the proposed rule was not. It had been the practice of the FPC, in the context of individual rate-setting proceedings, to prevent clearly identifiable costs resulting from

illegal discrimination (such as pay awards) from being passed on to consumers. Beyond this, however, the FPC was unwilling to go. Should the Supreme court uphold the FPC's position? Why? • *NAACP v. F.P.C.*, 425 U.S. 662 (1976)

7. Earth Sciences, Inc., conducted gold-leaching operations in Colorado. In the process used, a toxic substance is sprayed over gold ore, separating the gold from the ore. Earth Sciences collected the leachate in a small fiberglass-lined pool, called the primary sump. A reserve sump was available to catch excess leachate or runoff in emergency situations.

Warm April temperatures caused faster melting than expected of a blanket of snow covering the ore heap, and the primary and reserve sumps overflowed, discharging the toxic leachate into the Rito Seco Creek.

A state inspector visited the gold-leaching operation following reports of dead fish in the Rito Seco Creek. While the state inspector was present, the reserve sump overflowed a second time. When officials of the Environmental Protection Agency visited the site, they observed groundwater seeping below the sumps running into the Rito Seco and partially gathering into pools near the creek.

The United States brought suit, alleging that Earth Sciences had violated the Federal Water Pollution Control Act. The act defined the discharge of pollutants as "any addition of any pollutant to navigable waters from any point source." Earth Sciences argued that Rito Seco Creek was not a "navigable" water, since it is located entirely in Colorado and flows into two reservoirs which collect all the flow for recreational and agricultural uses.

How should the U.S. court of appeals resolve the issues? Why? • *United States v. Earth Sciences, Inc.*, 599 F.2d 368 (10th Cir. 1979)

Chapter 6   Consumer Protection and Bankruptcy Relief

Product safety, warranty, and strict product liability are considerations that are deeply imbedded in federal and state governmental regulation through consumer protection laws. Simply stated, those who manufacture products may be found liable for personal injury which the product causes. Recent federal laws, such as the Consumer Product Safety Act, require that defective products be recalled from the market. In addition to private lawsuits, manufacturers may be subjected to expensive legal contests with the government when consumer product liability is involved.

Central to the consumer protection movement is the debtor-creditor relationship which encourages easy credit and debt assumption. Liberal provisions in the bankrupty code allow debtors to be discharged from their debts, free from further liability.

6-1. Consumer Protection

Product liability laws provide that consumers who could reasonably be expected to be injured by a purchased product may recover damages. In most instances, this protection extends to consumers other than the purchaser. Coverage includes members of the consumer's household, guests, or service persons who might reasonably be expected to come in contact with a defective product. In some jurisdictions, however, there is still a requirement of *privity*. That is, a relationship between the injured party and the seller must be shown. In most cases, however, liability may be imposed on the seller or manufacturer on grounds such as breach of warranty or strict tort liability. Another body of consumer protection law is concerned with deceptive advertising, labeling, and marketing techniques. These consumer protection laws are discussed below.

A. Product Warranty

The term *warranty* applies to any promise or representation in the nature of a product guarantee. Under the UCC, the guarantee extends to title, merchantability, fitness, and against infringement of products, including those purchased solely for commercial or industrial use. A warranty may be either express or implied. The UCC states that a warranty is express when a seller or manufacturer makes a factual written or oral statement that relates to a product and becomes part of the basis of the bargain (2-313). Such warranties may not be made void by a *disclaimer* (denial of a claim) that is not consistent with the warranty itself. That is, any disclaimer must be explicit and should immediately follow this warranty. The code provides that a warranty may also be implied by law or by inference from the nature of the transaction or circumstances of the parties. For example, a seller who deals in watches impliedly warrants to purchasers that the time-pieces will tell time with a reasonable degree of accuracy. The implied warranty of fitness or merchantability can be made void only by a disclaimer that is written conspicuously and stated in specific language. Commonly understood expressions such as *as is* or *with all faults* make it plain that there are no implied warranties. The breach of a product warranty may provide grounds for a lawsuit and recovery of damages by the injured party.

In addition to the UCC's express and implied warranty provisions, the federal government has created an entirely new body of federal law with respect to consumer warranties. The Magnuson-Moss Act of 1975 applies to all consumer goods costing $5 or more for which a written warranty is provided by the seller. Quite specific requirements apply to certain warranties if the goods cost $10 or more. Consumer goods are defined as tangible personal property normally used for personal, family, or household purposes, including items to be attached or installed in real property. If the seller elects to give a written warranty, certain requirements must be met, including a prohibition against disclaimer. The Magnuson-Moss Act does not invalidate or restrict any right or remedy of a consumer under state law or other federal law. In bringing a civil suit, however, the buyer has the duty to notify the immediate seller within a reasonable time. As long as the seller has been notified of the breach of warranty, the buyer can sue others in the chain of distribution.

Warranties are discussed in more detail in Chapter 22.

B. Product Tort Liability

Section 402(a) of *The Restatement of Torts* governs most legal actions based on product liability. Its strict liability provision makes anyone who sells or produces a product in a *defective condition* (unreasonably dangerous to the user or consumer or to property) subject to liability for physical or emotional injury to the ultimate consumer and for physical damage to the user's property. The courts have regularly held that liability for defective products extends to the producer of the product, the wholesaler, and the retailer. The seller or producer must be engaged in the business of selling or manufacturing such a defective product. And the product manufactured or sold must be expected to reach the ultimate consumer without substantial change in specifications or conditions under which it was originally manufactured and sold.

The number of consumer lawsuits based on claims of product liability has increased sharply in recent years. The Consumer Product Safety Act of 1972 may be one factor accounting for this. The act established the Consumer Product Safety Commission with the power to protect consumers from unreasonable risk or injury from hazardous products. The act covers products or component parts, American-made or imported, which are manufactured or distributed for sale to a consumer for personal use, consumption, or enjoyment. The act, however, does not cover certain products such as tobacco goods, aviation and boating equipment, motor vehicles, and food or drugs.

The CPSC has the authority to establish and issue safety and performance standards. The standards generally consist of requirements as to performance, composition, contents, design, construction, finish, or packaging of a consumer product. Standards may also include requirements that a product be marked or accompanied by clear and adequate warnings or instructions.

The CPSC can order the recall of products found to be inherently unsafe and dangerous. It has the authority to impose civil fines for violations of its standards and cease and desist orders. Private citizens, acting in their own behalf, may bring suit to establish or enforce a safety rule if the CPSC fails to act. Commission findings must be supported by substantial evidence in the record as a whole. Rules and findings issued by the CPSC are subject to judicial review.

C. Deceptive Practices and Advertising

In addition to its antitrust authority, the FTC has wide-ranging authority over unfair or deceptive trade practices in commerce. Its Bureau of Consumer Protection investigates all business practices that harm the consuming public. The bureau advises the FTC on rules and proceedings and recommends cases for litigation. Statutes governing mail-order selling, unfair and deceptive advertising, and warranties are also monitored by the bureau.

1. Section 5, Federal Trade Commission Act. The FTC's power is extended by the Federal Trade Commission Act to false, misleading, or deceptive advertisements. Advertisers are required to prove the truth of any claim made in their commercials in newspapers, on radio and television, and in other media. Any untrue or misleading commercial may be removed from the market without a hearing, when consumer interests will be harmed by it. The offending advertiser can request a review of the commission's actions. In ordering an advertiser to cease and desist from continuing deceptive advertising, the FTC may also order the advertiser to engage in corrective advertising. A new advertisement can be ordered in which the former false or deceptive statements are contradicted and the truth stated.

● The Bristol-Myers Company, Sterling Drugs, Incorporated, and American Home Products Corporation ran advertisements claiming that certain of their products relieved nervous tension and similar symptoms and enabled persons to cope with the ordinary stresses of daily life. The FTC challenged these claims and issued complaints, stating that no reliable scientific evidence supported these advertisements. The FTC order would halt the misrepresentation. In addition, each company might be required to devote a percentage of its advertising budget for each product to advertising that would correct the challenged claims. Or, the companies might be ordered to cease and desist from advertising the products for two years.

2. Door-to-Door and Mail-Order Sales. The FTC has issued rules and regulations governing sales made in a customer's home. Buyers of products from a door-to-door salesperson are given a *cooling-off period* when they agree to buy merchandise costing more than $25. Under this policy, the buyer has three days within which to reconsider the purchase. At any time during this period, the buyer can rescind (cancel the purchase) and recover any money paid. Within ten business days after receiving a notice of rescission, the seller must refund all payments made, return any goods or property traded in by the buyer, and cancel and return any contract signed in connection with the sale.

FTC rules require that mail-order houses ship goods ordered by a customer within a reasonable time. If they do not, customers can request a refund of money paid, demand alternate products, or wait for delivery of the ordered merchandise. False or misleading advertisements are prohibited in mail-order catalogs.

● Jay Norris, Inc., does a gift and novelty business through mail-order catalogs and advertisements in national media such as *TV Guide.* It made false claims about a number of its products. It described a "flame gun" that would dissolve the heaviest snowdrifts and whip through the thickest ice; the product did neither. A roach powder was described as completely safe to use and as never losing its killing power, even after years; the powder was neither safe nor so deadly. Cars were listed as carefully maintained and thoroughly serviced; they were former New York taxicabs, many in poor condition. The FTC issued a cease and desist order prohibiting Jay Norris, Inc., from representing the safety or performance characteristics of any product unless such claims were fully and completely substantiated by competent and objective material available in written form.

3. **Bait-and-Switch Schemes.** Section 5 of the Federal Trade Commission Act prohibits acts engaged in by retailers to discourage the purchase of advertised products. Known as *bait-and-switch schemes,* they occur when a retailer advertises a low-priced product to entice customers into a place of business and then, according to a preconceived selling plan, discredits the low-priced item in an attempt to switch the customer to a higher-priced product. Customers are victimized in such a scheme because they patronize the advertiser's store rather than a competitor's outlet on the assumption that advertisements of low-priced products are made in good faith. Certain practices are considered in determining if an advertisement is a bait-and-switch scheme. One such practice is failure by outlets listed in the advertisement to have available sufficient quantities of the product to meet reasonably expected demands. The advertisement may disclose that the supply is limited and/or that the product is available only at designated locations. Another indication of a bait-and-switch tactic is refusal to take orders for the advertised product, if supplies are depleted, for subsequent delivery within a reasonable time.

D. **Food and Drug Safety and Packaging**
The Food and Drug Act of 1906 gave the federal government regulatory control over foods and drugs. The act prohibited interstate commerce in misbranded and adulterated foods, drinks, and drugs. The 1938 federal Food, Drug, and Cosmetic Act broadened the original legislation by extending the regulatory power of the Food and Drug Administration to cosmetics and medical devices such as mechanical hearts. Predistribution approval of new drugs was also required. A new drug, as defined in the act includes "any drug . . . not generally recognized . . . as safe and effective for use under conditions prescribed, recommended, or suggested in the labeling." Exceptions to this requirement include experimental drugs under limited investigational use. The 1958 Delaney amendment to the act forbids the use of new food additives until they are proved safe for public consumption. The amendment further provides that any food containing a substance shown to cause cancer in human or animals must be removed from the market, no matter how small the risk. Subsequent 1962 drug amendments required that all drugs be proved effective as well as safe before

they are marketed. The FDA was also given responsibility to regulate prescription drug advertising.

The Fair Packaging and Labeling Act of 1966 gave the FDA power to require that labels on packages of food, drugs, cosmetics, and medical devices be uniform and accurate. The act's major purpose is to make possible value comparisons among similar products. To this end, labels must indicate (1) who made the product, (2) what is in the package, (3) how much the package contains, and (4) the net quantity of one serving, if the number of servings is given. The use of qualifying words such as *jumbo* or *super* in statements of net quantity of contents is prohibited.

● Econ Home Products, Inc., included on the label of its detergent the statement "12 jumbo ounces of detergent." Under the provisions of the Fair Packaging and Labeling Act, the FDA should issue cease and desist orders to Econ Home Products for noncompliance with the prohibition of the addition of qualifying words or phrases to the net content statement. Had the label read "12 ounces of fast-acting detergent," it would have been allowed.

The FDA monitors compliance through its adminstration bureaus. Violations of the law can lead to a recall to remove defective products from the marketplace. If a voluntary recall is ineffective, the FDA may begin a civil action to stop the continued manufacture or distribution of a defective product. The FDA can carry out a seizure of the defective product by filing a complaint with the appropriate district court.

● One evening the Cochrans had vichyssoise, a cold potato soup made by Bon Vivant, Inc. The couple did not eat much because the soup tasted spoiled. The next morning Mr. Cochran felt ill. He began seeing double and had difficulty speaking. He was admitted to the hospital and by evening was dead. Mrs. Cochran was later admitted to the same hospital, totally paralyzed. Investigation soon revealed that the Cochrans were victims of botulism—deadly botulin toxin. As a result, the Food and Drug Administration went to court to obtain orders to seize and hold all Bon Vivant products. Bon Vivant also went to court—to file for bankruptcy.

6-2. Credit Laws

The credit laws that apply to consumer transactions resulted from Congress's efforts to remedy conditions which imposed an undue burden upon consumers. Four major laws were legislated.

A. Truth-in-Lending Act

The Truth-in-Lending Act of 1968 authorized the Federal Reserve Board to formulate regulations requiring full disclosure of credit terms before a consumer credit account is opened or a credit transaction is completed. The act also established limits on a consumer's liability for unauthorized use of a credit card. In 1969 Regulation Z, which told the public what must be done to comply with the Truth-in-Lending Act, was issued.

Chapter 6:
Consumer
Protection
and Bank-
ruptcy
Relief

81

1. Finance Charge. The Truth-in-Lending Act spells out how the *finance charge* in a credit transaction must be determined. Essentially, the finance charge is the sum of all charges which the consumer must pay in order to obtain credit. Such charges include, but are not limited to, service charges, carrying charges, interest, points (charge by a bank for taking a mortgage), and insurance premiums as required. The finance charge must be spelled out in dollars and cents and in total percentage to the closest quarter of 1 percent on the face of the credit statement.

2. Annual Percentage Rate. Central to the Truth-in-Lending Act is the determination and disclosure of the *annual percentage rate*. It is the effective or actual true cost of the credit to the consumer, computed by an elaborate set of statutory rules. For revolving charge accounts, the monthly rate is multiplied by the number of time periods used by the creditor in a year. For example, a $1\frac{3}{4}$ percent monthly charge on an unpaid balance has an annual percentage rate of 21 percent.

3. Open-End Consumer Credit Transactions. The Truth-in-Lending Act requires that the method of computing the interest on open-end credit transactions be spelled out for the consumer. Typical open-end transactions involve credit card or revolving charge accounts. The latter are agreements under which the consumer may keep on making new purchases, adding the amount of these purchases to the outstanding balance, up to an agreed ceiling. The consumer usually has the option of prepaying or of paying in stated installments. The disclosures are specified by Regulation Z, as described below.

4. Lending Disclosures. For all consumer-related installment sales that involve four or more installment payments, the following Truth-in-Lending disclosures are specified by Regulation Z.

○ The date on which the finance charge begins to accrue, if it differs from the date of the transaction.
○ The finance charge, expressed as an annual percentage rate except on small credit transactions when the amount financed does not exceed $75.
○ The number of payments, their total, and the respective amounts and due dates of the installments scheduled to repay the indebtedness.

> ● Healy financed a new car with National Finance Company. He was told before the agreement was signed that repayment of the $2,000 loan would be spread over a period of thirty-six months and that small regular payments would be required plus several substantially larger payments along the way. National Finance Company would not be in violation of Regulation Z as long as it gave Healy the number of installments and the amount and due date for each installment payment, as well as his obligation for default or late payment. Some states have laws that provide for a right of refinancing should the larger, or "balloon," payments prove too much for the consumer when due.

○ The amount or method of computing default, delinquency, or similar late payment charges.
○ A description of any secured interest held or to be acquired by the creditor and on what property
○ The method of computing penalty charges, if any, for prepayment.

○ Identification of the method of computing unearned finance charges which may be refunded, credited, or abated if prepayment is made.
○ Identification of any "balloon" payments.
○ Total amount of finance charge, identified by the term *finance charge.*
○ Notice of consumer's right of rescission, if applicable.

Disclosures must also be made when the installment payment purchase price is the same as a one-time purchase price. In such cases, the creditor is required to state that the cost of credit is included in the purchase price. *Acceleration clauses,* which give a creditor the right to speed up payment of the entire debt upon the debtor's default, are not a required disclosure.

5. Credit Cardholder Liability. The Truth-in-Lending Act sets the statutory limit of credit cardholder liability. For any unauthorized use of a credit card, the cardholder is liable for the first $50 of any charges. There is no liability for unauthorized use of a credit card after the card issuer has been notified by phone or letter of possible unauthorized use of the card. The $50 charge liability is also avoided if the credit card does not contain a method to identify the user of the card. A signature, photograph, or some electronic or mechanical confirmation method is required. The distribution of unsolicited credit cards is prohibited. Renewals and cards issued in response to a request or application are permitted.

● Pike's wallet, containing his American Express credit card, was stolen. He immediately notified American Express by mail that the card had been lost. In spite of Pike's prompt notice, the thief used the card for puchases totaling $980. Pike would be liable for $50 of the unauthorized use of his credit card if the use occurred before American Express received notice that the card had been stolen.

6. Wage Garnishment Restrictions. The Truth-in-Lending Act contains restrictions on *wage garnishment,* i.e., the withholding of wages to satisfy a creditor. The amount that may be garnished in any single workweek is limited to the lesser of 25 percent of an employee's disposable income (gross pay less all deductions required by law) or disposable income less thirty times the federal minimum hourly wage. The law applies to any business directly or indirectly involved in interstate commerce. It prevents employers from firing employees merely because their wages have been garnished "for any one indebtedness." Although the meaning of "any one indebtedness" is not entirely clear, the courts have held that the restriction does not prevent discharge because of several garnishments on different debts.

Creditors who are concerned about the limitations on garnishment can consider a wage assignment as an alternative course in debt collection. Many consumer credit arrangements contain a provision whereby the consumer assigns future wages to a creditor in the event of a default in payments. A wage assignment requires no court action by the creditor and thus differs from a garnishment. The creditor merely notifies the consumer's employer of the assignment and requests that wages be turned over to satisfy the debt.

A creditor armed with a garnishment, even though it is a court order, does not have collection rights superior to those of the holder of a wage assignment. The party who obtains the garnishment or wage assignment first may collect all the money from wages due him or her from the debtor first.

Chapter 6:
Consumer
Protection
and Bank-
ruptcy
Relief

B. Fair Credit Billing Act

To give consumers a fair and equitable means of correcting billing errors, Congress amended the Truth-in-Lending Act with the Fair Credit Billing Act. It established a billing dispute settlement procedure which permits consumers to question what they believe to be billing errors on their periodic statements. Creditors must acknowledge each inquiry and within ninety days correct any error or explain why the statement is correct. Open-end credit transactions are governed by the act, but not installment loans or purchases such as cars and homes which are paid according to a set schedule of installments.

The Fair Credit Billing Act also provides that if consumers purchase unsatisfactory goods or services on credit cards (including bank credit cards) they can assert against the card issuer any claims or defenses which they might have against the seller. For example, a cardholder who has a right to withhold payment from the seller for faulty merchandise may withhold payment for that merchandise from the credit card account. While the act does not help consumers to settle disputes, it does permit them to hold on to their money while matters are being settled. Before this statute provision can apply, the following conditions must be met:

○ The cardholder must make a good-faith effort to resolve the disagreement with the merchant honoring the card.
○ The amount of the initial transaction must exceed $50.
○ With certain exceptions, the place where the initial transaction in dispute was made must be in the same state as the address the cardholder has listed with the card issuer, or within a hundred miles of that address. Credit cards issued by nationwide chain operations such as Sears Roebuck or J. C. Penney are included in this condition regardless of the location of their stores or the place of residence of the cardholder.

Creditors may not penalize cardholders by impairing their credit rating because customers assert claims or rights under the act. A merchant or credit card issuer who feels that the customer's complaints are not justified may take to court any customer who refuses to pay the outstanding debt.

● Van Voorhies purchased a stereo system with a credit card. A few weeks after purchase, the unit stopped working, and Van Voorhies returned it to the merchant. Should the merchant refuse to settle the issue, Van Voorhies has the right to advise the credit card issuer that the conditions of the Fair Credit Billing Act have been complied with and further payments on the transaction are ceasing. It would then be left to the credit card issuer and the merchant to resolve the matter by either writing off the transaction or taking the dispute to court.

C. Fair Credit Reporting Act

The 1971 Fair Credit Reporting Act provided consumers with access to their credit worthiness files maintained by credit bureaus, in order to remedy any errors they might contain. Under this act, consumers can take steps to protect themselves if they have been denied credit, insurance, or employment.

Consumers who wish to know what information a credit bureau has collected can arrange either a personal interview at the bureau's office or an interview by telephone. The consumer can request that the bureau reinvestigate and correct or delete information that is found to be inaccurate, incomplete, or obsolete. When reinvestigation still produces information which the consumer feels is incorrect, the consumer's version of the facts must be inserted in the file. Credit bureaus must adhere to guidelines specifying how old information in the credit file may be and who is entitled to ask for information.

D. Equal Credit Opportunity Act

The Equal Credit Opportunity Act, as amended in 1977, prohibits discrimination in credit transactions because of sex, race, national origin, age, or marital status. Banks, small loan and finance companies, retail and department stores, credit card companies, and credit unions are governed by this act. Creditors are allowed to consider such factors as income, expenses, debts, and reliability of the applicant. Individuals are given the right to have credit in their own name (including their maiden name). They may get credit without a cosigner, if they meet the creditor's standards. Applicants have a right to know within thirty days whether their application for credit has been accepted or rejected. Creditors who violate any provisions of the act may be held liable for *punitive damages* (increased award in view of wrong done) and reasonable attorney's fees and court costs, plus any amount of actual damage (real loss).

6-3. Debtor Protection and Bankruptcy Relief

Most states have usury laws that attempt to protect debtors by limiting the amount of interest that may be charged for borrowed money. Other state and federal laws regulate the methods of debt collection in order to deter invasion of privacy and allow debtors to avoid undue financial hardship in discharging debts.

A. Fair Debt Collection Practices Act

The Fair Debt Collection Practices Act of 1977 protects consumers against abusive debt collective practices. Those who regularly collect debts owed or due another are required to identify themselves and to state that the person owes a debt when acquiring information about where a debtor is located. Collectors are prohibited from communicating with the debtor at any unusual time or place that is known to be inconvenient to the debtor. Harrassment or abusive techniques are outlawed. For example, debt collectors may not use obscene or profane language or publish a list of those who allegedly refuse to pay debts. The use of threats of violence or other creditor conduct that is so outrageous in character as to go beyond all bounds of decency is illegal under the act. Plaintiffs may recover actual damages, punitive damages, and attorney's fees.

B. Electronic Fund Transfer Act

The Electronic Fund Transfer Act of 1979 protects consumers from debts which arise from computer errors. The act also protects consumers in their use of computer-controlled electronic fund transfer (EFT) systems. Among others, automated teller machines which permit around-the-clock bank deposits and withdrawals and pay-by-telephone bill-paying systems are governed by the act.

The Electronic Fund Transfer Act limits a consumer's liability for unauthorized use of an EFT card to $50, provided notice of card loss or theft is given the issuer within two business days. Liability increases to $500 when notice is withheld beyond two business days; it is unlimited when notice is not given within sixty days. The unauthorized use of an EFT card is a violation in interstate commerce, a criminal offense punishable by a $10,000 fine and/or ten years' imprisonment.

The EFT legislation makes financial institutions liable for actual damages due to human or computer errors. Receipts for each EFT transaction and periodic statements of all fund transfers must be provided. Consumers have sixty days to report errors after receiving such notification. The financial institution has ten days to investigate alleged errors and to respond to the consumer. Errors found must be appropriately corrected.

C. Debtor-Creditor Relations

In debtor-creditor relations in general and bankruptcy in particular, it is important to understand a *secured transaction*. As generally defined, it is any transaction which is intended to create an interest in personal property which secures payment or performance of an obligation. Thus, a creditor who has a claim on property possesses a right over the property, even when the debtor has the right to possess and use the property.

Article 9 of the UCC describes the default rights of a secured party. Upon *default* (failure to pay according to the terms of the loan), the lender has the right to take possession of and sell the property or *collateral* (a value additional to the personal obligation of the borrower). The creditor may either sue for possession of the goods or simply remove the goods, provided the removal may be accomplished without breach of the peace. If the security agreement so provides, the secured party may require the debtor upon default to deliver the goods or collateral to a designated place. The secured creditor is also entitled upon default to render property serving as collateral unusable, without actually removing it.

After default of the debtor, a secured party is allowed to sell, lease, or otherwise dispose of any or all of the collateral. The debtor must be given notification of the time and place of sale. The UCC rules stating how the proceeds of a sale of collateral after default shall be applied are set forth in Chapter 41.

D. Bankruptcy Reform Act

Chapter 7 of the Bankruptcy Reform Act of 1978, dealing with liquidation or straight bankruptcy, and Chapter 13, dealing with adjustment of debts of individuals with regular income, contain provisions for individual debtors. These chapters afford *insolvent* individuals (those who are unable to pay their debts as they come due) an opportunity to wipe out their debts and at the same time provide equitable treatment for their creditors. (Business bankruptcy, especially corporate bankruptcy and reorganization, are discussed in Chapter 35 of this text.)

Chapter 13 provisions cover individuals with regular income whose unsecured debts are less than $100,000 and whose secured debts are less than $350,000. This includes individual debtors who own and operate a business.

The central feature of Chapter 13 is the provisions allowing individuals the means of paying off debts from future earnings over a three-year period under court protection from harassment by creditors. Once a Chapter 13 petition is filed, all of the debtor's property, including future earnings, is under the exclusive jurisdiction of the court. Unlike a straight bankruptcy under Chapter 7, a Chapter 13 filing is not a liquidation proceeding. In the event the debtor's position becomes hopeless, however, the right to convert to a Chapter 7 liquidation is preserved. Chapter 7 proceedings begin with the filing of a petition by the debtor (i.e., *voluntary petition*) or by the debtor's creditors (i.e., *involuntary petition*).

1. Voluntary Bankruptcy Petition. Any person or business other than banks, insurance companies, railroads, and municipalities may file a voluntary petition for bankruptcy. The petition may be filed jointly by husband and wife. The act of filing the voluntary petition automatically constitutes an order for relief; that is, creditors are prohibited from taking legal action against the debtor.

A voluntary bankruptcy may allow the debtor to repay creditors over a period as long as five years. The debtor is required to submit to the court a repayment plan which may or may not call for repayment of all the debts owed by the debtor. The plan may permit the debtor to retain even assets which are not exempt by law. The debtor must have a regular income or, in some instances, a reasonable prospect of a regular income. Property must be distributed to each unsecured creditor in an amount no less than would be paid in an involuntary liquidation. Approval of a distribution to a secured creditor is required, however, unless the debtor surrenders the property that secured the creditor's claim. A repayment plan must be proposed in good faith. Some courts have held that plans that propose to pay nothing or only token amounts to unsecured creditors are not meaningful. Other courts have held that payments must be substantial, but need not be the "best effort" of the debtor. In making good-faith interpretations, courts generally try to assess the debtor's budget, future income, payment prospects, outstanding indebtedness, and the nature of the debts being discharged.

2. Involuntary Bankruptcy Petition. Two types of involuntary bankruptcy petitions are available to debtors other than farmers, charitable organizations, and those excluded in voluntary bankruptcy proceedings. In cases where the debtor has fewer than twelve creditors, one or more creditors who hold a total of at least $5,000 of claims may file a petition with the court. In cases where there are twelve or more creditors, at least three with unsecured claims that total $5,000 or more must sign the petition. The debtor may elect to comply with the relief requested in the petition or contest the petition in a court action.

3. Debtor Exemptions. To give the debtor a fresh start, the law allows the debtor to exempt certain assets—property that need not be turned over for distribution to creditors. Exemptions include up to $7,500 in a residence; an interest up to $1,200 in one motor vehicle; and up to $200 in any household furnishings, wearing apparel, appliances, animals, crops, and musical instruments. These items must be held primarily for the personal, family, or household use of the debtor or a dependent and are doubled when husband and wife file joint petitions. Other items on the federal exemption list include up to $500 in jewelry and up to $750 in professional books or trade tools. Specified benefits such as social security, veterans' disability, and alimony support are also exempted. When the law was passed, Congress included a provision that allowed states to substitute their own often smaller exemptions for the federal exemptions, and many states have done so.

4. Trustee in Bankruptcy. A trustee in bankruptcy is elected at the first meeting of creditors by a majority of the unsecured creditors. The trustee's key role is to take over and reduce to money all the bankrupt's assets. The trustee is also responsible for uncovering debtor fraud and concealment and recovering fraudulent transfers of property and preference transfers. A *preference transfer* is defined as transfer of the debtor's property to a creditor made to satisfy a previous debt owed by the debtor to the creditor while the debtor was insolvent. In determining a preference transfer, the courts presume the debtor to have been insolvent during the ninety days preceding the filing of a bankruptcy petition. The courts also presume that preference transfers enable the creditor to receive more than a fair share in a bankruptcy proceeding. Creditors receiving a preference transfer must return it to the trustee.

● Henderson's creditors filed an involuntary bankruptcy petition. A month prior to the filing and while insolvent, Henderson secretly transfered title to an apartment building to a relative who was also an unsecured creditor, for a nominal consideration. The trustee who is responsible for collecting the property of Henderson for fair distribution to all creditors may recover the transfer. The trustee need only show that the preferred creditor received more than a fair share in the assets available for distribution.

The trustee also has the right to make void most *executory contracts*. These are contracts which have not been performed by all the parties to it.

5. Priority of Claims. After the trustee reduces the value of the debtor's assets to money, creditors who hold security interests are paid. The remaining classes of priority are:

○ Expenses related to the administration of the debtor's assets.
○ Claims arising in the ordinary course of the debtor's business following bankruptcy.
○ Claims for wages and employee benefits earned within 180 days before the petition filing, up to a maximum of $2,000 per individual.
○ Claims of $900 per individual for money deposited for undelivered goods or services.
○ Federal and state tax claims due within three years.
○ General creditors.

A creditor's rank on the list of priorities is important because all creditors of one priority must be paid in full before any creditors of a lower priority receive anything. If insufficient money exists to pay the creditors of a particular class in full, those creditors share what exists on a *pro rata* basis (i.e., proportionally according to fractional parts of the whole).

6. Discharge of Bankrupt's Debt. Individuals, but not partnerships and corporations, are entitled to discharge of debt as a matter of right, unless proper objections are sustained by the court. The discharge has the effect of ending the legal obligation of the debtor to pay those debts which have been discharged. A discharge bars creditors from commencing or continuing lawsuits to recover on discharged debts, unless the debtor has fraudulently concealed assets from bankruptcy proceedings. A discharge also permits the bankrupt to resume normal business relations and to enter into binding contracts.

Certain types of debts cannot be discharged. Generally, federal, state, or local taxes owing prior to bankruptcy continue after discharge. Other debts and liabilities that continue include alimony and child support payments and wages owed within a three-month period prior to bankruptcy. Government educational loans, unless they impose an undue hardship on the debtor, cannot be discharged.

Understanding Legal Terms

Define, identify, or explain the following terms:

acceleration clause	collateral cooling-off period	involuntary bankruptcy	punitive damages secured transaction
bait-and-switch scheme	default disclaimer	preference transfer privity	wage garnishment warranty

Questions for Review and Discussion

1. Contrast express and implied warranties.
2. Differentiate between the body of law created by the Magnuson-Moss Act and the UCC product guarantee provisions.
3. Describe the scope of the Consumer Product Safety Act and the powers of the Consumer Product Safety Commission.
4. Identify the product information that the Fair Packaging and Labeling Act requires displayed on consumer product labels.
5. Explain the finance charge and the annual percentage rate that are central to the Truth-in-Lending Act.
6. Under Federal Trade Commission rules, what are the buyer's rescission rights in respect to door-to-door sales?
7. What is the statutory limitation of a credit cardholder's liability in the event of a card's loss, theft, or unauthorized use?
8. Under the Fair Debt Collection Practices Act, what protection is given consumers against abusive debt collector practices?
9. Describe the two types of involuntary bankruptcy petitions available under the Bankruptcy Reform Act.
10. Explain the debtor's exemptions provided for under the Bankruptcy Reform Act.

Analyzing Cases

1. To deal with the risk posed by swimming pool slides, the Consumer Product Safety Commission (CPSC) required manufacturers to include warning signs on new slides. The sign requirements included language such as "Careless Belly Slides Can Cause Paralysis." The commission also required a ladder chain device to warn children to stay off large slides.

Aqua Slide 'N' Dive Corporation raised serious doubts about the effectiveness of the sign and ladder chain requirements. It also was concerned about the economic impact the signs would have on sales.

The testing of the effectiveness of the warning signs was done by a consultant on the commission's staff. The ladder chain device was tested only on the neighbors' children at a pool in the consultant's backyard. The consultant had concluded, "The device would serve as a warning, but probably would not prevent a child from climbing the ladder." The commission did conduct elaborate tests which demonstrated that a deep-water installation would prevent spinal injuries and paralysis.

Aqua Slide sought review of the CPSC's rule before the court of appeals. It argued that the rule was not supported by substantial evidence. Considering that courts traditionally defer to the expertise of regulatory agencies, how should the court dispose of this case? Why? ● *Aqua Slide 'N' Dive v. Consumer Prod. Safety Comm'n,* 569 F.2d 831 (5th Cir. 1978)

2. The California Department of Weights and Measures ordered the removal from sale of flour packaged by General Mills, Inc., and two other millers. The department acted after determining that the average weight of the packaged flour was less than the net weight stated on the packages. This was a violation of the California statute governing net weight labeling of flour which made no allowance for loss of weight resulting from moisture loss during distribution.

The millers sought injunctive relief in federal district court. They argued that the California statute authorizing removal of the flour was invalid.

It was undisputed that the packages of flour ordered off the market by the state authorities complied with the federal law governing net weight labeling of flour as contained in the Food, Drug, and Cosmetic Act and the Fair Packaging and Labeling Act.

Since the state statute did not permit weight variations resulting from loss of moisture during distribution, compliance would require the millers to pack more flour in each package. Congress had not expressly stated a requirement that the federal standard be exclusive. The millers prevailed in their request for an injunction against enforcement of the California requirements in the federal district court and also in the court of appeals. How would the U.S. Supreme Court dispose of this case? Why? ● *Jones V. Rath Packing Co.,* 430 U.S. 519 (1977)

3. The Federal Trade Commission issued a complaint charging that advertising conducted by Warner-Lambert Company (manufacturer of Listerine since 1921) had violated a provision of the Federal Trade Commission Act. The provision allegedly violated stated that "unfair methods of competition . . . and unfair or deceptive acts or practices . . . are declared unlawful. . . ." A hearing before an administrative law judge, in which substantial evidence was produced, sustained the allegations. Warner-Lambert appealed the decision to the FTC, which essentially affirmed the administrative law judge's finding. It ordered Warner-Lambert to cease and desist from representing that Listerine would cure, prevent, or have any significant beneficial effect on the symptoms of colds or sore throats. The commission further ordered Warner-Lambert to conspicuously include in the next ten million dollars of its advertising the following language: "Contrary to prior advertising, Listerine will not help prevent colds or sore throats or lessen their severity." Warner-Lambert sought review of the order before the U.S. court of appeals. Was the FTC's order a proper exercise of agency power? Why? ● *Warner-Lambert Co. v. F.T.C.,* 562 F.2d 749 (D.C. Cir. 1977), *cert. denied,* 435 U.S. 950 (1978).

4. The Federal Trade Commission filed a complaint charging the National Commis-

sion on Egg Nutrition (NCEN) with violating the Federal Trade Commission Act. It alleged that the NCEN had disseminated advertisements containing various false and misleading statements with respect to the relationship between eating eggs and heart and circulatory disease. At the FTC hearing the administrative law judge sustained the complaint and recommended that a cease and desist order be issued. The FTC directed the NCEN to cease and desist from disseminating advertisements containing such false statements as "There is no scientific evidence that eggs increase the risk of . . . heart disease. . . . " The NCEN sought review by the U.S. court of appeals, contending that even if the statement was misleading, the FTC's order infringed upon freedom of speech as guaranteed by the First Amendment. How should the court resolve these contentions? Why? ● *National Comm'n on Egg Nutrition v. F.T.C.,* 570 F.2d 157 (7th Cir. 1977), *cert. denied,* 439 U.S. 821 (1978)

5. A suit was brought against the United States seeking to forbid it from interfering with the interstate shipment and sale of Laetrile, a drug the plaintiff claimed was effective in treating terminally ill cancer patients. This is a drug not considered "safe and effective" within the meaning of the federal Food, Drug, and Cosmetic Act.

In a prior action, the district court had found that the "safety and effectiveness" requirements of the act had no reasonable application to terminally ill cancer patients. The act itself did not provide any exception for terminally ill patients. However, the court also reasoned that since a terminally ill patient would die regardless of what might be done, there were no realistic standards against which to measure the safety and effectiveness of a drug for that class of individuals. Thus, the court of appeals read an implied exception into the statutory language. How should the U.S Supreme Court dispose of this case? Why? ● *United States v. Rutherford,* 442 U.S. 544 (1979); *Rutherford v. United States,* 616 F.2d 455 (1980), *cert. denied,* 66 L. Ed.2d 160 (10th Cir. 1980)

6. Milhollin and others purchased automobiles from various dealers, financing their purchases through standard retail installment contracts. These contracts were assigned to Ford Motor Credit Company (FMCC). As required by the Truth-in-Lending Act and the Federal Reserve Board's regulation, the front page of each installment contract informed the buyer of the right to prepay the obligations under the contract in full at any time prior to maturity. Any buyer who did so would receive a rebate of the unearned portion of the finance charge. The front disclosure page of the installment contract did not mention a clause appearing in the body of the contract giving the creditor the right to accelerate payments of the entire debt upon the buyer's default.

In consumer suits against FMCC, the district court held that disclosure of this right on the front page was required by the provisions of the Truth-in-Lending Act that compels publication of "default, delinquency, or similar charges payable in the event of late payments."

Having agreed to review the case, how should the U.S. Supreme Court rule? Why? ● *Ford Motor Credit Co. v. Milhollin,* 444 U.S. 555 (1980)

7. Bellgraph, mother of seven children, owned a home in Elmira, New York, where she lived for thirty-four years. The home was worth $17,500. One minor daughter lived with Bellgraph, who was divorced. She received $50 a month for support of the daughter from her ex-husband. Her other income came from Social Security disability payments and public assistance and amounted to $390.74. She was totally disabled and was receiving treatment for several ailments.

Bellgraph had a great deal of trouble managing her money. A tax foreclosure proceeding was brought against her for back taxes owed to the city of Elmira. She filed a bankruptcy petition and plan in U.S. bankruptcy court. The plan proposed to pay 100 percent of the back taxes that she owed. The plan created classes of secured creditors, but did not call for any payments to unsecured creditors.

The plan was accepted by the secured creditors, including the taxing authority. No objections were filed by any creditor. At this point the court raised the question as to whether, in view of the fact that the plan did not call for payment to any unsecured creditor, the plan could be regarded as submitted in "good faith." How should the court resolve this question? Why? ● See *Matter of Bellgraph,* 4 B.R. 421 (Bankr. W.D.N.Y. 1980)

8. Byrd purchased a Ford Torino from Bassett Ford, Inc., of Citronelle, Alabama. The vehicle was purchased under a retail installment contract which was assigned to Ford Motor Credit Company (FMCC). The lender took a security interest in the automobile. Byrd was to make thirty-six monthly payments. Approximately thirty-four months later, Craig, a repossession agent, contended that the payments were in arrears. Craig requested that Byrd go to Bassett Ford to review the records of the account and to discuss the matter. Byrd drove there in the Torino. While Byrd was at Bassett Ford and engaged in arguing that his payments were not late, his vehicle was removed from where he had parked it. It was locked up in a storage area behind Bassett's building.

Byrd brought suit against FMCC, claiming conversion of his Torino. Byrd argued that FMCC had fraudulently lured him to Bassett Ford so that possession of the vehicle might be obtained without knowledge and consent, through stealth and trickery. Ford Motor Credit Company contended that a secured party has on default the right to take possession of collateral without judicial process if this can be done without breach of the peace. Should FMCC's arguments be accepted? Why? ● *Ford Motor Credit Co. v. Byrd,* 351 So.2d 557 (Sup. Ct. Ala. 1977)

9. Reno purchased a new Chevrolet from Wood Chevrolet Company in Birmingham, Alabama. The vehicle was purchased with a loan Reno obtained. The lender took a security interest in the Chevrolet. The note, assigned to General Motors Acceptance Corporation (GMAC), called for forty-two monthly payments of $141.45 each. Reno made payments on time for a period of twelve months, when he fell behind. Nevertheless, Reno continued to make some payments when he was able to do so. He received past due notices in the mail concerning the late payments.

Brewer, acting on behalf of GMAC, located Reno's Chevrolet. Using a duplicate key to the vehicle, which he had obtained from the seller, Brewer started the Chevrolet and drove it away.

Reno commenced suit against GMAC. He alleged that GMAC had unlawfully interfered with his right to possess his Chevrolet. GMAC defended on the ground that the UCC gives a secured party on default the right to take possession of collateral without judicial process if it can be done without breach of the peace. The trial court granted summary judgment in GMAC's favor. Reno appealed to the supreme court of Alabama. How should that court decide the case? Is this case any different from *Ford Motor Credit Co. v. Byrd?* Why? ● *Reno v. General Motors Accept. Corp.,* 378 So.2d 1103 (Sup. Ct. Ala. 1979)

Part 2

Case Briefs

Standard Oil v. F.T.C.,
577 F.2d 653 (1978)

Standard Oil Company of California broadcast several television commercials that promoted a gasoline additive known as F-310. The commercials included demonstrations which gave viewers a visual comparison of automobile exhaust before and after using the additive. A balloon attached to the exhaust of an automobile was shown inflating with opaque black vapor, while the announcer described it as "filling with dirty exhaust emissions that go into the air and waste mileage." The announcer then informed the viewers that "Standard Oil of California has developed a remarkable gasoline additive, Formula F-310." The viewers were further informed that the same car was run on six tankfuls of Chevron F-310 and the result was "no dirty smoke, cleaner air." A clear balloon was again shown being attached to the exhaust pipe of the car. This time the balloon inflated with transparent vapor. Another commercial focused on a meter dial labeled "exhaust emissions." The dial showed a scale of 0 (labeled "clean") to 100 (labeled "dirty"). A before-and-after sequence showed the meter pointing to 100 before use of F-310 and to 20 afterward.

The Federal Trade Commission advised Standard Oil that it objected to the advertisements. The commission pointed to, among other things, the fact that exhaust emissions are of two types: visible and transparent. The visible elements (black smoke and particulate matter) contribute less to pollution than the transparent elements, a fact that most members of the public are not aware of. While the additive reduced hydrocarbons and carbon monoxide (transparent pollutants) by 50 and 30 percent respectively, it had no effect at all on lead compound emissions. The commercial gave the public no indication whatsoever of the degree of reduction of invisible pollutants. Thus the disappearance of black smoke could well have been interpreted by the viewers to mean that the additive accomplished a greater pollution reduction than it actually achieved.

The FTC filed a complaint against Standard Oil. A hearing was held before an administrative law judge, who found in Standard Oil's favor. The commission, however, found that the advertisement were false, misleading, and deceptive representations in violation of the Federal Trade Commission Act and issued a cease and desist order. Standard Oil sought review by the U.S. court of appeals.

Petitioner's Position: The advertisements were truthful and were not misleading or deceptive. The FTC, in overturning the finding of the administrative law judge, disregarded the evidence which supported that decision.

Respondent's Position: The most literal truthfulness in advertising is the rule of trade under the Federal Trade Commission Act. If two meanings may be attributed to an advertisement, one of which is false, the advertisement is false.

Legal Issue: Does the record before the court support the commission's interpretation of the meaning the commercial would have to the average viewer and the commission's determination of the accuracy of that message?

Court Decision: There was substantial evidence to support the commission's finding that the F-310 commercials were misleading.

Court Reasoning: The Federal Trade Commission Act is intended to protect "that vast multitude which includes the ignorant, the unthinking, and the credulous." Standard Oil's error was to miscalculate the effect which the televised commercials would have on the public. Although the advertisements did not amount to a wholly false claim about an inferior product, they did misrepresent the extent of pollution reduction.

United States v. City of Chicago, 400 U.S. 8 (1970)

The Chicago and Eastern Illinois Railroad Co. sought to discontinue two passenger trains between Chicago and Evansville, Indiana. The railroad filed notice of its intention to discontinue service with the Interstate Commerce Commission as required by Federal law. The ICC began in investigation of the proposed discontinuance. It found that continued service was not required by public convenience and necessity. Continued operation would unfavorably affect the financial health of the railroad. Therefore, the ability of the railroad to serve other areas would be reduced and interstate commerce would be unduly burdened. The ICC entered an order terminating its investigation.

The city of Chicago brought suit before a federal district court to review the ICC's decision to terminate its investigation. The district court held that the ICC's decision was not an order, and for that reason it lacked jurisdiction to review the commission's proceedings. An appeal for review of the ICC's decision to terminate its investigation was then made to the U.S. Supreme Court.

Petitioner's Position: The decision of the ICC was not merely a decision not to investi-

gate *at all*. Rather it was a decision rendered after a hearing and investigation. There is a recognized presumption in favor of judicial review of final action by an administrative agency. Congress will not be presumed to cut off judicial review unless there is strong reason to believe that such was its intent. There is nothing in the legislative history of the relevant statutes to suggest Congress decided to prevent judicial review in a case such as this.

Respondent's Position: The relevant statute grants judicial review only in the case of orders of the ICC. A decision by the ICC to discontinue a pending investigation is not an order. The interests of all segments of the public are fairly protected under the statutory scheme without judicial review. The ICC represents the public.

Legal Issue: Is a decision of the ICC discontinuing an investigation of a railroad's proposed cessation of train service an order (hence judicially reviewable)?

Court Decision: The decision of the ICC to terminate its investigation was an "order" and hence was subject to judicial review.

Court Reasoning: Whether or not the ICC initiates an investigation in this type of proceeding is a matter within its sole discretion. A decision not to undertake an investigation is not subject to judicial review. However, a decision to investigate requires the ICC to believe that a substantial question exists. A decision to terminate an initiated investigation requires a commission report, and is considered a decision, on the merits of the case. A decision to terminate an investigation, therefore, is an order and is reviewable by the courts at the request of an aggrieved party.

Part 3   Contracts

Chapter 7   Nature and Kinds of Contracts

The study of contracts is basic to an understanding of all areas of business law. The law of contracts is the foundation of authority that gives the courts the power to enforce agreements by industry, government, business, and ultimately the consumer.

The right of individuals and business to contract, generally free of governmental interference, is protected under the Constitution. And the right to contract is central to the workings of the private enterprise system as it functions in the United States. Indeed, most of the business activity in this country depends on contracts in one form or another. Such contracts include promises to manufacture, sell, and deliver goods; perform services; pay salaries; pay rent or mortgage payments; insure life and property; transfer real estate; and undertake countless day-to-day transactions that are the very lifeblood of business and economic activity.

7-1. Contracts

A *contract* is a legally enforceable agreement between two or more competent parties to do or refrain from doing some particular thing that is possible and lawful.

● Esposito went into a department store and purchased a food processor for $85. She paid $15 down and promised to pay the balance when the processor was delivered. This agreement resulted in a contract enforceable at law because the parties mutually agreed to the terms and conditions of a legally enforceable transaction.

● Bingham Publishers, Inc., agreed to pay Davis $2.5 million for the exclusive right to publish and distribute her new novel, an expected bestseller. Davis, in turn, agreed to refrain from selling the publishing and distribution rights to anyone else, including the rights to any screenplay based on her work. This also resulted in a legally binding and enforceable contractual agreement between two competent parties.

In the Esposito case both parties agreed *to do* something they were legally entitled to do. In the Bingham case, Davis agreed to *refrain from doing* something she was legally entitled to do, that is, sell the right to her book to other publishers. In both cases, however, enforceable agreements arose because the parties assented to legal transactions.

The UCC further defines a contract as "The total legal obligation which results from the parties' agreement as affected by the Code or any other applicable law" [1-201 (11)].* Still another way to look at a contract is to consider it as a bargained-for exchange of promises or performances. The *Restatement (Second) of the Law of Contracts* defines a contract as "a promise or set of promises for the breach of which the law gives a remedy, or the performance of which the law in some way recognizes a duty." In this most basic sense, then, a contract is simply a legally binding agreement that the courts will enforce.

A contract must have the following four elements:

○ Mutual agreement (offer and acceptance of given terms)
○ Two or more parties who are capable of contracting
○ Consideration (promises, money, services, or other things of value)
○ Lawful subject matter and purpose

In certain circumstances the law also requires that particular types of contracts have a particular form, such as a written contract under seal.

A. Contracts and Agreements

All contracts contain agreements, but all agreements do not result in contracts. An agreement may or may not be legally enforceable. To be enforceable, it must conform to the law of contracts. The courts have never been agreeable to the enforcement of social agreements: dates, dinner engagements, or the like. These are classified as nothing more than agreements. Many states have extended this concept to include agreements to marry or engagements.

● Michelle Triola Marvin cohabited with actor Lee Marvin, giving up her career, she claimed, to devote her life to their mutual happiness. When they dissolved their relationship, she sued, claiming that because she had lived with him in a husband-wife relationship she should therefore be entitled to property rights and alimony allowed a divorced woman under California law. The court found that there was no marriage contract between them. What they had was nothing more than a social agreement. She was denied the property distribution and other rights that would have been forthcoming had there been a contract.

B. The Nature of a Contract

A contract is by nature a private law which the contracting parties create themselves and mutually agree will govern particular business and other relationships between them. As long as their private law does not violate public policy or public law and meets other requirements (to be discussed in later chapters), the courts will generally enforce this privately made law. In fact, an underlying principle of contract law is that the parties may usually agree to any terms they think fit so long as these terms do not upset the public order.

The subject matter of a contract is usually a promise, a thing, or an act of performance, although it can be almost anything of legal nature. The contract-

---

* Numbers in brackets and parentheses are numerical references to articles, sections, and subsections of the Uniform Commercial Code.

ing party who makes a promise is known as the *promisor;* the one to whom the promise is made is the *promisee.* The party who is obligated to deliver on a promise or undertake some act of performance is called the *obligor.* The contracting party to whom this party owes an obligation is called the *obligee.*

The general rule of contract law is that the parties to a contract must stand in *privity* to one another. That simply means that each must have a legally recognized interest or responsibility in the subject of the contract if they are to be bound by it. Outside parties who do not have such an interest or responsibility in the subject matter of a particular contract may not be bound by it. Their right to sue in the event that the contract is breached (broken) would also be called into question. This does not mean, however, that two or more parties who are in privity to one another cannot contract in such a way as to provide benefits to an outside third party. (An exception to the general rule of privity exists in cases involving warranties and product liability. See Chapter 22 for details.)

7-2. Kinds of Contracts

Contracts are of many kinds. The most common types of contracts are discussed in the paragraphs that follow.

A. Express Contracts

When contracting parties accept mutual legal obligations either through oral discussion or written communication, they have created *express contracts.* Oral negotiations will in many cases be reduced to written agreements before final acceptance.

1. Written Contracts. Most contracts are not written. There are far more oral and implied contracts than there are written ones. Written contracts include agreements evidenced by the exchange of letters, sales slips and receipts, and notations and memorandums signed or initialed by the parties. They may be typed, printed, scrawled, or written in beautiful penmanship. The law, including the UCC, is not specific in the definition of writing.

Reducing an agreement to writing does not make it a formal contract. Legal terms need not be used in expressing the parties' intentions. In fact, many states have passed statutes that require that so-called formal contracts be written in language familiar to and understood by the average person.

In specific situations, state laws require certain types of contracts to be in writing. And certain contracts should be in writing even though the law does not require them to be. When the parties agree to obligations that are complex, or when performance is not to be made until some future time, the parties should express these conditions and terms in writing. Such caution reduces the possibility of misunderstanding and dispute later on.

● Sharman, former coach of the Utah Stars basketball team, appealed to have his contract set aside. Although the contract was in writing, the matter of a pension arrangement was not spelled out fully. Sharman argued that failure to include the specific terms of the pension acted to excuse him from further performance. The court agreed, holding that a pension arrangement was an essential and material part of the contract and that failure to include the specific terms of the pension in the written agreement could lead to future dispute.

Had the parties been careful to write in all their terms and conditions, there might have been no dispute and the agreement might have been enforced.

2. Oral Contracts. When the law does not require a written agreement, an oral contract resulting from the spoken words of the parties will suffice. Parties to an agreement, however, must anticipate the difficulty of proving such agreements should disputes arise later.

● Richardson, a landowner, contracted in writing with J. C. Flood Company for the correction of a stoppage in Richardson's sewer line. In the course of the work Flood found a type of sewer pipe that did not meet the then existing requirements for sewer lines. Flood claimed that it informed Richardson orally of the matter and was instructed to replace the pipe. When Richardson refused to pay, claiming that he had not contracted for that work, Flood sued. Expensive litigation and appeal resulted in a judgment for the plumbing company, only because Richardson had stood by and watched the work being done.

Had the additional oral terms been reduced to writing and added to their contract, no dispute might have arisen. However, expressing every agreement in writing, in anticipation of future need of proof, would be impractical in the fast-paced modern world of business.

B. Implied Contracts

Contract obligations may arise from the acts or gestures of the parties. A respected legal axiom is: "One's actions speak so loudly one cannot hear what one says." Thus, one who knowingly accepts benefits from another may be obligated for their payment even though no express agreement has been made. Entering a bus and dropping a fare in the coin box, placing a quarter in a vending machine, and picking up a newspaper and depositing the money in the receptacle provided illustrate implied agreements. Agreements of this type may be *implied in fact* or *implied by law*.

1. Contracts Implied in Fact. Contracts may be implied by the direct and indirect acts of each party so obligated. Courts will follow the *objective concept* in interpretation of the acts and gestures of a party. Thus, the meaning of one's acts are determined by the impression they would have made upon any reasonable person who might have witnessed them, not by a party's self-serving claim of what was meant or intended.

● Smelgus watched Home Contractors as they installed a new fence at the back of his home. The fence was to have been installed at the rear of the home of a neighbor. The work crew was never interrupted even though Smelgus knew that a mistake had been made. Home Contractors were within their rights to believe that the work was being done with Smelgus's consent and approval. In assessing damages for the cost of the improvement, the court would accept the contractor's claim by applying the objective concept—the fact that demonstrable work was done on the fence in Smelgus's presence—rather than a defense by Smelgus, who might now orally deny any intention to contract.

In applying the objective concept, a court bases its decision on the failure of one party to act when that person has the opportunity and obligation to act. If

Smelgus, for example, had not intended to contract with Home Contractors, he was under an obligation to stop them from installing the fence. The fact that he did not do this even though he had the chance to would *imply* the existence of a contractual relationship with Home Contractors.

2. Contracts Implied in Law (Quasi-Contracts). The law will at times impose contract obligations in matters where it may be proved that the parties had never created written, oral, or implied agreements. Applying reasons of justice and fairness, a court may obligate one who has unfairly benefited at the innocent expense of another. Not to be confused with contracts implied in fact, such agreements are classified as *quasi-contracts*.

● A woman was found unconscious on the highway by a passing motorist who arranged to have her removed to a hospital for emergency treatment. When the injured woman regained consciousness, she denied any obligation to pay for treatment, claiming that she was not aware of what was going on and had not agreed to what had been done for her. The case illustrates a quasi-contractual situation wherein the injured person was unjustly benefitted at the innocent expense of the hospital, doctors, and others. In any suit that might arise over this episode, a court would require that the woman pay the fair value of the services rendered.

The quasi-contract concept may not be used, however, as a means of obtaining payment for an act that a party simply feels should be done. Nor will the concept be applied where one party bestows a benefit upon another unnecessarily or through misconduct or negligence.

● Klein, during a neighbor's absence, saw the need for mowing the lawn and doing other clean-up jobs on the neighbor's property. She did the work and billed the neighbor $50. Although there may have been an unjust benefit to the neighbor at Klein's innocent expense, the quasi-contract concept will not apply.

Quasi-contracts are not considered contracts in a true sense because they are entirely court-created; they do not arise as a result of the mutual understanding and assent of the parties as do other valid contracts.

C. Informal and Formal Contracts

The law requires in specific matters that contracts follow formalities prescribed by statute or the common law. These are defined as *formal contracts*. All others are classified as either informal or simple contracts.

1. Informal or Simple Contracts. Any oral contract or any written one that is not under seal or a contract of record is considered an *informal* or *simple contract*. Informal contracts generally have no requirements as to language, form, or construction. They comprise those obligations entered into by parties whose promises are expressed in the simplest and usually most ordinary nonlegal language.

2. Formal Contracts. By common law, formal contracts differed from other types in that they had to be (*a*) written, (*b*) signed, witnessed, and placed under the seal of the parties, and (*c*) delivered. The UCC removed the requirement for the seal in the sale of personal property. Many states, by statute, have eliminated the use of the seal entirely. Other states, however, still require the use of the seal in agreements related to the sale and transfer of real property.

● Kovach signed an agreement to buy ten acres of woodland located in the Adirondack Mountains. The seller found another interested buyer who would pay a higher price for the land. Kovach had signed the sales agreement without including any representation of the seal. Kovach would be helpless in attempting to enforce the contract in a state that required such formality in real estate agreements.

Today a person's seal may be any mark or sign placed after the signature intended to be the signer's seal. It does not, as in the time of early common law, require an impression in the document made by a ring or other mechanical device. In states still requiring the seal on formal contracts, it is sufficient to write the word *seal* after the signature. It is also acceptable to write the letters *L.S.* after the signature; they stand for the words *locus sigilli* ("place of the seal").

Formal agreements are usually prepared by attorneys or from model forms found in legal reference guides. Technical legal language which may be difficult for the average person to understand is often used. However, formal agreements need not be written in this fashion; simple, understandable English may be used. As stated previously, some states have passed legislation requiring all contracts to be written in language that the ordinary person can comprehend. In most cases it is the requirement of the seal that makes a contract formal, not the language used.

Classified as formal contracts today are agreements under seal, negotiable instruments and certain other types of documents, letters of credits, contracts of record, penal bonds, and recognizances. The latter two are not associated with business law and have to do with procedures related to the temporary release of a prisoner held on criminal charges.

Contracts of record are a special type of formal contract and have certain unique characteristics. For the most part, they are contracts that have been adjudicated and confirmed by a court, with an accompanying judgment issued in favor of one of the parties. The judgment is recorded, giving the successful litigant the right to demand satisfaction of the judgment. Contracts of record are not contracts in the true sense of the word because, for the most part, they are court-created. They usually do not have certain necessary requisites of a valid contract, such as mutual assent of the parties. Nonetheless, for public policy and other reasons they are enforced in the same way as any other valid contract.

● Kibler harvested wheat for Garrett and sent Garrett a bill for $826. Garrett sent Kibler a check for $444, on which was written "in full payment of all money owed." The condition was in very fine print and not seen by Kibler. Kibler sued Garrett for the amount still owed. The court ruled in favor of Kibler and entered a judgment against Garrett for the money owed. Entry of the judgment created a contract of record, which was enforceable against Garrett.

Also classified as contracts of record are consent decrees and other types of agreements entered into with government regulatory agencies. For example, a company might sign an agreement with an agency such as the Federal Trade Commission to cease and desist from falsely advertising a product. Such an agreement, like any other contract of record, would have the effect of a legally binding judicial decree.

JULIUS BLUMBERG, INC., LAW BLANK PUBLISHERS
80 EXCHANGE PLACE, AT BROADWAY, NEW YORK

Articles of Agreement,

Between Arthur Sparks of the City of Jersey City, County of Hudson, and State of New Jersey,--

---party *of the first part,*

and Donna Stevens of the City of Elizabeth, County of Union, and State of New Jersey,

---party *of the second part.*

The party of the first part, in consideration of ten Well-Known Brand No. 5 typewriters, sold to him this day by the said party of the second part, and by her agreed to be delivered to the party of the first part at Jersey City, New Jersey, free of all charges for delivery and other expenses whatsoever, on or before the first day of November next,--- *covenants and agrees to* pay to the party of the second part within sixty days after such delivery, the sum of Five Hundred Dollars ($500).-----------------------------

The party of the second part, in consideration of the foregoing agreement of the party of the first part,---

covenants and agrees to forward and deliver, on or before the first day of November next, all expenses to be paid by her, the said ten Well-Known Brand No. 5 typewriters, and hereby warrants the same to be new and in good order and condition for immediate use.---

This instrument may not be changed orally.

In Witness Whereof, *the parties hereunto have set their hands and seals the*

Nineteenth--------------------- *day of* October----------------- *in the year one thousand nine hundred and* ------.

Sealed and delivered in the presence of

Charles Blandovsky   *Arthur Sparks (L. S.)*

                              Donna Stevens (L. S.)

Figure 7-1. A formal contract.

D. Entire and Divisible Contracts

Contracts are either entire or divisible. Contracts that contain two or more parts that are dependent on one another for satisfactory performance are *entire contracts*. Those that contain two or more independent parts, each of which may be performed or breached without affecting the other, are *divisible contracts*.

1. Entire or Indivisible Contracts. All the terms and conditions in an entire contract must be performed. Otherwise the agreement is breached. Less than total performance results in cancellation of all other parts.

● Western Electronics contracted to deliver a tuner, amplifier, and stereo speakers to Kimmy. When delivery was made, the amplifier was missing. Without the amplifier the stereo set would be incomplete and of no practical use. Failure to deliver the amplifier resulted in a breach of the entire contract, relieving Kimmy of any obligation to Western Electronics.

Chapter 7:
Nature
and Kinds
of
Contracts

2. Divisible Contracts. By contrast, failure to perform any one part of a divisible contract would not necessarily invalidate the entire agreement. Those separate parts which are illegal and divisible from the whole may be rendered void or unenforceable; those that are valid may still be enforced by the courts.

● Mr. and Mrs. Willcher entered into a separation agreement when they accepted the fact that their marriage was breaking up. As it turned out, certain clauses in their contract were found to be void and not in conformance with state law. A question arose as to whether the entire contract, therefore, was void. The court ruled the contract agreement to be divisible, struck out the parts that were not legal, and enforced the rest.

E. Unilateral and Bilateral Contracts

The words *unilateral* and *bilateral*, as used here, refer to promises.

1. Unilateral Contracts. A *unilateral contract* is defined as "a one-sided agreement whereby one makes a promise to do, or refrain from doing, something in return for a performance, not a promise." In this type of agreement the offeree makes no promise to perform. However, as soon as the offeree does perform as requested by the offeror, that performance creates a binding agreement between the two.

● Tedesco promised, in writing, to pay Judd Realty, Inc., an 8 percent commission if the realty company would secure a purchaser for a property within a six-month period. Judd produced a purchaser within the six months, but Tedesco refused to pay the commission because final settlement did not occur until a short time thereafter. The court ruled that this was a unilateral agreement and that Judd, by producing a purchaser within the six-month period, had a right to the 8 percent commission promised.

2. Bilateral Contracts. A *bilateral contract,* by contrast, is one in which there is a promise by one party in return for a promise by the other. Bilateral agreements create binding obligations when the promises are made. Failure to perform by either party results in a breach of contract.

● Suppose that in the Tedesco case Judd Realty, Inc., was promised an 8 percent commission, and Judd promised to secure a buyer. Such an agreement would not be appropriate in sale of real estate, but if it had been, both parties would have been bound to their promises through a bilateral contract.

7-3. Status of Contracts

After a contract has been negotiated but until all obligations have been satisfactorily performed, it is *executory*. After performance is complete, the contract is *executed*.

A. Executory Contracts

Executory contracts are those that have been agreed to by both parties, are enforceable, and have promises and conditions still outstanding.

● Corley contracted to buy a new Volkswagen Rabbit. Terms of the sales were agreed to, and the VW Sales Company made the car ready for delivery on the date promised. Corley made payment except for $150, which was promised when the car was delivered. The contract is *executory*. All conditions and promises have not been met until Corley makes the $150 payment and the car is delivered to him.

B. Executed Contracts

Executed contracts are those whose terms and conditions have been completely performed by the parties. In executed contracts neither party remains obligated to the other in any way.

● In the previous case, delivery of the new car to Corley would complete the entire agreement. If the original contract contained a dealer's obligation to tune and adjust the engine after 500 miles, the agreement would continue to be executory until the engine adjustment had been made. When the engine adjustment had been made, the contract would then be executed.

7-4. Validity and Enforceability of Contracts

In addition to their other characteristics, contracts are also classified as valid, voidable, or void. Determination of validity depends upon laws that prescribe contract construction, operation, termination, and legality.

A. Valid Contracts

Agreements between two or more competent parties to carry out obligations that are legal in nature and enforceable through application of contract law are *valid contracts*. Failure of either party to perform accepted obligations provides grounds for the other party to seek damages for breach of contract.

● Feldman purchased a health and accident insurance policy, paying the premium for one year's coverage. Eight months later she was confined to a hospital after falling from a ladder. The agreement with the insurance company satisfied all the requirements of a valid contract. The insurance company's failure to make payments due under the policy could result in a complaint to the state insurance commission as well as a civil action for breach of contract.

B. Voidable Contracts

Voidable contracts are those that may be avoided (canceled) by one of the parties only. Contracts entered into by minors and contracts that are induced by fraud or misrepresentation are examples of such contracts.

● Volkes was enticed into signing a contract in which she agreed to pay for an expensive course of dancing lessons. Her agreement called for the payment of $31,000 over the period she would be so engaged. Arthur Murray, Inc., had continually informed her that she had great talent and would become a professional dancer. These representations were later found not to be true. The contract was voided in her favor, on grounds of misrepresentation.

Volkes in this case had the right of either demanding the fulfillment of the contract or avoiding her obligations, and she elected to do the latter.

C. Void Agreements

Void agreements are those that for many reasons are invalid from the moment the agreement is made. Such agreements may not rightfully be called contracts as no contractual obligations ever existed. Usually this is the case where the agreement lacks one or more of the requisites of a valid contract such as mutual assent, consideration, or legal subject matter.

● Zalis sued for a fee of $15,000, which Zalis claimed was owed in payment for having found a buyer for property being offered by Blumenthal. Blumenthal proved that Zalis had no state license either as a real estate sales representative or as a broker. The court denied recovery of the $15,000, basing its decision on law that required a license of anyone engaged in real estate practice. The carefully written agreement between Zalis and Blumenthal was declared void due to illegality.

Understanding Legal Terms

Define, identify, or explain the following terms:

bilateral contract	executed contract	informal contract	unilateral agreement
contract	executory contract	oral contract	valid contract
contract of record	express contract	quasi-contract	void agreement
divisible contract	formal contract	seal	voidable contract
entire contract	implied contract		

Questions for Review and Discussion

1. Explain the difference between a contract and an agreement.

2. Discuss the concept of contracts as being privately made laws.

3. How are the terms of an agreement in an implied contract ascertained? In an express contract?

4. How does a contract implied in fact differ from a contract implied in law, or a quasi-contract? Give an example of each.

5. What are the common-law requirements as to formal contracts?

6. Are contracts of record really contracts? Explain.

7. Explain the nature of promises in regard to (a) unilateral contracts and (b) bilateral contracts?

8. When is a contract considered (a) executed and (b) executory? Give an example of each type of contract.

9. What are the obligations of contracting parties under (a) a valid contract and (b) a voidable contract?

10. Why do void agreements not qualify as true contracts?

Analyzing Cases

1. Bloomgarden, a realtor, introduced Coyer and Guy to various parties with the result that Coyer and Guy were financed in a multimillion-dollar project along the Georgetown waterfront in Washington, D.C. At no time did Bloomgarden or the others involved mention that a fee was expected in return for Bloomgarden's assistance. Bloomgarden is now suing for $1 million, which he claims is due him under the usual custom of paying fees to one who promotes the financing of such projects. Bloomgarden claims the right of recovery through either an implied contract or a quasi-contract. Had either of these types of agreement been created? Explain. ● *Bloomgarden v. Coyer,* 479 F.2d 201 (D.C. 1973)

2. Wesley and Marjorie Kirk sustained damage to their home from high-altitude test flights of aircraft by United States government agencies. Before the tests began, advertisements and other public notices appeared stating that the United States would compensate any property owners for damages related to the tests. The Kirks contended that a contract implied in fact existed between them and the United States. Was there such a contract? ● *Kirk v. United States,* 451 F.2d (D. Okla. 1971)

3. Brookhaven Servicing Corporation, a mortgage lending company, sent a letter to Richman, a real estate broker. In the letter, Brookhaven promised a compensation of 3 percent on all mortgages placed if Richman would not seek mortgage money from any other company. Richman, relying on the letter, did as requested. The question now arises as to whether a unilateral contract had been created by the parties. Judgment for whom and why? ● *Richman v. Brookman Servicing Corp.,* 363 N.Y.S.2d 731 (1975)

4. B. L. Nelson & Associates, Inc., entered into a contract with the city of Argyle. They agreed to design and construct a sanitary sewer collection and treatment facility for the city. Payment for design services and construction was to be made as various segments of the work were completed. Was this a divisible or entire contract? ● *B. L. Nelson & Associates, Inc. v. City of Argyle,* 535 S.W.2d 906 (Tex. 1976)

5. Peters entered into a contract to purchase Dowling's business. The following terms were agreed to: (*a*) Peters would take over all Dowling's executory contracts; (*b*) Peters would purchase Dowling's tools at an agreed-to price; (*c*) Peters would accept full responsibility for all warranties made by Dowling on previous contracts; (*d*) Dowling would remain as a consultant to the new firm for a period of five years. Analyze each part of this contract and classify each term according to whether it is executed or executory. Is the contract entire or divisible? Explain your answer. ● *Wagstaff v. Peters,* 453 P.2d 120 (Kan. 1969)

6. Ruth Block asked J. B. Venable, Esq., an attorney, to represent her in a pending lawsuit. They reached an oral agreement in which Venable accepted Block's proposal. He agreed that he would be compensated out of any money they might recover in a judgment against the other party. Venable, through alleged negligence, failed to file certain documents that were vital to Block's suit, and as a result the judge threw the case out of court. Venable, now being sued by Block, contends that there was no contract because Block had never signed a written agreement and he never received a retainer fee. How would you decide this suit? ● *Venable v. Block,* 225 S.E.2d 755 (Ga. 1976)

7. American Store Equipment contracted to design and supply fixtures for extensive alterations to Jack Dempsey's Punch Bowl, Inc. Disagreements developed, and Jack Dempsey's canceled the entire contract. In a suit by American Store it was shown that American Store did not have the required architect's license for doing the design work. American Store then claimed a divisible contract, stating that supplying the fixtures was separate and distinct from the design function. Jack Dempsey's argued that this was an entire agreement, with the two parts so intertwined that they could not be considered as divisible. Is this a divisible or an entire contract? Do you think this is a valid contract? Explain. ● *American Store Equipment, etc. Corp. v. Jack Dempsey's Punch Bowl, Inc.,* 16 N.Y.2d 702 (1939)

8. Lawrence, a second cousin to Beck, took up residence in Beck's household, by Beck's invitation. He continued living there until his death twenty years later. Lawrence, on several occasions, had assured Beck that there were provisions in his will that would compensate Beck for the use of the room. Lawrence had also stated at different times that he would never accept charity from relative, friend, or stranger. Wilhoite, executor of the Lawrence estate, notified Beck that

there was nothing in the will concerning compensation for the twenty years' rent. Did a contract exist between Lawrence and Beck? If so, what kind? Discuss. ● *Beck v. Wilhoite,* 141 Ind. App. 543 (1967)

9. The Barretts signed a judgment note in the state of Delaware. (A *judgment note* is one which authorizes the holder to enter final judgment in a court against the maker without the maker's appearance or right of defense.) Failure to meet payment on the note resulted in a judgment against the Barretts in a Maryland court. The judgment was duly recorded and presented to the Delaware courts for execution and enforcement. At the time of the making of the note, Delaware law required the addition of the seal to the signatures of the payors, or promissors, on such an instrument. Would the judgment note be considered a formal contract? If so, what kind? Do you think the Delaware courts should enforce this judgment note? Explain. ● *South Orange Trust Co. v. Barrett,* 76 A.2d 310 (Del. 1950)

10. Anderson, a farmer, orally agreed to buy a used tractor from the Copeland Equipment Company for $475. Copeland delivered the tractor to Anderson, who used it for eleven days. During this period Anderson could not borrow enough funds to cover the purchase price. Anderson therefore returned the tractor to Copeland. Both parties agree that their sales contract was canceled when the tractor was returned. However, Copeland now claims that under the doctrine of quasi-contract Anderson is required to pay for the eleven days' use made of the tractor. Do you agree with Copeland? Explain your answer. ● *Anderson v. Copeland,* 378 P.2d 1006 (Okla. 1963)

Chapter 8 — Agreement: Offer and Acceptance

The first requisite of any contract is the agreement made by the parties. This is known as *mutual assent,* also commonly called the meeting of the minds. Mutual assent may be reached quickly, as in buying a newspaper at the local newsstand, or it may be the achievement of weeks of negotiation related to a multimillion-dollar undertaking.

Mutual assent develops from the expressed and implied obligations made by two or more consenting parties. The UCC states that "a contract for sale of goods may be made in any manner sufficient to show agreement, including conduct by both parties which recognizes the existence of such contract" [2-204(1)]. Although the UCC here refers to sales agreements, the courts usually take guidance from the UCC in interpreting other types of contracts. The agreement may be in writing, oral, or implied. Written agreements, of course, are preferred if the parties anticipate any future disputes as to the interpretation of the obligations they have accepted.

Mutual assent evolves through the communication of an offer and an acceptance between the contracting parties.

8-1. Definition and Requirements of an Offer

An *offer* is a proposal made by one party to another indicating a willingness to enter into a legally binding contract. The offer may be written, oral, or implied. One making an offer is the *offeror.* The one to whom it is made is the *offeree.*

An offer is valid only if it satisfies the following requirements:

○ Communication
○ Serious intent
○ Clarity and reasonable definiteness
○ Direction to a specific offeree

A. Communication to the Offeree

The proposed offer must be communicated to the offeree in order to be valid. The communication of the offeror's intentions may be by whatever means are convenient and desirable. It may be communicated orally, by letter, by telegram, or by any other means capable of transmitting the offeror's proposal. It may also be implied. Acts and conduct of the proposing party are in many cases successful in communicating an intention to make an offer to another party witnessing them. When acts and conduct are sufficient to convey an offeror's intentions, an implied offer results.

● A dealer in antique furniture attended an auction sale where many desirable items were offered. The dealer, getting the auctioneer's attention, nodded when asked for a bid at a certain price. Although no words were spoken between the auctioneer and the dealer, the nod by the dealer was sufficient communication to the auctioneer of an intent to make a valid offer. This, then, would constitute an *implied* offer.

A person signing a contract is *presumed* to have received communication of all its contents and therefore may be obligated by all its terms. It is inadvisable, therefore, to sign a contract without reading its contents very carefully.

B. Serious Intent

Offers made in obvious jest, during emotional outburst of rage or anger, or under other circumstances that might convey a lack of serious intent will invalidate what might have otherwise been a valid proposal. The offeror's words or actions must be such as would give the offeree assurance that a binding agreement is intended.

When offers are made in jest, it must be proved that both parties were in the same spirit of frolic and fun if a lack of serious intent is used as a defense. Serious intent is determined by what the offeree had the right to believe was intended by what was said and observed when the offer was made.

● McClurg and Terry, in company with friends, appeared before a justice of the peace, took their marriage vows, and were declared to be man and wife. The two never lived together, and now seek annulment, declaring that the marriage was never seriously intended. Both McClurg and Terry, supported by testimony of all others of their company, testified that the whole matter had been carried out as a joke, with no serious intent. The chancellor (judge) accepted the evidence presented, declared the marriage contract to have been without serious intent, and dissolved their marital obligations.

C. Clarity and Reasonable Definiteness of Terms

The communicated terms of an offer must be sufficiently clear to remove any doubt about the contractual intentions of the offeror. There will be no valid offer when terms are indefinite, inadequate, vague, or confusing.

● A building contractor wrote to Wendel, the owner of a 125-acre farm, stating, "Please consider this my offer to purchase 5 acres of your farm on which I propose to build a house. My offering price is $2,000 an acre. Reply by return mail." No binding agreement could result from this offer. It was both indefinite and inadequate; one could not tell from which of Wendel's 125 acres the contractor would select the 5 acres desired.

The UCC permits offers to omit certain information. It states that "even though one or more terms are left open a contract of sale does not fail for indefiniteness if the parties have intended to make a contract and there is a reasonably certain basis for giving an appropriate remedy" [2-404 (3)]. Under this section of the UCC as well as other applicable law, the following agreements are enforceable, although not complete in particular matters.

1. Cost-Plus Contracts. A *cost-plus contract* is one in which a final price is not included, but is to be determined by the cost of labor and materials plus an agreed-to percentage of markup. While the figure is not *certain,* it is *determinable* by a formula acceptable to both parties.

2. Requirements or Services as Needed. Courts will uphold contracts where the exact quantity to be delivered may not be known until there has been a determination of need. This type of contract, however, must be founded on the agreement of one party to supply and the other party to accept the needs or services in question.

● Peninsula Electric Company contracted to buy all the coal it might need from Chesapeake Fuel Company. The contract was written to cover a period of one year. The price of coal was to be determined by the price published under the commodity index on each date delivery was made. This agreement, while indefinite in its terms, did bind the parties to need and price factors that were reasonably definite and within the court's ability to make a determination of each.

3. Indefinite-Duration Contracts. Contracts that do not include definite terms as to beginning and ending dates are valid. It is held that these dates are subject to future determination by the parties.

● Scheider contracted with MGM to act and be a star in a pilot for a projected new television series. All terms were agreed to with the exception of dates for the filming of the series. Scheider sought to be relieved from the contract, claiming that failure to include the essential dates invalidated the agreement. The court upheld the agreement, holding that commercial practice, custom, or usage, as known to both parties, may be applied in supplying these missing terms.

4. First-Refusal Contracts. An offeror, such as a property owner, may enter a binding contract to give an offeree the right to first refusal, that is, the first right to purchase by matching any proposal terms made by a third party. Although the final terms are indefinite, they will be set by an offer made by a third party.

5. Current Market Price Terms. Agreements in which prices and terms are to be determined by future market price and general commercial usage are generally not invalid for want of indefiniteness.

● Swanson and King applied for a room in a college dormitory. At the time the college filed their dorm application, fees for the fall semester had not yet been set by the board of trustees. The resident director would make no commitment as to the dormitory building or the floor to which the two students would be assigned.

The agreement very clearly lacked definiteness of terms. However, the college would be obligated by the agreement to provide dormitory space. Terms to be added later must be within the bounds of reasonableness. Tripling dorm fees of the year before or assigning the students to an obviously undesirable room in an unsafe building would give the students grounds for voiding the otherwise valid agreement.

When it is agreed that the parties are not to be bound until after the price is fixed, neither party is bound until that is done. If, in anticipation of a satisfactory price, some goods are delivered and accepted, the buyer may return them if not satisfied with the final published price. If it is impossible to return the goods, the buyer is obligated to pay a price determined by the court to be reasonable.

● Suppose in the previous case Swanson and King moved in a suite in a dorm before final fees were announced. Their final acceptance would be determined by their willingness to abide by the not-yet-published fee schedule. Rejection of the new schedule would terminate their obligation except for negotiated payment for the time that they occupied the quarters.

D. Direction of Offers to Specific Offeree

A proposal to contract lacks validity unless the offer is intended for acceptance by a selected offeree. The offer, so made, may be accepted only by the one to whom it was made.

Offers may be directed to an individual or to an organized body such as a business or government agency. Offers may also be made to *collective groups*. These include such units as clubs, teams, social organizations, and other combines organized to serve the special interests of their membership. An offer made to a collective group is no different from an offer made to an individual.

● A music publishing house offered to provide the Colonial Marching Band with a series of new marches, to be published one each month over a period of one year. Each march, with full score, would cost the band $75. The Colonial Marching Band is a collective group. Acceptance of the offer could be made by a motion voted on by a majority of the members present at the meeting.

1. Public Offers. Offerors at times must communicate an offer to a party whose name, identity, or address is unknown. In such cases, the offer may be published or broadcast in any manner that might be considered likely to reach the one sought. Although accomplished through a public announcement, the offer is intended for only one person or a particular party. Although this is a *public offer*, it is no different legally from other types of offers.

● Hardesty was the victim of a burglary in which valuable paintings were taken from a studio. An advertisement appeared in the local newspaper offering a reward for information leading to the recovery of the paintings and the arrest of the burglar. This was a valid public offer. It was directed to an individual or party who might have the information requested by Hardesty, the offeror.

2. Invitations to Trade. By contrast, invitations to trade are not offers. An *invitation to trade* is an announcement published to reach many persons for the purpose of creating interest and attracting responses. Newspaper and magazine advertisements, radio and television commercials, and store window displays come within this definition. If invitations to trade were considered to be offers, an offeror would be at the mercy of untold numbers of persons who might respond and demand delivery of goods and services far beyond the advertising party's ability to supply them. In the case of an invitation to trade, no binding agreement develops until a responding party makes an offer which the advertiser accepts.

a. Advertisements. Most advertising is an invitation to trade. The usual intent of the advertiser is to attract, or tempt, readers, viewers, and listeners to contact the advertiser and make offers induced by the advertising. Advertisements usually state what the offeree must do but do not state what the offeror will be required to do. For example, advertisements do not normally indicate the number of items the offeror is willing to sell. In determining contractual obligations, however, the buyer must recognize the difference between offers and invitations to trade.

● The Dayton Shopping News carried an advertisement in which Elder displayed a $175 sewing machine for sale for only $26. The machine was advertised as the "Thursday Special." Craft entered Elder's store, tendered the $26, and demanded the machine. The court ruled that the advertisement was nothing more than an invitation to trade, not an offer. Craft's tender of the $26 was an offer which Elder could have either accepted or not, as he wished.

In a somewhat different case the decision was otherwise.

● Surplus Store published the following advertisement in a Minneapolis Newspaper: "SATURDAY 9 A.M. 2 BRAND NEW PASTEL MINK 3-SKIN SCARFS selling for $89.50. Out they go Saturday. Each . . . $1.00. 1 BLACK LAPIN STOLE Beautiful, WORTH $139.50 . . . $1.00. FIRST COME FIRST SERVED." Lefkowitz, the first customer admitted to the store on Saturday, tendered $1, demanding the Lapin stole. The store refused to sell, stating that the offer was intended for women only. Lefkowitz sued.

The court ruled in favor of Lefkowitz. It held that Surplus Store's proposal was clear, definite, and certain, leaving nothing further for the parties to negotiate. The advertisement was clear in expressing the store's intention to sell two mink scarfs, each for $1. Nothing in the advertised offer mentioned the later-added condition of a "women only" sale.

b. Auction Sales. The UCC confirms the common-law concept of auction sales. The UCC states that "a sale by auction is complete when the auctioneer so announces by the fall of the hammer or in other customary manner" (2-238). Thus it is indicated that the auctioneer's offering of goods is an invitation to trade and nothing more. In response to the auctioneer's *invitation,* bidders are encouraged to make offers in the form of bids. It is the auctioneer who makes final acceptance.

c. Bids or Estimates. Calls for bids or estimates for work to be done or materials to be furnished do not bind the person calling for the bids to give the work to the contractor submitting the lowest bid. Such calls for bids are not offers but rather requests for offers, to be accepted or rejected by the caller. The caller usually reserves the right to determine whether the lowest bidder has the necessary ability, skills, and financial stability to carry out the proposed agreement, and to reject a low bid if this is not the case. Statutes in some states, however, require that if a bid on a public contract is accepted, the offer of the lowest bidder must be the one accepted.

d. Printed Notices. Printed notices on steamship and railroad tickets, parking lot claim checks, insurance policies, telegraph blanks, and similar forms are considered to be part of the communicated offer, even if they are not read. The stipulations on baggage checks, however, must be called to the attention of the holders; and any printed statements on the letter paper on which an offer is written must be referred to in the body of the letter to be considered part of the communicated offer. Notices on parking lot claim tickets usually are considered part of the contract only if written or printed in a conspicuous manner.

● A wholesale stationery company wrote all contracts with supply houses and made all offers to retailers on letter paper on which was printed, in small type at the bottom of the paper, the following statement: "This company reserves the right to cancel the above offer, or contract, any time within five days from the date made, because of changing markets and demands." The court held that these statements had no legal effect because they were not specifically referred to in the body of the writing of the contract or offer and were not printed in a conspicuous manner.

8-2. Acceptance of Offers

Mutual assent is complete when the offeree has expressed or implied the intention of being bound by the agreement communicated in the offer. For an acceptance to be valid, the following conditions must be met:

○ Acceptance must be communicated to the offeror.
○ Terms of acceptance must be unqualified.

As will be shown later, the UCC makes an exception to the rule that there must be an unqualified acceptance.

A. Who May Accept an Offer?

Only the offeree, the one to whom the offer is directed, has the right to accept. If another party attempted to accept, that attempt would be viewed instead as a new and independent offer.

● Shuford sold machinery to the State Machinery Company. Concurrent with that sale Shuford also offered to sell another machine in stock. Lee, treasurer of Nutmeg State Machinery Corp., learned that the machine was available, called, inspected it, and bought it for $250. Shuford had mistakenly believed that Lee was from the State Machinery Co. He now refused delivery to Nutmeg. Nutmeg sued. The court held that no contract resulted. Only the party to whom an offer is made may accept an offer.

1. Acceptance in Unilateral Contracts. Unilateral contracts do not usually require communication of expressed acceptance. The offeror's promise is related to the offeree's performance rather than communication of intent. Performance commenced within the limits of time allowed by the offeror and with the offeror's knowledge constitutes acceptance.

● Fujimoto and Bravo were both employed by Rio Grande Pickle Company. When they expressed dissatisfaction with their jobs, their employer offered them a new contract whereby they would receive a 10 percent bonus on company profits if they remained with the firm. They did not respond with an expressed acceptance but remained on the job. At times they did discuss the terms of the new agreement with an official of Rio Grande. Rio Grande later refused to pay the 10 percent bonus, claiming that its offer had never been accepted. The court ruled this to be a unilateral agreement and that their performance in remaining with Rio Grande constituted acceptance.

The UCC places some responsibility upon the offeree in notifying the offeror of the commencement of performance. Notification of performance must be given within a reasonable time of commencement or the offeror may treat the offer as having lapsed [2-206(2)].

2. Acceptance of Bilateral Contracts. In bilateral contracts, unlike unilateral ones, the offeree must communicate acceptance to the offeror. Bilateral contracts consist of a promise by one party in return for a promise by the other. Until the offeree communicates a willingness to be bound by his or her promise, there is no valid acceptance.

● Suppose in the previous case Rio Grande Pickle Company had said to its two employees, "We will consider your written acceptance to this new proposal as binding us to the payment of the 10 percent bonus." There would have been the intention of creating a bilateral contract, supported by mutual promises by both Rio Grande and Fujimoto and Bravo.

B. Methods of Communicating Acceptance

The UCC says that "an offer to make a contract shall be construed as inviting acceptance in any manner and by any medium reasonable in the circumstances." [2-206(1) (a)]. The *Restatement (Second) of the Law of Contracts* in similar language says, "A medium of acceptance is reasonable if it is the one used by the offeror or one in similar transactions at the time and place the offer is received." Thus the offeree may choose any means of communication to make acceptance that is convenient, appropriate, and reasonable.

● The Electronics Development Corporation wrote the New England Battery Company, offering to purchase 100 high-ampere batteries at a quoted price. The battery company telephoned its acceptance of the offer, stating that written confirmation would follow. New England Battery's method of acceptance was reasonable and appropriate under the circumstances and conformed to the guidelines of the UCC, the *Restatement,* and general custom.

Communication of acceptance may be either express or implied. Where there is an express acceptance, at times the offer may stipulate that communication is to be made "by Western Union," or "by return mail" or in some other particular manner. Since these stipulations usually are interpreted as conditions of the offer, they should be followed. However, where such a stipulation is not a part of the offer, the general rule prevails: acceptance may be made in any manner and using any medium that is reasonable.

The effective date and timing of an acceptance can be quite important and, at times, may become the subject of dispute and litigation. This is so because when the acceptance has been communicated by the offeree to the offeror, the mutual assent of the parties is considered complete and the parties are thereby legally bound to a contract.

1. Face-to-Face and Telephone Communication. No special problem as to the timing of acceptance usually arises if the parties are dealing face-to-face. The acceptance becomes complete and effective as soon as the offeror hears the words of acceptance spoken by the offeree. In a similar vein, if the parties are negotiating over the telephone, the acceptance becomes effective when the offeree speaks the words of acceptance into the telephone receiver. When the parties must negotiate by writing letters or sending telegrams, problems may arise, and the law provides certain rules as to when acceptance occurs.

2. Communication by the Same Agent Used by the Offeror. Under common law if acceptance is made through the same agency or medium that communicated the offer, acceptance is complete and effective when it is delivered to that same agency or medium. Thus an offer made through the mail is accepted when the acceptance is mailed. Offers made by telegram are accepted and become effective when the acceptance is filed with the telegraph company. This ruling, of course, requires that the offeree properly address and deliver the acceptance to the forwarding agent. Otherwise, acceptance is not complete until actual delivery has been made to the offeror.

● Morrison sent Tholke a letter in which Morrison offered to sell certain described lands at a price quoted in the letter. Tholke decided to accept and mailed an acceptance the following day. Morrison changed his mind about selling the land and withdrew the offer before receiving Tholke's acceptance. In an action against Morrison the court ruled that acceptance was complete when Tholke mailed the acceptance and that Morrison's later decision to withdraw had no bearing on the negotiations.

Questions have arisen as to the status of the acceptance should the offeree successfully recover a letter from the post office before it is delivered to the offeror. No firm conclusion has been reached. Postal laws and regulations fail to provide a clear answer. It has been held that even though the offeree intercepts the letter, there was a valid acceptance when the letter was deposited in the mails. This view confirms the "accepted when mailed" doctrine long accepted at common law. Some courts, however, have taken an opposite view.

Anticipating disputes as to the date and time of acceptance, the offeree would be well advised to request receipt of mailing from the post office when returning acceptance to important agreements. Better still is the use of certified mail with signed receipt requested, available at an additional fee. Telegraph companies provide similar receipts of filed messages when requested. Proof of acceptance by telephone presents a more difficult problem, unless both parties agree to the use of tape recording devices that might later be used as evidence of a binding agreement.

3. Communication by Agent Different From That Used by Offeror. At common law when the offeree selects a means of communicating acceptance different from that used by the offeror, acceptance is not complete and effective until it actually reaches the offeror. Accepting by telegram when the offer is made by mail would be illustrative of using a different agent. In these situations delivery is complete when the acceptance reaches the offeror's home, office, or other return address. It need not be proved that the offeror personally opened and read the communicated acceptance.

● Coblentz Information Services sent a letter to Pettaway, offering to supply Pettaway's requirements for data processing services. Pettaway accepted by telegram. Pettaway's decision to accept by telegram rather than by mail meant that acceptance would not occur until the telegram actually reached Coblentz Information Services at its business offices.

To remove any doubts as to the date and time of acceptance, the offeror is permitted to include a condition in the offer to help resolve such problems. The condition usually states, "Acceptance will not be complete until your reply is received at our office," or words of a similar nature. This removes the possibility of an offer having been accepted without the knowledge of the offeror.

4. The Modern Trend. The common-law rules regarding the timing of an acceptance, as just described, have been applied quite stringently where contracts were for things or services besides personal property. However, the UCC has adopted more flexible rules governing the sale of personal property. The UCC adopts the standard that acceptance occurs *when it is sent,* as long as the method of communication is reasonable under the circumstances. A modern trend is developing in favor of applying this standard not only to the sale of personal property, but to contracts for other types of things and services as well.

5. Implied Acceptance. Acceptance may result from the conduct or actions of the offeree. Actions and gestures may indicate the offeree's willingness and intention to enter into a binding agreement.

● Through gross error, a work crew of Blair Construction Company replaced a roof on one of Zigmont's outbuildings. Zigmont was at home at the time, spoke to the workers, but made no effort to point out that no arrangements had been made for this work to be done. Zigmont was later billed for the reasonable cost of time and materials used on the job.

Although there has been no bilateral agreement between Zigmont and the firm replacing the roof, Zigmont demonstrated a willingness to accept the benefits accruing to the property. Zigmont's reaction to the activity of the work crew implies acceptance.

a. Mailing of Unordered Merchandise. Delivery of unordered merchandise through the mails is now considered nothing more than an offer to sell. In the past unethical sellers would attempt to treat the failure of the recipient to either return goods or send money as an implied acceptance of the offer to sell goods. Complaints were made that this practice allowed unethical firms to use the mails to defraud consumers and to saddle recipients with unwanted merchandise. This led to corrective regulations which are now incorporated into the Postal Reorganization Act of 1970. By this act recipients of unordered merchandise delivered through the mails may treat such goods as a gift. The receiver has no obligation to pay for or return the goods or communicate with the sender in any way.

● Daniels received a box of greeting cards in the mail from a firm in Georgia. Enclosed with the cards was a letter stating, "You may either send us $5 or return the cards within ten days." The Postal Reorganization Act relieves Daniels of any obligation whatsoever. The cards may be accepted as a gift.

Under the Postal Act and other applicable federal law only two kinds of goods may now be sent legally through the mails without the prior consent of the recipient: (1) manufacturer's free samples, and (2) merchandise mailed by charities asking for contributions. In the case of free samples, it is illegal for the senders to attempt to get the items back or send bills for them. In the case of charitable organizations, the recipient may feel a moral obligation to make a contribution or return the goods, but is under no legal compulsion to do so.

Chapter 8:
Agree-
ment:
Offer and
Accep-
tance

b. Unordered Goods Not Delivered by Mail. **When** unordered goods are delivered by agencies other than the post office, the common law is usually followed. The receiver generally is not obligated to contact the sender or pay for the goods. There is an implied obligation to retain the goods and give them reasonable care over a reasonable period of time. After that the receiver may consider that the sender no longer claims the goods and may use or dispose of them as desired.

● Paoletti received a set of stainless steel cookware, delivered by Stanley's Package Delivery Service. The merchandise had not been ordered. Instructions contained in the carton advised Paoletti to try them out for ten days without charge. The receiver then was to return them to the sender or remit installment payments of $23.99 a month over a twelve-month period. Paoletti is required to do neither. Keeping the cookware in a safe place for a reasonable time is Paoletti's only obligation.

It should be noted, however, that in recent years several states have supplanted the common law with statutes similar to the Postal Reorganization Act. These state statutes generally make it possible for consumers to treat as gifts unordered goods delivered by agencies other than the post office.

6. Silence as Acceptance. As a general rule, silence is not an acceptance. If, however, both parties agree that silence on the part of the offeree will signal acceptance, such acceptance is valid.

● A sales representative left a vacuum cleaner at the Johnsons' home. It was agreed that if the Johnsons did not call the representative after trying out the machine for three days, they would buy the cleaner and mail their check for $79.50. The Johnsons decided not to buy the cleaner but neglected to call the seller for two weeks. By their continued silence it would be implied that they had accepted the representative's offer and owed the $79.50.

An exception to the general rule occurs, also, when the parties have dealt in a particular way in the past. Prior dealings or customs of the trade can cause silence to be an acceptance.

8-3. Revocation and Rejection of Offers

In addition to being accepted, an offer may be revoked or it may be rejected. Revocation is done by the offeror. Rejection is the right of the offeree.

A. Revocation of an Offer

At any time prior to acceptance the offeror has the right to withdraw, or *revoke* the offer. Other than exceptions to be presented later, the offeror has this exclusive right despite what might at times appear to be a strong moral obligation to continue the offer. Offers may be revoked by the following:

○ Communication of revocation
○ Automatic revocation by terms of the offer
○ Passing of more than a reasonable length of time

○ Death or insanity of the offeror
○ Destruction of the subject matter
○ Subsequent illegality of the subject matter

1. Revocation by Communication. Offers may be revoked at the will of the offeror merely by communicating that intention to the offeree. Revocation is ineffective if acceptance has already been communicated, as by mailing the acceptance. Direct communication of revocation is not required if the offeree has knowledge of the offer's withdrawal through other means.

● Wagner offered to sell a thoroughbred trotting horse to Simpers for $125,000. It was mutually agreed that the offer would remain open for five days. Three days later Simpers read that Wagner's horse had been sold to Chambers' Stables for $150,000. Having learned of the sale, Simpers would be aware that the offer had been withdrawn.

● Suppose in this same case the offer had been made in a letter received by Simpers. Before any news of the sale to Chambers' Stables reached Simpers, a letter of acceptance was mailed to Wagner. Although the acceptance may not reach Wagner for another day, acceptance was complete upon the mailing of the letter, and revocation would not apply.

2. Automatic Revocation. When the terms of an offer include a definite time limit for acceptance, the offer is automatically revoked at the expiration of the time stated.

● Layton Realty Company entered into a unilateral agreement with Stearns whereby Layton agreed, for a 10 percent commission, to advertise and attempt to secure a buyer for Stearns' $150,000 property. The agreement was signed on June 25 and was conditioned to expire three months from that date. The agreement, by its terms, would expire (be revoked) at the end of the three-month period stated.

3. Revocation by Passing of Time. When no time limit has been set, an offer will revoke automatically after the passing of more than a reasonable length of time. The time element is determined through a review of all facts and surrounding circumstances. Perishable characteristics of goods, price fluctuations, supply and demand factors, and all other surrounding circumstances will contribute to establishment of the reasonable time factor. For example, communicating an offer by telegram rather than by letter would ordinarily imply the need for haste in making acceptance.

● Paramount Farms wired Acme Produce Brokers, offering 1,000 bushels of green bell peppers at the current market price. Produce Brokers waited for two days and then wired acceptance. Perishable qualities of the peppers, price fluctuation, and the fact that the offer was wired indicated the need for an immediate decision on Produce Brokers' part. The delay of two days revoked the offer.

The same rule applies to unilateral agreements where acceptance is made by commencement of performance.

● Holton offered to hire Gibson as a swimming pool guard if Gibson would take the Red Cross lifesaving course and work for the summer. Gibson returned two weeks

117

after the pool season opened, displayed the lifesaving certificate, and demanded the job. Holton had already hired another applicant. Gibson's delay revoked the offer.

4. Revocation by Death or Insanity. Death or insanity of an offeror automatically revokes an existing offer. Both death and insanity preclude the possibility of a meeting of the minds. Revocation in both situations is immediate. Communication to the offeree is not required.

5. Revocation by Destruction of Subject Matter. Destruction of subject matter related to an offer automatically revokes that offer. Destruction of the subject matter removes any possibility of performance of an anticipated agreement.

6. Revocation by Subsequent Illegality. The passing of restrictive legislation that would make performance of an anticipated agreement impossible automatically revokes an existing offer. Any agreement resulting from an attempted acceptance of such offers would be unenforceable.

● Community Construction Company offered to build a frame addition to the Station Hotel. Prior to acceptance by the hotel management the city council passed a local ordinance making it illegal to build new frame structures or frame additions to buildings within the city limits. The new ordinance automatically revoked Community Construction Company's offer.

B. Rejection of an Offer

An offeree's expressed or implied repudiation of an offer results in a *rejection* of an offer. Rejection terminates an offer and all negotiations associated with it. Further negotiation would commence with a new offer by the offeree or a renewal of the original offer by the offeror.

1. Communication of Rejection. Rejection is commonly achieved by communication of that intention by the offeree. The failure of the offeree to act within a reasonable time also conveys the intention of rejection. Rejection in unilateral agreements results from the offeree's failure to commence performance.

2. Counteroffers. Changing the terms and conditions of an offer by the offeree usually acts as a rejection of an existing offer. The offeror has the right to an acceptance without changes, additions, or deletions from the original proposal.

● Raughley offered DiCecco the position of office manager and auditor in Raughley's automotive import business. DiCecco agreed to accept the position if Raughley would add a $2,500 yearly end-of-year bonus to the salary offered. DiCecco's counteroffer acted as a rejection of Raughley's offer. Further negotiation would depend on new offers, emanating from either Raughley or DiCecco.

3. Counteroffers Under the UCC. The UCC takes exception to the above rule primarily when contract negotiations are being carried on between merchants. By *merchants* is meant parties other than consumers purchasing from retail outlets; thus, transactions between business people, such as wholesalers and retailers, are transactions between merchants. Under the UCC, additional terms proposed by the buyer or seller are to be "construed as proposals for addition to the contract." Between merchants such terms become part of the agreement unless (a) the original offer expressly limits acceptance to the terms of the offer, (b) the additional proposed terms materially alter the original offer, or (c) notification of objection to the additional proposed terms has already been given or is given within a reasonable time after notice of them is received.

● American Plastics Company forwarded a written offer to Keen Products Corporation offering to deliver a special type of plastic mold at 25 cents each in lots of five thousand. Included in the offer was a condition that any changes appearing in the offeree's anticipated acceptance would not be honored by American Plastics. Any counteroffer would, therefore, by UCC provisions result in a rejection.

If the negotiations are between nonmerchants or between merchants and nonmerchants, such additional proposed terms will not become part of the contract without the express agreement of the offeror. In the absence of the offeror's agreement, they will be considered proposals for addition to the contract. However, a contract comes about under the terms of the original offer.

8-4. Irrevocable or Firm Offers

Irrevocable or *firm offers,* under the UCC, are those made by merchants "in a signed writing which by its terms gives assurance that the offer will be held open." Only dealings between merchants are firm offers under the UCC. A wholesale house, for instance, may not revoke at will offers made to dealers when and if retailers are dependent on such offers in developing marketing plans for store merchandise. The rationale for the concept of irrevocable offers derives from the respected legal doctrine of *promissory estoppel.* This doctrine disapproves as unjust the revocation of an offer upon which another has already relied, acted, and made financial commitments.

● Red Owl Stores, Inc., through its representative, Lukowitz, promised Hoffman an agency store if he would follow instructions and advice in preparation for opening such a store. Hoffman entered into many ventures and financial obligations on advice of Lukowitz, always with Lukowitz's promise of securing an agency store. Further delay and financial demands led Hoffman to terminate negotiations and sue Red Owl for failure to secure the store. Red Owl claimed no obligation. Applying the concept of promissory estoppel, the court awarded damages stemming from his continued dependence on the offer that had been made through the agent, Lukowitz.

It has also been held that offers under seal are irrevocable. The UCC and special statutes in many states have nullified the use of the seal (2-203). In those states still using the seal the old rule of irrevocability continues to apply.

8-5. Options

An *option* is a contract that binds an offeror to a promise to hold open an offer for a predetermined or reasonable length of time. In return for this agreement to hold the offer open, the offeror receives money on something else of value from the offeree.

Money exchanged to bind the parties to an agreement, such as an option, is called *earnest money.* Parties to an option often agree that the earnest money may be credited toward any indebtedness incurred by the offeree in the event

Chapter 8:
Agree-
ment:
Offer and
Accep-
tance

that the offer is finally accepted. Should the offeree fail to take up the option, however, the offeror is under no legal obligation to return the earnest money.

Options remove the possibility of revocation through death or insanity of the offeror. The offeree who holds an option may demand acceptance by giving written notice of acceptance to the executor or administrator of the deceased offeror's estate or to the offeror's legally appointed guardian.

● Wrightson offered to sell Blackston a coin collection for $35,000. Blackston requested time to consider the offer, and Wrightson agreed to hold the collection for Blackston for two weeks in return for Blackston's payment of $50 earnest money. Wrightson died several days later. When Blackston tendered the $35,000 the executor refused to deliver the collection, claiming that death had revoked the offer. The court ruled otherwise, with judgment given to the offeree based upon the option agreement between Blackston and the deceased.

Understanding Legal Terms

Define, identify, or explain the following terms:

acceptance	counteroffer	merchant	revocation
automatic	implied acceptance	option	subsequent illegality
revocation	invitation to trade	public offer	unordered
collective group	irrevocable offer	rejection	merchandise
cost-plus contract			

Questions for Review and Discussion

1. Is mutual assent all that is needed to create a valid and enforceable contract? Explain your answer.

2. What is meant by serious intent when it is applied to a contract offer?

3. Must the courts automatically invalidate any contract that omits terms and conditions deemed important to the parties' obligations? Explain.

4. How does a public offer differ from an invitation to trade?

5. Explain the respective roles of the auctioneer and bidder in the process of making an offer and acceptance in an auction sale.

6. How does an acceptance evolve in the case of a unilateral offer? In the case of a bilateral offer?

7. Under common law, when does acceptance become effective if the offeree makes acceptance through the same agent used by the offeror in communicating an offer? When does it become effective if the offeree makes acceptance using an agent different from the one used by the offeror in communicating an offer?

8. Under the UCC, what is the effect and disposition of a counteroffer made during contract negotiations between merchants? What is the effect of counteroffers made by nonmerchants?

9. What are the two special qualities of an option? How does an option differ from an ordinary offer?

10. How important is mutual assent to the formation of legally binding and enforceable contracts? Explain your answer.

Analyzing Cases

1. Zinni visited Royal Lincoln-Mercury for the purpose of buying an automobile. The parties entered into an agreement that was evidenced by their filling out a written order form. The form contained the following language: "The order shall not become binding

until accepted by the dealer or his authorized representative." Below the statement was an appropriate line for affixing the signature. The form was never signed. Zinni is now suing for delivery of the car. Judgment for whom and why? ● *Zinni v. Royal Lincoln-Mercury Inc.*, 406 N.E.2d 212 (Ill. App. 1980)

2. Tockstein delivered a signed written offer to Rothenbuecher, in which Tockstein offered to purchase the offeree's house. Contained in the offer was the condition that the acceptance must be made within twenty-four hours to be valid. Rothenbuecher signed the agreement within the time limit and delivered it to his own real estate agent for delivery to Tockstein. Rothenbuecher now sues to enforce the agreement which Tockstein claims to be void. Judgment for whom and why? ● *Rothenbuecher v. Tockstein*, 411 N.E.2d 92 (Ill. App. 1980)

3. Moore, a repairer, gave a written proposal to Kuehn pertaining to a variety of repairs to be made to Kuehn's house. After reading the written proposal, Kuehn said, "The roof ought to be fixed, so get on with it." Moore proceeded to repair the roof and then, with full knowledge of Kuehn, completed all other work contained in the proposal. A question now arises as to whether Kuehn is liable to Moore for all the repairs. Judgment for whom and why? ● *Moore v. Kuehn*, 602 S.W.2d 713 (Mo. App. 1980)

4. Reserve Insurance Company sent out renewal notices to policy-holders, with stamped return envelopes enclosed. Duckett mailed her renewal on the day that her policy would have expired. She suffered an accident the following day while the renewal was still in the mail. Reserve claims that Duckett's acceptance did not occur until the renewal was received at it office after the accident. Is Reserve correct in this defense to Duckett's claim? Explain ● *Reserve Ins. Co. v. Duckett*, 238 A.2d 536 (Md. 1968)

5. The Board of Education of Independent School District #306 passed a resolution at a scheduled meeting to offer the administrative positions of superintendent, high school principal, and elementary principal "to our present administrative personnel respectively." Tatter, the superintendent at the time, stated that he did not feel the offer was binding but showed appreciation for the board's vote of confidence. He later had major disagreements with the board. At a subsequent meeting the board withdrew its offer, deciding not to retain Tatter. Tatter now sues for reinstatement, claiming that a contract had developed. Judgment for whom and why? ● *Tatter v. Board of Ed. of Independent School Dist. #306*, 490 F. Supp. 494 (Minn. 1980)

6. Thompson and his wife inspected new mobile homes being demonstrated by Sunnyland Mobile Homes, Inc. They selected the one they wished to buy and gave the dealer their $600 check as a down payment. At a later date the Thompsons refused to sign a prepared purchase agreement, claiming that the price contained was different from the one posted on the mobile home unit when they made their $600 payment. Suit is brought by the Thompsons to recover the $600 already paid. Will they recover the down payment? Explain. ● *Sunnyland Mobile Homes Inc. v. Thompson*, 384 So.2d 1111 (Ala. Civ. App. 1980)

7. Champagne Chrysler-Plymouth Inc. distributed flyers and ran thirty-second TV commercials advertising a free car for any 300 game bowled in a TV show called "Miami All-Star Bowling". The flyers stated that the car would be awarded if the game was bowled on the same day that the flyers were distributed. Giles bowled a 300 game and claimed his prize. Champagne refused, proving that Giles had not bowled his game on the day that the flyers were distributed. They claimed that even though the flyers were still being read days later, their offer had long since lapsed. Giles now sues for the car. Judgment for whom and why? ● *Champagne Chrysler-Plymouth Inc. v. Giles*, 388 So.2d 1343 (Fla. App. 1971)

8. Meister and Murphy proposed to purchase three grocery stores from Arden-Mayfair, Inc. Arden-Mayfair drew up a contract, listing the purchasers as the principals and their wives. Meister's attorney unilaterally changed the contract, deleting the wives as parties to the agreement. Other changes were also made, after which the principals signed the agreement and returned it to Arden-Mayfair, Inc. Meister and Murphy are seeking enforcement of the contract which Arden-Mayfair claims is void for want of an unqualified acceptance. Judgment for whom and why? ● *Meister v. Arden-Mayfair, Inc.,* 276 Ore. 517 (1976)

9. The Clamshell Alliance, an antinuclear group, requested the right to use the Portsmouth, New Hampshire, national guard armory on the night of April 29 for a fund-raising dance. Cushing, a member of the alliance, received a letter offer from the state attorney general, proposing to rent the armory as requested. Cushing's letter of acceptance was mailed the evening of April 4. Cushing received a telephone call from the attorney general that same evening, revoking the state's offer. The acceptance, according to Cushing, was in the mailbox before the attorney general's call was received. Cushing brought suit against Governor Meldrim Thomson, claiming a contract existed. Judgment for whom and why? ● *Cushing v. Thomson,* 386 A.2d 805 (N.H. 1978)

10. Miller, in Albuquerque, New Mexico, gave Kloepfer, a broker, a written offer for purchase of property owned by Mr. and Mrs. Pickett of Doylestown, Pennsylvania. Kloepfer relayed the offer by telephone. Shortly thereafter the Picketts wired Kloepfer that they accepted the purchaser's offer. Miller now seeks to remove himself from the agreement, claiming that acceptance could be made only by the Pickett's signing the purchase offer. The court is asked to decide whether a valid acceptance to sell was made. How would you decide this case? ● *Pickett v. Miller,* 412 P.2d 400 (N.M. 1966)

Chapter 9 Defective Agreement

The terms and conditions expressed or implied in any agreement should give clear and indisputable evidence of the rights and obligations of the contracting parties. However, what might appear to be mutual assent may have developed through less than the real consent of the parties. Real consent is not achieved when a party is induced to enter an agreement through the exercise of fraud, misrepresentation, undue influence, duress, or a mutual mistake.

The present chapter deals with the actions that may be taken to invalidate contracts in which one of the parties is able to prove a lack of real consent resulting from the wrongs of the other contracting party. It should be emphasized that these wrongs or defects that make contracts *voidable* are not usually discovered until after the fact, that is, until after the parties have entered into a seemingly binding agreement. In any event, the act of avoidance must be timely, or it is ineffective.

9-1. Fraud and Concealment

Fraud is either a wrongful statement or an intentional concealment pertinent to the subject matter of a contract knowingly made to the damage of the other party. Fraud, if proved, invalidates any contract and makes the wrongdoer liable to the injured party for all losses plus damages. Fraud is one of the more serious charges that permits rescission of an otherwise valid contract.

A. Elements of Fraud

Fraud is tinged with the elements of criminal wrong. In some situations the same facts that permit voidance of mutual assent may be sufficient for securing an indictment for criminal fraud. Five elements must be in evidence to prove fraud. The complaining party must prove the following:

○ There was a false statement or intentional concealment of a material existing fact.
○ The false statement or concealment was knowingly made.
○ The statement (or concealment) was made with the intent that the other party rely on it.
○ The other party did reasonably rely on it.
○ The wronged party was damaged by the false statement or intentional concealment.

● Hargrove contracted to install a heating system in Bower's house. Hargrove installed equipment that had been removed from another house, but represented to Bower to be new and in first-class condition. Hargrove had concealed pertinent facts that if known to Bower would have caused her not to accept the agreement. The facts of the case give evidence of all the requisites of fraud, and

Bower would have the right to sue for rescission of the contract, return of all money paid Hargrove, and any damages that resulted from Hargrove's intentional wrongdoing.

1. Statements of Fact, Puffing, and Professional Opinion. Fraud is founded on a claim of false statements and concealment of relevant existing material facts. False statements of material facts are those statements, statistics, and illustrations that specifically apply to the description and characteristics of the subject matter of a contract. Opinions and *puffing* consist of the persuasive words and arguments, as well as illustrations, that induce a person to buy. Opinions and puffing are not actionable even if grossly wrong and exaggerated.

● Dalton purchased a set of law reference books from Professional Books, Inc. The salesclerk made the following statements: (a) the set consists of five cloth-bound volumes, (b) all references are supported by recent court decisions or sections from the UCC, (c) the books are printed in easily readable type, (d) concentrated study of the five volumes would guarantee any student of success in passing examinations in business law, and (e) the books would add a professional decor to the new owner's library.

The first two statements are acceptable statements of material fact. The others are either opinions expressed by the seller or the persuasive puffing that might induce Dalton to make a purchase. Difficulty may be experienced in separating material fact from opinion, puffing, and exaggeration.

● Heat Products Company sold a device that it claimed would save 85 percent of the fuel if attached to any oil-burning furnace. The device cost $9.97 and could be installed by anyone in less than five minutes. Any person of ordinary prudence hearing or reading these claims would immediately react in disbelief. The statements would be accepted as nothing more than sales talk, puffing, or exaggeration.

However, when the offeror is an expert in a particular field, the courts can interpret that person's professional opinions not as sales talk or puffing, but as statements of material fact.

● Woerner, a navigator for Trans-Pacific Airways, sought advice from a reputable jeweler and horologist in selecting a watch that would be used in connection with her work. The seller showed Woerner an expensive watch, saying, "In my opinion this is the watch you will find dependable and will use with complete confidence in your work." Woerner bought the watch and discovered it to be a faulty timepiece that could not be depended on.

The seller, in this case, provided a professional opinion on which the buyer relied as one would rely on a statement of fact. Woerner might have grounds on which to bring an action of fraud.

2. *Caveat Emptor.* From the common law comes the doctrine of *caveat emptor:* "Let the buyer beware." *Caveat emptor* requires that a buyer examine the goods being purchased and be responsible for discovering obvious defects that might have prompted rejection of an offer. When the opportunity to examine is not given, *caveat emptor* will not prevail. Defects that one would not usually discover on ordinary examination may still be introduced as grounds for rescission of an agreement.

● Kallgren purchased a resort known as Bear Creek Lodge from Steele. The lodge was located on state lands by permit issued by the state forestry service. After the purchase, Kallgren was informed by the forestry service that the permit would be terminated at the end of five years because the lodge was too close to the state's right-of-way, Kallgren sued Steele for the return of money paid, claiming concealment of facts known to Steele. Steele defended, arguing that it was Kallgren's responsibility to examine and discover these facts for himself. The court refused to accept Steele's *caveat emptor* argument, awarding damages to Kallgren on grounds of concealment and fraud.

3. *Caveat Venditor.* Courts have slowly moved away from strict application of the *caveat emptor* doctrine to a newer concept of fairness placing greater responsibility upon the seller to divulge known and important material facts than upon the buyer to search them out. With increased frequency the courts are now applying the doctrine of *caveat venditor:* "Let the seller beware." Under this doctrine the buyer may have a remedy against the seller when the seller conceals an important defect at the time of the transaction.

B. Concealment

An offeror is not required to reveal every known fact related to the subject matter of an offer. Certain facts are accepted as confidential and personal to the offeror. For examples one offering a car, house, or used washing machine for sale need not disclose why it is being sold, how much profit will be realized, knowledge of an anticipated drop in the market price, and the like. Concealment becomes fraud, however, when a party intentionally prevents another party from discovering material matters that might otherwise have been discovered and have prompted a rejection. The law prohibits the concealment of facts and conditions that are material and relevant to the offeree's decision to buy.

● Sorrell contracted to purchase a residential lot from Young, paying $1,457.55 as a down payment. Young did not disclose that the lot had been filled, and the existence of the fill was not obvious to Sorrell. In an action to rescind the agreement Sorrell claimed that Young had concealed pertinent information that would have been important in his decision to buy. The court found Young guilty of intentional concealment, rescinded the contract, and awarded Sorrell the return of the $1,457.55.

9-2. Misrepresentation

Misrepresentation is a false statement made innocently and without intention to deceive. Such innocent misrepresentation usually arises from a *unilateral mistake* of facts; i.e., one party believing a fact exists when it does not exist.

● Leary, an auctioneer, described a set of Dalton china as "perfect, with no chips or cracks." Warner, the successful bidder, examined the dishes after taking possession of them and discovered several hairline cracks in the dinner plates. Leary's description arose from his mistaken belief that the set was in perfect condition. Leary is not guilty of fraud, but the sale may be rescinded because of misrepresentation.

Innocent misrepresentation renders an existing agreement voidable. The complaining party may either demand performance or rescission. If rescission is elected, both parties are returned to their original positions. No damages are generally awarded in a case of innocent misrepresentation.

● Henderson gave Bell's Book Barn $50, as down payment on what Bell had described as a first edition of Ryden's *History of Delaware*. Later, a more careful examination disclosed that the two-volume set was an unmarked second edition. Without any indication of wrongdoing, Bell would be guilty of nothing more than an innocent misrepresentation. Henderson may either rescind the agreement or demand delivery of the books. In cases of this kind the parties often renegotiate the purchase price if the agreement is affirmed.

9-3. Mistake as a Defect

When there has been no real meeting of the minds because of a mistake, mutual assent was never achieved and the agreement may be rescinded. As in misrepresentation, mistake permits either rescission or affirmation of the agreement.

A. Unilateral and Bilateral Mistakes

A mistake made by only one of the contracting parties is a unilateral mistake and does not offer sufficient grounds for rescission or renegotiation. When both parties are mistaken, it is a *bilateral mistake*. A bilateral mistake allows rescission by either the offeror or the offeree.

● Layton owned two farms in Sussex County. One of the farms was located near the waterfront and offered much potential for possible homesite and recreational development. The other was further inland and was equally valuable as a crop-producing venture. Baldt arranged to buy one of the properties, thinking that their agreement was for the waterfront farm. Layton understood that the sale was for the other property. There had never been a true meeting of the minds since both parties were mistaken as to the other's intentions. The circumstances would support an action for rescission of this agreement.

B. Nature of Mistakes

Actionable mutual mistakes are of many kinds. Some are universally accepted as grounds for rescission. Others are not grounds for rescission. Still others are actionable, but not in all courts or in all states.

1. Mistakes as to Description. When both parties are mistaken in the identification and description of subject matter, there is a real mutual mistake and rescission will be granted.

● Beachcomber Coins, Inc., bought a 1916 dime from Boskett. The dime had markings that showed it was from the Denver mint. Beachcomber accepted Boskett's offer to sell the coin only after making a very careful examination, paying Boskett $500. The American Numismatic Society later examined the coin and declared it to be a counterfeit. There was no evidence of any wrongdoing or fraud on the seller's part. Beachcomber sued for rescission and return of the $500. The court found in favor of Beachcomber because of a bilateral mistake in identification of the coin, granting rescission and the return of all money paid.

2. Mistakes as to Existence. Proof that the subject matter had been destroyed before agreement was made gives grounds for rescission. Thus, if one accepted an offer to purchase a boat that both parties mistakingly believed to be berthed at a specified marina, the agreement would be void if it were proved that moments before acceptance the boat had been destroyed. Had the boat been destroyed after final acceptance, there would have been no mutual mistake and an enforceable contract would have resulted.

3. Mistakes as to Value. When two parties agree on the value of the subject matter and later find they were both mistaken this is only a mutual mistake of opinion, not of fact. Mutual mistakes of opinion do not void an agreement.

● Hershey offered Di Sento a painting which both agreed to be worth $10,000. Di Sento paid Hershey $8,500 and took delivery of the painting. Di Sento later learned that the painting was worth no more than $300 to a knowledgeable collector. Although there had been a mutual mistake, it was of one of opinion and would not rescind the agreement. Interestingly, the same result would be forthcoming if it were learned that the painting were worth $1 million. Di Sento's right to the painting would not be disturbed.

4. Mistakes Through Failure to Read Document. Failure to read a document or the negligent reading of a document does not excuse performance on the grounds of a mistaken understanding of the document's contents. Exceptions may be made if there is a failure to read conditions in fine print or conditions not included in the body of the document. Also, exceptions may be made when conditions are printed on parking lot stubs, cleaner's tickets, hat check identifications, and the like. The law usually holds that these vouchers are given for identification purposes only. The courts generally are not favorable toward enforcing the fine-print conditions on the face or reverse side of such tickets.

5. Mistakes of Law. Misunderstandings of existing laws do not give grounds for rescission. As often quoted, "Ignorance of the law is no excuse." Rescission may be allowed, however, when there have been mistakes related to the law of another state. In this way the courts interpret mistakes of law of a different state as mistakes of fact, not of law. Some states have now adopted statutes that completely remove the so-called ignorance-of-law concept. In those states any mutual mistake of law is sufficient to bring about a rescission.

C. **Palpable Unilateral Mistake**
The law frowns upon one who knowingly and intentionally takes advantage of another's obvious mistake. Performance may not be demanded by one who was fully aware of a mistake being made by the other party.

● Miller, known by the seller to be color-blind, selected seat covers to go with the interior of her new car. The sales representative recognized a distasteful clash of colors in the selection but made no effort to correct or advise Miller at the time. Miller's was a palpable unilateral mistake, recognized and understood by the seller, giving sufficient grounds for rescission.

9-4. Undue Influence

Undue influence is the use of one's position of trust and superiority with another as a means of creating mutual assent. The use of undue influence makes it impossible to reach a true meeting of the minds, and a real consent is not achieved.

To prove undue influence, it must be shown that a *confidential relationship* existed between the parties. A confidential relationship, although not well defined in law, includes the relationships of parent to child, guardian to ward, husband to wife, attorney to client, physician to patient, pastor to parishioner, and so forth. It includes most relationships where there is a continued trust and confidence between the parties. In most cases involving undue influence one party, with strength and leadership, dominates the other, who is obviously weaker and dependent.

● NAB, an unwed mother whose identity was withheld as is custom in such cases, had her baby in the Methodist Mission Home of Texas. A counselor at the home spent five days convincing NAB that she should give the baby up for adoption. She was told, among other things, that she had no right to keep the baby, that she was selfish, and that an offer made by her parents to support her and the baby was made only to take advantage of her situation. She agreed to place the baby for adoption. She now seeks to revoke her consent, claiming it had been secured by undue influence. The court ruled that as an unwed mother, physically and emotionally weakened and having a confidential relationship with the mission counselor, NAB was the victim of undue influence, and ordered her consent revoked.

Undue influence should not be confused with persuasion or some subtle forms of coercion. Although one might be induced to enter agreements through the urging of an employer, professor, athletic coach, and the like, there is no undue influence in the absence of the required confidential relationship. Persuasion and subtle coercion, while at times unethical, are not considered undue influence in the eyes of the law and do not, in and of themselves, provide a basis for rescinding agreements.

9-5. Duress as a Defect

The use of force or the threat of force against a person or against that person's family or property, as the means of securing acceptance to an offer, is *duress*. In some cases it has been held that the definition also includes anyone in the threatened person's household, such as those employed in the operation of the home. As a defense against contract obligations it must be shown that the duress was such as to rob the party of freedom of choice through intimidation or fear of physical harm. The same force or threats may also constitute a tort or crime for which action may be brought against the wrongdoer.

● Albright obtained a deed to valuable real estate through threats made upon the aged parents of his deceased wife. During a period of their serious illness Albright threatened to burn the house down with them in it if they did not sign as ordered. They did sign the prepared deed and later sought to have the deed revoked. Albright's new deed would be revoked on proof of the duress used in securing the signatures of the aged couple.

A. Physical, Emotional, and Economic Duress

Duress may be physical, emotional, or economic. In each case the rescinding party must have been induced to enter an agreement through the use of violence or other threats by the other party.

1. Physical Duress. *Physical duress* embodies either violence or the threat of violence against an individual or against that person's family, household, or property. Physical violence and threats offer grounds for rescission of a contract. When threats alone are used, they must be of such intensity and seriousness as would induce a person of ordinary prudence to enter into the agreement, although without real consent. The Albright case presented above illustrates an agreement induced through physical duress.

2. Emotional Duress. *Emotional duress* arises from acts or threats that would create emotional distress in the one on whom they are inflicted. Duress of this kind may be far more serious than threats of physical violence. Exposure to public ridicule, threatened attacks on one's reputation in the community, or efforts to prevent employment might constitute emotional duress within the meaning of the law.

● Jordan worked as cashier for Highway Stores. Roberts, the store manager, told Jordan that if Jordan would not advance him $500 as a personal loan, he was going to report Jordan to the area supervisor for embezzlement of money handled in his job. Jordan had never taken anything from the store, had a good record, and was in every way an excellent worker. Any agreement to lend the $500 would be voidable on grounds of emotional duress committed by the manager. Although no physical threats had been made, the threatened injury to Jordan's reputation was real and serious.

3. Economic Duress. *Economic duress*, also known as business compulsion, consists of threats of a business nature that induce another, without real consent, to enter into commercial agreements. Historically, economic duress has not been widely accepted by the courts as grounds for voiding contracts. The courts are now, however, beginning to regard the concept of business compulsion as actionable economic duress.

● Loral Corporation contracted with Austin Industries, Inc., for production of precision parts to be used in radar sets being manufactured for the U.S. government. Midway into production of the sets, Austin Industries threatened to interrupt further delivery unless Loral agreed to an increase in price over what had been stipulated in the original agreement. Loral agreed, realizing the difficulties that would arise if the parts were not received. Loral sued to have the price increase agreement rescinded. The court ruled that the price boost was "voidable on the grounds of duress when it is established that the party making the claim was forced to agree to it by means of a wrongful threat precluding the exercise of free will."

B. Remedies in Case of Duress

The victim of duress has the option of either seeking rescission or demanding performance. Because of the intentional wrong associated with duress, the complaining party may also seek an award of damages.

Victims of duress must not delay making a complaint. If the action is not started within a reasonable time after the alleged acts of duress occur, a court will consider that the agreement, without change, has been reaffirmed. Victims of duress may not bring complaint if they knowingly and subsequent to the acts of duress permit a sale of property to an innocent third party.

● Stark Motors Company, seeking the purchase of Broadbent's Daimler Special, threatened that if Broadbent did not sell them the car for $25,000, they would use their "connections" to have the car declared illegal by the state motor vehicle division and barred from the road. Under fear of this threat Broadbent sold the car to Stark Motors. Then with Broadbent's complete knowledge, Stark Motors sold the car to Hinson, an innocent third party and collector of antique cars. Broadbent waived his right to claim duress against Stark Motors and have his agreement with Stark rescinded by knowingly allowing the car to be sold to Hinson.

9-6. Adhesion Contracts

Adhesion contracts are those that have been unilaterally drawn by the offeror and presented to the offeree for acceptance on a "take-it-or-leave-it" basis, allowing little or no room for negotiation between the parties. When specific terms and conditions are judged by a court to be unfair and unconscionable, the entire contract or those specific parts that are unfair may be rescinded. In disputes related to adhesion contracts, the courts are prone to favor the party who was obliged to accept another's terms without further negotiation or compromise.

● Randall signed a contract for the purchase of a used car from City Car Sales. The printed contract stated, among other things, that all financing had to be done through the seller's bank, the repairs and service for one year had to be done at the seller's shop, and that the car had to carry a brightly colored decal showing the name of City Car Sales as the dealer. The three imposed conditions constitute an unfair and unjust adhesion contract. They would be subject to rescission by a court if the subject of a lawsuit.

9-7. Unconscionability Under the UCC

The UCC gives protection to a party who claims damage through another's gross injustice. Under the UCC, agreements may be rescinded for reason of unconscionability (2-302). Although only recently introduced into statutory law, the doctrine of unconscionability is not new. It had its beginnings in the English case of *Earl of Chesterfield v. Janssen,* more than two hundred years ago. In that landmark case the judge held that one may not enforce an agreement that is so unconscionable "as no man in his right senses and not under delusion would make and no honest and fair man would accept. . . ." The UCC gives no precise definition of what is meant by *unconscionable. Webster's Dictionary* defines it as "not guided or controlled by conscience; . . . unscrupulous, excessive or exhorbitant; . . . shockingly unfair, harsh, or unjust." Modern case law through the use of this UCC concept is now providing greater definition and guidance as to the use and limitations of the doctrine of unconscionability.

Originally included in the UCC to apply to the sale of personal property, the doctrine of unconscionability now has been extended and applied to certain other types of agreements. Successful proof of unconscionability allows rescission in cases where there is no evidence of fraud, misrepresentation, mistake, undue influence, or duress. The doctrine has been particularly valuable in areas of consumer protection for the economically disadvantaged. It has special application to contracts binding persons with language difficulties, and where there is an obvious difference in the bargaining position of the parties. It has also been applied where a significant cost-price disparity or excessive price existed.

● Toker sold Westerman a refrigerator-freezer, as agent for People's Food. Westerman agreed to pay $900 for the unit; after interest and other fees were added, the sum due totaled $1,229. He paid $650 but refused to pay more, claiming that the contract was unconscionable. Westerman introduced evidence at the ensuing trial showing that the unit could have been purchased from other dealers for as little as $350. The court ruled the agreement unconscionable but permitted People's Food to retain the $650 already paid, as adequate compensation and full payment for a refrigerator-freezer of that make and class.

The UCC gives the courts much discretion and flexibility in applying remedies when a contract is held to be unconscionable. If the court as a matter of law finds the contract or any clause of the contract to have been unconscionable at the time it was made, then the court (a) may allow rescission and refuse to enforce the entire agreement; (b) may enforce the remainder of the contract by removing the unconscionable clause, if the contract is of a divisible nature; or (c) may so limit the application of any unconscionable clause as to avoid any unconscionable result [2-302(1)]. In *Toker v. Westerman*, cited above, the court chose the third of these remedies as being most appropriate to the circumstances in question.

Understanding Legal Terms

Define, identify, or explain the following terms:

adhesion contract	concealment	economic duress	puffing
bilateral mistake	confidential	fraud	unconscionability
caveat emptor	relationship	misrepresentation	undue influence
caveat venditor	duress	palpable mistake	unilateral mistake

Questions for Review and Discussion

1. What five essentials must be proved to establish that a contract is defective because of fraud?

2. Does a salesperson's typical opinion and puffing constitute grounds for an action based on fraud?

3. X has found defects in a digital watch that had been purchased and subsequently delivered to her. These defects would have been obvious to anyone who had the opportunity to examine the watch prior to its purchase. Y, the seller of the watch, gave X the opportunity to make such an examination. If X wants to rescind the contract for the digital watch, how will the doctrine of *caveat emptor* affect her rights? Explain.

4. What is the essential difference between fraud and misrepresentation?

5. Does a unilateral mistake give grounds to a party to rescind a contract? Does a bilateral mistake give grounds for rescission? Explain.

6. Do the courts look favorably or unfavorably upon a situation whereby one party takes advantage of another's unilateral palpable mistake?

7. What is the meaning of confidential relationship in respect to a charge that a contract

was obtained through undue influence? Give examples of parties who usually enjoy a confidential relationship and who may be particularly susceptible to charges of exercising undue influence.

8. Why do the courts typically grant damages to parties who are victims of fraud or duress, but not to the victims of contracts made defective by mistake or misrepresentation?

9. What are the essential characteristics that make an adhesion contract different from an ordinary contract? What is the general attitude of the courts toward the enforcement of adhesion contracts?

10. Under what circumstances does the UCC permit a court to apply the doctrine of unconscionability to a contract?

Analyzing Cases

1. Price retained the Todd Auction Company to sell his property. Mitchell was the high bidder and signed an agreement to close the sale within thirty days. At the time of the auction Mitchell paid a $37,000 deposit to Todd and accepted right of possession to the property. A dispute arose, and Mitchell refused to go through with the deal as promised. Mitchell claimed that he purchased the property relying on Price and Todd's representations that a generator for backup electricity would be installed. Such a generator had not been installed, nor had a road been relocated as had been promised by the sellers. Mitchell is suing for recission and the return of the $37,000 deposit. Judgment for whom and why? ● *Price v. Mitchell*, 268 S.E.2d 743 (Ga. App. 1980)

2. Woodstock Village, a land development partnership, entered into a contract to purchase a 12-acre tract of land from Fowler. Woodstock purchased the land and began development of a shopping center. Subsequently, Woodstock learned that a 5,000-square-foot piece of the property had been deeded away twelve years earlier by Fowler to the state. Woodstock is claiming fraud and is seeking a reduction in the purchase price reasonable to what was actually sold. Fowler claims that there can be no fraud because he did not realize that the document he signed twelve years before was a deed and therefore his actions were not intentional. Judgment for whom and why? ● *Woodstock Village v. Fowler*, 267 S.E.2d 558 (Ga. 1980)

3. John Libel and Janet Libel were divorced. Janet threatened to cut off her husband's child visitation rights unless he signed a post-divorce agreement extending alimony. Only a court has the right to alter or modify child visitation right pursuant to a decree of divorce. John signed the agreement and now seeks to have it rescinded on grounds of duress related to his former wife's threats. Will the court rescind the agreement? Explain. ● *Libel v. Libel*, 616 P.2d 306 (Kan. App. 1980)

4. Golden was the lessee of a certain property. He entered into an agreement to sublease the property to Newberry Wrecker Service, Inc., from September 1, 1970, to December 31, 1975. In fact Golden's lease was to expire July 31, 1972. Newberry could have discovered this fact had he made inquiry. Soon after July 31, 1972, the lessor who owned the property sought to regain it from Newberry. Newberry sued Golden for fraud. Golden claims innocence of ever having made any statements pertaining to either ownership of the property or the length of his lease. Judgment for whom and why? ● *Golden v. Newberry Wrecker Service, Inc.*, 267 S.E.2d 763 (Ga. App. 1980)

5. American Imagination Corp. of Texas (AICT) entered into a contract with W. R. Pierce & Associates in which Pierce was to install two ice machines and AICT was to pay Pierce $6,793.20. Although Pierce made oral statements to the effect that his company would repair the machines, if needed, the written agreement stated that AICT would keep the machines in "first class condition and repair." AICT in a suit on the contract argued that Pierce's oral statements as to repairs were not being fulfilled. Pierce pleaded *caveat emptor* and AICT's failure to read and abide by the written contract. Judgment for whom and why? • *American Imagination Corp. of Texas v. W. R. Pierce & Assocs., Inc.*, 601 S.W.2d 147 (Texas Civ. App. 1980)

6. Walker, who was in the gravel business, advertised a piece of property as having 580 feet of frontage on the highway and claimed to have an engineer's report certifying that the tract contained at least 80,000 cubic yards of gravel. Cousineau, a contractor also in the gravel business, purchased the property on these representations. Cousineau, after the purchase, found that the property had only 415 feet of highway frontage, and the gravel ran out after only 6,000 yards had been excavated. Cousineau is now seeking rescission of the contract. Judgment for whom and why? • *Cousineau v. Walker*, 613 P.2d 608 (Alaska 1980)

7. Stein, founder and president of Stein Egg and Poultry Company, Inc., retired from the firm after thirty years' experience. Upon retirement he executed an agreement, for consideration paid him, selling the business and agreeing not to compete with the new owners. In making the agreement he questioned the new owners about the not-to-compete clause and was told not to worry about it. He was told that if he wished, he could open up again "across the street." This assurance was given by the firm's new president. Stein now attempts to open a new and similar business and the new owners of Stein Poultry & Egg Company are suing to stop him. Judgment for whom and why? • *Stein v. Stein Egg & Poultry Co., Inc.*, 606 S.W.2d 203 (Mo. App. 1980)

8. Maxine Stetzel was involved in an auto accident with John Dickerson. Stetzel sustained personal injuries. The insurance adjuster was boorish and persisted in invading Stetzel's privacy until she finally signed a written release in return for a cash settlement of $400. Having reconsidered, she now seeks to rescind the agreement with the insurance company. On what grounds may she seek to do so? Is she likely to have the agreement set aside? Why or why not? • *Stetzel v. Dickerson*, 174 N.W.2d 438 (Iowa 1970)

9. Jack and Jenny Montgomery owned a tract of land which they agreed to sell to William Strickland. The terms of the sale were to be $41,500 for the property. No per acre charge or the like was specified. The Montgomerys had believed that the tract consisted of twenty-one or twenty-two acres, but when the land was surveyed they found it to contain thirty-five acres. The Montgomerys now refuse to go through with the deal. Strickland sues. Judgment for whom and why? • *Montgomery v. Strickland*, 384 So.2d. 1085 (Ala. 1980)

10. Mary Elizabeth Saunders was injured while riding a bus owned and operated by the defendant, New Orleans Public Service, Incorporated. She went to a doctor provided by the bus company and was assured that she had nothing more than a bruise and would be all right in a week or so. Relying on the doctor's statements, she accepted a $100 settlement and signed the customary release exempting the bus company from further claims. It later developed that her injuries were more severe. She is now suing for damages, claiming that settlement was made and induced by mutual mistake on the part of herself and the examining physician. It was determined on testimony that the doctor had never touched Saunders, but only observed her condition from across the room. Judgment for whom and why? • *Saunders v. New Orleans Public Service, Inc.*, 387 So.2d 603 (La. 1980)

Chapter 10   Contractual Capacity

Historically, the common law has protected vulnerable and defenseless persons from their liability and answerability to contracts to which they may have agreed. The English courts in their early decisions absolved minors, insane persons, married women, and certain others parties of obligation to contracts they had already entered. Unless a party was *capable*, that is, had legal competence to contract, promises were not enforceable against that party. This concept of contractual competency, or capacity, survived into the law of the American colonies and is an integral part of the law of each of the fifty states today.

Contractual capacity is the second requisite of every enforceable agreement. Minors, insane persons, those suffering temporary mental debility from alcohol or drugs, and enemy aliens are ordinarily excused from contractual liability due to incapacity. State statutes and court decisions have given further definition to capacity. In special areas the U.S. Constitution and federal agencies have also adopted specific laws and regulations that affect the rights and liabilities of individuals and corporations with regard to their legal and contractual capacity.

10-1. General Presumptions About Contractual Capacity

In the formation of contracts, there is a general presumption that anyone entering into a contractual relationship has the legal capacity to do so. Thus, one enforcing an agreement is not required to prove that the other party was competent in creating mutual assent. However, this is a *rebuttable presumption;* that is, a defending party has the right to try to refute the presumption and thereby prove an incapacity to contract.

● Garrett and DeMont entered a contract that obligated Garrett to sell her Piper Cub aircraft to DeMont for $2,500. Garrett at the time was only seventeen years of age. Should Garrett change her mind and refuse to respect their agreement, it would not be necessary that DeMont prove that Garrett was legally competent to enter into this agreement. Garrett, however, would be permitted to introduce evidence to show that she lacked capacity to contract. If successful in her defense, Garrett would be excused from any and all promises made to DeMont.

10-2. Minors' Rights and Obligations

The English courts very early understood the harm done young persons by those who took advantage of their lack of maturity and understanding of contract obligations. The courts adopted what was known as the *harm-benefit test*. If a minor could prove that the harm created by an agreement was greater than the benefits that would be received under it, the court could rescind the agreement. Each separate case was judged on its own merits, however, at times exposing minors to contracts in spite of their immaturity. In adopting the concept of incapacity, therefore, the courts in the United States replaced the harm-benefit concept with a more general blanket of protection accorded all persons who were incapable of contracting. Thus, the minor was relieved of having to prove more harm than benefit in order to avoid contractual obligations.

A. Definition of Minority

Minority, under common law, was a term that described persons who had not yet reached their twenty-first birthday. After attaining age twenty-one, one was said to have reached *majority*. Ratification and adoption of the Twenty-sixth Amendment to the U.S. Constitution in 1971 lowered the voting age in federal elections from twenty-one to eighteen. Following this lead, the states started to enact new laws that enabled eighteen-year-olds to vote in state and local elections. Then, accepting the logic that if eighteen-year-olds were sufficiently mature to be drafted into military service and vote they were mature enough to make certain contracts, states began to lower the age of majority for certain types of contracts to eighteen years. However, differences still exist within and between states as to the age requirements for achieving majority; this is so particularly in matters related to the use of alcoholic beverages, marriage, and the operation of motor vehicles.

1. Legal Age. To provide some uniformity in establishing a person's age, the common law has defined one's legal age (i.e., majority) as beginning at 12:01 a.m. of the day immediately before the day one celebrates one's natural birthday. Thus, for the purpose of counting one's legal age, the count is said to start on the last day of one's present year rather than the first day of the next year.

● Katz was born on November 5. Federal and state elections were scheduled for November 4th of Katz's seventeenth year. Election laws required persons to be eighteen years old to vote. As Katz's legal birthday would fall at 12.01 a.m. on November 4th, there would be no question as to Katz's right to register and vote in the November 4th elections.

2. Emancipation and Abandonment. Minors who are married are said to be *emancipated,* that is, freed from observing the laws regulating rights and obligations of minors on contracts. Similarly, when minors leave home and give up all rights to parental support, they are said to have *abandoned* the usual protective shield given them. Although minors in these two categories are no longer protected from liability on their contracts, merchants are usually reluctant to deal with them on a credit basis, fearing that they may still attempt to repudiate their contracted debts. When approving credit, merchants as a rule require that minors procure the signature of a responsible adult who will agree to guarantee payment of money owed.

B. Misrepresentation of Age

Minors, at times, knowingly and intentionally misrepresent their age when making contracts that they later choose to disaffirm or repudiate. Absent a corrective statute, the courts will not deny disaffirmance when there has been either an express or implied misrepresentation. Statutory remedies, however, may allow recovery against a minor when misrepresentation of age can be proved or when the minor is engaged in a business. Some states, for example, will deny disaffirmance if the minor has signed a written statement falsely asserting adult status. Courts of equity have also denied the right of disaffirmance on ground of what is called *estoppel*. The doctrine of estoppel denies rights to complaining parties that are shown to be the cause of their own loss or injury. Under estoppel, a court of equity will usually permit disaffirmance only when the minor restores to the other party all consideration or value received through the minor's misrepresentation.

At times the tort of *deceit,* which in a tort action requires basically the same proof required of fraud in a contract action, has been used to recover damages brought by a minor's misrepresentation of age. However, the alleged tort of deceit usually must be one that can be clearly established. If it cannot be, and the contract secured by the alleged misrepresentation is one that the law usually allows a minor to disaffirm, the courts tend to give the minor the benefit of doubt. In such circumstances, the courts have frequently denied claims by adults against minors based on the tort of deceit. Only in those states where corrective statutes have been adopted, and which clearly deny a minor the right to disaffirm a contract when there is misrepresentation of age, is the adult contracting party well protected.

● Danby, a minor whose appearance camouflaged her youth, purchased a fur-trimmed cloth coat from Avenue Style Shop for $235. She paid $75 and signed a contract agreeing to pay the balance in five installments over the next five months. Included in the body of the contract that she signed was the statement, "At the time of signing this contract I have reached the age of eighteen and am obligated herein as an adult." Danby later attempted to disaffirm her contract and was sued by Avenue Style for the balance owed. In states without special statutes disallowing minors' disaffirmance if there is misrepresentation of age, it is doubtful that the Avenue Style Shop would be successful in its suit against the minor.

10-3. Contractual Capacity of Minors

Minors said to be in their *tender years,* below the age of seven, do not have the understanding and comprehension required in creating enforceable mutual assent. Any agreements they might make may be declared void; the matter is in the discretion of the court. After age seven, minors generally are not denied the right to make contracts. Their contracts however are *voidable,* not void. They may elect either to accept or to repudiate their contract obligations in most circumstances. As a consequence, those dealing with minors run the risk of their electing to void their contractual obligations, giving no other grounds than age.

A. Executory Contracts

Executory contracts, those that have not been fully performed by both parties, may be repudiated by a minor at any time. A promise to deliver goods or render services at some future time need not be carried out by the minor who so decides. This privilege is not available to one who contracts with a minor. If goods delivered to a repudiating minor are still in existence, it is the minor's duty to return them to the other party.

● Wroten, sixteen years of age, bought a motorcycle from Hurka's Cycle Shop, paying the seller $800 cash with the rest to be paid in ten monthly installments. Two weeks after taking delivery of the bike Wroten wrecked it. Its value after the accident was nil. Wroten sued for the return of the $800 already paid and the cancellation of the outstanding balance owed. In most states, Hurka's Cycle Shop would be required to make the full $800 refund and cancel the outstanding debt.

A minority view expressed by some courts allows a party to seek a judgment for the use or depreciation of goods while in a minor's possession. Even in such cases the minor is not obliged to pay any more than what the court feels would be a reasonable amount in view of all the surrounding circumstances and the particular goods in question.

B. Executed Contracts

Courts usually apply the same general rule to executed contracts as to those that remain executory. As you may recall, an executed contract is one that has been fully carried out by both parties. The minor usually has the option of repudiating or accepting such contracts. Likewise, a minority view allows a recovery against a minor in an amount equal to the reasonable value for the use or depreciation of goods delivered to the minor under such an agreement.

C. Contracts for Necessaries

Necessaries are those goods and services that are essential to a minor's health, education, and welfare. A minor's contract covering necessaries is enforceable against the minor. The minor, however, is not required to pay the price or value agreed to on a contract for necessaries, but only a *reasonable price or value*, as determined by the court. If the necessaries had already been provided the minor by parents or others, they will not qualify under this rule.

Classified as necessaries are food, clothing, shelter, medical and dental services, tuition and books, and other goods and services reasonably required in protecting the minor's health and welfare, and in providing a necessary basic education or vocational training. In determining whether goods and services qualify as necessaries, the court will inquire into the minor's family status, financial strength, and social standing or station in life. Necessaries, then, are not the same to all persons.

● Morgan, a minor, was a commuting student at the local community college. She purchased textbooks and study guides for her courses in accounting, management, and business math. Any attempt to repudiate this purchase and recover her money would likely fail. The supplies purchased were all necessary to her education.

● Thompson attended an exclusive boarding school that catered to the children of wealthy parents. She purchased a formal gown that she planned to wear to a spring dance arranged by the school for all its students. To a person of another station in life, the gown might be viewed as a nonessential luxury. But to a person of Thompson's station in life, the gown would represent a necessary. She would likely be denied any right to return it and demand a refund from the store.

The rulings related to necessaries, in any case, apply only to executed contracts. Wholly executory contracts calling for a future delivery or rendering of services may be repudiated by the minor. Thus, in the foregoing cases had the books and the gown only been ordered, and not delivered and paid for, it would have been possible for the minors in question to repudiate their agreements with no damages or monetary losses being assessed against them.

Technically, parents are not liable for contracts executed by minors, even for necessaries, unless the parents have cosigned the contracts. An exception exists, however, if the parent has neglected or deserted the minor. In such a situation, the parent may be held liable to a third person for the reasonable value of the necessaries supplied by the third party to the minor.

D. Other Contracts Not Voidable

By statute and court decision certain other types of contracts have been excepted from the general rule that the contracts of minors are voidable at the minor's option. For public policy reasons, minors may not at their option disaffirm a valid contract of marriage or repudiate an enlistment contract in the armed forces based on a claim of incapacity to contract. Neither may a minor repudiate a contract for goods and services required by law; for example, minors may not repudiate payments for innoculations and vaccinations required for attendance at a university or college or required in securing a visa for travel in certain foreign lands.

● Joan Williams, fourteen years old, moved in and lived with Earl Johnson, Jr. Joan later testified at a trial for an unrelated cause that she was Johnson's common-law wife. Earl objected to her testimony, arguing that as a minor she could not consent to a marriage. Marriage laws in their state, Kansas, provided that a female must be at least twelve years old, and males at least fourteen, to marry. The court validated the marriage and would not permit rescission, as Kansas respected common-law marriage, and both parties were of ages that permitted marriage within their state.

Some states have given special recognition to a minor's contracts associated with the operation of a business if the minor is self-supporting. In these states, such contracts have been held not to be voidable. A minor who is a partner in a business is not permitted to withdraw or disturb any investment made in the partnership that might financially weaken the partnership or the rights of its creditors.

E. Affirmance and Disaffirmance of Minors' Contracts

Minors may affirm or disaffirm their contracts on reaching their majority—eighteen, twenty-one, or other age set by statute—or within a reasonable time thereafter. *Affirmance,* the willingness to abide by the contract obligations, may be implied by making an installment payment, paying off the balance of money owed on a previously voidable contract, or continuing to accept goods and services being provided under a contract. Affirmation may also result from the minor's oral or written declaration to abide by the contract. These acts as well as others ratify an existing agreement and elevate it to the status of one enforceable against an adult.

A minor, on attaining adulthood, may likewise *disaffirm,* or repudiate, an agreement made during minority. Disaffirmance, however, must be made within a reasonable (usually short) period of time after a minor reaches majority. The exact period of time will vary depending on the nature of the contract and applicable state and local law. Failure to make disaffirmance within a reasonable period of time would imply that the contract had been affirmed, or ratified, by the minor. The method of disaffirmance is fundamentally the same as the method of affirmance. Disaffirmance may be implied by the acts of the minor after achieving majority, as by a failure to make an installment payment due on a sales contract. Similarly, an oral or written declaration of disaffirmance would achieve the same end.

1. Disaffirmance Related to Innocent Third Parties. The UCC permits one having a voidable title to transfer good title to an innocent third-party purchaser of those goods (2-403). Thus, disaffirmance by a minor will not require the innocent purchaser to return the goods.

● Jones, when a minor, sold her car to Caldwell Motor Sales. Caldwell, in turn, sold the car to Bromley, an innocent third-party purchaser. When Jones reached her majority she sought to recover the car from Bromley by disaffirming the original contract with Caldwell. Jones would be denied the right of recovering the car through disaffirmance.

The UCC rule refers only to sale of personal property. In cases where a minor has sold real estate to one who subsequently sells it to an innocent third party, the minor, on reaching adulthood, may disaffirm the sale and recover the real property.

2. "Shield or Sword" Doctrine. Disaffirmance of a contract may not be used by a minor as a means of taking obvious advantage of the other party. The right to disaffirm an agreement was given to minors as a protective device or "shield" against those who might try to take unfair advantage of their immaturity and inexperience. The courts have denied the right of disaffirmance when it has been clearly shown that the minor used this privilege as a weapon or "sword" against the other contracting party.

● Rawlins, seventeen years of age, purchased an airline ticket for travel between Chicago and Los Angeles. On arrival at Los Angeles he demanded the return of all money paid, claiming such rights as a minor. Obviously, Rawlins was using his rights as a minor to take advantage of the airline. He was not using his rights as a minor as a protective device, as the law intended. It is doubtful that Rawlins would be permitted to recover the money for his passage to Los Angeles.

10-4. Capacity of Mental Incompetents

Persons deprived of a mentality sufficient to comprehend and understand contractual obligations have the right to disaffirm their contracts. Their rights are, in many respects, but little different from the rights of minors. Agreements of mental incompetents are either voidable or void, depending on the seriousness of their disability and on whether they have been declared insane.

A. Contracts of Persons Not Legally Declared Insane

Contracts of persons lacking mental competence, but not legally declared insane, are *voidable*. Such persons may disaffirm all contracts except those for necessaries. The incompetent must return all consideration received or its equivalent value in money. However, where a party is aware of the other's mental incapacity and takes unfair advantage of the situation, the infirm party may repudiate the agreement without any obligation of returning consideration or reimbursing the other party for its reasonable value.

● Homan had married Ward, and Ward was seeking rescission of their marriage contract on grounds of Homan's incapacity. He was weak of mind, suffered from schizophrenia, and was not lucid 100 percent of the time. The court, on inquiry, found that at the time of the marriage he was lucid and understood what was going on. Because he was lucid on his marriage day, the court would not invalidate the marriage. The court further stated that Homan's mental state at times other than the day of the marriage had no relevance on what was concluded to be a valid marriage.

B. Agreements of Persons Legally Declared Insane

Persons declared to be insane by competent legal authority are denied the right to enter contracts. Any contractual relationship with others results in nothing more than an unenforceable agreement. Such agreements, sometimes incorrectly called "contracts," are *void*. In most states persons who knowingly take advantage of one declared insane are subject to criminal indictment and prosecution.

10-5. Contractual Incapacity of Others

Questions arise as to the contractual capacity of persons under the influence of alcohol or drugs, enemy aliens, married women, and corporations. Their contractual capacity is described in the paragraphs that follow.

A. Persons Under Influence of Alcohol or Drugs

Contracts agreed to by persons under the influence of alcohol or drugs are voidable. Incompetence related to either alcohol or drugs must be of such degree that a contracting party would have lost the ability to comprehend or be aware of obligations being accepted under the contract. One who contracts while in this condition may either affirm or disaffirm the agreement at a later time. Disaffirmance here requires full and complete restitution to the other party of all consideration that had been received. However, restitution may be refused when evidence indicates that one party took advantage of the other's drunken or weakened condition. Statutes in some states protect persons who have been declared to be habitual drunkards. Contracts of such persons, like persons declared insane, are void in those states.

● Danvers, a purchasing agent for Alloway Corporation, was entertained at luncheon by a representative of Holden Hardware Supply Company. During lunch, Danvers was treated to three cocktails, which materially lowered his sales resistance. He did, however, continue to be alert and aware of all going on around him. During lunch Danvers signed an agreement for delivery of hardware supplies for his employer. As Danvers was aware of what he was doing, was not drunk, and understood the seriousness of the contract, the agreement was valid and enforceable.

B. Enemy Aliens

Enemy aliens are citizens of another country living within the United States who maintain an allegiance to their native country when the two countries are at war. Contracts made with enemy aliens that give aid and comfort to the enemy or imperil the safety of the United States are void. Contracts of enemy aliens are valid and enforceable when they do not afford aid or comfort to the enemy or do not pose a threat to the United States.

● Stoltzburg lived in the United States. During the years he had lived in this country he had never renounced his citizenship in his native land, nor had he applied for U.S. citizenship. War broke out between his country and the United States. Stoltzburg was employed as a violinist in a symphony orchestra. His contract with the orchestra would be enforceable by Stoltzburg. His professional activities in no way contributed to the enemy's efforts, nor did they pose any threat against the United States.

C. Married Women

By early common law married women were denied the right to contract. Only single women had the capacity for making enforceable agreements. Upon marriage the wife gave up all contract rights and the husband received a life estate in the real property of the wife.

Commencing with the married-women's statutes adopted by New York in the 1890s, all states have adopted statutes giving married women the right to contract in their own name. Federal and state laws have given added protection to married women in contracts for employment, loans, buying or leasing real property, and the like. Efforts at eliminating discrimination against married women in their right to contract have had considerable success over the past fifty years, and as a result, all prior laws in this area are of little more than historic interest. Efforts to eliminate discriminatory practices against single women in their contractual and other legal rights have become the subject of more recent attention, and these efforts are continuing at present.

D. Corporations

Corporations may not perform acts that are outside the express or implied powers granted by a corporate charter. Such acts are called *ultra vires* acts. The common law treated *ultra vires* acts as void and without legal authority. The Modern Business Corporation Act, Section 7, removed this defense in cases where a corporation is being sued for a breach of contract. (Chapter 35 of the text provides a further discussion of *ultra vires* acts.)

Decisions of some courts have allowed rescission of an executory *ultra vires* contract. When performance has not commenced and no damage has been incurred, these decisions have been accepted as fair and just.

Understanding Legal Terms

Define, identify, or explain each of the following terms:

abandonment	emancipation		
affirmance	enemy alien	insanity	majority
contractual capacity	harm-benefit test	intoxication	minority
disaffirmance	incapacity	legal birthday	necessaries

Questions for Review and Discussion

1. What test did the early English courts introduce to determine whether a minor could avoid a contract? How does this test differ from the rules regarding repudiation of minors' contracts that the courts of the United States apply today?

2. How has the Twenty-sixth Amendment to the U.S. Constitution affected the age at which minors achieve majority? How has the amendment affected rights and obligations of minors in regard to contracts?

3. Contrast the legal responsibilities of minors for (a) contracts for necessaries and (b) contracts for other than necessaries.

4. Are minors excused from liability on contracts in connection with business ventures in which they are engaged? Explain.

5. How does the law differentiate between contractual obligations of persons declared to be legally insane and those suffering from less serious mental illness, but not declared insane?

6. What is the intent and meaning of the "shield or sword" doctrine?

7. When may a party use intoxication or drug addiction as a defense against performing contractual obligations? May habitual drunkards have their contracts declared void? Explain.

8. What was the status of the contractual and property rights of married women as compared to that of their husbands under early common law? How have the contract and property rights of women changed in modern times?

9. What limitations are imposed by law upon the rights of corporations in making contracts?

Analyzing Cases

1. In 1969 Vassayl A. Lonchyna, age nineteen, entered into an enlistment contract with the U.S. Air Force. At age twenty-one he accepted his commission, and later accepted promotion to first lieutenant. Three times he applied for educational delays that prolonged the start of his actual duty. He was finally called to active duty in 1980. He is now claiming that since he was a minor when he originally signed the enlistment contract, it is voidable. Judgment for whom and why? ● *Lonchyna v. Brown (Secretary of Air Force)*, 491 F. Supp. 1352 (N.D. Ill. 1980)

2. Karen Taylor was involved in an automobile accident while riding in a car driven by John Avi. Following the accident she suffered from occasional impaired memory, decreased ability to concentrate, and irritability. She was hospitalized from late November 1975, when the accident occurred, until December of the same year. After three meetings Taylor received a check for $400 from the insurance company in return for which she signed a document that released the insurance company or Avi of any further claims. The signing was witnessed by Taylor's sister and mother-in-law. The release was fully explained before Taylor signed it. Soon after cashing the $400 check Taylor brought suit claiming more damages. The insurance company defended itself, claiming that the release was valid. Judgment for whom and why? ● *Taylor v. Avi*, 415 A.2d 894 (Pa. 1979)

3. Carol Scherer sought a divorce from her husband, Howard, in the Dominican Republic. She met all jurisdictional requirements and even had her husband sign a power of attorney, allowing for his appearance in the matter. Howard Scherer is now trying to overturn the divorce through an action in his own state of Indiana, which is permitted. He contends that at the time of signing the power of attorney he was drunk and had taken Valium. Could Howard's intoxication

be a defense against the divorce decree? Explain. ● *Scherer v. Scherer,* 405 N.E.2d 40 (Ind. 1980)

4. Charles Edward Smith, Jr., while seventeen years old, purchased a car. He continued to use the car, making payments for ten months after reaching his eighteenth birthday. He has now returned the car and is seeking a rescission of the contract. Does Bobby Floars Toyota, Inc., the seller, have to return Smith's money? Explain. ● *Bobby Floars Toyota, Inc. v. Smith,* 269 S.E.2d 320 (N.C. 1980)

5. James Halbman, a minor, entered into an agreement with Michael Lemke, the manager of a gas station, to purchase an automobile. A number of months later, after the engine was found to be totally defective, and after vandalism had caused such damage as to make the car useless, Halbman, who was still a minor, disaffirmed the contract and demanded the return of his money. May he do so? Explain. ● *Halbman v. Lemke,* 298 N.W.2d 562 (Wis. 1980)

6. Darwin Kruse was a construction worker. He was injured while working for Coos Head Timber Company. Subsequent to the accident Kruse signed an agreement with his employer that granted Kruse compensation in exchange for his promise not to sue. Kruse is now trying to have the agreement voided. Evidence introduced proved that Kruse had an IQ of 83 and that he dropped out of school at age eighteen. When he dropped out of school, he was in the eighth grade but was doing less than fifth-grade-level work. Is Kruse's "slowness" sufficient reason to invalidate the contract? Explain. ● *Kruse v. Coos Head Timber Co.,* 432 P.2d 1009 (Ore. 1967)

7. The Logan County Bank loaned Taylor the money to buy a car. Taylor, at the time of making the loan, was a minor. Soon afterward when eighteen, Taylor was drafted into the armed forces. He wrote to the bank and told it to pick up the car. The bank sold the car for junk and received only $30. The bank is now suing Taylor on the note that he signed when making the loan. Is Taylor liable? Explain. ● *Logan County Bank v. Taylor,* 295 N.E.2d 743 (Ill. 1973)

Chapter ll   Consideration

Mutual assent provides the foundation in the creation of binding agreements. Contractual capacity of the parties determines whether agreements are valid, void, or voidable. Consideration, the third requisite, is the incentive that leads an offeror to make a proposal and the inducement that prompts the other party to accept. It distinguishes a contract from a mere gift or an empty promise.

11-1. Requirements of Consideration

Consideration requires a combination of mutual promises or, as in unilateral contracts, a promise for an anticipated act. A one-sided promise, not supported by the promise or act of the offeree, merely creates an unenforceable agreement.

A. Definition of Consideration

The *Restatement (Second) of the Law of Contracts* defines consideration as (1) an act other than a promise; (2) a forbearance; (3) the creation, modification, or destruction of a legal relation; or, (4) a return promise *bargained for* and given in exchange for the promise. Summed up, all *consideration* is either:

○ Doing or promising to do a legal act or service that yields pleasure or benefit to a party when one is under no legal or contractual obligation to provide the benefits so given or promised.
○ Or, refraining or promising to refrain from doing that which one is otherwise free to do and has a legal right to do. This act or promise of refraining is called *forbearance*.

1. Bargained-for Promises. Consideration has two requisites: (1) bargaining between the parties must take place with the motive being that a promise made be dependent on the consideration to be received and (2) the consideration must have value. Thus, an agreement to exchange gifts would not be a bargained-for promise. Two persons contemplating the exchange of gifts are not bound by bargained-for promises. Likewise, acts done without the expectation of reward lack any semblance of bargained-for consideration and create no obligations between the one performing and the one being benefited.

● Harrington agreed to loan Taylor a chain saw which Taylor planned to use in removing small trees from a recently purchased homesite. There was no understanding that Taylor would pay for the use of the chain saw. Harrington now refuses to allow Taylor to use his saw. Although Harrington might have a moral obligation to carry out the offer of the saw, their agreement was not an enforceable one in that it contained no bargained-for promise.

144

2. Consideration in Bilateral Contracts. Consideration consists of a mutual exchange of benefits and sacrifices (detriments) between contracting parties. In this exchange, what is a benefit to the offeree is at the same time a sacrifice to the offeror. Likewise, the benefit bargained for by the offeror will finally result in a sacrifice by the offeree. Unless each promise in a bilateral agreement has created obligations by providing benefits and sacrifices to each party, no enforceable agreement is achieved.

● Dorton offered to sell a real estate lot to Sidway for $5,800. Sidway was interested but needed more time to consider the proposition. Dorton agreed to continue the offer for three days. To "bind the bargain," Sidway gave Dorton $25 in earnest money. Dorton's benefit was the $25 he received, which also was Sidway's sacrifice or detriment, since she had to give up the $25. In return, Sidway was benefited by Dorton's promise to hold the offer open for three days. Dorton's sacrifice or detriment consisted of giving up the right to advertise and sell the real estate lot to anyone else for a period of three days.

3. Consideration in Unilateral Agreements. In unilateral agreements, the offeror's promise is nothing more than an offer. There is no mutuality of consideration until the offeree commences performance of the requested act.

The option of performance (acceptance) rests entirely with the offeree. Once performance is started, however, a mutuality of benefits and sacrifices arises, establishing mutual agreement and consideration.

● The Carbolic Smoke Ball Company advertised a reward to anyone who used its smoke ball and thereafter contracted any ailment resulting from taking cold. Carbolic Smoke Balls were popularly used as an inhalant to the cure of asthma and other pulmonary complaints. Carill purchased and used a smoke ball, following all instructions provided by the manufacturer. Shortly thereafter he suffered from an attack of influenza. Carbolic Smoke Ball Company, when sued by Carill for the promised reward, contended that there had been no mutuality of promises and that therefore there was no consideration in support of Carill's claim. The court held that the seller's advertising contained enforceable promises to anyone who accepted its proposition. Consideration was achieved when Carill acted on the unilateral promise made in the seller's advertising.

B. Nature of Consideration

Common law established the concept that some promises, even when seriously made by competent parties, would not be binding and enforceable. Only bargained-for promises were valid and resulted in enforceable obligations. The typical friendly promise to help another repair a car, prepare for a final examination, or the like, gives no grounds for legal action if the promise is not carried out. Such promises are nothing more than an expression of intent to perform some gratuitous act or service, not supported by mutual obligations.

1. Something of Value. There are no specific requirements or qualifications, other than being legal, as to what one may promise in return for another's offer to deliver goods and services. The promise itself is consideration when it represents something of value. Thus, the promise to assist another to repair a car would be *something of value* promised. It would not be consideration, however, if it had not been bargained for. The value placed on goods and services need not be the street or market value. It is important only that the parties concerned had freely agreed on the value and price.

● Chapman negotiated with Martin as to how much Chapman might charge to paint Martin's house. They concluded their bargaining session when Martin agreed to pay Chapman $900 to do the job. Court enforcement of their promises will in no way depend on what other painters might have charged for the same job, whether that be more or less than $900.

2. Money as Consideration. Money is the usual consideration offered by one seeking another's promise or performance. The parties are free to negotiate privately the amount of money to be paid except when price structures have been established through administrative rulings or legislation. Historically, rent, fuel oil, natural gas, and other goods have been the subject of price controls. Likewise, employers engaged in interstate commerce may not bargain with qualified employees for a wage rate less than guaranteed by the federal Fair Labor Standards Act.

3. Goods and Services as Consideration. Before money was accepted as a medium of exchange, consideration consisted of goods and services. In modern times, especially during recessionary or inflationary cycles, parties have sometimes found it more beneficial to enter into barter agreements than to base their promises on cash payments. The courts have held that barter agreements do contain valid consideration. Thus, for example, the exchange of services in return for the use of another's car or a promise to trade a watch for a typewriter represent benefits and sacrifices that consitute valid consideration to support a legally binding contract.

4. Illusory Promises. An *illusory promise* is one that does not obligate the promissor to anything. One who makes an illusory promise is the only one with any right to determine whether the other party will be benefited in any way. Illusory promises fail to provide the mutuality of promises required in establishing consideration.

● Lancaster Apartments agreed to buy such fuel oil as it "might desire" for one heating season from Economy Oil Company. In return for this promise, Economy negotiated terms whereby it would give Lancaster a special schedule of discounts for the oil. The promise to buy as much as it "might desire" had actually obligated Lancaster to do nothing. Its promise was illusory because Lancaster "might desire" absolutely no fuel oil and still keep its promise. The benefits that Lancaster was to derive from the schedule of discounts were not supported by a real or enforceable promise on Lancaster's part. A suit brought by either party to enforce this agreement would fail for want of consideration.

5. Output and Requirements Contracts. When an agreement provides for the purchase of a buyer's requirements or is based on a supplier's output, the UCC takes another view. The UCC limits each party's obligations in such an agreement to *what might be reasonable* compared with requirements and output under normal and comparable conditions [(2-306(1)]. The UCC also requires good faith in determination of the meaning of these terms. Thus, occurrence of good-faith actions by either or both parties in furtherance of their obligations gives evidence that an output and requirements contract was intended and in fact exists. In contrast to illusory promises, specifications of output and requirements may be determined by the court, if necessary, and do constitute real obligations.

● International Health Assurance Company hired Furrer as its agent to select and train new agents for a planned sales group. The contract stated that Furrer was to spend as much time as she personally felt necessary to do the job successfully. Furrer, in good faith and reliance on this agreement, carried out her obligations and produced an effective sales force. International refused to honor the contract, claiming her promise to be illusory. International argued that Furrer had never accepted any specific obligation as to the amount of time she would spend in performance of her assigned job. The court ruled in favor of Furrer, basing its decision on the *good-faith* and *requirements* concepts of the UCC. Although the UCC itself did not govern this transaction, which was for services rather than goods, the court followed UCC principles. There was a mutuality of valid consideration.

11-2. Special Types of Consideration

In most commercial and consumer transactions a mutual exchange of benefits and sacrifices signifies that the essential ingredient of consideration is present. There are certain special kinds of agreements and promises, however, where the benefits and sacrifices are unique in some manner and for some particular reason. Significant among these are promises not to sue, options, and subscriptions and pledges.

A. Promises Not to Sue

A promise not to sue, when there is the right to sue, is enforceable when supported by consideration. Promising not to sue is a forbearance. A promise not to sue, supported by consideration, is a customary solution to claims by persons who threaten suit for damages resulting from another's tort or a breach of an enforceable contract. Settlements of this type are often preferred to expensive and time-consuming litigation.

● Chambers was fired from a job under questionable circumstances. She discussed her legal rights with an attorney who suggested that she might be reinstated in the job if suit were brought against the employer. Her former employer agreed to pay Chambers $2,400 if she would accept their decision to terminate her job and if she would give up her intentions to bring suit against the firm. A court would uphold this agreement based on a mutuality of promises between the parties.

Acceptance of an agreement not to sue, supported by consideration, terminates one's right to continue any action, presently or in the future, on grounds described in the agreement. Promises not to sue are commonly called *releases*. Agreements of this kind are frequently negotiated between attorneys even after a lawsuit has been filed and trial begun. In such event the settlement is arranged in cooperation with the court and presiding judge.

B. Options

An *option* is the giving of consideration to support an offeror's promise to hold open an offer for a stated or reasonable length of time. The UCC has made an exception to the rule requiring consideration when the offer is made by a merchant; in such cases, an offer in writing, stating the time period over which the offer will remain open, is enforceable without consideration (2-205). The offer must be signed by the offeror, and time allowed for acceptance may not exceed three months. When the time allowed is in excess of three months, firm offers by merchants must be supported by consideration in order to be enforceable.

C. Subscriptions and Pledges

The dependence of charitable institutions and nonprofit organizations upon solicitation of contributions has encouraged the courts to enforce pledges as though they were contractual obligations. When pledges are made to fund a specific project, the pledgee's sacrifice is the carrying out of that project. Pledges, in this sense, are considered unilateral agreements, enforceable only when accepted by commencement of the proposed project.

● All Saints Church launched a campaign to fund expansion of the church sanctuary. One million dollars was pledged by members and friends of the church. Relying on these pledges, the church started work on the building program. Each of the pledges, however small, became an enforceable agreement through a mutuality of benefits to be derived by the pledgors to the fund. Carrying out the proposed plan, as outlined to the pledgors, was therefore valid consideration supporting their pledges.

At times pledges and subscriptions are to be used for general operation and maintenance, as of a school or college. When there is no promise to carry out a specific project, the courts have held that each pledge made is supported by the pledges of all others who have made similar pledges. This concept of consideration is used in support of all promises of money for undefined causes.

11-3. Issues and Problems Regarding Consideration

The consideration supporting a contract is at times challenged on the basis of its adequacy or legality, and disputes may arise involving the settlement of debts. Cases in both law and equity and statutes give guidance to the courts in dealing with these problems.

A. Adequacy of Consideration

Contracting parties at times complain that the benefits promised are not commensurate to the sacrifices accepted. A party obligated to sell a property for $50,000 may, prior to carrying out the agreement, complain that $50,000 is far too little in return for the property being sold. It is generally not the responsibility of a court to review the fairness or terms of a bargain in the absence of evidence of fraud, misrepresentation, mistake, undue influence, or duress. However, courts of equity will at times give a party relief when the consideration is such as might shock the conscience of the court. Thus, if in the sale of the property it were shown that the real value was ten times that which the owner agreed to accept, a court of equity might set aside the agreement on grounds of unfairness and injustice. In very specific matters, usually related to taxes, some states have adopted statutes dealing with adequacy. In general, however, courts are reluctant to disturb the promises made by parties to an enforceable contract. Indeed, the courts have consistently held that the advantages or profits gained through skillful bargaining are the basis of free trade and competition.

B. Legality of Consideration

Consideration requires that the benefits and sacrifices promised between the parties be legal. Absence of legality renders the consideration invalid.

● Custom Builders agreed to construct a frame addition to Baldt's home. All terms and conditions were agreed to by both parties. Zoning laws related to fire protection restricted all new buildings and additions to masonary construction. The consideration, therefore, was illegal, and neither party may demand performance of the agreement.

A more complete study of illegal agreements will be presented in Chapter 12.

C. Liquidation of Claims and Debts

Problems arise between creditors and debtors in agreements pertaining to payment of debts. Disputed amounts, undisputed amounts, accord and satisfaction agreements, and general releases are all related to the *liquidation,* or settlement, of existing claims and debts.

1. Disputed Amounts. *Disputed amounts* are those on which the parties never reached mutual agreement. Final settlement of disputed claims may lead to misunderstanding, dispute, and lengthy negotiation. Tender of an amount less than that claimed by a creditor, if accepted in full payment, is an *accord and satisfaction. Accord* is the implied or expressed acceptance of less than what has been billed the debtor. *Satisfaction* is the agreed-to settlement as contained in the accord. Only if the dispute is honest, made in good faith, and not superficial or trivial will the courts entertain arguments based on accord and satisfaction.

● Britz had her car repaired by Hillside Mechanics. No agreement had been made as to charges to be made for contracted engine work to be performed. When the job was finished, Britz received a bill for $695. She thought this to be excessive. She mailed a check to Hillside for only $550, writing on the check "in full payment for all services and parts used in repair of my car." Hillside cashed the check and later sued Britz for the $145 balance. Hillside would fail in this action, having accepted a lesser amount which was offered in good faith by Britz, in full payment of a disputed amount.

2. Undisputed Amounts. *Undisputed amounts* are those on which the parties mutually agreed. Although a party may have second thoughts about the amount promised for goods or services rendered, the amount that was agreed to by the parties when they made their contract remains an undisputed amount. A part payment in lieu of full payment when accepted by a creditor will not cancel an undisputed debt.

● Owens had four new tires mounted on a car, agreeing to pay $59 for each tire, or a total of $236 for all four tires. A few days later, but before paying the $236, Owens saw the same tires advertised by another dealer for $43, or $172 for four tires. Owens sent a check for only $172, with a notation on the check reading, "In full payment for four tires purchased October 4, 1982." The seller deposited the check and demanded payment of the balance of $64.

There was no *good-faith dispute* in Owens' dealings with the tire company. The buyer was merely attempting to get the tires at the lower price that she could have paid another dealer. The sum of $236 was an undisputed amount, and the balance is owed the seller.

3. General Release. Statutes in most states permit the cancellation of a debt, in whole or part, when the creditor gives the other party a statement in writing expressing intent of releasing the other of indebtedness. Such a statement is called a *general release*. States that still use the seal require that such releases contain the creditor's seal.

● Benedito owed Acme Printing Company $85. The account was long overdue and predictably uncollectible. As a friendly gesture, Acme prepared the release shown in Figure 11-1, which removed the account from its books and assured Benedito's continued goodwill toward Acme.

4. Composition of Creditors. Creditors may join together and enter into an agreement with a financially distressed debtor wherein the creditors jointly agree to accept amounts less than owed. This bargained-for agreement is sufficient to bind the creditors to liquidation of the debts owed to each one of them. Both the creditors and debtor are benefited by the avoidance of bankruptcy proceedings which would further reduce the debtor's assets and leave less available for distribution to the creditors.

11-4. Promises Not Requiring Consideration

State laws sometimes eliminate the requirement of consideration in specific types of agreements. There is no uniformity among states as to the types of

---

October 15, 19--

The Acme Printing Company hereby releases Sandra Benedito from all obligations on her account as of this date.

ACME PRINTING COMPANY

Elissa King (L. S.)
President

Figure 11-1. A general release.

agreements subject to such laws. The following are the principal types of agreements that do not require consideration.

A. Promises Bearing a Seal

Where state law requires that contracts bear a seal, the seal retains its historical significance. It gives a written contract the presumption of consideration; that is, promises expressed in a signed and sealed agreement are enforceable even though the consideration is not recited in the agreement itself. The presumption favors one seeking the enforcement of a sealed agreement in that there is no necessity to prove consideration. The UCC has eliminated the use of the seal in contracts for the sale of personal property (2-203). However, statutes in many states still require the use of the seal in real property and certain other types of transactions. Since there is no uniformity in this regard, it is advisable to research and consult individual state requirements.

B. Promises After Discharge in Bankruptcy

Persons discharged from indebtedness through bankruptcy may reaffirm and resume their obligations, prompted perhaps by moral compulsion. In the past, reaffirmation has been the subject of abuse by creditors who used pressure against those whose debts have been excused. Under the new and far-reaching Bankruptcy Reform Act of 1978, Congress included measures that make it more difficult for creditors to extract such promises. The bankruptcy court now must hold a hearing when a reaffirmation is intended, informing the bankrupt that reaffirmation is optional, not required, and of the legal consequences of reactivating a debt. If consumer debts are to be reaffirmed, the court can review the conditions of the reaffirmation to guard against a creditor imposing unjust hardships on the debtor.

State laws, in most cases, provide that no new consideration need be provided in support of reaffirmation. Most states require that a reaffirmation be supported by contractual intent. Some states require the new promise to be made and evidenced in writing. However, when there is no such provision, an oral promise or reaffirmation is usually sufficient.

C. Debts Barred by Statute of Limitations

State laws known as statutes of limitations limit the time within which a party is allowed to bring legal action against another for breach of contract, an action in tort for recovery of damages, and the like. The time allowed for the collection of a debt varies from state to state, usually from three to ten years. Some states allow more time for collection when the document of indebtedness is under seal, as in the case of a promissory note containing the seal of the maker. Debtors may revive and reaffirm debts barred by the statutes without the necessity of new consideration. Affirmation may result from the part payment of the debt or an expressed intention to pay. When a debt is revived, the creditor again is permitted the full term, as provided by the statute, to make collection.

● McBride had owed Jansen's Market $125 for more than five years. No legal action had even been initiated by Jansen's, and there was no judgment against McBride for that amount. State law allowed five years from the date a debt was made for its collection. Although McBride's indebtedness has been outlawed by the statute of limitations, a part payment on the debt will revive the account for an additional five years, during which it may be collected by legal action in court.

D. Promises Enforced by Promissory Estoppel

Promissory estoppel is a legal doctrine that restricts an offeror from revoking an offer, under certain conditions, even though consideration, such as earnest money, has not been paid to bind an agreement. To be effective, promissory estoppel requires that the offeror know, or be presumed to know, that the offeree might otherwise make a definite and decided change of position in contemplation of promises contained in the offer. Courts, in reaching this doctrine, have accepted the principles of justice and fairness in protecting the offeree from otherwise unrecoverable losses.

● Geremia borrowed money from East Providence Credit Union for use in the purchase of a car. The agreement required that Geremia keep the car insured. The credit union promised, in the agreement, that if Geremia was late in making premium payments, it would make payment and add the amount to Geremia's indebtedness. Geremia was late with premium payments, and East Providence Credit Union failed to keep up the policy as promised. Subsequently the car was damaged in an accident, and demand was made for immediate and full payment of money owed the credit union. In a suit brought by the credit union Geremia pleaded the defense of promissory estoppel as related to the lender's promise to pay the insurance premiums. The court ruled in favor of Geremia.

Although the credit union had received no consideration supporting the promise to pay late premiums, Geremia had accepted the promise and had placed himself in a very different and difficult position through his reliance upon the promise. Had the credit union not made such a promise, Germia would no doubt have made other arrangements for making regular and prompt payments to the insurer.

11-5. Agreements Lacking in Consideration

The promises just described are exceptions to the general rule that consideration must support an enforceable contract. The exceptions are allowed by state statute or because the courts, in the interest of fairness or justice, find it inappropriate to require consideration. There are certain promises, however, which the courts will not enforce because they lack even the rudimentary qualities of valid consideration. Included in this category are barren promises, promises of future gifts, legacies, past consideration, and moral consideration.

A. Barren Promises

A *barren promise* is a promise to do nothing more than one is already bound to do either by law or by contract. Because neither party has been benefited by any promise or act other than what is already required, there is no consideration. Barren promises may be divided into three kinds.

○ Promises to do that which one is already required by law to do or promises to refrain from doing that which one is restricted by law from doing are unenforceable.

● Velex promised to buy her daughter a new car on her twenty-first birthday if she would observe all traffic laws and not be arrested for traffic violations during the ensuing six-month period. The parent would have no contractual obligation through this promise. The daughter's careful driving is no more than she is required by law to do. The promise of a new car would not be enforceable as it is supported by nothing more than the daughter's barren promise.

○ Promise to do nothing more than one is already pledged or obligated to do by contract are unenforceable.

● Vignola Furniture Company sold a love seat to Stephen Trisko. When it was delivered, Trisko discovered it had been damaged. Vignola promised to fix the love seat if Trisko refrained from suing them. When Trisko did sue, Vignola defended by claiming they had an agreement not to sue supported by consideration. The court held that Vignola Furniture had an implied warranty to deliver an undamaged love seat and that the agreement to repair the one delivered involved nothing more than fulfilling an already existing contractual obligation. Vignola's promise was thus a barren promise.

The same rule applies to police officers, firefighters, and other public servants and officials who may promise some special service for monetary or other reward for doing what is actually their job. Suppose, for example, a police officer promises to provide a store owner additional protection against crime by making additional rounds of the store in return for some money. Neither the police officer nor the store owner could enforce such an agreement in a court. It is based on the officer's barren promise to do what the law already requires.

○ Promises to pay part of an existing debt.

● Stranger owed Heald's Body Shop $300, which Heald had difficulty in collecting. Heald called Stranger and offered to cancel the entire debt if Stranger would send the body shop $200. There was no dispute as to the amount of money owed. Payment of the $200 would not obligate Heald to refrain from seeking the balance of $100. By paying the $200, Stranger had done nothing more than she was already obligated to do. Thus, Stranger's barren promise would not support Heald's agreement to cancel the entire debt.

B. **Gifts**

A promise of a gift to be given at some future time is not enforceable for want of consideration. Included here are promises to provide gratuitous services or to lend one's property without expectation of any benefits in return.

● Julia, Ruth, and Kathryn Magee are elderly sisters. They had made promises to convey all their property to Barbara and John Stacey. At no time had Barbara and John Stacey made any promises or performed any services for the sisters. The Magee sisters sought to annul the promises on which the Stacey's demanded performance. The court ruled that in the absence of any consideration the promises by Julia, Ruth, and Kathryn were not enforceable. The promise of a gift without supporting consideration is nothing more than an unenforceable agreement.

C. **Legacies**

A *legacy* is a bequest of personal property, money, or the like contained in the last will and testament of a deceased person. The promise of a bequest is unenforceable for lack of consideration. An exception to this rule is a legacy promised as consideration in exchange of benefits previously bargained for between the deceased and one to whom a legacy was promised.

D. **Past Consideration**

A promise to give another something of value in return for goods or services rendered and delivered in the past, without expectation of reward, is *past consideration*. Only when goods or services are provided as the result of bargained-for present or future promises is an agreement enforceable.

● Huntley, without expectation or promise of payment, worked for more than sixteen hours helping Craven, a friend, frame out a new garage on Craven's property. When the job was finished, Craven said, "I'll never forget what you have done for me. When I get paid, you're going to get $100 for all you have done." Craven's promise would not be enforceable as it was nothing more than past consideration.

E. Moral Consideration

Demands of the conscience prompted by the good deeds or loyalty of others may generate promises of future rewards. Such promises are supported by strong *moral consideration,* but not the required bargained-for promises that qualify as valid consideration. Promises derived from allegiance, friendship, honor, and the like are in the nature of moral consideration and unenforceable for want of valid consideration.

● Stanton's parents owed more than $500 to Kings' Market for groceries sold to the Stantons during the past few months. They were unable to pay, and on one occasion Stanton talked with the Kings' Market manager, saying, "I'd like to help my parents out, and sometime, if I'm able, I'm going to send you a check for the money they owe you." There was no bargained-for promise here, and therefore no consideration to support Stanton's implied promise. Had Kings' manager agreed to refrain from any collection effort against the parents, Stanton's promise would have been enforceable through a mutuality of benefits and sacrifices.

11-6. Benefits to Third Parties

The benefits promised under consideration need not be bestowed on the parties making the agreement. When a party expresses an intention to be obligated for benefits that will go directly to an outside third party, the agreement still provides sufficient consideration to support the promise.

● Griffith made formal application to Highland College for a son who was graduating from high school. After reviewing the young man's academic records and other documents, the college mailed a letter of acceptance to the son. Although the benefits requested by Griffith were to accrue to the son, the promise of the college to accept the young man as a student was valid consideration for any obligations accepted by Griffith to pay the college fees related to their agreement.

Understanding Legal Terms

Define, identify, or explain each of the following terms:

adequacy of consideration	disputed amount forbearance	moral consideration output and	past consideration seal
barren promises	general release	requirements	undisputed amount
consideration	illusory promises	contract	

Questions for Review and Discussion

1. What are the two types of promises and acts under which all valid consideration may be classified?

2. Explain the meaning of a bargained-for promise as it applies to valid consideration. What is required for all bargained-for prom-

ises if they are to be considered valid consideration? How does a bargained-for promise differ from a gratuitous promise?

3. Explain what is meant by the statement: "Where consideration is concerned, one contracting party's benefits are the other party's sacrifices, and vice versa."

4. Illustrate by example what is meant by an illusory promise.

5. Why are options accepted as having all the requisites of a valid and enforceable contract? What is the consideration given for an option?

6. Explain the position of the courts in reviewing the agreements of parties to determine whether the consideration exchanged was fair and adequate for both parties.

7. How does an accord and satisfaction operate to liquidate debts where there is a disputed amount? Does it serve to liquidate a debt where there is an undisputed amount? Explain.

8. What are the most common agreements that are enforceable without proof of consideration?

9. Explain why the courts do not accept barren promises as valid consideration to support a contract.

10. Why will the courts refuse to enforce agreements supported by promised gifts, past consideration, or moral consideration?

Analyzing Cases

1. Casmir Lesnick married his wife Anastasia in 1971. In 1975, with her own money, Anastasia purchased a home which she and Casmir lived in until her death in 1976. The home was conveyed, when she purchased it, into a land trust with her children as the beneficiaries. Casmir now claims that this was invalid because it deprived him of his rightful share of the property as Anastasia's husband. Prior to her death Anastasia had orally promised to convey the land to her husband. May the surviving husband enforce this agreement? Explain. ● *Lesnick v. Estate of Lesnick,* 403 N.E.2d 683 (Ill. 1980)

2. Mr. and Mrs. Pickles entered into a contract to purchase land at a price of $25,000. The land was to be used for a new home. Soon after the sale an inspection disclosed that raw sewage was backing up into the property. As a result the board of health condemned the property. The Pickleses have stopped payment on their mortgage, and the board of health is seeking to close off the area. In defending themselves in an action in equity against them, the Pickleses contend that the contract for purchase of the property was an unconscionable agreement such that a promise to pay $25,000 for the property may justifiably be rescinded on grounds of inadequacy of consideration. How will the court of equity treat this defense? Explain. ● *Lenawee County Board of Health v. Messerly,* 295 N.W.2d 903 (Mich. App. 1980)

3. August Koedding entered into a contract with N. B. West Contracting Co., Inc., in which N. B. West was to repave Koedding's parking lot. After the job was completed, there was a dispute as to the quality of the work, and Koedding threatened a lawsuit. N. B. West promised to reseal the lot and guarantee the work for two years if the suit was dropped. Koedding agreed. There is still a problem, and the court is asked to decide whether the agreement not to sue N. B. West is enforceable. How would you decide? Explain ● *Koedding v. N. B. West Contracting Co.,* 596 S.W.2d 744 (Mo. 1980)

4. Carlton Beall owned a farm upon which he allowed Cecelia Beall to live. Carlton offered to sell the property to Cecelia, and they both signed an option covering a period of three years in return for Cecelia's payment of $100. Just prior to the option's expiration, an extension in the form of a new and separate option was added. No consideration was tendered by Cecelia. Now Cecelia wishes to buy the property. Carlton refuses to sell, claiming that the second option was no good. Who is right? Why? ● *Beall v. Beall*, 413 A.2d 1365 (Md. 1980)

5. Tim W. Koerner and Associates, Inc., was a distributor for electrosurgical products for Aspen Labs, Inc. Zimmer U.S.A., Inc., purchased Aspen and replaced Aspen's distribution system with its own. Aspen remained in business as a subsidiary. Koerner is suing Aspen and Zimmer, joined as defendants, trying to force them to honor a contract that Aspen and Zimmer had made, designed to compensate old Aspen dealers for their past efforts. Zimmer has refused to honor the agreement. Judgment for whom and why? ● *Tim W. Koerner & Assocs., Inc. v. Aspen Labs, Inc.*, 492 F. Supp. 294 (U.S. Dist. Ct., S.D. Texas, Houston Div. 1980)

6. After their divorce, Husband (PLO) and Wife (LO) signed a sealed agreement in which the wife was to transfer her interest in their co-owned house to the husband so that he might more easily sell it. She subsequently changed her mind and refused to follow through on the agreement. The husband sued the wife for specific performance in a court of equity. He further claimed that because the contract was under seal she could not repudiate it. Was the husband correct in this claim? Explain. ● *Husband (P.L.O.) v. Wife (L.O.)*, 418 A.2d 994 (Del. 1980)

7. Following a lengthy trial involving community property with regard to real estate, a settlement was worked out. Under the settlement that was accepted and signed by all parties, Hunt was to receive nothing. Lee, executor of the estate involved, argued that Hunt had agreed in the settlement that other third parties named in the settlement would be the beneficiaries of the estate. Hunt claimed that he had accepted a sacrifice for which no benefits had accrued to him and that since no consideration was given him under the agreement, it was unenforceable as to his promise. Judgment for whom and why?

● *Lee v. Hunt*, 631 F.2d 1171 (5th Cir. 1980)

8. A. J. Whitmore lived with his brother, R. Lee Whitmore, and his brother's wife, Lillie Mae. A. J. and R. Lee got along very well, and one day R. Lee, in the presence of Lillie Mae, said to A. J., "When we're gone this (land) is yours." After their deaths, A. J. claimed ownership on grounds of a gift. From the time of R. Lee's statement until his and Lillie Mae's deaths, A. J. bestowed no benefits on them. Is A. J. entitled to the property? Explain. ● *Whitmore v. Watkins (Executor)*, 267 S.E.2d 6 (Ga. 1980)

9. Lloyd Hurley and his wife Zenobia were experiencing marital difficulties. They finally reached a compromise in which Zenobia promised not to sue for divorce if Lloyd would refrain from infidelity and be a faithful and loving husband. She has now changed her mind about their agreement and is bringing a divorce action. Will Zenobia's agreement that she would not divorce her husband prevent her from carrying out her present intentions? Why? ● *Hurley v. Hurley*, 615 P.2d 256 (N.M. 1980)

10. A representative of the Prudential Life Insurance Company had sold the decedent a life insurance policy, stating that the policy covered loss of life through risk of war or aviation accident. After getting the new coverage, the insured canceled a life policy with another insurer that did cover aviation and war risks. The insured was killed while serving as a pilot of a helicopter in Vietnam. Prudential paid the claim entered on the policy. The insurer is now suing to recover what was paid, claiming that the new policy did not cover war and aviation risks. The executor of the estate argued that under the doctrine of promissory estoppel the deceased was covered because of promises made by the company's representative upon which the deceased relied. Judgment for whom and why? ● *Prudential Life Ins. Co. of America v. Clark*, 456 F.2d 932 (U.S. Ct. of App., Fla. 1972)

Chapter 12   Illegality

Closely related to the doctrine of consideration is the fourth requisite of binding contracts: legality of subject matter. Did the consideration involve a promise to commit an act prohibited by law? Was the consideration of a kind that would be harmful to the public good? Were promises made that would not be enforceable because of statutes or ordinances that prohibited or limited their performance, such as zoning laws, billboard advertising regulations, and the like? Even though parties may have entered into agreements that satisfy the legal requirements of mutual assent, competent parties, and consideration, the agreement will not be enforced if the subject matter is illegal.

● Remington Builders contracted to build a service station in the vicinity of Windtop Acres, an exclusive residential development. When plans were presented to the county development authority, the project was disapproved. Zoning regulations in the area prohibited any type of commercial enterprise. The decision invalidated Remington Builders' contract for want of valid subject matter.

12-1. The Requirements for Legal Subject Matter

The subject matter, or consideration, of an enforceable agreement must conform to the following:

○ Applicable common law
○ Statutes and local ordinances
○ Principles related to the welfare and security of the public at large

Agreements that go beyond what the law will permit are void and unenforceable. Since they are usually void from their very creation, such agreements are not contracts in the truest sense. Were the courts to enforce such agreements in disregard of their illegality, that would in effect give such agreements greater authority than the law itself.

12-2. Agreements Contrary to Common Law

In the absence of statutes or ordinances on any specific matter, common law is the legal authority followed in determining rights and duties of persons. When statutes have been adopted supplanting or changing the common law, such statutes govern. Agreements contrary to common law, when the common law governs, are unenforceable.

● At common law one found to be grossly negligent toward the safety of others could be held liable for any resulting injuries and could not be released or given waiver of such liability. In a state that adhered to this common-law principle, Zener agreed not to sue Longo if Longo caused an accident through his gross negligence while Zener was riding in Longo's car. It is doubtful that in this state Zener's agreement would be enforceable if she were injured owing to Longo's negligent driving. Certain states, however, have *guest statutes* giving further definition of the duty of care owed a passenger in one's vehicle and setting guidelines for liability for reckless or negligent driving.

12-3. Agreements Contrary to Statutory Law

It has been estimated that at the present time there are 17 million statutory laws in force in the United States. Agreements made in opposition to any of them would be technically unenforceable. Fortunately, a large number of these statutes are no longer enforced owing to the changing of times and new economic and social standards, and the statutes are rarely used to defeat the effectiveness of otherwise legal agreements. Agreements presented here are the ones that presently have the greatest importance in determining the validity of contracts.

A. Sunday Agreements

State statutes and local ordinances regulate the making and performing of contracts on Sunday. Varying application and enforcement of restrictive blue laws in different geographical areas have materially changed the status of Sunday agreements in recent years. Certain states have eliminated uniform statewide laws regulating Sunday activities, but permit their separate counties and incorporated cities, towns, and villages to adopt their own special ordinances under a concept known as *local option*. Thus, adjoining counties may have opposing laws, with one opting, by popular referendum, to permit Sunday sales while the other opts to make such sales illegal. However, where laws do restrict business dealings on Sunday, the following two rules are usually observed:

○ Agreements made on Sunday or any other day requiring that performance be on Sunday *may be* ruled invalid. Exceptions to this rule are those agreements held to be necessary to the health, welfare, and safety of the community and its residents.

● In a county that prohibited the sales of alcoholic beverages on Sunday, the owners of a roadside tavern agreed to open their establishment for a gathering of a college fraternity. The owners further agreed to open the bar from two to six o'clock that afternoon. The agreement to sell the alcohol would be void. However, the agreement to make the tavern available for the meeting might be valid if considered necessary to the welfare and well-being of the community at large.

○ Agreements made on Sunday for work to be done or goods to be delivered on a business day are valid and enforceable. However, some states still require that there be an affirmation of such agreements on a day other than Sunday if such agreements are to be enforceable.

● Owens entered into an agreement on a Sunday to return to Simpers' house the following Tuesday to excavate and pour foundations for an addition to Simpers' house. The agreement would be enforceable, except in states that would require a weekday affirmation.

The enforcement of Sunday laws varies widely from state to state, county to county, and village to village. Some localities have restrictive laws but prefer not to enforce them, permitting all types of commercial activity without interference. Religious influences have been of major importance where enforcement is strict. The highly populated urban areas have almost entirely succumbed to the pressures of commercialism and have removed the Sunday blue laws from the books.

B. Agreements Made on Legal Holidays

Legal holidays in any state or community are those days specified by the national, state, or local governing bodies. Religious holidays and days of celebration set aside by fraternal orders are not included in the meaning of the term.

Legal holidays have never received the same close attention as Sundays in the matter of contracts. Generally, contracts entered into or to be performed on legal holidays are valid and enforceable. If the payment of money or the performance of certain acts is to be made on a holiday, the courts will permit such payments to be made and such acts to be performed on the next regular business day. Suppose you signed a promissory note dated April 4, payable in three months. Since the date of payment falls on July 4, a national holiday, payment may be made on July 5 or the next business day following July 4.

C. Usurious Agreements

The practice of charging more than the amount of interest allowed by law is called *usury*. To protect borrowers from excessive interest charges, each state has passed laws which specify the rate of interest that may be charged in lending money. The legal interest rates vary from state to state. The obvious intent is to set a rate that will be equitable for both the borrower and the lender.

The *legal interest rate* is the amount of interest that will be applied in those cases where the loan agreement does not specify the amount of interest charged. The *maximum rate* may be greater than what is called the *legal rate*. Special statutes provide higher interest rates for small loan companies, pawnshops, and other lending agencies accepting high-risk applicants for credit.

● In a state where the legal interest rate restricted consumer loans to interest of no more than $1\frac{1}{2}$ percent per month (18 percent per annum), Edwards borrowed $1,000 from Golden Finance Associates, agreeing to repay the loan in ninety days, with interest at 5 percent each month. The interest being charged Edwards was usurious. In effect, the interest rate for this loan was 60 percent computed on a per annum basis (12 months × 5 percent per month). The penalty that might be imposed upon Golden Finance Associates for this illegal practice would depend on that individual state's statutes or upon local laws setting forth such penalties.

D. Wagering Agreements

Any agreement or promise concerning gambling or a wager is invalid and may not be enforced. States make exceptions when bets are placed in accordance with laws that permit horse racing, lotteries, church-related or charitable games of bingo, and gambling casinos regulated by state authority.

1. Insurance Contracts. When insurance was first introduced, contracts written on the life or property of others were looked upon as a kind of wagering agreement. Today, however, such contracts are upheld in view of the great benefits to be derived through the spreading of individual losses over large groups of policyholders. The dictates of public policy show that such agreements are in public interest.

● The Dickinson School District purchased insurance covering all schools in the district against loss by fire. Although a return from this agreement with the insurance company would depend upon the outcome of an uncertain event (that is, a possible fire), the policy is valid in that it is in the public interest and for the common good.

2. Futures Contracts. A futures contract is an agreement for the sale of a certain commodity or security for future delivery for a certain price. Thus, a party may, in October, purchase options for delivery of commodities or securities several months later. Such an agreement is valid and enforceable when the agreement gives either party the right to insist on delivery of the items described in the agreement. Otherwise such an agreement might be considered a gambling device and therefore unenforceable.

E. Unlicensed Transactions

Certain businesses and professions are required to be licensed for the following reasons:

○ To provide a source of income, a part of which will be used in the supervision of the business or profession being licensed
○ To provide supervision and regulation of businesses and professions that might inflict harm upon the general public if allowed to operate without controls

Contractors, undertakers, doctors, dentists, restaurateurs, and others in public service must be closely supervised and controlled for the protection of the general public. Services rendered and goods sold in the absence of a required license result in invalid contracts. Such agreements are not enforceable.

● Fosky worked as an industrial electrician at the Apex Steel Company. He agreed to spend a weekend wiring Truby's house. As an industrial electrician, Fosky already possessed an electrician's license. If he did not have one, neither Fosky or Truby could enforce this agreement or obtain relief for any alleged breach.

F. Agreements to Commit a Crime or Tort

Any agreement to commit a crime or tort in return for consideration promised would be void. Crimes include both felonies and misdemeanors, which are illegal by either common law or statute. Torts are those acts or malicious statements that result in injury to another or another's reputation or property.

● Steuber promised to pay the *Daily Banner*, a local newspaper, $500 if it would print a story alleging dishonest practices by Ivy, a competitor of Steuber's. The story was libelous and threatened to be injurious to Ivy. Even if the *Daily Banner* had agreed to publish the story, the agreement would be void because it involved the promise of a tort.

12-4. Agreements Contrary to Public Policy

Case law has established a catalog of agreements that are generally ruled to be void because of their opposition to good morals, welfare, and safety of the people. States have adopted statutes defining such agreements and rendering them void. Administrative branches of federal and state governments have also established regulations which, under the definition of public policy, make agreements or acts that are injurious to the public unenforceable. Following are the agreements most commonly invalidated as contrary to public policy:

A. Agreements to Obstruct Justice

In this group are included the following agreements: to protect another from arrest, not to prosecute a criminal, to suppress evidence, not to serve as a witness in a trial, to encourage lawsuits (known as *champerty*), to give false testimony, to bribe a juror. These acts are not only sufficient to render a contract void but they also usually carry penalties because they are considered criminal offenses.

● Anderson was a witness to an accident involving two cars. One of the drivers paid Anderson $50 in return for her promise to forget all that she had seen. Anderson later changed her mind and testified truthfully about the facts concerning the accident. Is she responsible for damages resulting from her breach of the agreement to remain silent?

The agreement Anderson made with the driver is void because it is considered against public policy, and any effort to hold her to it will be unsuccessful.

B. Agreements Interfering With Public Service

Contracts in this group include agreements to bribe or interfere with public officials, to obtain political preference in appointments to office, to pay an officer for signing a pardon, requiring one of the parties to the agreement to break a law or commit a tort, and to illegally influence a legislature for personal gain.

● Benjamin entered into an agreement with the state highway engineer in which the engineer agreed to use his influence to have the new state highway run adjacent to Benjamin's farm. Benjamin paid the engineer $5,000 for his promise to attempt to grant this request. This agreement is void and may not be enforced. The failure of the engineer to exert his influence would give Benjamin no rights in seeking the return of the $5,000 paid.

C. Agreements With Enemy Aliens

Agreements that may give aid and comfort to the enemy during wartime are illegal and therefore void.

● A naval base was located within an area inhabited by citizens of an unfriendly foreign power who had migrated into the area. To relieve naval personnel from arduous labor, workers were chosen from among civilians living within the area. Should hostilities break out between the two governments, the employment of these civilian workers would likely be considered contrary to the public good, and hence invalid and improper, because of financial aid and intelligence that might thereby be made available to the enemy.

D. Agreements in Restraint of Marriage

The courts will not enforce agreements wherein a party agrees to give up the right to marry in consideration of promises of money or other rewards by the other party.

● Johnson's father wished her to remain single and offered her $50,000 if she would not marry. The agreement is void. She would be permitted to marry at any time even though she has agreed to her father's request. Even if Johnson did keep her promise, her father would have no legal obligation to pay the money promised.

● Suppose, however, that Johnson had agreed to a request made by her father not to marry an undesirable young man with whom she had been keeping steady company. This contract would be valid and enforceable. In this case she had not given up the right of marriage, but had agreed not to marry a particular person (which constitutes valid subject matter).

E. Agreements to Defraud Creditors

Agreements that tend to remove or weaken the rights of creditors are void as contrary to public policy. Thus a debtor's agreement to sell and transfer personal and real property to a friend or relative for far less than actual value would be void if done for the purpose of hiding the debtor's assets from creditors with a legal claim to them.

● Harvey, before filing for voluntary bankruptcy, agreed to sell all his shop equipment to his brother for $250. His intent was to shield these assets from the bankruptcy proceedings so they could not be sold to pay off debts owed to creditors. When the bankruptcy proceedings were completed, he hoped to buy back the property for the same $250. Since this agreement was made with the intent to defraud creditors, it would be void.

F. Agreements to Induce Breach of Contract

Any agreement made with the intent of disrupting performance of another's obligations under an executory contract is against public policy and void. Thus, an agreement that would induce employees under contract to leave their employment for another position would be void. In this category also would come any promises made to induce another to leave a spouse or seek a divorce. Such inducement, known as *alienation of affections,* permits an action against the offending party, sometimes known as a corespondent.

G. Agreements to Pay Officials for Existing Legal Duties

Any agreements to pay an official additional consideration in return for services for which the official is already compensated is void as contrary to public policy. These agreements are also void under the concept of barren promises.

12-5. Agreements in Restraint of Trade

The law tries to be a constant protector of the rights of persons to make a living and to do business freely in a competitive market. If persons enter into contracts that take away these rights, the law will restore the rights to them by declaring such contracts void. Agreements which have the effect of removing competition or denying to the public services they would otherwise have, or which result in higher prices and resulting hardship, can be declared void.

A. Agreements to Suppress Competition

Any agreement made with the intent of suppressing competition, fixing prices, and the like is void as an illegal restraint of trade. Such agreements are unenforceable because they deprive the public of the advantages guaranteed in an economy based on freedom to contract, laws of supply and demand, and fair and honest business dealing. (See the discussion of restraint of trade regulation in Chapter 5 for more on anticompetitive agreements.)

● Cramer and Cole, used-car dealers, conspired by agreement to reduce prices, offer special trade-in inducements, and adopt other methods that would ultimately result in financial ruin to a competitor, Dobb's Auto Sales. If either Cramer or Coles failed to live up to the agreement, court action could not be sought for enforcement.

Agreements of this type may be legal and enforceable, however, if they do not violate the so-called rule of reason that is usually applied by the courts. That is to say that such agreements are enforceable when they do not unreasonably restrict businesses from competing with one another.

● The Topps Chewing Gum company and the Major League Baseball Players Association entered into exclusive five-year contracts for the services of baseball players. For the five-year period covered by the agreements, photographs of major league baseball players were to appear exclusively on baseball cards distributed by Topps with the sale of its chewing gum. The Fleer Corporation, a rival of Topps, brought suit for $16 million, alleging that the exclusive contracts were an effort to freeze out competition in this area and thus constituted "an illegal restraint on trade." A court ruled otherwise, however, holding that the Topps agreement "cannot be said to restrain trade unreasonably." The court said that Fleer could have competed with Topps by seeking licenses with baseball players while they were still in the minor leagues to appear in photographs on Fleer's baseball cards when and if they reached the major leagues.

B. **Sale of Business or Profession**
It is common practice and good business to restrict the seller of a business or profession from entering the same type of business or opening a professional office within a prescribed geographic area over a stated period of time. The buyer of the business or professional practice is contracting not only for the assets of the business but for the goodwill and reputation of the former owner. Conditions of this kind, when made part of a contract, must be reasonable if they are to be enforced. What is reasonable must be determined by a careful examination of the business or profession. Thus, a neighborhood luncheonette would be severely restricted in placing geographic limitations on the seller. However, the sale of a widely spread and patronized chain-store business would permit a much greater territorial restriction.

● Morris sold a silk-screening business to Gann. A condition in the contract prohibited Morris from entering a similar business over a period of ten years. Morris sought to have this condition invalidated as being contrary to public policy. It was found that Morris's former business was well-known and had clients in all parts of the state. The court ruled that in view of his reputation and influence over such a wide area, ten years was reasonable. The agreement was declared to be valid.

C. **Employment Contracts**
The most valuable assets of many large business houses are the secret methods of production and the formulas used in the manufacture of highly competitive consumer goods. The success of certain advertised soft drinks, cleaning fluids,

chemicals, and automotive equipment depends upon keeping production methods confidential. Such companies must protect themselves from the loss of trade secrets through persons in their employ. Employees may be required to sign contracts which restrain them from working for competitors for a reasonable time after leaving their present job. Employees may also be required to assign to an employer all patents taken out during their term of employment and for a period of some years thereafter if the patents in any way relate to the work of the employer. Contracts for the protection of trade secrets, while in restraint of trade, are valid if reasonable. They serve to encourage and protect firms engaged in research and development which result in ultimate public good.

● Yarnall, a research scientist of many years' experience in nuclear physics and exploration, was offered a position in the research and development laboratories of International Fuels Ltd. The contract covered a period of five years, with substantial salary increases each year. As part of the agreement Yarnall was to be restricted from working with any other firm or government agency engaged in the same areas of nuclear development for a period of five years subsequent to fulfillment of the International Fuels agreement.

Considering the work to be done and the possible exposure to International's secret processes and research projects, the time covered was reasonable. Given the abilities and knowledge possessed by an individual such as Yarnall, the agreement would not take away his freedom and capacity to secure employment in other research fields.

D. Illegal Monopolies

Illegal monopolies are business arrangements that are made with the intent to restrain competition and free trade or that result in such restraint. Agreements among manufacturers, wholesalers, and retailers of goods and services to divide territories within which each will confine its operations or to eliminate or restrain competition are illegal and therefore void. Agreements of this kind tend to force up prices by restricting output or availability of goods or by fixing or controlling prices.

● Harcum Fuel Company combined with two other fuel oil suppliers in Harcum County, plotting out a division of the county each would serve and agreeing on prices to be charged consumers, the amount each would allot to advertising expenses, and wages each would pay to employees in the fuel oil trade. The arrangement was illegal, against public policy, and in no way enforceable should one of the three suppliers repudiate the tripartite agreement.

E. Legal Monopolies

Not all monopolies are illegal. Public policy recognizes that in certain circumstances a monopoly may be a valuable instrument which gives incentive to talented persons and enterprises and benefits society as a whole. The law grants recognition to the following categories of monopolistic agreements.

1. Patents. *Patents* are valid enforceable monopolies granted by the federal government to inventors, who are given exclusive rights to their inventions, usually for a period of seventeen years. *Ordinary patents* give protective coverage to inventors of processes, machines, chemical formulas, and articles of manufacture. *Design patents* cover "any new original and ornamental design for an article of manufacture," such as a newly designed toy. Design patents, unlike ordinary patents, may be granted for a period of less than seventeen years. The use of a patent without the owner's permission gives the patent holder the right to demand all profits from the unauthorized use of the patent. All patents are registered for a fee with the U.S. Patent and Trademark Office in Washington, D.C.

2. Copyrights. *Copyrights* protect the writings of authors, the works of artists, painters, and sculptors, and the musical scores of composers from unauthorized reproduction, republication, and sale. Under the Copyright Revision Act, which took effect on January 1, 1978, a work created after that date is protected for the duration of the creator's life plus fifty years. Copyrights are registered with the Library of Congress in Washington, D.C.

3. Trademarks. *Trademarks* consist of unusual and unique symbols and trade names that are distinctive and novel and are adopted for goods sold in more than one state. The registration of a trademark or trade name with the U.S. Patent and Trademark Office establishes the priority of its use and gives the owner its exclusive use for twenty years. Trademarks are also known as *logos*—artistic renditions of an easily recognizable and unique design of a firm's initial or special markings that identify the manufacturer's or seller's name or products.

4. Franchises. *Franchises* are a type of legal monopoly that may be either public or private. They are businesses ventures that are given protection against competition through authorization of federal, state, or local government franchising agreements or under agreement with a privately owned parent company.

a. Public Service Franchises. When franchised by public authority, such monopolies are called *public service franchises.* Public utilities, such as an electric company or a telephone company, and state and interstate bus lines and railroads are illustrative of public franchises. Public service ventures are usually supervised by public service commissions overseeing virtually their entire operation. The commissions usually make decisions on rate changes and may render a final decision on the franchised corporation's rights in serving the public. Thus they can decide to extend, reduce, or even discontinue such services. Usually, however, this is done only after public hearings are held on the matter.

b. Private Investment Franchises. Franchises granted and regulated by privately financed parent companies are a different type of legal monopoly. For example, fast-food outlets may be operated under franchises granted by the owner of the name, with restrictions on use of trade names, distinctively designed and architecturally registered roadside stands, and other characteristics. One accepting a fast-food franchise is usually obligated to purchase supplies from the parent organization, use standard advertising, and follow menus prepared for all franchise owners. Should an independent operator infringe on the parent organization's patented and copyrighted names and designs, such a party could be enjoined (stopped) from continuing such an operation by a court of proper jurisdiction. Although monopolistic in a sense (more so from the viewpoint of their internal operation), such franchises are legal and are protected by the courts. They do not restrain trade unreasonably because one franchise, such as a McDonald's restaurant, can compete with another, such as a Burger King.

12-6. Consequences of Illegality

Illegality of contract, as in promises to commit criminal acts, not only serves to void existing agreements but may lead to indictment and prosecution when sufficient evidence warrants such action. Persons who agree to commit criminal acts for a promised consideration are involved in what criminal law defines as a *conspiracy*. Agreements that do not violate criminal laws may still be invalid. Thus, many agreements considered contrary to public policy have been declared invalid as against the public good, but not illegal in terms of criminal liability. Both types of agreements fail to have the characteristics that permit legal enforcement.

A. Illegality in Entire Agreements

In cases where the entire agreement is tainted with illegality, no binding contract will result. Even though specific sections of the agreement may have been legally enforceable, illegality of any part of an *entire* contract will render it void.

B. *In Pari Delicto* and Divisible Contracts

When an agreement is divisible and the illegal promises and acts are completely segregated from other promises and acts that are not tainted by illegality, courts may order performance of those parts that are legal and rescind those parts ruled illegal and invalid. Enforcement of that part determined to be valid and enforceable, of course, is tempered by the extent of illegality of the other divisible parts.

● Harkness, a truck driver, agreed to drive a sixteen-wheeler from the orange groves of Florida into Boston. Interstate Commerce Commission rules prohibit drivers from driving more than eight hours without layover and rest. Harkness's straight-through trip required longer than the ICC eight-hour limit. Harkness would still be able to sue for the wages promised, separating the illegal driving time from the main purpose of the agreement.

● However, suppose Harkness had agreed to drive the rig knowing that bales of marijuana were to be secreted among the crates of oranges. The courts would then declare the agreement to be illegal in its entirety and would deny Harkness any rights whatsoever under the contract.

1. Rule of *in Pari Delicto*. When both parties to an illegal agreement are equally wrong in the knowledge of the operation and effect of their contract, they are said to be *in pari delicto* (in equal fault). In such cases no aid will be given to either party in an action against the other, and the court will award no damages to either. When the parties are not *in pari delicto,* relief will often be allowed if sought by the more innocent of the two. While this rule is not applicable where one may be less guilty of premeditation and intent to achieve a gain through known illegal acts, it may be applied when one party is not aware that a law is being broken and where there is no intent to do a wrong.

● Haines agreed to remodel Kronski's house so that it might be used as a public restaurant. Haines accepted $500, with Kronski's promise to pay an additional $2,000 when the job was done. Haines was aware that zoning laws would not permit commercial use of any property in the area. Kronski was not aware of this fact, and in an action against Haines the court would rule that Kronski might recover his $500 as the parties were not *in pari delicto.*

2. Exculpatory Clauses. *Exculpatory clauses* are those terms within a contract that tend to free one of the parties from any blame for injuries to the other because of negligence or neglect. Exculpatory clauses are at times included in employment contracts, exempting the employer of any responsibility in the event that the employee is injured on the job, even when the injury resulted from the employer's negligence. Clauses of this kind may at times be rescinded as contrary to public policy. The courts, however, may elect to separate the exculpatory clause from the otherwise valid contract, voiding only the objectionable terms. Additional defenses against enforcement of such clauses may be found in the application of rules related to adhesion agreements (see Chapter 9).

● Peoples was injured in a fall from a scaffold erected by Donar Systems, his employer. The work was being done for the city of Detroit. Detroit claimed no liability because of a clause in Donar's employment contract that absolved the city of any liability in claims of this kind. The court ruled that this clause was void as contrary to public policy. In doing so, the court separated the exculpatory clause from the rest of the contract, holding that the other parts of the agreement were valid and enforceable.

Understanding Legal Terms

Define, identify, or explain each of the following terms:

blue laws	local option	private investment	trademark
copyright	legal monopolies	franchise	usury
exculpatory clauses	illegal monopolies	public service	wager
in pari delicto	patents	franchise	

Questions for Review and Discussion

1. What is the underlying rationale of the courts in voiding agreements that are contrary to either common law or statutory law?

2. Why do the states differ in their attitude toward and enforcement of Sunday contracts? What usually determines whether Sunday contracts will be enforced in a particular state or locale?

3. Why do most states have usury laws to regulate the interest rate that may be charged in consumer transactions?

4. Distinguish between the legal interest rate and the maximum rate of interest which is permissible in a consumer transaction.

5. Why do the courts not classify insurance contracts as wagering agreements even though such contracts seem to fit the legal definition of wagers?

6. X, a professional person, failed to secure a license as required by licensing statute yet rendered services in connection with her occupation. What is the legal effect of such a transaction? Explain.

7. What is meant by the term *public policy* in relationship to the enforcement of contracts? How do the courts normally treat agreements found to be contrary to public policy?

8. Describe the rule of reason which the courts use to determine whether contracts are in restraint of trade. How do courts normally treat contracts found to be in restraint of trade?

9. Why does the law permit the existence of certain legal monopolies? Give some examples of so-called legal monopolies.

10. Two types of contracts—one a divisible contract and the other an entire contract—

are before a court for consideration as to their legality and enforceability at law. Each agreement contains clauses which are partly legal and partly illegal. How is the court likely to treat the enforcement and disposition of these two types of contracts?

Analyzing Cases

1. The owners of an apartment complex entered into an agreement with the city of Chattanooga in which certain lands were to be rezoned in consideration of the apartments' owner creating a buffer zone of 200 feet between the apartments and the nearest property. Hayman, a new owner of the complex, is now attempting to have the agreement rescinded on grounds that it is contrary to public policy. Is Hayman likely to succeed in this action? ● *Hayman v. City of Chattanooga*, 513 S.W.2d 185 (Tenn. 1974)

2. Betty, a teacher, and James, an engineer, maintained an intimate relationship. Betty got pregnant. James refused to help, and Betty threatened a paternity suit and publicity that would injure James's reputation. Betty was also frightened that a nonmarital pregnancy would threaten her job. They agreed on a temporary marriage and wrote an antenuptial contract. The agreement specified that they would remain married for fourteen months and defined the rights of each one to any property they would then hold together. Nine years passed, at which time they were divorced. What effect if any does this agreement have on the property settlement as related to their divorce? ● *Marriage of Dawley*, 551 P.2d 323 (Ca. 1976)

3. Emco, Inc., and Healy entered into an agreement whereby Healy issued a promissory note to Emco, Inc., the proceeds from which were to be used to purchase Emco stock. This transaction was in violation of a statute of the state of Texas. Emco is now suing Healy for nonpayment of the note, and Healy defended that the agreement was illegal and therefore not enforceable. Judgment for whom and why? ● *Emco, Inc. v. Healy*, 602 S.W.2d 309 (Tex 1980)

4. Blakeslee agreed to construct a sewer line for Mattabassett. When a claim arose due to faulty pipes delivered by another company, Mattabassett started suit against the contractor, asserting that their contract contained a right to indemnification from damages resulting from the agreement. The clause stated that Mattabassett was to be protected against "all costs for any claim to which the owner may be put out. . . ." Blakeslee argued, in defense, that this was an exculpatory clause attempting to excuse Mattabassett even when damages resulted from his own negligence, pointing out that such a clause was contrary to public policy. Judgment for whom and why? ● *Leonard Concrete Pipe Co. v. C.W. Blakeslee & Son*, 424 A.2d 277 (Conn. 1979)

5. Rhoads signed an employment contract with Clifton, Gunderson & Co., in which he promised not to deal with any of Clifton's clients for a period of five years after his present employment was terminated. No geographic limitations were included in their agreement. Is this clause in their contract enforceable? Explain. ● *Rhoads v. Clifton, Gunderson & Co.*, 411 N.E.2d 1380 (Ill. 1980)

6. Ingrassi, an oral surgeon, was hired by Karpinski. Karpinski opened a second office and gave that office over to Ingrassi's professional management. Included in the Karpinski-Ingrassi employment contract was a condition that prohibited Ingrassi from opening his own office in a five-county geographic area should their employment agreement be terminated. Three years later, and within one week of termination of their agreement, Ingrassi opened his own office within the restricted territory. The court is asked to rule on the validity of the restrictive

covenant in the Karpinski-Ingrassi employment contract. Judgment for whom and why? ● *Karpinski v. Ingrassi,* 268 N.E.2d 751 (N.Y. 1971)

7. Lachman, a landowner, engaged Sperry-Sun Well Surveying Company to make a directional survey of an oil well located on Lachman's property. The agreement between the parties, among other things, prohibited the surveying firm from releasing any details of the survey to anyone other than Lachman. The survey showed that the well actually penetrated the subterranean area beneath a neighboring property, from which location Lachman was extracting oil. Sperry-Sun informed the neighbor of Lachman's trespass. Lachman brought suit against Sperry-Sun for damages resulting from its disclosures and for not abiding by the terms of their agreement. Sperry-Sun argued that the restrictive clause served to protect Lachman's illegal acts and was therefore not enforceable. Judgment for whom and why? ● *Lachman v. Sperry-Sun Well Surveying Co.,* 457 F.2d 850 (10th Cir. 1972)

8. James Crawford, with others, formed a "last man's club." The members purchased land in upstate New York to be used as a hunting lodge and their headquarters for club activities. The ground was purchased in 1935, with the members agreeing that the land and improvements would finally belong to the last surviving member of the club. Crawford survived the others and claimed exclusive title to the property. Quinn, the daughter of a member who died in 1969, contested Crawford's right to the property, claiming it to be an illegal "gamble-till-death" agreement, a wagering contract, and not enforceable. Was Quinn correct in her claim as an heir to Quinn's estate? Explain your answer. ● *Quinn v. Stuart Lakes Club, Inc.,* 439 N.Y.S.2d 30 (1981)

9. Arnow borrowed money from Giventer, an attorney. The lender prepared a promissory note whereby Arnow agreed to repay the principal at $7\frac{1}{2}$ percent interest, compounded quarterly. The annual rate allowed by law in the state of New York at that time was $7\frac{1}{2}$ percent. Giventer sued for collection on the note and Arnow argued that $7\frac{1}{2}$ percent interest compounded quarterly exceeded the rate of interest allowed by law and therefore was usurious. Judgment for whom? Explain why. ● *Giventer v. Arnow,* 333 N.E.2d 366 (N.Y. 1975)

10. The Orthopedic Equipment Company entered into a contract with Streetman in which Streetman was to promote and sell Orthopedic's equipment in the state of Florida. According to the terms of their contract, Streetman was prohibited from selling anyone else's product during the period of the contract. Streetman wishes to sell other products and is claiming the Orthopedic agreement to be in restraint of trade. He sues. Judgment for whom and why? ● *Orthopedic Equipment Co. v. Streetman,* 390 So.2d 134 (Fla. 1980)

Chapter 13   Form of Agreement

Contracting parties have a wide choice in selecting the form of agreement that will best serve their needs. Oral, written, implied; bilateral, unilateral; entire and divisible—all are acceptable in creating binding agreements. Where no specific type of agreement is required, parties are free to determine the form of agreement they use. It is, however, essential to be acquainted with state laws that dictate when a contract must be in writing, or under seal. The UCC and separate statutes prescribe these requisites when applicable.

13-1. Legality of Oral Agreements

Most people have a mistaken belief that only written contracts may be enforced. It is true that a party may experience difficulty in proving the existence of an oral or implied agreement. Samuel Goldwyn, of MGM fame, once said that "oral contracts aren't worth the paper they're written on." Goldwyn was responsible for contracts made in Hollywood under which film stars were paid millions of dollars for their performances. Anticipating the need of proving oral agreements should prompt the parties to remember the names of others who were present during their negotiation or to keep carefully recorded notes for future reference.

● Kohler talked with a plumber about the installation of a new hot water heating system that could save him hundreds of dollars during one heating season. The name of the new system, certified test results in fuel efficiency, cost of the system and installation, and when installation was to be made were all agreed to by both parties in their negotiations. No written contract was used. Kohler kept detailed notes of all that both agreed on during their negotiating session. Kohler would be permitted to refer to these notes should a dispute develop through either a good-faith misunderstanding of their agreement or an intentional breach by the plumber.

Once an oral contract has been executed, even in those cases where written contracts are required, nonconformance to the "in writing" requirement will not be acceptable grounds for rescission. Only oral contracts that are executory, with conditions still to be performed, may be rescinded if there was a requirement that they be in writing.

13-2. Factors Favoring Written Form

Accepting the premise that oral agreements are as enforceable as those in writing, there are situations that strongly favor an agreement in writing. Although either oral or written form would be legally acceptable, written agreements are preferred in the following situations.

170

A. Complexity of the Agreement

Recall of terms and conditions in oral agreements becomes increasingly difficult as the number of terms and conditions increases. Human weakness in listening and concentrating on another party's statement sometimes makes recall impossible, leading to misunderstandings, dispute, and possible legal action. Reducing the terms and conditions to some form of memorandum, signed or initialed by the parties, lessens the possibility of later dispute.

● Jordan purchased a 1961 Corvette which she intended to restore to mint condition. Meyers' Restoration Specialists examined the car, detailed all of the labor and parts required for the job, and gave her a final estimate of $6,700, which Jordan accepted. No written estimate or memorandum was used to support their agreement. A week after work had commenced, Meyers told Jordan that rust-proofing would be necessary if the job were to be done correctly and that this would add $385 to the bill. Jordan argued that rust-proofing had been included in their original agreement. Without anything in writing it would be difficult to prove or disprove the contentions of either party.

B. Future Performance

Perfect recall of agreed-to conditions and terms becomes increasingly difficult with the passing of time. When performance is to be delayed for days, weeks, or months, a written agreement or memorandum should be made.

● Formal Wear Associates orally agreed to supply proper men's wear for Borden, his best man, and ushers for a June 16 wedding. These arrangements were made by Borden's telephone call on April 19. Recognizing the possibility of unintentional conflicts and confusion during that busiest of all wedding months, June, Borden would be foolish not to demand a confirmation in writing from Formal Wear Associates.

13-3. The Parol Evidence Rule

In general, the *parol evidence rule* restricts the use of oral evidence in any move to change, delete, or add to the terms of a written agreement. Following oral discussion and negotiations it is customary for parties to reduce their agreements to some written form. Of the terms, conditions, and promises discussed, only those included in the writing will be enforced. Exceptions to the general rule are discussed in this section.

● Hathaway purchased a mobile home from Ray's Motor Sales. Subsequent to signing all documents related to the sale, the seller stated that if Hathaway had any troubles with the unit, Ray's would take care of them. The present action resulted from the seller's refusal to take care of problems that Hathaway claimed should be adjusted under Ray's expressed warranty. The court ruled that there was no enforceable warranty as Ray's promise was not contained, with other conditions, in the written sales agreement.

A. When the Rule Applies

The parol evidence rule applies to agreements that, in the absence of any indication of fraud or mistake, the parties carefully and intentionally put into writing. The courts, under what is called the *best-evidence rule* will accept only the original of a writing, not a copy. Under this rule, a written instrument is regarded as the primary or best possible evidence. Thus the best-evidence rule concurs with and supports the parol evidence rule.

B. When the Rule Does Not Apply

The parol evidence rule will not apply when unfair and unjust decisions might result from its application. The courts are in general agreement on the exceptions described below:

○ In those cases where, through neglect of the parties, the written agreement is not complete, and oral evidence may be used. When a written agreement is complete in all matters other than price, oral evidence may be used to determine the price. For example, this may be done by reference to the current market price of a product or by determining charges considered proper and reasonable by custom of the marketplace.

○ When a written agreement is obscure or indistinct in certain of its terms, oral evidence may be used to clarify those terms.

● Bowser purchased a television set from City TV Sales and Service. A written agreement of sale contained an express warranty whereby the seller promised to make repairs and replacement of parts to the set over a period of six months from date of purchase. Subsequently the picture tube burned out. City TV contended that the warranty did not cover the picture tube. Oral evidence, through other dealers in the area, would be accepted by the court in determining what was generally included in such a warranty.

○ When one of the parties to a written agreement offers the defenses of fraud, misrepresentation, mistake, undue influence, or duress in a suit on the contract, oral evidence may be used in establishing proof of those defenses.

○ Oral evidence may be used to prove that the parties, after entering into a written contract, orally agreed to rescind or modify its terms. However, proof of such oral mutual rescission or modification must be clear-cut and convincing to a court.

13-4. The Equal-Dignities Rule

The *equal-dignities rule* provides that when one appoints an agent to negotiate an agreement which itself must be in writing, the appointment and authorization of the agent must also be in writing. Similarly, the appointment of an agent to negotiate an agreement that the law does not require to be in writing may be accomplished through an oral agreement.

● A state statute required that all agreements for the sale of real property must be in writing, signed, and under seal. Layton orally agreed to sell William's house and lot on promise of a 10 percent commission and the exclusive right to represent Williams for ninety days. Layton did secure a buyer and delivered a purchase agreement to Williams, signed and sealed by the prospective buyer. By application of the equal-dignities rule, the contract of sale is voidable by Williams due to Layton's failure to secure a signed and sealed authorization to sell the property.

13-5. Writing Required by Statutes of Frauds

Early English law permitted the enforcement of all oral contracts when they could be proved through testimony of witnesses. Witnesses were required to prove or disprove the existence of an oral agreement, the parties themselves being barred from testifying on their own behalf. Perjury was not uncommon at the time, opening the door to enforcement of numerous alleged contracts that a defendant was unable to disclaim. To correct this matter, the English Parliament in 1677 passed the Act for the Prevention of Fraud and Perjuries, later called the *Statute of Frauds*. The provisions of the English Statute of Frauds were adopted into practice in the courts of the several states after the Colonies separated from England on July 4, 1776.

Sections 4 and 17 of the Statute of Frauds named six types of agreements that required written evidence if they were to be enforced by either party. While Parliament rescinded the Act for Prevention of Frauds and Perjuries in 1954, no change has been made in laws of virtually any American states that would permit the six named agreements to be oral. Each state now has its own statute of frauds. Only one type of agreement mentioned in the original act has found its way into the UCC.

A. Writing as Defined by Statutes of Frauds

Statutes of frauds require that any of the specified agreements be supported by a *memorandum*. This does not mean a completely written contract. To be acceptable, the memorandum should generally include the following:

○ The names of the parties to the agreement
○ A brief description of the subject matter
○ The terms and conditions agreed to
○ The consideration promised
○ Signature(s) of the party or parties obligated to the agreement

The information required of the memorandum may be contained in a letter, a sales slip, telegrams, and any other type of writing or communication. There is no requirement for formality. The intent of the statutes is only that written evidence of some kind be available as proof of each party's rights and obligations.

Signatures of both parties are not required. However, in the event of a dispute only the party whose signature actually appears may be held liable. To assure that both parties are held liable, therefore, it is vitally important that both signify their intention to be so bound by signing the written memorandum.

● Storms contracted to rent pastureland from Weaver for grazing her horses. The agreement was for two years, and the state statute of frauds required that it be in writing to be enforceable. Storms noted the conditions and terms of the agreement on the back of an envelope and handed it to Weaver, who then approved what had been written and signed it. Storms returned the envelope to her briefcase without adding her signature. The information contained in the memorandum would satisfy the statute. However, Weaver alone could be held liable, because Storms had never added her signature to the agreement.

B. Contracts Requiring Written Form

The following are the six types of agreements that must be in writing to be enforceable, according to the modern statutes of frauds applicable in most states today. The first five of these agreements were contained in section 4 of the old English Statute of Frauds; the sixth listed below was found in section 17 of the original act, and is now incorporated into the UCC. In fact, it is often called the UCC statute of frauds to distinguish it from other statutes of frauds.

1. Contracts of Executor or Administrator. Agreements by executor or administrator to pay debts of deceased out of his or her own personal estate must be committed to writing. An *executor* may be either a person or a corporation named in a will to oversee the distribution of the deceased's estate according to the provisions contained in a will. An *administrator* is one named by a court to do the work of an executor if none is named in the will or if the executor either refuses to perform or is incapable of performing the duties. Persons having the responsibility of executor or administrator often make promises for the protection of the survivors, under emotional stress. Such promises must be in writing to be enforceable, thus removing the possibility of enforcing unintentional or ill-advised oral statements.

● Jones is named as the executor of his brother's estate. A creditor demands the payment of $500 owed by the deceased. To protect his brother's wife from the claim, Jones promises to pay the bill himself. This promise would not be enforceable against him unless it were reduced to a written agreement.

2. Guaranty of Debts or Against Wrongdoing of Third Parties. A promise to pay another's bills or to settle for any of another's wrongful acts, *if that party does not settle them personally,* is an obligation that must be in writing if it is to be valid and enforceable. This is a *guaranty of payment.* A guaranty is thus distinguished from a suretyship, which is a primary obligation and which would be enforceable even though made orally. A *surety* is liable with the principal debtor on the original contract.

● In a state where parents were not liable for torts of children over seven years of age, Cinski, seventeen years of age, bought a used car and attempted to have it registered in his name. When application was made for tags, Cinski was required to secure a written statement from his parents or other responsible adults guaranteeing liability for any damages that might result from Cinski's use of the car.

An oral agreement by parents or others would not be enforceable against the one who made such an agreement in the event that the minor were involved in an accident causing another party physical injuries or damages to property.

3. Contracts in Consideration of Marriage. Agreements made *in consideration of marriage* must be in writing. This section does not relate to the *marriage contract* itself, which in almost all cases is oral. It refers to those promises made by parties prior to marriage in which they accept additional obligations not ordinarily included in the implied obligations of marriage itself. Such promises are enforceable only if they are in writing and are agreed upon prior to the marriage.

● DelCampo was engaged to Adams, with the wedding scheduled for March. In November, DelCampo urged Adams to marry him during the Christmas holiday, promising to give her a new car if she would give up her job and change the wedding plans. Adams did exactly as her fiancé requested. This was a contract in consideration of marriage and would be enforceable only if written evidence were available to prove their agreement.

4. Contracts Not to Be Completed Within One Year. If the terms of an executory agreement make it impossible to complete the agreement within one year of the date of the agreement, the contract must be in writing.

● You are offered a position as a salesperson for a firm that desires your services in calling on all prospective customers in the fifteen counties of the state. It is planned that you are to spend one month in each county. When you report for work, the manager informs you that the position is no longer open to you, although you had accepted the offer. Any action against the company would fail in that the contract could not be completed within one year and there had been no written agreement.

In situations where an agreement could possibly extend beyond one year, but where performance need not require more than one year, an oral agreement is sufficient.

● In May 1969, Whipple loaned Frigon $1,500. It was orally agreed that Frigon would repay the money in January 1970, or when he received a refund from his 1969 taxes. Frigon argued, when sued for the $1,500, that his financial condition would have made it impossible to pay back the $1,500 within one year and that therefore the statute of frauds would have required the agreement to be in writing. The court ruled that the agreement allowed performance within one year, removing it from any obligation to present a written agreement in support of the claim.

It is generally held that contracts of employment intended to be for the life of the employee need not be in writing. There is no certainty that the employee might live beyond the one-year limitation of the statute. To clarify claims of this kind, some states have enacted statutes which require *lifetime agreements* to be in writing, thereby following the different concept that both employer and employee intended the agreement to continue for more than one year.

Under statutes of frauds, the time period commences on the date on which a contract is made, not on the date when performances is to begin. An agreement entered into on Wednesday in which a person agrees to start working the following Monday for one year would therefore have to be in writing.

5. Contracts for Sale of Real Property. All contracts for the transfer or sale of any interest in real property must be in writing. In many state in which the seal is still in use, these contracts must be under seal. Real-property transactions have always been looked upon as formal and of a most serious nature because of the finality of transfer of irreplaceable rights by the owner. A lease for the renting of another's real property must be in writing unless it is for a period of less than one year.

● Miller orally agreed to sell Black a vacant lot adjacent to properties owned by each party. Written agreements were dispensed with because of their lasting friendship as neighbors over more than twenty years. Without either one's previous knowledge, the area was rezoned for light industry, and the value of the lot fell drastically. Provisions of the statute of frauds would allow Black to rescind the purchase agreement without any right on the seller's part to demand performance.

6. Contracts for Sale of Personal Property Worth $500 or More. Originating in section 17 of the English Statute of Frauds, this provision has been included in the UCC (2-201). Oral agreements not supported by a memorandum may not be enforced in sales agreements where the value placed on goods being sold is $500 or more. (There are, however, four exceptions to this rule. These are discussed in Chapter 20.) It has been held that the buyer's check given in partial payment provides sufficient evidence to prove a contract of sale in an action where a written memorandum is required by the UCC statute of frauds.

● Fisher offered to sell his sailboat to Cohen for $4,650. Cohen gave Fisher his check for $2,325. Noted on the check were words to the effect that the check was a deposit on the sailboard *D'Arc Wind* as part of the purchase price of $4,650. In a subsequent dispute on the agreement Cohen did not deny the oral agreement but argued that the contract was not enforceable as the price exceeded the $500 set forth in the UCC Statute of Frauds. The court held that the check was sufficient evidence of a contract of sale since it was signed by the one obligated to make the purchase and it described the subject matter and the consideration to be paid.

Each state has enacted special statutes outlining other agreements that must be in writing. Other contracts usually required by special statutes to be in writing include the release of a party from debt (general release) and the resumption of obligations after a bankruptcy. However, the diversity of these special statutes makes it impractical to list them here. Reference to the statute of frauds of the individual state is recommended in determining what additional special agreements be in writing in a particular state.

13-6. Formalities of Contract Construction

Certain formalities are usually followed in the formation of other than the simplest kinds of written agreements. While statutes of frauds may necessitate nothing more than the briefest written disclosure of promises, conditions, and terms, plus the signature(s) of the obligated party or parties, contracts in general commercial and consumer use usually are carefully written, researched for legal compliance, signed, and often sealed, acknowledged, and recorded. And leases and contracts for the sale of real property may have additional requirements of content and formality extending beyond even these formalities.

A. Signatures

Written agreements should be signed by both parties. As mentioned previously if signed by only one party any obligation on the agreement would be limited to that party alone. Parties should use their usual signatures, that is, the signatures used in other matters in the regular course of business. One may, although it is unusual, adopt any name desired in creating a contractual obligation as long as the party intends to be bound by that signature. Thus, a well-known actress may sign a hotel register using a name other than her real name as a means of protecting her privacy. A signature may be the full name or initials, and it may be printed, typewritten, or stamped, as with a rubber stamp. However made, it must be made with the intent to be bound thereby.

1. Physical Incapacity. In cases where a party is not able to sign owing to illness, physical handicap, or other physical reason, another may sign for that person. The signature should be followed by a statement similar to the one shown in Figure 13-1 and signed by a witness.

2. Illiterate's Signature. Persons who are totally lacking in the ability to read or write are often obliged to sign documents. Literacy is not always the test of career and financial success, and contracts involving great sums of money may

Signature: *Thomas Stewart*

WITNESS: I hereby attest that Thomas Stewart was
physically unable to sign his name and that
his name was signed by me in his presence
and at his request.

Alice O'Neal

Figure 13-1. Signature for an incapacitated person.

require the signature of one who never learned to write. The law accepts that person's *mark,* usually an X, properly witnessed, as a valid signature (see Figure 13-2).

3. Corporate Signatures. Corporations are themselves legal entities, bestowed with certain rights, powers, and obligations by a charter issued by state authority. While officers may act in behalf of a corporation, the corporation itself must have its own signature. The signature of a corporation is the *corporate seal.* This is usually a specially designed seal, giving the name of the corporation and the date of incorporation, sometimes embellished by an artistic design. The corporate seal is usually impressed into the documents to be signed, with witnesses attesting to its being placed there by a responsible officer of the corporation or other authorized person.

B. Witnesses and Acknowledgment
Witnesses are required in the signing of a will, but in most other documents their signatures are at the option of the contracting parties. To assure that no misunderstanding will arise as to the acceptance and signing of a written agreement, the use of a witness is advised.

Certain official documents, such as a certificate of title to a motor vehicle, require the owner's signature and an *acknowledgment* by a notary public when

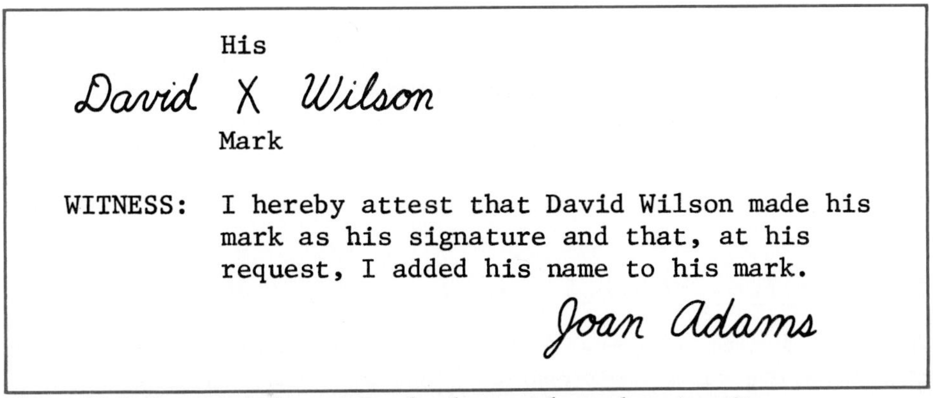

His

David X *Wilson*

Mark

WITNESS: I hereby attest that David Wilson made his
mark as his signature and that, at his
request, I added his name to his mark.

Joan Adams

Figure 13-2. Signature of a person who does not know how to write.

Chapter
13:
Form of
Agree-
ment

177

transferring ownership. In most states a notary public may be anyone over the age of twenty-one appointed by the secretary of state to perform this service. The notary witnesses the signing of the document and then *acknowledges* this act by signing the document and adding the official seal to it. A notary is not authorized to read the document being signed and may be prevented from doing so. The notary's legal authority is limited to the act of acknowledging another's signature to be the result of his or her own free act and deed before the notary.

C. Seal

Some states still require the use of one's seal when signing a formal contract. Contracts for the sale and transfer of real estate come within this category. Historically the seal was a carefully designed coat of arms or other suitable design, mounted in a ring and used to impress markings in melted sealing wax placed on the document. Modern practice has dispensed with this custom, and today's seal is usually nothing more than the word *seal* or the *L.S.* (*locus sigilli*, meaning "place of the seal") printed or written next to the signature.

D. Recording for Protection of the Parties

As a protection to lenders, persons selling goods through installment contracts, and the like, the law provides that certain documents be recorded in a public office for inspection by those who have a legitimate right to seek the recorded information. Thus, when money is loaned on a motor vehicle, the lender may establish a lien on the vehicle and the lien will be recorded as a protection to the lender. A *lien* is a possessory claim held against a party for goods or services rendered. Recording of agreements is a privilege accorded persons who have established rights in property belonging to another or property to which another has been given nothing more than possession. Such recording, however, has no effect on the enforceability of the document as between the original contracting parties.

● Stewart borrowed $2,500 from First State Loan Company. As security for the loan the lender demanded that a lien be recorded in its favor against Stewart's late model car. The lien was recorded with the state motor vehicle department against Stewart's title to the car. In the event that Stewart sold the car to another without mentioning the lien, the buyer would learn of the claim when a new title were issued. The new owner would be, then, liable for the amount of the recorded lien.

Understanding Legal Terms

Define, identify, or explain each of the following terms:

acknowledgment	equal-dignities rule	memorandum	recording
administrator	executor	parol evidence rule	statutes of frauds
corporate signature			

Questions for Review and Discussion

1. What are the different classes of contracts that parties may use to give expression to their mutual assent?

2. Should all contracts be in writing? Explain.

3. How does the parol evidence rule operate

if a party seeks to include, by oral statement and proof, additional terms and conditions not mentioned in a written contract? When and how will the courts allow the introduction and use of parol evidence?

4. How does the equal-dignities rule apply to the appointment of contracting agents?

5. What do the courts say about the enforceability of contracts which are not in writing as required by statutes of frauds? According to statutes of frauds, what essential information should a written memorandum usually contain?

6. Name the types of contracts that must be in writing under statutes of frauds.

7. How do a contract of marriage and a contract in consideration of marriage differ? Which of the two must be in writing in order to be enforceable under statutes of frauds?

8. How may a person who is physically handicapped sign a contract? How may an illiterate sign?

9. How should a corporation sign a contract?

10. What are the duties and obligations of a notary public regarding the acknowledgment of a signature on a contract or other document?

Analyzing Cases

1. Aaron Butler and Frances Wheeler entered into an agreement for the lease of a piece of property with an option to buy. Their agreement was handwritten and consisted of two separate documents, each with part of the transaction listed. When Butler exercised his option to buy, Wheeler claimed that the agreement was void under the statute of frauds. Wheeler specifically argued that since the agreement was contained in two separate documents the intent of the statute was not followed. Judgment for whom and why? ● *Butler v. Lovoll*, 620 P.2d 1251 (Nev. 1980)

2. Maturo signed a contract with Scranton in which Scranton agreed to sell certain property to Maturo. The contract contained a condition that would release Maturo if a mortgage could not be obtained. Scranton then sold the property to another party. Maturo is suing for specific performance. Scranton offered the defense that the agreement was void because of the mortgage contingency clause. Scranton further claimed that the agreement did not conform with the requirements of the statute of frauds because the contingency clause did not contain all the material terms and conditions. Judgment for whom and why? ● *Maturo v. Scranton*, 418 A.2d 918 (Conn. 1979)

3. Prior to their marriage Henry orally promised Wilma that if she would marry him and take care of him he would leave all his property to her. She did marry and take care of Henry as requested. Just before his death Henry made a will naming others as beneficiaries of his property, completely excluding Wilma. Wilma now sues the estate to overthrow the will and get what had been promised her by Henry. Judgment for whom and why? ● *Tatum v. Tatum*, 606 S.W.2d 31 (Tex. Civ. App. 1980)

4. The president and board of directors of Georgetown College are being sued by Madden and others for breach of contract and negligence arising from a variety of problems. Among other problems, the court was asked to determine whether the contract was under seal as it affected the statute of limitations. In this case the word *seal* was printed on the page. However, it was not on the signature lines, but an inch above and to the left, over the word *attest*. Was this a sealed contract? Explain. ● *President of Georgetown College v. Madden*, 505 F.Supp. 557 (U.S. Dist. Ct., D. Md. 1980)

5. Baker was a home builder who engaged in home remodeling. He was hired to reconstruct a portion of a home. Material worth

$7,311.34 had been purchased when the home owners went bankrupt. Suit was brought on the contract. The home owners claim the statute of frauds as a defense, proving that no written contract had ever been made or signed by the parties. Judgment for whom and why? ● See also *Clark v. Cloud Brothers, Inc.,* 406 N.E.2d 260 (Ind. App. 1980).

6. Trimmer, on December 5, contracted to work for Short for one year, performance to commence on January 1 of the following year. Short repudiated the contract, and Trimmer is now suing for damages. Short's defense relies on the absence of a written agreement between the parties. Judgment for whom and why? ● *Trimmer v. Short,* 492 S.W.2d 179 (Mo. 1973)

7. Both the plaintiff and defendant were manufacturers and distributors of dental products. Eastern Dental Corporation supplied many products to Isaac Masel Company which were incorporated in Eastern's goods. Eastern now wishes to terminate all sales to Isaac, and Isaac is suing, claiming that they have a contract. The contract was oral and never had been reduced to writing. No quantity terms were ever expressed, since they changed constantly. Isaac claims that the agreement would come under the UCC statute of frauds related to sale of personal property over $500. Judgment for whom and why? ● *Eastern Dental Corp. v. Isaac Masel Co.,* 502 F. Supp. 1354 (U.S. Dist. Ct., E.D.Pa. 1980)

8. Burden agreed to rent a truck from Ryder for one year. Burden signed a contract which contained a clause which said "this agreement is not binding on Ryder until executed at its general offices in Miami." It was never so executed. Burden now claims the statute of frauds as a defense to the argument, showing that no written agreement was in evidence and there can be no contract without signatures of the parties. Judgment for whom and why? ● *Burden Pallett Co. v. Ryder Truck Rental, Inc.,* 271 S.E.2d 96 (N.C. 1980)

9. Sydney Advocat entered into an oral agreement with Nexus in which he promised to work for Nexus until he was sixty-five, with certain pension benefits guaranteed at the time of retirement. He was fifty-eight at the time he entered Nexus's employment. When Advocat retired, Nexus refused to carry out the pension promise, and Advocat is suing for those benefits. Judgment for whom and why? ● *Advocat v. Nexus Indus., Inc.,* 497 F. Supp. 308 (U.S. Dist. Ct., D.Del. 1980)

Chapter 14

Operation, Performance, and Assignment

Contracts are created for the purpose of gaining some benefit in return for sacrifices promised. Once a contract has been created, both parties look forward to the performance of this exchange of benefits and sacrifices. Whether a contract relationship is successful will depend on each party carrying out the agreed-to acts and promises. Performance means just one thing: complete performance. Anything less is nonperformance. Nonperformance, also called a breach, must lead to an amicable settlement of differences, rescission of the contract, a suit for damages, or, in equity, a request for specific performance.

14-1. Determination of Contract Performance

Whether a contract has been performed will depend on how the parties executed the acts and promises, known as conditions and terms, of the agreement. Determination of performance may be a matter left entirely to the contracting parties, or it may, by agreement, be left to the decision of an outside third party. Third parties such as architects, engineers, lawyers, and the like are often selected for their expertise. At inception both parties agree to abide by the decision of the third party as to whether performance has been complete and satisfactory. In most contractual situations, however, the determination of performance is left to the contracting parties themselves.

● Hempill agreed to pay County Motors $250 for a general overhaul and tune-up of her car's engine. When the work was complete, Hempill took a test drive with the shop mechanic and supervisor. Everything appeared to be satisfactory, and Hempill paid County Motors the promised $250. But had the car shown defects of workmanship, the parties would then have had to mutually determine what had to be done to achieve satisfactory performance before there would be an acceptance of County Motor's promised performance.

A. Definition of Performance

Performance may be defined as the fulfillment or accomplishment of a promise, contract, or other obligation according to its terms. Performance, then, is directly related to the conditions and terms of the contract and whether they have been satisfactorily carried out by each party. The possibility of nonperformance should be anticipated when drawing up contract terms and conditions. Terms should be sufficiently clear that no misunderstanding or dispute might develop before, during, or subsequent to performance. Too often a failure by the parties

181

to define their respective obligations adequately means that the courts must step in to sort the matter out for them, sometimes with unforeseen outcomes for the parties.

B. Relationship to Contractual Conditions and Terms

Conditions, or terms, expressed or implied, will determine the rights and duties of the parties prior to performance, during performance, and following performance. Conditions may, therefore, be classified as (1) conditions precedent, (2) conditions concurrent, or (3) conditions subsequent.

1. Conditions Precedent. A *condition precedent* is a condition that requires performance of certain acts or promises *before* the other party is obligated to pay money or give other consideration agreed to. In a unilateral contract, the performance of a condition precedent serves as the offeree's acceptance of the offer. In a bilateral contract, it is a promise which if not performed leads either to rescission or to termination of the entire agreement.

● O'Neal, a senior medical student, signed an agreement to accept an internship in Doctors' Hospital. The hospital agreed to give her that position on condition that she receive her M.D. degree from the local medical college at graduation in June. Earning the medical degree was a condition precedent to Doctors' Hospital's performance of its obligation to give O'Neal the promised position on its staff.

Similarly, a condition precedent would be imposed upon a manufacturer or wholesaler who, in April, promises delivery of gift wares and toys to a department store in October. Until the gift wares and toys are delivered in October, the department store is not obligated to pay for the promised goods.

2. Conditions Concurrent. A condition which requires both parties to perform at the same time is a *condition concurrent*. A promise to deliver goods supported by the buyer's promise to pay on delivery is a very common condition concurrent. Real estate sales agreements, by custom, usually state that the owner-seller will deliver a good and complete deed to the real property on the buyer's presentation of either cash or a certified check for the amount of the purchase price. Failure of either to do as promised concurrently would be a breach of the express contract condition.

3. Conditions Subsequent. A *condition subsequent* is one in which the parties agree that the contract will be terminated on a prescribed event occurring or not occurring. A contract between a builder and a client stating that contract performance would terminate if a required building permit were not obtained from the issuing public authority within sixty days *after* the signing of their agreement is a condition subsequent. Some warranties included in contracts are also illustrative of such conditions.

● Jordan agreed to build a house and garage for Ravena for $85,000. The agreement was signed by both parties. Among other terms included in the agreement was one that stated that Jordan would warrant the house and garage free from any construction defects for one year subsequent to having completed and being paid for the work. The warranty constituted a condition subsequent—a condition that applies *after* both parties have performed their primary obligations on the contract.

Another common condition of this kind is the one contained in a fire insurance policy. The insured typically agrees in the policy that the report of a fire loss must be made within thirty days of the loss or the insurer will be free of obligation to reimburse the insured for loss.

4. Express and Implied Conditions. The conditions illustrated to this point have all been express conditions. *Express conditions* are those that have been accepted by both parties through either an oral or a written contract. *Implied conditions* are those that may be reasonably inferred because they are necessary for performance of a promised act. Implied conditions may be implied in fact or implied in law.

Conditions implied in fact are those that are part of the agreement but not expressly stated or written. Thus a service agency agrees to repair a car at a price quoted. An implied condition to the agency's promise to repair would be the other party's delivery of the car to the agency's place of business.

Conditions implied in law are those which the law recognizes as being customary or required for fairness in the dealing of the parties, even in the absence of an express agreement. Thus a store's promise to deliver goods implies *by law* that cash be paid on delivery. If the seller and buyer have agreed on a credit arrangement, that would be an express condition. However, in the absence of credit or other arrangements, sales always imply cash payment.

C. Performance and Nonperformance

Performance always means complete performance. Only when there has been complete performance has an obligation been executed. Only then is the party discharged from further performance. When both parties have executed all promises, both parties are discharged. When there is a wrongful performance by one or more of the parties, there is a breach of contract. However, nonperformance is not always wrongful nor does it always result in a breach. A court may take into account the degree of nonperformance in determining the consequences for the parties.

1. Complete Performance. Complete performance occurs when all parties to a contract have fully and satisfactorily met all the conditions and terms related to their agreement. The contract is then discharged and fully executed. Only a condition subsequent, such as a warranty or guarantee, would continue to bind the parties until the warranty period has expired.

2. Substantial Performance. *Substantial performance* occurs when a party, in good faith, completes all obligations except for minor and unimportant details. It is usually possible to correct the minor defects easily and inexpensively, and the lack of performance does not truly impair the intent of the agreement. Substantial performance is not nonperformance to the degree that allows the other party to claim a breach of contract. This concept does not permit a deviation from the original plan of the agreement that might in any way defeat the purpose of the contract. One who has rendered substantial performance may demand payment of the contracted price, less what might be required to correct the minor defects or omissions in performance.

Hadden, after working for Consolidated Edison Company for thirty-seven years, was forced into retirement by his employer on grounds that he had received bribes over the past few years in the amount of $16,000. Consolidated Edison, because of these findings, revoked Hadden's pension rights. Hadden argued that he had *substantially performed* and earned his pension through the thirty-seven years of employment. The court held that Hadden had substantially performed his employment obligations, which were conditioned only on the number of years worked. Although the court found a lack of loyalty and good faith toward the employer, it held that Consolidated Edison had substantially received the consideration from Hadden on which his pension right was earned.

3. Satisfactory Performance. A condition of satisfactory performance is often made an express condition of a contract. However, even when not specifically expressed in an agreement, there is an implied condition of satisfactory performance. Satisfaction may be related to *personal satisfaction* of the parties, or it may be determined by the *custom of the marketplace.* Satisfactory performance will be presented in greater detail in Chapter 15.

4. Nonperformance. Nonperformance, sufficient to support a charge of breach of contract, may result from either complete or partial failure to perform or may be performance that does not fulfill requirements of quality or quantity as either expressed or implied in the contract. Nonperformance permits rescission whereas substantial performance only permits a claim for damages for the minor obligations left undone.

5. Partial Performance. *Partial performance* is nonperformance resulting from a contracting party's abandonment of contracted obligations once performance has commenced. Abandonment occurs at some point during performance with either an express or implied intention that indicates a decision to do nothing more. This is not to be confused with substantial performance, which, as pointed out previously, continues to bind both parties to their original agreement. Partial performance gives the nonbreaching party the option of treating the contract as canceled, with no obligation to the other party, or of paying for labor and materials already contributed to the partial performance.

● Harley contracted to have his Farmall tractor rebuilt by County Farms Machine Company. Work was commenced on the job, but after it was only partly completed the mechanics were put on other work that promised greater profits to the firm. County Farm left the job unfinished over a three-week period, indicating no intention to return to it for several more weeks. Harley may treat the contract as breached and demand possession of his tractor without any obligation to reimburse County Farm Machine Company for what has been done.

6. Determination by Third-Party Referees. Good-faith differences of opinion over whether a contract's terms and conditions have been performed can and do occur. Anticipating such differences of opinion, the parties may agree to let a third party study the matter and make a final judgment on the question. For example, contractors usually agree to accept the final judgment of an architect or engineer whose professional opinion in the matter they respect. The architect or engineer, acting as a third-party referee, will issue what is called a *certificate of performance* at specified intervals during the construction. Awarding of each certificate of performance to a party usually obligates the other contracting party to make payment for the work completed and approved.

D. Time of Performance

The time within which a contract is to be completed may or may not be essential to the obligation of performance. Whether performance is so dependent upon a time limit that time becomes a materially important condition of the contract must be determined from the facts surrounding the individual agreement.

1. **When Time Is of the Essence.** The phrase "time is of the essence" may be inserted as a condition precedent associated with a time limit given a party for performance. This phrase implies that the time element is of the utmost importance in satisfaction of a promise of performance. The courts, however, look at the surrounding circumstances of an agreement and the intent of the parties to determine whether time is actually of the essence. Only when time is actually of the essence will one party's failure to render performance within the time specified discharge obligations of the other party.

● Klein contracted with RV Supply Associates for a recreational vehicle to be used by Klein and his family for a tour of the United States, with other RV owners, to start on July 15. The seller agreed to deliver the vehicle on July 10, to give Klein time to prepare and stock the vehicle for the tour. RV Supply was aware of the necessity of making delivery on the date contained in their agreement. Time is of the essence in this agreement. Delivery of the RV at a later date would defeat the purpose of Klein's purchase of the vehicle.

2. **When Time Is of Secondary Importance.** Often agreements stipulate a time limit for delivery of goods and services when the passing of such a time limit, in fact, has little or no real consequence. In such cases, where time is of secondary importance, the courts may disregard the time stipulations in determining whether there has been performance.

● Steven Development Corporation agreed to build a house for String. The completion date was to be within 130 days after performance was commenced. The contractor was thirty days late in completing the house, and String sued to rescind the agreement, demanding back his deposit and claiming that time was of the essence and Steven's failure to deliver in the promised 130 days discharged him from any further liability to Steven. The court ruled that time was not of the essence and had not been clearly established as essential to satisfactory performance. String was held to his purchase agreement for the house.

14-2. Liability for Contract Nonperformance

Liability on a contract permits a claim for damages against the party or parties who failed to perform agreed-to promises. A contracting party may be one person, partnership, or corporation, or two or more joined together. When two or more are joined together, they may be jointly liable, severally liable, or jointly and severally liable.

A. Several Liability

When two or more persons acting on one side of an agreement hold themselves out as *individually responsible*, they are said to have *several liability*. This type of agreement usually reads, "I promise. . . ." or "Either of us promises. . . ." The injured party in this type of agreement has the right to sue the others individually. Since each one has complete liability on the agreement, a release of one will not release the other.

● Wingate Engineering Co., Inc., and Electronic Sales Company entered an agreement in which they agreed to be severally (individually) liable to the Turnpike Tunnel Corporation as subcontractors for all electrical work on a job being done by that firm. In the event of a breach of their agreement, Turnpike Tunnel Corporation would have the option of a suit for damages against either Wingate Engineering or Electronic Sales.

B. Joint Liability

Joint contracts are those usually preceded by the words "We promise to. . . ." They are agreements in which two or more persons, acting as one, contract with another party and are said to have *joint liability*. Joint parties are usually sued together, although more modern decisions indicate that they may be sued individually.

● O'Connor and Green enter into an agreement with Cohen, in which they say, "We promise to deliver 10 tons of coal to you on December 15." This is a joint contract, and failure to deliver the coal would permit Cohen to sue both O'Connor and Green.

Judgments by a court against persons with joint liability may be collected from all the parties, share and share alike, or they may be collected from only one of them. When the damages are collected from only one, a *contribution* may be sought by that individual from the others for their proportionate share of the judgment.

● Suppose, in the action by Cohen against O'Connor and Green, the court awarded a judgment in favor of Cohen, who collected the entire amount from O'Connor. O'Connor, in turn, may demand from Green a share of one-half the judgment.

C. Joint and Several Liability

When two or more persons sign a contract using the expression "We jointly and severally agree and promise . . ." they have *joint and several liability*. They may be sued collectively or individually, at the option of the injured party. Payments by the ones not joined in the suit may be demanded by the one against whom the judgment is collected.

● O'Connor and Green enter into an agreement with Marcello in which they state, "We jointly and severally agree and promise to pay Marcello $600 when he delivers to us one used 3-ton truck." Failure to pay could result in an action against either O'Connor or Green or against the two of them at the same time.

14-3. Third Parties and Operation of Contracts

Third parties, also known as *outside parties,* are at times given benefits through a contract made between two other parties. Although not obligated by the agreement made between those in privity, the third party may have the legal right of enforcing the benefits availed them through such agreements.

A. Intended Beneficiaries

Beneficiaries in whose favor a contract is made are *intended beneficiaries*. Those most frequently recognized to be intended beneficiaries, with the right to demand and enforce the benefits promised, are (1) creditor beneficiaries, (2) donee beneficiaries, and (3) insurance beneficiaries.

1. Creditor Beneficiaries. A *creditor beneficiary* is an outside third party to whom one or both contracting parties owe a continuing debt of obligation arising from a contract. Frequently the obligation results from the failure of the contracting party or parties to pay for goods delivered or services rendered by or for the benefit of the third party at some time in the past. The key thing to remember, then, is that a creditor beneficiary is owed some *debt of performance*.

● McDonald owed Hinkson $750 for work that Hinkson had done on McDonald's house. McDonald, in another agreement, audited the books for Henley's Service Station, on condition that the $250 fee charged would be given Hinkson toward payment of the $750 debt. Hinkson would be a creditor beneficiary, with the right to demand payment from Henley's Service Station if the $250 were not paid.

2. Donee Beneficiaries. At times the contracting parties may agree to make a *gift of performance* to an outside third party. The recipient of such a gift is called a *donee beneficiary*. Such a third party does not provide any consideration for the benefits received, and this party owes the contracting parties no legal duty. However, the contracting parties owe the donee beneficiary the performance promised, and if it is not forthcoming, the donee beneficiary may bring suit. The consideration that supports this type of agreement is the consideration evolving from and exchanged by the parties in privity to the contract.

● Suppose, in the above case, Hinkson directed Henley's Service Station to pay the $250 fee to Hinkson's daughter. The daughter would be the donee beneficiary. If Henley failed to pay her the $250, she would have the right to bring suit for collection.

3. Insurance Beneficiaries. One named as the beneficiary of an insurance policy is considered a donee beneficiary. The beneficiary does not have to furnish the insured with consideration as a requisite of enforcing payment of the face value of the policy. In some cases an insurance beneficiary may also be a creditor beneficiary. For example, this occurs when in consumer and mortgage loans the creditor requires the debtor to furnish a term life insurance policy naming the creditor as the beneficiary, so that the policy will liquidate the debt if the debtor dies before the loan has been repaid. Insurance beneficiaries, and the properties of an insurance contract generally, are discussed in greater detail in Part 10.

B. Incidental Beneficiaries

An *incidental beneficiary* is an outside party for whose benefit a contract was not made, but who would substantially benefit if the agreement were performed according to its terms and conditions. Through interpretation of facts a court might be called upon to determine whether in any particular case a third party was an intended or an incidental beneficiary. Incidental beneficiaries, as opposed to intended beneficiaries, have no legal grounds for enforcing the contract made by those in privity of contract.

● Iowa Beef Processors, Inc., entered a consent decree agreement with the U.S. government to continue full operation of one of its packing plants pending the sale of the plant, which had been declared to be part of a monopoly under the Clayton Antitrust Act. Bailey brought suit against Iowa Beef Processors on behalf of a meat packers' union, arguing that the purpose of the Clayton Act was to benefit employees in divestiture proceedings like this one. The court held that the members of the union were nothing more than incidental beneficiaries, that the Clayton Act had not been legislated to benefit labor unions, and that they had no rights as would have been allowed a creditor or donee beneficiary.

C. Third-Party Interference with Contractual Relations

Third parties who intentionally interfere with the performance of a contract to which they are neither a party or a beneficiary may be held responsible in an action for resulting damages. An action of this kind is *in tort* rather than *in contract,* and the defendant is called an *intervenor.*

● Kenshaw was employed by Electronic Research Corporation under a contract that was to continue for five years. Kenshaw was involved in research projects related to long-term planning of a new type of radio transmission. Radio Development and Research Associates heard of the work being done by Kenshaw and was successful in luring her away from Electronic Research by offering salary and bonuses that far exceeded her pay at Electronic Research. Electronic Research Corporation has the right to seek damages against the other employer in a tort action resulting from interference with an already existing contract with Kenshaw.

14-4. Assignment of Contracts

Contracts represent intangible property rights which a party in privity may wish to sell or transfer to another. Transfer of such a right to an outside third party may be accomplished through an *assignment.* In its simplest terms an assignment is a transfer of a contract right.

● Owens Development Corporation held an option to purchase 38 acres of land near the intersection of Routes 95 and 7. Two weeks before the option was to expire American Marketing Associates approached Owens and offered to purchase its option at a price that would assure Owens of an excellent profit. Owens assigned the option to American Marketing Associates, which immediately exercised the option, purchasing the property as assignee of Owens Development Corporation's rights to the property.

A. Assignment and Delegation Distinguished

Generally, rights are *assigned* and duties are *delegated.* Both are governed by the rules applicable to assignment. If A is owed money by B, A may assign to C the right to collect the money. On the other hand, if A has agreed to pay B to harvest 200 acres of wheat for a price, B may delegate the duty of harvesting to C. There are restrictions against delegation of duties that will be presented later in this chapter.

● Donovan agreed to build a standard two-car garage for Kingsley for $9,000. Plans and specifications were provided by Kingsley. Donovan would have the right to delegate to another builder the duties involved in building the garage. Likewise, the new party might later assign to another the right to collect the $9,000 from Kingsley, after the job was finished.

B. Parties to Assignment

Three parties are associated with any assignment. Two of the parties are the ones who entered the original agreement. The party who assigns rights or delgates duties is the *assignor*. The outside third party to whom the assignment is made is the *assignee*. The remaining party to the original agreement is the *obligor*.

● Thomas owed Rawlins $500 for work that Rawlins had done on her home. Rawlins, who owed Stevens $500, authorized Stevens to collect the $500 owed by Thomas. Rawlins, here, is the assignor, Stevens the assignee, and Thomas the obligor.

C. Consideration in Assignment

Consideration is not required in the creation of an assignment. When there is no supporting consideration, however, the assignor may repudiate the assignment at any time prior to its execution. In the previous illustration there was consideration supporting Rawlins's assignment. In consideration of the right to make the collection from Thomas, Stevens sacrificed the right to collect money owed by Rawlins. If the assignment had been likened to a gift of the $500, it could have been rescinded.

D. Method of Assignment

To be valid, an assignment must follow certain accepted procedures designed to protect all the parties. Form of assignment, notice of assignment, and the rights of parties in successive or subsequent assignments must conform to practices established by case law and state statutes.

1. Form of Assignment. In the absence of a statute, assignment may be accomplished through written, oral, or implied agreements between the assignor and the assignee. Parties to an assignment, however, must observe the requirement provided by the equal-dignities rule. If the law requires that the agreement by the original parties be in writing, the assignment, too, must be in writing. If the original agreement was one included in the statute of frauds, the assignment must be evidenced by a written memorandum.

● Buckwood agreed in writing to purchase an antique automobile, in mint condition, from Healey for $35,000. The written agreement satisfied the requirements of the statute of frauds for such sales of personal property. Buckwood later made an oral assignment of the contract to Vanderver. The assignment would require a written memorandum to be valid.

2. Notice of Assignment. An assignment is valid at the time it is made. As a measure of protection against subsequent assignments, the assignee should give notice immediately to the obligor. This is an obligation of the assignee, not the assignor. If notice is not given, it would be normal practice for the obligor to render performance to the other original contracting party—the assignor in this case. If, after due notice has been given, the obligor makes payment to the assignor, the obligor is not excused from making payment to the assignee.

● Van Waters & Rogers, Inc., were assignees of a debt owed by Interchange Resources, resulting from construction work done by the assignor for Interchange, the obligor. Notice of the assignment, and a demand for payment was made by Van Waters & Rogers. The notice and demand were disregarded, and payment was made to the assignor instead. In a suit against Interchange Resources the court held that the firm was liable to the assignee, as notice and demand had been made prior to their decision to make payment to the assignor.

3. Subsequent Assignments. Should the assignor make a subsequent assignment of the same right, the courts must decide which of the two assignees has a superior right and claim against the obligor. Conflicting decisions in different states have provided the two following rules.

○ The majority view holds that the assignee to whom the first assignment was made has a superior right and claim even if a subsequent assignee was the first to give notice of assignment to the obligor.
○ A minority view has held that whichever assignee gives notice of assignment first has a superior right and claim to any assigned benefits.

E. Rights and Duties of the Assignee

The rights and duties of the assignee are exactly the same as those previously held by the assignor under the original contract agreement. It is fair to say that "the assignee steps into the shoes of the assignor." Any claims the assignor may have had against the obligor now belong to the assignee. Any defenses the obligor may have had against the assignor's claims may now be used against the assignee.

● Custom Builders contracted to make repairs to Stoner's house. Other opportunities opened to Custom Builders, and it assigned its contract with Stoner to Hall's Alterations Company. By this assignment, Hall's "stepped into the shoes" of Custom Builders. Any rights or claims that previously existed between Stoner and Custom Builders now have been shifted over to Hall's. Hall's has the rights and obligations descending from Custom Builder's contract. Likewise, Stoner may now hold Hall's liable for all terms and conditions in the agreement made with Custom Builders.

The assignee's duty in the process of assignment is to give notice of the assignment to the obligor. The obligor, in turn, is allowed a *reasonable* time to seek assurance that an assignment has been truly made. Making the assignment in writing reduces the possibility of one's fraudulent representation as an assignee.

● Jurgenson presented himself to the paymaster of Highway Trucking Services Company, stating that O'Malley, one of its drivers, had made an assignment to him of $75 of the money owed O'Malley. Highway Trucking Company, the obligor, need not pay the $75 to Jurgenson until the paymaster has time to ascertain the validity of the assignment.

F. Liabilities and Warranties of the Assignor

The assignor is obligated to any express and implied warranties that serve to protect either the assignee or the obligor. A warranty is a guarantee.

1. Warranties to the Assignee. The assignor is bound by an implied warranty that the obligor will respect the assignment and make performance as required by the original agreement between the assignor and the obligor.

● Suppose in the Jurgenson-O'Malley assignment that Highway Trucking Company either refused or was not able to pay Jurgenson the $75. O'Malley would be bound by an implied warranty to Jurgenson that the $75 would be paid. If the assignment were nothing more than a gift to Jurgenson, there would be no enforceable warranty in the absence of any consideration between the assignor and the assignee.

2. Warranties to the Obligor. If through an assignment the assignor delegates to an assignee duties owed the obligor, there is an implied warranty that the duties delegated will be carried out in a complete and satisfactory manner.

● Sunbrite Painting Contractors assigned a contract for the painting of Jenkin's Bridge to Fitzhugh. Fitzhugh's work was far below that deemed to be satisfactory in the painting trade. The managers of the bridge operation could sue Sunbrite for damages due to Sunbrite's breach of the implied warranty.

G. Restrictions on Assignments

While most contracts may be assigned, those for personal and professional services may not be. The right of assignment may also be restricted by agreement of the parties in privity and in certain cases by law.

1. Restrictions on Personal and Professional Service Contracts. One may not assign, or delegate, duties that are of a personal or professional nature. By *personal* is meant *other than routine*. Services of a custom tailor, a musician, an artist, or a hair stylist are of a personal nature. In each case, parties rendering such services are chosen for a special ability, artistic talent, or the like. Professional services are those rendered by physicians, lawyers, certified public accountants, ministers, and the like. People in these occupations are selected because of their special abilities, and their services are not considered routine. Routine services are those performed by electricians, mechanics, plumbers, waitresses, and others whose skills and abilities are judged according to the usual custom and standards of the marketplace.

● McDonald's System, Inc., granted a franchise to Copeland for a fast-food outlet in Omaha. McDonald's later agreed to give Copeland first-refusal rights in any plans to open other outlets in the Omaha area. After opening several additional franchise outlets, Copeland sold his franchises to Schupack, together with the right to new McDonald outlets in the area. McDonald's Systems, Inc., refused to honor the assignment, claiming that its relationship with Copeland developed through a special confidence in Copeland's ability in managing and promoting its new franchise outlets. The court held that Copeland's ability and skill were not of a routine nature, but were unique owing to Copeland's personal qualifications, and that his contract with McDonald's Systems, Inc., therefore implied a restriction against any assignment.

2. Restrictions Imposed by Original Contract. Parties to a contract may include a condition that will restrict its assignment. Some courts have held that a restriction against assignment of a debt owed by the obligor robs the assignor of a property right guaranteed by law, and would be contrary to public policy. Other courts have permitted this restrictive condition. If, in the Sunbrite Painting Contractors case, Jenkin's Bridge management had included a condition against assignment, the assignment to Fitzhugh would have been void.

3. Restrictions Imposed by Law. Assignment, in special situations, may be restricted by law or declared void because it is contrary to public policy. Thus, members of the armed services may not assign any part of their pay, except to a spouse or family member. Police officers, persons elected or appointed to public office, and others are likewise restricted from making assignment of their pay or of duties which they have been especially chosen and appointed to perform.

14-5. Novations

When two contracting parties agree to some material change in their executory agreements, the change creates what is known as a *novation*. The change may relate to the parties themselves, the consideration, the subject matter, or any other provision of their original agreement. A novation is actually a new contract, based upon a former one but containing one or more significant changes.

● Kemp has a two-year contract with the Smith Electric Company as credit manager. Kemp wishes to accept a position in another state. He introduces another competent credit manager to Smith, the president of the firm. Smith then agrees to release Kemp if this new person will take over Kemp's contract for the rest of the two-year period. This is a novation, and the release of Kemp creates a complete separation of the original contracting parties from their original contract.

Novations differ from assignments in the following four ways:

○ Assignments may be made without the mutual consent of both contracting parties. Novations, on the other hand, require the mutual assent of both the original offeror and the offeree.

● Rugg, a painting contractor, contracted to paint the offices of the Johnson Electric Company. He now finds that he has undertaken more contract obligations than his firm can handle. If he decides to assign this contract to another reputable painter, he would not be required to have the Johnson Company's permission. He may also seek to have the contract turned over to the other firm with the consent of the Johnson Company. In the first case, Rugg would remain a guarantor; in the second, he would be fully released because, by the company's consent, a novation had taken place.

○ Assignments may not release assignors of their obligations. Assignors may assign only their rights. Novations transfer *all rights and obligations,* giving the replaced party complete freedom from the original contract.

○ In an assignment the "assignee steps into the shoes of the assignor." This is not true in a novation. The new member of the contract has a new agreement with the other party, not necessarily with the previous obligations.

Had the Rugg painting contract in the above case been assigned, the rights of the assignee would have been exactly the same as Rugg's; also the responsibilities would not have changed. Had there been a novation, the Johnson Electric Company and the substituted painting contractor might decide on far different terms from those in the Rugg agreement.

○ The assignor of an executory contract is never fully released until the contract is executed. In a novation the former party steps out free of any and all obligations on the original agreement.

● Vandegrift had a maintenance contract with the Larken Company to do all adjustments and repairs to its electric motors over a five-year period. After two years, the Vandegrift assigned this contract to the Johnson Electric Company. Although the assignment has been made and all parties are in agreement, Vandegrift will remain a guarantor of all work done by the Johnson Electric Company for the three years that the contract still has to run.

Understanding Legal Terms

Define, identify, or explain each of the following terms:

assignment
condition precedent
condition
  subsequent

incidental
  beneficiary
joint liability
nonperformance

novation
satisfactory
  performance
several liability

substantial
  performance
third-party referee

Questions for Review and Discussion

1. What kind of performance may a promisee demand from a promissor in execution of contracted terms and conditions?

2. Give examples that illustrate conditions (a) precedent, (b) concurrent, and (c) subsequent, in contract performance.

3. Contrast conditions that are implied in fact with those that are implied in law.

4. Distinguish between nonperformance, substantial performance, and complete performance of one's contractual obligations.

5. When will a court permit nonperformance of a contract containing the phrase "time is of the essence"?

6. When may an outside or third party bring an action based on nonperformance against the parties who have made a contract?

7. List the kinds of contracts that may not be assigned.

8. After an assignment has been made, what are the obligations of (a) the assignor, (b) the assignee, and (c) the obligor?

9. In what way is the equal-dignities rule applicable to an assignment?

10. In what ways does a novation differ from an assignment?

Analyzing Cases

1. Dr. Waterhouse, while on call, was involved in an automobile accident. Several insurance companies were parties to the settlement, including INA Commercial Union and the Chicago Insurance Company, which had insured Waterhouse for professional liability. Chicago Insurance Company now claims that it is a third-party beneficiary of the contracts between Dr. Waterhouse and the other insurance companies and that those contracts should protect its interests. Was Chicago Insurance Company correct in its claim? ● *Insurance Co. of North America v. Waterhouse*, 424 A.2d 675 (Del. 1980)

2. Shaeffer contracted to build a quadruplex building and sell the completed building and property to Kelton. All financing arrangements were made. When the building was near completion, Kelton started advertising the rental of the units. Upon completion of the building Kelton sought to rescind the agreement because of some minor but unimportant deviations from the building plans. Shaeffer is now suing Kelton, arguing that Kelton has breached the contract for purchase of the building. Judgment for whom and why? ● *Shaeffer v. Kelton*, 619 P.2d 1226 (N.M. 1980)

3. A contract was entered into containing the following language: "Goodman Properties, Inc., hereinafter called 'owner'. . . and Melvin Clayman, Stanley Clayman, and David Hillman, jointly hereinafter called 'purchaser'. . . . " A dispute has arisen and there is a question as to whether the three men are severally or jointly liable. What decision would be made on this point? ● *Clayman v. Goodman Properties, Inc.*, 518 F.2d 1026 (D.C. Cir. 1973)

4. Butkovich & Sons contracted to do extensive alterations and repairs to a house owned by Grane, against which State Bank of St. Charles held a first mortgage. Butkovich & Sons are now suing for money they claim is owed on the contract. The defendants refused payment owing to serious defects in the contractor's work, including a failure to reinforce a concrete floor and installing the new main floor 9 inches below that called for in the plans and specifications. Butkovich & Sons claim substantial performance of the contract. Judgment for whom and why? ● *Butkovich & Sons v. State Bank of St. Charles*, 379 N.E.2d 837 (Ill. 1978)

5. Byrnes and others entered into a contract with Faulkner, Dawkins, and Sullivan in which 44,000 shares of stock were to be sold by Byrnes to Faulkner and the others. Faulkner later repudiated the contract. Byrnes brought suit for breach. Faulkner claimed that there could be no breach because Byrnes had never shown that he was actually prepared to tender delivery of the stock. At no time had Faulkner and the others indicated their readiness to pay for the 44,000 shares. Judgment for whom and why? ● *Byrnes v. Faulkner*, 413 F.Supp. 453 (U.S. Dist. Ct., S.D.N.Y. 1973)

6. Farmers Insurance Exchange issued uninsured motorist coverage to Nixon. A condition of the policy required that any claims against the policy must be made within one year of any insurable accident. Nixon was involved in an accident, but suit was not brought against him until more than one year had elapsed. A statute exempted insured motorists from the one-year rule. Farmers argued that the one-year limit in the policy was a condition subsequent to its obligations on the policy. Judgment for whom and why? ● *Nixon v. Farmers Ins. Exch.*, 201 N.W.2d 543 (Wis. 1972)

7. Bombay Broadcasting Company sold radio station KMOP to Clayton. Clayton was given an option in the method to be used in payment for the station. He could either issue a promissory note signed by him personally or form a corporation which would then issue and sign a note in the corporation's name. Clayton opted to form a corporation, which duly issued a note signed by the corporation. The note was later assigned to the Communications Capital Corporation. The note is now in default, and Clayton is being called on to pay it. Clayton offers the defense that he did not personally sign the note. Judgment for whom and why? ● *Clayton v. Communications Capital Corp.*, 440 P.2d 330 (Ariz. 1968)

8. King Brothers entered into a contract to construct a house for McMullen. A completion date was a condition to their contract. Due to the unavailability of certain materials required by McMullen, modification in the original plans by McMullen, and heavy rains, King Brothers were twenty-nine days late in completing construction. McMullen is suing for damages because of the delay. Judgment for whom and why? ● *King Bros. Bldg. Contractors, Inc. v. McMullen*, 393 So.2d 413 (La. 1980)

Chapter 15

Termination and Discharge

Although some contracts continue in effect for years, the law does not look upon a contract as being effective permanently or forever. Even the so-called perpetual-care agreements given with lots sold in a cemetery are subject to possible termination if circumstances or conditions require it. Termination occurs when either party to an agreement concludes the contract according to its terms; when performance becomes impossible due to some permissible circumstance; or when the law intervenes, making the agreement inoperative. The law differentiates between termination and cancellation. *Cancellation* results from one party's failure to perform, giving the other the right to put an end to the agreement. The canceling party has the right to seek damages against the other for the breach of agreement. On the other hand, when a contract is *terminated*, there is no resulting recognizable suit for damages by either of the parties.

When a contract is *discharged*, one or more of the legal relations between the parties has been terminated. This chapter discusses the circumstances and conditions under which contractual obligations may be terminated and the parties discharged from the responsibility of performance.

15-1. Discharge by Agreement

Parties to a contract may stipulate the time and conditions for termination and discharge as part of their agreement. Or they may subsequently agree not to do what they had originally promised to do. The latter is the case when there is a mutual rescission of the contract, a waiver of performance by one or more of the parties, a novation, or an accord and satisfaction to liquidate an outstanding debt or obligation.

A. Termination by Terms of the Contract

Parties, during contract negotiation, may agree to certain terms that provide for automatic termination upon the occurrence or nonoccurrence of stated events. You may recall from Chapter 14 that these are defined as conditions subsequent. For example, a professional athlete may contract with management that their agreement will be terminated if for any reason the player becomes either physically or mentally incapable of rendering full performance. Such an agreement may also spell out management's obligations should there be a termination of the agreement before full performance has been made. In other situations the clause providing for automatic termination may be related to a promissor's success in acquiring the raw materials or other supplies upon which performance will depend.

● Naudain Oil Company agreed to furnish 500 gallons of heating oil to Bancroft Academy, an amount necessary to take care of the academy's requirements during the heating season. Naudain and Bancroft agreed that in the event that Naudain could not obtain heating oil through its suppliers, the contract would be terminated. Thus, they had mutually agreed to a condition subsequent that would free both parties of continuing obligations should the predetermined eventuality, the failure to obtain the oil, occur.

1. Conditions Implied in Fact. As you may recall, a condition implied in fact is one that the parties would reasonably understand to be a part of an agreement, although not expressed. Failure to adhere to such implied conditions may result in termination of a contract. Thus, a party agrees to chauffeur another's car from New York to Chicago for a fee of $100, the date of departure to be determined by the owner of the car. The owner's selection of a date is an implied condition of the contract, and failure to set a date will terminate the agreement.

2. Notice of Termination. Contracts often permit either party to terminate an executory contract by giving proper notice to the other of the intention to terminate. Contracts may be written without containing any agreement as to when termination is to occur. In such cases the agreement may be terminated at will by either the promissor or the promisee. In that event, termination takes place at the time notice is given. Leases for real estate usually contain a condition that requires the tenant to give notice of termination sixty or ninety days before the lease expires. Failure to give this notice gives the landlord the option of either terminating the lease on the date of expiration or extending it for a time equal to the time covered by the lease.

B. Mutual Rescission

Contracting parties may, either before or after performance commences, rescind their contract as a result of further negotiation and by their mutual assent. *Mutual rescission,* in the majority of cases, requires both parties to return to the other any consideration already received or pay for any services or materials already rendered. Mutual rescission may be effected through an oral, written, or, at times, implied agreement. Following the requirement of the equal-dignities rule, if the original agreement required a contract in writing, the rescission agreement must also be written.

C. Termination by Waiver

Termination by waiver occurs when a party with the right to complain of the other party's unsatisfactory performance or nonperformance fails to complain. It is a voluntary relinquishing (waiver) of one's rights to demand performance. A waiver differs from a discharge by mutual rescission in that a waiver entails no obligation by the parties to return any consideration that may have been exchanged up to the moment of rescission. Discharge by waiver, when made, is complete in itself.

● O'Leary was hired by Accounting Consultants, under a five-year written contract. Five months after starting the new job, O'Leary failed to report for work. Accounting Consultants made no effort to locate O'Leary, either to demand that she fulfill her contract or to demand that she pay the firm damages resulting from her breach of the agreement. Thus a termination by waiver resulted from Accounting Consultant's voluntary relinquishing of its rights, thereby discharging both parties from further obligation.

D. Novation

By a novation the parties to a contract mutually agree to the termination of an existing contract, replacing it with a new one. Through a novation all parties are discharged from further obligation to the former agreement.

E. Accord and Satisfaction

As previously stated, an accord and satisfaction is a resulting new agreement arising from a bona fide dispute between the parties as to the terms of their original agreement. The mutual agreement to the new terms is the accord; performance of the accord is the satisfaction: thus, accord and satisfaction. The accord, although agreed to, is not a binding agreement until the satisfaction has been made. The original agreement is not discharged, therefore, until the performance or satisfaction has been provided as promised.

● Lockyear agreed to repair Johnson's typewriter. It was agreed that Johnson would pay Lockyear for any time spent on the job, plus any new parts needed. Lockyear submitted a bill for $118. Johnson felt that the charges were excessive and contacted Lockyear, expressing her dissatisfaction. Lockyear insisted on full payment of the $118. Johnson mailed Lockyear a check for $100, on which was written, "In full payment of all services and parts used in repairing my typewriter." This was the agreement or accord. Lockyear then cashed the check. Cashing of the check was the satisfaction that Lockyear received from Johnson, liquidating the original amount billed.

F. General Release

A general release is a document expressing the intent of a creditor to release a debtor from obligations on an existing and valid debt (see Figure 11-1 on page 150). A general release terminates a debt and excuses the debtor of any future payment without the usual requirement that consideration be given in return.

15-2. Discharge Through Performance

Most contracts are discharged through performance. Generally, discharge is permitted only if there has been complete performance in a manner satisfactory to the party being served. Courts allow exceptions to complete performance and may allow discharge when there has been substantial performance.

A. Complete and Substantial Performance

Complete performance occurs when both parties fully accomplish every term, condition, and promise to which they agreed. Substantial performance results when a party, in good faith, executes all promised terms and conditions with the exception of minor details that do not effect the real intent of their agreement. Complete performance terminates an agreement, discharging the parties of any further obligation to one another. Ordinarily substantial performance also serves to discharge the agreement, but with a difference. A party who complains that performance has been substantial, but not complete, has the right to demand reimbursement from the offending party to correct those details that prevented complete performance.

● Rago purchased a tour package from All World Tours, Inc. The brochures advertising the tour stated that scheduled stops and guided tours would be made in sixteen different cities and historic areas during the three-week trip. Fifteen of the scheduled stops were made, but the sixteenth was canceled for reasons beyond the control of All World Tours. Rago demanded the return of the entire $4,300 paid to the tour operators, claiming that there had been less than complete performance of their contract. A court would hold that there had been substantial performance, allowing a refund to Rago only in the amount All World saved by not making the sixteenth stop.

B. **Satisfactory Performance**

Satisfactory performance is either an express or implied condition of every contract. Sales agreements for consumer goods often express this condition by including the words "money back if not entirely satisfied." In other contracts satisfaction may be carefully defined according to the expectations of the parties. When there is no express agreement, the law implies that work will be done in a skillful manner and that the materials or goods will be free of defects. Ordinarily the parties may be discharged from a contract only if there has been satisfactory performance. What is satisfactory performance, however, is something that is not always easy to ascertain. Therefore, the courts are often called upon to determine whether there has been a breach of the guarantee of satisfactory performance.

1. **Satisfaction Determined by Personal Taste.** Many articles and services are sold on the understanding that only the one buying them will be allowed to determine what is meant by *satisfaction*. Services rendered in a beauty salon or barbershop, photographs taken at a studio, and portraits painted by an artist are in this classification. Regardless of the skill and application of the person doing the work, customers may, on the basis of their personal judgment and satisfaction, refuse payment.

● Betty Montalvo made an appointment with a reliable beauty salon to have her very expensive wig trimmed and styled. The manager told her that unless she was satisfied with the results of their work she would not have to pay them for their services. The customer's personal taste and judgment alone will be the determining factor as to satisfaction in this case.

The beauty salon in the Montalvo situation will not be discharged from its obligations or freed from its liability until it has performed satisfactorily in accordance with the personal taste and preferences of Montalvo.

2. **Satisfaction Unrelated to Personal Taste.** Satisfactory performance of contracts for those goods and services not involving *personal taste* does not permit the arbitrary judgment of the parties in ruling on the matter of satisfaction. Contracts for the sale of mechanical devices and services offered by tradespeople are of this type. Both parties may introduce expert witnesses in determining whether satisfaction has been achieved. Since even expert witnesses may disagree on satisfaction, a jury is often required to make the final decision after

sifting the opinions offered on both sides of a case. The jury's decision would also determine whether a discharge is permissible.

3. Satisfaction Determined by Outside Parties. Contracting parties may delegate the decision of satisfactory performance to an unbiased, disinterested, but competent outside party. Both contracting parties must agree to the appointment of an outside party who will determine whether there has been satisfactory performance. In effect, it is this outside third party who determines whether the contracting parties are discharged from their contractual obligations.

C. Tender of Performance

To *tender* means to offer. A *tender of performance* is an act or overture showing that a party is ready, willing, and able to perform an obligation. Tender may relate to the payment of money, the performance of a promised act, or any other matter stipulated in the terms of an agreement. The tender must be unconditional, without reservation, and without qualification.

1. Tender of Cash. Contracts requiring the payment of money are not complete until the amount agreed upon has been paid. Unless the agreement provides that payment may be made by check or some other means, *payment in cash is implied.*

When payment is made, *legal tender* must be offered. Legal tender consists of all coin and currency that Congress has declared must be accepted when presented in payment of all debts public and private. United States currency carries the words "This note is legal tender for all debts public and private." The United States Code, Section 462 of Title 31, states that there shall be no limitation imposed on the debtor as to the number of coins of any denomination that may be used in payment of a debt. When tender of cash payment is refused, the debtor is relieved of the obligation to make tender a second time. It then becomes the obligation of the creditor to seek out and request payment from the debtor.

● Holliday owed Central National Bank $500, due on an installment car loan. Holliday tendered $350 in small bills and the balance in pennies, nickels, dimes, and quarters. The bank is obligated to accept payment in this manner, although the bank will be allowed a reasonable time, at its convenience, to count and determine the exact amount of money received before issuing a receipt to Holliday.

2. Tender of Check or Other Commercial Paper. Tender of a check or other commercial paper, when agreed to by the creditor, does not act as a full discharge of the debtor's obligations. Payment by check is implied to be only a conditional payment. The debtor is not discharged until the check is accepted and paid by the bank on which it has been drawn. The same is true when payment is made through the assignment of a right to collect money owed by another to the assignor-debtor. Until the money is paid by the obligor, the debtor is not discharged.

3. Conditions Accompanying Tender. In making tender of performance, one owing performance must observe certain rules that determine when and how tender is to be made.

○ Tender must be made in the manner required by the terms of the contract, at the proper time and place, and to the proper person.

○ Tender of a past-due debt must include the interest from the due date up to the date that tender of payment is made.

○ Tender of money must be for the exact amount due and in legal tender.

○ Present ability to perform must be shown by an actual tender, or offer, of the money or goods promised. A mere expression of willingness to perform is not sufficient.

● Svenson owed Turner Lumber Company $350. A 2 percent discount was allowed if the bill was paid within ten days. Svenson sent Turner Lumber Company his personal promissory note for the $350, discounted 2 percent. The note is nothing more than a promise to pay and is not a tender of the amount due. The creditor may either accept the note, with the discount, or return it to Svenson as unacceptable.

○ Tender of goods is acceptable only when the contract calls for goods rather than money. Goods tendered must meet the requirements of the contract to be valid.

15-3. Discharge by Impossibility of Performance

Performance of a promised act may become impossible owing to conditions existing at the time the agreement was made. Such impossibility will render the contract void. Impossibility of performance due to reasons that arise subsequent to the creation of a contract may render an agreement either void or voidable.

A. Conditions Making Performance Impossible

Conditions that would defeat performance, existing at the time of making a contract, automatically void an otherwise enforceable agreement.

● Harris contracted to purchase Steele's 35-foot cruiser for $38,000. The contract was signed, and Harris tendered payment which Steele accepted. Neither party knew at the time that the cruiser had burned the night before at its anchorage located many miles away in another state. At the time of making their contract, performance was already impossible. Both parties are discharged of any promise of performance, and Steele is obligated to return the $38,000 to Harris.

Conditions that arise subsequent to the making of a contract may either void the agreement or make it voidable by one of the parties. Discharge through impossibility of performance may, in some situations, be allowed only if the specific and anticipated impossibility has been made a condition to the agreement.

1. Acts of God. An *act of God,* in contract law, is any natural disaster that is not reasonably foreseeable. This includes floods, cyclones, hurricanes, lightning, earthquakes, volcanic eruptions, and the like. Courts will not excuse a party from performance based on an act of God unless:

○ There was an act-of-God clause in the contract excusing performance in the event of the unforeseeable natural disaster.

○ The natural disaster (act of God) was in fact not reasonably foreseeable.

● Continental Construction Company agreed to furnish all the steel necessary for constructing the Hance River Bridge. The contract contained the usual act-of-God clause. Performance was made impossible by flooding of Continental's holding yard, where the completed steel had been stored. Continental had been warned of the anticipated flooding days before it occurred. Continental is not excused as it had sufficient time before the flooding to move the steel from its endangered location.

○ The party claiming a defense under the act-of-God clause was not negligent.

● Loden shipped cucumbers from Nogales, Arizona, to Los Angeles, over the Southern Pacific Railroad. En route, the car containing the cucumbers was side-tracked owing to heavy rains and a washout. Shipment was delayed for more than a week, and Loden claimed damages of $10,000. The railroad defended itself under the act-of-God clause in the bill of lading. The court held that the railroad could have used alternate routes which were then available. The railroad was held liable due to its own negligence.

Statute law in most states now provides interpretation of termination through acts of God. Courts in those states have repeatedly held that, when substantial performance of a contract is possible, the impossibility of precise performance due to an act of God does not excuse either party to the contract.

● American Builders contracted with the Stewart Lumber Company for 1 million board feet of No. 2 dressed white pine. Prior to delivery, Stewart Lumber Company's lumberyard was destroyed by a hurricane. Although an act of God would seem to have made performance impossible, the lumber company would be obligated to secure lumber elsewhere, which may be done through proper negotiation. Stewart must deliver the lumber to American Builders under their agreement.

2. Destruction of Subject Matter. When the subject matter of an executory contract has been selected by the parties and later is destroyed, the performance obligation is discharged. When the contract is not specific in the description or the location of the subject matter, a promissor is not discharged if the subject matter *intended* for delivery is destroyed. In this case the promissor is obligated to locate and deliver subject matter of the same kind and quantity that could be secured elsewhere. Any financial losses due to the misfortune must be borne by the promissor. If, however, the subject matter of the contract is specific as to location and description, the obligor may be excused from performance when that subject matter is destroyed.

● Rockefeller contracted to supply International Paper Company with pulpwood to be taken from specified lands owned by Rockefeller. The paper company demanded performance of delivery after fire had destroyed the woodlands from which the pulpwood was to be taken. The court ruled that both parties had agreed that the pulpwood was to come from a specific tract, the one that was destroyed. Rockefeller was discharged of any obligation to perform.

3. Existing or Subsequent Illegality. When performance of contract promises requires execution of acts declared illegal because of existing common law, statute, or public policy, the contract is unenforceable from its inception. When the performance of a contract is made illegal through the passing of laws subsequent to the formation of the contract, the contract is likewise declared unenforceable.

● Exquisite Home Builders, Inc., started construction of a house for Quagliana. Quagliana, through his designer, demanded that the house be built in such a way as to provide a desired view. The builder discovered that to do so would violate subsequently enacted building restrictions. Further demands by Quagliana resulted in the contractor abandoning the job. In a suit against Exquisite Builders for damages, the court ruled in favor of the contractor, stated that performance was impossible without violating the building code.

4. Death, Insanity, or Disability of Contracting Party. Death, insanity, or disability of one obligated to performance of a promise that requires a special talent or skill terminates and discharges an agreement. Musicians, artists, writers, and certain professionals are included here. When promised services are to be performed for the *personal benefit* of a promisee, death of the promisee will also terminate the agreement.

When contract promises relate to services that may be performed by others, and do not demand the personal services of the contracting party, performance is not excused through death, insanity, or disability. The guardian of the party involved or the estate of the deceased may be held liable for performance.

● Armour, a farmer, agreed to harvest wheat growing in Woodward's 40-acre field. Before the wheat was ready for harvest, Armour died. Performance here did not require the personal services of Armour. The work could be performed by others engaged in contract harvesting. Armour's estate could be held to the agreement if Woodward opted to do so.

5. Certain Acts of the Parties. Impossibility of performance may result from negligence or wrongful intentional acts of one of the parties. Impossibility of performance of this kind does not discharge the contract. The injured party may seek damages on grounds of an inexcusable breach. Thus, in the previous illustration, had Woodward, prior to Armour's death, barred Armour from coming on his property to harvest the wheat, that act would have discharged Armour of any further obligation to tender performance and given him the additional right to seek damages from Woodward for a breach. The same rule is applied when wrongful acts or negligence of one of the parties makes performance more difficult and expensive to the other or causes unanticipated delays in tendering full performance of the contract.

B. **Effect of Frustration-of-Purpose Doctrine**

Courts at times apply a principle of fairness and justice in cases where it would be thoroughly impractical and senseless to fulfill promised acts. This concept has given rise to the *frustration-of-purpose doctrine,* or *economic frustration doctrine.* The doctrine is applied only in those cases where a party recognizes and understands possible risks and accepts them in contemplation of performance.

● Wright contracted to play for Alabama Football, Inc., for the 1977, 1978, and 1979 seasons. Alabama Football was then a member of the World Football League, which had been formed to compete with the well-established American and National Football Leagues. At the time of signing, Wright was aware, as were most others, of the new league's instability and questionable future. Before any scheduled games were played, the World Football League was dissolved and the Alabama team thereby ceased to exist. Wright's claim under the contract was dismissed and the contract discharged. Applying the frustration-of-purpose doctrine, the court held that demanding performance would be impractical, unfair, and unjust to Alabama Football, Inc., in this situation. Wright knew of and accepted the risks that might frustrate the team's intent to perform its obligations under the agreement.

15-4. Discharge by Operation of Law

A contract is discharged by operation of law when one of the parties has made a material alteration in a written contract, has intentionally destroyed the contract document, or has been declared bankrupt.

A. Material Alteration of a Written Contract

A material alteration of a written contract will discharge a contract. For discharge, the following conditions must be met:

○ The alteration must be *material,* changing a party's obligations to the agreement.

● A written contract signed by Harvey and Kitchen did not show the date on which it was signed. Harvey, who held the document, filled in the date. This was not a material alteration. It merely completed an agreement to which both parties had signed their names.

○ The alteration must have been made by one of the contracting parties, not by an outside third party who is in no way related to the contract.
○ The alteration must have been knowingly and intentionally made, not the result of negligence or mistake.
○ The alteration must be unilateral, made without the agreement and consent of both parties.

A contract is not materially altered if one of the parties, without consent of the other, fills in blank spaces; writes in implied obligations, not initially reduced to writing; or adds words to do no more than fortify in writing that to which the parties have already agreed.

B. Physical Destruction of the Contract.

The destruction, by burning or otherwise, of a written agreement may serve to discharge the agreement. Destruction by the obligee with the intent that the other party be discharged would act to discharge that party when the written contract is under seal. An implied agreement by both parties to the destruction may be evidenced by the obligee's reluctance to complain, resulting, then, in discharge by mutual agreement. The status of a contract and the obligations of the parties usually depend on proof of an existing written agreement. The original contract or a certified copy should be placed in the hands of an impartial party or an attorney or in another safe place of keeping, and each party should be provided with original signed copies of their agreement.

C. Bankruptcy of a Contracting Party

Through the provisions of the Bankruptcy Reform Act of 1978 (see Chapter 6), a discharge in bankruptcy from a court will be allowed as a defense against collection of most, but not all, debts of the bankrupt.

D. Release Through Statute of Limitations

State statutes providing time limits within which suit may be brought are known as *statutes of limitations*. Each state sets its own time limits. Generally, actions for collection of open accounts (charge accounts) must be brought within three to five years, written agreements usually within ten years, and judgments from ten to twenty years. Those states requiring the seal on certain contracts have still other limitations and requirements, much broader than applied to simple contracts. The statute of limitations does not technically void the debt but gives the debtor a defense against any demand for collection. In cases where the debtor is absent from the state for a valid reason, becomes a member of the armed forces, or is serving time in prison, and in other special cases, the time so spent in not included. These interruptions in the running of the statute are known as *moratoriums*. Thus, a creditor's rights are not to be denied against a debtor who knowingly and intentionally leaves the jurisdiction of the court in which collection would ordinarily be enforced.

● Norris owed several creditors a total of $38,000 at the time she was sent to prison for ten years for commiting a felony. The ten years spent in prison will not be included in the time span allowed the creditors, who may bring legal action against Norris to collect the debt.

Understanding Legal Terms

Define, identify, or explain the following terms:

act of God	legal tender	statute of	termination by
cancellation	material alteration	limitations	waiver
discharge	moratorium	tender of	
frustration-of-	mutual rescission	performance	
purpose doctrine			

Questions for Review and Discussion

1. What is the difference between the termination and cancellation of a contract?

2. What is meant by a condition implied in fact? Does failure to abide by such a condition terminate a contract? Explain.

3. What is the difference between a termination by mutual rescission and a termination by waiver?

4. What is required if tender of performance is made by cash?

5. Give examples to illustrate what is meant by acts of God. What is the general rule in law regarding whether an act of God will excuse contract performance?

6. Does the negligence or intentional wrong of a contracting party serve to discharge contract obligations? Explain.

7. When is the frustration-of-purpose doctrine applicable? Can it serve to terminate a contract?

8. Do you think that the time restrictions imposed by the statute of limitations upon the collection of overdue accounts is fair and reasonable to creditors? Explain your viewpoint pro or con.

9. Will the physical destruction of a contract document result in the discharge of the parties' contractual obligations? Why is it important to put a contract in a place of safe keeping?

10. Under what circumstances is a contract terminated through additions or alterations made to a written agreement after its acceptance by both parties?

Analyzing Cases

1. Neal offered to sell certain lands to Damazo. Just prior to settlement, the city of Frederick imposed certain administrative regulations on Neal, the seller, which made the sale quite impossible. The new regulations were totally unprecedented and unforeseeable. Neal repudiated the agreement and suit is brought by Damazo. Judgment for whom and why? ● *Damazo v. Neal*, 363 A.2d 252 (Md. 1976)

2. Mr. and Mrs. Burke agreed to purchase property from Patrick. On the day before settlement Mr. Burke died. Mrs. Burke is now trying to rescind the contract on grounds of impossibility of performance resulting from her husband's death. Patrick is now suing in an effort to enforce the contract. Judgment for whom and why? ● *Burke v. Patrick*, 366 A.2d 1070 (Md. 1976)

3. Music Inc. agreed to furnish music services to Henry B. Klein Company for a sixty-day period. It was agreed that the service would be given for subsequent sixty-day periods unless Music Inc. were given notice of termination of the agreement by Klein Company at least sixty days prior to the date of anticipated termination. One day prior to the sixty-day limit, Klein informed Music Inc. that it was giving notice of termination as allowed in their contract. A written note containing the same information was mailed by Klein but was not received by Music Inc. until the first day into the next sixty-day period. Music Inc. argued that termination had not been made in time and that the contract was, then, automatically extended for an additional sixty-day period. Judgment for whom and why? ● *Music Inc. v. Henry B. Klein Co.*, 245 A.2d 650 (Pa. 1968)

4. Kenison contracted for the purchase of property from Baldwin. A condition of their contract required that Baldwin personally execute the new deed for Kenison. At settlement Kenison willingly accepted a deed executed by a third party. Kenison is now suing to rescind the contract, claiming that Baldwin had breached their agreement in not personally executing the new deed. Kenison, in his complaint, argued that by accepting the deed from the third party Baldwin had waived any right to complain and that there had been a novation of the terms from the original agreement. Judgment for whom and why? ● *Kenison v. Baldwin*, 351 P.2d 307 (Okla. 1970)

5. Intracostal Sales and Service, Inc., entered into a plumbing subcontract with Cheezum, a general contractor, in which Intercostal agreed not to file any liens against the job. The promise was included in the written contract. Intracostal did, in fact, file liens. Cheezum subsequently breached its agreement, and Intracostal sued. Cheezum argued that Intracostal's own breach, in filing liens, forfeited its right to complain. Judgment for whom and why? ● *Cheezum Dev. Corp. v. Intracostal Sales and Service, Inc.*, 336 So.2d 1210 (Fla. App 1976)

6. The Pete Smith Company entered into a contract with El Dorado to build a golf course. The contract specifically expressed the intent that Pete Smith Company would bear the risk of unfavorable weather conditions during construction. A torrential rainfall caused erosion immediately before completion of the golf course. Smith wishes to rescind the agreement based on the concept of frustration of purpose, claiming that it was unfair and unjust to require performance since the rainstorm was unforeseeably severe. Judgment for whom and why? ● *Pete Smith Co. v. El Dorado*, 529 S.W.2d 147 (Ark. 1976)

7. Parker signed a number of learn-to-dance contracts with Arthur Murray, Inc. Each contract was deemed noncancelable and stated that no refunds would be made. Parker subsequently suffered a permanent disability as a result of an automobile accident and was not physically able to continue the lessons. He is now seeking to have the contracts rescinded on grounds of impossibility of performance. Judgment for whom and why? ● *Parker v. Arthur Murray, Inc.*, 295 N.E.2d 487 (Ill. 1973)

8. Strauss, representing a number of season ticket holders, is suing Long Island Sports, Inc., for breach of conditions implied in fact in conjunction with their ticket contracts. Long Island Sports, Inc., as owners of the Long Island Nets basketball team, had traded one of the team's star players. Strauss held that the tickets had been purchased, in part, to see this star play. It was claimed that nonperformance of that player would be justified only if there had been a physical injury making it impossible for him to play. Long Island Sports argued that trading players was a "custom of the market place," an accepted practice among professional teams, and that the trade could have been anticipated by Strauss and the other ticket buyers. Judgment for whom and why? ● *Strauss v. Long Island Sports, Inc.*, 401 N.Y.S.2d 233 (1978)

9. American Trading and Production Company agreed to transport lubricating oil from a port in Texas to Bombay, India, for Shell International Marine, Ltd. Owing to war conditions at the time, the Suez Canal was closed to shipping and American Trading Company was forced to reroute the chartered ship, resulting in great additional expense and the loss of any expected profits from the venture. American Trading sought to rescind the agreement, giving the required route change and added expense a grounds for nonperformance. Judgment for whom and why? ● *American Trading and Prod. Co. v. Shell Int'l Marine, Ltd.*, 453 F.2d 939 (2d. Cir. 1973)

10. Walker was employed by the American Optical Company. Compensation to Walker, under the employment contract, included the payment of a bonus. Payment of employees' bonuses was conditioned by their continued employment and by their being employed at the time the bonuses were paid. Prior to the date set for payment of the promised bonus, Walker quit his job. He is now suing American Optical Company for payment of the bonus. The defendant argued that payment of the bonus was an obligation only if Walker had continued to work for them and had been an employee at the time set for bonus payments. Judgment for whom and why? ● *Walker v. American Optical Co.*, 509 P.2d 439 (Or. 1973)

Chapter 16   Breach of Contract and Remedies

Chapter 15 dealt with discharge of contracts through termination. This chapter deals with cancellation resulting from *breach of contract*. Whereas discharge by termination is brought about by mutual agreement, performance, or intervening legal restrictions, breach of contract evolves from negligent or intentionally wrong performance, expressed repudiation of contract obligations, or an abandonment of performance some time after performance has commenced. While discharge by termination would rarely result in the award of damages to either party, when there is a breach of contract the injured party has the right to seek damages.

16-1. Deliberate Wrongful Performance or Nonperformance

A breach of contract results if performance is not begun within a reasonable time of the date scheduled for performance. When time is of the essence, there is a breach if performance is not completed within the time limits agreed to by the parties. A breach also results if the performance has been negligent and unskillful. The services rendered must adhere to the standards of skill as determined by the custom of the marketplace. Wrongful performance or nonperformance discharges the other party from further obligation, permitting rescission and a claim for damages.

● Polsky, a tax specialist, contracted to prepare federal and state income tax returns for Central Garage. It was agreed that all completed forms and documents were to be delivered to Central five days before the date they were to be submitted to the respective tax collection agencies. Polsky delayed preparation of Central's returns, making Central liable for interest and fines levied for failure to submit the returns on the dates set by law. Through Polsky's nonperformance the contract between Polsky and Central Garage is discharged. Central Garage may now seek damages from Polsky on grounds of breach of a valid contract.

16-2. Repudiation and Anticipatory Breach

An *anticipatory breach* occurs when a party to an executory, bilateral contract either expresses or clearly implies an intention not to perform agreed-to obligations even before being required to act. The repudiation must be clear and absolute. It must also indicate a deliberate and complete refusal to perform according to the terms of the contract. Breaches of this kind are also called *constructive breaches*. Injured parties may seek damages by showing that in reliance on the contract they have materially changed their position. The injured party may commence suit at the time of the anticipatory breach or await the date agreed to for performance, thus giving the breaching party time to reconsider and begin performance. It is not possible to have an anticipatory breach in a unilateral contract, since in that case the parties are not actually bound to any agreement until performance begins.

● Plein hired Flowers as manager of an antique mart to be opened on August 1. Flowers moved from her home area and rented an apartment conveniently located near her new job. Two weeks before August 1, Plein informed Flowers that she would not be needed and canceled their contract. In reliance on the contract with Plein, Flowers had materially changed her position. She had obligated herself to an apartment lease and other expenses in anticipation of her new job. Flowers may either bring suit and seek damages immediately or await August 1, in hope that Plein will reconsider and hire her as promised.

16-3. Abandonment of Contract Obligations

Cessation of performance, once performance is begun, is treated as an *abandonment* of contracted obligations. Leaving or deserting one's obligations discharges the other party from any promises made and permits a suit for damages. A temporary or short-lived interruption of performance is not deemed to be abandonment. To constitute abandonment, the promissor must have inexcusably interrupted performance with the obvious intention of not returning to complete the obligations promised.

● McVeigh left a television set with Academy Electronics for needed repairs. Academy promised that the set would be ready for McVeigh in ten days. Technicians started work on McVeigh's set, but after dismantling the tuner and other parts of the set, they left it unfinished, started other jobs, and showed no intention of completing the McVeigh job. After three weeks had elapsed, McVeigh demanded the return of his unrepaired set. Academy Electronics had obviously abandoned performance on McVeigh's television. McVeigh was thereby discharged of any obligation to Academy Electronics. He has the right to receive back the set without the desired repairs and the right to seek damages resulting from Academy's breach.

16-4. Liability and Effect of Breach

A breach of contract gives the injured party a relief from any obligations to the contract and the right to seek damages related to the breach. A breach may arise through a failure of either conditions precedent or conditions subsequent, as expressed or implied in the parties' agreement. Thus, in the sale of a car there is an implied condition precedent (in fact, an implied warranty) that the buyer will receive a good and sufficient title to the car. A breach of such an implied condition releases the purchaser of any obligations on the contract.

A. Liability for Damages

One who breaches a contract obligation automatically discharges the other party of any further obligation and becomes liable for damages. The different types of damages related to a breach are detailed later in this chapter.

B. Attempts to Limit Liability

Contracts may contain conditions that expressly limit the liability of one or both parties. Depending on the intent of such conditions and their degree of fairness and justice, courts may either enforce the conditions or declare them to be void.

1. Effect of Hold Harmless Clauses. A contract may contain hold harmless conditions that will serve to relieve a party or parties should eventualities arise over which they have no control. It is common for contracts to include hold harmless clauses that cover nonperformance due to acts of God, fire, mob violence, strikes, walkouts, war, and numerous other acceptable exclusions that the courts have ordinarilly permitted. Hold harmless clauses must be fair, reasonable, and not so protective of a party's obligations as to remove all possibilities of recovery in the event of negligence or nonperformance.

● Eastern Fabricators, Inc., contracted to fabricate and deliver to a road construction project all the steel required for the building of a high-level bridge over the Delaware River. Eastern's contract, agreed to by both parties, excluded the right to seek damages against Eastern in the event of a railroad or truckers' strike that might interfere with delivery of the steel ordered. The exclusion would be deemed fair and reasonable should performance be interrupted for the reasons stated.

2. Effect of Exculpatory Clauses. An exculpatory clause is one that serves to excuse a contracting party of liability, fault, or guilt arising from the party's own negligence or failure to perform up to acceptable standards of work. Courts tend to disregard clauses of this kind when they favor only one of the parties. As previously pointed out, when part of an adhesion contract these clauses are often judged to be unconscionable as well as contrary to public policy and therefore void.

● Fulenwider accepted a job as yard electrician and lineperson for Marshallton Mills. The work was hazardous and required Fulenwider to maintain and repair high-voltage lines even in the severest weather. The contract of employment signed by Fulenwider contained a clause that exempted Marshallton Mills from any legal action whereby their employee might seek recovery for injuries received while carrying out assigned duties. Although Fulenwider questioned this exculpatory clause when hired, the contract was offered to him on a "take it or leave it" basis. Should Fulenwider be injured on the job, a court would doubtless void the clause as being unfair, unconscionable and part of an adhesion agreement.

16-5. Damages for Nonperformance and Breach

Damages is a term that describes money awarded to parties who have been victimized or have suffered injury to their legal rights by others. Damages are awarded a successful plaintiff in civil actions arising from the breach of a contract or from a tort. Damages are of different kinds, and the nature of a claim usually determines what type of damages will apply. In some states, by statute or judicial rule, juries are charged with two decisions: (1) which party is to be given favorable judgment, and (2) how much damages are to be awarded. Appeals to a higher court are allowed when the amount of damages awarded appears to be unreasonably low or excessively high.

● Linsky worked as chemist for Research Chemicals, doing routine testing under the direction of those involved in research projects. Although working under a written employment contract covering one year, Linsky was laid off after only four months without justifiable cause. His salary at the time was $18,000 a year. In an action for damages against the employer, Linsky was awarded damages of $30,000 by a sympathetic jury. Research Chemicals would be within its rights in appealing this judgment as being excessive in consideration of Linsky's type of employment and the salary agreed to under Linsky's contract.

A. Actual or Compensatory Damages

Actual damages are a sum of money equal to the real financial loss suffered by the injured party. Since they are intended to compensate the injured party, actual damages are also called *compensatory damages*. Thus, damages awarded for nondelivery of promised goods or services would be an amount equal to the difference between the price stated in the contract and what the promisee would have to pay elsewhere. Should the same goods or services be conveniently available elsewhere at the same or at a lower price, no actual loss could be claimed.

● Harvey agreed to build a house for Grover for $87,500. When performance was to commence, Harvey refused to go through with the contract, claiming that inflationary costs of labor and materials made it impossible for him to build the house for the agreed price without suffering great financial loss. Should Grover sue Harvey for breach of the contract, actual damages would be the difference between $87,500 and what Grover would be charged by other equally competent and reputable builders for the same house.

B. Incidental and Consequential Damages

Incidental damages and *consequential damages* are awarded for losses indirectly but closely attributable to a breach. They differ from actual damages in that the losses are not the direct result of a breach or tort, but might reasonably be expected to derive from a breach. To be liable for such damages, a party must have been aware that such losses might accrue from the breach.

● Kirkwood Rolling Mills was forced to shut down owing to a broken shaft that connected the plant's diesel engines with operating machinery related to the plant's manufacturing processes. Phillips Machine Company agreed to make needed repairs for Kirkwood for $28,000. After the contract was awarded to Phillips, Phillips abandoned the job without cause. In addition to actual damages related directly to the repairs, Phillips might also be charged with any incidental charges resulting from the failure to repair the main shaft as had been agreed. For example, he might be charged with any incidental losses incurred by Kirkwood owing to delays in reopening the plant.

Courts do not generally award incidental damage based on emotional distress, anxiety, embarrassment, or humiliation in a contract action, although they may do so in a tort action.

C. Punitive or Exemplary Damages

Punitive damages, also called *exemplary damages*, are damages awarded in excess of actual or incidental damages where it is shown that the wrongful party acted with malicious intent and willful disregard for the rights of the injured party. They are in the nature of court-ordered punishment rather than compensation for a known loss. They are usually awarded in cases involving torts rather than contracts. However, they have been awarded when a defendant in a contract action is found to be guilty of abusive and dishonest practices in consumer transactions that are unconscionable and contrary to the public good.

D. Nominal Damages

Nominal damages are only token damages awarded to parties who have experienced an injury to their legal rights but no actual loss. The common law usually awarded 6 cents to the successful plaintiff when no actual losses were shown. In today's practice the award is usually $1.

● Steinberg, on several occasions, warned Oberly, a neighbor, about trespassing over Steinberg's yard. As a last resort, Steinberg sued Oberly on the tort of trespass. Although successful in proving that a tort had been committed, Steinberg showed no actual loss, and he was awarded $1 in nominal damages against Oberly.

E. Present and Future Damages

Damages may be awarded for present injuries and for others that might reasonably be anticipated in the future. Thus, one charged with fraud in the sale of a building infested with termites may be held liable for all damages revealed at the time of the suit and for damages that would reasonably be forthcoming as the result of the undisclosed and concealed infestation of the property.

F. Speculative Damages

Speculative damages are damages computed on losses which have not actually been suffered and which cannot be proved; they are damages based entirely on an expectation of losses that might be suffered from a breach. They differ from future damages in that speculative damages are not founded on fact but only upon hope or expectation. Their basis is nothing more than a *calculated guess* as to the gains one might have gotten had there not been a breach. Courts do not allow speculative damages.

G. Damages Under *Quantum Meruit*

The doctrine of *quantum meruit* ("as much as one had earned") is important in the assessing of damages in cases founded on contracts implied in law, or quasi-contracts. Thus, where there has been no express or implied mutual agreement, a court will at times impose an obligation against a party who has been unjustly rewarded at the innocent expense of another. Damages awarded will be in an amount considered reasonable in return for the benefits one derived through the quasi-contract relationship.

● Hertz rented premises from Ficus for the purpose of opening a restaurant. While the lease was being negotiated, Hertz did extensive remodeling of the premises. Ficus had agreed to the changes being made. Hertz now contends that reimbursement should be made to him under the doctrine of *quantum meruit*, claiming that a quasi-contract existed between himself and Ficus. The court agreed and ruled that Hertz should be awarded damages equal to the cost of the renovations and improvements which had accrued to and so unjustly benefited Ficus.

16-6. Mitigation of Damages

The injured party has an obligation to do what is reasonably possible to *mitigate the damages,* that is, to keep damages to a minimum. One who has been wronged by another's breach must exercise reasonable precautions to prevent the damages from becoming unfairly and unreasonably burdensome to the other party.

● Cann performed certain construction services for the First National Bank of Akron. There were signs of caulking failure from Cann's work, first observed by First National in 1976. Within a year First National awarded a painting contractor the job of remedying these defects. Cann, in conjunction with some new work, offered to provide the necessary engineering services to repair the old, defective caulking. Cann's offer was refused. In an action by First National against Cann for damages caused by the faulty caulking, the court ruled that First National had failed to mitigate the mounting damages by refusing to accept Cann's offer to correct the defects.

Had Cann been permitted to provide the engineering services offered, the damages sought by First National Bank would have been considerably less than the bank claimed as its actual damage.

16-7. Liquidated Damages

Parties may stipulate as a condition of their contract the amount of damages that might be assessed if there is a breach. Damages agreed to in the initial contract are called *liquidated damages.* Liquidated damages must be realistic and in proportion to the losses that might be reasonably anticipated should there be a breach. When liquidated damages are found to be excessive or unfair, a court will disregard them and leave the matter of setting damages to the discretion of a jury.

A. Anticipatory Mutual Consent

Liquidated damages clauses are most often included in agreements where the parties anticipate great difficulty in determining the losses that might be suffered if there were a breach. By mutual consent the parties predetermine what damages might be applicable.

● American Construction Company contracted to design and construct an office building for the Marcus Corporation. During initial deliberations it was mutually agreed that the project be completed within a period of 210 days from the date performance was scheduled to begin. It was further agreed that if American Construction Company failed to complete the project in that time, $500 would be assessed the builder for each day beyond 210 days that the office building was not finished. The $500-a-day assessment represents liquidated damages.

B. Liquidated Damages or Penalty?

Courts will enforce liquidated damages only if they are reasonable and if they bear an approximate relationship to what would be considered the probable damages resulting from a breach. Liquidated damages are intended to be nothing more than reasonable compensation and should not be far greater than the actual damages suffered. They may not be punitive or exemplary. When the liquidated damages are construed to be unreasonable, punitive, or exemplary, they are looked upon as a penalty and may be declared void. Even though the parties or their attorneys may loosely refer to such provisions as "penalty clauses," the courts are unlikely to enforce them if they are of an actually punitive nature.

● Lingle applied for admission as a student at the Moss Technical Institute and received notice that her acceptance had been approved for the fall semester. As part of the admissions procedure Lingle was required to sign an agreement in which she would become liable to the school in the amount of a full year's tuition and all dormitory and meal costs should she fail to enroll for classes. The liquidated damage clause signed by Lingle would be considered excessive and unreasonable in consideration of any actual loss Moss Technical Institute might suffer should she fail to enroll.

16-8. Rescission Upon Breach

The breach of a contract gives the wronged party the right to rescind the agreement, treating the contract as discharged. An injured party who has already tendered partial performance or has paid money in support of the contract may bring an action to recover money paid or for payment for goods or services rendered. Rescission itself may constitute a breach of contract when the one claiming to having been wronged failed to show that a breach in fact existed.

16-9. Remedies Through Equity

Generally, a court of equity will entertain actions only in situations where it is conclusively known that an award of a money judgment from a court of law would not provide fair and just satisfaction to the complainant. Equity is founded on principles of fairness and justice rather than the dictates of common law, statutes, and judicial decision.

A. When Equitable Relief Is Granted

Equitable relief as a solution to contract disputes is granted only when the following conditions are met:

○ There is proof of an existing contract.
○ There is no satisfactory remedy available at law.
○ Specific performance will not inflict an unfair or unjust hardship on the other contracting party.
○ The contract in dispute is legal in nature.

● Padley and Home Builders, Inc., entered into a written agreement whereby Home Builders contracted to sell Padley a house and lot for $125,000. When time arrived for settlement, Home Builders repudiated its agreement and refused to make the sale, tendering back to Padley a deposit of $2,500 which was refused. Padley sought relief through a petition to the state court of equity.

The Padley case presents all requisites of equity for acceptance of the contract dispute for decision. The parties had entered into a legal agreement, in writing as specified by the statute of frauds. Padley's interest was in purchasing and getting the deed to the house, not in money damages that could have been obtained in an action at law. Enforcement of the agreement would not inflict any unfair or unjust hardship upon Home Builders. And there is no question as to the legality of their agreement.

B. Decrees of Specific Performance

A *decree of specific performance* is a command from a court of equity that a promissor execute an agreement under an enforceable contract. A decree of specific performance differs from a judgment at law in that it calls for the party to perform rather than to pay damages. Specific performance is almost always granted the injured party in disputes related to the promised sale and transfer of title to real estate, since each piece of real estate is unique.

● Duane Sales, Inc., secured an option to purchase a certain building being offered by Carmel. The option came into dispute when Carmel refused to go through with the sale after the purchase price was tendered by Duane Sales. The court issued a decree of specific performance. Since each parcel of real estate is different and distinct from all others, money damages would not provide a satisfactory remedy to Duane Sales, Inc., whose contractual intent was to secure ownership of the building.

1. Contracts for Personal Property. Contracts for the sale of personal property will be enforced through a decree of specific performance only when the subject matter is unique, for example, when it has artistic, sentimental, or historical value or other qualities not available elsewhere. Obviously, an award of money damages in any of those situations would not provide the complainant with satisfaction. By contrast, specific performance would not be decreed if a contract for delivery of a new automobile of a common model and design had been breached. The same model and design would be available to the victim of a breach elsewhere. On the other hand, an agreement to sell a car that had been previously owned and driven by a famous person would be of unique value and could be enforced through specific performance.

2. Contracts for Personal Services. Contracts for personal services are rarely enforced through specific performance. Demanding that an unwilling party perform promised personal services would be contrary to the Thirteenth Amendment to the U.S. Constitution, which prohibits human servitude. A remedy in cases of this kind, however, may be found through injunctive relief.

C. Injunctive Relief

An *injunction* is an order issued by a court of equity directing that a party do or refrain from doing something. An injunction may be either *temporary* or *permanent*. A temporary injunction is issued as a means of delaying further activity in any contested matter until the court is able to determine whether a permanent injunction should be entered or the injunction removed entirely. One who disobeys an injunction does so under penalty of contempt of court.

1. Mandatory Injunctions. A *mandatory injunction* is a command from a court of equity that requires a party to perform an obligation arising from a statute, common law, or a contract. Mandatory injunctions may not be decreed against those who breach promises to perform personal services. To do so would be impractical and would defy the Thirteenth Amendment of the U.S. Constitution. Mandatory injunctions are at times used to enforce completion of other types of agreements, for example to pressure property owners into carrying out contract obligations to maintain buildings or correct hazardous conditions associated with real property, and the like.

● Layton and Williams, real estate developers, erected all the steel frame required for a new office building in Stanton Acres Center. Financial difficulties interfered with completing the building, and it presented a hazard to children and others who trespassed onto the property. A mandatory injunction was decreed, commanding Layton and Williams to either finish the building as their building permit allowed them to do or remove the unfinished structure from the land.

2. Restraining Injunctions. A *restraining injunction* is a mandate from a court of equity commanding a party to cease and desist from carrying out or continuing some specified act. Injunctions of this kind may be used to restrict breaching parties from performing personal services for others which they have failed to perform for the victim of a breach. Thus, whereas a decree of specific performance or a mandatory injunction may not be used to demand performance of personal services, a restraining injunction can be used to *prevent* a party from performing certain professional or personal services for others.

Understanding Legal Terms

Define, identify, or explain each of the following terms:

abandonment	incidental damages	nominal damages	specific performance
anticipatory breach	liquidated damages	punitive damages	temporary
breach of contract	mandatory	restraining	injunction
compensatory	injunction	injunction	
damages	mitigation of		
constructive breach	damages		

Questions for Review and Discussion

1. In what three ways does a breach of contract usually evolve?

2. When may the victim of an anticipatory breach commence legal action against the other party?

3. Under what circumstances may a party declare a breach of contract under the concept of abandonment?

4. What test is used to determine the validity of a hold harmless clause?

5. How do exculpatory clauses differ from hold harmless clauses? Give an example of each.

6. What proof is required of a party claiming punitive damages of one who has breached a contract or committed a tort?

7. Under what circumstances will a court award nominal damages?

8. How is the principle of mitigation of damages applied in the event of a breach?

9. Under what condition does a party seek relief from a court of equity rather than a court of law?

10. When will a court of equity decree a temporary injunction rather than a permanent injunction?

Analyzing Cases

1. Hedges Manufacturing Company signed a lease for the rental of a building owned by Mrs. Geschke. The lease contained a clause that allowed the landlord to relet the premises in case the tenant abandoned the lease. Soon after occupying the building, Hedges experienced serious financial reverses and informed Mrs. Geschke that the firm would have to give up the lease and vacate the building. Geschke made no attempt to find a new tenant and on occasion grossly discouraged those who would have rented the premises. She is now suing, claiming that it was impossible to find new tenants. Hedges argued, however, that it is freed from liability on its lease because Geshke made no attempt to relet the building and thereby mitigate the damages. Judgment for whom and why? ● *Chicago Title and Trust Co. v. Hedges Mfg. Co.*, 414 N.E.2d 232 (Ill. App. 1980)

2. Simon, landlord of an apartment house, leased apartments to tenants who then occupied all apartments in the building. The leases contained the standard language making tenants responsible for certain upkeep and maintenance of their own apartments. Subsequently, Simon fired both the building superintendent and the janitor and maintenance man. As a result, from time to time there was no heat, hot water, or elevator service. Routine maintenance was almost nonexistent, and all the hall and lobby furniture was removed. The tenants are now suing for breach of their lease contracts and are seeking punitive damages from Simon. Simon defended that it was the tenants' obligation to look after maintenance. Judgment for whom and why? Is the court likely to award punitive damages to the tenants? ● *111 East 88th Street Partners v. Simon*, 434 N.Y.S.2d 886 (1980)

3. Fogleman was hired by Peruvian Associates and for no reason was subsequently fired. Fogleman is now suing for breach of contract, seeking actual damages. He is also claiming incidental damages for emotional stress, anxiety, embarrassment, and humiliation. Judgment for whom and why? ● *Fogleman v. Peruvian Assocs.*, 622 P.2d 63 (Ariz. App. 1980)

4. Ralston Purina Company, producers and marketers of cat food, entered into a contract with Custom Canners to can Purina's products. After a time it was discovered, through customer complaints, that Custom had been deliberately short-weighting the cans. Purina is now seeking damages. What type(s) of damages would Purina be entitled to if successful in this case? ● *Ralston Purina Co. v. Custom Canners, Inc.*, 500 F. Supp. 218 (U.S. Dist. Ct., N.D. Ga. 1980)

5. Duden and Pontchartrain State Bank entered into financing arrangements in which Duden was to build certain condominiums. Even with the bank's help there was a question as to whether the condominiums could be built and, if they could, how profitable the venture would be. The bank subsequently repudiated its agreement with Duden. Duden is suing for the lost profits anticipated had the condominiums been built. Judgment for whom and why? ● *Pontchartrain State Bank v. Duden*, 503 F. Supp. 764 (U.S. Dist. Ct., E.D. La. 1980)

6. Hernandez entered into a contract with Leive in which Leive agreed to sell his house to Hernandez. Leive later, without any reason, refused to go through with the sale, and Hernandez is suing for specific performance. Hernandez is asking that the court award a decree giving him the house and damages for attorney's fees due to the breach. Judgment for whom and why? ● *Hernandez v. Leive*, 391 So.2d 292 (Fla. App. 1980)

7. Smith, in violation of deed restrictions, erected a 40-foot CB antenna on his property. The community objected to the antenna and demanded that it be removed. A decision

now must be made whether to sue Smith for breach of the contract restrictions contained in the deed to his property or seek an injunction against permitting the antenna to remain. Which would better serve the desire of those living in Smith's community? Why? ● *Meierhenry v. Smith,* 302 N.W.2d 365 (Neb. 1981)

8. Martin Bloom Associates, Inc., as part of its contract with Manzie, assured Manzie that financing would be easily obtainable on the basis of its past architectural work and reputation. Manzie was thereafter denied financing owing to the absence of feasibility studies and the inadequate drawings supplied by Bloom Associates. Martin Bloom Associates is now suing for payment for work already completed. Manzie's defense is that Martin Bloom was the party that actually breached the contract. Judgment for whom and why? ● *Martin Bloom Assocs., Inc. v. Manzie,* 389 F. Supp. 848 (U.S. Dist. Ct., D. Nev. 1975)

9. Popik was employed by Iroquois Industries Corporation. As part of the employment contract, Popik promised not to compete with Iroquois after leaving Iroquois's employment. Popik disregarded his convenant, going to work for a competing firm after finishing the Iroquois contract. Iroquois is now seeking a restraining injunction against Popik, petitioning the court to bar Popik from continuing his employment with the competing firm. Is Iroquois Industries Corporation likely to get the relief sought? Why? ● *Iroquois Indus. Corp. v. Popik,* 415 N.E.2d 4 (Ill. App. 1980)

10. Christy entered into a written contract whereby Pilkinton, the owner of an apartment house, agreed to sell the building to Christy for $30,000. At the time scheduled for settlement Pilkinton tendered to Christy a full and sufficient deed to the property. Christy was not able to secure the money needed for purchase and repudiated the agreement. Pilkinton is now suing for breach of contract. Christy presented evidence that showed that the income from his business had fallen to a point that made it impossible for him to get the needed funds. Pilkinton argued that the impossibility claimed by Christy was a foreseeable one and does not therefore excuse him from performance. Judgment for whom and why? ● *Christy v. Pilkinton,* 273 S.W.2d 553 (Ark. 1954)

Part 3

Case Briefs

Barnes v. Treece,
549 P.2d 1152 (Wash. 1976)

Treece was vice president of a corporation engaged in the manufacture and sale of punchboards (boards with holes containing slips; the slips, punched out by players, entitle them to various prizes). On one occasion, Treece made the announcement that he would pay $100,000 to anyone who could prove that any of the firms's punchboards were fraudulent, crooked, or dishonest. Barnes later read the offer, discovered punchboards that had been rigged, delivered them to Treece, and demanded the promised $100,000. Treece refused to pay the $100,000 promised, and this suit was brought on that alleged breach of contract.

Plaintiff's Position: Barnes contended that Treece had made a unilateral offer and that it had been accepted, acted upon, and performed in good faith. Barnes argued that he had every reason to believe that Treece's offer was seriously intended as made and communicated and that a contractual relationship did develop at the time he delivered the rigged boards to Treece.

Defendant's Position: Treece argued that the alleged offer of $100,000 was not seriously intended, that it was made as a joke, in jest, and that at no time was there an intention of creating a contract that would obligate him to the payment of the $100,000 now sought.

Legal Issue: When an offer is made, will the subjective or objective test of the intent of the offeror be accepted in determining if an offer is valid in terms of serious intent?

Court Decision: The objective test of the intent of the offeror will be accepted. Judgment for Barnes, plaintiff.

Court Reasoning: The court held that sufficient grounds existed to determine formation of a valid contract. The court concluded that an offer made in a manner that the offeree would perceive to be serious, and without any indication as to jest or joking, should be considered as having been seriously made. Even though the offeror claims no serious intent, there was no evidence of that fact at the time the offer was made, and the plaintiff had every reason to believe that the defendant made the offer with no reservations as to an intention to enter a binding agreement.

Manasquan Savings and Loan Assoc.
v. Mayer,
236 A.2d 407 (N.J. 1967)

Mayer joined with her husband in borrowing $22,000 from the Manasquan Savings and Loan Association. The money was to be used for building a house, and the loan was secured by a mortgage on the land and the new house. Mayer was nineteen, a minor, when she signed the loan agreement and supporting documents. After the house was built, Mayer and her husband separated, abandoned the property, and defaulted on the mortgage payments. The plaintiff foreclosed the mortgage, and Mayer sought to be relieved of all her obligations on grounds that she was a minor at the time the loan agreement was signed by her. She gave up all rights to the property but sought the return of all money that she had personally contributed toward repayment of the mortgage loan. The plaintiff, as evidence of their agreement, introduced the loan documents which, in three separate places contained affadavits signed by the defendant in which she attested to the fact that she had reached her majority at the time of signing the documents.

Plaintiff's Position: The plaintiff contended

that in approving the $22,000 loan it rightfully relied on Mayer's written representations in which she stated that she had reached her majority and that the lender had the right to reasonably depend on the defendant's representations. The lender further argued that Mayer's misrepresentation of her age denied her of any rights she may have otherwise had in demanding the return of money she had contributed toward the payment of the mortgage debt.

Defendant's Position: Mayer relied entirely on the defense of incompetency, that she was a minor when signing the agreement, and that she had the right to void her obligations thereto. She contended that she had willingly given up all her rights, if any, in the mortgaged property, in anticipation of being able to recover money personally paid the plaintiff.

Legal Issue: May a minor void an agreement in which the minor has knowingly misrepresented his or her age in the documents associated with a written contract? Does such an intentional misrepresentation, relied on by a lender, remove the minor's usual right to rescind a contract?

Court Decision: Mayer may not void the agreement. In circumstances where a minor knowingly misrepresents his or her age, the usual right to rescind a contract may not apply. Judgment for the plaintiff, Manasquan Savings and Loan Association

Court Reasoning: The court held that the plaintiff's position would be unreasonably eroded if it were required to reimburse Mayer for money contributed toward the mortgage payments. The Manasquan Savings and Loan Association had a right to be made whole (meaning it should suffer no loss

through this forfeited mortgage). The court held that the only possibility of the defendant being paid any money would be in the event that the foreclosure sale brought in an amount sufficient to repay the mortgage, accrued interest, and other expenses, and leave a surplus above the $22,000 amount borrowed that could be divided between Mayer and her husband.

Meyer v. Benko
55 Cal. App. 3d 937 (1976)
Benko advertised a property for sale at a price of $24,950. In an effort to conclude a possible sale, he agreed to accept Mayer's offer of $23,500. Meyer gave him a deposit, and Benko gave Meyer a receipt for the deposit. Then Benko refused to go through with the contract, stating that the receipt for the deposit was not a written contract as required by the statute of frauds and that the price agreed upon was not adequate. Meyer brought this action in equity for specific performance. The lower court would not issue a decree of specific performance, and this appeal was made.

Appellant's Position: Meyer contended that the seller's receipt contained the information outlining the obligations of seller and buyer and was signed by Benko, who is being charged with this breach. The statute of frauds asks for nothing more. Meyer held that Benko was anxious to sell the property and had reduced the price in order to bring about the sale. He argued that the seller was not coerced into selling the property but had entered into an agreement that was fair and equitable to both parties.

Appellee's Position: Benko contended that receipt, although containing detailed information and his signature, did not result in a written contract. He held that the price agreed upon ($23,500) was inadequate and that the property was actually worth between $29,000 and $30,000. The appellee argued that on these two grounds the alleged contract should be rescinded.

Legal Issue: Two issues were involved in this appeal: (1) Did the receipt, signed by Benko, provide the necessary written contract as required by the statute of frauds? (2) Does a seller's complaint and defense of inadequacy of consideration give grounds for rescission of an existing contract?

Court Decision: On the first issue the court held that the deposit receipt, with information contained and signature of seller in place, was sufficient to constitute a written contract between the parties. As to the second issue, the court held that the price offered by Meyer and accepted by Benko need not be equal to what might be the full value of property being sold. The decision of the lower court was therefore reversed and specific performance was decreed, as requested by Meyer.

Court Reasoning: The court reasoned that a receipt was sufficient to meet the requirements of the statute of frauds. Further, the court said that the price of $23,500 was fair and reasonable, all facts being considered. Benko made a free choice in accepting Meyer's offer, in that Benko had an immediate desire to sell the property and was willing to accept the reasonable offer made by the appellant, Meyer.

Parker
v. Twentieth Century Fox Film Corp.,
474 P.2d 689 (Cal. 1970)
On August 6, 1965, Shirley MacLaine

Parker agreed, in a written contract with Twentieth Century Fox Film Corporation, to play the leading female role in a musical, *Bloomer Girl*. Parker was to be paid $750,000, agreeing to work for fourteen weeks, over which time the film was to be produced in Los Angeles. Work was scheduled to commence on May 23, 1966. A letter delivered to Parker, dated April 4, 1966, informed Parker of Fox Films' decision to cancel the filming of *Bloomer Girl*. Fox Film informed Parker that it would "comply with our obligation" under the written contract. As a substitution, Fox Film offered Parker the lead part in another film, *Big Country*. Unlike *Bloomer Girl*, the substitute film was a dramatic production, not a musical that would have relied on Parker's special abilities and talents in singing and dancing. Further, *Big Country* was to be filmed in Australia rather than Los Angeles. Parker refused to accept Fox Film's offer of the lead in *Big Country*. Action was brought, seeking damages of $750,000, as guaranteed under Parker's original contract. The lower court gave judgment to Parker. Fox Film appealed the lower court's decision.

Appellant's Position: Fox Film offered no denial of its breach of the contract to produce *Bloomer Girl*. The appellant protested that Parker made no effort to mitigate damages arising from the breach. The opportunity to mitigate was afforded Parker through the proposal that she play the lead in *Big Country*, which she refused. The film studio contended that any judgment against it should be reduced by the amount she would have received had she accepted the role offered in *Big Country*. Fox Film offered no evidence or argument showing Parker's failure to procure other employment as a means of mitigating damages. This appeal was based entirely on Parker's refusal to mitigate by refusing to accept the lead in *Big Country*.

Appellee's Position: Shirley MacLaine Parker argued that the obligation to mitigate damages did not require her to accept employment of an inferior or different kind than her abilities and skills had prepared her for. The original film was a musical, the type of production for which she was trained and had established a reputation. *Big Country* was a dramatic production, inferior to other films to which she had been a part and demanding a type of performance to which she was not accustomed and had not been trained. Further, *Bloomer Girl* was to have been filmed in Los Angeles, whereas *Big Country* was scheduled to be produced in Australia, which would have required her to have absented herself from the Los Angeles film center. Parker contended that she was under no obligation to accept employment so different, and unrelated to areas of dancing and singing in which she was outstanding in her profession.

Legal Issue: Must a party accept alternative employment outside the scope of his or her professional skills and talents in order to fulfill an obligation to mitigate damages?

Court Decision: No. The court held that the lead in *Big Country* was an inferior role to that which Shirley MacLaine Parker had contracted for in *Bloomer Girl*. The Supreme Court of California thus affirmed the lower court decision and judgment awarding Shirley MacLaine Parker $750,000 damages.

Court Reasoning: The court noted that Shirley MacLaine Parker's special training, skills, and talents were in musical productions, whereas the role offered her in the substitute film called for the talents of a dramatic actress. Further, the demand that she relocate in Australia for many weeks, removing her from Los Angeles, imposed additional burdens which Parker had no obligation to accept. Had she been offered the lead in another film that called for her to use her special talents, training, and experience, her obligations under the doctrine of mitigation would have been different. However, Fox Film based its appeal solely on its offer of a role in *Big Country,* and therefore the court denied any claim that Parker had not observed the legal obligations to mitigate the $750,000 damages already awarded.

Part 4   Personal Property and Bailments

Chapter 17   Personal Property

The term *property* is broadly interpreted. It includes everything that one might own—for example, a car, a shirt, a building, and the land on which a building is built. There are other types of property that one cannot see, such as a patent for an invention, a franchise to sell something, and the goodwill of a brand name. Property is more than ownership. It includes the *legal right* to use and enjoy, to dispose of, and to bestow property in the event of death.

The Fifth and Fourteenth Amendments to the U.S. Constitution protect the individual's right to life, liberty, and property.

Certain physical things, such as air, light, and running water, because of their very nature, cannot be owned and are not the subject of personal property. Likewise, wild animals, birds, and fish, in their natural state, cannot be owned by private individuals unless they are brought under their control.

17-1. Real and Personal Property Distinguished

All property (things and rights) is generally divided into two classes: personal property and real property. The terms *personalty* and *realty* may also be used.

Personal property includes all property that is movable. Known also as *chattels,* personal property embraces such items as automobiles, furniture, animals, clothing, aircraft, and boats. Personal property which may be seen or touched and which may be given an actual physical description is known as *tangible personal property.*

Spaneas purchased the Valley Hardware Store from Fingold. The purchase included the building, the store inventory, the display cases and shelves, a cash register, a built-in air-conditioner, and miscellaneous store equipment. Spaneas also bought the accounts receivables that were owed to Fingold and a franchise to sell a particular line of merchandise. The store inventory, display cases, cash register, and miscellaneous store equipment were tangible personal property.

On the other hand, certain other types of property are valued for the *rights* they assure their owners. Thus a document of title guarantees the right of ownership. The document is not valued for itself, but for what it represents. Such

222

rights are defined as *intangible property*. Stock certificates, the deed to a house, a bond and mortgage, and even a dollar bill are examples of intangible personal property. The value of the dollar bill is not the dollar itself, but what it might buy for the owner in the marketplace. Another legal term that describes this type of personal property is *chose in action*. A chose in action is a personal right not reduced into possession, but recoverable by a suit at law. In addition to the items mentioned above, choses in action include money due on a note or contract, damages due for breach of contract or for tort, and insurance policies.

Such things as patents, copyrights, and trademarks are other examples of intangible personal property. The accounts receivables and the franchise that Spaneas purchased from Fingold in the above example are also considered intangible personal property.

Real property embraces all land extending downward to the center of the earth and items intended to be permanent improvements to the land. Houses, buildings, trees, shrubbery, and permanent fixtures installed in houses and buildings are real property. Also included in real property is a right-of-way over someone else's property and the air space over land. Real property is explained in depth in Chapter 36.

A. Things Severed From Real Property

Real property becomes personal property when separated from land or from houses or other buildings. When a tree is cut down, it becomes personal property. Fruit harvested from trees loses its identity as real property when detached from the tree and placed in a waiting basket.

● Woodworth paid real property taxes on a house and small barn built on a 5-acre tract of land. The barn was of no further use to Woodworth, and it was taken down. Having reverted to personal property, the materials were sold to a firm that dealt in used building materials. Woodworth's real property taxes would be reduced, reflecting the reduction in the value of the remaining real property.

B. Things Added to Real Property

Personal property becomes real property when attached to or made a permanent part of land or buildings. Bricks, lumber, concrete, and other building materials are personal property when delivered to a building site. When these materials are combined with others in the creation of a permanent building, they become real property.

C. Fixtures

Chattels lose their identity as personal property when attached to the real property with the apparent intent that they are not to be detached at some later time and removed. When so attached, chattels become *fixtures* and are considered part of the real property, or realty. Arguments often arise between landlords and tenants about the rightful ownership of such items at the end of the tenant's lease. The following questions are useful in determining whether a chattel is personal property belonging to the tenant or is real property subject to the landlord's demand of ownership.

○ Has there been a *temporary* or *permanent* installation of the chattel?
○ Has the chattel been *adapted* to the intended use of the real property?

○ What was the apparent *intent* of the party at the time of affixing the chattel to the real property?

● Franklin complained to her landlord that the kitchen in her apartment needed to be modernized. The landlord gave her permission to improve the kitchen as long as it could be done without cost to him. Franklin installed modern cabinets, a built-in stove, and an under-the-counter dishwasher. She also bought a new refrigerator. Even though Franklin paid for them, the cabinets, stove, and dishwasher would be considered fixtures and would belong to the landlord. The refrigerator, which was not built in, would remain the personal property of the tenant.

Trade fixtures are those items of personal property brought upon the land by the tenant which are necessary to carry on the trade or business to which the land will be devoted. Contrary to the general rule, trade fixtures remain the personal property of the tenant or occupier of the land and are removable at the expiration of the term of occupancy.

17-2. Acquiring Title to Personal Property

Title (ownership) of personal property may be acquired in many different ways. Sales agreements, which are governed under special rules of the UCC, will be examined in greater depth in Chapter 20. Although sales agreements are the most common means of transferring title to personal property, there are other methods, as described below.

A. Finding Personal Property

A finder does not get title to another's lost property. An effort must be made to discover the identity of the real owner. State laws provide, however, that if a reasonable effort is made to locate the owner, without success, the finder may claim ownership of the goods. Different states have different time limits beyond which the finder will be recognized as the actual owner.

A finder of personal property must also exercise reasonable care in handling, using, and preserving the property. The rules governing the use of reasonable care by a finder of lost property are discussed in detail in Chapter 18.

1. Misplaced Property. There is an exception to the rule that the finder holds the property until the true owner can be found. If the lost property is found on the counter of a store, on a table in a restaurant or hotel, on a chair in a washroom, or in some similar public or semipublic place, it is considered not to be *lost* but to have been *misplaced*. It is reasonable to suppose that the owner will remember leaving it there and return for it. For this reason, the finder may not keep possession of the article but must leave it with the proprietor or manager to hold for the owner. If the property is found on the floor or in the corridor or any other place that would indicate that it was not placed there intentionally, the finder may retain possession of the article. In this case, it is not likely that the owner would recall where it was lost.

● Dyjak, a customer, found a purse on a small shelf in a fitting room of the Village Dress Shop. She gave the purse to the owner of the store, but later, when she learned that it had not been claimed, she sued the store for its return.

Dyjak could not regain possession of the purse. It was found in an area used

Part 4:
Personal
Property
and
Bailments

224

only by customers of the shop. The proprietor owed his customers a duty of guarding any property that was left there. He was therefore entitled to retain possession of the purse.

2. Responsibility of Finder. The finder of lost property has a legal responsibility, usually fixed by statute, to make an effort to learn the identity of the owner and return the property to that person. Advertising the property in a general-circulation newspaper is usually evidence of the finder's honest effort to locate the owner. Statutes in many states provide that, if the finder of lost property has made an effort to locate the owner and has not been successful within a period specified by law, the property then belongs to the finder.

● While on a hike through a wooded area, Blotner kicked a cardboard box which broke open and disclosed a bundle of currency of various denominations. Blotner picked up the box, examined its contents, and discovered a bank deposit slip made out in the name of a local merchant. As soon as he took possession of the box containing the currency, the finder accepted the legal responsibility of taking care of the money and returning it to its rightful owner.

Suppose the bank deposit slip had not been in the box and Blotner was unsuccessful in an attempt to find the rightful owner. After making a sincere effort to locate the real owner, and after a period of time set by statute, Blotner would become the owner of this find.

3. Escheat of Lost and Abandoned Property. When property is found and turned over to officials of a state, without any claim registered by the finder, the property becomes the property of the state after a period of time set by statute. The same rule applies to bank deposits and other claims which have been abandoned by persons in whose names such claims were registered. In these latter instances, a period of up to twenty years is usually required to establish the right of the state to take title. When property reverts to the state, it is said to *escheat*.

4. Offer of Reward. Finders of lost property are entitled to any reward offered if they have not surrendered possession of the property before learning of the reward. A finder who learns about a reward after returning a lost article cannot legally enforce payment of the reward, having returned the article without expecting any. But a finder who learns about a reward before returning the property need not surrender possession until the reward is paid. If a reward has not been offered, the finder is entitled to be reimbursed for any expenses incurred in connection with the possession of the property.

B. Gifts

Title may be transferred by a gift. There are three requirements for a gift to be completed: (1) the *donor* (the one giving the gift) must intend to make a gift, (2) the gift must be delivered to the *donee* (the one receiving it), and (3) the donee must accept the gift. Once all three requirements are met, the gift cannot be taken back by the donor. It is known as an absolute gift, or *gift inter vivos* (gift between the living).

1. Gifts *in Causa Mortis*. A gift given during one's lifetime, in contemplation of death from a known cause, is a *gift in causa mortis*. Gifts *in causa mortis* are conditional. The donor may reclaim the property if death does not come as expected or is caused by circumstances other than those feared.

● Rossano was seriously ill following an abdominal operation. Realizing that death might be near, Rossano signed over a savings account to Hall, giving Hall the savings book with necessary notations of assignment. Rossano did die three weeks later, not because of the surgery but because of pneumonia. Rossano's executor may declare the gift *in causa mortis* void and demand the return of Rossano's savings for benefit of the estate.

2. Federal Gift Tax. As part of the federal estate tax, which imposes a tax on the estates of people whose gross estate exceeds $225,000 (gradually increasing to $600,000 by 1987), the federal government levies a tax on the sum total of gifts made during one's lifetime. This is known as the *federal gift tax*. The value of all taxable gifts made during the decedent's lifetime is added to the value of the decedent's property at the time of death and, along with life insurance, is included in the taxable gross estate. Not included in the gift tax are gifts up to $10,000 in value made to each donee per calendar year. This gift tax exclusion per donee per calendar year was increased from $3,000 to $10,000 by the Economic Recovery Act of 1981.

● A donor who has two married children and four grandchildren can give away as much as $80,000 a year without being subject to the federal gift tax. This may be done by giving $10,000 each to the two children, their spouses, and the four grandchildren.

Gifts to charitable institutions are exempt from the tax, as are gifts to a donor's spouse. In addition, everyone is entitled to a unified tax credit which may be applied against both estate and gift taxes to help exempt or shield property transfers from taxation. Since a tax credit is a direct reduction of taxes due, it is considerably more beneficial than a tax deduction. For example, everyone is entitled to a unified tax credit of $62,800 beginning in 1982; this is actually the equivalent of $225,000 being exempted from estate and gift taxation. Table 17-1 shows how the increased credit will be phased in over the six-year period from 1982 to 1987 and the corresponding exemption equivalents.

Table 17-1. Phase-In of Unified Gift and Estate Tax Credit

Year	Unified Credit	Exemption Equivalent
1982	$ 62,800	$225,000
1983	79,300	$275,000
1984	96,300	$325,000
1985	121,800	$400,000
1986	155,800	$500,000
1987 and after	192,800	$600,000

Part 4:
Personal
Property
and
Bailments

226

3. **Uniform Gifts to Minors Act.** Problems arise when gifts are given to minors. Parents or guardians sometimes use such gifts for unauthorized purposes. Donors sometimes revoke gifts to minors. The Internal Revenue Service may not recognize a gift to a minor. Instead, it may tax the income from the gift to the donor, who is usually taxed at a higher tax rate than the minor.

As of 1977, all states in the United States except Georgia and Louisiana had adopted the Uniform Gifts to Minors Act or an amended version of it.

The purposes of the act are to make it easier to make gifts to minors, to standardize the procedure, and to satisfy the provisions of the Internal Revenue Code relating to the annual gift tax exclusion of $10,000 and have the income from the gift taxable to the minor.

● Planchard placed $50,000 in a joint certificate of deposit with his ten-year-old daughter, Danielle. He claimed that the money was a gift to his daughter and that the interest from the certificate should be taxable to her rather than to him. The Internal Revenue Service required Planchard to declare the interest from the joint certificate of deposit on his tax return as part of his gross income. Planchard would have avoided taxation by following the provisions of the Uniform Gifts to Minors Act.

C. Inheritance

Title to personal property may be transferred by a will or by law when the deceased dies without a will. Title to personal property passes, on the owner's death, to the personal representative of the estate. Later, it is distributed to the heirs. This is discussed in detail in Chapter 38.

D. Court Judgment

A court may award title to goods owned by one against whom there is an unpaid judgment on file. Through a court order, a debtor's goods may be sold to satisfy such judgments. A court of equity may issue a decree of specific performance ordering a party to transfer title to goods which have been sold but to which the seller has denied the buyer both title and possession.

● Lee bought an eighteenth-century blanket chest from Olde Towne Shop. Payment was to be made in thirty days, as permitted under Lee's charge account. When Lee returned to get the chest, Olde Towne's owner rescinded the sale. Lee may seek a decree for specific performance, requiring the owner to give up title and possession of the chest as agreed to in the contract.

E. Original Production

Ownership may derive from one's efforts in writing a book, painting a picture, inventing a new gadget, and the like. The one who creates an original product or work may have title to it protected under the copyright, patent, or trademark laws. These laws are explained later in this chapter.

F. Accession

The offspring of animals, the proliferation of growing plants, and so on are owned by the person who has title to parent animals or plants. The owner of goods also takes title to their *accessions*—i.e., any additions to or modification of presently owned goods.

G. Confusion of Goods

Negligent or intentional *confusion* (mixing together) of goods with goods belonging to another may transfer title. Making it impossible to separate and identify the property belonging to each gives the innocent party title to the combined mass of goods.

● Union Stamp and Coin Company loaned coins to Szot. The coins were then mixed with other coins owned by Szot. It was impossible to then determine which were Szot's coins and which belonged to Union Stamp and Coin.

Unless the coins could be separated according to their real owners, Union Stamp and Coin would be permitted to claim all the coins.

17-3. Ownership of Goods

A. Title to Stolen Goods

Although a presumption of title to goods usually follows possession of them, it is possible for a person to have possession of goods without having title, just as it is possible for a person to have title without having possession. Thus, a thief acquires no title to goods that are stolen and, therefore, cannot convey a good title. The true owner never relinquished title to the goods, and even an innocent purchaser, who acquired the goods in good faith and for value, would be obliged to return the goods to the owner. Title to stolen goods never left the true owner, and possession can always be regained by that owner if the goods can be found, no matter in whose possession they may be at the time.

● Dooling purchased a typewriter from Jarvis, paying a fair price for it. Later, Tyron demanded that Dooling return the typewriter to him, claiming that Jarvis had stolen the machine from him. Tyron proved ownership by a bill of sale.

It was held that Dooling must return the typewriter to Tyron. Dooling can acquire no better title than Jarvis had. Jarvis could not convey title to Dooling, for he had no title himself.

B. Single or Multiple Title

Title may be transferred to one or more new owners. Rights and obligations, whether of one or several persons, depend on the definition of the type of ownership accepted. Many of the following general classifications of single or multiple ownership apply to real property as well as personal property. (Real property ownership will be discussed in Part 9 of this book.)

1. Severalty Ownership. Ownership by one person alone is known as *severalty ownership*. Title is not shared with any other person.

2. Joint Tenancy. When two or more persons own personal property as joint tenants, they each own an equal share, and the death of one joint owner (tenant) transfers that individual's interest to the surviving joint tenant(s). This is known as a *joint tenancy*. Each individual has an *undivided interest* in the entire chattel, or property. In addition, all joint owners must obtain title at the same time.

Part 4:
Personal
Property
and
Bailments

228

● Jevins, Cantwell, and Swift were members of a flying club, and together they bought a Piper Comanche. Title to the aircraft was put in all three names as joint owners. Neither one, then, had complete ownership of any specific part of the aircraft. Each member had an undivided interest in the entire plane.

3. Tenancy in Common. *Tenancy in common* differs from joint tenancy in the right of survivors. Death of one of the co-owners passes title to that one person's share to the beneficiaries named in that person's will or to the heirs if there is no will.

● Clark and Tatman purchased two CB transceivers and a base station. They owned them as tenants in common. Should either Clark or Tatman die, that co-owner's share would not go to the other owner. It would go to person(s) named in the will of the deceased or to the deceased's heirs.

Tenants in common need not own equal shares in the property and they are not required to obtain title to the property at the same time as the other tenant(s) in common. The terms used in describing joint tenancy and tenancy in common are very similar. Attorneys generally use the expression *with right of survivorship* if joint tenancy is intended. When courts are unable to determine whether ownership is joint or in common, there will be a presumption in favor of tenancy in common. This assures the surviving heirs, rather than an outsider, of receiving complete title to the deceased's personal property. This presumption is sometimes applied in cases in which one of the parties acted in bad faith.

● Allen, who had a savings account in his own name, closed the account and placed the money in a joint account with his son. Sometime later, without Allen's permission, the son closed the joint account and placed the money in a new account in his own name individually. Allen was surprised and angry when he discovered his son's actions and attempted, without success, to retrieve the bankbook. When Allen died, the court held that the son's withdrawal of the money was in bad faith. The act of bad faith had the effect of terminating the joint tenancy and creating a tenancy in common. One-half of the funds in the bank account went to Allen's son, the other half went to Allen's estate.

4. Community Property. Some states have legislation with regard to *community property* rights. These usually give each spouse a one-half title interest in personal property owned by the other. Excepted from this right are goods owned by either party prior to marriage or property acquired by gift or inheritance during marriage.

● Prior to marriage Jennings owned a car, sewing machine, fur coat, and valuable jewelry. Her husband owned a motorcycle, a complete set of mechanic's tools, and a part ownership, with others, in an airplane. After marriage, individually and together, they made numerous purchases for the home and for themselves personally. Only those things purchased after marriage are included in their community property.

Most states now have laws or court decisions providing for some form of equitable distribution of marital property when a couple is divorced. *Equitable distribution laws* allow judges to distribute property equitably (fairly) between the husband and wife regardless of who has title.

17-4. Patents, Copyrights, Trademarks

Patents, copyrights, and trademarks, in addition to being special types of monopolies (see Chapter 12), give valuable property rights to their owners.

A. Patents

A patent, as you may recall, is an official document, sometimes referred to as *letters patent,* which gives the owner the exclusive right to make, use, or sell an invention for a term of seventeen years. To be patentable, a device must consist of some new idea or principle not known before. It must be a discovery as distinguished from mere mechanical skill or knowledge. The device may be a process, an article of manufacture, or a composition of matter.

● A microbiologist invented a bacterium capable of breaking down crude oil. The U.S. Patent and Trademark Office denied a patent on the bacterium, claiming that it was alive and therefore not patentable. On appeal, the U.S. Supreme Court held that the live, human-made bacterium is patentable. The court said that such a microorganism is a "manufacture" or "composition of matter" within the meaning of the patent law.

A patent may not be obtained if the subject matter of the patent would be obvious to a person having ordinary skill in the field.

In the past, organizations which had been awarded federal contracts for research sometimes had difficulty obtaining patents on their discoveries. Some agencies of the federal government granted patent rights; others did not. In 1980, Congress amended the patent law, allowing federal contractors greater control over the results of their research. The amendment permits universities, small companies, and nonprofit organizations to retain ownership of patents gained as a result of federal grants and contracts. Large corporations are excluded from the provisions of the amendment. Prior to this change in the law, every government agency supporting private research had its own patent policy. There was no uniformity among agencies. Many worthwhile inventions were never marketed because the government retained title to them. It is expected that this amendment to the patent law will have far-reaching effects in the marketplace.

B. Copyrights

Copyrights are intangible property rights granted by statute to authors or originators of literary, musical, or artistic productions. They give to their owners the exclusive legal right to reproduce, publish, and sell their work for a specific time period. Works created after January 1, 1978, when the present copyright law came into effect, are protected for the life of the author plus fifty years. The law allows some copying to be done without permission under the *doctrine of fair use.* This doctrine provides that copyrighted material may be reproduced without permission if the use of the material is reasonable and not harmful to the rights of the copyright owner. Copying items for such purposes as criticism, comment, news reporting, teaching, scholarship, and research is permissible. In addition, libraries and archives may reproduce single copies of certain copyrighted materials for noncommercial purposes without obtaining permission of the copyright owner.

The Computer Software Copyright Act, passed in 1980, amended the copyright law by including computer programs among "writings" to which exclu-

Part 4:
Personal
Property
and
Bailments

230

sive rights can be granted. The act defines a computer program as "a set of statements or instructions to be used directly or indirectly in a computer in order to bring about a certain result." Under the act, it is not an infringement for the owner of a copy of a computer program to make another copy provided that its duplication is essential in the use of a particular machine.

C. Trademarks

A trademark, as you may recall, is any word, name, symbol, or device adopted and used by a manufacturer or merchant to identify the goods and distinguish them from those manufactured or sold by others. It is different from a patent in that it does not apply to an invention or manufacturing process. Rather, it applies to the name or mark used to identify a product. The function of a trademark is to identify the source of a product, that is, the one who makes it. Coke, for example, is made only by the Coca-Cola Company, and Wheaties are made only by General Mills. Owners of trademarks have the exclusive right to use the particular word, name, or symbol that they have adopted as their trademark. Trademarks can be established in three different ways: under the common law, under a state statute, or under the Federal Trademark Act of 1946.

1. Common-Law Trademarks. Under the common law, trademarks may be established by usage rather than by registration with the state or federal government. To claim such a mark, the party must demonstrate that use of the mark has been of such quality and for such a duration that it has come to identify goods bearing it as originating from that party. The mark must have developed a secondary meaning—not merely identification of the product, but rather identification of its producer.

● Powers, who published a small newspaper, decided to name the paper the *Daily Planet*. D.C. Comics, Inc., publishers of the Superman comic book, brought suit to stop Powers from using that name. Evidence was introduced to show that the *Daily Planet* first appeared in the Superman story in 1940. Since then it has played a key role, not only in the Superman story, but also in the development of the Superman character. In addition, D.C. Comics, Inc., has utilized the Superman character in connection with many products born of the Superman story. These products have included school supplies, toys, costumes, games, and clothes. The court enjoined Powers from using the name *Daily Planet*. It held that D.C. Comics, Inc., had demonstrated an association of such duration and consistency with the *Daily Planet* that it had established a common-law trademark in that name. The *Daily Planet* has over the years become inextricably woven into the fabric of the Superman story.

2. State Trademark Statutes. Although the U.S. Constitution gives exclusive control to the federal government over patents and copyrights, it is silent about trademarks. Therefore, federal laws apply only to trademarks that are used in interstate commerce. Each of the fifty states has statutes that regulate the use of trademarks in intrastate commerce, that is, within the boundaries of the state. Although there has been an attempt to make the trademark laws of each state uniform, in general they differ substantially.

3. The Federal Trademark Act of 1946. The Federal Trademark Act of 1946, called the Lanham Act, provides for registration of trademarks with the U.S. Patent and Trademark Office. To be eligible for registration, the goods or ser-

Figure 17-1. Marks at issue in the Spangler case.

vices must be sold or used in more than one state or in this and a foreign country. A trademark cannot be registered if it consists of:

○ Immoral, deceptive, or scandalous matter.
○ Matter which may disparage or falsely suggest a connection with persons, living or dead, institutions, beliefs, or national symbols, or bring them into contempt, or disrepute.
○ The flag or coat of arms or other insignia of the United States, or of any state or municipality, or of any foreign nation, or any simulation thereof.
○ The name, signature, or portrait of any living individual, except with that person's written consent.
○ The name, signature, or portrait of a deceased President of the United States during the life of a surviving spouse, if any, except by the written consent of the spouse.
○ A mark which so resembles a mark registered in the Patent and Trademark Office or a mark or trade name previously used in the United States by another and not abandoned, as to be likely, when applied to the goods of the applicant, to cause confusion, or to cause mistake, or to deceive.

● Spangler Candy Co., makers of Dum Dums lollipops, claimed that its competitor, Crystal Pure Candy Co., copied its trademark. Crystal Pure produced a candy called Pop Pops. The makers of Dum Dums claimed that the makers of Pop Pops copied precisely the type of font and logo of its trademark (see Figure 17-1). The court allowed Pop Pops mark, holding that it does not resemble the Dum Dums mark so as to be likely to confuse or to deceive purchasers.

Anyone who registers a trademark may give notice that the mark is registered by displaying with the mark the words "Registered in U.S. Patent and Trademark Office" or "Reg. U.S. Pat. & Tm. Off." or the letter R enclosed within a circle, thus: ®.

A trademark registration remains in force for twenty years and may be renewed for additional twenty-year periods, unless it is canceled or surrendered.

Understanding Legal Terms

Define, identify, or explain the following terms:

accessions	donee	gift *in causa mortis*	severalty ownership
chattels	donor	gift *inter vivos*	tangible personal
chose in action	escheat	intangible property	property
confusion	fixtures	personal property	trade fixtures

Questions for Review and Discussion

1. In what way does intangible personal property differ from tangible personal property?

2. Describe five ways one can acquire title to personal property other than by a sales agreement.

3. When may someone who finds lost property claim ownership of it?

4. Distinguish between an ordinary gift and a gift *in causa mortis*.

5. Explain the purposes of the Uniform Gifts to Minors Act.

6. Describe the kind of title that is given by a thief who sells stolen goods to an innocent person.

7. Differentiate between owning property as a joint tenant with another person and owning property as a tenant in common.

8. Discuss the rights of husband and wife in states that have community property. Are all goods covered by these rights?

9. What are protected by (*a*) patents, (*b*) copyrights, and (*c*) trademarks?

10. Describe the protection given by the Computer Software Copyright Act of 1980.

Analyzing Cases

1. In his will, Gavegnano left all his tangible personal property to his daughter, Caroline. At the time of his death, he owned nineteen thoroughbred horses. In addition, a cashier's check made payable to him for $33,000 was found among his belongings. The lower court judge held that the horses and the check were tangible personal property and should be given to Caroline under the terms of the will. Caroline's brothers appealed the decision, claiming that neither the horses nor the check were tangible personal property. Are Caroline's brothers correct? Explain. ● *Pagiarulo v. National Shawmut Bank*, 233 N.E.2d 213 (Mass. 1968)

2. Mrs. Bisset leased a commercial garage building to Briggs Motor Company for a period of eight years. After using the garage for about four years, Briggs Motor Company assigned its lease to Delaney, Inc., and moved out. It left behind some equipment, which was not attached to the building. Delaney, Inc., used the equipment, and after three years, sold the business to Goss. When Goss moved out, Mrs. Bisset claimed that the equipment left behind by Briggs Motor Company was mislaid property and belonged to her, not to Goss. Do you agree with Mrs. Bissett? Why or why not? ● *Goss v. Bisset*, 411 S.W.2d 50 (Ky. 1967)

3. While walking home from church, two boys, aged nine and twelve, came upon some trash in the parking lot of a supermarket. In the trash, they found a large envelope containing a gun and $12,300 in cash. The boys became excited and confused and sought the advice of some friends who were also walking home from church. One of the friends, a fifteen-year-old girl, took the envelope containing the gun and the money to her house to show her mother. The boys followed and waited outside the girl's house. The girl's mother telephoned the police and turned the money and the gun over to them. The police gave the girl a receipt and listed her as the finder. The boys (through their parents) seek a determination from the court that they are entitled to the money if the true owner is not found. Who do you believe is entitled to the money? Why? ● *Edmonds v. Ronella*, 342 N.Y.S.2d 408 (1973)

4. Pollard found a valuable first edition that someone had dropped on the street. She took the book home, placing it with others in a collection of first editions. The owner's name could not be found in the lost book, and Pollard made no effort to locate the owner. Does she now have title to the book? Explain. ● See also *Doe v. Oceola*, 270 N.W.2d 254 (Mich. 1978)

5. Texas Hydraulic and Equipment Co. welded and bolted a new dump body and hoist onto a truck owned by Lane. Later, the holder of a chattel mortgage on the truck took possession of it from Lane for nonpayment of the mortgage. Texas Hydraulic claims that the mortgage holder is not entitled to the body and hoist because it had attached those items to the truck after the mortgage was placed on it. Do you agree with Texas Hydraulic? ● *Texas Hydraulic & Equipment Co. v. Associates Discount Corp.*, 414 S.W.2d 199 (Tex. 1967)

6. Haddad Shoe Store terminated its present lease and made plans to move to another nearby building. Preparations were made to remove shelving and other fixtures that had been built into the store when Haddad's lease first started. The landlord warned Haddad to desist in any act of removing these things from the property. May Haddad remove the shelves that were paid for and installed by him during his tenancy? Explain. ● See also *George v. Town of Calais*, 373 A.2d 553 (Vt. 1977)

7. Sakraida obtained a combination patent on a water flush system to remove cow manure from the floor of a dairy barn. The individual elements of the patent had been used before in the dairy business for many years. The only new feature was a provision for the abrupt release of water from storage tanks directly onto the barn floor. This caused the flow of a sheet of water washing all animal waste into drains without the use of hand labor as had been required in the past. It was argued that the patent was void because the invention was obvious to people having ordinary skill in the field. Do you agree? ● *Sakraida v. Ag Pro, Inc.*, 96 S. Ct. 1532 (1976)

8. Union Carbide Corp. sells Eveready batteries, flashlights, and small automobile bulbs. It has used the Eveready trademark since 1901. In 1969, Ever-Ready Incorporated, which had conducted a fluorescent light maintenance service for twenty-five years, began importing and selling miniature lamp bulbs. The company stamped the term *Ever-Ready* on the base of each bulb and on the package containing them. Carbide sought an injunction to bar Ever-Ready's use of the term *Ever-Ready* on its product. The lower court refused to issue the injunction, holding that the term *Eveready* had not acquired a secondary meaning in the eyes of the public. Union Carbide Corp. appealed the lower court's decision. It argued that it is not necessary for the public to be aware of the name of the manufacturer of a product for the trademark to have acquired a secondary meaning. It is sufficient that the public be aware that the product comes from a single, though anonymous, source. How would you decide? Explain. ● *Union Carbide Corp. v. Ever-Ready, Inc.*, 531 F.2d 366 (7th Cir. 1976)

9. Alabama Custom Tape, Inc., was popularly known as a "tape pirate." When it became apparent that a particular musical composition (copyrighted by someone else) was destined to become a hit, the company would purchase a copy of the recording and reproduce it hundreds of thousands or millions of times and sell the copies to the public. A federal law provided that, after the first mechanical recording of a composition, others might make similar use of the composition upon payment of 2 cents per recording. Alabama Custom Tape, Inc., argued that it was making similar use of the compositions that it recorded and that it, therefore, came within the law. Do you agree? Why or why not? ● *Fame Publishing Co. v. Alabama Custom Tape, Inc.*, 423 U.S. 841 (1975)

Chapter 18

Bailments of Personal Property

A student rents a typewriter. A pedestrian finds a briefcase. A neighbor borrows a friend's ladder. In each of the three situations, possession of tangible personal property has been given to someone other than the owner, but in no case was there an intent to give title. Each situation illustrates a transaction known as a bailment.

A *bailment* is the transfer of possession of personal property by the owner, know as the *bailor,* to another person, called the *bailee.* In a bailment neither the bailor nor the bailee intends that title to the property should pass. The bailee has an obligation to return the same property to the bailor at a later time or on demand.

● Rent-A-Car leased a station wagon to Havian. Havian signed a rental agreement that listed rights and obligations of Rent-A-Car and Havian, the bailee. Havian paid a security deposit and a fee for insurance, and he agreed to return the car in forty-eight hours. Through the lease, these two parties created a bailment.

18-1. Characteristics of a Bailment

Bailments are distinguished from other agreements by several characteristics.

A. Possession

A bailment is created at any time a bailee takes rightful possession of another's personal property. Good judgment must be exercised by the bailee in the care, use, and preservation of the other person's goods. Possession should not be confused with custody. One who has the physical control of another's goods, but is under the constant supervision of the owner in their use and care, has only *custody. Possession,* in a bailment relationship, implies that the bailee not only has physical control of another's goods, but also has the responsibility of personal supervision and care as well.

● Weeks agreed to drive Tarlow's car during a trip they were making together. Tarlow sat beside the driver during the trip, making decisions on routes to be taken, speeds traveled, and stops made. Weeks was not a bailee. Tarlow has possession; Weeks had nothing more than custody.

Suppose, at the end of the first day, Tarlow asked Weeks to take the car to a service station to get gas and an oil change and Weeks went alone. This would be a bailment. Weeks, as bailee, had physical control of the car and had to make decisions as to its care and protection.

B. Retention of Title

The owner of bailed property never passes title to a bailee. Agreements by which title does pass from one person to another would come within the law of sales, gifts, exchanges, and the like.

● Agnes Simpkins, a horse breeder, transferred a thoroughbred racehorse to Kate Ritter. The certificate for the foal named Ritter as the transferee. Under the arrangement, Ritter was to pay the entire cost of the horse's upkeep. In return, she would receive the horse's earnings. The horse was to be returned ultimately to Simpkins, although the time for the return was disputed. When Simpkins brought suit for the return of the horse, Ritter claimed that she had title to it because the certificate for the foal named her as transferee. The court said that an agreement to return the identical property is a bailment, not a sale. It held that Simpkins, the bailor, retained title to the racehorse.

C. Delivery and Acceptance

Bailments require a delivery of goods by the bailor and acceptance by the bailee. Only when the goods are accepted is a bailment actually created.

D. Obligation to Return Goods

Another requirement is that, when the bailment relationship ends, the bailee return to the bailor the same goods as were delivered and accepted. Goods may be returned either in their original form or in an altered form, depending on the conditions of the bailment agreement.

When the owner of property loans goods to another with the intention that the goods may be used and later replaced with an equal quantity of the same quality of goods, there is no bailment. A transaction of this kind is known as a *mutuum*.

● Mead's Stationers borrowed six typewriter ribbons from the Typewriter Service Company. It was agreed that Mead's would replace the ribbons with six others when its order was received from the manufacturer. In this case, Typewriter Service Company gave up both possession and title to its six ribbons. This was a mutuum, not a bailment transaction.

18-2. The Bailment Contract

The validity of a bailment is generally governed by the rules of contracts. To be legally enforceable, a bailment contract must contain all the elements of any valid contract: mutual assent, capable parties, consideration, and valid subject matter. The contract may be express or implied. Subject to statutory regulations, it may be either written or oral.

● Glover purchased a truck from Spencer for $5,500. Spencer agreed to install a winch on the vehicle at a later date. Glover paid $5,000, took possession of the truck, and agreed to pay the balance when the winch was installed. Sometime later, Spencer took the truck from Glover to have the winch installed, saying that he would "take good care of it" and that if anything happened to it he would "stand behind it." The truck was stolen from Spencer. In his defense, Spencer argued that the bailment contract was oral and therefore not enforceable. The court disagreed,

Part 4:
Personal
Property
and
Bailments

236

saying that a bailment may be written or oral and that no formal language is required for its creation.

18-3. Principal Types of Bailments

There are three principal types of bailments: bailments for the sole benefit of the bailor, bailments for the sole benefit of the bailee, and mutual-benefit bailments. The first two types are called gratuitous bailments. In *gratuitous bailments*, property is transferred to another person without either party's giving or demanding payment of any kind. Such bailments lack consideration; therefore, they may be rescinded at any time by either party. Parties to such agreements usually consider them only as favors. In reality, however, definite legal responsibilities are placed upon both the bailor and the bailee.

A. Bailments for Sole Benefit of Bailor

When possession of personal property is transferred to another for purposes that will benefit only the bailor, a *bailment for the sole benefit of the bailor* results.

● Conte agreed to deliver Higgins's watch to a jewelry shop which she would pass on the way to work. Higgins gave her the watch, and she placed it in a briefcase with other valuables. Conte was promised no reward for this act. It was a favor. It was also a bailment for the sole benefit of the bailor.

B. Bailments for Sole Benefit of Bailee

Transactions in which the possession of personal property is transferred for purposes that will benefit only the bailee are gratuitous *bailments for the sole benefit of the bailee.*

● Martin asked Kahn if she might use the latter's car for a trip she planned to make to Kansas City. Kahn agreed to lend the car, asking nothing in return for this favor. The bailment was created for the sole benefit of the bailee, Martin.

C. Mutual-Benefit Bailments

When personal property is transferred to a bailee with the intent that both parties will benefit, a *mutual-benefit bailment* results. The ordinary bailments involving business transactions are usually mutual-benefit bailments in which the business person is a *compensated bailee.*

● In preparing for a trip to Detroit, Cassidy left a suit at the Valet Shop to be cleaned and pressed. The agreed-upon price for these services was $8. Both Cassidy and the Valet Shop will benefit from the transaction. This is a mutual-benefit bailment. The Valet Shop is a compensated bailee.

Four basic kinds of mutual-benefit bailments exist. These are (1) pledge, or pawn; (2) contract for use of goods; (3) contract for custody of goods; and (4) contract for work or service on goods. In addition, a bailment by necessity, also described below, may be implied by law.

1. **Pledge, or Pawn.** A person wishing to borrow money must often give the

lender possession of personal property as security for repayment of the debt. The property thus left as security is called the *pledge*, or *pawn*. The borrower, or debtor, is the *pledgor*, or bailor. The lender, or creditor, is the *pledgee*, or bailee. The pledgee may be a bank, a loan company, a credit union, a pawnbroker, or another person.

● Cohen borrowed $7,400 from the American Arlington Bank. As security for the loan, the parties signed a bailment agreement making the bank the bailee of Cohen's valuable painting of King George III of England, alledgedly one of three portraits of the king by the eighteenth-century painter George Ramsey. The painting was hung in the office of the bank's vice president. This was a pledge because the bank had possession and complete control over the painting while the loan was outstanding.

The UCC sets out the rights and duties of pledgors and pledgees (9-207). These rights and duties are explained in detail in Chapter 41.

2. Contracts for Use of Goods. A mutual-benefit bailment results when an agreement is made for renting goods for a fixed sum or at a definite rate. Examples are renting a tool from a rental store or hiring a horse from a riding academy or an automobile from a drive-it-yourself firm.

The bailee has the right to the exclusive possession and use of the article during the period of the contract. The bailee must exercise reasonable care in the use and protection of the property. *Reasonable care* means that degree of care which a reasonably prudent person would have used under the same circumstances and conditions. Damages resulting from causes outside the bailee's control will not make the bailee liable. However, damage or destruction caused by the bailee's use of the article in a way different from that agreed upon makes a bailee absolutely liable to the bailor.

3. Contracts for Custody of Goods. Contracts for the storage of property are mutual-benefit bailments when a fee is charged. Garages, warehouses, grain elevators, and similar businesses are engaged in bailments of this kind.

The bailee, except by special agreement, is not an insurer. The bailee must exercise reasonable care and has no implied authority to use the bailed property unless use is necessary to maintain the property's value.

● Zerke boarded a valuable racehorse as Oxley Stables. Oxley had full responsibility for the care of the horse during Zerke's absence. The horse was not taken from its stall over a period of three weeks, and lack of exercise crippled it. Reasonable care, in this case, required that the animal be exercised. (Exercise does not necessarily mean use.)

Suppose Oxley Stables had entered Zerke's horse in a race at the county fair grounds. If the horse won a purse, the money would belong to Zerke. If the horse were injured, Zerke could hold the stable responsible as an insurer, having exceeded its rights as bailee.

a. Parking Lots and Garages. When a car is parked in a parking garage or lot, the relationship may be a license to use the parking space or a lease of the parking space. (Licenses and leases are defined and compared in Chapter 37.) It may also be a bailment. In the event the car is damaged or stolen, the difference is

Part 4:
Personal
Property
and
Bailments

238

important. If the transaction is a license or lease, there is no duty imposed on the garage or lot owner to safeguard the car from damage or theft.

● Baughman leased an apartment from Broadview Apartments. Under a separate agreement, he paid Broadview $15 a month to park his car in the basement of the building. There was no requirement to check the car in or out, and each tenant was provided with a key to the garage door. Baughman parked in an assigned spot, locked the car, and took the keys with him. When he returned for the car, it was gone. This was a lease of a parking space. Baughman could not recover from Broadview Apartments for the loss of the car. The burden was on him to prove some specific act of negligence on the part of Broadview or its employees. He could not meet this burden.

If the transaction is a bailment, however, the burden of proof shifts from the bailor to the bailee. Once the bailor proves delivery of the car to the bailee, the bailee must prove that he or she was not negligent if the car is damaged or stolen. An exception to this rule may apply in the case of airport parking lots, since all courts do not agree that a bailment exists in airport parking lot cases. The courts of some states have held that a bailment does not occur because the garage does not take control of the vehicle.

● Ellish parked her Cadillac car at the airport parking lot. She had entered the lot by means of an entrance gate where she obtained a ticket from an automatic vending machine. Upon her taking the ticket, a gate opened and permitted her car to enter the lot. A sign at the entrance stated, "This contract licenses the holder to park one automobile in this area at holder's risk . . . only a license is granted hereby and no bailment is created." She selected her own parking space, locked the car, and took the keys with her. Upon returning to the lot four days later, she discovered that her car was missing. In a suit brought against the garage, the court held that there was no bailment. The court said that Ellish had not transferred control of the vehicle to the airport garage. Since she could not prove a negligent act on the part of the airport garage, she lost the case.

The courts have uniformly held that the surrender of car keys to a parking lot or garage attendant is a sufficient delivery of possession and control to create a bailment. Other factors which have been considered to be important in determining a bailment relationship are whether there are attendants at the entrances and exits of the lots, whether the car owner receives a claim check that must be surrendered before the car can be removed, and whether the parking lot is enclosed.

b. *Safe-Deposit Boxes.* A bank operating a safe-deposit-box service has the possession of the property placed in the box by the customer. The legal relationship created by this transaction, under the prevailing view, is that of bailor and bailee.* The fact that the bank does not know the character or description of the property that the customer places in the safe-deposit box does not change that relationship. It has been argued that a bailment cannot exist because the bank does not have exclusive possession of the property that is left in the safe-deposit

---

* Courts in a few states, such as Delaware, have held the the safe-deposit-box holder is a renter of space and that therefore the lessor-lessee relationship applies.

box. Most courts, however, have rejected this argument, saying that the bank has exclusive access to the property. The depositor cannot gain access to the safe-deposit box without the consent and active participation of the bank.

4. Contracts for Work or Service on Goods. Agreements in which property is transferred to another for work, repairs, or other service—for which the owner agrees to pay a fee—are mutual-benefit bailments. Cleaners, repair shops, and persons developing photographic film, for example, are engaged in bailment transactions of this kind. The bailee is not an insurer, but must exercise ordinary care. Losses by fire, theft, or other causes beyond the control of the bailee do not excuse the bailor from paying for the bailee's services if the work is completed prior to the time of loss and if the bailor is notified that the property is ready for delivery.

● Ricotta left a car at Modern Paint Shop for a new paint job. When the car was ready to be picked up, she was notified. Two days later, before she took delivery of the car, the shop was burned out, together with the newly painted car. The fire resulted when burglars entered an adjoining building, where they started a fire.

Modern Paint Shop has no obligation to compensate Ricotta for the loss. This was a bailment requiring ordinary care. The loss did not result from negligence or lack of care on the part of Modern Paint Shop.

5. Bailments by Necessity. A common type of mutual-benefit bailment, implied by law, is the *bailment by necessity*. This arises when one purchases a suit or dress and is required to give up possession of one's own property while being fitted; when one receives services in a barber or beauty shop, where one must give up possession of a hat or other articles of apparel; and in other similar situations which require a customer to give up possession of property for the benefit of both parties. In such cases the bailee is required to accept the other's property and to exercise ordinary care in its protection.

● Cook had an appointment at a hairdresser's. The day was cold and rainy, and she wore a heavy coat, overshoes, and a storm hat. The operator asked Cook to put her things on a rack outside the booth, which was out of sight. There was no other place to leave them.

This is a typical bailment by necessity. It would have been inconvenient, improper, and perhaps impossible for Cook to have remained clothed in her rainwear while being served by the shop. Even though the shop had placed a sign reading "Not Responsible for Articles Left Here" over the rack, it did not remove the shop's responsibility as a bailee of her things.
    Restaurants are not always responsible for property left in a cloakroom.

● Meisnere hung his coat in an unattended cloakroom at the request of a waitress after the coat had fallen from his chair. No claim check was given to Meisnere, and there was no charge for the service. A notice was posted in the cloakroom disclaiming any responsibility for lost belongings, but Meisnere did not see the notice. His coat was stolen. The court held in favor of the restaurant, saying that no bailment took place. There had been no delivery which resulted in a change of possession and control of the coat.

Part 4:
Personal
Property
and
Bailments

240

18-4. Bailments Imposed by Law

The law recognizes two types of bailments where the obligation of the bailee is imposed by law rather than by mutual agreement of the parties. In these situations, the bailee must exercise the same degree of care as in other bailments for the sole benefit of the bailor. (See the earlier discussion in this chapter.)

A. Involuntary Bailments

In an *involuntary bailment,* personal property is delivered to a stranger through some agency beyond the control of either party, as by an act of God. The law implies delivery of the property to the one who comes into possession.

● During a hurricane, personal property of many kinds was blown onto Vail's land. An involuntary bailment resulted, and Vail had the implied obligation to give some care, though slight, to the property until the real owners were located and the property returned.

B. Lost Property

By implication, the finder of lost property who takes possession of the goods becomes the bailee. The rights and duties of the finder are those of a bailee. Thus, the finder of a purse or of any other property acquires an ownership that is second only to the real owner's right to the property. The finder is considered to be the bailee of the property, holding it for the true owner until that person can be located. The situation is the same when someone comes into possession of property by mistake.

18-5. Duties of Bailor and Bailee

As in other legal relationships, the law gives specific rights to and imposes specific duties on the parties to a bailment. Generally, the duties of the bailee are closely related to (and in a sense the opposite of) the rights of the bailor. The duties of the bailor and bailee are discussed here.

A. Duty of Bailor

The bailor must deliver a safe chattel to the bailee. If the chattel is not safe and if the dangerous conditions are not apparent upon ordinary examination, the bailor has an obligation to call such facts to the bailee's attention.

● Clark, a bus driver, volunteered to repair ceiling tiles at a church. Scaffolding was rented by a church employee from Rental Equipment Company, Inc., but guardrails were not selected by the employee to go with the scaffolding. Clark fell off the scaffolding and was seriously injured. An expert witness testified at the trial that scaffolding equipment is not safe without a guardrail. Clark recovered money damages from the rental company. The court said that the rental company owed a duty to warn the inexperienced volunteer that scaffolding without guardrails is inherently dangerous.

In a bailment for the sole benefit of the bailee, the bailor is not responsible for injuries to the bailee caused by defects in the bailed property unless the bailor had actual knowledge of the defect at the time of the bailment.

In a bailment for the sole benefit of the bailor, the bailor has a duty to reimburse the bailee for any expenses the bailee might have in the care of the property. The bailee has a corresponding duty to keep such expenses within a reasonable amount, depending upon the circumstances.

B. Duty of Bailee

Bailees must use care in handling a bailor's property.

1. Degrees of Care. The bailee's duty of care has changed in recent years. Formerly, three degrees of care were generally recognized in the law of bailments: great care, ordinary care, and slight care. Some states still recognize these degrees of care as part of their bailment law.

In a bailment for the sole benefit of the bailee, the bailee was required to use *great care* because possession of the goods was solely for the bailee's benefit. The bailee was responsible for *slight negligence,* which is the failure to use that degree of care which persons of extraordinary prudence and foresight are accustomed to use.

● Williamson borrowed her aunt's car and used it to drive 500 miles for a job interview. At no time during the entire trip did she check the oil in the engine. This carelessness resulted in some damage to the motor. Williamson did not exercise extraordinary care, and she will be responsible for any repairs resulting from her slight negligence.

In a mutual-benefit bailment, the bailee owed a duty to use *ordinary care.* The bailee was responsible for *ordinary negligence,* which is failing to use that amount of care that a reasonable person would use under the same circumstances.

● Levasseur stored his boat, motor, and trailer in Field's building for the winter for $10. Levassaur expressed some doubts about the soundness of the building, particularly concerning the structure of the roof. Field assured him that the building was safe. The roof collapsed after a winter snowstorm, damaging Levasseur's boat. In allowing Levasseur to recover from Field, the court said that the relationship imposed a duty on the bailee to use ordinary care, which he failed to do.

In a bailment for the sole benefit of the bailor, the bailee owed a duty to use only *slight care* since the bailee was receiving no benefit from the arrangement. The bailee was required only to refrain from *gross negligence.* This is very great negligence—much more serious than ordinary negligence.

● The Martins asked two girls, Bell and Christian, to occupy their home during the Martins' vacation. The Martins did not pay the housesitters but left a few dollars for groceries. The contents of the house were badly damaged by fire when one of the girls left a pan of grease unattended on a range burner. This was a gratuitous bailment for the sole benefit of the bailor. The court held that Bell and Christian were not liable for damage to the Martins' personal property because they were not grossly negligent.

2. Modern Theory. The modern theory, adopted by many courts and applied to bailees generally, is that there are no degrees of care or negligence. These

Part 4:
Personal
Property
and
Bailments

242

courts hold that it is the duty of all bailees to exercise *reasonable care*. What is reasonable care, these courts say, depends upon the nature and value of the property and the circumstances under which the bailment occurs.

● Edwards took her late-model Cadillac automobile to the Crestmont Cadillac garage to have a tire changed and the wheels aligned. When she returned later to pick up the car, she learned that it had been stolen from the garage. The court held Crestmont responsible. It had not used reasonable care in preventing the car from being stolen. The court said that a bailee is presumed to be negligent when it fails to redeliver the bailed property unless it can prove that it was not negligent.

3. Use of Bailor's Property. In a bailment for the sole benefit of the bailee, the bailee has the right to use the property for the purposes for which the bailment was created. Use for other purposes or use over a longer time than provided for in the agreement will make the bailee responsible for any damages that may result to the property, regardless of the amount of care exercised.

● Robbins used Castro's chain saw to cut up a small tree that fell during a storm. The cutting of the tree was all that Castro had agreed to allow Robbins to do with the saw. Robbins decided to cut up other timber awaiting the fireplace. The saw's engine caught fire. Even though Robbins was in no way responsible for the fire, he is obligated to reimburse Castro for the damage.

Any *ordinary* and *expected expense* incurred in the use of another's property must be borne by the bailee.

On the other hand, repairs and adjustments not caused by ordinary use or damages not attributed to the bailee's negligence become the responsibility of the bailor. The bailee is not obligated to replace parts which break down because of the gradual use and depreciation of the other's property over a long period.

● Swanson, with Oberly's permission, took Oberly's motorcycle on a trial ride. Every precaution was taken to avoid damage. Nevertheless, on the way home, the front tire blew, and Swanson found it necessary to buy a new tire. The old tire had been badly worn in many places. The blowout was not caused by Swanson's negligent use. Oberly, the bailor, would be responsible for any *unusual* and *unexpected* expenses resulting from the tire blowout, including the obligation of reimbursing Swanson for the tire.

In a mutual-benefit bailment, the bailee must use the property only for the express purposes permitted by the bailor as provided for in the contract of bailment. The rental of a car, tools, or formal wear, for example, implies the right of reasonable use. Failing to use the property as agreed makes the bailee responsible for any damages that might result, regardless of the degree of care that was exercised.

● Smith rented a formal suit from the Valet Shop. While wearing it, he crawled under a friend's car to make an adjustment to the brakes. Smith was liable to the Valet Shop for the resulting damage to the suit. The bailed property had not been used for the purposes permitted by the bailor.

In a bailment for the sole benefit of the bailor, the bailee has no implied right to use the bailor's property. Use without permission is technically a tort of conversion on the part of the bailee; it would make the bailee fully liable for any damages that might result, even if the bailee had used great care and was not guilty of negligence. (Conversion, you may recall, is the civil wrong that arises when one unlawfully treats another's property as one's own.)

● Lindstrom agreed to care for Holbart's car while Holbart was absent from the city. Although permission to use the car had not been given, Lindstrom drove the car many times to save having to walk.

Should Lindstrom become involved in an accident as a result of the unauthorized use of Holbart's car, he would be fully and indefensibly liable to Holbart for damages. In a case like this, it is not even necessary that the bailor prove lack of care by the bailee.

Some property, however, requires use or exercise to maintain its value. If the property is of a type that might depreciate from nonuse, the bailee would have an implied obligation to perform the services necessary to maintain the property in proper condition.

18-6. Termination of Bailment

Either party may terminate a gratuitous bailment. Lacking consideration, the bailment agreement is not enforceable. A bailee who terminates must return the property to its owner at a proper time and place. Termination by the bailor requires the giving of notice of such intention of termination and a request that the property be returned.

In the case of a mutual-benefit bailment, the parties may anticipate termination in their original agreement. They can specify the length of time the bailment is to extend. The parties may also end their agreement by mutual assent at any later time.

18-7. Tortious Bailees

Persons who have *wrongful possession* of another's property are said to be *tortious bailees*. There are four types of tortious bailees:

○ One in possession of stolen property
○ One wrongfully retaining possession of the lost property of another

● Bradshaw found a wallet belonging to Compton. Intentionally and knowingly, she refused to either return the wallet or contact Compton about the matter. Bradshaw placed herself in a vulnerable position because of her failure to return Compton's property; she would be fully responsible for the wallet and contents, regardless of the circumstances under which Comptom himself might have lost it. Such failure to act would also make her criminally liable on a complaint made to the police.

○ One using a bailed article for a purpose other than agreed upon
○ One refusing to return property at the termination of the bailment

Part 4:
Personal
Property
and
Bailments

244

Tortious bailees are fully and unconditionally responsible for any and all damage that results to property in their possession, regardless of the degree of care that they might exercise or the cause of the damage.

18-8. Lawful Recovery of Property

Owners of personal property, when deprived of its possession, may not recover possession by "taking the law into their own hands." Lawful means are available through either civil or criminal complaints filed with the proper courts. Even in cases where a tortious bailee refuses to give up possession, it is not the owner's right to use force or any other illegal means to recover possession.

A person who is deprived of the right of possession by a tortious bailee may seek one of two actions against the offender: replevin or conversion.

A. Replevin

Replevin is a common-law action used to get recovery of personal property that is wrongfully held by the one in possession. Replevin commands the bailee to return property to the owner. The action is taken through a court of law. The proper name, used by the courts, is a *writ of replevin*. This action is used when the owner seeks the return of the property, rather than its value.

● The University Library loaned books to Keaveny. They were first editions, and part of a set that had been out of print for a hundred years or more. It would have been impossible to replace the volumes without making a search throughout the country for volumes in the same good condition.

The University Library would seek a writ of replevin, to be served against Keaveny, demanding the return of the books.

Some states have done away with this common-law action and allow suit to be brought for the return of the goods in an ordinary tort action.

B. Conversion (or Trover)

Conversion is a tort action used when the bailor prefers to recover the *value* of property held by a tortious bailee rather than the property itself. This tort is discussed in detail in Chapter 2. The value awarded is the value of the goods at the time the bailment was created, not the value at the time that the action is taken.

● Whittington, who owned many fine horses, loaned a saddle horse to Charles for the afternoon. Charles did not return the horse, but stabled it in his own barn and made no move to call Whittington or to indicate an intention to return it later. Whittington learned that the horse had been injured while being ridden by Charles.

The owner would be better rewarded by demanding the value of the horse according to its worth at the time it was delivered to the bailee. The condition of the animal would not encourage Whittington to seek its return. Charles would be liable for all damages as well as for the animal's value.

The courts of some states refer to this tort action by its common-law name of *trover.*

Understanding Legal Terms

Define, identify, or explain the following terms:

bailee

bailment

bailment by
  necessity

bailment for the
  sole benefit of the
  bailee

bailment for the
  sole benefit of the
  bailor

bailor

gratuitous bailment

involuntary
  bailment

mutual-benefit
  bailment

mutuum

pawn

pledge

pledgee

pledgor

reasonable care

replevin

tortious bailee

Questions for Review and Discussion

1. Distinguish between the words *possession* and *custody*. Which one is associated with bailment?

2. Discuss the requirements of a bailment contract.

3. Describe the principal types of bailments, and give an example of each.

4. Explain the relationship between (*a*) a bank and one keeping valuables in a safe-deposit box and (*b*) between the owner of a car parked in a parking lot and the owner of the lot.

5. Give an example of (*a*) a bailment by necessity and (*b*) an involuntary bailment.

6. Explain the duty of the bailor. What additional duty is imposed upon the bailor in a bailment for the bailor's sole benefit?

7. How much care is reasonable care in a mutual-benefit bailment?

8. How does the modern theory of care imposed on a bailee differ from the degrees of care recognized in former years?

9. Distinguish between termination of gratuitous bailments and that of mutual-benefit bailments.

10. Discuss tortious bailees. Generally, what two actions may an owner bring against a tortious bailee having possession of the bailor's property?

Analyzing Cases

1. Donovan, seventeen, was hired by Schlesner as a gas station attendant. This job included pumping gas, keeping the station clean, washing windows, and taking care of customers. Donovan was also required to keep the books to reflect the sale of such items as gas, milk, and candy. Schlesner deducted money from Donovan's pay each week for shortages that appeared from the books. In a suit which Donovan brought to recover the money so deducted, Schlesner claimed that Donovan was a bailee of the goods that were sold in the gas station. Do you agree with Schlesner? Why or why not? ● *Donovan v. Schlesner*, 240 N.W.2d 135 (Wis. 1976)

2. F-M Potatoes, Inc., stored potatoes for Suda. The oral agreement provided for a storage rental price of 40 cents per hundredweight to February 1 and an additional 10 cents per hundredweight to April 1. F-M Potatoes, Inc., controlled the temperature and atmospheric conditions of the warehouse. Suda stored 13,000 hundredweight of potatoes in the warehouse. The potatoes spoiled because F-M Potatoes failed to maintain the proper temperature and atmospheric conditions. F-M Potatoes, Inc., argued that the arrangement was a lease rather than a bailment, and hence it was not liable for the spoilage. Do you agree? Explain. ● *F-M Potatoes, Inc. v. Suda*, 259 N.W.2d 487 (N.D. 1977)

3. Capezzaro reported to the police that he was robbed of $7,500 at gunpoint by a woman. The following day Henrietta Winfrey was arrested. Capezzaro positively identified her as the woman who robbed him. The police found $2,480.66 hidden in her girdle. The money was impounded by the police as evidence of the crime. Several months later, Winfrey was indicted for armed robbery. Two years later, the indictment was dismissed based on medical opinion that Winfrey was unable to know right from wrong at the time she allegedly committed the crime. When the police were notified of the dismissal, they returned the $2,480.66 to Winfrey. Capezzaro claimed that the money should have been given to him. Do you agree with Capezzaro? Why or why not? ● *Capezzaro v. Winfrey*, 379 A.2d 493 (N.J. 1977)

4. Rabinovitzch's husband delivered her motor vehicle to Sea Crest Cadillac-Pontiac, Inc., for service and repair. When he returned that evening to pick it up, the motor vehicle was missing from the garage. When suit was brought against Sea Crest to recover the value of the car, Sea Crest argued that Rabinovitzch had the burden of proving that Sea Crest had not exercised due care to prevent the loss of the automobile. Who has the burden of proof in this case? ● *Rabinovitzch v. Sea Crest Cadillac-Pontiac, Inc.* 335 N.E.2d 698 (Mass. 1975)

5. Nash's motorcycle, valued at $2,400, was seized and impounded by the police and held in police custody. An investigation was being made concerning the motorcycle's engine, which was believed to have been stolen. While in police custody, the motorcycle was stolen from the city pound. Can Nash recover from the city for the loss of the motorcycle? Why or why not? ● *Nash v. City of North Platte*, 288 N.W.2d 51 (Neb. 1980)

6. Judith Lissie and Annette Pillion were employed by the Southern New England Telephone Company in its commercial department on the second floor. They were not permitted to leave their coats by their desks or in their working area. Instead, they were assigned an area on the first floor to place their coats. Members of the general public had access to that coatroom until 5:00 p.m., and a security guard checked the building between 5:00 and 10:00 p.m. One evening, after working until 8:00 p.m., Lissie and Pillion discovered that their coats were missing. Can they recover the value of their coats from their employer? Explain. ● *Lissie v. Southern New England Tel. Co.*, 359 A.2d 187 (Conn. 1976)

7. Nelson rented a space to park and tie down an airplane at Schroeder's airport. Nelson, however, held onto the keys to the plane. To comply with federal regulations, the airport was required to move the plane to another location. Schroeder tried to reach Nelson by telephone to explain the change, but Nelson's telephone had been disconnected. Schroeder's employees moved the plane to another position and tied it down. Some time later, the weather bureau issued a storm warning. Other airplane owners went to the airport to check the security of their planes. Nelson did not do so. Schroeder's employees, however, checked Nelson's plane before the storm and found it to be securely tied down. The high winds turned the plane upside down causing it to be damaged. Can Nelson recover from the airport? Why or why not? ● *Nelson v. Schroeder Aerosports, Inc.*, 280 N.W.2d 107 (S.D. 1979)

8. Trosclair purchased a 42-acre farm. He allowed his wife's parents, Mr. and Mrs. Mudd, to live on the farm free in exchange for taking care of it. Trosclair left his two-year-old riding mower on the farm for Mr.

and Mrs. Mudd to use. While using the mower, Mrs. Mudd came upon a bucket and hose that were in her path. She stopped the mower by shifting the gears to neutral and got out to remove the obstacles. The mower jumped from neutral into forward gear and struck her from behind, injuring her severely. Trosclair had used the mower for two years and admitted that when encountering heavy grass, the mower on occasion slipped from forward to neutral gear causing it to stop. It had never jumped from neutral to forward gear, however. Did Trosclair have a duty to warn Mrs. Mudd of the defect? Why or why not? ● *Mudd v. Travelers Indemnity Co.* 309 So.2d 297 (La. 1975)

9. Masonic Manor Apartment Hotel agreed in writing to rent space to Peck for the storage of Peck's boat for a monthly fee. The hotel reserved the right to move the boat from the spot first designated to "another spot in the garage for the convenience of the Masonic Manor." The agreement further stated that the hotel "shall not be held liable for any damage to these boats and equipment while on the premises." Entrance to the garage was through two large overhead doors. Many of the residents of the hotel had either keys or electronic opening devices for the garage doors, but Peck did not. Peck's boat was stolen from the garage. Was this a bailment or a lease? Was the hotel responsible for the loss of the boat? Explain. ● *Peck v. Masonic Manor Apartment Hotel,* 278 N.W.2d 589 (Neb. 1979)

Chapter 19   Carriers, Warehousers, and Innkeepers

May a bus refuse to stop for someone waiting at a bus stop? May an airline refuse to take on a passenger? Is a furniture mover responsible to the owner when the furniture it is carrying is damaged in an accident? May goods that are stored in a warehouse be delivered to someone other than the owner? May a motel with a vacancy refuse to accept a guest? All these questions relate to bailments that are considered to be special or extraordinary. They include bailments by carriers, warehousers, and innkeepers. Special rules apply to each of these bailments.

19-1. Carriers

Individuals, partnerships, and corporations in the business of transporting goods and passengers are known as *carriers*. The carrier of goods is a bailee of the personal property that it transports. The carrier of passengers is a bailee only of the passenger's luggage given into its possession. Both are bailees of goods belonging to another, but the obligations, rights, and responsibilities of the two types of carriers are very different. Carriers are either private carriers or common carriers.

A. Private and Common Carriers Distinguished

Persons and firms engaged in the transport of goods and passengers under private contract arrangements are known as *private,* or *contract, carriers.* They are permitted by law to select those with whom they want to do business. They do not operate on regular schedules and are not regulated by state or federal authority as to rates charged and services offered. The acceptance of merchandise by them creates a bailment for mutual benefit. They are required to exercise ordinary care, as in all other mutual-benefit bailments, and are responsible for any losses arising from their negligence. They are not considered to be insurers of the goods that they ship.

● Garvin moved to a different apartment after the expiration of her lease. Larimore Moving and Storage Company contracted to move Garvin's furniture and belongings. The charge for the van and a moving crew was $35 an hour. As a private carrier, Larimore was entitled to adjust its rates depending on the nature of each job accepted. Any damage to Garvin's belongings, if due to the negligence of the company's work crew, would be Larimore's responsibility entirely.

Common carriers of passengers and freight are public-service ventures operating under government-granted franchises. Their rate schedules and operations are regulated and inspected by federal, state, or local public authority. Interstate carriers have double scrutiny, from both federal and state commissions. All rate and schedule changes require approval by the public authority before being placed in effect. Common carriers are a kind of quasi-public operation. *Quasi-public businesses* must satisfy strict rules promulgated by public officials while at the same time operating for a profit through private investment.

● Red Sky Taxi Company operated under a franchise granted by the city of Ashmont. It served the public, maintaining cab stands at railroad stations, leading hotels, and the municipal airport. The franchise gave Red Sky exclusive rights to operate a taxi service within the city of Ashmont.

In consideration of the special privileges allowed under the franchise, a common carrier must accept all persons seeking transportation. It may not, as with a private carrier, select its own passengers, make its own rate schedules, and use its own discretion in determining where to operate and provide services.

B. Common Carriers of Goods

Railroads, trucking companies, boat and steamship lines, and air carriers are all franchised as common carriers of goods. If a common carrier does all its business within the boundaries of one state, it is an *intrastate carrier*. Such carriers are franchised by state authority, usually a public service commission. *Interstate carriers*, those operating between states, receive their franchises from a federal agency, the Interstate Commerce Commission (ICC). Regulation of air carriers and the granting of franchises for airline service come under the jurisdiction of the Civil Aeronautics Board (CAB).

1. Duty of Care and Other Obligations. Common carriers of goods are insurers of all goods accepted for shipment. They are liable as insurers regardless of whether they have or have not been negligent.

● Whitehall Packing Co. engaged Safeway Truck Lines to transport forty barrels of fresh meat from its plant in Wisconsin to Howard Johnson's in New York. The federal government required plastic liners in the barrels, and Howard Johnson's would not allow dry ice in them. The refrigerator unit in Safeway's truck operated properly. The truck experienced delays and took longer than its normal running time for the trip. When it arrived in New York, the meat in the barrels had an off or gassy odor and was not considered acceptable by the U.S. government inspector. An expert meat inspector testified that the barreled meat was smothered because of the use of the plastic liners and the absence of dry ice. Some hanging meat in the same truck was found to be in perfect condition. Although there was no evidence that Safeway was negigent, the court held it responsible, saying that it was an insurer of the meat.

The Carmack Amendment to the Interstate Commerce Act, passed in 1978, codified this common-law rule. It states that a carrier is liable for damage to goods transported by it unless there is proof that the damage comes within one of the following exceptions:

○ Acts of God (floods, tornadoes, cyclones, earthquakes, etc.)
○ Acts of the public enemy (wartime enemies, saboteurs, and the like)

Part 4:
Personal
Property
and
Bailments

250

○ Acts of public authorities
○ Acts of the shipper
○ The inherent nature of the goods (perishable goods, evaporating and fermenting liquids, diseased animals, etc.)

This extraordinary duty of care is imposed upon common carriers, not private carriers. Private carriers are liable only for their negligent acts.

In addition to being insurers, common carriers of goods must accept *without discrimination* all goods offered to them for shipment. Under the Interstate Commerce Act, discrimination either through the selection of customers or through the use of preferential rates is illegal. Exceptions to the rule against discrimination are as follows:

○ A common carrier is not required to accept goods of a type it is not equipped to carry.
○ The carrier may refuse goods which are inherently dangerous and which would create hazards beyond the control of the carrier's usual safety facilities.
○ The common carrier may refuse goods that it does not represent itself as hauling.
○ The carrier may refuse goods that are improperly packed. Proper packaging is determined by the type of goods being shipped, the length of the haul, and the usual custom of the trade.
○ The carrier may refuse goods that are not delivered at the proper place and time.

Common carriers will not be excused from liability for losses due to strikes, mob violence, fire, and similar causes. Labor unions are required to give notice of impending strikes weeks in advance of the strike dates to allow carriers to reject shipments that might be damaged by delays caused by strikes.

The carrier is required to ship goods by the proper route, protect them during shipment, and deliver them to the proper person.

2. Limitation of Liability in Bill of Lading. Carriers may limit the amount of their liability to the value stated in the *bill of lading* (the written contract between a common carrier and a shipper).

● Mrs. Bratton hired Allied Van Lines, Inc., to transport her household goods from Ohio to Florida. When the goods were picked up, Mrs. Bratton signed a bill of lading which contained a provision limiting the carrier's liability to $1.25 per pound (which amounted to $4,500) or the actual value of the goods as written on the bill of lading. There was a place on the bill of lading for Mrs. Bratton to fill in the actual value of the goods ($10,630). She failed to do this. The shipment was destroyed in transit. Mrs. Bratton argued that since she did not read the document and was unaware of any provision affecting the carrier's liability, she was not bound by the words in the bill of lading. The court held that a bill of lading containing a limitation of the carrier's liability is binding even though the shipper had not read the limitation and even though her attention had not been called to it by the carrier. She received only $4,500.

3. Rights of Common Carriers. A common carrier has two rights which it may enforce against shippers of goods.

Chapter 19:
Carriers,
Ware-
housers,
and Inn-
keepers

○ The right to the payment of fees agreed upon for the shipment of the goods.
○ The right of lien on all goods shipped for the amount of the shipping charges due. This right of lien is terminated when payment is received by the carrier. Should the consignee (the one receiving the goods) fail to pay the charges, the shipper has the right to sell the goods at public sale, placing the receipts from the sale to the credit of the consignee.

● Hanlon Book Company ordered paper from Maine Paper Company. The paper was shipped from Bangor, Maine, under terms that transferred title to the paper when delivered to the carrier. Hanlon Book Company refused to pay shipping costs when informed of the arrival of the shipment. Notice was finally given to both firms of the carrier's intention to sell the paper to recover shipping charges. At a public sale, the paper brought a high bid of $237. The carrier deducted shipping costs and turned over the balance to the Hanlon Book Company.

4. Bills of Lading. The shipper usually makes out the bill of lading on forms supplied by the carrier. When the goods are accepted by the carrier, its agent signs triplicate copies, giving evidence of receipt of the goods. One copy of the bill of lading is kept by the carrier. The other two are for the shipper and the consignee, respectively. A bill of lading may be used as proof of ownership by the shipper or buyer, depending on the terms of the contract. One who has a bill of lading has the right to demand delivery of the goods from the carrier after the goods reach their destination.

The party shipping goods under a bill of lading is known as the *consignor;* the one to whom the goods are shipped is the *consignee.* When the bill of lading does not contain the words "to the order of," or "to bearer," it is called a *straight bill of lading* and is not negotiable. Conversely, when a bill of lading contains the words "to the order of" in front of the consignee's name or contains the words "to bearer," it is negotiable and is commonly called an *order bill of lading.*

If an employee of a common carrier issued a bill of lading without actually receiving the goods described in the bill, the carrier would be completely liable to any innocent third party who might have given value to the fraudulent holder. The one giving value for the bill of lading has a right to depend upon the carrier's position in issuing a bill that would from all intents and appearances give the impression of being genuine.

● Ace Appliances shipped eight freezers to Kaufman Stores over the Rio Grande and Eastern Railroad. The bill of lading called for ten freezers. The freight agent accepting the order signed the document without checking the number of crates. If the order bill of lading were sold to a buyer in the belief that there were ten freezers en route, the carrier would be liable for the two missing freezers.

5. Connecting Carriers. Common carriers often accept goods for shipment to points beyond the terminus of their own lines. The goods are then transferred to *connecting carriers* in order to complete delivery. Losses during shipment over the facilities of the connecting carriers will be determined according to the following rules:

○ The initial carrier will be responsible for damages while the goods are in the custody of connecting carriers if the shipment is an *interstate shipment*— one that goes beyond the borders of the state in which it originated.

Part 4:
Personal
Property
and
Bailments

252

○ The initial carrier is relieved of any liability for losses that may occur while the goods are in the possession of connecting carriers if the shipment is an *intrastate shipment*—one entirely within a single state.

6. Termination of Carrier's Liability as Insurer. A common carrier ceases to be an insurer of goods after they have been delivered to their destination. The bill of lading, which is the carrier's contract, usually states that forty-eight hours after the goods have arrived at their destination and the consignee has been notified of their arrival, the carrier's status will be reduced to that of a mutual-benefit bailee. This change reduces the carrier's liability from that of an insurer to one required to exercise ordinary care. A delay by the consignee beyond the forty-eight-hour limit also permits the carrier to charge additional fees for the storage of the goods still remaining in its possession. The fee is known as a *demurrage charge*.

Many carriers are willing to contract for what is called *door-to-door delivery*. Under these terms the carrier continues to be an insurer until the goods have been deposited at the street address or plant of the consignee.

C. Common Carriers of Passengers

Common carriers offering passenger service include buses, railroads, airlines, and taxicabs.

A *passenger* is a person who enters the premises of a common carrier with the intention of buying a ticket for a trip. One continues to be a passenger as long as one continues the trip. This relationship is terminated after one has reached the destination printed on the ticket and left the premises of the carrier.

1. Duties of Carriers of Passengers. A common carrier has an obligation to accept all persons who may seek passage over its lines. Carriers may not discriminate in the selection of passengers. There are, however, exceptions to this general rule.

○ Common carriers may refuse passengers when all available space is occupied or reserved.
○ Passengers may be refused if they are disorderly, intoxicated, insane, or infected with a contagious disease. To accept such persons would be to endanger the health and welfare of the other passengers. If these persons were accepted for passage, the carrier would be liable for any resulting injuries to the other passengers.

2. Obligations to Passenger's Person. A carrier must exercise reasonable care in the protection of passengers. Injuries which are reasonably foreseeable or preventable and result from the carrier's negligence give a passenger a right to sue for damages. However, if injuries are not reasonably foreseeable or preventable, the carrier is not responsible.

● Three men who were intoxicated boarded a commuter train around midnight. They were talking loudly and making a lot of noise. A conductor saw them and told them not to bother passengers. At the next stop, while the conductor let passengers on and off the train, the men went to another car. There, they assaulted, hit, and kicked a passenger. As soon as the conductor reboarded the train, he sought out the three men, discovered what they had done, and had them arrested. In a suit brought by the injured passenger against the carrier, the court held in favor of the carrier. The court said that the incident occurred so quickly and unexpectedly that the conductor acting with the highest degree of care under the circumstances could not have averted it.

3. Obligation of Carrier for Baggage. In conjunction with the carrying of passengers, a carrier is obliged to accept a reasonable amount of baggage. Baggage includes those things necessary for the comfort of the passenger and for the purpose of the trip. Excess baggage may be shipped by a passenger on payment of additional fees. Personal luggage carried aboard an airline and kept at one's seat does not generally come within the weight limits permitted each passenger.

When a baggage car or baggage compartment is available for checking luggage, the carrier is considered an insurer of the luggage checked by the passengers and left in these places. Property kept by passengers at their seats or in overhead compartments places upon the carrier the obligation of exercising ordinary care for its safety. The Carmack Amendment to the Interstate Commerce Act expressly permits the common carrier to limit its liability in connection with baggage carried in interstate commerce.

● Godlewski kept in her possession, during the flight, a briefcase containing many valuable papers and company directives for her trip. When she left the plane at Chicago, she discovered she had forgotten to pick up the briefcase, which was on the seat beside her. Investigation did not disclose the whereabouts of the case. Loss was due to Godlewski's own negligence, and the airline is not responsible to Godlewski or her firm.

Had Godlewski checked the briefcase with her other luggage in the baggage compartment of the plane, the airline would have been an insurer, and she would have been able to recover her loss.

The carrier is excused from liability for losses when the loss results from the passenger's negligence.

19-2. Warehousers

When goods are stored in a warehouse, the relation of bailor and bailee is created between the owner of the goods and the warehouser. The law discussed in Chapter 18 applies generally to such transactions. Some particular law relating to warehousers is also found in Article 7 of the UCC. The UCC defines a *warehouser* as a person engaged in the business of storing goods for hire. A *warehouse* is a building or structure in which any goods, but particularly wares or merchandise, are stored. A *warehouse receipt* is a receipt issued by a person engaged in the business of storing goods for hire.

Although both common carriers and warehousers are mutual-benefit bailees, they perform different functions. Common carriers are engaged in moving goods. Warehousers keep goods in storage. At times, however, one or the other will perform both functions.

A. Classes of Warehousers

Warehousers are sometimes classified as public and private warehousers. A *public warehouser* is one who owns a warehouse where any member of the pub-

Part 4:
Personal
Property
and
Bailments

254

lic who is willing to pay the regular charge may store goods. Grain elevators in the Midwest, used to store farmers' grain, are sometimes established as public warehouses. A warehouser whose warehouse is not for general public use is a *private warehouser*. Most warehousers fall into this latter category.

Sometimes business people will borrow money using goods that they have stored in a warehouse as security for the loan. The one who lends the money is given the warehouse receipt. If the debt is not paid, the holder of the receipt may obtain possession of the goods that are in storage. This practice is called *field warehousing*.

B. Duties and Rights of Warehousers

The duties and rights of warehousers are set forth in Article 7 of the UCC.

1. Duty of Care. A warehouser must use that amount of care that a reasonably careful person would use under similar circumstances. Failure to use such care is negligence and makes the warehouser liable for losses or damages to the goods.

● Bekins warehouse stored Keefe's household goods in its warehouse beneath some sprinkler system pipes. It did not inspect the area before placing the goods there. One of the pipes was unconnected, and water from the pipes leaked onto Keefe's goods, damaging them. Bekins's failure to inspect the area before placing goods there was a negligent act which made it responsible for the loss.

The parties may limit the amount of liability of the warehouser by including terms to that effect in the storage agreement or warehouse receipt.

● The warehouse receipt given by Bekins to Keefe in the above case limited Bekins's liability to 10 cents per pound per article. The limitation was enforceable even though it was not specifically called to Keefe's attention when the warehouse receipt was signed.

Such a limitation is not effective, however, if a warehouse converts the goods to its own use.

2. Duty Not to Commingle Goods. Unless the warehouse receipt provides otherwise, a warehouser must keep goods covered by each receipt separate from other goods. This is required so that the goods may be identified and delivered to the owner at any time. However, fungible goods may be *commingled* (mixed together). Fungible goods are goods of which any unit is, by nature, the equivalent of any other like unit.

● Fifty farmers stored their grain in the same grain elevator. The grain was mixed together. It was owned in common by all fifty owners. The warehouser was liable to each owner for that owner's share of the grain.

3. Right to Sell Goods. If, at the end of a storage period, goods are not removed from a warehouse, the warehouser may sell them. Before doing so, however, the warehouser must notify the owner that they are going to be sold and give that person the right to redeem them. If no time for storage is fixed in the agreement, the warehouser must give at least thirty days' notice to the owner before selling them. Goods may also be sold by the warehouser if they are hazardous to persons or to other property, and the warehouser had no knowledge of the hazard when the goods were placed in the warehouse. After warehouse charges are deducted, all proceeds from any such sale must be turned over to the person to whom the goods were to be delivered.

4. Warehouser's Lien. The UCC states that a warehouser has a lien on the goods that are in the warehouser's possession (7-209). A *warehouser's lien* is the right to retain possession of the goods until the satisfaction of the charges imposed upon them. The lien is for the amount of money owed for storage charges, transportation charges, insurance, and expenses necessary for the preservation of the goods. The lien is a possessory one. It is lost when the warehouser voluntarily delivers the goods or unjustifiably refuses to deliver them. If the owner of the goods owes the warehouser money for the storage of other goods, the warehouser has a lien for the other debt only if it is so stated in the warehouse receipt.

If the person who stored the goods is a merchant in the course of business, the warehouser's lien may be enforced by a public or private sale at any time or place and on any terms which are commercially reasonable. Notice must be given to all persons known to claim an interest in the goods. The notice must include a statement of the amount due, the nature of the proposed sale, and the time and place of any public sale.

C. Warehouse Receipts

A warehouse receipt may be issued by any warehouser. It need not be in any particular form, although it should include such essentials as the location of the warehouse, the date of issue, the rate of storage charges, and a description of the goods.

Such a receipt is negotiable, like a bill of lading, if by its terms the goods are to be delivered to *bearer* or to *the order of* a named person. A *negotiable warehouse receipt* may be transferred from one party to another by indorsement and delivery. When this is done, ownership of the goods which are stored in the warehouse is transferred to the transferee of the warehouse receipt.

19-3. Innkeepers

Among facilities available to those who travel or live away from home are hotels and convenient roadside motels. Dormitories are available to college students. An important function performed by those operating such facilities is the safekeeping of a guest's or resident's property. Thus, the responsibilities of hotelkeepers come within the study of bailments.

A. Types of Accommodations

The legal duties and rights of those owning and operating such facilities will vary depending on whether the particular facility is classified as a private accommodation or a public accommodation.

1. Private Accommodations. Dormitories, rooming or lodging houses, and clubs that offer living facilities on a contract basis are *private accommodations.* They are not regulated under the same laws provided for hotels and motels. In private accommodations, owners are given the right to select guests, and they may require contracts covering a week, a month, or longer periods.

Part 4:
Personal
Property
and
Bailments

256

The owner or manager has an obligation to exercise ordinary care in protection of the guest's personal property. A mutual-benefit bailment relationship exists between the guest and the one operating such a facility.

● Students living in dormitories at Northshore College signed contracts obligating them to a full semester's residence. Rooms were assigned by the resident director. Typewriters, clothing, and other personal property of the students which they left in their rooms established a mutual-benefit bailment with the college. Ordinary care by the resident director would require that security services be installed to restrict strangers from entering rooms of students.

Negligence on the part of management makes the owner of private accommodations liable for losses of a guest's personal property. Open entrances, unguarded hallways, or unrestricted movement of strangers through the facility could be regarded as negligence.

2. Public Accommodations. *Public accommodations* are those that hold themselves out to the public as willing to accept persons for unspecified periods of residence. They may not select their guests, and they may not require long-term contracts of residence. Their guests are *transients,* persons whose length of stay is not regulated by contract. Although a transient may remain for one, two, ten, or more days, the obligation may be terminated at will by the guest.

Included in the category of public accommodations are hotels and motels, which have rights and responsibilities respecting guests, lodgers, licensees, and business guests.

B. Classes of Transients

A *guest* is a transient who enters a hotel in proper condition and is willing and able to pay for accommodations. A *lodger,* on the other hand, is one who is a permanent resident. A lodger's living accommodations are usually referred to as a *boardinghouse.* While the hotelkeeper has common-law liability for luggage and other property brought into the hotel by a guest, the boardinghouse keeper's liability with boarders is limited to ordinary care of property. Persons not living at a hotel but entering it to enjoy the other facilities offered to the public are either business guests or licensees. A *business guest* is one coming on the premises with the intention of transacting some business with the hotel or its occupants. Other persons coming on the hotel premises for their own convenience and without invitation are *licensees.* To such persons the management owes only the minimum degree of care.

C. Rights and Obligations of Innkeepers

The hotelkeeper's obligations to a guest and the guest's property are imposed by common law and state statute. The obligations and rights are not by contract with the guest.

1. Obligation to Accept All Transients. A hotelkeeper is required to accept all guests who apply for accommodation. By the Civil Rights Act of 1964, and other federal and state legislation, the hotel may not discriminate in selection of guests for reasons of race, creed, color, sex, or ethnic background.

● Andrews-Caplan sought accommodations at the Atlantis Hotel. The clerk refused accommodations, saying that the hotel catered only to members of the medical and legal professions and their families. Excluding Andrews-Caplan as a guest made the hotel liable to Andrews-Caplan for any damages he might prove resulting from the hotel's actions.

A hotelkeeper may refuse accommodations to persons whose presence might imperil the health, welfare, or safety of other guests, or of the hotel itself. In addition, would-be guests may be turned away when all rooms are occupied or reserved. State laws which gave public accommodations other rights of refusal in past years were invalidated completely by the Civil Rights Act of 1964. Unless accommodations are refused for one of the two reasons given above, the hotelkeeper is subject to liability on a complaint made by a would-be guest.

2. Duty of Care to Guest's Person. A hotelkeeper must exercise reasonable care in protecting its guests. Guests may claim damages resulting from a lack of care or from negligence on the part of the hotel or its employees.

● Chalmers occupied a room as a guest of the Central Hotel. During the night an intruder entered her room, closed the door, and assaulted and raped her. Chalmers suffered both physical and mental injury from the experience. The hotel was negligent in permitting strangers to use an elevator that took them to the sleeping floors. No security guards were employed, and the elevator operators were not required to ask for identification of those going to the upper floors of the hotel. The Central Hotel is liable for damages resulting to Chalmers from its own negligence.

A hotelkeeper must respect and guard the guest's *right of privacy*. Guests are guaranteed, by law, exclusive and undisturbed privacy of rooms assigned by the hotel. Interruption of the guest's privacy through unpermitted entry by hotel employees or other guests, or through negligence, creates a liability under a tort action for *invasion of privacy*.

● Tuck occupied a room in the Lakeside Hotel. While he was watching television, a stranger opened the door and entered the room. The hotel clerk had negligently assigned the occupied room to this late guest. Tuck may seek damages against the hotel for invasion of privacy.

3. Duty of Care to Guest's Property. A hotelkeeper has a greater duty of care toward a guest's property than is imposed in the usual mutual-benefit bailment. Hotelkeepers are held by law to be insurers of the guest's property. The insured property includes all personal property brought into the hotel for the convenience and purpose of the guest's stay. In the event of loss, the hotelkeeper may be held liable, regardless of the amount of care exercised in the protection of the guest's property.

● Upon checking into the Concord Hotel, Mr. and Mrs. Modell placed two diamond rings in the hotel's safe-deposit vault. Later, Mrs. Modell withdrew the rings from the vault to wear that evening. When she went to return them later that night, she was told by the desk clerk that the vault was closed until the next morning. That night, the Modells' room was broken into, and the rings were stolen. The hotel was held liable for the loss of the rings because it did not provide a place for their safe-keeping.

4. Limitations of Innkeeper's Liability. As protection to hotelkeepers, the

Part 4:
Personal
Property
and
Bailments

258

common law has provided exceptions to the rule that the hotelkeeper is an insurer. Hotelkeepers are not liable as insurers for the following:

○ Losses caused by a guest's own negligence.

> ● Locks were installed on all sleeping rooms in the Mainline Hotel. Bellhops instructed guests in the use of the locks, and they were advised to lock their doors whenever leaving their rooms. Hamlin left the hotel without locking the room door, and property was stolen from his room. The hotel is not liable for this loss.

○ Losses to the guest's property due to acts of God or from acts of the public enemy

○ Losses of property due to accidental fire in which no negligence may be attributed to the hotelkeeper. This exception also includes fires caused by other guests staying at the hotel at the same time. Such persons, even though on other floors, are called *fellow guests.*

○ Losses arising out of characteristics of the property that cause its own deterioration.

In most states, hotelkeepers are further protected by laws limiting the amount of claim any guest may make for a single loss. The limit is usually $500 or less, depending upon the state in which a hotel is located. These laws also give the hotelkeeper the right to provide a safe or vault for the better protection of the guests' valuables. A guest who does not use the safe provided for valuables will be personally responsible for losses and may not seek recovery from the hotelkeeper. The hotel gives notice to guests of the prevailing statutes by posting copies of the statutes in each room.

● MacDonald, a professional photographer, was assigned to cover a national political convention. Many cameras, valuable lenses, and flash equipment were stored in his room. One evening a thief entered the room and removed cameras and lenses valued at $3,500. Under most state laws, the hotel is liable for no more than $500 of the loss reported.

A reasonable interpretation of the law permits a guest to keep in the room those valuables that one would ordinarily have on or about one's person at all times. These would include a watch, cufflinks, rings worn, and a reasonable amount of cash.

5. **Innkeeper's Right of Lien.** Hotelkeepers are permitted a right of lien on the property of a guest. If a guest cannot pay the bill, the hotelkeeper is permitted to take possession of the guest's property as security for payment at some later date. Payment of the bill releases the property and terminates the right of lien.

● When Isaksen completed her hotel stay, she discovered that she did not have sufficient cash to pay her bill at the Park Hotel. The hotel would not accept her check and took possession of her luggage as security until the bill was paid. After cash was wired to Isaksen, by her firm, she paid the bill. This terminated the hotel's right of lien on her property.

Some courts have recently held that before a hotelkeeper may make claim to a guest's luggage or property, the guest must have a hearing before a magistrate. In such cases, the magistrate reviews the available evidence. If it is warranted, the magistrate issues a writ permitting the hotel to exercise its right of lien.

Understanding Legal Terms

Define, identify, or explain the following terms:

bill of lading

carrier

common carrier

consignee

consignor

field warehousing

licensee

negotiable

   warehouse receipt

order bill of lading

private

   accommodations

private carriers

private warehouser

public

   accommodations

public enemy

public warehouser

straight bill of

   lading

transient

warehouse receipt

warehouser

warehouser's lien

Questions for Review and Discussion

1. Distinguish between private and common carriers.

2. Discuss the amount of care required of a common carrier in event of damage to freight. What degree of care must a carrier use in protecting passengers from injury?

3. How does an order bill of lading differ from a straight bill of lading?

4. When does a person become a passenger? When does that relationship terminate?

5. What duty of care is owed by a warehouser to the owner of stored goods?

6. Explain the warehouser's lien. For what amount of money is it? When is it lost?

7. Discuss the exceptions to a hotelkeeper's obligation to accept all persons.

8. How has the federal Civil Rights Act of 1964 affected a hotelkeeper's obligations to accept persons for accommodations?

9. What are the two obligations owed by a hotel to a guest's person?

10. Enumerate the common-law exceptions to a hotelkeeper's obligation to act as the insurer of a guests's property.

Analyzing Cases

1. Naughton Disposal Service was engaged in the business of recycling garbage. The company rented containers to its customers and bought from them the garbage that the customers stored in the containers. The company operated under specific contracts with its customers. It did not have a permit to operate as a common carrier. That state's statute defined a common carrier as "any person engaged in transportation by motor vehicle who carries or holds himself by advertising or otherwise to carry the property of those choosing to employ him." The Public Utilities Commission attempted to stop Naughton from operating because it did not have a permit. Naughton argued that it was a private carrier, not a common carrier, and was not under the jurisdiction of the Public Utilities Commission. Do you agree with Naughton? • *New Hampshire Pub. Util. Comm'n v. Naughton,* 394 A.2d 311 (N.H. 1978)

2. Faribault Woolen Mill Co. shipped 120 bales of New Zealand "greasy wool" (uncleaned, freshly shorn wool) from New Zealand to its factory in Minnesota. The wool was shipped in a large metal ocean cargo container roughly the size of a semitrailer. The container was designed so that wheels could be attached for hauling it over the road. The container left New Zealand aboard an ocean vessel which docked in Norfolk, Virginia. It was then converted into a trailer and hauled over the road to a railway terminal. The railroad's inspection reports stated that the outside of the container was in good condition at that time. A railroad flatcar took the container to its destination in Minnesota. When it was opened, an unpleasant odor and rotted condition of some bales announced that the cargo had been water-damaged. A hole 4 to 5 inches in diameter was discovered in the container's metal top. It had jagged edges as if it had been punched in, and was covered from the outside with tape. One side of the tape was loose, allowing a sliver of light to enter through the hole. Is the railroad responsible for the damaged cargo? Why or why not? ● *Faribault Woolen Mill Co. v. Chicago, Rock Island and Pacific R.R.,* 289 N.W.2d 126 (Minn. 1980)

3. W. J. Casey Trucking & Rigging Co. was engaged by General Electric Co. to transport a rotor from its North Bergen, New Jersey, plant to a generating station in Burlington, New Jersey. A crane was used by G.E.'s personnel to load the rotor onto Casey's truck. G.E.'s employees helped Casey's truck driver secure the rotor onto the truck. They directed the exact placement of the chains used to hold the rotor in place and rejected suggestions made by the truck driver. The rotor was damaged during transit when it shifted on the bed of the truck. Was the carrier responsible for the damage to the rotor? Give reasons for your answer. ● *W. J. Casey Trucking & Rigging Co. v. General Elec. Co.,* 376 A.2d 603 (N.J. 1977)

4. The snow from a severe winter storm was still on the road when Mlynarchik, a sixty-five-year-old woman, stepped off the bus on which she had been riding. A high snowbank was piled about $2\frac{1}{2}$ to 4 feet from the side of the bus. Mlynarchik stepped back and faced the bus, waiting for it to go by so that she could cross the road. As the bus started up, it began to skid. The back of it moved toward Mlynarchik. She stepped back against the snowbank but slipped and fell down with her feet pointing out into the road. The bus continued to skid toward her, and although she moved her legs to the right against the snowbank, the right rear wheel rolled over her left leg. Was Mlynarchik still a passenger at the time of the accident? What duty of care was owed to her by the bus company? Was the bus company liable for her injuries? Explain. ● *Mlynarchik v. Massachusetts Bay Transp. Auth.,* 322 N.E.2d 433 (Mass. 1975)

5. Poroznoff was living in a room at the YMCA on a week-to-week basis. It was his only residence. While there, he became drunk and disorderly and was arrested by the police. On his return to the YMCA, he found that his room was locked. He was told by the management not to reenter the building. Poroznoff argued that since the room at the YMCA was his only residence, he was not a transient guest. He claimed that he had rights of a tenant. Do you agree with Poroznoff? Why or why not? ● *Poroznoff v. Alberti,* 401 A.2d 1124 (N.J. 1979)

6. A state agency attempted to inspect Blair Academy's dormitories as hotels under the state's hotel and multiple-dwelling law. The law of that state defined a hotel as any building "which contains 10 or more units of dwelling space or has sleeping facilities for 25 or more persons and is kept, used, maintained, advertised as, or held out to be, a place where sleeping or dwelling accommodations are available to transient or permanent guests." Did Blair Academy's dormitories come within that state's definition of a hotel? Explain. ● *Blair Academy v. Sheehan,* 373 A.2d 418 (N.J. 1977)

7. I.C.C. Metals, Inc., delivered three separate lots of an industrial metal called indium to the Municipal Warehouse Company for safekeeping. Municipal gave I.C.C. a warehouse receipt for each lot. Each receipt contained a clause limiting the warehouser's liability to $50 per lot. The metal was worth $100,000. Two years later, when I.C.C. requested the return of the metal, it was informed by Municipal that the metal could not be found. Although it could offer little evidence to support its position, Municipal suggested that the metal had been stolen through no fault of its own. Municipal claims that its responsibility is limited to $50 per lot. Do you agree? Explain. ● *I.C.C. Metals, Inc. v. Municipal Warehouse Co.,* 409 N.E.2d 849 (N.Y. 1980)

Part 4

Case Briefs

Andrews
v. Ohio State Teachers Ret. Sys. Bd,
404 N.E.2d 747 (Ohio 1980)

Edith W. Andrews had been a member of the Ohio State Teachers Retirement System for twenty-two years before being employed by the University of Cincinnati. During her employment with the university, she was not entitled to contribute to the Ohio State Teachers Retirement System. Instead, she came under certain private pension plans with Teachers Insurance and Annuity Association of America (TIAA) and College Retirement Equities Fund (CREF). At a later date, Andrews became employed by the Bowling Green State University and again became eligible to contribute to the Ohio State Teachers Retirement System.

Andrews applied to the Ohio State Teachers Retirement System to purchase credit for the six years of service with the University of Cincinnati. She discovered that she could not do so unless she divested herself of any interest she might have under the annuity contracts with TIAA and CREF. She then sent the following letter to TIAA and CREF: "This letter is to advise you that I hereby, for myself, my heirs, administrators and assigns, renounce any and all interest that I may have at the present time, or in the future, in and to the above-described pension plans. If I have any other monies or plans with the Teachers Insurance & Annuity Association of America, or the College Retirement Equities Fund, I hereby renounce on behalf of myself, my heirs, administrators and assigns, any and all interest I may have presently or in the future to the same. I am completely divesting myself of any interest, of any payments from said funds presently or in the future. Under no conditions whatsoever, will I accept any payments from these funds."

On the same day, Andrews sent a $5,900.85 check to the Ohio State Teachers Retirement System in an effort to purchase service credit for her six years of service with the University of Cincinnati. The retirement system returned the check and refused to allow Andrews to purchase the requested service credit because TIAA and CREF had rejected Andrews's renunciation of her annuity contracts. They were afraid that any acceptance of her renunciation would jeopardize the favorable tax status which the annuity contracts received under the Internal Revenue Code.

Andrews brought suit seeking a mandatory injunction to allow her to purchase service with the University of Cincinnati.

Plaintiff's Position: Andrews contended that her unequivocal letter to TIAA and CREF effectively divested her of any rights under the annuity contracts and that such letter constituted either a release, discharge, waiver, renunciation, or gift of any rights which she may have had under such contracts.

Defendant's Position: TIAA and CREF contended that rescission and cancellation of the annuity contracts or renunciation or waiver by Andrews of her rights thereunder required consideration, which was not present in this case.

Legal Issue: May a gift be made to someone who does not accept it?

Court Decision: No. One may make a gift, as donor, only if the gift is accepted by the donee.

Court Reasoning: Clearly, one does not have to accept an unwanted gift which another attempts to make to that person. Whether viewed as a rescission, release, discharge, renunciation, waiver, gift, or otherwise, and whether or not supported by consideration, Andrew's attempted renunciation by way of the letter was ineffective so long as it was not accepted or agreed to by TIAA and CREF.

Sony Corporation of America v. Universal City Studios, Inc., 104 S.Ct. 774 (1984)

Sony Corporation of America manufactures and sells Betamax, a videotape recorder which can record a telecast off the air and make a copy of the audiovisual material which can be viewed at another time. Universal City Studios, Inc. and Walt Disney Productions, Inc. own the copyrights on some of the television programs that are broadcast on the public airways. Earlier, the U.S. Court of Appeals had ruled in favor of Universal's claim that Sony and others were liable for contributing to the infringement of their copyrights. Sony appealed to the U.S. Supreme Court.

Some members of the general public use the videotape recorders to record various television programs. At the trial several witnesses testified as to how they used the videotape recorder. Among them were William Griffiths and Marc Wielage. Griffiths owned a Betamax videotape recorder which he used to videotape television programs in his home. He kept some videotapes of the programs he recorded and erased others in order to reuse the tapes. Griffiths testified that he copied about 20 minutes of a Universal motion picture called *Never Give an Inch,* and two episodes from Universal television series entitled "Baa Baa Black Sheep" and "Holmes and Yo Yo." He also testified that he had copied but already erased Universal films called *Alpha Caper* and *Amelia Earhart.* He did not intend to keep any Universal film in his library. He had also recorded documentaries, news broadcasts, sporting events, and political programs such as a rerun of the Nixon-Kennedy debate.

Wielage, in addition to recording programs, has traded tapes with from twenty-five to thirty people, most of whom he contacted through a magazine. He exchanged "want lists" of films with these people. All the tapes that he made or acquired were for his own personal use, and he watched them either alone or with a few friends.

Surveys conducted by Sony and Universal showed that the primary use of the Betamax machine for most owners was "time-shifting"—the practice of recording a program to view it at a later time, and thereafter erasing it. The surveys also showed that a substantial number of people interviewed had accumulated libraries of tapes.

Petitioners' Contention: The petitioners (Sony and others) contended that home-use copying with the videotape recorder is not an infringement of the copyright law. They argued that the fair-use doctrine of the copyright law allows home-use copying of copyrighted audiovisual materials. In addition, they pointed out that since the copyright law of 1971 allows home-use sound recording, it also allows home-use audiovisual recording, even though the statute does not expressly so state.

Respondents' Contention: The respondents (Universal and Disney) contended that the activity of the parties in recording their copyrighted works off the air was copyright infringement. They asserted that the involvement of Sony and the retail stores in the manufacturing, distributing, advertising, and selling of Betamax recorders made the petitioners liable as direct or contributory infringers of their copyrights.

Legal Issue: Does off-the-air copying of copyrighted audiovisual materials by owners of videotape recorders in their homes for private, noncommercial use constitute an infringement of the copyright law?

Court Decision: The U.S. Supreme Court reversed the decision of the U.S. Court of Appeals. Noncommercial home use recording of material broadcast over the public airwaves is a fair use of copyrighted works and does not constitute copyright infringement.

Court Reasoning: The Copyright Act describes a variety of uses of copyrighted material that are not infringements of copyright. One of these is the doctrine of "fair use." Timeshifting, as occurs here, merely enables viewers to see works that they had been invited to witness free of charge. If the Betamax were used to make copies for a commercial or profit-making purpose, such use would be unfair. But a use that has no effect upon the potential market for the copyrighted work need not be prohibited in order to protect the author's incentive to create. Moreover, the purpose of this use serves the public interest in increasing access to television programming, an interest that is consistent with the First Amendment policy of providing the fullest possible access to information through the public airwaves.

Rosier
v. Gainesville Inns Assoc., Ltd.,
347 So.2d 1100 (Fla., 1977)
The Rosiers were guests at the Gainesville Holiday Inn. Before retiring for the night, they locked their outside door but did not secure the chain latch. Later, they awoke to find a ski-masked burglar in the room at the foot of their bed. In attempting to subdue the burglar, Mr. Rosier was stabbed twice, and Mrs. Rosier received a shattered right finger. The intruder escaped through the open outside door. The type of lock used in the door was a normal residential lock rather than a lock with a dead bolt as used in most hotels. Evidence showed that persons had entered guests' rooms in the past, probably with the aid of passkeys.

Plaintiffs' Position: The Rosiers claimed that the motel breached a duty in that (1) a passkey was available to the assailant and (2) the locks provided were inadequate.

Defendant's Position: The motel contended that since no passkeys were missing, they were not negligent in that respect. Also, since the Rosiers failed to secure the chain latch to the outside door, they were negligent.

Legal Issue: Could the motel foresee that the failure to use adequate locks would lead to the sort of injury sustained here?

Court Decision: Yes. The motel could have foreseen this occurrence.

Court Reasoning: The motel had knowledge of prior burglaries of guests' rooms carried out in a manner similar to that shown by the plaintiffs. A registered guest in a hotel or motel is a business invitee to whom the innkeeper owes a duty of reasonable care.

Part 5   Sales

Chapter 20   The Sales Contract

The great majority of all contracts today have to do with the sale of goods. Consider each item of food in the supermarket, each car on the sales lot, each newspaper, each book, and each magazine on the newsstand. Then contemplate the millions of items sold at the variety stores. So great is the importance of the sale of goods that special uniform laws have been enacted by the various states for the regulation of such sales.

The sale of goods often involves the laws of more than one state. Many years ago the legal problems arising from sales involving more than one state were so complicated that people hesitated to make such contracts. To overcome this difficulty, all the states except Louisiana have adopted the UCC, thus bringing about uniformity of customs and practices in sales contracts. Louisiana has adopted portions of the UCC.

Today, when anyone enters into a contract for the sale of goods, Article 2 of the UCC governs the transaction. Other kinds of contracts, such as those for services and for the purchase and sale of real property are governed by the law of contracts, discussed in Part 3 of the text.

● Bennett bought a parcel of land, on which a well had been dug, from Columbus Land Co. The well failed to produce water. In a suit brought by Bennett against Columbus, the court held that the UCC did not apply. The sale of land upon which a well has been dug does not involve the sale of goods.

20-1. Goods

Since goods are the subject matter of all sales contracts, it is important to define the term at the outset. *Goods* mean all things (including specially manufactured goods) which are movable at the time of identification to the contract for sale [2-105(1)]. Goods also include the unborn young of animals, growing crops, timber, and minerals if they are to be sold separately from the real property [2-107(1)]. Office furniture, mobile homes, human blood, milk, numismatic coins, wedding pictures, electricity, waste paper, kerosene, Christmas trees, ships, airplanes, horses, soybeans, polyethylene film, a printing press, and a book of recipes have all been held to be goods by the courts.

Goods that are not yet in existence or not yet under the control of people are called *future goods* [2-105(2)]. They include fish in the sea, minerals in the grounds, goods not yet manufactured, and commodities futures.

● A. G. Estes, Inc., contracted to sell its cotton crop to Cone Mills Corp. before the crop has been planted. This was a legally enforceable agreement to sell a commodity at a certain time in the future for a certain price.

20-2. The Contract for Sale

A contract for sale may be for a present sale of goods or it may be a contract to sell goods at a future time. A *sale,* as defined by the UCC, is the passing of title from the seller to the buyer for a price [2-106(1)]. Thus, every time anyone buys goods, either for cash or on credit, and receives title to them, a sale occurs.

● Calloway traded horses with Manion, a horse trader. Later, when a dispute arose, it was argued that the UCC did not apply to the transaction. The court, in holding that the UCC did apply, said, "a sale is defined as the passing of title from the seller to the buyer for a price, and the price may be payable in goods or otherwise."

If title is to pass at some future time, the agreement is a *contract to sell* rather than a sale [2-105(2)].

● Rubenstein paid a $100 deposit and signed a contract to buy a new car from Boulevard Motors. The car was to be ordered from the manufacturer and would be delivered in about forty-five days. This was a contract to sell because title was to pass at a future time.

A gift is not considered a sale because, although title passes, it is not given for a price. Similarly, a bailment does not meet the definition of a sale because title does not pass between the parties. The rules governing the passing of title from the seller to the buyer are discussed in detail in Chapter 21.

20-3. Special Rules Pertaining to Sales

One of the purposes of the UCC is to simplify, clarify, and modernize the law governing commercial transactions. With that in mind, the authors of the UCC used the fundamental rules of contract law as a base but made them less rigid. For example, sales contracts may be formed by any manner of expression—oral, written, or otherwise. Strict rules regarding the method of communication of offers and acceptances are relaxed. Firm offers are binding without consideration. The price may be omitted from a sales contract, and the amount of goods to be sold need not always be definite. Additional terms may sometimes be added by an offeree when accepting an offer. No consideration is necessary to modify a contract for the sale of goods. These special rules relating to sales contracts are discussed in more detail below.

A. Formation of Contract for Sale

A contract for sale may be made in any manner that shows that the parties reached an agreement. It may be oral (with some exceptions) or in writing, or it may be established by the conduct of the parties. An enforceable agreement may come about even though the exact moment of its making cannot be determined and even though some terms are not completely agreed upon [2-204(1)(2)].

● Advance Steel Co. agreed orally, in a series of telephone conversations, to sell some steel to Harlow & Jones, Inc. The steel company sent a form to the buyer confirming the sale, and the buyer sent a purchase order for the steel containing different terms. When the buyer received the seller's confirmation form, it telephoned the seller, objecting to the shipping and delivery terms stated in the form. The seller made two partial shipments of steel. Later, when suit was brought, the seller argued that its sales confirmation form was the offer which the buyer accepted by mailing back its purchase order form. The buyer argued that it had rejected the seller's confirmation and that its purchase order was a counteroffer which the seller accepted by making two partial shipments. The court held that the agreement was in fact made during the series of telephone conversations. The fact that the shipping and delivery terms were not completely ironed out was unimportant.

B. Offer and Acceptance

As explained in Chapter 8, it is a general rule of contract law that if the offeror sends an offer by one method of communication (such as by mail) and the offeree accepts by the same method (mail), the contract comes into existence when the acceptance is sent. On the other hand, under contract law still followed in some states, if the offeree accepts by a different method (such as by telegram in the above example), the contract comes into existence when the acceptance is received by the offeror rather than when sent by the offeree. The UCC does away with this distinction [2-206(1)(a)]. To establish a contract for the sale of goods, unless otherwise indicated by the offeror or the circumstances, the offeree may accept the offer in any manner and by any medium that is reasonable. A contract for the sale of goods comes into existence when the acceptance is sent, so long as the method used to send it is reasonable.

● Goodwin sent a letter to Callaghan offering to buy ten file cabinets for $700 if Callaghan would ship them promptly. Callaghan accepted the offer by telegram. The contract came into existence when the telegram was sent.

Unless the buyer indicates otherwise, an order or other offer to buy goods for prompt shipment may be accepted by either a prompt shipment or a prompt promise to ship [2-206(1)(b)]. Under this rule the goods that are shipped may be either conforming or nonconforming goods. According to the UCC, goods are conforming when they are in accordance with the obligations under the contract [2-106(2)]. In the example given above, Callaghan could have accepted the offer by promptly shipping the file cabinets instead of by promising to ship them.

C. Firm Offer

Another rule of law that has been modified by the UCC is the rule that requires consideration in an option contract. An option contract is a binding promise to hold an offer open. Consideration is required to make it binding on the parties. No consideration is necessary, however, if the offeror is a merchant, that is, one who deals in goods of the kind being sold or who has special knowledge of those goods (2-205). The offer must be in the form of a signed writing and is limited to a period of three months. It is called a *firm offer*.

● Janke Construction Co. obtained a price quotation from Vulcan Materials Co. for some pipe to be used on a construction project on which it intended to bid. Later, when a dispute arose, the court held that Vulcan's quotation was not a firm offer under the UCC because it had not stated that the price was irrevocable.

D. Open-Price Terms

Another change that the UCC has made is that a contract for the sale of goods may be made even though the price is not settled. Such *open-price terms* may occur when the parties intend to be bound by a contract but fail to mention the price or decide to set the price later. Under the non-UCC law, no contract would come about because the terms are not definite. The UCC allows such a contract to come into existence [2-305(1)]. If the parties cannot agree on the price at the later date, the price will be a reasonable price at the time for delivery of the goods.

● Ayers contracted to buy chicken feed from Sparton Grain & Mill Co. As part of the contract, Sparton agreed to buy and market all Ayer's eggs. The price that Ayers was to pay for the feed was not mentioned. The court held that the UCC requires the price to be a reasonable one when no price is quoted (2-305).

E. Output and Requirements Terms

Sometimes a seller will agree to sell "all the goods we manufacture" or "all the crops we produce" to a particular buyer. This is known as an *output contract*. At other times a buyer will agree to buy "all the oil we need to heat our building" (or some similar requirement) from a particular seller. This is called a *requirements contract*. Such contracts were often not allowed at common law because the quantity of the goods to be bought or sold is not definite. The UCC allows output and requirements contracts for the sale of goods as long as the parties deal in good faith and according to reasonable expectations [2-306].

● Spencer Oil Co. agreed to sell to Lopaz Manufacturing Co. all the heating oil Lopaz would need during the next year. Spencer knew that Lopaz used about 5,000 gallons of oil each year. Over the summer, Lopaz enlarged its building to an extent that it would require 25,000 gallons of heating oil during the next year. Spencer would not be bound to supply that amount of oil to Lopaz because it was far beyond the amount it expected to supply.

F. Additional Terms in Acceptance

Under the general rules of contract law, an acceptance of an offer must be an absolute, unqualified, unconditional assent to the offer. If the acceptance differs in the slightest from the offer, it operates as a rejection. The UCC changes this rule somewhat (2-207). A contract for the sale of goods comes into existence even though the acceptance states terms additional to or different from those offered or agreed upon (unless acceptance is made conditional on assent to the additional terms). The additional terms are treated as proposals for additions to the contract if the parties are not both merchants. If both parties are merchants, the additional terms become part of the contract unless they materially alter it, or the other party objects within a reasonable time, or the offer limits acceptance to its terms.

This rule is intended to deal with two typical situations. The first is where an agreement has been reached either orally or by informal correspondence between the parties and is followed by one or both of the parties sending formal acknowledgments or memos which contain additional terms not discussed earlier.

● The Gateway Co. reached an oral agreement with Charlotte Theatres, Inc., for the sale of an air-conditioning system. Later, Gateway put the agreement in writing, signed it, and sent it to Charlotte for its signature. Charlotte signed the writing but added additional terms relative to the date of completion of the contract. Since both parties were merchants, the additional terms would become part of the contract unless Gateway objected to them within a reasonable time. Had one of them not been a merchant, a contract would have come into existence without the additional terms, and the added terms would have been treated as proposals for additions to the contract.

The second situation in which this rule applies is one in which a telegram or letter which is intended to be the closing or confirmation of an agreement adds further minor suggestions or proposals such as "ship by Thursday" or "rush."

● Cal-Cut Pipe and Supply, Inc., offered in writing to sell used pipe to Southern Idaho Pipe and Steel Co., specifying a delivery date. Southern Idaho accepted by sending a check but changed the delivery date. Cal-Cut mailed a confirmation containing the original delivery date with the postscript, "We will work it out." The court held that there was a binding contract between them despite the conflicting delivery terms.

G. Modification
Under the general rules of contract law, if the parties have already entered into a binding contract, a later agreement to change that contract needs consideration to be binding. The UCC has done away with this rule. An agreement modifying a contract for the sale of goods needs no consideration to be binding [2-209(1)]. Any such modification may be oral unless the original agreement is in writing and provides that it may not be modified except by a signed writing. Any such clause in a form supplied by a merchant to a nonmerchant, however, must be separately signed by the nonmerchant to be effective [2-209(2)].

20-4. Oral and Written Contracts
Of the millions of sales contracts made every day, by far the greatest number are oral or implied. Sales through vending machines, self-service counters, and the like are implied; sales made by clerks over the counter are usually oral. In some situations a written memorandum of the sale is desirable to avoid future misunderstanding.

● Ruocco agreed to buy a set of the *Encyclopaedia Britannica* from Conti Book Stores. The salesperson described the set to be of "a recent edition." Ruocco took this to mean they were of the current edition. When the books were delivered, it was found that they were of a former edition. A written agreement that named the edition in exact terms would have resolved the dispute that followed between Ruocco and the seller.

A. Statute of Frauds
As was discussed in Chapter 13, a statute of frauds requires certain contracts to be in writing to be enforceable. The UCC contains such a statute. A contract for the sale of goods for the price of $500 or more must be in writing to be enforceable [2-201(1)].

● Ultra Fashion Stores agreed to purchase surplus jeans owned by Evangeline's Specialty Shop. The agreement was oral and called for cash payment of $850 upon delivery of the jeans thirty days from date of agreement. In the absence of any written agreement, the sale cannot be enforced by either party.

The UCC Statute of Frauds is much more flexible, however, than statutes of frauds under the non-UCC law. The UCC has four exceptions to the general rule. These are discussed below.

1. Sales Between Merchants. An exception to the general rule is made when the sale is made between merchants. If either merchant delivers a confirmation of the oral agreement to the other within a reasonable length of time and if the receiver is aware of the contents of the correspondence, this will satisfy the requirements of a written contract [2-201(2)]. The receiver, however, may avoid any commitment or obligation by giving written notice of any objection to the contents of the confirming letter within ten days of its receipt.

● Suppose, in the previous illustration, Ultra Fashion Stores had written a confirmation of the order and delivered it to Evangeline's Specialty Shop two days later. Unless Evangeline's communicated a written objection to Ultra Fashion's confirmation within ten days, the agreement would be construed as a valid enforceable agreement.

2. Specially Manufactured Goods. Another exception to the general rule is made if the goods are to be specially manufactured for the buyer and are not suitable for sale to others in the ordinary course of the seller's business. In such a case, if the seller has made either a substantial beginning in manufacturing the goods or has made commitments to buy them, the oral agreement will be enforceable [2-201(3)].

● Associated Lithographers agreed orally with Stay Wood Products, Inc., to print brochures and other materials advertising Stay Wood's products. The price amounted to more than $500. When suit was brought on the oral agreement, the court held that Stay Wood could not assert the UCC Statute of Frauds as a defense. The printed materials were specially manufactured and were not suitable for sale to others. Associated had made a substantial beginning in printing the goods.

3. Admissions in Court. If the party against whom enforcement is sought admits in court that an oral contract for the sale of goods was made, the contract will be enforceable [2-201(3)(c)]. The contract is not enforceable under this exception, however, beyond the quantity of goods admitted.

● Anderson admitted in court that he orally agreed to sell 18,000 bushels of durum wheat to Farmer's Elevator Co. Because of the admission, Anderson could not use the UCC Statute of Frauds as a defense.

4. Executed Agreements. When the parties carry out their agreement in a satisfactory manner, the law will not render the transaction unenforceable for want of an agreement in writing. Executed contracts need not be in writing; the writing requirements apply only to contracts which are *executory*, that is, not yet performed. This means that contracts for goods which have been received and accepted need not be in writing.

If there has been a part payment or a part delivery in conformance with the contract terms, the law will enforce only that portion of the agreement that has been performed [2-201(3)(c)].

● Gilmore orally agreed to sell Nash three electric guitars and a powerful amplification system for $900. Delivery was to be made in ten days, at which time Nash agreed to have the money ready for payment. If Gilmore had delivered one of the three guitars to Nash, the court would enforce payment for that one instrument.

B. Requirements of Writing

The writing that is required to satisfy the UCC Statute of Frauds must indicate that a contract for sale has been made between the parties [2-201(1)]. It must also be signed by the party against whom enforcement is sought (the defendant). A writing is acceptable even though it omits or incorrectly states a term agreed upon. However, a contract will not be enforceable beyond the quantity of goods shown in such writing. For that reason, it is necessary to put the quantity of goods to be bought and sold in the written agreement. An informal note, memorandum, or sales slip will satisfy the writing requirements.

● Had Gilmore, in the previous case, noted the terms of the agreement on the back of an envelope and had Nash signed it, the requirements of a written agreement would have been met, thereby obligating Nash to the sales contract. Only the defendant in a lawsuit must have signed the writing.

20-5. Auction Sales

In *auction sales* the auctioneer presents goods for sale. This is similar to an invitation to trade. Bidders in the crowd respond with their offers. The highest bid (offer) is accepted by the auctioneer, usually by the drop of the hammer together with the auctioneer's calling out "Sold."

If, while the hammer is falling, a higher bid comes from those in the crowd, the auctioneer has two options: to declare the goods sold or to reopen the bidding [2-328(2)].

Such a sale is with reserve unless the goods are in explicit terms put up without reserve. In an auction *with reserve* the auctioneer may withdraw the goods at any time before announcing completion of the sale. In an auction *without reserve,* after the auctioneer calls for bids on an article or lot, that article or lot cannot be withdrawn unless no bid is made within a reasonable time. In either case, a bidder may retract a bid until the auctioneer's announcement of completion of the sale. A bidder's retraction does not revive any previous bid [2-328(3)].

● Swenson, an auctioneer, was silent as to whether a sale would be with or without reserve. Durocher bid $1,500 on an Oriental vase. She was the highest bidder. Swenson refused to sell the vase at that price. Durocher demanded that the $1,500 bid be accepted. Swenson was justified in withdrawing the vase from the auction because the terms were not announced, making it a sale with reserve.

The practice of planting persons in the crowd for the purpose of raising bids by innocent purchasers is not allowed. Except in a forced sale, if a seller (or the seller's agent) makes a bid at an auction without notifying other bidders, a buyer has two options. Under the UCC, a buyer may either avoid the sale or take the goods at the price of the last good-faith bid prior to the completion of the sale [2-328(4)].

● In the above example, if the owner of the Oriental vase had bid against Durocher, Durocher could have purchased the vase for the price of the last bid other than the owner's that had been made before her final bid.

20-6. Bulk Transfers

Over the years, bulk transfers have caused special problems for business people. Merchants, owing debts, would sometimes sell out their entire stock in trade for less than what it was worth. This practice left creditors with no way of reaching and selling the goods to obtain the money owed them. Article 6 of the UCC protects creditors from this practice. It is called the Bulk Transfer Article of the UCC. As defined by the UCC, a *bulk transfer* is any transfer in bulk and not in the ordinary course of the transferor's business of a major part of the materials, supplies, merchandise, or other inventory of an enterprise [6-102(1)].

The UCC lists four requirements that must be followed whenever a bulk transfer is made. If the four requirements are not met, any transferee of the goods (such as a buyer) can lose all ownership rights to them. Creditors who have suffered damages may demand the return of all goods bought, with no obligation to reimburse the transferee [6-104(1)]. The four requirements of the bulk transfer law are as follows:

○ The transferee must require the transferor to furnish a list of any existing creditors.
○ The parties must prepare a schedule of the property being transferred so that it can be identified.
○ The transferee must preserve the list and schedule for six months following the transfer and make it available for inspection.
○ The transferee must give notice of the transfer to all the creditors at least ten days before taking possession of the goods or paying for them, whichever happens first (6-105).

After observing these four requisites, the transferee may pay for and take title and possession of the inventory. Creditors who have not, to that time, taken any action to interrupt the transfer have lost their right to do so.

The bulk transfer law is applicable to businesses whose principal activity is to sell merchandise from stock. It also includes firms which manufacture the goods they sell.

If the bulk transfer is an auction, the auctioneer must meet the obligations of the transferee that are listed above (6-108). An auctioneer who knows that the auction is a bulk transfer and fails to meet the requirements will be liable to the creditors up to the amount of the net proceeds of the auction.

Understanding Legal Terms

Define, identify, or explain the following terms:

auction with reserve	bulk transfer	future goods	open-price terms
auction without reserve	contract to sell	goods	sale
	firm offer		

Questions for Review and Discussion

1. Name three items that are goods and one item that is a future good.

2. Explain in what way a sale is different from a contract to sell.

3. Describe six ways in which the UCC is less rigid than the fundamental rules of contract law.

4. Compare an option contract with a firm offer. How do they differ?

5. How does the UCC change the general rule of contract law requiring an acceptance to be an absolute, unqualified, unconditional assent to an offer?

6. Explain in what way an agreement to modify a contract for the sale of goods differs from an agreement to modify other kinds of contracts.

7. Explain how the UCC Statute of Frauds regulates executory sales agreements.

8. Describe the four exceptions to the UCC Statute of Frauds relating to contracts for the sale of goods.

9. Compare an auction with reserve with an auction without reserve and explain when each comes about.

10. Discuss the reason for the bulk transfer provision of the UCC. What does this law require?

Analyzing Cases

1. O'Brien placed a telephone order for twenty shipments of lettuce from Soroka Farms. Soroka Farms shipped the lettuce to a cooler, where it was held under cold storage. It was later shipped directly to O'Brien's customers. O'Brien refused to pay for the lettuce, arguing that the contract was not enforceable because it was not in writing as required by the statute of frauds. Evidence clearly showed that although O'Brien had not paid for the lettuce, he had accepted and effectively received the shipment. Do you believe that the oral contract was enforceable in this case? Why? ● See also *O'Day v. George Arakelian Farms, Inc.*, 540 P.2d 197 (Ariz. 1975)

2. Seigel, while shopping at the Giant Food Store, took a six-pack carton of Coca-Cola from the shelf. One of the bottles in the carton exploded as he was carrying the carton to a shopping cart, causing him to fall and be injured. When Seigel brought suit for breach of warranty, Giant Food argued that no warranty was made because no sales contract took place. Seigel argued that the retailer's act of placing the bottles on the shelf for a price indicated an intent to offer them for sale and that, as a customer, his act of taking physical possession of them indicated his intent to accept the offer. Since Giant Food was a self-service store, Seigel argued, this was the only reasonable way to accept the store's offer. Did a contract for sale occur? Why or why not? ● *Giant Food, Inc. v. Washington Coca-Cola Bottling Co.*, 332 A.2d 1 (Md. 1975)

3. Barclay wrote to Interstate saying that it would be able to manufacture fiberglass panels. The letter quoted a price and said, "The price quotation is based on orders of 75,000 sq. ft. or more (truckload quantities) freight prepaid. Order less than 75,000 sq. ft. add $.01/sq. ft. f.o.b. Lodi." When Interstate ordered some panels, Barclay replied that it could not fill the order. Interstate claims that Barclay breached a contract by refusing to deliver the goods. Do you agree? Why or why not? ● *Interstate Indus., Inc. v. Barclay Indus. Inc.*, 540 F.2d 868 (7th Cir. 1976)

4. Norma J. of California, a California corporation, placed two orders with Avila Group, Inc., a New York corporation, to purchase 80,000 yards of fabric. The purchase orders were on Avila's standard order form and were signed by Norma J.'s president. When the first shipment of fabric was delivered, Norma J. rejected it on the ground that

the fabric that was delivered did not conform to samples it had seen earlier. Norma J. also refused to accept delivery of later shipments. In a lawsuit that followed, Norma J. claimed that no contract came into existence because Avila did not return countersigned copies of the order form showing acceptance of the order by Avilla. Do you agree with Norma J.? Explain. • *Avila Group, Inc. v. Norma J. of California,* 426 F. Supp. 537 (N.Y. 1977)

5. Ferguson agreed to sell to R. L. Kimsey Cotton Co., Inc., all the cotton produced by Ferguson on a specified parcel of land at an agreed price. The agreement was in writing and contained other terms. Later, Ferguson argued that the agreement was invalid because the quantity and subject matter were vague and indefinite. Is Ferguson correct? Why or why not? • *R. L. Kimsey Cotton Co., Inc. v. Ferguson,* 214 S.E.2d 360 (Ga. 1975)

6. On July 23, Cargill, Inc., telephoned Stafford about buying some wheat. Stafford said that he had 40,000 bushels of wheat which he might let them have. He told Cargill to send a confirmation, saying, "If it looks right, I will sign it and send it back." Cargill prepared and mailed a confirmation but sent it to the wrong address. Stafford received the confirmation on August 17, almost four weeks after it had been sent. On August 21, Stafford wrote Cargill objecting to a cancellation clause in the confirmation, saying "thus contract void." Cargill argued in court that the contract was enforceable under the provision of the UCC which says that between merchants, if either merchant delivers a confirmation to the other within a reasonable time, an oral contract is enforceable. How would you decide? • *Cargill, Inc. v. Stafford,* 553 F.2d 1222 (10th Cir. 1977)

7. Carolina Transformer Co., Inc., brought suit against Anderson for several thousand dollars owed them for the purchase of transformers. In his testimony, Anderson said that he had made a trip to North Carolina, where he had orally negotiated the contract and had reached a final agreement with Carolina for the purchase of the transformers. Later, when he was sued on the contract, Anderson argued that he was not responsible because, under the UCC, a contract for the sale of goods of $500 or more is not enforceable unless it is in writing. Do you agree with Anderson? • *Carolina Transformer Co. v. Anderson,* 341 So.2d 1327 (Miss. 1977)

8. Representatives of a fish marketing association (AIFMA) and a fish company (NEFCO) met at Bristol Bay, Alaska, to negotiate a marketing agreement for the forthcoming fishing season. At this meeting, NEFCO's agent, Gage, signed an agreement that contained the price that was to be paid for the fish and other details about the transaction. It omitted the quantity of fish that was to be purchased. Later, when suit was brought on the agreement, NEFCO argued that is was unenforceable because the agreement failed to mention the quantity. Do you agree with NEFCO? Explain. • *Alaska Ind. Fish Mktg. Ass'n v. New England Fish Co.,* 548 P.2d 348 (Wash. 1976)

9. Coleman bid $2,050 for a D-7 tractor at a public auction. Nothing was stated that the auction was with reserve. The auctioneer yelled "Sold," accepting Coleman's bid. Later, the owner of the tractor refused to sell it for $2,050, saying that the auction was with reserve and that therefore he could refuse to accept the bid. Must the owner sell the tractor to Coleman for $2,050? Why or why not? • *Coleman v. Duncan,* 540 S.W.2d 935 (Mo. 1976)

10. Ireland, who owed money to West Denver Feed Co., sold his entire business to Hall. Ireland did not comply with the Bulk Transfer Act. Two years later, Hall filed for bankruptcy. The West Denver Feed Company brought suit against Ireland for the money owed. May it recover under the Bulk Transfer Act from Ireland? Explain. • *West Denver Feed Co. v. Ireland,* 551 P.2d 1091 (Colo. 1976)

Chapter 21   Title and Risk

A private party sells a car to a buyer who agrees to pick up the car the next day. That night, the car is stolen. A boat dealer contracts to sell a yacht to a private party. The yacht sinks before the buyer takes possession. A seller ships goods to a buyer, and the goods are destroyed by a tornado before reaching their destination. A city levies a personal property tax on goods that were sold by the owner the previous day. An attaching creditor sues the owner of a piece of construction equipment two days after the owner had agreed to sell it to a third party. In some of these situations, it is necessary to determine who must bear the risk of loss, the buyer or the seller. In others, it is important to determine who has title to the goods. Earlier law followed the rule that whoever had title also had the risk of loss. The UCC separates risk of loss from title, treating them differently.

21-1. Passage of Title From Seller to Buyer

Title is the right of ownership to goods. People who own goods are said to have title to them. Sometimes, in the case of a sale or a contract to sell, it becomes necessary to determine whether title has passed and, if it has, to know the exact time and place of passage. For example, when someone files a petition in bankruptcy, a trustee is appointed by the court to take legal title of all goods owned by the bankrupt for distribution among the bankrupt's creditors.

In the absence of an agreement, title passes from the seller to the buyer at different times, depending on whether the goods are to be moved. If the contract calls for the goods to be moved, title passes when the seller completes delivery obligations. If the goods are not to be moved and a document of title (warehouse receipt or bill of lading) is used in the transaction, title passes when the document is delivered. If the goods are not to be moved and no document of title is used, title passes at the time and place of contracting. Title to goods cannot pass under a contract for sale before they have been identified to the contract. These rules are explained in detail below.

Table 21-1. Passage of Title From Seller to Buyer

Terms of Contract	Title Passes
Agreement of parties	At time and place agreed upon
Shipment contract	At time and place of shipment
Destination contract	On tender of goods at destination
No movement—with document of title	At time and place of document delivery
No movement—without document of title	At time and place of contracting

A. Identification of Goods to Contract

Before title can pass from the seller to the buyer, goods must be *identified* to the contract. This means that specific goods have to be selected as the subject matter of the transaction [2-501(1)].

● North Central Community College's bookstore ordered 150 copies of *Introduction to Management* from the Superior Book Company. The books became identified to the contract when Superior employees at the company's warehouse selected the particular 150 books that were to be sent to the college bookstore.

The parties may enter into an agreement setting forth the time and manner of identification of goods to the contract. If no such agreement is made, identification occurs in the following ways.

1. Existing Goods. If the goods are already in existence and have been selected as the subject matter of a contract, identification occurs when the contract is made.

● While visiting a pet shop, Roderick noticed that one particular dog stood out from all the others. It was friendly toward Roderick and had distinct markings. He decided to buy it. Since he was going away on vacation that afternoon, it was agreed that he would pick up the dog and pay for it in two weeks. Identification occurred when the contract was made.

2. Future Goods. If the contract is for the sale of future goods (goods not yet in existence or not yet under the control of people), identification occurs when the goods are either shipped or selected by the seller as goods to which the contract refers.

● Procopio agreed to sell ten dozen lobsters from her next haul to Captain Dan's Harborside Restaurant. Identification will occur when Procopio hauls in and sets aside ten dozen lobsters for that particular restaurant.

In the case of crops, identification occurs when they are planted if they are to be harvested within twelve months or the next normal harvest season after contracting. If the contract is for the sale of unborn young of animals, identification occurs when they are conceived provided birth occurs within twelve months after the contract is made [2-501(1)(c)].

3. Fungible Goods. *Fungible goods* are "goods of which any unit is, by nature or usage of trade, the equivalent of any like unit" [1-201(17)]. Wheat, flour, sugar, and liquids of various kinds are examples of fungible goods. They are usually sold by weight or measure. Title to fungible goods may pass without the necessity of separating goods sold from the bulk. Under the UCC, "an undivided share of an identified bulk of fungible goods is sufficiently identified to be sold although the quantity of the bulk is not determined" [2-105(4)].

● Cashway Oil Company owned a large fuel storage tank which was partially filled with diesel fuel. The exact quantity of fuel in the tank was not known. The company was going out of business. McAllister contracted to buy half the oil in the tank, and O'Donnell contracted to buy the other half. Identification occurred when the contracts were made even though the exact quantity of each sale was unknown at that time and neither party had taken a share of the oil from the entire lot.

B. Agreement of the Parties

The parties to a sales contract may, if they wish, enter into an agreement stating when and where title will pass from the seller to the buyer. In such a case, title will pass at the time and place agreed upon. However, if the agreement allows the seller to retain title after the goods are shipped, title will pass at the time of shipment regardless of the agreement, and the seller will have a security interest in the goods [2-401(1)]. A security interest (see Chapter 41) gives the seller a right to have the property sold in the event the buyer fails to pay money owed to the seller.

● Raymond agreed to sell Glover her Datsun 280Z for $4,000. The agreement called for Glover to pay $2,000 down and the balance in monthly installments for two years. Under the agreement, title to the vehicle would not pass to Glover until the $4,000 was paid in full. Since Raymond delivered the car to Glover on the day the agreement was signed, title passed to Glover at that time regardless of the terms to the contract. The effect of those terms was to give Raymond a security interest in the vehicle for the balance of the money owed to her.

C. Physical Delivery of the Goods

If the goods are to be delivered by the seller, title passes when the seller completes delivery obligations according to the terms of the contract. Some contracts require sellers to turn the goods over to a carrier. These are known as *shipment contracts*. Other contracts, called *destination contracts*, require sellers to deliver the goods to the buyer's location and tender them to the buyer there.

1. Shipment Contracts. If the contract requires the seller to send the goods to the buyer but does not require the seller to deliver them directly to the place of destination, title is transferred at the time and place of shipment [2-401(2)(a)].

● Underwood was employed by Kentucky Cardinal Dairies to pick up milk from various farmers and deliver it, in the farmers' cans, to the dairy. When no one was looking, he poured some of the milk from the farmers' cans into his own cans and sold it to another dairy. He was charged with the unlawful conversion of milk "which was the property of Kentucky Cardinal Dairies." In his defense, he argued that the milk was still the property of the farmers because it had not yet reached the dairy. The court disagreed, holding that title to the milk passed to the dairy the moment it was picked up by Underwood because that was the time and place of shipment.

2. Destination Contracts. If the contract requires the seller to deliver the goods to a destination, title is transferred when the seller tenders the goods at the place of destination [2-401(2)(b)].

D. Delivery Without Moving Goods

Sometimes delivery is made without moving the goods. This may occur when the goods are in the possession of a bailee. It may also occur when the buyer agrees to pick up the goods directly from the seller. Passage of title in such cases depends upon whether a document of title was used in the transaction.

1. Delivery With Document of Title. If the seller is to deliver a document of title, title passes to the buyer when the document is delivered [2-401(3)(a)]. A *document of title* is a paper which evidences that the person who possesses it is entitled to receive the goods named in the document [1-201(15)]. The document must be either issued by or addressed to a bailee. Bills of lading and warehouse receipts are examples of documents of title.

● Sawyer was given a negotiable warehouse receipt when she stored a large quantity of beans in a grain elevator. Later, in exchange for an agreed price, she negotiated the receipt by indorsing it and delivering it to Moradian. Moradian received title to the beans when the document was delivered to him.

Automobile title certificates generally have not been given the legal status of documents of title as that term is used in the UCC.

2. Delivery Without Document of Title. When delivery is to be made without moving the goods and no documents are to be delivered, title passes at the time and place of contracting [2-401(3)(b)].

● Tetrault gave Whatley a check for the purchase of a boat and trailer to fulfill the terms of their contract. No title documents were passed. The person with whom the items were stored was notified of the sale, and Tetrault arranged to pick them up the next day. Title passed from the seller to the buyer when the contract was made.

E. Revesting of Title in Seller

Buyers, after entering into sales contracts, sometimes refuse to accept the goods that are delivered or are otherwise made available to them. In all such cases, title to the goods revests in the seller [2-401(4)]. This is true whether or not the buyer's rejection of the goods was justified. Similarly, title to goods revests in the seller when the buyer accepts goods and then, for a justifiable reason, decides to revoke the acceptance. A justifiable reason for revoking an acceptance would be the discovery of a defect in the goods after having inspected them.

21-2. Transferring Imperfect Title

Sellers occasionally do not have perfect title to the goods that they sell. The goods may have been stolen, obtained by fraud, purchased from a minor or incompetent, or entrusted with the seller by the true owner and sold by mistake. The question that arises in such cases is whether an innocent purchaser for value receives good title to the goods. The answer to this question depends on whether the seller's title to the goods was void or voidable and whether the goods had been entrusted to a merchant.

A. Void Title

With the exception of voidable title, discussed below, buyers of goods acquire whatever title their sellers had to the property. If a seller has void title (no title at all), as does a seller of stolen goods, a buyer of the goods obtains no title to them either.

● A thief entered Dobeck's apartment and stole her brand-new 21-inch color television set, which had just been purchased that day and had not yet been removed from its original carton. The thief sold the set to Guthrie, an innocent purchaser, who believed that the thief was the real owner of the set. Dobeck would have the legal right to the return of the television set from Guthrie if its whereabouts were located. Guthrie's only right of recourse would be against the thief for the money paid for the set.

The continued sale of the stolen property through several innocent buyers would not in any way defeat the real owner's right in the property. The rights of possession and title of successive buyers of stolen property can never be any better than the rights of the thief.

B. Voidable Title

Anyone who obtains property through fraud, misrepresentation, mistake, undue influence, or duress holds only voidable title to the goods. This kind of title is also received when goods are bought from a minor or person who is mentally ill. *Voidable title* means title that may be voided if one of the parties elects to do so. Some people refer to voidable title as title which is valid until voided.

Anyone with voidable title to goods is able to transfer good title to others. The UCC provides, "A person with voidable title has power to transfer a good title to a good faith purchaser for value" [2-403(1)].

● Reed bought an expensive television set from Merchandise Mart on a thirty-day charge account. In making the purchase, Reed made several fraudulent statements to the store's credit department. Although the set was bought by fraudulent means, a resale by Reed to an innocent purchaser for value would cut off the right of Merchandise Mart to demand the return of its former property.

Although the store cannot recover the goods, it may bring an action against Reed for any loss suffered due to the fraud or other wrongdoing.

C. Entrusting Goods to a Merchant

People often entrust goods which belong to them to merchants. For example, they leave their watches with jewelers and their television sets with stores to be repaired. When this occurs, if the merchant sells the goods in the ordinary course of business to a third party who has no knowledge of the real owner's rights, the third party receives good title to them [2-403(2)]. The original owner who entrusted them to the merchant loses title to the goods altogether, but may bring an action against the merchant for money damages caused by the loss.

● Enright took his late-model Trans Am automobile to a garage to have the muffler and tail pipe replaced. He was told that he would be able to pick up the vehicle at about five o'clock that afternoon. The garage sold used cars as part of its regular business. By mistake, a salesperson who worked at the garage sold Enright's Trans Am to Reilly, who was unaware that the vehicle belonged to Enright. Reilly will receive good title to the car. Enright's cause of action will be against the garage for the conversion of his vehicle.

The reason for this rule of law is to give confidence to people who buy in the marketplace. People can be assured that they will receive good title to property (except stolen property) which they buy from a merchant who deals in goods of that kind in the ordinary course of business.

21-3. Risk of Loss

It is not unusual for goods to be stolen, damaged, or destroyed while awaiting shipment, while being shipped, or while awaiting pickup after a sales contract has been entered into. When this occurs, it becomes necessary to determine who must suffer the loss, the seller or the buyer. The UCC rules for determining this are as follows (2-509).

A. Agreement by Parties

The parties may, if they wish, enter into an agreement setting forth the time that risk of loss passes from the seller to the buyer. If they do so, the rules that follow do not apply.

B. Shipment and Destination Contracts

Like the passage of title, if the contract calls for the goods to be moved, the risk of loss passes when the seller completes the delivery obligation. If the contract requires the seller to send the goods to the buyer but does not require the seller to deliver them directly to the place of destination (a shipment contract), the risk of loss passes to the buyer when the goods are delivered to a carrier. If the contract requires the seller to deliver the goods to a destination (a destination contract), the risk of loss passes to the buyer when the goods are tendered at destination. Shipment and destination contracts are often distinguished by the shipping terms *f.o.b. the place of shipment* and *f.o.b. the place of destination*.

1. F.o.b. the Place of Shipment. The abbreviation *f.o.b.* means "free on board." When goods are sent *f.o.b. the place of shipment,* they will be delivered free to the place from which the goods are to be shipped (2-319). The buyer must pay all shipping charges from there to the place of destination. More important to this study, the terms indicate that title to the goods and the risk of loss passes at the point of origin. Delivery to the carrier by the seller and acceptance by the carrier complete the transfer of both title and risk of loss. Thus the buyer accepts full responsibility during the transit of the goods.

● Marcus Manufacturing of Boston, Massachusetts, shipped goods to Harlan, Inc., in Memphis, Tennessee. Terms of the shipment were f.o.b. Boston, Massachusetts. During shipment the goods were destroyed by fire. Harlan, not Marcus, would suffer the loss. Undoubtedly, Harlan would place a claim against the carrier in its obligation as insurer of goods accepted for shipment.

2. F.o.b. the Place of Destination. Goods shipped under the terms *f.o.b. the place of destination* belong to the seller until they have been delivered to the destination shown on the bill of lading. Similarly, the risk of loss remains with the seller until the goods are tendered at destination. Tender at destination requires that (*a*) the goods arrive at the place named in the bill of lading, (*b*) the buyer is given notice of their arrival, and (*c*) a reasonable time is allowed for the buyer to pick up the goods from the carrier.

● Suppose, in the previous example, the shipment to Harlan, Inc., had been made under terms of f.o.b. Memphis, Tennessee. Title and risk would not have passed at the shipping point. The seller would have had to suffer the loss, and Harlan would have had no obligation for payment.

3. Miscellaneous Shipping Terms. When terms of shipment do not specify shipping point or destination, it is assumed to be f.o.b. the place of shipment. Adding the term *c.o.d.* (cash on delivery) instructs the carrier to retain possession until the carrier has collected the cost of the goods.

The term *c.i.f.* (cost, insurance, and freight) instructs the carrier to collect all charges and fees in one lump sum. This includes the cost of goods shipped, insurance, and freight charges to the point of destination. The term *c.f.* means that insurance is not included.

The term *f.a.s. vessel* (free alongside vessel) at a named port requires sellers to deliver the goods at their own risk alongside the vessel or at a dock designated by the buyer.

C. Goods Held by Bailee

When the goods are held by a bailee to be delivered without being moved, the risk of loss passes to the buyer when the buyer receives a document of title describing the goods. The risk of loss also passes to the buyer when the bailee acknowledges the buyer's right to possession of the goods.

● Kobuc, a cattle farmer, stored a large supply of corn in a vacant silo owned by his neighbor, Durfee. Several months later, Kobuc sold the corn to a third party who wanted it to remain in Durfee's silo until it was needed. Durfee agreed to store the corn for the new owner. Risk of loss passed to the new owner when Durfee acknowledged the new owner's right to possession of the corn.

D. Goods to Be Picked up by Buyer

When the contract calls for the buyer to pick up the goods, the passage of risk of loss from the seller to the buyer depends on whether the seller is a merchant. If the seller is a merchant, the risk of loss passes when the buyer receives the goods. If the seller is not a merchant, the risk of loss passes to the buyer when the seller tenders delivery, that is, offers to turn the goods over to the buyer.

● Wagstaff agreed to sell her travel trailer to Barton for $1,500. Barton paid for the trailer and arranged to pick it up from Wagstaff the next evening. She became preoccupied, however, and even after several telephone calls from Wagstaff, failed to pick up the trailer, which had been made ready for her. The trailer was stolen five days later from Wagstaff's driveway. Barton must suffer the loss because the trailer had been tendered to her. Had Wagstaff been a merchant, she would have had to assume the loss because Barton had not yet received possession of the trailer.

E. When There Is a Breach

When the seller sends goods to the buyer which do not meet the contract requirements and are, therefore, unacceptable, the risk of loss remains with the seller [2-510(1)]. In situations where the buyer accepts the goods but later discovers some defect and rightfully revokes the acceptance, the passage of risk of loss depends upon whether the buyer is insured. If the buyer has insurance, that insurance will cover the loss. To the extent there is no insurance, the risk of loss remains with the seller from the beginning [2-510(2)].

When the buyer breaches the contract as to goods which have been identified to the contract, the seller may, to the extent of having no insurance coverage, treat the risk of loss as resting with the buyer [2-510(3)].

Table 21-2. Passage of Risk of Loss From Seller to Buyer

Terms of Contract	Risk of Loss Passes
Agreement of parties	At time and place agreed upon
Shipment contract	On delivery of goods to carrier
Destination contract	On tender of goods at destination
No movement—goods held by bailee	On receipt by buyer of document of title or on acknowledgment by bailee of buyer's right to possession
No movement and no bailee—seller is a merchant	On receipt of goods by buyer
No movement and no bailee—seller is not a merchant	On tender of delivery to buyer

21-4. Sales With Right of Return

Because of competition and a desire to give satisfaction, goods are sometimes sold with the understanding that they may be returned even though they conform to the contract. Determination of ownership and risk of loss while such goods are in the buyer's possession is sometimes necessary. Sales with the right of return are of two kinds.

A. Sale on Approval

A sale which allows goods to be returned even though they conform to the contract is called a sale on approval when the goods are primarily for the buyer's use (2-326). When goods are sold on approval, they remain the property of the seller until the buyer's approval has been expressed. The approval may be indicated by the oral or written consent of the buyer or by the buyer's act of retaining the goods for more than a reasonable time. Using the goods in a reasonable and expected manner on a trial basis will not imply an acceptance. Grossly careless use and a failure to inform the seller of the buyer's intent to return, however, could constitute an acceptance.

Goods held by the buyer on approval are not subject to the claims of the buyer's creditors until the buyer decides to accept them. In addition, the risk of loss remains with the seller until the buyer has accepted the goods (2-327).

B. Sale or Return

A sale that allows goods to be returned even though they conform to the contract is called a *sale or return* when the goods are delivered primarily for resale (2-326). When such a sale occurs, the buyer takes title to the goods with the right to revest title in the seller after a specified period or reasonable time. In such cases, the buyer must accept all the obligations of ownership while retaining possession of the goods. Goods held on sale or return are subject to the claims of the buyer's creditors.

● Butcher owned a gift shop in which she sold other people's goods on consignment. Pedro delivered a dozen handmade braided rugs to Butcher with the understanding that he would be paid for any that were sold. Any rugs that did not sell after three months would be returned to him. This was a sale or return because the rugs were delivered primarily for resale.

While in the buyer's possession, the goods must be cared for and used in a reasonable manner, anticipating their possible return in the same condition as when received, after making allowance for ordinary wear and tear. Also, the goods must be returned at the buyer's risk and expense.

21-5. Insurable Interest

Buyers may place insurance on goods the moment a contract is made and the goods are identified to the contract. It is then that buyers receive an insurable interest in the goods they buy [2-501(1)]. They obtain an insurable interest even though they later reject or return the goods to the seller. Notwithstanding the buyers' right to insure the goods, sellers retain an insurable interest in goods so long as they still have title to them.

● While shopping on vacation in an antique store in Connecticut, Maniff, who lived in Nevada, came upon a dining room set that she liked. She decided to buy the set on the condition that the antique dealer would ship the goods f.o.b. Winnemucca, Nevada. The dealer agreed. Maniff received an insurable interest in the goods when they were identified to the contract. At the same time, the dealer retained an insurable interest in the goods until they were tendered at their destination in Winnemucca. Both Maniff and the antique dealer could insure the goods.

Understanding Legal Terms

Define, identify, or explain the following terms:

c.f.	document of title	f.o.b. the place of	sale on approval
c.i.f.	f.a.s. vessel	shipment	shipment contracts
c.o.d.	f.o.b.	fungible goods	title
destination	f.o.b. the place of	identified	voidable title
contracts	destination	sale or return	

Questions for Review and Discussion

1. Discuss the general rules that determine when title passes.

2. Compare identification to a contract of existing goods with identification to a contract of future goods. Why is identification to a contract important?

3. Explain title as it refers to fungible goods.

4. Distinguish between shipment contracts and destination contracts and describe the passage of title and risk of loss in each. When do title and risk of loss pass when the terms are (a) f.o.b. the place of shipment? (b) f.o.b. the place of destination?

5. In what two situations does title revest in the seller after having passed to the buyer?

6. Discuss the rights of an innocent purchaser of stolen goods.

7. When may a seller recover goods to which the buyer had no more than a voidable title?

8. What are the rights of a person whose goods have been wrongfully sold by a merchant to whom they were entrusted?

9. When does the risk of loss pass to the buyer when the contract calls for the buyer to pick up the goods?

10. Distinguish between a sale on approval and a sale or return.

Analyzing Cases

1. The state of Alabama levied a sales tax on sales that took place within its borders. Delta Air Lines served meals on some, but not all, of its flights departing from Alabama, and the ticket price for a flight was the same whether or not meals were served. No meals were served while the aircraft was in Alabama airspace. By the use of a mathematical formula, the state of Alabama levied a sales tax on meals served to Delta's passengers. Delta objected, arguing that no sale of goods took place in Alabama. Did the sale of the meals occur when passengers bought their tickets in Alabama or when their meals were served outside of the state? Explain. ● *State v. Delta Air Lines, Inc.*, 356 So.2d 1205 (Ala. 1978)

2. Brown, who operated Jack's Skelly Service Station, was sued by his former wife for child support payments. During the trial, the question arose as to who owned the gasoline in the service station tanks, Brown or Brown's supplier, Martin. Brown had entered into a "special Keep-Full motor fuel sales agreement" under which Martin agreed to deliver to Brown's place of business Skelly motor fuel. The agreement stated that title to the fuel "shall be and remain in Martin until removed from the tanks through and by means of computing pumps." Who owned the gas in the tanks, Brown or Martin? Why? ● *Stewart v. Brown*, 546 S.W.2d 204 (Mo. 1977)

3. Gallo entered into a contract in October to deliver 3,500 heifers to Weisbart's ranch between May 1 and October 1 of the next year. Gallo experienced difficulty in raising the heifers due to rising costs and a severe winter, and his bank foreclosed on the cattle before they could be delivered to Weisbart. Weisbart claims that a sale of the cattle occurred in October when the contract was made and that title passed to him at that time. Do you agree with Weisbart? Why or why not? ● *Weisbart & Co. v. First Nat. Bank*, 568 F.2d 391 (5th Cir. 1978)

4. Droukas read an advertisement for the sale of two marine engines in a nautical magazine. He telephoned the seller, Divers Training Academy, Inc., spoke to its president, and ordered the engines. He sent a check for the purchase price, and the academy shipped the engines from Florida to Massachusetts. The bill of lading stated that "shipping charges are to be collect." On receipt of the engines, Droukas discovered that contrary to the representations made by the academy's president, the engines had sustained saltwater damage before shipment. In determining which state had jurisdiction over the case, the question arose as to whether this was a shipment contract or a destination contract. How would you decide? Why? ● *Droukas v. Divers Training Academy, Inc.*, 376 N.E.2d 548 (Mass. 1978)

5. Mann bought a Lincoln Continental Mark IV automobile from Kilbourn American Leasing, Inc., for $6,500 cash. He received by mistake from Kilbourn a title certificate for a similar but different vehicle. Kilbourn later borrowed money from a bank and gave the correct title certificate for Mann's car to the bank as security for the loan. The bank claims that Mann does not have title to the car because he did not receive the title certificate. Is the bank correct?

Why or why not? ● *National Exch. Bank v. Mann*, 260 N.W.2d 716 (Wis. 1978)

6. Moon bought a wrecker truck from Hollowell, a truck dealer, paying $8,840 and receiving a certificate of title. Moon did not see the wrecker truck or know where it was but understood from Hollowell that it would be delivered after the wrecker equipment was mounted on it. Four and a half months later, when the truck was in the possession of another company having the wrecker equipment installed, Hollowel sold the same truck to Simson. The latter took delivery of the vehicle from the company that installed the wrecker equipment. Hollowell absconded with the proceeds of both sales. Moon brought suit to recover the vehicle from Simson. Will he succeed? Why or why not? ● *Simson v. Moon*, 222 S.E.2d 873 (Ga. 1975)

7. Estes purchased a late-model Chevrolet Caprice sports coupe from Howard, an automobile dealer in Mississippi. Later, it was discovered that the vehicle had been stolen from a Chevrolet dealership in Florida and, after a circuitous route, eventually had come to rest in Mississippi. The bill of sale to the vehicle had been forged. Estes contends that he has good title to the vehicle because he bought the auto from a dealer. Is Estes correct? ● *Allstate Ins. Co. v. Estes*, 345 So.2d 265 (Miss. 1977)

8. Eberhard Manufacturing Company sold goods to Brown Industrial Sales Company without agreeing on who would bear the risk of loss. The contract contained no f.o.b. terms. Eberhard placed the goods on board a common carrier with instructions to deliver them to Brown. The goods were lost in transit. Who will suffer the loss, Eberhard or Brown? Why? ● *Eberhard Mfg. Co. v. Brown*, 232 N.W.2d 378 (Mich. 1975)

9. Henry Heide Incorporated received a warehouse receipt for 3,200 100-pound bags of sugar which it bought from Olavarria. The corporation withdrew 800 bags of the sugar from the warehouse (which had thousands of pounds stored there), but when it returned for the balance, it discovered that the warehouse was padlocked and empty. Some 200,000 pounds of sugar had mysteriously disappeared from it. Henry Heide Incorporated carried insurance for such a loss, but its insurance company refused to pay, claiming that the corporation had no insurable interest in the sugar. Do you agree with the insurance company? Why or why not? ● *Henry Heide, Inc. v. Atlantic Mut. Ins. Co.*, 363 N.Y.S.2d 515 (1975)

Chapter 22

Warranties and Product Liability

Because of the broad provisions of the UCC, the majority of business and consumer transactions today are covered by some kind of warranty. Statements and promises made by the seller often become warranties even though they were not meant to be such. Samples and descriptions of goods create warranties. Unless excluded, merchants who sell goods warrant that the goods are merchantable, that is, fit for the purpose for which they are sold. Similarly, when a seller selects the product for a buyer to be used for a particular purpose, the seller warrants that it will be fit for that particular purpose.

Along with the law of warranties, court decisions and state legislatures have developed the doctrine of product liability. The law at one time restricted damage actions to persons who were in privity, or had a direct relationship through a contract with the other party. Today, however, manufacturers and others in the chain of distribution may be liable to consumers with whom they have not dealt directly.

22-1. Express Warranties

Express warranties are warranties created by the seller's explicit statements, descriptions, or samples. They arise in three ways: by an affirmation of fact or promise, by a description of the goods, or by a sample or model (2-313).

A. Affirmation of Fact or Promise

Whenever a seller of goods makes an affirmation (positive statement) of fact about the goods to the buyer, an express warranty is created. The seller warrants that the goods will live up to the affirmation, which must relate to the goods and be part of the basis of the bargain.

● Alby went into a furniture store and told the clerk that he was interested in buying a cherry coffee table. The clerk showed Alby a table and said that it was made of solid cherry. Shortly after buying it, Alby discovered that the table was stained cherry but was actually made of pine. The statement by the store clerk that the table was made of solid cherry was an affirmation of fact which created an express warranty. Alby would be entitled to his money back since the store breached its warranty.

Similarly, an express warranty occurs whenever a seller makes a promise about the goods to the buyer. Here, also, the promise must relate to the goods and be part of the basis of the bargain.

● Boehm, a farmer, purchased 50 pounds of feed additive called Proto-Tone 316 Medicated from Triple F Feeds. The salesperson from Triple F had told Boehm that the additive would not hurt the dairy cattle and that milk production would increase by 25 percent. In fact, the additive caused milk production to decline, and the cattle refused to eat. The cows had to be sold at half their value. The court held that the promises made by the salesperson were express warranties, which were breached when they failed to come true.

Manufacturers often include express warranties with the products they sell. They are usually found inside the package containing the product and are sometimes referred to as guarantees.

● Scanlon bought an electronic insect killer from a department store. In the package with the product was a card that said, "Full one-year warranty. If, within one year from the date of purchase, this electronic insect killer fails due to a defect in material or workmanship, this company will repair or replace it, free of charge." This promise by the company was an express warranty.

1. Formal Words Not Necessary. It is not necessary to the creation of an express warranty that the seller use formal words such as *warrant* or *guarantee*. Similarly, it is not necessary for the seller to have a specific intention to make a warranty. If the language used amounts to an affirmation of fact or promise about the goods and becomes part of the basis of the bargain, an express warranty is created. Advertisements often contain promises which amount to express warranties.

● Twentieth Century Auto Polish was advertised as a safe, noncorrosive polish, manufactured to the highest standards required of finishes. Rankin bought a can of the polish, and it ruined the finish of her new car. Rankin could seek damages against the manufacturer, claiming that the advertised statements were warranties made to any prospective purchaser.

2. Opinion and Puffing. Warranties are based on statements of fact. Opinions of salespersons, exaggerated and persuasive statements, and the like are not included. Courts have long recognized the temptation of salespersons to indulge in puffing, or extolling their wares beyond the point of fact. Buyers must use good judgment in separating a seller's statements of fact from those statements that are only opinion or puffing.

B. Description of the Goods

Any description of the goods which is made part of the basis of the bargain creates an express warranty that the goods will be as described [2-313(1)(b)].

● Salem University ordered textbooks to be used in a psychology course. The publisher's descriptive literature showed the text to be ideal for second-year college classes. Sample copies were not made available for inspection. When delivered, the book proved to be for the high school level and not applicable to Salem's psychology course.

The publisher's description constituted an express warranty. The books were purchased as a result of that description, which proved to be inaccurate. Salem University may enforce its warranty rights by rescinding the contract and returning the books to the seller.

C. Sample or Model

It is a common practice of salespeople to show samples of their products to prospective buyers. When this is done, and a sample or model becomes part of the basis of the bargain, an express warranty is created. The seller warrants that the goods that are delivered will be the same as the sample or model [2-313(1)(c)].

● A company which manufactured sausage-stuffing machines contracted to buy various castings from a foundry. The castings were to conform to samples which the foundry had made according to plans submitted by the manufacturing company. When the castings were delivered, the company rejected them because they were not the same as the samples. The foundry had breached its express warranty, giving the company the right to rescind the contract.

22-2. Implied Warranties

An *implied warranty* is a warranty imposed by law rather than by statements, descriptions, or samples given by the seller. It arises independently and outside the contract. The law annexes it or writes it, by implication, into the contract which the parties have made. Implied warranties are designed to promote high standards in business and to discourage harsh dealings. There are two types of implied warranties: the implied warranty of fitness for a particular purpose and the implied warranty of merchantability.

A. Fitness for a Particular Purpose

Sometimes buyers will have the seller select goods for them rather than select them themselves. They rely on the seller's knowledge and experience to chose the product after telling the seller of the particular use they have for the goods. This creates the implied *warranty of fitness for a particular purpose*. In such circumstances sellers, whether or not they are merchants, impliedly warrant that the goods they choose will be fit for the purpose for which they are to be used (2-315).

● Cantania asked Brown, a paint retailer, to recommend a paint to cover an exterior stucco wall which was in a chalky condition. Brown recommended and sold Cantania a certain product, advising him to wire-brush any flaky particles before painting. Cantania followed these instructions, but the paint did not adhere owing to the poor condition of the wall. Since Brown knew the particular purpose for which the paint was to be used and that Cantania was relying on his skill and judgment to select the proper paint, the implied warranty of fitness for a particular purpose arose and was breached. The fact that Brown had acted in good faith in recommending the goods did not prevent the implied warranty from coming into existence nor excuse the breach.

B. Merchantability

One of the most beneficial warranties, from the point of view of a buyer, is the implied *warranty of merchantability*. The warranty is this: Unless excluded in one of the ways discussed below, whenever a merchant sells goods, the merchant warrants that the goods are merchantable [2-314(1)]. This warranty is given only when the seller is a merchant.

● Lobue bought a second-hand car for $2,000 from Magliozzi, a private party who had advertised the car for sale in the newspaper. She drove the car home, parked it in her driveway, and turned off the engine. The next morning, the car would not start. The automobile mechanic who was called to try to start the car informed

Lobue that it would cost $1,200 to repair the car so that it would start properly. Lobue has no remedy against Magliozzi for breach of warranty of merchantability because Magliozzi was not a merchant.

To be merchantable, goods must at least (1) pass without objection in the trade under the contract description; (2) if fungible goods, be of fair average quality; (3) be fit for the ordinary purposes for which such goods are used; (4) be of the same kind, quality, and quantity if more than one item is involved; (5) be adequately contained, packaged, and labeled as the agreement may require; and (6) conform to any promises or statements of fact made on the container or label [2-314(2)].

● If Magliozzi had been a merchant, in the above case, Lobue would have had a remedy against him for breach of warranty of merchantability. An automobile that will not start is not fit for the ordinary purposes for which automobiles are used.

The serving for value of food or drink to be consumed either on or off the premises is considered to be a sale for the purposes of the warranty of merchantability. (Some cases held to the contrary prior to the adoption of the UCC.)

The courts have held the following to be nonmerchantable: day-old chickens that had bird cancer; contaminated blood received in a blood transfusion; applesauce that was inedible because of poor taste and smell; contaminated cheese; and any food containing impurities, such as bits of wood, metal, or glass.

C. Usage of Trade

Other implied warranties may arise from ways in which the parties have dealt in the past or by usage of trade [2-314(3)]. For example, when a person sells a pedigreed dog, there is an implied warranty that the seller will provide pedigree papers to evidence conformity of the animal to the contract. The reason this implied warranty arises is that providing such papers has become a well-established custom or practice of the trade.

22-3. Warranty of Title

Whenever goods are sold, the seller warrants that the title being conveyed is good and that the transfer is rightful. The seller also warrants that the goods shall be delivered free of any security interest (see Chapter 41) or other lien about which the buyer had no knowledge [2-312(1)(a)(b)]. This warranty is known as the *warranty of title*. It is not designated as an implied warranty and, hence, is not excluded or modified by such words as *as is* or *with all faults,* as is discussed later in this chapter.

● Garcia bought a 30-foot cabin cruiser with a 318-cubic-inch Chrysler engine from Broadbine for $15,000. Just as he was about to go on a first cruise, Garcia was notified by the police that the boat had been stolen from another person. Garcia was required to turn the boat over to the rightful owner. His remedy was against Broadbine for breach of warranty of title.

The warranty of title is not made when the buyer is aware that the person selling does not personally claim title, as in a sheriff's sale or a sale by the personal representative of an estate.

22-4. Magnuson-Moss Warranty Act

The Magnuson-Moss Warranty Act was passed in 1975 to prevent deceptive warranty practices and to provide consumers with more information about warranties that are made on products they buy. The act applies only when written warranties are made voluntarily on *consumer products*. These are defined as tangible personal property normally used for personal, family, or household purposes. Because it is a federal law, the act affects only warranties on products that are sold in interstate commerce.

Under the act, when a written warranty is given to a consumer on goods costing more than $10, all the following must be done:

○ The written warranty must be made available before the consumer decides to buy the product.
○ The writing must express the terms and conditions of the warranty in simple and readily understood language.
○ The warranty must disclose whether it is a full warranty or a limited warranty.

A *full warranty* is one in which a defective product will be repaired without charge within a reasonable time after a complaint has been made about it. If it cannot be repaired within a reasonable time, the consumer may have either a replacement of the product or a refund of the purchase price. The consumer will not have to do anything unreasonable to get warranty service, such as ship a heavy product to the factory. A full warranty is conferred upon anyone who owns the product during the warranty period, not only the original buyer. A full warranty must also state its duration, as, for example, a "full one-year warranty."

● Kienitz bought an electric range manufactured by a well-known firm. Attached to the box containing the range were several papers, one of which read: "Full one-year warranty. If your range fails because of a manufacturing defect within one year from the date of original purchase, we will repair the product without charge to you. Parts and service labor are included. Service will be provided in your home in the forty-eight contiguous states, the state of Hawaii, or in the District of Columbia." This was a full warranty. The range would be repaired or replaced at no cost to the consumer if it turned out to be defective.

A *limited warranty* is any written warranty that does not meet all the requirements for a full warranty. The consumer is not given the absolute, free-of-charge repair or replacement of a defective product as is given in the full warranty. Something less than a complete remedy is given to a consumer.

● Farver, who lived in Alaska, bought an electric range similer to the one bought by Kienitz in the above example. Attached to the box containing the range was a paper which read: "Limited warranty applicable to the state of Alaska. In the state of Alaska free service, including parts, will be provided to correct manufacturing defects at our nearest service shop location or in your home, but we do not cover the cost of transportation of the product to the shop or for travel costs of a technician to your home. You are responsible for these costs. All other provisions of this limited warranty are the same as those stated in the above warranties [referring to full warranties]." This was a limited warranty because it included a charge to the consumer.

Other examples of limited warranties are those which (*a*) cover only parts, not labor (*b*) allow only a pro-rata refund or credit in the case of a defect rather than a full refund, (*c*) require the buyer to return a heavy product to the store for service, or (*d*) cover only the first purchaser.

22-5. Exclusion of Warranties

Except when express warranties are made under the Magnuson-Moss Warranty Act, sellers may exclude or modify implied warranties by stating that no warranties are given when a contract for sale is made. Special rules, however, must be followed. To exclude the implied warranty of merchantability, the word *merchantability* must be used in the disclaimer. If the exclusion is in writing, it must be in large, bold type so that it is conspicuous. To exclude the implied warranty of fitness for a particular purpose, the exclusion must be in writing and also be conspicuous [2-316(2)].

● Valdez bought a used car from Kinkaid Motors, Inc., for $2,095. Printed on the sales slip, which Valdez signed, were the following words in large, bold capital letters: "THE SELLER HEREBY EXCLUDES THE WARRANTY OF MERCHANTABILITY AND FITNESS FOR A PARTICULAR PURPOSE." Two days later, when the car broke down, Valdez had no recourse against the car dealer for breach of either of the implied warranties.

A common practice in the sale of used cars, lawnmowers, electrical appliances, and similar merchandise is for the seller to stipulate that the goods are being sold as is. The use of such expressions as *as is, with all faults,* and others is another way to exclude implied warranties [2-316(3)(a)].

Implied warranties may also be excluded under the UCC by having buyers examine the goods. When buyers have examined the goods or the sample or model as fully as they desire (or have refused to examine them when given the opportunity), there is no implied warranty as to defects which an examination would have revealed [2-316(3)(b)].

Under the Magnuson-Moss Warranty Act, any clause purporting to exclude or limit consequential damages for breach of warranty must appear conspicuously on the face of the warranty. *Consequential damages* are losses which do not flow directly and immediately from an act but only from some of the consequences or results of the act.

● Souci bought a freezer made by a reputable manufacturer, carrying a full one-year warranty. The following sentence appeared in boldface type on the face of the warranty: "In no event shall this company be liable for consequential damages." Shortly after buying the freezer, Souci filled it with $1,500 worth of meat. Several days later, the freezer stopped working owing to a defect in its manufacture. Under the warranty, the company will have to either repair or replace the freezer, but it is not responsible for the loss of the meat. This loss is considered to be a consequential damage, which the company had effectively disclaimed.

The Magnuson-Moss Warranty Act places limits on the exclusion of implied warranties to consumers. Under the act, if either a full or limited express warranty is made to a consumer, the implied warranties of merchantability and fitness for a particular purpose may not be excluded during the warranty period. This law also applies if the seller gives the buyer a service contract.

22-6. Duty to Notify Seller of Defective Product

In order to recover money damages for breach of warranty, buyers of defective goods must notify the seller of the defect within a reasonable time after the discovery or after the defect should have been discovered. Failure to do so will prevent them from recovering damages for breach of warranty [2-607(3)(a)].

● Shortly after buying an electric stove from an appliance store, Schloss discovered that the self-cleaning unit of the stove did not work. She did not get around to notifying the store of the defect until seven months later. Because of the delay in notifying the store of the defect, Schloss lost the right to recover from the store for breach of the implied warranty of merchantability.

22-7. Privity Not Required

Under earlier law, warranties extended only to the actual buyer of the product, that is, the one with whom the seller had dealt or was in privity. People who were injured by defective products had no remedy against the seller for breach of warranty unless they themselves had purchased the goods. Thus, if children were injured by foreign objects in food that had been bought by their parents, the children could not recover for injuries because they had not purchased the goods. The UCC has abolished the requirement of privity Under today's law, for example, a child injured by an impure product would be able to recover money damages from the seller even though the child's parents had purchased the goods.

22-8. Product Liability

One of the most important areas of law for consumers today is known as *product liability*. Under this law, which is a tort rather than a breach of contract, a buyer or user of a product who is injured because of the product's unsafe or defective condition may recover damages from the manufacturer, the seller, or the supplier of the goods. Injuries to persons or damage to property caused by defects in design and manufacture give consumers a right to seek recovery under the law of product liability.

Obligations under product liability run concurrently with implied or express warranties. Liability is extended to the manufacturer, the seller, and all others in the normal marketing chain. It extends to the retail store or seller, to manufacturers, growers, packers, and all others engaged in the marketing process. In addition, liability can extend to all users and others who might be injured by another's use of a product.

● O'Daniel purchased a new car from Boulevard Motors. The car operated without any problem for six months. At that time the right front wheel collapsed. The car turned over, injuring O'Daniel, two passengers, and a pedestrian and wrecking a parked car.

Proof of defective construction would give all of the injured parties a right to seek damages from the manufacturer and Boulevard Motors under product liability. The owner of the wrecked car could also seek recovery under product liability. In a legal action, it would be normal procedure to name both the manufacturer and the seller as joint defendants. Product liability suits are usually based on either negligence or strict liability, both of which are tort actions.

A. Negligence

As discussed earlier, negligence is the failure to exercise that degree of care that a reasonably prudent person would have exercised under the same circumstances and conditions. In order to recover for negligence in a product liability case, it is necessary to prove all of the following: (1) that there was a negligent act on the part of the manufacturer or supplier of the goods, (2) that injuries occurred, and (3) that the injuries were caused by the negligent act. It is difficult for injured parties to obtain actual evidence of a negligent act on the part of the manufacturer, since they were not present when the goods were made and normally they have very little information about the manufacturing process. There is usually insufficient evidence to win the case. Injured parties are often more successful in bringing suit for breach of implied warranty of merchantability rather than for negligence.

● Valez was driving on an interstate highway in a brand-new automobile she had purchased a week earlier. She was traveling at the speed limit of 55 miles per hour. Suddenly she heard something snap. The car veered off the highway and smashed into a tree. Valez was thrown out of the car and received back, leg, and neck injuries. A mechanic who inspected the vehicle after the accident discovered that there was no fluid in the car's steering mechanism and that there was a strong burning odor. There was no evidence, however, as to why the fluid was missing. Valez could not recover on the theory of negligence because she was unable to prove a negligent act on the part of the manufacturer or seller of the automobile. She would be able to recover for breach of warranty because an automobile with a defective steering mechanism is not merchantable.

B. Strict Liability

Under the doctrine of strict liability, it is not necessary to prove a negligent act on the part of the manufacturer or seller when someone is injured by a defective product. *Strict liability* is a legal theory, adopted by two-thirds of the states, which imposes liability on manufacturers or suppliers for selling goods which are unreasonably dangerous, without regard to fault or negligence. Under this rule of law, manufacturers have the duty to design reasonably safe products. To recover from a manufacturer in this type of action, the injured party must prove that (1) the product was in an unreasonably dangerous condition, (2) the condition existed at the time the product left the manufacturer's control, and (3) the condition was the proximate cause of the injuries. Privity between the seller and user of the product is not necessary. The manufacturer's and seller's liability extends to all persons who may be injured by the product. Injured bystanders, guests, or others who have no relationship with the product, the seller, or the manufacturer may seek damages caused by defects in the offending product.

● Ryder Truck Rental rented a truck to Jackson. While he was waiting for a light to change, the truck moved forward owing to a faulty brake system. Martin, in another car, was injured when the truck hit her car. The Delaware Supreme Court ruled, on an appeal, that Ryder could be held liable even without proof of its negligence. It was only necessary for the injured party to prove that the truck had an unreasonably dangerous product design which caused personal injury or property damage to the plaintiffs.

1. Duty to Warn. Sometimes a duty is placed upon manufacturers to warn consumers that harm may result from a product. Unavoidably unsafe products may require a warning to inform the consumer of possible harm. If the warning is adequate, consumers may be required to use the product at their own risk. A warning must specify the risk presented by the product and give a reason for the warning.

● Palmer, an eleven-year-old boy, received injuries necessitating the amputation of his leg well above the knee when his left leg got caught in the agitator of the fertilizer spreader on which he was riding. The following warning was placed by the manufacturer in front of the spreader near the operator's controls:

> BE CAREFUL
> 1. Keep all shields in place.
> 2. Stop machine and adjust oil.
> 3. When mechanism becomes clogged, disengage power before cleaning.
> 4. Keep hands, feet, and clothing away from power-driven parts.
> 5. Keep off implement unless seat or platform is provided. Keep others off.

The court held this warning to be inadequate because it did not specify the danger presented by the agitator. It was too general. It did not detail the extent of the risk it posed to life and limb.

2. Punitive Damages. In addition to recovering damages to compensate them for their losses, injured parties in strict liability cases sometimes recover punitive damages. These are a monetary penalty imposed as a punishment for a wrongdoing.

● Four-year-old Lee Ann Gryc was clothed in pajamas made from a cotton material manufactured by Riegel Textile Corporation. The material was commercially known as flannelette. It was not treated and did not meet the minimum federal standards of product flammability. Lee Ann reached across the electric stove in her home to shut off a timer. Her pajamas were instantly ignited, and she received severe burns over her upper body. The jury found Riegel Textile Corporation liable for these injuries and awarded Lee Ann $750,000 in compensatory damages and $1,000,000 in punitive damages.

Understanding Legal Terms

Define, identify, or explain the following terms:

consequential damages	implied warranty	warranty of fitness for a particular purpose	warranty of merchantability
consumer products	limited warranty		
express warranties	merchant		warranty of title
full warranty	product liability		
	strict liability		

Questions for Review and Discussion

1. In what three ways may express warranties arise?

2. Distinguish between statements of fact and puffing, as related to express warranties.

3. When does the implied warranty of fitness for a particular purpose arise? When and by whom is the warranty of merchantability given?

4. What six requirements are necessary for goods to be merchantable?

5. Describe the warranty of title that is made by a seller of goods.

6. Differentiate between a full warranty and a limited warranty under the Magnuson-Moss Warranty Act.

7. What special rules must be followed to exclude the warranties of merchantability and fitness for a particular purpose? In what other ways may warranties be excluded?

8. Describe the buyer's duty to notify the seller of a breach of warranty.

9. What is the purpose of today's product liability laws and decisions?

10. What three things must an injured party prove to recover from a manufacturer in tort for strict liability?

Analyzing Cases

1. McCoy bought an antique pistol from the Old Fort Trading Post for $1,000. Later, the gun was taken from McCoy by the police when they learned that it was stolen property. The police turned the gun over to the rightful owner. McCoy notified the Old Fort Trading Post of what had happened and asked for the return of his money, but the owner of the business refused to give him a refund. What remedy, if any, does McCoy have against the owner of the trading post? Explain. ● *Trial v. McCoy*, 553 S.W.2d 199 (Tex. 1977)

2. Werner purchased a sloop from Montana for $13,250. During the negotiations before the sale, Montana had told Werner that the sloop would "make up" when placed in the water and become watertight. Werner placed the sloop in the water and allowed sufficient time for the planking to swell, or "make up," to form a watertight hull, but it still leaked and could not be sailed. He then discovered extensive dry rot in the hull and learned that the cost of repairs would be substantial. Montana refused to take the sloop back and refund Werner's purchase price. Does Werner have a cause of action against Montana? If so, on what grounds? Explain. ● *Werner v. Montana*, 378 A.2d 1130 (N.H. 1977)

3. Associated Grocers delivered a pallet of produce to the back room of the Thriftway Market. On top of the stack of produce was one cardboard box of Chiquita brand bananas. The bananas were unwrapped, and the box contained breather holes. There was nothing wrong with the bananas; they were edible and saleable. Later that morning, Anderson, the produce manager, removed the box of bananas from the top of the stack. When he reached for a lug of radishes that had been under the bananas, a banana spider, 6 inches in diameter, leaped from some wet burlap onto his left hand and bit him. The spider did not come from the bananas or the container. Nine months later, Anderson died of heart failure. His widow, as the personal representative of the estate, brought suit against Associated Grocers on strict liability and breach of warranty theories. She claimed that the bananas delivered to the Thriftway Market and handled by her deceased husband were defective and thereby unfit for the ordinary purpose for which the bananas were to be used. Do you agree with her contention? Why or why not? ● *Anderson v. Associated Grocers, Inc.*, 525 P.2d 284 (Wash. 1974)

4. Mr. and Mrs. Benfer bought a mobile

home from Thomas, a mobile home retailer. Prior to the purchase, Thomas had told them that the type of mobile home he carried had a ¼-inch sheathing on the siding that made it better than cheaper units. The Benfers were interested in this feature as their neighbor had a mobile home with plywood underneath it. Thomas showed them a model of the mobile home that he carried and pointed out to them the grade of plywood sheathing that was on the model. When the mobile home was delivered to them, they were given several written warranties signed by the manufacturer, Town & Country Mobile Homes, Inc., including one which specifically warranted that the mobile home was sheathed with ¼-inch plywood beneath the prefinished aluminum exterior wall surface. Later, the Benfers discovered that their mobile home did not contain this sheathing. Do they have a cause of action against the retailer, Thomas? Why or why not? • *Town & Country Mobile Homes, Inc. v. Benfer,* 527 S.W.2d 523 (Tex. 1975)

5. Romedy bought a car from Willett Lincoln-Mercury, Inc. He did not inspect it until four or five days after it was delivered to him. Three weeks later, he notified the dealer that the car did not contain the equipment that the dealer had said it would contain. He did, however, continue to make payments on the car. Later, he brought suit against the dealer for breach of warranty. Will he recover? Explain. • *Romedy v. Willett Lincoln-Mercury, Inc.,* 220 S.E.2d 74 (Ga. 1975)

6. Shaffer ordered a glass of rosé wine at the Victoria Station Restaurant. As he took his first sip of wine, the glass broke in his hand, causing permanent injuries. Shaffer brought suit against the restaurant for breach of warranty of merchantability. The restaurant's position was that since it did not sell the wineglass to Shaffer (only its contents), it was not a merchant with respect to the glass, and therefore made no warranty. Do you agree with the restaurant? Why or why not? • *Shaffer v. Victoria Station, Inc.,* 588 P.2d 233 (Wash. 1978)

7. Haven Hills Farm, Inc., purchased a tire from Sears, Roebuck & Co., Inc., for a truck used in the transportation of eggs sold in its wholesale egg business. On a trip from Jackson, Mississippi, to Mobile, Alabama, the tire blew out, causing the truck to turn on its side, destroying 11,862 dozen eggs. At the time of the blowout, the tire was $4\frac{1}{2}$ months old and had been driven 30,000 miles. Haven Hills Farm, Inc., claimed that Sears was liable to it for damages under the theory of strict liability and also for breach of the implied warranty of merchantability. It argued that Sears sold the tire in a defective condition unreasonably dangerous to consumers or other persons likely to be exposed to potential hazard. How would you decide? Why? • *Sears, Roebuck & Co. v. Haven Hills Farm, Inc.,* 395 So.2d 991 (Ala. 1981)

8. Stewart, while working for a bearing manufacturing company, stood on the lifting platform of a forklift and caused it to raise him to a rack 16 feet above the floor level so that he could inventory some ball bearings. Suddenly, the lift apparatus failed. The platform fell to the floor, and Stewart was seriously injured. The cause of the failure was attributed to negligent repair work performed a few days earlier by Scott-Kitz Miller Co., a company responsible for maintenance of the equipment. Scott employees had removed some bolts holding the lift guide and reinserted them backward. In this position, the bolts protruded in such a way that when an attempt was made to lower the raised platform, the lift assembly would hang at the top of the mast, then fall to the floor. Stewart claims that the forklift was defectively designed because the manufacturer failed to fashion the guide bolts and their housing in such a way that maintenance personnel could not later insert them backward. Explain whether or not you agree with Stewart. • *Stewart v. Scott-Kitz Miller Co.,* 626 P.2d 329 (Okla. 1981)

Chapter 23

Performance and Breach of Contract

A contract for sale is performed when the parties do what they have agreed to do under the contract terms. The seller performs by making *tender of delivery,* that is, offering to turn the goods over to the buyer. The buyer performs by making *tender of payment,* which means offering to turn the money over to the seller. A breach of contract occurs when one of the parties fails to do that which has been agreed to under the terms of the contract for sale. The UCC has special rules governing tender of delivery and tender of payment. Similarly, the UCC provides particular remedies for the seller and the buyer when the other party breaches a contract.

23-1. Guidelines for Performance

All parties to a contract for sale must act in good faith. If they have dealt together in the past, their prior dealings may give meaning to a contract that is in dispute. Often, traditional ways of doing things within a particular occupation or trade become important in determining the meaning of contract terms.

A. General Obligations of Parties

The obligations of the parties to a contract for sale are relatively simple and straightforward. The seller is obligated to transfer and deliver the goods; the buyer is obligated to accept and pay for them, both in accordance with the terms of the contract (2-301). In addition, all parties must act in good faith, which means that they must act honestly (1-203). The court need not enforce a contract or part of a contract which it finds to be unconscionable. An unconscionable contract, as you recall, is one that is so one-sided that it causes oppression and gives unfair advantage to one of the parties (see Chapter 9).

B. Course of Dealing and Usage of Trade

When disputes arise between parties who have dealt together in the past, the court often looks to their past dealings to give meaning to the disputed transaction. Similarly, the court will look to any usage of trade in the vocation in which the parties are engaged for assistance in interpreting the meaning of their sales contracts. Although terms which are expressly stated in a contract will usually control the contract's meaning, the parties' course of dealing and usage of trade are often looked at to supplement or qualify the express terms (1-205).

● Associated Hardware Supply Co. negotiated with Big Wheel Distributing Company for the purchase of merchandise. The parties could not agree on pricing the goods. Associated Hardware wanted to pay cost plus 10 percent while Big Wheel insisted on dealer-catalogue less 11 percent. Although the parties exchanged letters, there was never any formal agreement on pricing. Over a two-year period, Associated Hardware ordered goods from Big Wheel amounting to more than $850,000, paying for them on a dealer-catalogue-less-11-percent basis. Thereafter, when an additional $40,000 was owed for merchandise purchased, Associated Hardware refused to pay, claiming that no agreement had been reached as to the pricing of the goods. Finding in favor of Big Wheel, the court attached great weight to the course of dealing of the parties. It held that the parties' course of dealing for the two-year period governed the sale of the remaining merchandise.

23-2. Tender of Performance

An offer by the parties to a contract for sale to do that which they have agreed to do is known as *tender of performance*. The seller offers to turn the goods over to the buyer; the buyer offers to turn the money over to the seller. Tender of performance is necessary in order to test the other party's ability and willingness to perform his or her part of the bargain. If tender is not made and the other party fails to perform, the one not making tender cannot bring suit.

A. Tender of Delivery

Although the buyer is obligated to accept and pay for the goods after a contract for sale has been made, this obligation is conditioned upon the seller making tender of delivery. Failure of sellers to do this is an excuse for buyers not to perform their part of the bargain (2-507).

1. Manner of Seller's Tender. Tender of delivery requires the seller to put and hold conforming goods at the buyer's disposition. In addition, the seller must give the buyer notice that the goods are being tendered. Tender of delivery must be at a reasonable hour of the day to allow the buyer to take possession of the goods. It is the responsibility of the buyer, unless the parties agree otherwise, to furnish facilities that are suitable for receiving the goods (2-503).

● Henderson agreed to sell 500 cases of tomato juice to Wholesale Grocers for $38 a case. Just before shipping the goods, however, she was offered $48 a case from another company. She delivered the 500 cases to Wholesale Grocer's loading platform at three o'clock in the morning. Finding no one there, she left with the goods and sold them to the other company at the higher price. She claimed that Wholesale Grocers had breached the contract by not accepting the goods when they were tendered at the loading platform. The court held in favor of Wholesale Grocers. Henderson did not put and hold the goods at the buyer's disposition during a reasonable hour of the day.

2. Shipment by Seller. When the contract for sale is a shipment contract, the seller must put the goods in the possession of a carrier and contract with the carrier for their transportation (2-504). Any necessary documents must be sent to the buyer, who must be promptly notified of the shipment.

3. Goods in Possession of Bailee. Sometimes the goods are in the possession of a bailee and are to be delivered to the buyer without being moved. When this occurs, tender requires that the seller either tender a negotiable document of title covering the goods or obtain an acknowledgment by the bailee of the buyer's right to possession of them.

● Spiegel purchased 5,000 cases of canned onions from Ingalls at a price that was much lower than the wholesale market price of the same product. The cases of onions had been stored by Ingalls at the East Side Storage Warehouse. Spiegel wished to continue storing the onions at the same warehouse, as she had no immediate use for them. Ingalls notified East Side Storage Warehouse that the onions had been sold to Spiegel. Tender occurred when the warehouse acknowledged to Spiegel that it was now holding the cases of onions for her instead of for Ingalls.

B. Tender of Payment

Although the seller is obligated to deliver the goods to the buyer, this obligation is conditioned upon the buyer making tender of payment, unless the parties otherwise agree [2-511(1)]. Tender of payment may be made by any means or in any manner that is commonly used in the ordinary course of business. The seller, however, may demand payment in legal tender but must give the buyer a reasonable time to obtain it. *Legal tender* is money that may be offered legally in satisfaction of a debt and that must be accepted by a creditor to that end when so offered. (See Chapter 15, page 199.)

● Atwell agreed to sell a large piece of computer equipment to Cummings for $7,500 on c.o.d. terms. When the equipment was delivered, Cummings offered to pay Atwell with a check. This was a sufficient tender of payment because checks are commonly used in the ordinary course of business. Atwell did not have to accept Cummings's check if she did not wish to do so. If she refused to take it, however, she would have to give Cummings a reasonable time to obtain legal tender.

1. Payment by Check. Payment by check is conditional under the UCC. If the check clears the debt is discharged. If the check is dishonored, the debt is revived [2-511(3)].

2. Payment Before Inspection. When a contract requires payment before inspection, as when goods are shipped c.o.d., the buyer must pay for them first, even if they turn out to be defective when they are inspected. Of course, if the defect is obvious, the buyer would not have to accept or pay for the goods. Payment by the buyer before inspecting the goods does not constitute an acceptance of them. Upon discovering a defect, the buyer may use any of the remedies that are mentioned later in this chapter against the seller for breach of contract (2-512).

23-3. Buyer's Right to Inspect Goods

Except when goods are shipped c.o.d. or when the contract provides for payment against a document of title, the buyer has the right to inspect the goods before accepting them or paying for them (2-513). The inspection may take place after the goods arrive at their destination, when shipped by the seller. Expenses of inspection must be borne by the buyer but may be recovered from the seller if the goods do not conform to the contract and are rejected by the buyer.

● Engelbach agreed to sell Lawner a diamond ring of a particular size and value. Lawner, however, refused to pay for the ring when it was delivered without first having it appraised by a third party. Engelbach would not allow this. The court would hold that the buyer had the right to inspect the ring and have it appraised before paying for it.

23-4. Buyer's Rights and Duties Upon Delivery of Improper Goods

When defective goods or goods not of the kind specified in the contract are delivered, the buyer may elect to reject them all, accept them all, or accept any commercial unit or units and reject the rest. A *commercial unit* is a single whole for the purpose of sale, the division of which impairs its character or value on the market. For example, a commercial unit may be a single article (as a machine) or a set of articles (as a suite of furniture or an assortment of sizes). It may be a quantity (as a bale, gross, or carload) or any other unit treated in the marketplace as a single whole item.

A. Rejection

A rejection occurs when a buyer refuses to accept delivery of goods tendered.

1. Manner of Rejection. A rejection of goods must be done within a reasonable time after their delivery or tender to the buyer. After a rejection, the buyer may not claim ownership of them. In addition, the buyer must notify the seller of the particular defect in the goods so as to give the seller an opportunity to cure the defect (2-605). If the goods are in the buyer's possession, the buyer must hold them with reasonable care long enough for the seller to remove them [2-602(2)(b)]. A buyer who is not a merchant has no other obligation as to goods that are rightfully rejected.

2. Buyer's Duties Generally. If the seller gives no instructions within a reasonable time after being notified of the rejection, the buyer may store the goods for the seller, reship them to the seller, or resell them for the seller. In all cases, the buyer is entitled to be reimbursed for expenses (2-604).

● Cleary ordered a case of grapefruit to be shipped to her from a Florida-based fruit company. When she opened the package soon after it arrived, she discovered that it contained oranges rather than grapefruit. Cleary is obligated to notify the company of its error and hold the oranges with reasonable care long enough for the seller to remove them from her possession. If Cleary receives no instructions from the fruit company and it does not remove them, she may take any of the three actions listed above and be reimbursed for her expenses.

3. Merchant Buyer's Duties. A special duty comes into existence when a buyer who is a merchant rejects goods. Merchant buyers are under a duty after the rejection of goods in their possession or control to follow any reasonable instructions received from the seller with respect to the goods. If there are no such instructions, they must make reasonable efforts to sell the goods for the seller if they are perishable or threaten to speedily decline in value [2-603(1)].

Merchants who sell rejected goods are entitled to be reimbursed either by the seller or from the proceeds of the sale for reasonable expenses of caring for and selling the goods. They are also entitled to such commission as is usual in the trade or, if none, to a reasonable sum not exceeding 10 percent of the proceeds of the sale [2-603(2)].

● If Cleary had been a merchant, in the above case, and unless she had been notified to do something else by the seller, she would have had a duty to try to resell the oranges. Any proceeds from the sale, less expenses and a sales commission, would have to be turned over to the fruit company.

B. Acceptance

Acceptance of goods takes place when the buyer, after a reasonable opportunity to inspect them, does any of the following (2-606):

○ Signifies to the seller that the goods are *conforming*, that is, that they are in accordance with the obligations under the contract.
○ Signifies to the seller a willingness to take them even though they are not conforming.
○ Fails to reject them.
○ Does any act that is inconsistent with the seller's ownership.

> ● Kandy Corp. bought concrete-forming equipment from Economy Forms Corp. Kandy used the equipment for six months before notifying Economy that it was inadequate. The court held that the use of the forms in construction was an act inconsistent with the seller's ownership and constituted an acceptance of the goods by Kandy Corp.

Once goods have been accepted, they cannot be rejected. A buyer who accepts goods with knowledge of a nonconformity cannot revoke the acceptance unless the acceptance was on the assumption that the nonconformity would be cured.

C. Revocation of Acceptance

If a buyer has accepted goods on the assumption that their nonconformity would be corrected by the seller and the seller does not do so, the buyer may revoke the acceptance. This may also be done in cases in which the nonconformity is difficult to detect (2-608). The revocation must be made within a reasonable time after the buyer discovers the nonconformity. A revocation of an acceptance is not effective until the buyer notifies the seller of it. Buyers who revoke an acceptance have the same rights and duties with regard to the goods involved as if they had rejected them.

23-5. Seller's Right to Cure Improper Tender

Sellers may sometimes *cure* an improper tender or delivery of goods; that is, they may correct the defect which caused the goods to be rejected by the buyer. When the time for performance has not yet expired, the seller has the right to cure the defect and make a proper tender within the contract time [2-508(1)]. In cases where the time for performance has expired, the seller is allowed to have an additional amount of time to substitute a conforming tender if the seller had reasonable grounds to believe that the goods that were delivered were acceptable [2-508(2)]. In all cases, sellers must notify buyers that they are going to cure the improper tender or delivery.

> ● Caravan Motel ordered ten dozen bath towels from samples shown by Fleming Towel Company's representative. The representative made a mistake in writing up the order. As a result, the towels that were delivered were inferior to those shown to Caravan at the time the order was given. Caravan rejected them. Because the Fleming Towel Company had reasonable grounds to believe that Caravan Motel would accept the towels that were delivered, it would have additional time to substitute correct towels for the ones that were delivered. When it learned of the rejection, Fleming Towel Company would be required to notify the motel that it intended to cure the nonconforming delivery.

The seller does not have the right to cure when a buyer accepts nonconforming goods, even though the buyer later sues the seller for breach of contract. The seller has this right when the buyer either rejects the goods tendered or revokes an acceptance of the goods.

23-5. Breach of Contract

As discussed previously, breach of contract occurs when one of the parties fails to do that which was agreed upon in the contract. When this happens, the other party to the contract has specific remedies available under the UCC.

A. Anticipatory Breach

Sometimes, one of the parties will notify the other party before the time for performance that he or she is not going to perform. This is known as anticipatory breach. It is a breach committed before there is a present duty to perform the contract. Under older contractural law, the injured party in such a case would have to wait until the actual time for performance before bringing suit or taking some other action. It was necessary to wait for the actual time for performance in order to know for sure that the other party was, indeed, not going to perform. Under the UCC, when either party repudiates the contract before the time for performance, the injured party may take action immediately if waiting would be unjust or cause a material inconvenience (2-610). Any of the remedies (discussed below) for breach of contract are available to the aggrieved party in addition to the right to suspend his or her own performance.

● Baily ordered ten steel I-beams to be made to order from Midwest Steel Co. for use in a building which Baily was going to begin building in six months. Midwest Steel agreed to deliver the I-beams on or before that date. Two months before the delivery date, Midwest Steel notified Baily that it would not be able to fill the order. Baily could treat the contract as having been breached and use any of the buyer's remedies that are available to him under the UCC.

People who repudiate contracts are sometimes allowed to change their minds and retract the repudiation. This may be done if the other party has not already canceled the contract, changed obligations, or treated the repudiation as final.

B. Seller's Remedies

When a buyer breaches a contract by rejecting conforming goods or wrongfully revoking an acceptance or refusing to make a payment due on or before delivery, the seller may select from the remedies listed here.

1. Withhold Delivery of the Goods. If the goods have not been delivered, the seller has a right to retain possession of them upon learning of the buyer's breach [2-703(a)].

2. Stop Delivery of Goods. *Stoppage in transit* is a special right permitted a seller who discovers the insolvency of the buyer after the shipment of goods has been started by a common carrier but before the goods have been delivered to such an insolvent buyer. This right is available on both f.o.b. shipping point and f.o.b. destination shipments. The seller must satisfy the carrier that the buyer is insolvent and must accept all responsibility for any damage that may result to the carrier if shipment of goods is interrupted. Should this action be taken against a buyer's goods, both the seller and the carrier may be subjected to a suit for damages if the insolvency information is unfounded.

The seller may also stop delivery of a carload, truckload, planeload, or larger shipments of express or freight when the buyer repudiates or fails to make a payment that is due before delivery or otherwise breaches the contract (2-705). If the seller has issued a negotiable bill of lading, the seller can stop delivery only by surrendering the document to the carrier. If the buyer has received the document, delivery of the goods cannot be stopped in transit.

3. Resell the Goods. The seller may resell the goods or the undelivered balance of them [2-706(1)]. In the case of unfinished manufactured goods, a seller may either complete the manufacture and resell the finished goods or cease manufacture and resell the unfinished goods for scrap or salvage value. In such cases, the seller must use reasonable commercial judgment to avoid losses [2-704(2)]. After the sale, the injured party may sue the other for the difference between what the property brought on resale and the price the buyer had agreed to pay in the contract.

● Owens Motors sold a new car to Hudson three weeks before the announcement of new models. Hudson refused to take delivery when the car was ready. In anticipation of a decrease in price when new models appeared, Owens Motors sold the car to another interested buyer. The second deal, however, brought $200 less than would have been realized had Hudson not breached the contract.

Owens Motors could have demanded $200 from Hudson to cover its proved loss. In situations like this, the seller must act in good faith in making the second sale. If Owens Motors, to benefit a friend, had sold the car at a ridiculously low price, Hudson would not have been obligated to make up the difference.

Resale may be at public or private sale. If it is a private sale, the seller must give the buyer reasonable notice of intention to resell the goods. If it is a public sale, it must be made at a place that is normally used for public sales, if such a place is available. In addition, if the goods are perishable or threaten to decline in value speedily, the seller must give the buyer reasonable notice of the time and place of resale [2-706(4)(b)].

A purchaser who buys in good faith at a resale takes the goods free of any rights of the original buyer. Furthermore, the seller is not accountable to the buyer for any profit made on the resale. The seller who chooses to do so may buy the goods at the resale [2-706(4)(d)].

4. Recover Damages. The seller may retain the merchandise and sue the buyer for either (*a*) the difference between the contract price and the market price at the time the buyer breached the agreement or (*b*) the profit (including overhead) that the seller would have made had the contract been performed (2-708). In either case, the seller is also entitled to incidental damages. These are reasonable expenses that indirectly result from the breach, such as expenses incurred in stopping delivery of goods, transporting goods, and caring for goods that have been rightfully rejected.

5. Sue for Price. The seller may sue the buyer for the price of any goods which the buyer has accepted. Similarly, upon the buyer's breach, the seller may bring suit for the price of goods that cannot be resold at a reasonable price [2-709(1)]. In addition, the seller may sue the buyer for the price of any lost or damaged goods after the risk of their loss has passed to the buyer. The seller who sues the buyer for the price must hold for the buyer any goods that are under the seller's control. The goods may be sold, however, at any time resale is possible before the collection of a judgment in the case. The net proceeds of any resale must be credited to the buyer. Any goods that are not resold become the property of the buyer if the buyer pays for them as a result of a court judgment [2-709(2)].

6. Cancel the Contract. The seller can cancel the contract. This occurs when the seller puts an end to the contract because the other party breached. When this occurs, the seller may use any of the remedies mentioned above for breach of contract (2-106).

C. Buyer's Remedies

When the seller breaches the contract by failing to deliver goods or by delivering improper goods, the buyer may cancel the contract and recover any money paid out. The buyer may also choose any of the following remedies (2-711).

1. Cover the Sale. The buyer may *cover* the sale, that is, buy similar goods from someone else and sue the seller for the difference between the agreed price and the cost of the purchase. Cover must be made without unreasonable delay (2-712).

● Flamme Bros. contracted to deliver a specific quantity of corn to Farmers' Union Co-op Co., a cooperative grain elevator. When Flamme Bros. failed to deliver the corn, Farmers' Union bought corn from its members over a two-week period. The court held that this was cover of the contract without unreasonable delay. Farmers' Union recovered the difference between the agreed price of the corn from Flamme Bros. and the price it paid to the farmers for the corn it bought.

2. Recover Damages for Breach. If the buyers chose to do so, they may keep nonconforming goods. In such a case, they must notify the seller to that effect, and if they choose to, they may ask for an adjustment. If no adjustment is made, they may sue the seller for either breach of contract or breach of warranty, as the case may be. Damages would be an amount equal to the difference between the value of the goods ordered and the value of those received. In a proper case, incidental and consequential damages may also be recovered (2-714). Consequential damages include any loss (such as profits) which resulted from the breach and which the seller had reason to know might occur. They also include injury to person or property resulting from a breach of warranty (2-715).

● Orlowski ordered five dozen pairs of jeans for resale in her clothing store. When the jeans arrived, they were not the same quality as those that the company representative had shown Orlowski when he visited her. She needed jeans for the spring trade and decided to accept them. If no adjustment is made by the company upon notice that the jeans were nonconforming, Orlowski can sue the company for the damages (including loss of profits) she suffered because of the breach of the express warranty.

3. Recover Damages for Nondelivery. The buyer may deduct all or any part of the damages resulting from breach of contract from any payment still due under the same contract. The buyer must notify the seller first, however, of an intention to do this (2-717). In addition, the buyer may sue the seller for damages for nondelivery of goods. Damages sought would be the difference between the contract price and the price of the same goods in the marketplace on the date of the breach. Here also, the buyer may claim incidental or consequential damages resulting from the breach (2-713).

● Acme Restaurants ordered four sides of choice beef from Haldas Wholesale Butchers. Haldas failed to deliver the beef when promised. The quoted wholesale price on choice beef had advanced 9 cents a pound since the date of contract. Acme Restaurants would be justified in demanding damages of 9 cents a pound for the weight of beef not delivered. Any other incidental damages could be added to the claim.

4. Bring Action for Specific Performance. When the goods are unique, the buyer may ask the court to order the seller to turn the goods over to the buyer under the contract terms [2-716(1)]. This is known as an action in equity for specific performance of the contract. A decree of specific performance, if granted by the court, would require the seller to deliver to the buyer the goods described in the sales agreement. This type of action is permitted only when an award of money will not give the buyer sufficient relief. Contracts for objets d'art, rare gems, antiques, and goods described as one-of-a-kind come within the scope of this type of action. Under the UCC, the decree of specific performance may include the payment of the price, damages, or other relief as the court may deem just. Specific performance is discussed in more detail in Chapter 16.

5. Bring Action for Replevin. Buyers have a right of replevin for goods that have been identified to the contract if, after a reasonable effort, they are unable to buy the goods elsewhere [2-716(3)]. A court-ordered *writ of replevin* would require the seller to convey the goods to the purchaser.

D. **Liquidated Damages**
Damages for breach by either party may be liquidated, that is agreed upon in advance so that the amount is stated in the sales agreement. Such damages will be allowed by the court if they are reasonable [2-718(1)]. Liquidated damages are discussed in more detail in Chapter 16.

E. **Statute of Limitations**
Nearly all lawsuits have a time limit within which suit must be brought. If the time limit is exceeded, the action is forever barred. Generally, an action for breach of contract for sale must be commenced within four years after the date of the breach (2-725). The parties may, if they wish to do so, provide for a shorter time period, not less than one year, in their sales agreement. They may not, however, agree to a period longer than four years.

Understanding Legal Terms

Define, identify, or explain the following terms:

commercial unit	cover	tender of delivery	tender of
conforming goods	cure	tender of payment	performance

Questions for Review and Discussion

1. Describe in general terms the obligations of parties to a contract for sale.

2. Why is tender of performance necessary?

3. What is required of the seller in making tender of delivery? What form of payment may be used by the buyer in making tender of payment? When may the seller demand legal tender?

4. Explain the right of the buyer to inspect goods that are received under a contract for sale.

5. What three choices does a buyer have when defective or nonconforming goods are delivered?

6. Describe the manner in which buyers must reject goods if they decide to do so. After a rejection, what may buyers do with goods in their possession? What special duty applies to a merchant buyer?

7. When may buyers revoke their acceptance?

8. Compared older contractual law with the UCC as it applies to an anticipatory breach.

9. Explain the remedies that are available to a seller when a buyer breaches a contract for sale.

10. Explain the remedies that are available to a buyer when a seller breaches a contract for sale.

Analyzing Cases

1. Halverson, a potato farmer, entered into a written contract to sell to Pet, Inc., 10,000 hundredweight of potatoes suitable for processing into high-quality potato chips. The potatoes were to be grown during the next growing season, and delivery was to be made to Pet, Inc., "as needed." It was agreed that Pet, Inc., would furnish the vehicles for loading and transporting the potatoes to its plant. Halverson grew the potatoes and, in the fall, harvested them and stored them in his warehouse. He received no orders from Pet, Inc., to ship the potatoes and, in March, was forced to dump them in a field. When sued for the price of the potatoes, Pet, Inc., argued that since Halverson failed to make tender of delivery, it was not liable. Do you agree with Pet, Inc.? Why or why not? ● *Halverson v. Pet, Inc.*, 261 N.W.2d 887 (N.D. 1978)

2. Herman Googe agreed to buy an automobile from Irene Schleimer. Later, Googe changed his mind and refused to buy the car. Schleimer, without making tender of delivery, brought suit against Googe for breach of contract. Will Schleimer recover? Explain. ● *Schleimer v. Googe*, 377 N.Y.S.2d 591 (N.Y. 1975)

3. Dehahn agreed to sell and Innes agreed to buy for the price of $35,000 a 35-acre gravel pit, a back hoe, a bulldozer, a loader, two dump trucks, and a low-bed trailer. Since Dehahn had recently lost his bid for re-election as road commissioner in the town, he was required to remove the equipment from town property. He moved the equipment to a field owned by Innes across from the driveway to Innes's home and left the keys in the vehicles. Later, Innes canceled the contract and refused to make any payments. When sued, Innes argued that Dehahn failed to make tender of delivery of the equipment. Do you agree with Innes? State why or why not? ● *Dehahn v. Innes*, 356 A.2d 711 (Me. 1976)

4. Formetal Engineering Co. placed an order with Presto Manufacturing Co., Inc., for 250,000 polyurethane pads to be used in making air-conditioning units. The pads were to be made according to samples and specifications supplied by Formetal. When the pads arrived, Formetal discovered that they did not conform to the sample and specifications in that there were incomplete cuts, color variances, and faulty adherence to the

pads' paper backing. Formetal notified Presto of the defects and said that it was rejecting the goods and returning them to Presto. The goods, however, were never returned. Was the rejection proper? Explain. ● *Presto Mfg. Co. v. Formetal Eng'r Co.*, 360 N.E.2d 510 (Ill. 1977)

5. Mr. and Mrs. Aldridge bought a motor home from Sportsman Travel Trailer Sales, located in Texas. Two years later, after traveling more than 14,000 miles on trips to Louisiana, Colorado, and California, they attempted to reject the motor home, claiming that it was defective. Can they return the vehicle and recover damages? Explain. ● *Explorer Motor Home Corp. v. Aldridge*, 541 S.W.2d 851 (Tex. 1976)

6. City National Bank of Crete agreed to sell and deliver to Goosic Construction Company a set of concrete forms for the sum of $200, which Goosic paid. The forms had been repossessed at an earlier time by the bank and were stored at another location. When Goosic arrived at the storage location to pick up the forms, a Mr. Roberts claimed a storage lien and refused to allow Goosic to take possession of them. Goosic never received the forms, which had a fair market value of $1,500. Did the City National Bank make proper tender of delivery? If Goosic Construction Company wins the case, how much will it recover? Give reasons for your answers. ● *Goosic Const. Co. v. City Nat. Bank*, 241 N.W.2d 521 (Neb. 1976)

7. Carolyn McQueen bought a new Fiat Spider for $5,995.80 from American Imports, Inc. The deal included a $500 trade-in allowance on McQueen's Oldsmobile, and McQueen borrowed the money to buy the car from a credit union. She took possession of the Fiat on November 21, paying with checks totaling $5,495.80, and promising to deliver the Oldsmobile for trade-in the next week. Two days later, the Fiat overheated.

McQueen had also discovered that neither the speedometer nor the odometer functioned properly. American Imports, Inc., towed the car to its garage, replaced a broken fan belt, and tightened a nut on the speedometer which also controlled the odometer. After the repairs were made, McQueen refused to take the car, saying that she wanted a new one. She stopped payment on the checks. When sued for the purchase price, McQueen claimed that she had revoked her acceptance of the Fiat and could, therefore, cancel the contract. Is McQueen within her rights? Why or why not? ● *American Imports, Inc. v. G. E. Emp. West. Region Fed. Credit Union*, 245 S.E.2d 798 (N.C. 1978)

8. Ronald and Sally Berube agreed to buy a mobile home from Mobile Homes Sales and Service for $8,600. They were to pay a deposit of $500 and planned to obtain the balance of $8,100 by borrowing from Navy Federal Credit Union. When their loan was approved, the Berubes asked the mobile home salesperson if the company would set up the mobile home for them upon their paying the $500 deposit. According to the Berube's testimony, the salesperson obtained approval of the company's president to do this, took the $500 from the Berubes, and agreed to have the mobile home set up on the following Monday. The mobile home was not set up then, however, as the company claimed that it could not do so until it received payment. The Berubes asked for their $500 back. When it was not returned, they brought suit in small-claims court. In its defense, the mobile home company argued that tender of payment is a condition precedent to the seller's duty of delivery, and therefore the company did not breach the contract by refusing to install the mobile home until the full purchase price was paid. Is the company's contention correct? Why or why not? ● *Berube v. Mobile Homes Sales and Services*, 220 S.E.2d 636 (N.C. 1975)

Part 5

Case Briefs

Guess v. Lorenz,
612 S.W.2d 831 (Mo. 1981)

Kathy Lorenz advertised her Datsun 260Z for sale in a newspaper in November, and Allen Guess answered the ad. He examined and drove the car and asked Lorenz questions about its condition. Lorenz told him that she really liked the car and was selling it because she was buying another car. She pointed out the broken radio antenna, which she said could probably be replaced for about $12, and that the car needed paint and interior repair. Guess asked Lorenz about the shocks, brakes, transmission, engine, rear end, etc., and said, "She assured me that the car was in good shape at that point." During the test drive, Guess noticed a noise in the back which Lorenz said was "just something the car does." Guess also asked about the 90,000 miles on the car, and Lorenz told him that these were mostly highway miles and not a lot of city driving. Lorenz said she told Guess "the engine was sound and everything was running well for me, but I had not replaced anything on the car, except for the alternator."

Guess purchased the car for $2,995. Within two weeks, he replaced the rear tires, which were of odd sizes, for $104. Shortly thereafter, he took the car in for $218.35 of rear-end work. He had the car tuned up for $93 and both carburetors adjusted for $137. Guess said that when he took the car in for repairs, he was told the car needed shocks and a clutch. He said he also learned that a new aerial would cost between $70 and $110 instead of the $12 mentioned by Lorenz.

Guess telephoned Lorenz in late February or early March and asked her if she would be willing to help pay for repairs to the car. She was not willing. Guess then brought suit against Lorenz.

Plaintiff's Position: Guess contended that the statements made by Lorenz at the time of the sale were express warranties of the car's good condition.

Defendant's Position: Lorenz argued that Guess had failed to allege and prove a breach of express warranty.

Legal Issue: Can a seller's statements to the effect that a car was "in good shape" and that the noise in the rear end was "just something the car does" be taken as express warranties of its condition at the time of the sale?

Court Decision: No. Under the circumstances here, the statements "the car is in good shape" and "that's just something the car does" are not express warranties of its condition.

Court Reasoning: The statements of the seller in this case were very general. A seller may puff his or her wares or express an opinion as to the quality and value of the goods even to the point of exaggeration without incurring a warranty obligation. Lorenz was neither a car dealer nor a person who gave any impression of knowledge about cars. Considering all the circumstances, it would not be reasonable to find that her statements were express warranties of the car's condition.

Even if the statements could be construed as warranties of the car's condition at the time of sale, the evidence presented by the buyer is insufficient to support the finding of a breach. Guess testified to the cost of work done on the vehicle, but no evidence was offered to show that these repairs were necessary. The mere fact of subsequent repair does not demonstrate that at the time of sale the car was not "in good shape" for a used car which had been driven 90,000 miles. The buyer could not expect new-car performance, particularly when he was told by the seller that she had replaced nothing but the alternator.

Society National Bank v. Pemberton
409 N.E.2d 1073 (Ohio 1979)

Pemberton desired to supplement his income as a landscape laborer by plowing snow during the winter. Accordingly, he visited Chapel Hill Dodge and informed the sales manager, Mr. Green, that he wished to purchase a used truck which could be used to plow snow on a commercial basis. Mr. Green, who testified that he had thirty years of experience in selling vehicles, showed Pemberton a two-year-old four-wheel-drive pick-up truck which showed 20,000 miles on the odometer. The testimony disclosed that Green advised Pemberton that this truck would be just right for the purpose of commercial snowplowing, that it was a one-owner vehicle, and that it was in good shape after having been serviced and inspected by a Chapel Hill Dodge mechanic who specialized in the servicing of used trucks for resale. Pemberton drove the truck around the parking lot of Chapel Hill Dodge, raised and lowered the snowplow blade, and decided to make the purchase.

Pemberton executed a sales contract which contained a clause in very fine print stating that all used cars and trucks are sold as is and without any express or implied warranties. Chapel Hill Dodge also required that Pemberton sign a warranty document which conspicuously disclaimed any warranties on the vehicle. Pemberton stated he only remembered signing several papers and did not understand the significance of these provisions.

Also testifying was the previous owner of the truck, a construction corporation that appeared in court through its president. He testified that he knew from experience that after two years of very hard use, the truck would soon require major part replacements. Therefore, he traded it in toward a new truck, which was also purchased from Chapel Hill Dodge.

Approximately one month after Pemberton purchased the truck, the brakes failed while he was crossing a large intersection. Pemberton was forced to lower the snow blade for some distance in order to stop the vehicle. Later, over a four-month period, various other components failed. The drive shafts, starter, and transmission all required repair or replacement. The carburetor failed to function properly, both inner and outer axles required replacement, the electrical system caught fire, and, finally, the snow blade would not raise or lower.

Mr. Pemberton plowed the first snowfall in November of that year for his various contract customers. He was unable to plow during the remainder of the winter due to the innumerable mechanical failures. However, the truck was used for transportation to and from work, a distance of 60 miles per day, despite its total unfitness for the purpose for which it was purchased—commercial snowplowing. Pemberton refused to pay the $2,500 balance owed to the bank for the purchase of the truck, and the bank brought suit. The bank acknowledged at the trial that any defenses available against Chapel Hill Dodge would also be available against the bank.

Plaintiff's Position: The bank argued that all warranties, express or implied, were disclaimed in the sales agreement.

Defendant's Position: Pemberton contended that the seller expressly warranted that the truck would be fit for snowplowing and that this express warranty was not disclaimed by the written contract.

Legal Issue: The issue in this case is whether the express oral warranties as to fitness for a particular purpose were effectively disclaimed in the subsequent written contract.

Court Decision: They were not disclaimed. Although the general disclaimer clause in the warranty agreement was effective to disclaim the implied warranty of fitness for a particular purpose, and the as-is clause was sufficient to disclaim all implied warranties, these did not disclaim the express warranties.

Court Reasoning: Express warranties were given as to the condition and performance ability of the truck. Pemberton was told unequivocally and specifically by Chapel Hills' salesperson that the truck was "just right for plowing snow." Such statements by salespeople can become a sufficient basis on which to find the creation of express warranties. These are in addition to those warranties implied by law and are not so easily withdrawn from the parties' agreement.

The UCC specifically provides for the situation in which express warranties are made during the negotiation of a sale, but then are allegedly disclaimed in the actual sales contract. In these cases, preference is given to the express warranties, and inconsistent disclaimers are inoperative to the extent they are unreasonable [2-316(1)]. In interpreting this provision of the UCC, courts have been uniform in holding disclaimers which are in-consistent with an express warranty to be inoperative. The rationale for these decisions is succinctly expressed in the official comments to the UCC: that express warranties rest on negotiated aspects of the individual bargain, and go so clearly to the essence of that bargain that words of disclaimer in a form are repugnant to the basic negotiated terms.

Accordingly, when a written contract for the sale of goods provides that the goods are sold as is and also disclaims all warranties, either express or implied, and such provisions cannot reasonably be construed as consistent with the seller's oral express warranty, the express warranty will predominate, and the inconsistent provisions are inoperative to the extent they are unreasonable.

In this case, the disclaimer provisions in the sales contract and warranty document are hopelessly inconsistent with Chapel Hill's oral express warranties. The latter must predominate in that it would be unreasonable to allow the printed form disclaimers to withdraw from the parties' agreement all the prior affirmations made as to the truck's ability to be used for commercial snowplowing.

Prior to the signing of these forms, it is clear that the parties had agreed on the sale of a truck fit for this purpose. This is what the defendant thought he was buying and what he was entitled to receive. Being in the business of selling used vehicles, Chapel Hill should have known of the numerous defects in the truck and that it would be unfit for the hard use certain to result if used for snowplowing. For the breach of this express warranty, Pemberton is entitled to recover damages.

Part 6   Commercial Paper

Chapter 24   Nature and Kinds of Commercial Paper

The huge expansion of credit buying and the many new credit plans have resulted in many more payments by check than by cash. The explosion of credit buying also means that more and more people and businesses signed promissory notes than ever before. These instruments, checks and promissory notes, are examples of commercial paper that is used conveniently and safely as a substitute for money and to obtain credit in today's society. The rules governing commercial paper are found in Article 3 of the UCC.

24-1. Purpose of Commercial Paper

Throughout history there has been a need to transact business without carrying around large sums of money. In the Middle Ages, for example, merchants at first carried gold and silver with them as they traveled from one fair to another buying goods. They were in constant danger of being robbed, however, and needed a safer and more convenient method of exchanging their gold and silver for the goods they bought. A system was developed by which merchants could deposit their precious metals with goldsmiths or silversmiths for safekeeping. When the merchants bought goods, instead of paying for them with gold or silver, they simply filled out a piece of paper, called a bill of exchange. The bill of exchange ordered the goldsmith or silversmith to give a certain amount of the precious metal to the person who sold the goods. That person would then take the bill of exchange to the goldsmith or silversmith and receive payment. There also developed a need to borrow money in order to buy things at one time and pay for them at a later time. Today, commercial paper circulates freely in the business world as an instrument of credit, allowing millions of people to borrow money easily. The law of commercial paper has developed in recognition of the need to transact business without carrying around large sums of money and to borrow money easily. This law is also referred to as the law of negotiable instruments.

24-2. The Concept of Negotiability

The concept of negotiability is one of the most important features of commercial paper. Largely because of this feature, negotiable instruments are highly trusted and used daily by millions of people. The concept is simple: When an instrument is transferred by negotiation, the *transferee* (person to whom transfer is made) receives more protection than the *transferor* (one who transfers) had under the instrument. The transferee is able, in many instances, to recover money on the instrument even when the person from whom the instrument was received could not have done so. These special rights that are sometimes available to transferees of negotiable instruments are discussed in detail in the chapters that follow.

24-3. Kinds of Negotiable Instruments

There are three basic kinds of negotiable instruments: drafts (including checks), notes, and certificates of deposit. These are described below.

A. Drafts

A *draft* (also known as a *bill of exchange*) is an instrument by which the party creating it orders another party to pay money to a third party. The one who draws the draft (that is, the one who orders the money to be paid) is called the *drawer*. The one who is requested to pay the money is called the *drawee*. The one who is to receive the money is known as the *payee*.

● Ahearn owed Bickum $500, payable in sixty days. Bickum owed Connors the same amount. Bickum wrote out a draft ordering Ahearn to pay Connors $500 in or within sixty days and gave the draft to Connors. When the sixty days elapsed, Connors presented the instrument to Ahearn for payment.

Drafts may be presented to the drawee for payment, as above, or for *acceptance*. When a draft is presented for acceptance, the drawee is requested to become liable on the instrument. To accept a draft, the drawee usually writes "accepted" across the face of the instrument and dates and signs it. By doing this, the drawee agrees to pay the instrument at a later date when it becomes due. An acceptance must be written on the draft, but it may consist of the drawee's signature alone (3-410). Instead of waiting for the sixty days to elapse before mak-

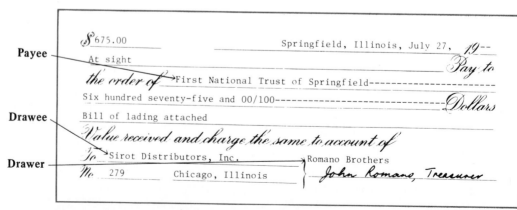

Figure 24-1. A sight draft.

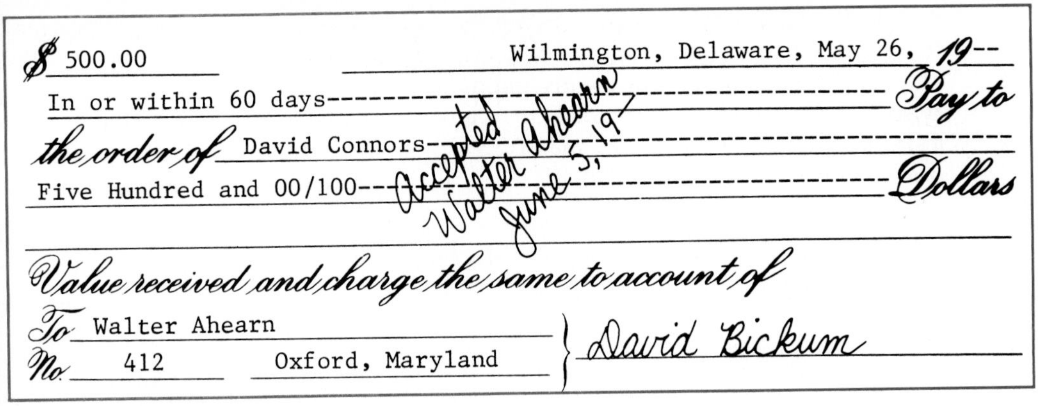
$ 500.00 Wilmington, Delaware, May 26, 19--

In or within 60 days Pay to the order of David Connors

Five Hundred and 00/100 Dollars

Accepted Walter Ahearn June 5, 19--

Value received and charge the same to account of

To Walter Ahearn

No. 412 Oxford, Maryland

David Bickum

Figure 24-2. An accepted time draft.

ing presentment, in the above case, Connors could have asked Ahearn to accept the instrument at any time before its due date. A draft is said to be *dishonored* when a drawee refuses to accept it before its due date or to pay it on its due date.

1. Sight and Time Drafts. A *sight draft* is a draft that is payable as soon as it is presented to the drawee for payment. A *time draft* is a draft that is not payable until the lapse of a particular time period stated on the draft. Drafts that are payable "thirty days after sight" and "sixty days after date" are examples of time drafts.

2. Trade Acceptances. A *trade acceptance* is a draft used by a seller of goods to receive payment and also to extend credit. It is often used in combination with a bill of lading, which is a receipt given by a freight company to someone who ships goods. For example, a seller ships goods to a buyer and sends a bill of lading, with a trade acceptance attached, to a bank in the buyer's city. The trade acceptance is drawn by the seller ordering the buyer to pay the money either to the seller or to someone else. If it is a sight draft, the buyer must pay the draft immediately to receive the bill of lading from the bank. If it is a time draft, the buyer must accept the draft to receive the bill of lading from the bank. The freight company will not release the goods to the buyer unless the buyer has the bill of lading.

In Figure 24-3, Walker is the seller and drawer of the trade acceptance,

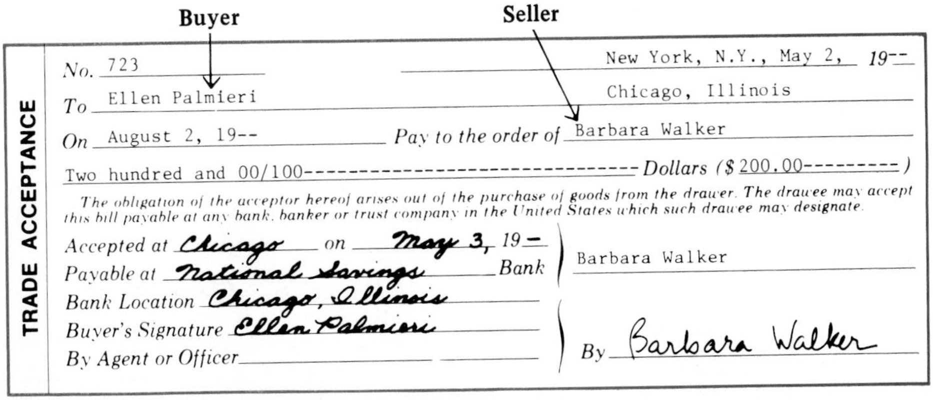

TRADE ACCEPTANCE

No. 723 New York, N.Y., May 2, 19--

To Ellen Palmieri Chicago, Illinois

On August 2, 19-- Pay to the order of Barbara Walker

Two hundred and 00/100 Dollars ($ 200.00)

The obligation of the acceptor hereof arises out of the purchase of goods from the drawer. The drawee may accept this bill payable at any bank, banker or trust company in the United States which such drawee may designate.

Accepted at Chicago on May 3, 19--

Payable at National Savings Bank

Bank Location Chicago, Illinois

Buyer's Signature Ellen Palmieri

By Agent or Officer

Barbara Walker

By Barbara Walker

Figure 24-3. A trade acceptance.

Chapter 24: Nature and Kinds of Commercial Paper

which is a time draft because it is not due until August 2. Palmieri, the buyer, has accepted the trade acceptance by signing and dating it. Thus, she will be able to receive possession of any goods accompanying the trade acceptance. Walker may discount the instrument at a bank for cash or use it as collateral on a short-term loan. *Discounting* means that the bank will buy the instrument at a price below its face amount with the aim of ultimately collecting the face amount.

3. Domestic and International Bills of Exchange. A *domestic bill of exchange* is a draft that is drawn and payable in the United States. A draft that is drawn in one country but payable in another is called an *international bill of exchange* or *foreign draft.*

4. Checks. A *check* is a special kind of draft which is drawn on a bank and payable on demand. Since a check is also the most common type of draft, it is discussed in more detail in Chapter 27.

B. Notes

A *note* (often called a *promissory note*) is a written promise by one party, called the *maker,* to pay money to another party, called the payee. In contrast with drafts, notes are promise instruments rather than order instruments and involve only two parties instead of three. They are used by people who loan money or extend credit as evidence of debt. When two or more parties sign a note, they are called *comakers.*

A *demand note,* as its name implies, is payable whenever the payee demands payment. A *time note,* on the other hand, is payable at some future time, on a definite date named in the instrument. Unless a note is payable in installments, the principal (face value) of the note plus interest must be paid on the date that it is due. In an *installment note,* the principal together with interest on the unpaid balance is payable in installments (series of payments) at specified times.

C. Certificates of Deposit

A *certificate of deposit* is an acknowledgment by a bank of the receipt of money and a promise to pay the money back on the due date, usually with interest. Certificates of deposit generally pay more interest than regular savings accounts because the depositor cannot withdraw the money before the due date without penalty.

No. __381__   __Boston, Massachusetts, October 1,__ 19--

On demand, the undersigned, for value received, promise(s) to pay to the order of
CAMBRIDGE TRUST COMPANY

__Two thousand four hundred and 00/100--------------------__ Dollars,
at its offices in Boston, Massachusetts, together with interest thereon from the
date thereof until paid at the rate of __11__ percent per annum.

Address __100 Bedford Street__   *Victor Powell*

__Waltham, Massachusetts__

Figure 24-4. A demand note.

24-4. Parties to Commercial Paper

In addition to drawers of drafts and checks, makers of notes, and payees of both types of instruments, there are other parties to commercial paper. They are the bearer, the holder, the holder in due course, the indorser, the indorsee, and the acceptor.

○ A *bearer* is a person who is in possession of a negotiable instrument that is payable to bearer or to cash. A person who is in possession of an instrument that has been indorsed in blank (by the payee's signature alone) is also a bearer.

○ A *holder* is a person who is in possession of a negotiable instrument which is issued or indorsed to that person's order or to bearer.

○ A *holder in due course* is a holder of a negotiable instrument who is treated as favored and is given immunity from certain defenses. A detailed discussion of holders in due course can be found in Chapter 26.

○ An *indorser* is a person who indorses a negotiable instrument. This is done in most cases by signing one's name on the back of the paper. The different kinds of indorsements are discussed in Chapter 25.

○ An *indorsee* is a person to whom a draft, note, or other negotiable instrument is transferred by indorsement.

○ An *acceptor* is a drawee of a draft who has promised to honor the draft as presented by signing it on its face.

24-5. Requirements of Negotiability

To be negotiable, an instrument must include the following (3-104):

○ It must be in writing and have the signature of the maker or drawer.
○ There must be an unconditional promise or order to pay.
○ It must designate a sum certain in money.
○ It must be payable on demand or at a definite time.
○ It must be payable to order or bearer.

● Aetna Acceptance Corp. signed a promissory note which stated, "Buyer agrees to pay to seller" a certain amount of money. The note was not negotiable because it lacked certain requirements of negotiability (it was not payable to order or to bearer). The person to whom the note was transferred was not entitled to the special protection that would have been available had the note been negotiable.

The essentials of negotiability, illustrated in Figure 24-5, are discussed in the following paragraphs.

A. Written Instrument

A negotiable instrument must be in writing. This is broadly understood to include printing, typewriting, pen or pencil writing, or even painting. A negotiable instrument written in pencil is, however, an invitation to alteration by forgery. If this should happen, the person who drew the instrument would be responsible for any loss caused by the negligent drawing of the instrument.

Most negotiable instruments are written on paper, but this is not a requirement. Oddly drawn checks are sometimes presented to and paid by banks. Since negotiable instruments must be capable of circulating, they should not be

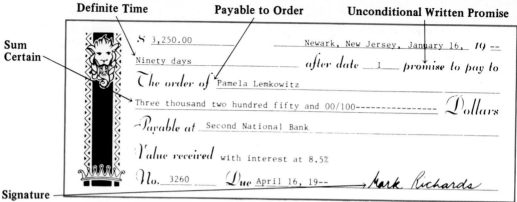

Figure 24-5. Requisites of negotiability.

written on any nonmovable object. Neither should they be written on anything unstable and unable to retain writing for a lasting period of time.

B. Signature of Maker or Drawer

To be negotiable, an instrument must be signed by the maker or drawer. Any writing or executed symbol is accepted as a signature. It may be handwritten, typewritten, printed, or produced in any way that will make a lasting impression. The writing can be done with ink or with anything that makes a mark. For proof of authority or genuineness, however, it is good judgment on the part of the receiver of an instrument to insist on a written signature.

A signature may be made by an *agent* (one who represents and acts for another) or other representative. No particular form of appointment is necessary to establish such authority. Agents who sign their own name to an instrument are personally obligated if the instrument neither names the person represented nor shows that the agent signed in a representative capacity. The signature may appear in the body of the instrument as well as at the end (3-401).

C. Unconditional Promise or Order to Pay

To be negotiable, an instrument must contain no conditions that might in any way affect its payment. Statements requiring that certain things be done or that specific events take place prior to payment make the instrument a simple contract rather than negotiable paper.

● Ingalsby wrote the following note to Security Credit Union: "I promise to pay to the order of Security Credit Union $400 sixty days after the delivery of my new automatic washing machine from the Atlantic Appliance Center." This instrument is not negotiable because it is conditional upon the delivery of the washing machine.

An instrument is conditional, and thus not negotiable, if it states that it is subject to any other agreement. The same is true if an instrument states that it is to be paid only out of a particular fund. This latter rule does not apply to instruments issued by government agencies. An instrument may state that it "arises out of" another agreement without being conditional. Similarly, a negotiable instrument may indicate a particular account that is to be charged.

● Eleanor Hess accepted a friend's note which read, "Ninety days after date, I promise to pay to the order of Eleanor Hess $150 out of the proceeds of a garage sale." The promise is conditional since payment will be made only if the garage sale takes place and the proceeds of the sale are sufficient. Hess should insist on rewording the last part of the note to read, "to be charged to the proceeds of a garage sale." This wording does not affect negotiability, since the neighbor's general credit is relied upon and the reference to the garage sale is simply a recordkeeping instruction following payment.

In addition to being unconditional, a negotiable instrument must contain a promise (as in a note) or an order (as in a draft). A writing that says "due Martha Charett $400" or "IOU $400" is not negotiable because it is neither a promise nor an order to pay.

D. Sum Certain in Money

A negotiable instrument must be payable in a *sum certain* in money. This means an amount of money that is clearly known. *Money* is defined as a medium of exchange adopted by a domestic or foreign government as part of its currency (1-201). Thus, a sum certain in money need not be money of the United States.

● Security Loan held a note which it had received from a branch of the National Bank of France. The note specified payment in French francs. On the due date the note would probably be paid in dollars and cents according to the exchange rate of francs and dollars on the date of maturity and payment.

The sum payable is a sum certain even though it is to be paid (1) with stated interest or by stated installments, (2) with stated different rates of interest before and after default or a specified date, (3) with a stated discount or addition if paid before or after the date fixed for payment, (4) with exchange or less exchange, whether at a fixed rate or at the current rate, or (5) with costs of collection or an attorney's fee or both upon default (3-106).

E. Payable on Demand or at a Definite Time

Negotiable instruments must be made payable on demand or at a definite time. This requirement makes it possible to determine when the debtor or promisor can be compelled to pay. Without this information, the present value of an instrument cannot be determined.

1. Demand Paper. An instrument is payable *on demand* when it so states, or when it is payable "on sight" or "on presentation." The key characteristic of demand instruments is that the holder can require payment at any time by making the demand upon the person who is obligated to pay.

2. Definite-Time Paper. Certainty as to the time of payment of an instrument is satisfied if it is payable on or before a definite date. Instruments payable at a fixed period after a stated date or at a fixed period after sight are also considered to be payable at a definite time. In each instance, a simple mathematical calculation makes the maturity date certain. The expressions "one year after date" and "thirty days after sight" are definite as to time. An undated instrument payable sixty days after date is negotiable as a demand paper.

A promise to pay only upon an act or event, the time of whose occurrence is uncertain, is not payable at a definite time. Thus, an instrument payable when a person marries, reaches a certain age, or graduates from college, or one payable within a specific period of time after a named person's death, is not negotiable.

3. Acceleration. An *acceleration clause* on the face of an instrument hastens the maturity date. For example: "In case of default in payments of interest (or of an installment of the principal), the entire note shall become due and payable." Instruments payable at a fixed time but subject to acceleration are negotiable.

4. Extension. *Extension clauses* give the maker of a note the opportunity to extend the payment date to a further definite time. For example, a maker may make a note payable in six months, but may include the right to extend it to one year without loss of negotiability.

F. Payable to Order or to Bearer

The chief characteristic of a negotiable instrument is its capacity to circulate freely as an instrument of credit. This function is achieved, and the intention of the maker (i.e., ease of transferability and payment of the amount indicated to a holder) is expressed, by the words "to the order of" or "to bearer." They are called the words of negotiability. Instruments not payable to order or to bearer are not negotiable.

1. Payable to Order. An instrument is *payable to order* when by its terms it is payable to the order of any person with reasonable certainty. The maker or drawer may state, "Pay to the order of . . . ," "Pay to . . . or his (her) order," or "Pay to . . . or his (her) assigns." An instrument may be payable to the order of the maker or drawer; the drawee; a payee who is not the maker, drawer, or drawee; two or more payees; an estate, trust, or fund; an office or an officer by title; or a partnership or unincorporated association (3-110).

2. Payable to Bearer. An instrument is *payable to bearer* when by its terms it is payable to bearer or the order of bearer; a specified person or bearer; cash or the order of cash; or another indication which does not designate a specific payee (3-111). An instrument made *payable to order and to bearer* is payable to order unless the bearer words are handwritten or typewritten. The omission of these or similar words destroys the negotiability of the instrument, making it a simple contract, valid only when legal consideration is present. The basic characteristic of bearer instruments compared with order instruments is that they can be negotiated by delivery without indorsement. Whether an instrument is a bearer instrument may be determined either by what appears on the face of the instrument or by the last indorsement. A special indorsement which designates the name of the indorsee ("pay to Paul Minor") transforms a bearer instrument into an order instrument. A blank indorsement consisting of the indorser's signature transforms an order instrument into a bearer instrument. Thus, a check payable "to the order of Olga Pirina" becomes a bearer instrument if it is indorsed "Olga Pirina." Since bearer instruments are similar to cash and can be negotiated by delivery, caution in their handling is required.

● Pet 'n' Poodle received a check payable to the order of cash. The proprietor indorsed it "Pay to Cedar Products, Inc., in partial payment of a shipment of red cedar shavings." Any further transfer of the check will require an indorsement by Cedar Products, Inc.

24-6. Omissions, Ambiguity, and Nonessentials

The omission of the date does not affect the negotiability of an instrument. When the date is omitted, the date on which the instrument is received is considered to be the date of issue. An instrument may be antedated or postdated without affecting its negotiability (3-114). Any instrument lacking one or more elements of negotiability, however, cannot be enforced until it is completed. Handwritten terms control typewritten and printed terms, and typewritten ones control printed. Words control figures, except where words are ambiguous (capable of being understood in more than one way). The numbering of, or the failure to number, an instrument does not affect its negotiability.

Understanding Legal Terms

Define, identify, or explain the following terms:

acceptance	demand note	holder	note
bearer	dishonored	indorsee	payee
bill of exchange	draft	indorser	sight draft
certificate of deposit	drawee	installment note	time draft
comaker	drawer	maker	trade acceptance

Questions for Review and Discussion

1. What is the purpose of commercial paper?

2. Describe the concept of negotiability. What protection is available in many instances to a transferee of an instrument that has been negotiated?

3. Name the three basic kinds of negotiable instruments. Which of these are order instruments and which are promise instruments?

4. How may a trade acceptance be used in combination with a bill of lading? Give an example of this.

5. Explain how the following notes differ from each other: (a) demand note, (b) time note, and (c) installment note.

6. Contrast a bearer of a negotiable instrument with a holder.

7. Name the essential requirements for an instrument to be negotiable.

8. Explain the manner in which the maker or drawer or a negotiable instrument may sign it.

9. When is an instrument payable to order? To bearer? To whom is an instrument payable that is made payable to order and to bearer?

10. How would each of the following affect the negotiability of an instrument: (a) omission of the date; (b) failure to number the instrument.

Analyzing Cases

1. Nestrick, who was associated with the *Liberty Advertiser*, borrowed money from the Bank of Viola. The promissory note that he signed read: "For value received, the undersigned promises to pay to the Order of Bank of Viola, Viola, Illinois, the principal sum of $15,884.54 payable in installments Or as follows: Or payable $80.00 per week from Jack & Jill contract with interest at the rate of 8.00 per cent per annum from date until paid." The Jack & Jill contract referred to in the note was a contract entered into by the Jack & Jill store for advertising space in the *Liberty Advertiser*. Was the note conditional? Explain ● *Bank of Viola v. Nestrick*, 390 N.E.2d 636 (Ill. 1979)

2. In exchange for certain plumbing fix-

tures and materials, the Hotel Evans gave A. Alport & Son, Inc., a promissory note in the amount of $1,600. The note stated that it was "with interest at bank rates." Did these words in the note affect its negotiability? Why or why not? ● *A. Alport & Son, Inc. v. Hotel Evans, Inc.*, 317 N.Y.S.2d 937 (1970)

3. William R. Van Dusen and Betty Van Dusen signed one of their personal check forms which had their names printed at the top. The name of the bank and the account number were crossed out. The remainder of the form was filled in as a check would be and was payable to the order of Frank Kaminsky in the amount of $12,000. It was dated, and the following notation was written at the lower left-hand corner: "note—6% Int." Was the instrument negotiable? Explain your answer. ● *Kaminsky v. Van Dusen*, 390 N.Y.S.2d 544 (1976)

4. Barton signed a promissory note promising to pay to the order of Scott Hudgens Realty & Mortgage, Inc., the sum of $3,000. The note stated, "This amount is due and payable upon evidence of an acceptable permanent loan . . . and upon acceptance of the loan commitment." Was the note negotiable? Why or why not? ● *Barton v. Scott Hudgens Realty & Mortg.*, 222 S.E.2d 126 (Ga. 1975)

5. The following instrument, containing many blank spaces, was signed by Leo H. Fabacher: "Freeport, Texas, 15 April 1971 $6002.19. For value received, I, we, or either of us, the undersigned, promise to pay to the order of _____ In _____ monthly installments of $_____ each and one installment of _____, the first installment to become due and payable on or before the 16 day of July, 1971, and one installment to be due and payable on the _____ day of each succeeding month until the whole of said indebtedness is paid with interest from date at the rate of 10 per cent per annum."

Hoss, who is in possession of the paper, claims that it is an enforceable negotiable instrument. Do you agree with Hoss? Explain. ● *Hoss v. Fabacher*, 578 S.W.2d 454 (Tex. 1979)

6. In exchange for legal services rendered to her by the law firm of Westmoreland, Hall, and Bryan, Barbara Hall wrote the following letter: "I agree to pay to your firm as attorney's fees for representing me in obtaining property settlement agreement and tax advice, the sum of $2,760, payable at the rate of $230 per month for twelve (12) months beginning January 1, 1970. Very truly yours, Barbara Hall Hodge." Was the letter a negotiable instrument? Give the reason for your answer. ● *Hall v. Westmoreland, Hall & Bryan*, 182 S.E.2d 539 (Ga. 1971)

7. Jon and Rita How gave the Fulkersons a postdated check for $2,000 as their acceptance of an offer to sell a trailer park. The Fulkersons claim that no contract came into existence because the postdated check created a qualified acceptance. Is the negotiability of an instrument affected by the fact that it is postdated? Explain. ● *How v. Fulkerson*, 528 P.2d 853 (Ariz. 1974)

8. Gray, the owner of a wholesale grocery company, delivered $4,800 worth of cigarettes to Ernie's Truck Stop. The manager of Ernie's gave the cigarettes to Joseph Faillance of New York. Faillance paid the manager with $4,800 worth of American Express traveler's checks. Gray saw Faillance sign and countersign the checks. They were not dated or made payable to anyone. The manager gave Gray the checks in payment for the cigarettes without indorsing them or filling in the name of a payee. Payment was refused on the checks as they turned out to be stolen. Must the payee's name be filled in for a check to be negotiable? Explain. ● *Gray v. American Exp. Co.*, 239 S.E.2d 621 (N.C. 1977)

9. Locke gave two promissory notes to Consumer Food, Inc., which stated, "Buyer agrees to pay to seller. . . ." Consumer Food, Inc., assigned the notes to Aetna Acceptance Corporation. Were the notes negotiable? Explain. ● *Locke v. Aetna Accept. Corp.*, 309 So.2d 43 (Fla. 1975)

Chapter 25

Issue, Transfer, and Negotiation

Commercial paper is passed freely from one person or business to another almost in the same way as money for the payment of debts and the purchase of goods and services. It begins its journey through life by being issued by the maker or drawer. An instrument is *issued* when it is first delivered to a holder (3-102). From then on it is often transferred by delivery to other people. *Delivery* is the voluntary transfer of possession from one person to another (1-201). *Transfer* is the act by which the owner of an instrument delivers it to another with the intention of passing rights in it to the other. The rights that a person holds in commercial paper may be transferred either by assignment or by negotiation.

25-1. Assignment Versus Negotiation

Commercial paper that does not meet all the requirements of negotiability cannot be negotiated. It can only be transferred by assignment, which is governed by the ordinary principles of contract law. People who receive instruments by assignment are not given the special protection given to those who receive instruments by negotiation.

A. Assignment

Commercial paper is *assigned* either when a person whose indorsement is required on an instrument transfers it without indorsing it or when it is transferred to another person and does not meet the requirements of negotiability. In all such transfers, the transferee has only the rights of an assignee and is subject to all defenses existing against the assignor. (See Chapter 14.)

● Arnette sold 100 cases of beans to Brodie for $12 a case. In exchange, Brodie gave Arnette a promissory note, promising to pay the $1,200 in six months at 14 percent per annum interest. The note was not negotiable, however, because it read "I promise to pay to Arnette" instead of "I promise to pay to the order of Arnette." To obtain needed cash, Arnette transferred the note to her bank. This transfer was an assignment rather than a negotiation because the note did not contain the proper words of negotiability. Brodie refused to pay the bank the amount due on maturity because the beans he had received from Arnette were defective. They were not merchantable. Since the transfer of the note was an assignment rather than a negotiation, the bank was subject to the same defense as Arnette and could not enforce payment of the note. Its only recourse is against Arnette. Had the note been negotiable, the bank could have received greater rights than its transferor had. It could have forced Brodie to pay the note even though Brodie received bad beans.

An assignment of commercial paper also occurs by operation of law when the holder of an instrument dies or becomes a bankrupt. In such cases, title to the instrument vests in the personal representative of the estate or the trustee in bankruptcy.

B. Negotiation

Negotiation is the transfer of an instrument in such form that the transferee becomes a holder. A holder, you will remember, is a person who is in possession of an instrument issued or indorsed to that person or to that person's order or to bearer or in blank.

● Mildred Liles sold Myers some restaurant equipment for $5,000. In payment for the equipment, Liles received $500 cash and a promissory note payable to her order for $4,500. Liles was a holder because she was in possession of an instrument issued to her.

If an instrument is payable to order, such as "pay to the order of," it is known as *order paper*. To be negotiated, order paper must be indorsed by the payee and delivered to the party to whom it is transferred. If an instrument is payable to bearer or cash, it is called *bearer paper* and may be negotiated by delivery alone, without an indorsement. When order paper is indorsed with a blank indorsement (defined below), it is turned into bearer paper and may be further negotiated by delivery alone.

25-2. Negotiation by Indorsement

An instrument is indorsed when the holder signs it, thereby indicating the intent to transfer ownership to another. Indorsements may be written in ink, typewritten, or stamped with a rubber stamp. They may be written on a separate paper (rider or *allonge*) so long as the separate paper is so firmly affixed to the instrument that it becomes part of it. Although the UCC does not require indorsements to be on any particular side of the paper, for convenience purposes they are usually placed on the back of the instrument. Anyone who gives value for an instrument has the right to have the unqualified indorsement of the person who transferred it unless it is payable to bearer.

Negotiation is effective to transfer an instrument even though it is: (*a*) transferred by an infant, a corporation exceeding its powers, or any other person without capacity; (*b*) obtained by fraud, duress, or mistake of any kind; (*c*) part of an illegal transaction; or (*d*) made in breach of duty. Any such negotiations, however, may be rescinded except as against a holder in due course (defined and explained in Chapter 26).

A. Types of Indorsements

There are four commonly used types of indorsements. They are blank indorsements, special indorsements, restrictive indorsements, and qualified indorsements.

1. Blank Indorsements. A *blank indorsement* consists of the signature alone written on the instrument. No particular *indorsee* (person to whom an instrument is indorsed) is specified. When a holder indorses an instrument in blank, it then becomes payable to bearer and may be transferred by delivery alone. Figure 25-1 shows a blank indorsement.

● Iris Honig received a check from a client which she delivered to her bank and indorsed in blank. Use of the blank indorsement would be proper, since there is no likelihood the check would become lost or stolen. In the event the check indorsed in blank is lost or stolen and gets into the hands of another holder, the new holder can recover its face value by delivery alone. The bank that cashes the check can require the new holder's indorsement, however.

When an instrument is made payable to a person under a misspelled name or a name other than that person's own, the payee may indorse in the incorrect name or in the correct name, or in both. Signatures in both names may be required by a person paying or giving value for the instrument (3-203).

2. Special Indorsements. A *special indorsement* (or *full indorsement*) is made by writing the words "pay to the order of" or "pay to" a specified person, followed by the signature of the indorser. When indorsed in this manner, the instrument remains an order instrument and must be indorsed by the specified person before it can be further negotiated.

The holder of an instrument may convert a blank indorsement into a special indorsement by writing the same words ("pay to the order of" or "pay to") over the indorser's signature.

● Suppose in the case of the special indorsement in Figure 25-2 Fern Lowry had borrowed $1,200 from her bank to repay a debt owed to Charles Rutz and the bank loaned Lowry the $1,200 by giving her a check in that amount payable to her. Fearful the check might get lost in the mail, Lowry indorsed it as shown. Since the check cannot be legally transferred or negotiated until Rutz indorses it, Fern Lowry is protected.

3. Restrictive Indorsements. A *restrictive indorsement* limits the rights of the indorsee in some manner in order to protect the rights of the indorser. An indorsement is restrictive if it (*a*) is conditional, (*b*) purports to prohibit further transfer of the instrument, (*c*) includes the words "for collection," "for deposit," "pay any bank," or like terms signifying a purpose of deposit or collection, or (*d*) otherwise states that it is for the benefit or use of the indorser or of another person (3-205).

Figure 25-1. Blank indorsement.

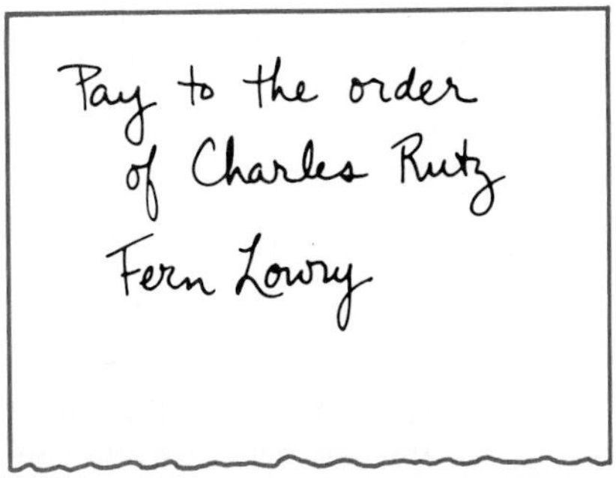

Figure 25-2. Special indorsement.

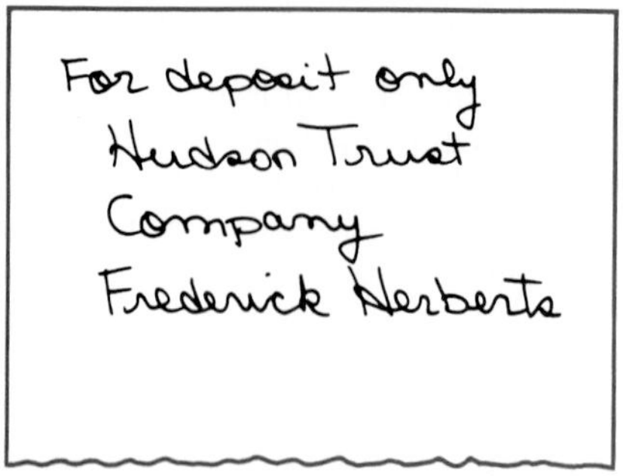

Figure 25-3. Restrictive indorsement.

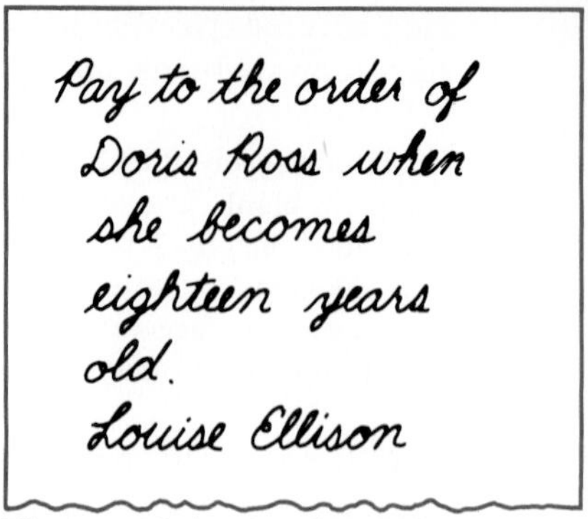

Figure 25-4. Conditional indorsement.

A *conditional indorsement* makes the rights of the indorsee subject to the happening of a certain event or condition.

● Ellison wished to transfer a check to her granddaughter, Doris Ross, as a birthday gift. Since Ellison did not want Ross to cash the check before her eighteenth birthday, a conditional indorsement such as the one illustrated in Figure 25-4 was used. Until the condition presented in the indorsement has been satisfied, Ross has possession of the check, but she does not have the right to cash it.

Indorsements for deposit or collection are designed to get an instrument into the banking system for deposit or collection. When a check is indorsed "for deposit only," as in Figure 25-3, the amount of the instrument will be credited to the indorser's account before it is negotiated further. Retail stores often stamp each check "for deposit only" as it is received. This provides protection in the event the check is stolen.

An indorsement that purports to prohibit further transfer, such as "pay Olga Peterson only" may be further negotiated after the directions in the indorsement are carried out. Thus, after Olga Peterson is paid, any holder of the instrument may continue to negotiate it. A restrictive indorsement does not prevent further transfer or negotiation of the instrument.

4. Qualified Indorsements. In a *qualified indorsement,* the indorser disclaims (refuses to accept) liability for payment of an instrument should the maker fail to pay it. The manner of disclaiming the indorser's liability is to add the words "without recourse" before or after the signature, as shown in Figure 25-5. Qualification of an indorsement limits the indorser's liability. It does not affect the transfer of title to the instrument or its negotiability.

● Chappell, a lawyer, receives a $10,000 check payable to his order in payment of a client's claim. Chappell indorses the check to the client "without recourse." In doing so Chappell disclaims liability as a guarantor of payment of the check.

B. Accommodation Party

An *accommodation party* is one who signs an instrument in any capacity for the purpose of lending his or her name to another party to the instrument (3-415). Thus, an accommodation party who signs on the front of a promissory note below the signature of the maker, assumes the same liability as the maker. On

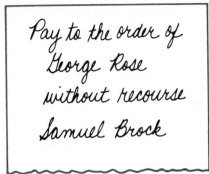

Figure 25-5. Qualified indorsement.

the other hand, an accommodation party who signs on the back of the instrument assumes the same liability as an indorser. An accommodation party is not liable to the party accommodated. The party accommodated is liable to the accommodation party if the latter pays the instrument.

● Callaghan applied for a loan at his local bank. The bank would agree to loan the money to him only if someone else would sign the promissory note along with Callaghan. Williamson agreed to do this and signed the instrument on the front. She was an accommodation party. Callaghan was the party accommodated. The bank could demand payment from either Callaghan or Williamson. Callaghan would be liable to Williamson for the amount of the note if she should pay the amount to the bank.

C. Significance of Indorsements

Indorsements have a threefold significance. In addition to being necessary to negotiate order paper, they create obligations on the part of the indorser. These obligations come in the form of implied warranties and a contractual promise to pay subsequent holders of the instrument.

1. Warranties of Indorsers. An indorser who receives consideration for an instrument makes five warranties to subsequent holders of the instrument (3-417). These warranties are as follows:

○ The indorser has good title to the instrument. This warranty gives assurances to subsequent holders that the person indorsing it did not steal it or come into possession of it in an unlawful manner.

● State National Bank accepted a check from Lawless for deposit to her account. The check contained a blank indorsement by Anthony Fiore. The bank later discovered that Lawless had found the check in a supermarket. A stop payment order had been issued by the real owner, Anthony Fiore. Lawless, by her indorsement, had warranted that she was the true owner of the check. She would be held liable on this warranty for any loss suffered by the bank.

○ All signatures are genuine or authorized.

● A check made payable to Jones was indorsed by his stepmother, who forged his signature and cashed the check at the Commonwealth Bank & Trust Co. The bank has a cause of action for the recovery of the money from Jones's stepmother on the ground of breach of warranty that all signatures are genuine or authorized.

○ The instrument has not been materially altered. The indorser warrants that there has been no alteration or other irregularity.

● Cushing wrote a check payable to the order of Daly for $5 and delivered it to Daly. Daly altered the check to read $500, indorsed it, and cashed it at a bank. Cushing will have to pay only the original amount of the check ($5) unless it can be shown that she was negligent in writing it so that it could be easily altered. The bank's recourse is against Daly for breach of this warranty.

○ No defense of any party is good against the indorser.

● Emerson, who was seventeen years old, bought a boat from Flynn for $300, paying for it by personal check. The transaction took place on Friday afternoon. Flynn kept the check over the weekend. On Monday morning she indorsed the instrument and cashed it at her local bank. Meanwhile, Emerson had used the boat over the weekend and had decided that he did not like it. He stopped payment on the check, and it was returned to the bank that had cashed it marked "payment stopped." The bank could not recover the $300 from Emerson because he was a minor when he entered into the contract. He may use the defense of minority against anyone who sues him on the contract. The bank, however, can recover the $300 from Flynn. By indorsing the check, she impliedly warranted that there were no defenses that she could use to defend herself, including Emerson's defense of minority.

A qualified indorser (one who uses the words "without recourse" as shown in Figure 25-5) does not make this warranty. Such an indorsement warrants only that the indorser has no knowledge of a defense that may be used, such as Emerson's defense of minority in the above case.

○ The indorser has no knowledge of any insolvency proceeding instituted with respect to the maker, acceptor, or drawer of an unaccepted instrument.

2. Contract of Indorsers. Unless an indorsement states otherwise (as by such words as "without recourse"), every indorser agrees to pay any subsequent holder the face amount of the instrument if it is *dishonored* [not paid by the maker or drawee (3-414)]. To enforce this obligation, it is necessary for the holder to do two things. The holder of an instrument must first present it for payment to the maker or drawee when it is due. If that person refuses to pay the instrument, it is said to be dishonored. The holder must then notify the indorser or indorsers of the dishonor. The notice must be given before midnight of the third full business day after the date of the dishonor. Failure by the holder to make presentment and to give timely notice of dishonor to an indorser has the effect of discharging that indorser from liability on the contract to pay subsequent holders of the instrument.

Unless they otherwise agree, indorsers are liable to one another in the order in which they indorse. This is presumed to be the order in which their signatures appear on the instrument.

● The Security Loan Company received a check indorsed and delivered to it by Diana Sklar in payment of a loan. When presented for payment at the drawer's bank, the check was returned for want of sufficient funds. Security Loan would have the right to demand payment from any or all of the indorsers shown on the back of the check (see Figure 25-6), if it gave them proper notice, starting with Diana Sklar. To be assured of maximum safety, the holder should demand payment from the indorsers in reverse of the order in which their names appear—Sklar, Allen, Jones, and Brownlee—until payment is received from one of them.

Figure 25-6. Indorsers are liable to subsequent holders of the instrument.

D. Banks Supplying Missing Indorsement

A depositary bank which has taken an item for collection may supply any indorsement of the customer which is necessary to title (4-205). This rule is designed to speed up bank collections by eliminating the necessity to return to a depositor any items that were not indorsed. Such an indorsement may not be supplied by a bank, however, if the instrument contains the words "payee's indorsement required."

E. Multiple Payees

If an instrument is payable to two or more payees in the alternative, as in "pay to the order of Eric Foss *or* Betty Foss," the indorsement of only one of the payees is necessary to negotiate it (3-116). On the other hand, if an instrument is payable to two or more payees and is not payable in the alternative, as in "pay to the order of Eric Foss *and* Betty Foss," the indorsement of all payees is necessary for a proper negotiation.

● Middle States Leasing Corporation drew a check payable to the order of two payees, Interpace Corporation and United Leasing Services, Inc., in the sum of $150,000. United Leasing Services, Inc., indorsed the check and received the entire proceeds from the drawee bank without the indorsement of Interpace Corporation on the instrument. Because the instrument was not indorsed by both payees, the bank was held responsible to Middle States Leasing Corporation for the entire amount of the check.

25-3. Forged or Unauthorized Indorsements

An unauthorized signature or indorsement is one made without actual, implied, or apparent authority (1-201). With three exceptions and unless ratified (approved afterward), an unauthorized or forged signature does not serve as the signature of the person whose name is signed (3-404). It has no effect. In addition, when an instrument is paid on a forged indorsement, the tort of conversion takes place (2-419). To illustrate, when a bank pays proceeds to a forger and the payee's wishes are not carried out, the bank is held liable for converting the payee's funds.

Chapter 25:
Issue,
Transfer,
and
Negotia-
tion

327

● Seventeen checks payable to the Mott Grain Company, totaling $40,520.93, were deposited to the personal bank account of Baszler, the company's manager. Baszler disappeared with the money but was later found and convicted of embezzlement. Nine of the checks contained restrictive indorsements, requiring them to be deposited in the company's bank account. The remainder of the checks bore blank indorsements, such as "Mott Grain Co./Verson Baszler." Baszler's only authority was to deposit the checks in the Mott Grain Co.'s account. The bank was held liable to the grain company, in conversion, for the amount of the checks.

There are three exceptions to the general rule that an unauthorized indorsement has no effect (3-405). The exceptions are designed primarily to promote negotiability of commercial paper. They are as follows.

A. Imposters

An imposter is someone who impersonates another. When an instrument is issued to an imposter on the false belief that the imposter is the payee, the indorsement by any person in the name of the payee is treated as an effective indorsement. This rule places the loss, in such a case, on the one who is in the best position to prevent it—the maker or drawer of the instrument.

● Covington was induced in a fraudulent oil-land scheme to issue a cashier's check to an imposter under the false belief that the imposter was a person named Baird. The imposter's indorsement of the name "Baird" on the check was held by the court to be effective to negotiate the instrument. The bank that paid the check was not held liable in conversion, and the check was considered to be properly negotiated. The indorsement by the imposter was treated as an effective indorsement.

B. No Interest Intended

When the maker or drawer of an instrument intends the payee to have no interest in the instrument, an indorsement by any person in the name of the payee is effective.

● Gordon loaned $5,000 to Wolf, intending Wolf to have the entire interest in the money. He made the check payable jointly, however, to Wolf and Wolf's wife Norma. When the check was cashed, Norma's indorsement was forged. The court held that the forged indorsement was valid because Gordon did not intend Norma to have any interest in the instrument.

C. Padded Payrolls

When an agent or employee of the maker or drawer pads the payroll by supplying the employer with fictitious names, an indorsement by any person in the name of each fictitious payee is effective. This rule places the burden of preventing this type of fraud on the drawer or maker, the party in the best position to prevent it.

● Harrison, the payroll clerk for Industries, Inc., made out payroll checks for ten employees who did not exist and had her employer sign them. She negotiated the ten checks by indorsing them in the names of the fictitious payees. The indorsements by Harrison were effective. Industries, Inc., not Harrison, had the burden of preventing this type of fraud, which it was in a position to avoid. Industries, Inc., would be liable for any losses suffered as a result of the padding of the payroll.

Understanding Legal Terms

Define, identify, or explain the following terms:

accommodation
  party
allonge
assigned
bearer paper

blank indorsement
conditional
  indorsement
delivery
issued

negotiation
order paper
qualified
  indorsement

restrictive
  indorsement
special indorsement
transfer

Questions for Review and Discussion

1. Differentiate between an assignment and a negotiation of commercial paper.

2. What indorsement is used by a holder who wishes to be relieved of responsibility on a negotiable instrument in the event it is not paid when due because of insufficient funds? Explain.

3. Identify two ways an instrument may be negotiated so that the transferee becomes a holder.

4. What must a holder of a dishonored negotiable instrument do to hold prior indorsers liable on the instrument?

5. Is a blank indorsement unsafe when the instrument is being carried in the holder's pocket or sent by mail? Explain.

6. What does the indorser of a negotiable instrument warrant to an indorsee?

7. What agreement does an indorser (other than a qualified indorser) of a negotiable instrument make with subsequent holders of the instrument?

8. What indorsements are necessary to negotiate an instrument that is payable (a) to two or more persons in the alternative? (b) to two or more persons not in the alternative?

9. Explain the legal consequences that arise when a check is paid on a forged indorsement. What are the three exceptions to the general rule that any unauthorized indorsement is not effective?

10. Who may indorse an instrument that is issued to an imposter on the false belief that the imposter is the payee?

Analyzing Cases

1. Powell, intending to write a check to Thompson Electric, Inc., instead made it payable to the order of "Thompon Electric." Thompson Electric, Inc., indorsed the check with its name correctly spelled. Was the indorsement valid? Why or why not? ● *State v. Powell*, 551 P.2d 902 (Kan. 1976)

2. When checks were received by Palmer & Ray Dental Supply, Mrs. Wilson, a company employee, indorsed them with a rubber stamp reading: "Palmer & Ray Dental Supply" (followed by the company's address). Mrs. Wilson deposited some of the checks in the company's account but cashed the rest, keeping the money for herself. The company contends that the indorsements were restrictive and, therefore, that the bank should not have cashed them. Were the indorsements restrictive? Explain. ● *Palmer & Ray Dental Supply, Inc. v. First Nat'l Bank*, 477 S.W.2d 954 (Kan. 1972)

3. Higgins delivered a promissory note payable to the Westerly Hospital for $527.58 in payment for services rendered by the hospital during the birth of Higgin's child. The hospital indorsed the note in blank and delivered it to the Industrial National Bank at a discount. When Higgins did not pay the note at maturity, the hospital paid the bank and amount due and took the note back. Higgins

claims that the hospital was not a holder when it took the note back because the bank did not indorse it. Do you agree with Higgins? Why or why not? ● *Westerly Hosp. v. Higgins,* 256 A.2d 506 (R.I. 1969)

4. Tufi forged the payee's name on the front of a U.S. Treasurer's check. When convicted of forgery he appealed, contending that a signature on the front of a check cannot be an indorsement. May an indorsement be written on the front of an instrument? Explain. ● *United States v. Tufi,* 536 F.2d 855 (Hawaii 1976)

5. Halloway executed and delivered a note for $2,551 payable to Madison Bank and Trust Company. He signed the note on the lower right-hand corner. On the lower left-hand corner were the words "Indorsed without recourse," followed by the signature of a person named Wolfram. When Halloway defaulted on the note, Wolfram claimed that he made no warranties when he signed the note. Do you agree with Wolfram? Why or why not? ● *Wolfram v. Halloway,* 361 N.E.2d 587 (Ill. 1977)

6. Alan D. Smathers and his wife, Josephine, signed two promissory notes payable to the order of Alan's father, John H. Smathers. After the death of John, the unindorsed notes were in the possession of another daughter-in-law, Joy I. Smathers, who claimed that John had given them to her husband, who had subsequently died. Joy contends that she is a holder of the notes. Do you agree with her contention? Why or why not? ● *Smathers v. Smathers,* 239 S.E.2d 637 (N.C. 1977)

7. Commercial Credit Corporation issued a check payable to Rauch Motor Company. Rauch indorsed the check in blank and delivered it to a bank. The bank typed a very long special indorsement payable to Lamson on two legal-size sheets of paper and stapled them to the checks. May an indorsement be written on a separate paper and stapled to the checks? Explain. ● *Lamson v. Commercial Credit Corp.,* 531 P.2d 966 (Colo. 1975)

8. The indorsement of the payee of a check drawn by Funding Systems Leasing Corporation was forged. Below the forged indorsement was added the signature of another person which was not forged. The check was deposited with the Sumiton Bank, which claims to be a holder. Was the bank a holder? Why or why not? ● *Sumiton Bank v. Funding Sys. Leasing Corp.,* 512 F.2d 774 (1975)

9. The United States of America issued a check of the U.S. Treasury in the amount of $49,314.47 payable to two companies, Floors, Inc., and American Fidelity Fire Insurance Company. Floors, Inc., indorsed the check with a rubber stamp indorsement, "For Deposit Only, Floors, Inc.," deposited it in its account in the Peoples National Bank, and later withdrew the money. Was the check properly negotiated? Why or why not? What tort, if any, did the Peoples National Bank commit? Explain. ● *Peoples Nat'l. Bank v. American Fidelity Fire Ins.,* 386 A.2d 1254 (Md. 1978)

10. As part of a business transaction, Tubin purchased a $14,250 cashier's check from a bank and had it made payable to Rueckhaus. Rueckhaus indorsed the check: "Pay to the order—Consumers Investment Co. and Charles D. Wyche, Sr. . . ." Wyche's signature was forged on the back of the check, and it was deposited in Consumers Investment Co.'s account in the Fair Park National Bank. Consumers Investment Co. withdrew the money for its own use. Does the owner of the cashier's check have recourse against anyone for the payment that was made on the forged indorsement? If so, against whom? Explain. ● *Tubin v. Rabin,* 533 F.2d 255 (Tex. 1976)

Chapter 26

Holders in Due Course, Defenses, and Discharge

In Chapter 24, the concept of negotiability was discussed. It was stated there that when an instrument is transferred by negotiation, the transferee may, in many instances, receive more protection than the transferor had under the instrument. This special protection occurs when the transferee is a holder in due course. Certain defenses, discussed below, cannot be used against such a holder.

26-1. Holder in Due Course

The UCC defines a *holder in due course* as a holder who takes the instrument for value, in good faith, and without notice that it is overdue or has been dishonored or of any defenses against or claim to it on the part of any person (3-302). A payee may be a holder in due course.

A. Holder

To be a holder in due course, the person in possession of the instrument must first be a holder. This means that the instrument must have been issued or indorsed to that person or to that person's order, to bearer, or in blank.

● John and Nancy Augustine contracted with Hanover Homes Corporation for the construction of a house. They obtained a commitment for a mortgage loan from a bank, which issued checks periodically as the construction progressed. The checks were made payable to John, Nancy, and Hanover Homes Corporation. The last check that was issued was deposited in Hanover's bank account without Nancy's indorsement on it. The bank that received the check for deposit was not a holder because, without Nancy's indorsement, the check was not issued or indorsed to it or to bearer or in blank.

B. Value

A person must give value for an instrument in order to qualify as a holder in due course. Thus, if an instrument is transferred to a person as a gift, that person would not qualify as a holder in due course.

A holder who purchases an instrument for less than its *face value* can be a holder in due course only to the extent of the interest purchased.

● Cruz makes a $1,500 note payable to the order of Jessup. Jessup borrows $1,000 from Teal, who requests Cruz's note to secure repayment of the loan. Since Teal has advanced $1,000, she has given value to this extent and qualifies as a holder in due course to this extent. If Jessup cannot repay the loan, Teal can foreclose on the note by collecting it from Cruz. Should Cruz have a personal defense against Jessup, Teal is free and clear of the defense to the extent of $1,000. The defense may be asserted with respect to the $500 balance.

C. Good Faith

To be a holder in due course, the holder must take the instrument in good faith. *Good faith* is defined as "honesty in fact" [1-201(19)]. It requires that the taker of a commercial instrument act honestly in its acquisition. If the taker is negligent in not discovering that something was wrong with the paper, this does not establish lack of good faith.

● Leo's Used Car Exchange purchased three cars at a car auction from Villa, paying for them with two checks totaling $15,150. Villa presented the checks to a bank and asked the teller to give him cash, since he was going to another auction and needed it. The teller did so without obtaining the bank manager's approval, which was against the bank's policy. Shortly thereafter, Leo's Used Car Exchange stopped payment on the checks because title to the three cars was not clear. The lower court held that the bank that cashed them was not a holder in due course because of the teller's negligence in not obtaining the manager's approval before cashing the checks. The appellate court reversed the lower court's decision, holding that good faith means honesty in fact. The court said, "Nothing in the definition suggests that in addition to being honest, the holder must exercise due care to be in good faith." Since the bank was a holder in due course, it was able to recover the $15,150 from the drawer of the checks, Leo's Used Car Exchange.

D. Without Notice

To be a holder in due course, a holder must not have notice of any claim or defense to an instrument or notice that an instrument is overdue or has been dishonored. A holder has notice of a claim or defense if the instrument bears visible evidence of forgery or alteration. The same is true if the instrument is so incomplete or irregular as to make its legal acceptance doubtful. Notice of a claim or defense is also considered given if the holder notices that the obligation of any party is voidable. Thus, the maker of a note has the right to avoid an obligation on the instrument in the event of a fraud carried out by the payee.

● Hinkson gave Carlo $175 for a note signed by Lambert. A casual inspection of the note showed that the amount had been erased and altered. Hinkson would not be a holder in due course. It would be useless for her to argue that she did not see the obvious erasure and alteration.

The holder has notice that an instrument is overdue when there is reason to know that (1) any part of the principal amount is overdue, (2) an acceleration of the instrument has been made, or (3) an unreasonable length of time elapsed after demand for the payment had been made or after the instrument was issued. What is an "unreasonable time" is determined by a consideration of the nature of the instrument, the usage of the trade or business, and the circumstances and facts involved in each case. A reasonable time to negotiate a check drawn and payable within the states and territories of the United States is presumed to be thirty days.

● Travers received a check from Thawley, placed it in a desk drawer, and rediscovered it three months later. Collins, a local merchant, offered to cash the check for Travers for value. Collins is on notice that the check is overdue for an unreasonable time, and so he is not a holder in due course.

The holder with knowledge of an overdue installment on principal has notice that the instrument is overdue and therefore cannot be a holder in due course. Past-due interest, however, does not give notice of any defect in the instrument.

Knowledge of some facts does not of itself give the holder notice of a defense or claim. For example, the fact that an instrument is postdated or antedated does not prevent someone from being a holder in due course; neither does completing an incomplete instrument constitute having such notice, unless the holder has notice of any improper completion.

E. Holder Through a Holder in Due Course

A holder who receives title to an instrument from one who is a holder in due course receives all the rights of the former party. This is called a *shelter provision*. It is designed to permit the holder in due course, who is free from personal defenses, to transfer all rights in the paper. However, should the transferee be party to a fraud or other illegal act which affects the instrument, that person would not have the rights of a holder in due course.

● Riverbank Motors defrauded Ashwell in the sale of a used Toyota for which Ashwell gave a note for $1,400. The note was transferred to Cerreta for value. Cerreta had no knowledge of the fraudulent sale to Ashwell and became a holder in due course. The note was later purchased by Sayer, a Riverbank Motors salesperson who was involved in the fraudulent sale to Ashwell. Sayer would not have the rights of a holder in due course, since he was party to fraud and thus not allowed to improve his status by purchasing the note from a later holder in due course.

26-2. Rights of a Holder in Due Course

A holder in due course takes an instrument free from all claims to it on the part of any person and free from all personal defenses of any party with whom the holder has not dealt. *Personal defenses* (sometimes called *limited defenses*), discussed below, are defenses that can be used against a holder but not a holder in due course of a negotiable instrument. When a negotiable instrument is negotiated to a holder in due course, all personal defenses are cut off; that is, no one can use personal defenses against a holder in due course (3-305).

A. Personal Defenses

Personal defenses include (1) all valid claims to an instrument; (2) all defenses which would be available in any action on a simple contract; (3) defenses that the holder (or the person through whom the holder holds the instrument) acquire it by theft; and (4) defenses of want or failure of consideration, nonperformance, or nondelivery. The most common personal defenses are illustrated in the following paragraphs.

1. Breach of Contract. Negotiable instruments are often issued in exchange for property, services, or some other obligation as part of an underlying contract. Sometimes, when this occurs, the party to whom the instrument was issued breaches the contract by failing to perform or by doing so in an unsatisfactory manner. If suit is brought on the instrument by a holder against the maker or drawer, the latter may use breach of contract as a defense. Since this is a personal defense, however, it may not be used if the holder of the instrument is a holder in due course.

2. Lack or Failure of Consideration. *Lack of consideration* is a defense that may be used by a maker or drawer of an instrument when no consideration existed in the underlying contract for which the instrument was issued. The ordinary rules of contract law, discussed in Chapter 11, are followed to determine the presence or absence of consideration in such a case.

● Gruel executes a note in favor of Searle as a birthday gift. Searle indorses the note to Chard in payment of an obligation. As against Searle, Gruel has a defense of lack of consideration. Chard has furnished value and can enforce the note against Gruel in spite of his defense.

Failure (want) of consideration is different. This is a defense that the maker or drawer has available when the party dealt with breaches the contract by not furnishing the agreed consideration.

● National Radio Company, Inc., sold to Frequency Electronics, Inc., its product line known as Atomichron, an atomic clock said to be the most accurate commercially available means for keeping time. The sale included certain patent rights valued at $325,000. As part of the purchase price, Frequency Electronics gave National Radio a $325,000 promissory note. The note was subsequently acquired by Lerner, who was chairperson of the board, treasurer, and principal stockholder of National Radio Company. When one of the patents turned out to be void, Frequency Electronics refused to pay the note. The court held that a note given in payment for an invalid patent is void for failure of consideration. In addition, the court said that Lerner was not a holder in due course because he had knowledge of the invalid patent. He was subject to the defense of failure of consideration. Had Lerner been a holder in due course, the defense would have been cut off.

Both lack of consideration and failure of consideration are limited defenses. They may not be used against a holder in due course.

3. Fraud in the Inducement. There are two kinds of fraud: fraud in the inducement and fraud as to the essential nature of the transaction, sometimes called fraud in the factum. The first is a personal defense, discussed here; the second is a real defense, discussed below. The five elements of fraud are explained in depth in Chapter 9. When someone is induced by a fraudulent statement or act to enter into a contract, that person may have the contract rescinded. Likewise, the defense of fraud in the inducement may be used against a holder of a negotiable instrument issued as part of the transaction. Since the defense is limited, it may not be used against a holder in due course.

4. Lack of Delivery. Every commercial instrument may be revoked by its maker or drawer until it has been delivered to the payee. Delivery is the transfer of possession from one person to another. If the transfer of possession is not intended to give the transferee rights, delivery is made in a physical sense, but the instrument has not been "issued." Thus, in the event a payee forcibly, unlawfully, or conditionally takes an instrument from a drawer, the drawer has the defense of conditional delivery. The payee therefore may be denied the right to collect on the instrument. If the payee negotiates the instrument to a holder in due course, however, this defense is cut off.

● Castro drew a check in favor of Rush and delivered it with the express understanding that it was to be negotiated only on condition that Rush first paint her car. Rush negotiated the check to Bee-Line Auto Center in violation of this understanding. Only in the event that Bee-Line is not a holder in due course can Castro assert against Bee-Line a defense of conditional delivery and Rush's failure to perform.

5. Payment. When a commercial instrument is paid, its indebtedness is discharged. Payment of an instrument before maturity discharges the maker from further liability to immediate parties. The maker is not relieved, however, should the instrument come into the possession of a holder in due course. The maker or acceptor of an instrument should demand the return of the instrument when it has been paid. If the instrument is payable on demand, it should be marked "paid." Partial payments should be recorded on a note. Unless such precautions are taken, a defense of payment would not prevail against any subsequent holder in due course.

● Tropsa executed a promissory note on February 1 for $2,500 due October 1, with interest at 9 percent from date, payable to Ingersoll. On May 1, Tropsa paid $500 and obtained a receipt. On August 5, Ingersoll indorsed the note to Byram and received $2,300 in value. Byram, in taking the note in good faith, became a holder in due course and could recover $2,500 from Tropsa.

B. Real Defenses

Some defenses are available against everyone, including holders in due course. These are known as *universal* or *real defenses* [3-305(2)]. They are as follows:

1. Infancy and Mental Incompetence. A minor need not honor a negotiable instrument if it was given in payment for a contract which the minor may disaffirm on the grounds of minority. This is true even if the instrument comes into the hands of a holder in due course. Similarly, persons who have been found insane by a court are not liable on a negotiable instrument since their contracts are void.

2. Illegality, Duress, or Other Incapacity. An instrument which is associated with an illegal act—such as gambling or smuggling—would be void from its beginning and would not be valid or collectible by anyone. This would be true even though the holder was unaware of the illegal acts or conditions.

● The Condado Aruba Caribbean Hotel loaned Tickel, who resided in Colorado, $20,000. The money was loaned for the purpose of gambling at the hotel's casino in Aruba, Netherlands Antilles, where gambling is legal. Tickel wrote two checks to repay the debt, each of which was returned for insufficient funds. When suit was brought on the checks, the Colorado court held that gambling debts are unenforceable in that state even against a holder in due course. Tickel was not liable on the checks that he had written to the hotel.

3. Fraud as to the Essential Nature of the Transaction. A party who is defrauded as to the essential nature of the transaction may use that as a defense against all persons, even a holder in due course.

● Hartsook was asked to sign what his brother explained was a letter being sent to a close friend. Hartsook, who was extremely ill and had poor eyesight, signed the paper as instructed without reading it. The paper was actually a promissory note payable to the order of Hartsook's brother. Such fraud is a real defense.

4. Discharge in Insolvency Proceedings. Anyone ruled a bankrupt is relieved of all obligations on a commercial instrument. The holder will receive equal treatment with other creditors when the assets of the bankrupt are collected and divided according to the bankruptcy law. An exception would be in those cases where the note is secured by a recorded mortgage on personal property (i.e., chattel mortgage).

5. Unauthorized Signatures. Any unauthorized signature of another's name on a commercial instrument is totally inoperative unless approved by the person whose name is signed. An unauthorized signature, however, would operate as the signature of the unauthorized signer in favor of any person who in good faith pays the instrument or takes value for it.

● Ochoe paid value for a promissory note held by Baum, who was a holder in due course. Originally the instrument was drawn by Becwar, who forged the name of Fulmer to the note. When the note is presented for payment, Fulmer may refuse to honor it, inasmuch as the forgery is an unauthorized signature and a real defense against all holders. Becwar would be liable in favor of any person who paid for the note or took value for it.

6. Material Alteration. Any alteration of an instrument is material if it changes the contract of any party thereto in any respect. Included are changes in the number or relations of the concerned parties, completion of an incomplete instrument, and the adding to or removal of any part of the writing as signed. Fraudulent and material alteration by the holder discharges any party whose contract is changed thereby, except that a subsequent holder in due course may enforce the instrument according to its original terms (3-407).

● McWalters wrote out a check for $175 and presented it to Eastman in payment for a used Canon AE-1 camera. Eastman altered the check to read $375, then presented it for payment at McWalters's bank. The bank honored the altered check. McWalters may demand that the bank reimburse his account for $200, the difference between the original and the altered amount.

Any person who negligently contributes to a material alteration of an instrument or an unauthorized signature may not exercise the defense of alteration or lack of authority against a holder in due course, a drawee, or other payor who pays the instrument in good faith. For example, using a pencil to write a check or not being careful to keep the figures compact and clear gives a dishonest holder an opportunity to alter the amount. The careless writer would be without defense (3-406).

C. Consumer Credit Protection

Federal Trade Commission rules substantially limit the effects of the so-called holder-in-due-course doctrine. This doctrine placed the person to whom an installment contract was assigned in a better position than the original seller. Under the doctrine, third parties (such as banks and finance companies) who purchased installment notes were formerly not obligated in any way to customers who had been sold shoddy merchandise. Thus, the holder-in-due-course doctrine allowed sellers a simple means to avoid accountability to consumers by separating a buyer's duty to pay for goods and services from the seller's comparable duty to perform as promised.

In 1976 the Federal Trade Commission ruled that holders of consumer credit contracts are subject to all claims and defenses that the buyer could use against the seller. Thus, credit contracts used by sellers and transferred to holders in due course will retain their character as sales agreements. In addition, the rule expressly preserves the buyer's option of asserting legitimate claims against the seller by making it unlawful to include a waiver-of-defense clause. Finally, sellers may not accept the proceeds from a buyer's loan directly from a lender unless the contract authorizes the consumer to assert claims and defenses against the lender too.

● Gruner bought a washing machine under an installment sales contract and found that it broke down repeatedly during the first two months. When the store that sold it refused to exchange it, Gruner refused to continue paying for it. Then the real troubles began. The store had already sold the sales contract to a financial institution which disclaimed any responsibility for the operation of the washing machine. It threatened to sue Gruner for nonpayment, with further threats of repossession and garnishment of salary. Previously, under the holder-in-due-course doctrine, Gruner had little practical alternative but to pay. Under the FTC rule, however, such actions by sellers involving breach of contract and fraud are prohibited. Gruner may therefore successfully avoid payment to the financial institution in question.

26-3. Liability of the Parties

No person is liable on an instrument unless that person's signature or the signature of an authorized agent appears on the instrument. Parties to negotiable instruments are either primarily or secondarily liable.

A. Primary Liability

Primary liability is an absolute liability to pay. A party with primary liability promises to pay the instrument without any reservations of any kind. Two parties have primary liability: the maker of a promissory note and the acceptor, if any, of a draft [3-413(1)].

B. Secondary Liability

Secondary liability is a liability to pay only after certain conditions have been met. Two types of parties are secondarily liable on negotiable instruments: the drawer of a draft (a check, you will remember, is the most common kind of draft) and the indorser or indorsers of either a note or a draft. The conditions that must be met before either the drawer or the indorser has a liability to pay are as follows:

○ The instrument must be properly presented to the primary party or drawee and payment must be demanded.
○ Payment must be refused (dishonored) by the primary party or drawee or be impossible.
○ Notice of the dishonor must be given to the secondary party within the time and in the manner prescribed by the UCC.

1. Presentment for Payment. In order to be sure that a secondary party (drawer or indorser) will be liable on an instrument, the holder must make proper presentment for payment unless excused. This means that the holder must present the instrument to the maker or drawee and ask for payment. If such presentment is not made at the proper time, all indorsers are discharged from their obligations. They will not have to pay the holder of the instrument. In addition, if such presentment is not properly made and the drawee cannot pay because of insolvency (inability to pay debts), the drawer is discharged from all obligation. Presentment must be made on the date that the instrument is due.

● Novak indorsed a note as an accommodation to a friend. When the note became due, the holder did not present it to the maker for payment. Two weeks after the date of maturity, when the note was dishonored, the holder attempted to hold Novak liable. Because the holder delayed presentment beyond the time when the note was due without excuse, Novak's liability as an indorser would be discharged.

If no due date is stated on the instrument, presentment must be made within a reasonable time after the maker or drawee became liable on it. The definition of a reasonable time for instruments other than checks will vary, depending on the circumstances and banking and trade practices. A reasonable time for a check is thirty days with respect to the liability of the drawer and seven days with respect to the liability of an indorser.

● A check was drawn by Sarr on June 15. It was indorsed and delivered to Stabler on June 22 by the payee. Stabler then indorsed it to Roche on June 28. When Roche presented the check to Sarr's bank for payment on July 18, he learned that the bank had been ordered closed by bank examiners. Should the bank be unable to pay off its depositors and other liabilities, Roche would have no recourse against either Sarr, the drawer, or Stabler, an indorser. A reasonable period of time within which to initiate bank collection had been exceeded.

When the date that an instrument is payable is not a full business day for either the person making the presentment or the party paying, presentment is due on the next following full business day for both parties. To be sufficient, presentment must be made at a reasonable hour. If presentment is made at a bank, it must take place during the banking day.

The party from whom payment is demanded can request to see the instrument. If payment is made, the instrument must be handed over then and there. This is important because if the party paying does not get the instrument back, it might show up later in the hands of a holder in due course, and the holder would have to pay it again.

2. Presentment for Acceptance. A draft may be presented to the drawee for acceptance as well as for payment. This is particularly important when a draft is not yet due. The holder is given the opportunity to test the drawee's willingness to honor the instrument. When a draft is presented for acceptance, the drawee is asked to become primarily liable on the instrument. The drawee is asked to agree now to pay the amount of the draft when it is presented for payment at a later date. To accept a draft, the drawee signs the instrument (usually perpendicularly) across its face. It is customary, also, to write the word "accepted" and the date along with the drawee's signature. When a drawee bank accepts a check, it stamps the word "certified" across the face of the instrument and signs it. This is known as a certified check (see Chapter 27).

Although in most cases a draft may be presented for either payment or acceptance, there are three situations in which a draft must be presented for acceptance. They are where the draft states that it must be presented for acceptance, where the draft is payable elsewhere than at the residence or place of business of the drawee, and where the date of payment depends upon presentment, for example, when the draft contains a statement like: "Thirty days after sight pay to the order of. . . ."

3. Dishonor. An instrument is dishonored when presentment is duly made and acceptance or payment is refused or cannot be obtained within the prescribed time. Dishonor also occurs when presentment is excused and the instrument is past due and unpaid. The presenting party has recourse against indorsers or other secondary parties after notice of dishonor has been given.

A note was presented to Czarnecki for payment on the date specified. Czarnecki refused to honor it, claiming the note was a forgery. The holder would have to proceed against the indorsers in order to obtain payment. The note was dishonored when Czarnecki refused to pay it.

4. Notice of Dishonor. If an instrument has been dishonored, the holder must give notice of the dishonor to the drawer and to the indorsers before midnight of the third full business day after the date of dishonor. Unless notice is excused, any indorser who is not given notice within the specified time is discharged. A drawer who is not given notice within the specified time is discharged if the drawee cannot pay because of insolvency. Notice of dishonor may be given, by or on behalf of the holder, to any person who may be liable. It may also be given by any party who has received notice or by any other party who can be compelled to pay the instrument. Also, an agent or bank in whose hands the instrument is dishonored may give notice to the principal or customer or to another agent or bank from which the instrument was received. Necessary notice must be given by a bank before its midnight deadline and by any other person before midnight of the third business day after dishonor or receipt of notice of dishonor. These time provisions are viewed as adequate for making decisions and for sending notice.

Notice may be given in any reasonable manner that conveys the information to the liable parties. It may be given orally or in writing. Written notice is effective when properly sent, even though it is not received. In the event the party to be given notice is involved in insolvency proceedings, notice may be given either to the party or to the court-appointed representative of the estate. The banking practice of returning an instrument bearing a stamp to the effect that acceptance or payment has been refused is sufficient notice of dishonor.

Proper notice operates for the benefit of all parties who have rights on an instrument against the party notified.

● Karl, Kalish, Janik, and Kunes are indorsers of a dishonored note in that order. The holder gave notice only to Karl and Janik. Janik is not required to give additional notice to Karl. Should Janik be compelled to pay, he would have recourse against Karl. Both Kalish and Kunes are discharged if they are not notified by the holder or by one of the indorsers.

Delay in giving notice of dishonor or in making presentment is excused when the holder has acted carefully and the delay is due to circumstances beyond the holder's control. The conditions of giving notice or making presentment must be complied with as soon as the cause of the delay ceases.

Unless excused, protest of any dishonor is necessary to charge the drawer and indorsers of any draft which on its face appears to be drawn or payable outside the states and territories of the United States and the District of Columbia (3-501). A *protest* is a certificate of dishonor which states that a draft was presented for acceptance or payment and was dishonored. It also states the reasons given for refusal to accept or pay. It is required for drafts drawn or payable outside the United States and optional in all other cases with the holder. A protest is made under the hand and seal of a United States consul or vice consul, or of a notary public or other person authorized to certify dishonor by the law where dishonor occurs.

An indorser who has written "demand and notice waived" or "protest waived" above his or her indorsement or across the face of the instrument is liable for payment without subsequent presentment or notice of dishonor. Prior indorsers are excused from their liability to such an indorser.

If a waiver of notice or protest is stated on the face of the instrument, it is binding upon all parties; when written above the signature of an indorser, it binds only the indorser.

26-4. Discharge of Parties

Any party may be discharged from liability on an instrument by any one of the following methods (3-601).

A. Payment or Satisfaction

The most frequent method of obtaining a discharge from liability is for the primary party to pay the amount of the instrument. This can be accomplished even though the payor knows that some third party has a claim on the instrument.

B. Tender of Payment

If the maker or acceptor is ready and able to pay at the place(s) specified in the instrument when it is due, an offer to pay has been made. This rule of tender gives a limited discharge to the obligor (person liable) on an instrument. The obligor is discharged to the extent of subsequent liability for interest, costs, and legal fees. In this manner, makers and acceptors of notes and drafts payable at a bank have made a tender of payment if they maintain an adequate balance in the bank as of the due date of the instrument.

C. Cancellation and Renunciation

The holder of an instrument may discharge any party on the face of the instrument or an indorser even without consideration. This can be accomplished intentionally by striking out the party's signature. Renunciation of the holder's rights can also be achieved by a writing signed and delivered or by surrender of the instrument to the party being discharged.

D. Impairment of Recourse or Collateral

A party to an instrument is discharged to the extent the holder releases or agrees not to sue any person against whom the holder has recourse. A similar discharge takes place when the holder agrees to suspend his or her rights in any collateral or impairs any collateral. *Impairment of recourse* takes place when the holder strikes out the name of one of the indorsers on an instrument. Such an act discharges not only that indorser, but also all parties who have a right to recourse against the discharged indorser.

E. Reacquisition of the Instrument

Where an instrument is returned to or reacquired by a prior party, any indorsement which is not necessary to the holder's title may be canceled. In any subsequent reissue or further negotiation of the instrument, any intervening party is discharged as against the reacquiring party.

F. Fraudulent and Material Alteration

Except for a subsequent holder in due course, any fraudulent and material alteration by the holder discharges any person whose contract is thereby changed.

G. Certification of a Check

Certification of a check is acceptance. Where a holder procures certification, the drawer and all prior indorsers are discharged.

H. Acceptance Varying Draft

Where the drawee's acceptance of tender in any manner varies the draft as presented, the holder may refuse the acceptance and treat the draft as dishonored. In such a case, the drawee is entitled to have the acceptance canceled. Where the holder assents to an acceptance varying the terms of the draft, each drawer and indorser who does not agree to the assent is discharged.

I. Unexcused Delay

Any indorser is discharged from an instrument when any necessary presentment or notice of dishonor is delayed beyond the time when it is due without excuse. Similarly, where without excuse a necessary protest is delayed beyond the time when it is due, any drawer or indorser is discharged.

Understanding Legal Terms

Define, identify, or explain the following terms:

failure of
   consideration
good faith
holder

holder in due course
lack of
   consideration
limited defense

personal defense
presentment
primary liability
protest

real defense
secondary liability
shelter provision
universal defense

Questions for Review and Discussion

1. What are the requirements for being a holder in due course?

2. What is the purpose of the shelter provision, and when will it not apply?

3. Why are personal defenses sometimes called limited defenses? Identify the most common personal defenses.

4. Explain the significance of real defenses. Identify the real defenses.

5. What effect do Federal Trade Commission rules have on the holder-in-due-course doctrine—that is, the doctrine placing the person to whom a negotiable instrument is assigned in a better position than the original seller?

6. Under what circumstances is presentment of an instrument for acceptance required?

7. (a) Indicate the time when presentment of a negotiable instrument must be made when there is a due date on such an instrument. (b) Indicate the time when presentment of a negotiable instrument must be made in the event that there is no due date on such an instrument.

8. When is an instrument dishonored, and what is meant by prompt and proper notice of dishonor?

9. Explain the method of giving notice of dishonor of an instrument drawn or payable outside the United States. How is it accomplished?

10. Under what circumstances will the holder of an instrument be excused from giving notice of dishonor to prior indorsers or to a drawer?

Analyzing Cases

1. Refrigerated Transport Co., Inc., employed a collection agency to collect some of its overdue accounts. The collection agency indorsed without authority checks made payable to Refrigerated and deposited them in the agency's own checking account. Was the bank that accepted the checks for deposit a holder in due course? Why or why not?
● *National Bank v. Refrigerated Transp.*, 248 S.E.2d 496 (Ga. 1978)

2. Delores Gentry applied to an employment agency for a job as a clerk-typist. She asked for a job in which the placement fee would be paid by the employer. The agency referred her to a particular employer and told her that she would have to pay the fee but

that the employer would repay it in six months. She accepted a job at $135 per week and signed a monthly installment note promising to pay $500 to the employment agency. After making two payments on the note, totaling $163.80, Gentry discovered that her employer had not agreed to repay the employment agency fee and that it would not do so. Gentry quit her job and sued the agency for the recovery of the $163.80. The agency argued that it was a holder in due course. Do you agree with the agency? Explain.
● *James Pair, Inc. v. Gentry*, 215 S.E.2d 707 (Ga. 1975)

3. Rutherford purchased real property from Ethel Stokes for $35,000. He paid $5,000

down and signed a promissory note for the balance. The note was secured by a deed of trust (a type of security interest, discussed in detail in Chapter 41). When payments on the note were overdue, Stokes considered foreclosing on the property. Prior to doing so, however, she negotiated the note to Craig, who purchased it at a discount with notice that it was in default. Was Craig a holder in due course of the note? Why or why not? ● *Matter of Marriage of Rutherford,* 573 S.W.2d 299 (Tex. 1978)

4. As part of the purchase price for a 9,040-acre ranch, Kirby gave Bergfield a $20,000 check drawn on the Bank of Bellevue. Bergfield had her banker telephone the Bank of Bellevue to inquire about Kirby's account balance to be sure that the check was good. It was learned that there was not enough money in Kirby's account to cover the check. Bergfield continued to hold the check and did not present it to the Bank of Bellevue for payment. Later, Bergfield argued that the telephone call to the bank was a presentment and demand for payment of the check. Do you agree? Why or why not? ● *Kirby v. Bergfield,* 182 N.W.2d 205 (Neb. 1970)

5. Carolyn Brazil wrote a check to a contractor who agreed to make certain improvements on her home. She wrote the check in reliance on the contractor's false representation that the materials for the job had been purchased. They, in fact, had not been purchased. Brazil had the bank on which the check was drawn stop payment on it. Another bank, which cashed the check and became a holder in due course of the instrument, attempted to recover the amount of the check from Brazil. Can it do so? Explain. ● *Citizens Nat'l. Bank v. Brazil,* 233 S.E.2d 482 (Ga. 1977)

6. David L. and Nettie L. Weiner signed seven promissory notes, totaling $89,000, in their capacity as president and secretary of NMD Realty Co. In addition, they indorsed each note on the reverse side with their individual signatures. Each note contained the following provision: "The Maker and endorser or endorsers each hereby waives presentment, demand and notice of dishonor." The Weiners claim that, because they are secondarily liable, the bank may not proceed against them individually until after presentment, notice of dishonor, and protest have occurred. Do you agree with the Weiners? Explain. ● *Bank of Delaware v. NMD Realty Co.,* 325 A.2d 108 (Del. 1974)

7. Haik transferred his stock in Petrocomp, an oil exploration company, to Rowley in exchange for five $10,000 promissory notes. The notes were signed by Rowley and indorsed by Rowley's son, Stephen. Rowley failed to pay the notes when they became due. No presentment for payment was made by Haik on the due date nor was a timely notice of dishonor given to Rowley's son, Stephen. May Haik hold Stephen liable on the notes as an indorser? Explain. ● *Haik v. Rowley,* 377 So.2d 391 (La. 1979)

8. The Aurora Bank had loaned money to Lewis Hamlin without any security. The bank's board of directors asked its loan officer to have both Mr. and Mrs. Hamlin sign a deed of trust on their farm to secure the payment of the debts because the directors felt that the bank was not adequately secured. When Mrs. Hamlin refused to sign a renewal note and a deed of trust, the loan officer told her that she was responsible for her husband's debts and that the bank would foreclose on the farm if she did not sign. (These statements were not true, and the bank could not legally foreclose on the farm.) Mrs. Hamlin was very upset and crying when the loan officer talked to her. She testified that she was told, "If I didn't sign these papers he had no alternative but to go after our land, our home." Two or three days later, she signed the notes but not the deed of trust. Is Mrs. Hamlin liable on the notes that she signed? Why or why not? ● *Aurora Bank v. Hamlin,* 609 S.W.2d 486 (Mo. 1980)

Chapter 27

Checks and Bank Collections

The use of checks, instead of cash, to pay bills has become a way of life for most people in the United States. The number of checks written each year in this country has increased at an average rate of 7 percent annually since 1970, and it is expected that in the near future over 60 billion checks will be written and processed each year in the United States. To handle this huge volume of activity, regional check-processing centers have been established in different parts of the country. In addition, the latest computer technology is being used to speed up the process of bank deposits and collections.

27-1. Checks

A *check* is a draft drawn on a bank and payable on demand [3-104(2)(b)]. It is the most common form of a draft. It is drawn on a bank by the drawer, who has an account with the bank, to the order of a specified person named on the check, or to the bearer. A check is a safe means of transferring money, and it serves as a receipt after it has been paid and canceled by the bank.

In the check shown in Figure 27-1, Evans is the drawer; she has an account in the Western National Bank. Alicia Adams Fashions, Inc., is the payee. Western National Bank, on whom the check is drawn, is the drawee.

Ownership of a check may be transferred to another person by indorsement

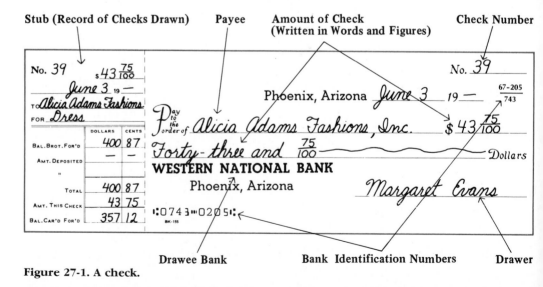

Figure 27-1. A check.

by the payee. In this manner, checks may circulate among several parties, taking the place of money. A bank must honor a check when it is properly drawn against a credit balance of the drawer. Failure to do so would make the bank liable to the drawer for resulting damages.

A. Requirements as to Form

Banks provide regular and special printed check forms. These display a series of numbers printed in magnetic ink, which makes it possible to process checks speedily and accurately by computers. The first set of figures is the bank's Federal Reserve number. This is followed by the bank's own number. The second set of numbers is the depositor's account number. The use of printed forms is not required. Any writing may become a negotiable check if it is a draft drawn on a bank and payable on demand.

● Martinez, when checking out of a motel, discovered she had lost her checkbook and credit cards, and there were no blank checks available. She wrote out a check on a 5- by 8-inch index card, taking care to comply with the requirements of negotiability. When signed by Martinez, this writing would constitute a valid check.

B. Special Types of Checks

Special types of checks have been developed for use in particular situations. Some of these checks are bank drafts, traveler's checks, and cashier's checks.

1. Bank Drafts. A *bank draft* is a check drawn by one bank on another bank in which it has funds on deposit, in favor of a third person, the payee. Many banks deposit money in banks in other areas for the convenience of depositors who depend upon the transfer of funds when transacting business in distant places. When the buyer is unknown to the seller, such checks are more acceptable than personal checks.

2. Traveler's Checks. *Traveler's checks* are similar to cashier's checks in that the issuing financial institution is both the drawer and the drawee. The purchaser signs the checks when they are purchased, in the presence of the issuer. To cash a check, the purchaser writes the name of the payee in the space provided and countersigns it in the payee's presence. Only the purchaser can negotiate traveler's checks, and they are easily replaced by the issuing bank if they are stolen.

Traveler's checks are issued in denominations of $10 and up, and the purchaser of the checks ordinarily pays a fixed fee to the issuer.

3. Cashier's Checks. A *cashier's check*, sometimes called an *official check*, is a check drawn by a bank upon itself. The bank, in effect, lends its credit to the purchaser of the check. Courts have held that payment cannot be stopped on a cashier's check because the bank, by issuing it, accepts the check in advance. In that sense, it is similar to a certified check, discussed below. People who will not accept personal checks will often accept cashier's checks. Such a check may be made payable either to the depositor, who purchases it from the bank, or to the person who is to cash it. If the check is made payable to the depositor, it must be indorsed to the person to whom it is transferred.

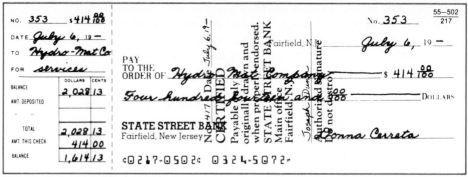

Figure 27-2. A certified check.

C. Certified Checks

Check certification is an action of a bank in which, at the request of either the depositor or the holder, the bank acknowledges and guarantees that sufficient funds will be withheld from the drawer's account to pay the amount stated on the check. A prudent person would request a certified check when involved in a business transaction with a stranger rather than accept a personal check.

The UCC provides that "certification of a check is acceptance (3-411). This means that a drawee bank that certifies a check becomes primarily liable on the instrument just the same as an acceptor of a draft. The bank has absolute liability to pay. Whether anyone is secondarily liable depends upon who had the check certified. If the drawer had the check certified, the drawer and all indorsers remain secondarily liable on the instrument. If, on the other hand, the holder had the check certified, the drawer and all prior indorsers are discharged. The UCC places no obligation on a bank to certify a check if it does not want to do so [3-411(2)]. Figure 27-2 illustrates a certified check.

D. Postdated Checks

A check may be *postdated* (dated ahead) when the drawer has insufficient funds in the bank at the time the check is drawn but expects to have sufficient funds to cover the amount of the check at a future date. Postdating is also practiced when some act or performance is to be completed before the date for payment of the check. Such a check, at the time it is drawn, has the effect of turning a demand instrument into a time instrument. This is because it is an order to pay a specified amount of money at a future date stated.

● In 1969, Gentilotti wrote a check payable to the order of his five-year-old son for $20,000. The check was postdated to 1984. It was delivered to the child's mother, who kept it for the child. The check was indorsed by the father as follows: "For Edward Joseph Smith Gentilotti / My Son / If I should pass away / The amount of $20,000.00 dollars / Shall be taken from / My Estate at death. / S. Gentilotti 11-25-69." Gentilotti died in 1973. The court held that the negotiability of the check was not affected by the fact that it was postdated fifteen years. In addition, the court said that the indorsement modified the check by providing for acceleration (advancement) of the time for payment. The court, therefore, ordered that the $20,000 be paid to the son.

27-2. Bank Deposits and Collections

The tremendous number of checks handled by banks and the countrywide nature of the bank collection process require uniformity in the law of bank collections. For this reason, Article 4 of the UCC contains rules and regulations for handling bank deposits and collections.

A. Bank Descriptions

During the bank collection process, banks are described by different terms depending on their particular function in a transaction. Sometimes a bank takes a check for deposit. At other times, it pays a check as a drawee. At still other times, it takes a check for collection only. The different terms that are used to describe banks and their meanings are as follows (4-105):

○ *Depositary bank* means the first bank to which an item is transferred for collection even though it is also the payor bank.
○ *Payor bank* means a bank by which an item is payable as drawn or accepted. It includes a drawee bank.
○ *Intermediary bank* means any bank to which an item is transferred in the course of collection except the depositary or payor bank.
○ *Collecting bank* means any bank handling the item for collection except the payor bank.
○ *Presenting bank* means any bank presenting an item except a payor bank.
○ *Remitting bank* means any payor or intermediary bank remitting for an item.

B. A Check's Life Cycle

The life cycle of a check begins when the drawer writes a check and delivers it to the payee. The payee may take the check directly to the payor bank (the bank on which it was drawn) for payment. If that bank pays the check in cash, its payment is final, and the check is returned to the drawer with the next bank statement (4-213). However, it is more likely that the check will be deposited in the payee's own account in another bank. That bank, known as the depositary bank, acts as its customer's agent to collect the money from the payor bank (4-201). Any settlement given by the depositary bank in this case is *provisional* (not final). It may be revoked if the check is later dishonored. The check is sent (sometimes through an intermediary bank) to a collecting bank, which presents the check to the payor bank for payment. If it is honored by the payor bank, the amount will be deducted from the drawer's account, and the check will be returned to the drawer with the next bank statement. If the check is dishonored for any reason, it will be returned to the payee via the same route that it was sent and all credits given for the item will be revoked.

27-3. The Bank-Depositor Relationship

The relationship between the drawee bank and its customer is that of both (*a*) debtor and creditor and (*b*) agent and principal. The relationship arises out of the express or implied contract that occurs when the customer opens a checking account with the bank. The bank becomes a debtor when money is deposited in the bank by the customer. At this time, the customer is owed money by the bank and is therefore a creditor. When an *overdraft* occurs, that is, when the bank pays out more than the customer has on deposit, the debtor-creditor role reverses, and the bank becomes the creditor.

The bank acts as the customer's agent when it collects or attempts to collect checks or other negotiable instruments made payable to the customer (4-201). If the items are deposited in the customer's account, any settlement made by the bank with the customer is provisional. A provisional settlement may be revoked by the bank if an item that the bank is attempting to collect is dishonored. The bank may charge back the amount of any credit given for the item to its customer's account or obtain a refund from its customer (4-212).

● Tuttle indorsed and deposited in his checking account a check that had been made payable to him by Ralby. Tuttle's bank credited his account for the amount of the check and sent it through the clearinghouse for collection. The check was returned to the bank because of insufficient funds in Ralby's account. Tuttle's bank charged back (debited) the amount it had credited to Tuttle's account.

A. The Bank's Duties

The bank's duties to its customers are as follows:

1. Duty to Honor Orders. The drawee bank is under a duty to honor all checks drawn by its customers when there are sufficient funds on deposit in the customer's account. If there are not sufficient funds on deposit, the bank may charge the customer's account even if it creates an overdraft (4-401). If a bank fails to honor a check because of a mistake on its part, the bank is liable to the customer for any actual damages the customer suffers (4-402).

● Rougier, who had $178 in her checking account, wrote out a check for 78.42 and mailed it to the telephone company in payment of a telephone bill. Due to a mistake on its part, Rougier's bank dishonored the check and returned it to the telephone company marked "insufficient funds." As soon as the error was discovered, the telephone company was notified and the check was redeposited and honored by the bank. Since Rougier suffered no loss, the bank was not liable for dishonoring the check. Had Rougier's telephone been disconnected because of the dishonored check, the bank would have been liable to her for the cost of restoring service. The bank would also be responsible for any other damages to Rougier caused by the loss of telephone service.

A bank is under no obligation to a customer to pay a stale check unless it is certified. A *stale check* is a check which is presented for payment more than six months after its date. A bank, however, may honor a stale check without liability to its customer if it acts in good faith (4-404).

● The Chemical Bank paid a check that had been written by New York Flameproofing Co. ten years earlier on a check form no longer used by that company. The account on which the check was drawn had been closed for seven years, and the company's address written on the check had changed seven years earlier. In holding against the bank for paying the check, the court said that such payment was a reckless disregard of due care so as to constitute bad faith. The bank was liable for the amount paid.

The drawee bank is not liable to a holder of a check for dishonoring the instrument unless it is certified. The holder's recourse is against the drawer or indorsers on their secondary liability.

2. Death or Incompetence of Customer. The drawee bank is not liable for the payment of a check before it has notice of the death or incompetence of the drawer. In addition, a bank may continue to pay or certify checks for ten days after the date of death of the drawer even though it has notice (4-405). This rule permits holders of checks that are drawn shortly before the drawer's death to cash them without the necessity of filing a claim with the court handling the deceased's estate.

3. Forged Checks and Depositor Protection. A *forgery* is committed when a person fraudulently makes or alters a check or other form of commercial paper to the injury of another. The *intent to defraud* and the *creation of a liability* must be proved by the prosecutor.

● Wheeler applied for a $400 loan from Home Finance Company and received its check for that amount. He painstakingly altered the amount to read $4,000. Later he presented the check, properly indorsed, to a building contractor in partial payment of an outstanding debt. In transferring the check, Wheeler was guilty of forgery.

If a bank, in good faith, pays an altered amount of a check to a holder, it may deduct from the drawer's account only the amount of the check as it was originally written. Thus, in the above case, if the bank pays the full $4,000 to the building contractor, it can deduct $400 from Home Finance Company's account, but no more. The bank would be able to deduct the full $4,000 from Home Finance Company's account if the alteration was caused by that company's carelessness in writing the check.

The depositor is also protected against a signature's being forged. When a checking account is opened, the depositor must fill out a signature card, which is permanently filed at the bank. Thereafter, the bank is held to know the depositor's signature. The bank is liable to the drawer if it pays any check to which the depositor's signature has been forged.

4. Midnight Deadline. Payor banks are required to either settle or return checks quickly (4-302). If they do not do so, they are responsible for paying them. If the payor bank is not also the depositary bank, it must settle for an item by midnight of the banking day of receipt.

● LaPierre wrote a check to Kimberly Motors for $2,500 in payment for a second-hand car. The payor of the check (the bank on which it was drawn) was the National Bank & Trust Co. Kimberly Motors deposited the check into its account in the Southwest Mutual Bank (the depositary bank), which sent it on for collection. LaPierre's car broke down before she reached home that evening. She immediately stopped payment on the check. The National Bank & Trust Company must return the check to the Southwest Mutual Bank, with a notation that payment has been stopped, before midnight of the day that it received the check. If it keeps the check longer than that, it will be liable for payment.

If the payor bank is also the depositary bank, it must either pay or return the check or send notice of its dishonor on or before its midnight deadline. A bank's *midnight deadline* is midnight of the next banking day following the banking day on which it receives the relevant item [4-104(h)].

● In the above case, if the National Bank & Trust Company had also been the depositary bank, it would have had an extra day to handle the check. The bank would have had until midnight of the next banking day to return the check to Kimberly Motors with the notation that payment had been stopped.

B. The Depositor's Duties

Depositors, in general, owe a duty to the banks in which they have checking accounts to have sufficient funds on deposit to cover checks that they write. They must also examine their bank statements and canceled checks promptly and with reasonable care and notify the bank quickly of any discrepencies.

1. Responsibilities Regarding Bad Checks. Most states have statutes making it larceny or attempted larceny for a person to issue a check drawn on a bank in which the person has insufficient funds. Such statutes usually have the following provisions, which must be observed in the prosecution of anyone issuing a bad check:

○ The payee has the obligation of informing the drawer of the nonpayment of the check, together with notice of the provisions of the bad-check law and of the party's legal rights and obligations.
○ After receiving notice of nonpayment, or dishonor, the drawer is given a specified number of days, usually five or ten, in which to make the check good, without fear of prosecution.
○ Failure to make full payment of the check within the number of days allowed by statute serves as presumption of guilt that the drawer issued the check with full knowledge of the facts and with intent to defraud.

● State National Bank received Yoder's check for $120 due on an installment note it held. After it was deposited, the check was returned to State National with the notification "insufficient funds." The bank's collection department sent a registered letter to Yoder in which responsibility under the bad-check statute was explained. Failure on the part of Yoder to make the check good within the period of time indicated would result in a criminal complaint being lodged against Yoder through the office of the state's prosecuting attorney.

Needless to say, bad-check statutes are effectively used as a means of collection. Most bad-check writers make an effort to make full payment of the check when advised that they are subject to prosecution.

Many banks now offer overdraft protection service to their depositors which cover small overdrafts that are usually caused by the mistake of the drawer in balancing the checkbook. With this service, the bank honors small overdrafts and charges the depositor's account. This saves the drawer the inconvenience and embarrassment of having a check returned to a holder marked "insufficient funds."

2. Duty to Examine Accounts.

The UCC imposes a duty on depositors to examine their bank statements and canceled checks promptly and with reasonable care when they are received from the bank (4-406). They must report promptly to the bank any forged or altered checks. If they do not do so, depositors cannot hold the bank responsible for losses due to the bank's payment of a forged or altered instrument.

The exact time within which a depositor must notify a bank is not established except in the case of the same wrongdoer forging or altering more than one check. In that case, the bank must be notified of the wrongdoing within fourteen days after the depositor receives the bank statement and canceled checks.

● Applegard's checkbook was stolen from her desk without her knowledge. The thief filled out three of the stolen checks, forged Applegard's signature, and cashed them. Applegard must notify the bank of the forgery at least within fourteen days after she receives the bank statement and canceled checks. If she does not do so, her bank will not be liable for paying the forged checks.

The absolute limit for notifying a bank of a forged or altered check is one year from the time the depositor receives the bank statement. The limit is three years, however, in the case of a forged indorsement on a check.

C. Stop-Payment Rights

Drawers may order a bank to stop payment on any item payable on their account (4-403).

1. Manner of Stopping Payment.

The *stop-payment order* must be received in time and in such a manner as to afford the bank a reasonable opportunity to act on it. An oral order is binding upon the bank for fourteen calendar days only, unless confirmed in writing within that period. A written order is effective for only six months, unless renewed in writing. The burden of establishing the fact and amount of loss resulting from the payment of an item contrary to a binding stop-payment order is on the customer [4-403(3)].

2. Bank's Right of Subrogation.

If a bank fails to stop payment on a check, it is responsible for any loss suffered by the drawer who ordered the payment stopped. The bank, however, may take the place of any holder, holder in due course, payee, or drawer who has rights against others on the underlying obligation (4-407). This right to be substituted for another is known as the bank's right of *subrogation*. It is designed to prevent loss to the bank and unjust enrichment to other parties.

● Jervey was induced by fraud to enter into a contract with Glidden. As part of the transaction, Jervey wrote and delivered a check to Glidden for $1,500. When Jervey discovered the fraud, she immediately ordered her bank to stop payment on the check. The bank, by mistake, ignored the stop-payment order and paid the $1,500 to Glidden. The bank must return the $1,500 to Jervey but may sue Glidden for fraud under its right of subrogation.

Understanding Legal Terms

Define, identify, or explain the following terms:

bank draft	depositary bank	payor bank	remitting bank
cashier's check	forgery	postdated	stale check
check	intermediary bank	presenting bank	subrogation
check certification	midnight deadline	provisional	traveler's check
collecting bank	overdraft		

Questions for Review and Discussion

1. Describe the primary characteristics that justify the use of checks, rather than any other negotiable instrument, as a means of making payments.

2. Explain the procedure whereby a check is certified.

3. Distinguish between a bank draft and a personal check. Explain why a bank draft is considered more acceptable in payment of a debt than a personal check.

4. Describe the life cycle of a check that is deposited in the payee's bank which is not also the payor bank.

5. What is the relationship between the drawee bank and its customers when money is deposited in the bank? When an overdraft occurs?

6. Explain the liability of a bank for dishonoring an uncertified check due to a mistake on its part (a) to its customer, (b) to a holder of the check, (c) in the case of a stale check.

7. What is the bank's responsibility as to the payment of checks after the death of the drawer?

8. How are bad-check statutes used as a means of collection?

9. To what extent is a bank liable to a depositor for paying a check that has been altered after being written by the drawer?

10. How does an oral stop-payment order compare with a written stop-payment order as it affects the bank's obligations?

Analyzing Cases

1. Fitting wrote an $800 check on her account with Continental Bank. A bank employee had mistakenly placed a "hold" on the account, causing the bank to dishonor the check when it was presented for payment. Fitting was unable to prove that she suffered damages because of the dishonor. Can she recover from the bank? Explain. ● *Continental Bank v. Fitting,* 559 P.2d 218 (Ariz. 1977)

2. SCI Equipment, Inc., gave Taboada a personal check in the amount of $2,732.99 for the repair of its tractor trailer. Taboada took the check to the bank on which it was drawn, cashed it, and with the proceeds purchased an official bank check payable to his business name. A dispute arose over the quality of the repairs on the tractor trailer. SCI attempted to stop payment on its personal check but could not do so because the check had been cashed. Instead, the bank refused to honor its cashier's check which it had given to Taboada. May the bank dishonor its cashier's check? Why or why not? ● *Taboada v. Bank of Babylon,* 408 N.Y.S.2d 734 (1978)

3. Templeton received a $5,000 check payable to his order drawn on the First National Bank of Nashville. He deposited the check for collection in his own bank on June 18. The check reached the First National Bank of Nashville through normal banking channels on June 22. That bank had received a stop-payment order on the check on May 15 and, therefore, refused to honor it. It kept the check until June 28, when it returned it to Templeton with the notification that payment had been stopped. Is the First National Bank of Nashville liable for the amount of the check to Templeton? Explain. ● *Templeton v. First Nat'l. Bank*, 362 N.E.2d 33 (Ill. 1977)

4. A man purporting to be R. E. Merriman cashed three checks at Payroll Check Cashing, a division of Lou's Liquors. Each check was drawn on the account of Allied Construction Company in the amount of $298.84. Each was payable to the order of R. E. Merriman, and bore the signature of Steven Snider. Payroll Check Cashing indorsed the checks and deposited them in its own bank, which sent them through the collection process to the New Palestine Bank on which they were drawn. That bank inspected the checks and paid them. When the canceled checks were sent to Allied Construction Company in its monthly statement, Allied notified New Palestine Bank that the three checks bore forged signatures of Steven Snider. Who is responsible for the loss? Explain. ● *Payroll Check Cashing v. New Palestine Bank*, 401 N.E.2d 752 (Ind. 1980)

5. Granite Equipment Leasing Corp. drew a check on the Hempstead Bank payable to the order of Overseas Equipment Co., Inc. Five days later, Granite notified its bank in writing to stop payment on the check, as it had apparently been lost. Granite then sent the money to Overseas Equipment Co. by wire. Thirteen months later, the check was sent to the Hempstead Bank for collection. The bank paid the check and charged Granite's account for its amount. Granite, in seeking the return of the money from the Hempstead Bank, claims that the bank violated its duty to stop payment on the check. Is Granite correct? Why or why not? ● *Granite Equip. Leasing Corp. v. Hempstead Bank*, 326 N.Y.S.2d 881 (1971)

6. Ragusa drew a $5,000 check on its account in the Community State Bank payable to the order of Southern Masonry and delivered it to that company. Later, Ragusa was advised by Southern Masonry that the check had been lost. A replacement check was drawn and delivered to Southern Masonry, and a verbal stop-payment order on the lost check was given to the bank. Three years later, the lost check was presented for payment to the Community State Bank, paid, and the amount was deducted from Ragusa's account. Was the bank liable for paying the check after it had received the stop-payment order? Did the bank violate a duty owed to its customer for paying the stale check? Explain. ● *Charles Ragusa & Son v. Community State Bank*, 360 So.2d 231 (La. 1978)

7. While in the hospital during his final illness, Norris signed and dated a blank check and inserted figures "3.300" after the word "For" on the lower left-hand corner of the check. He gave the incomplete check to a friend with instruction to give it to his sister and to have her complete it for the amount he had written on it. Later, the check was filled in with Norris's sister's name as payee in the amount of $3,300 and deposited in her account. The check was dishonored because the drawer died before it cleared the payor bank. May a bank honor a check when it knows of the death of the drawer? Explain. ● *In Re Estate of Norris*, 532 P.2d 981 (Colo. 1975)

8. In payment for services rendered, one of Stewart's clients gave him a check for $185.48 which had been drawn by the client's corporate employer and made payable to the order of the client. Although properly indorsed by the client, the drawee bank flatly refused to cash the check for Stewart. The bank acknowledged that the check was good, that is, that there were sufficient funds in the account. Can Stewart sue the bank for refusing to honor the check? Why or why not? ● *Stewart v. Citizens & Nat'l Bank*, 225 S.E.2d 761 (Ga. 1976)

9. The Summit County Clerk of Court's office drew a check on its alimony and support account with Firestone Bank for $45 payable to Leona C. Brechbill. Brechbill placed it for deposit with Arlington Trust Co. That bank encoded the check (so that it could be read mechanically) to read $10,045. That amount was later paid to Brechbill. The check was sent for collection to the Riggs National Bank of Washington, D.C., which in turn sent it to the Federal Reserve Bank of Cleveland. The Federal Reserve Bank sent it to the Firestone Bank, which paid the check by deducting $10,045 from the clerk of court's office alimony and support account. No examination of the canceled checks was made by the clerk of court's office. Almost eight months later, the error was discovered by the state auditor. Is the Firestone Bank responsible to the county for the $10,000 overcharge? Explain your answer. ● *State ex rel. Gabalac v. Firestone Bank,* 346 N.E.2d 326 (Ohio 1975)

10. Ussery, a former convict, was hired by Nu-Way Services, Inc. as its night manager. Part of his duties entailed obtaining parts from parts companies. Nu-Way's president, on several occasions, dated and signed checks and filled in the names of the payees, leaving the amounts blank for Ussery to fill in later. Ussery substituted his name for the name of the payee on seven of the checks and cashed them. He also obtained access to the company's checkbook and removed some checks. Over a six-month period, he wrote out and cashed forty-three checks on which he named himself as payee and forged the company president's signature. No one in the company examined the monthly bank statement or canceled checks for forgeries or alterations nor compared the checks with the company checkbook. Is the drawee bank liable to Nu-Way Services, Inc., for paying the forged checks? Why or why not? ● *Nu-Way Services, Inc. v. Mercantile Trust Co.,* 530 S.W.2d 743 (Mo. 1975)

Part 6

Case Briefs

St. Paul Fire & Marine Ins. Co.
v. State Bank,
412 N.E.2d 103 (Ind. 1980)

Stephens, a farmer, delivered and sold 184 bushels of corn to Aubrey for $478.23. The following day, Aubrey prepared its check payable to Stephens in payment for the corn and mailed it to Stephens. The check was prepared in the following fashion: the amount 478.23 was typewritten upon the line customarily used to express the amount of the check in numbers, abutting the printed dollar sign. On the line customarily used to express the amount in words there appeared "The sum of $100478 and 23 cts," which was imprinted in red by a checkwriting machine. The line ended with the printed word "Dollars."

Stephens presented the check and two other items worth $5,604.51 to a branch of the State Bank of Salem. By this time, someone had typed on the check the figure 100 immediately before the typed figure 478.23. This was rather crudely done, and involved typing the 100 in an uneven line. The second 0 was typed directly over the printed dollar sign on the check. Stephens told the branch manager that he wished to apply these funds to the amount of his indebtedness to the bank. He also wished to withdraw $2,000 in cash and to deposit the balance in his checking account.

The branch manager questioned Stephens about the Aubrey check since Stephen's prior dealings with the bank had not involved transactions of that size. The manager also knew that Stephens had filed a voluntary petition in bankruptcy several months prior, but had subsequently reaffirmed his obligations to the bank. Stephens explained that he had purchased a large quantity of corn in

northern Indiana and had sold it in Kentucky at a higher price. Evidently satisfied with his explanation, the manager stamped "paid" on nine promissory notes of which Stephens was maker and returned them to Stephens. The manager then directed a teller at the bank to fill out a deposit slip for the transaction. At that time, neither the manager nor the teller noticed the typewritten modification on the check. The transaction consisted of applying the funds represented by the three items in the deposit ($106,082.74) to Stephens's debt represented by the nine promissory notes ($31,851.81), an installment payment, of which Stephens was a joint obligor, of $27,599.27, accrued interest owed the bank by Stephens in the amount of $5,265.65, and the $2,000 cash given to Stephens. The balance was credited to Stephens's account.

Later that afternoon, the branch manager began thinking about the transaction and examined the items in the deposit. He noted that Aubrey's check bore signs of possible tampering and contacted Aubrey's office in Louisville to inquire about the validity of the check. An Aubrey representative told the manager that a check in that amount was suspicious. The manager "froze" the transaction. The next day, Aubrey stopped payment on the check. Thereafter, the bank attempted to recover possession of the nine promissory notes from Stephens but was unsuccessful. Stephens subsequently left town. The bank claims a loss of $28,193.91. It brought this action to recover that amount from Aubrey.

Plaintiff's Position: The bank contended that it was a holder in due course of the check and, therefore, that it was not subject to defenses claimed by Aubrey. The bank argued that it gave value to Stephens by applying the Aubrey check to his indebtedness and by surrendering the promissory notes to him. It also contended that it took the check without notice of any defenses of Aubrey.

Defendant's Position: Aubrey contended that the bank did not take the check for value since it froze Stephens's account the moment it became suspicious of the check. In addition, it canceled the amounts it had credited against Stephens's debt. Aubrey argued that the bank's action in crediting Stephens's debt on the notes merely constituted a bookkeeping procedure. Aubrey claimed that the bank did not change its position by doing this, particularly since it could still maintain an action against Stephens on the promissory notes.

In addition, Aubrey contended that the bank was not a holder in due course of the check because the bank took the check with notice of a defense to the check on the part of Aubrey. Aubrey claimed the following should have put the bank on notice of a defense: the small size of Stephens's farming operation; Stephens's banking history, including frequent indebtedness and overdrawals; the bank's knowledge of Stephens's petition in bankruptcy; the size of the Aubrey check in relation to typical transactions undertaken by the bank; and the implausibility of Stephens's explanation to the bank manager, himself familiar with farming, of the transaction underlying Stephens's receipt of the check.

Legal Issue: Did the bank give value and take the check without notice of any claims or defenses, making it a holder in due course?

Court Decision: Yes. The court held that the bank was a holder in due course of the check. It could enforce the check against the drawer, Aubrey, to the extent it gave value for it.

Court Reasoning: Value is given for an instrument when the instrument is taken in payment for a prior debt. The bank gave value when it credited Stephens's account and surrendered the promissory notes.

In upholding the finding that the bank took the check without notice, the court noted that the bank's branch manager admitted that he took the check without comparing the amount expressed by the checkwriting machine with the amount expressed in typewritten figures; indeed, he testified that he did not even look at the figures. He relied, instead, upon the amount expressed by the checkwriter that was entered upon the line generally used to express the amount of a check in words. When there is a conflict between the two amounts on a check, the UCC states that words control figures. Arguably, the amount imprinted by the checkwriting machine is expressed in figures upon the line customarily expressing the amount in words. The court felt, however, that the purposes of the UCC are best served by considering an amount imprinted by a check-writing machine as "words" for the purpose of resolving an ambiguity between that amount and an amount entered upon the line usually used to express the amount in figures. The purpose of making a sum payable when expressed in words controlling over the sum payable expressed in figures is the fact that words are much more difficult to alter. The perforated imprinting by a checkwriting machine, while expressing the sum payable in figures, is even more difficult to successfully alter than a sum payable in written words.

The court did not agree with Aubrey's contention that the circumstances surrounding the transaction were so irregular as to put a reasonably prudent banker on notice of a defense to Aubrey's check. The mere knowledge of the questionable financial position of the transferor of an instrument does not in itself defeat holder-in-due-course status.

Lialios v. Home Ins. Cos.,
410 N.E.2d 193 (Ill. 1980)
In settlement of a workers' compensation claim with Moulopoulos, Home Insurance Companies issued a draft drawn on itself, payable through Citibank, New York, and made payable to Moulopoulos. The draft stated on its face "upon acceptance pay to the order of Costas Moulopoulos $1,275.00." A week later, Moulopoulos went to the insurance company and stated that he had lost the draft. The insurance company issued a stop-payment order on the draft and issued another to Moulopoulos. In fact, Moulopoulos had not lost the first draft. Instead, he had negotiated it to Lialios. When Lialios's bank presented the draft to Citibank, payment was refused due to the stop-payment order. Lialios brought this action against Home Insurance Companies for the amount of the draft.

Plaintiff's Position: Lialios claimed that he was a holder in due course of the draft and thus not subject to Home Insurance Companies' defense that the workers' compensation claim had been paid.

Defendant's Position: The insurance company argued that the draft was conditional and, therefore, not a negotiable instrument. It contended that the words "upon accept-ance" indicated a conditional promise to pay. It further argued that the draft was not payable on demand or at a certain time.

Legal Issue: Is the draft a negotiable instrument, thereby allowing Lialios to be a holder in due course?

Court Decision: Yes. The draft was a negotiable instrument, and Lialios was a holder in due course, entitled to the face amount of the draft.

Court Reasoning: The instrument indicates that Citibank is merely the collecting bank and that the insurance company is both the drawer and drawee. The words "upon acceptance" do not destroy the negotiability of an instrument. They are only a restatement of an "implied or constructive condition" of any draft or check which must be accepted to charge the drawee. A promise or order otherwise unconditional is not made conditional by the fact that the instrument is subject to implied or constructive conditions.

The UCC, however, provides that a draft drawn on the drawer is effective as a note. When a draft is drawn by one party on that party, which has the effect of a promissory note or an accepted bill of exchange, it is considered to be accepted by the very act of issuing it. Presentment and acceptance are not necessary to make the draft a liability of the drawer to the payee or holder. The use of "upon acceptance" on the instrument is superfluous for this reason. Finally, because the draft is drawn on the drawer, it is effective as a note, and because no definite time for payment is stated in the instrument, it is payable on demand. Neither the language "upon acceptance" nor the absence of a definite time for payment destroyed this instrument's negotiability.

Part 7

Agency and Employment

Chapter 28   Creation of Agency

The job placement agent, the service station attendant, the attorney—all represent someone else in their business dealings with third parties. The complexities of business today often cause us to delegate to others things we cannot conveniently do for ourselves. Even someone operating a sole proprietorship has to delegate authority to other people at times. Thus, the agent-principal relationship is created. This relationship is regulated by the law of agency.

The law of agency is common law as expressed in the *Restatement (Second) of Agency*, an authoritative gathering of court decisions and opinions. This body of law defines *agency* as a legal relationship between two persons who agree that one is to act on behalf and under the control of the other in dealing with third parties. The relationship is *fiduciary* in that the person with the duty to act does so in trust for the benefit of another. The agency relationship may or may not arise as a result of an actual contract.

28-1. Agency and Other Business Relationships

To resolve disputes between parties in business transactions, the courts often are called upon to distinguish among an agent, an employee, and an independent contractor.

A. Principal-Agent Relationship

When one person is represented by another in business dealings with third parties, their relationship is called a principal-agent relationship. The person who is authorized to represent the other is known as the *agent*. The person or business for whom the agent performs and whom the agent represents is called the *principal*. The person with whom the agent deals or contracts is called the *third party*. The *contract of agency* between principal and agent, by which the agent is vested with authority to represent the principal, establishes the principal's liability for the agent's acts in dealings with third parties.

● Berk Associates, Inc., an employment agency, hired three salespersons to recruit top-flight employees for client companies. The three agents screened and tested job applicants for nationwide placement. They arranged interviews between job applicants and potential employers, which frequently resulted in employment agreements. The relationship between Berk Associates, Inc., and the three salespersons was one of agency; the principal was liable for the acts of the agents in their dealings with the third-party job applicants and the client companies seeking qualified employees.

1. Delegation of Agent's Authority. Agents are appointed by principals because of assumed fitness to perform assigned tasks. Because principals rely on the agent's personal skill and integrity, they do not ordinarily give agents the power to delegate authority or to appoint subagents. A *subagent* is a subordinate employed by an agent, with the knowledge of the principal, to assist the agent in the conduct of the principal's affairs. In those instances where the agent is permitted to delegate authority, the acts of the subagent are binding on the principal as if they had been performed by the agent. Should the agent delegate authority without authorization, the acts of the subagent do not impose any obligation or liability on the principal to third parties.

In some instances, the agent is permitted to delegate authority even though the agreement between the principal and agent does not contain an express power of delegation. Such an intention may be implied from the nature of the employment. For instance, general authority to manage a business for a principal implies the agent has authority to perform to the extent usual and customary in such operations. Unless agreed otherwise, the agent has authority to employ, supervise, or discharge employees as the course of business may reasonably require. An agent is also authorized to appoint a subagent for the principal, unless otherwise agreed, if an unforeseen situation arises which makes such an appointment reasonably necessary for the protection of the principal's interests. However, authority that requires the exercise of discretion or judgment, such as receiving money for the principal and issuing receipts for it, cannot be delegated.

The delegation of personal or confidential acts is not ordinarily allowed. These include, but are not limited to, the acts of voting, serving on juries, rendering professional services, and holding public office.

2. Minors and Agency Law. A principal may not cite the infancy of an agent as a reason for avoiding a contract made by that agent. The principal who is a minor may generally avoid or accept a contract made by an agent to the same extent as if the contract had been made by the minor. However, state statutes are not universal in the way they treat the business contracts of minors. Some state courts have held that a minor who is sufficiently mature to run a business may not avoid business-related contracts made while running the business.

● Davis, a minor who owned a stationery store, hired Craig, an adult, as store manager. Craig contracted with a supply house to purchase a new cash register for the store. Davis refused to accept delivery or to pay for the register. In the event the court interprets this transaction to be reasonably related to the carrying on of Davis's business, it could hold that the purchase agreement was binding on Davis.

3. Business Organizations and Agency Law. Agency law applies to the operation of corporations and partnerships. A *corporation* is a legal entity created by state statute authorizing an association of persons to carry on an enterprise. It is authorized to conduct business transactions by means of agents acting in its behalf. Its agents include the officers of the enterprise as well as other designated employees. All aspects of agency law relating to wrongful acts committed by agents against third parties or their property also apply to corporations. Corporate liability also extends to acts of fraud committed by its officers or employees within their actual or apparent authority.

● Sanchez claimed that Chou, president of Haase Equipment, Inc., made an oral contract appointing Sanchez the national sales manager of the corporation. His compensation was to be based on a straight salary and a percentage of any increased volume of sales. The corporation directors later refused to pay the percentage of compensation based on increased sales volume and argued that Chou had no authority to make such an agreement. The agreement would be binding on the corporation, however; Sanchez would not be expected to know that Chou's agreement with him required approval by the board of directors. Thus, the corporation is liable for the acts of its president within the scope of the business it is empowered to engage in.

The Uniform Partnership Act specifies that every partner is an agent of a *partnership* (i.e., an association of two or more persons to conduct a business for profit) for the purpose of its business. The appointment of an agent by one partner is binding on all other partners. Likewise, partners as agents are liable for contracts each makes in behalf of the business.

● Bianco and Gilman operated the Polka Dot Shop as partners. During Bianco's vacation, Gilman ordered a large selection of pantsuits, skirts, coordinated separates, and blouses for the spring selling season. Although Bianco was not present and might disagree with the selection, she will be liable for her share of the expense. Gilman was acting as agent for the partnership, representing both herself and Bianco.

B. Employer-Employee Relationship

The legal principles governing the relationship of principal and agent and of employer and employee are basically the same. The main difference between the two relationships is the employer's power to control the activities of the employee. While an agent brings about a relationship between a principal and a third party that results in a contract, an employee has no such rights or powers. An employee merely performs mechanical acts for the employer under the employer's direction and subject to the employer's control. The employer controls not only what shall be done by the employee but also how it shall be done.

A person who is an employee, however, may be required to perform duties for the employer that require the exercise of judgment and discretion and that result in the establishment of a contractual relationship between the employer and a third party. The employee then has the status of an agent even without a formal contract of agency.

● Mayer, an estate manager, frequently sent an employee to a building supply center for needed hardware, with instructions to charge them to the estate's account. These purchases were paid for without question. When the employee charged

Part 7:
Agency
and
Employ-
ment

360

items for personal use, without Mayer's knowledge or consent, the building and supply company could collect from the estate. The employer was liable for the acts of the employee performed within the scope of the employee's apparent duties.

1. Employment Contract. Like other contracts, employment agreements require capable parties, valid subject matter, consideration, and mutual assent. They are generally expressed in words and may be either oral or written.

● Sutton was hired by Hudson Pharmacy as a licensed pharmacist. He was to be paid a salary of $1,680 a month and would work eight hours a day, six days a week. Sutton agreed to dispense drugs only on prescriptions signed by physicians. All the requirements of contract law were satisfied.

Under the statute of frauds, if a contract of employment is to last more than one year from the date of the making of the contract, it must be in writing.

Both employer and employee have duties to each other in the employment relationship. An employee is obligated to render those services agreed to with the same degree of care, skill, and attention characteristic of others engaged in similar work. An employee is forbidden to reveal to third parties trade secrets valuable in the employer's business. Obligations to an employer for inventions resulting from work done within the scope of employment depend on the conditions agreed to in the employment agreement. In the absence of a stipulation regarding such rights, the employer has a nonexclusive right to the use of such inventions without payment of royalty or license rights.

● Employed as a chemical engineer, Diaz developed an inexpensive process that reclaimed polluted chemicals. In the absence of conditions in his employment contract, Diaz's discovery is his own, even though it resulted from work done within the scope of employment. The employer, however, may use the process without obligation to Diaz.

An employer must pay an employee the amount agreed on for services rendered. An employer also has an obligation to provide safe working conditions and to point out to employees any hazards of employment that are not otherwise obvious. And, as discussed in subsequent chapters, federal and state laws provide additional protection to employees.

2. Termination of the Employment Contract. Employment contracts are terminated in the same way as other contracts. Failure to carry out assigned duties is the most common cause of employee discharge. Others include disobedience to proper instructions, misrepresentation or fraud exercised in obtaining the job, and lack of loyalty toward the employer.

A failure of the employer to carry out obligations to the employee is a breach of the employment contract. Additional legal grounds for abandoning employment are mistreatment of employee by the employer, unsanitary employment conditions, and employer demand for services not included in the employment contract.

For decades the courts have honored the common-law doctrine of *employment-at-will*. This principle says that persons hired without a fixed term of employment serve at the pleasure of their employers. The only exceptions have been a few cases involving public policy questions and discrimination based on race, sex, age, and union activity. Recently, the courts and sympathetic juries of California, Illinois, Kansas, Maryland, Michigan, New Jersey, and Pennsylvania have weakened or set aside the time-honored doctrine of employment-at-will. They have found that employers have sometimes created implied contracts with their noncontract employees. Such obligations are found in the wording of employee handbooks, personnel policy manuals, and even oral statements made by persons who did the hiring prior to an employee's termination. In addition, government employees, including those of public school systems, usually may not be discharged by the employer without notice and a hearing.

C. Master-Servant Relationship

In statutes dealing with relations between two parties, the word *employee* has largely displaced *servant*, and the word *employer* has replaced *master*. In general, then, *employee* is synonymous with *servant*, and *employer* with *master*. In the master-servant relationship, the servant generally performs duties that are specifically prescribed. There is very limited authority, if any, to enter into contracts on behalf of the master or employer.

The word *servant* retains significance in tort liability cases where the employee serves as a borrowed servant. This condition arises when an employee of one employer is loaned to another employer. Who should bear the loss caused by the employee's tort depends on which employer had control of the worker when the tort occurred.

In dealing with the borrowed-servant doctrine and the general master-servant relationship, the courts refer to the appropriate section of the *Restatement (Second) of Agency*. There a servant is defined as an agent who is employed to perform service in the affairs of a master and who with respect to the physical conduct in the performance of the service is controlled or is subject to the right to control by the master. The same *Restatement* also states various circumstances that are helpful in applying this definition. Circumstances such as whose work is being performed and who supplies the tools and the place of work are relevant. The skill of the worker and the manner in which the worker is paid may also be relevant to the ease with which control over a worker may be shifted from one master to another. And the length of time that the nominal servant of one master has been aiding in the business of another is indicative of a shift in control.

● Shenker was employed as a janitor for the B&O Railroad. In addition to his work for the B&O, Shenker maintained a nearby rail station and performed various services for the P&LE Railroad. While on the station premises and doing P&LE work, Shenker was injured. The facts showed that Shenker was at all times paid by the B&O Railroad and under the sole supervision of B&O employees. The court should find that Shenker was not a borrowed servant of the P&LE Railroad but rather a servant of an independent concern; that is, the B&O Railroad. The B&O Railroad, therefore, should be held liable for the injuries Shenker sustained.

D. Independent Contractor Relationship

Independent contractors are persons who contract to do work for others according to their own judgment and method. Normally, independent contractors are paid by the job and not by the hour. They generally have control over the job

Part 7:
Agency
and
Employ-
ment

362

and perform a specialized service. In this capacity, independent contractors are neither employees nor agents. They maintain all required business licenses and permits, pay all job-related expenses, and are obligated only to get the job done.

The degree of control or supervision over the matter and means by which work is performed is the principal element that differentiates independent contractors and employees. Employers have the right to control employees. They do not have the right to control independent contractors.

Other guidelines are helpful in establishing an independent contractor relationship. Independent contractors, not the principal, have the power to choose their own workers and to discharge them on the job. They provide their own equipment and tools and are responsible for performing the entire job, including cleaning up. Architects, painters, physicians, nurses, and plumbers are examples of independent contractors when they are in business for themselves. They can lose this status and become agents, however, if they are hired as members of an employer's staff. The independent contractor and not the hiring party is liable to third parties for negligence.

● National Development Corp. awarded a contract to Case Utility Equipment to transport temporary structures and erect them on a new building site. Owing to Case Utility's negligence, one of the trailers broke loose in route and crashed into a passenger bus. The bus was heavily damaged, and a number of passengers were injured. Since Case Utility was using its own truck and exercised complete control over the loading and transport of the structures, it was operating as an independent contractor. Case Utility rather than National Development Corp. should be held liable for the property damage and injuries caused by this act of negligence.

By definition, a person cannot be an employee and independent contractor at the same time. An employee, however, can act as an agent for another. Similarly, an independent contractor can serve as an agent of another in respect to a particular business dealing. Thus an independent contractor who is authorized to make contracts or enter into transactions for the principal is an agent. For example, the lawyer who is retained to try a case is an independent contractor, but simultaneously acts as an agent when authorized to negotiate with a third party for settlement of the case.

28-2. Kinds of Agents

Agents are generally classified according to the scope of their employment or the manner of their appointment.

A. General Agent

A *general agent* is a person who has been authorized, on behalf of a principal, to conduct all the principal's particular kind of business activity on a daily basis. In the exercise of the authority, the agent is expected to use discretion and judgment in performing delegated acts.

● Semlak, manager of a Reliable Oil Company service station, hired A-1 Painting Company to paint the interior office and work areas. Semlak also employed two extra attendants to monitor the self-service pumps. As a general agent for Reliable Oil Company, Semlak has the authority to take these independent actions which protect and promote the interests of Reliable Oil Company. He thereby binds his employer.

B. Special Agents

A *special agent* is a person who is authorized by an employer to carry out a single business transaction or a series of transactions without continuity of service. Examples are real estate brokers, lawyers, and auctioneers who are retained to do a specific job and whose authority is restricted to those acts necessary to accomplish it. A bailee may become an agent if authorized to buy or sell the bailed property on behalf of the bailor. A more detailed discussion of bailments is found in Chapter 18.

A *factor,* or commission merchant, is a special agent employed to sell merchandise consigned for that purpose. The factor has possession of the goods and sells them for and in behalf of a principal. A factor who guarantees the credit of a third party to a principal and guarantees the solvency of the purchaser and performance of the contract is known as a *del credere agent.* In the event of default, the *del credere* agent is liable to the principal.

● Lutz employed Saverine to act as her agent in selling merchandise. The contract of agency was for one year, and it included a guaranty by Saverine that Lutz would not suffer loss because of sales on credit that Saverine made with third persons. Merchandise valued at $12,000 was delivered to Malloy, who presented $2,000 in down payment and signed a promissory note for $10,000, payable in ninety days at 15 percent interest. Malloy declared bankruptcy fifteen days after the sale. Lutz sued Saverine. As a *del credere* agent, Saverine guaranteed the credit of Malloy and is liable to Lutz for the $10,000 balance.

A *gratuitous agent* is a person who promises to act for a principal without pay for service rendered, loss, or expense. Unlike an agency supported by a contract with consideration, in this form of employment or appointment, performance is not enforceable. Once gratuitous agents undertake the promised act, however, they become obligated to carry it out properly and completely.

28-3. Authority of Agent

Agents may perform only acts that have been authorized by the principal. Agents who exceed their delegated authority become personally liable. Unauthorized actions do not bind the principal unless they can be reasonably assumed by a third party to be within the scope of the agent's authority. Authority granted an agent may be express, implied, or apparent.

A. Express Authority

Express authority refers to the authority of an agent to perform the duties that are specifically stated in the contract of agency. It is voluntarily conferred on the agent by the principal, orally or in writing. Express authority may also be indicated by conduct, such as when a sales representative informs the principal of travel plans for the week and no objection to them is expressed.

B. Implied Authority

Implied authority is the authority of an agent to perform acts which are necessary or customary to carry out expressly authorized duties. It stems from a rea-

Part 7:
Agency
and
Employ-
ment

364

sonable effort of an agent to understand the meaning of the principal's words describing what the agent is to do. Implied authority can be described as *incidental authority* when the acts performed are reasonably necessary to carry out an express authority. For example, an agent would have incidental authority to contract for the repair of the principal's van that broke down while being used to deliver perishable products that the agent had express authority to sell and deliver. Implied authority may be described as *customary authority* when the agent acts in conformity with the general trade or professional practices of the business.

● Merritt, a real estate broker and general agent for Ventura Realty Company, has the express authority to represent property owners in contractual relations with potential buyers. Merritt then delegates this authority to three full-time and one part-time subagents, or salespersons. Although an agent generally does not have the authority to delegate authority to subagents, the custom and nature of the real estate business are such that the seller is presumed to expect that the authority given to Merritt will be exercised through salespersons.

C. Apparent Authority

Apparent authority refers to circumstances whereby a principal, by virtue of words or actions, leads a third party to believe that an agent has authority but no such authority was intended. It is a well-settled principle of agency law that actions of an agent taken within the scope of the agent's apparent authority are binding on a principal for purposes of liability to third parties. Section 8A of the *Restatement (Second) of Agency* confirms that this is so even when the agent disregards contrary instructions by the principal. Of course, the person with whom the agent is dealing must reasonably believe the agent has authority to so act, must have no notice of a lack of such authority, and must act or rely upon the agent's appearance of authority. Thus, once a principal clothes an agent with the semblance of authority, the principal cannot deny that the authority exists to the harm or prejudice of third parties who have acted or relied upon that appearance.

● Meeks parked his car in Poole's garage. Wishing to sell the car, Meeks gave the necessary title papers to Poole, but instructed Poole not to make a final sale without first consulting him regarding the price. Having found a prospect who offered a good price, Poole sold the car and transferred the title papers. Meek's act of giving the title papers to Poole would be viewed by the court as conduct that would reasonably lead a third party to conclude that Poole had apparent authority to sell the car. Thus Meeks could not rescind the sale, because he is bound by the contract made by his agent.

28-4. Creation of Agency Relationships

An agency is usually created by appointment or consent. It is sometimes created, however, by necessity, operation of law, estoppel, and ratification.

A. Agency by Appointment or Consent

The appointment of an agent may be oral or by conduct, unless required by state statute to be in writing. In a few states, the agent is required to have written authority where the contracts to be made by the agent come within the statute of frauds. This, as you recall, is a statutory provision requiring that certain kinds of contracts be proved by a proper writing. A written authorization of agency may be in the form of a letter, contract, or *power of attorney*. The latter is a written authority by a principal to an agent. The person holding a power of attorney is known as an attorney in fact. The major purpose of a power of attorney is to evidence the authority of the agent to third parties with whom the agent may deal.

A *universal agency* gives an agent the broadest powers. The agent is authorized by the principal to do every act which can be lawfully delegated during the term of the agency. The authority given is equivalent to an unrestricted power of attorney.

B. Agency by Necessity, Operation of Law, and Estoppel

An agency relationship may be created in several instances when there is no contractual relationship or mutual consent between parties. One such relationship arises from necessity. This form of agency is sometimes necessary to prevent loss to the principal due to unusual and emergency circumstances.

● Before departing on a vacation, Mosely left Owens in charge of his store, the House & Garden Shop. While Mosely was away, a severe wind and rain storm blew away part of the roof of the store. To protect the merchandise in the store from weather damage, Owens hired a contractor to make necessary roof repairs. A though this action was not within the scope of Owens's ordinary authority, it would be considered reasonable and appropriate in his capacity of agent by necessity.

The courts may rule that an agency by operation of law exists if it appears from the facts that a necessity or desired social policy is involved. A child to whom a parent has failed to provide the necessities of life may be declared by the court an agent of the parent for the purpose of purchasing necessaries the parent failed to provide. Under such an agency relationship, the parent would be bound by such contracts as long as they are reasonable.

● Gustavson, the father of three children, abandoned his family after placing an advertisement in the classified section of the local newspaper stating that he would no longer be responsible for any bills unless contracted by himself. Mrs. Gustavson bought food, clothing, and medical care for the children and herself, charging everything to her husband. Mrs. Gustavson is an agent by necessity, and her husband is responsible for contracts made by her for all reasonable necessaries of life.

The marital relationship does not, in itself, establish authority for one spouse to act for the other. However, if a wife or husband customarily permits the other to purchase items needed in the household, the appearance of authority to make such purchases can be implied, even though actual authority does not exist.

An *agency by estoppel* is created when one person is falsely represented to be an agent by the alleged principal, and a third party is injured by relying on this representation.

● Semlak, manager of the Reliable Oil Company service station, permitted an employee of A-1 Painting Company to use one of the uniforms worn by his station attendants. Without authority, the painter sold a new car battery to a customer at a

Part 7:
Agency
and
Employ-
ment

366

reduced price that was excessively low. Since he had let the painter give customers the impression that he was a regular employee, Semlak would be estopped from denying that the service station was liable on the contract for the battery or its replacement warranty.

An *agency by implication* exists when an agent performs acts that clearly indicate or imply to third parties that the agent is acting with the apparent authority of the principal. For example, if a restaurant manager asks an employee to look after the business in the manager's absence, a third party would assume the employee was the manager's agent in carrying out this function. The employee's acts, such as collecting bills or directing other restaurant workers in their duties, would clearly imply that the employee was acting with the apparent authority of the principal. On the surface, an agency by implication and an agency by estoppel appear much alike. Technically, however, they differ. An agency by implication is a real agency. Its existence is proved by the acts of the parties rather than by spoken words. An agency by estoppel is not an actual agency. The alleged principal has falsely misrepresented that an agency exists, and the law binds the principal for the representation.

C. Ratification

When a person approves an unauthorized act performed by an agent or an act done in the principal's name by a person who had no authority to act as an agent, *ratification* of the agent's actions results. Although ratification does not create agency, it has the effect of agency. It is the assertion by a person that an act which was not binding was done on his or her account and is viewed as if originally authorized. Certain conditions must be fulfilled for the ratification to be valid. The principal must intend to ratify, have the legal capacity to ratify, and have knowledge of all the material facts. The ratification must apply to the entire act, and the act must have been done in behalf of the principal.

The principal cannot accept the benefits of such a transaction and refuse to accept the obligations that are part of it. The principal becomes bound as though the agent had authority to so act.

● Cerone contracted for the purchase of a used car for Seymour, without her knowledge or consent. Cerone instructed the dealer to hold the car until directed to deliver it. When Seymour learned of the purchase, she notified the dealer to deliver the car at once. By this act, Seymour ratified the unauthorized purchase. Seymour could not subsequently refuse to accept the car. She is bound on the contract just as if Cerone had possessed full authority to make it.

Understanding Legal Terms

Define, identify, or explain the following terms:

agency	general agent	power of attorney	servant
agency by estoppel	incidental authority	principal	special agent
del credere agent	independent	ratification	third party
employee	contractor		
employer	master		
employment-at-will			

Questions for Review and Discussion

1. How is agency defined in the *Restatement (Second) of Agency?*

2. Explain the function of the three parties involved in the principal-agent relationship.

3. What is the main difference between the relationship of principal-agent and that of employer-employee?

4. Explain the principal element that differentiates an independent contractor from an employee.

5. Discuss the exceptions to the time-honored common-law doctrine of employment-at-will and the reason why courts and sympathetic juries have recently weakened the doctrine or set it aside.

6. Describe a special agent and the conditions under which a bailee may become a special agent.

7. Distinguish between express, implied, and apparent authority.

8. What is the extent of the principal's responsibility for third-party damages caused by an agent's disregard of a principal's instructions, while working within the scope of employment.

9. Explain the circumstances under which a principal may be estopped from denying an agency relationship.

10. Describe the conditions that must be fulfilled for an agency by ratification to be valid.

Analyzing Cases

1. Food Caterers, Inc., had a franchise agreement with Chicken Delight, Inc. The agreement permitted Food Caterers to use the name and the methods of operation of Chicken Delight and in turn regulated the manner in which Food Caterers could do business. However, while the franchise agreement regulated the standards under which business could be conducted, the two businesses otherwise were independent corporations with separate ownership, management, and employees.

Carfiro was employed by Food Caterers for the purpose of delivering hot chicken. There was no evidence that Carfiro was hired, paid, instructed by, or even known by Chicken Delight. However, the franchise agreement between Chicken Delight and Food Caterers did require the franchisee, Food Caterers, to deliver hot packaged food bearing the trademark "Chicken Delight" free of charge. In the course of making a delivery, Carfiro was involved in an accident that killed McLaughlin. The administrator of McLaughlin's estate brought suit naming Chicken Delight, Inc., the franchisor, as defendant. It was argued that Carfiro should be found to be an agent of Chicken Delight because Carfiro was acting for the benefit of that corporation.

Chicken Delight contended that the delivery of its hot food products by the employee of the franchisee was not sufficient to establish liability on its part. How should the court rule? Why? Is the question as to whether Carfiro was an agent of Chicken Delight one of fact or law? ● *Estate of McLaughlin v. Chicken Delight, Inc.,* 321 A.2d 456 (Conn. 1973)

2. The Caro Construction Corporation was awarded a contract to build a post office building in Golden, Colorado. At the time the contract was awarded, Nicholas Caro was sole stockholder. Shortly afterward, however, he was divorced from his wife, Betty, who was awarded ownership of 50 percent of the stock in the business.

Nicholas Caro contacted First National Bank of Denver to obtain financing in order to construct the post office building. The bank approved the loan on condition it would be signed by the corporation and by Nicholas and Betty Caro individually, as a guaranty against default. After the promissory note and personal guaranty were executed, the bank learned that the Caros had recently been divorced. To ensure that Betty Caro understood she had made herself personally liable, the bank requested she review the documents with her attorney. Although the attorney advised her that it had been a mistake to sign the guaranty, Betty Caro made no protest of her liability. The lawyer wrote to the bank that he had discussed the guaranty with Betty Caro and that she understood its significance. Betty Caro also signed another letter accepting the bank's request for an increase in the interest rate. The Caro Corporation then requested and received financing from the bank and proceeded with construction. While in the process of being built, the building collapsed. The bank sued Nicholas and Betty Caro as well as the Caro Construction Company.

At trial, Betty Caro contended that her husband had misrepresented the facts to her when he incorrectly told her she was bound by the guaranty and had no choice but to sign the bank's request modifying the terms of the agreement. She argued that her husband, in obtaining her signature on the original note and on the interest rate modification letter, through misrepresentation had acted as agent for the bank. Hence, the bank was chargeable with Nicholas Caro's misrepresentation. How should the court rule? Why? ● *First Nat. Bank of Denver v. Caro Const. Co., Inc.*, 508 P.2d 516 (Kan. 1973)

3. Hogan was the proprietor of Deep Woods Camp for Boys, Incorporated, which he operated in Brevant, North Carolina. While visiting Georgia, Hogan arranged to purchase a two-ton truck from Bill Walker Pontiac, located in Brunswick, Georgia. To save delivery charges, Hogan arranged with Walker Pontiac to pick up the truck himself from General Motors in Pontiac, Michigan. General Motors would not sell directly to a customer and insisted that if Hogan were to pick up the truck he must do so as an agent for Walker Pontiac. Telephone calls between Walker Pontiac and General Motors accomplished this result. After Hogan signed a receipt for the truck as agent of Walker Pontiac, it was released to him.

While driving the truck home and passing through Kentucky, Hogan fell asleep at the wheel. An accident ensued which took the life of Grant. Grant's estate sued, naming Bill Walker Pontiac among other parties. Kentucky statutes require that a master-servant or principal-agent relationship exist between the owner and the operator of a vehicle before liability can be imposed upon the owner. It was argued in district court that Hogan was Walker Pontiac's agent at the time of the accident and thus Walker Pontiac and its insurance company were liable for Hogan's admitted negligence. In this diversity-of-citizenship action, the court rejected this argument. On appeal, how should the court rule? Why? ● *Grant v. Bill Walker Pontiac-G.M.C., Inc.*, 523 F.2d 1301 (6th Cir. 1975)

4. The National Aeronautics and Space Administration (NASA) underwent a reduction in force for budgetary reasons. The reduction in force required that a specified number of employees be laid off. NASA's enabling act authorized it to use the services of both civil service employees and independent contractors, who in turn hired their own employees (contractor employees). The work provided by independent contractors included not only technical and scientific work but also such support functions as fire protection, security, and food and janitorial services. The independent contractors, not NASA, furnished the necessary management and personnel. Civil service regulations require that when a federal installation undergoes a reduction in force, employees of that installation be laid off only if they cannot be placed in alternative available positions. The reduction-in-force procedure resulted in the dismissal of NASA's own employees, while employees of independent contractors were retained.

Dismissed civil service employees and their union brought suit in district court. They contended that NASA employed many technical service workers as independent contractors, but exercised a degree of control which made them functionally employees of the United States. They alleged that such an arrangement violated the civil service laws (which specified the order of retention of employees during a reduction in force) and NASA's own statute (which provided that officers and employees be appointed in accordance with civil service laws). Thus, if the contracts with the independent contractors were for these reasons illegal, civil service employees should be permitted to take over the positions filled under the agreements with the contractors. The district court ruled favorably for the displaced civil service employees in a number of instances. The administrator of NASA brought an appeal to the court of appeals. How should the court of appeals hold? Why? ● *Lodge 1858, Am. Fed'n of Gov't Emp. v. Webb*, 580 F.2d 496, *cert. denied* 439 U.S. 927 (1978)

5. Stahl was having trouble with her Volkswagen. She brought it to the service station of LePage, where it was examined and the trouble diagnosed. LePage informed Stahl that he would not be able to do the work, but that his employee Donley wanted to take the job on his own and could make use of the garage facilities for this purpose. A new engine was required, and Donley installed the wrong engine. The entire job had to be done over at a cost of hundreds of dollars. Stahl brought suit against LePage. She argued that she should be allowed to recover against LePage for the misdeed of Donley, because Donley had apparent authority to act as LePage's agent. LePage disputed this, arguing that the facts did not warrant a finding of agency under any theory. How should the court find in this dispute? Why? ● *Stahl v. LePage*, 352 A.2d 682 (Vt. 1976)

6. An election was held at the Georgetown Dress Corp. to determine whether the employees of that corporation would be represented by a union. By a 184-105 vote, the union forces prevailed. Georgetown claimed the election was held in an atmosphere of coercion and intimidation which made a fair election impossible. An administrative law judge of the National Labor Relations Board

(NLRB) found that a series of coercive events had indeed taken place. Employees were threatened with violence, destruction of their property, and even death if they did not vote for the union. Under applicable law, these threats would require the election be held invalid if the union initiated the threats or was chargeable with them.

Testimony before the judge showed, however, that the threats originated not from the union but from a group called the In-Plant Organizing Committee. That committee consisted of a group of employees of the Georgetown Dress Corp. seeking to gain unionized status. The union itself did not organize or attempt to organize the workers of the plant. Instead, the In-Plant Organizing Committee, which was independent of the union, was formed for this purpose. It was, however, assisted by the union with some literature, occasional (but not regular) payment of expenses, and instructions on how to organize and obtain votes. The latter included specific instructions not to use violence or intimidation. The NLRB found the election proper. On appeal to the court of appeals, should the union be held chargeable with the misconduct of members of the In-Plant Organizing Committee and the election held invalid? Why? ● *NLRB v. Georgetown Dress Corp.*, 537 F.2d 1239 (4th Cir. 1976)

7. Castle Fabrics, Inc., engaged in a complicated series of transactions with Fortune Furniture Manufacturers, Inc., in which the former sold fabric to the latter. In the course of their dealings, a dispute arose as to the acceptability of the fabric received by Fortune. Fortune returned the fabric to Castle for credit. It believed it would receive full credit for the returned fabric. In fact, Castle resold the fabric at a loss of approximately $20,000. It gave Fortune only partial credit and sued for recovery of its loss.

While a number of UCC issues were presented, one of the major issues concerned the sending of a credit memorandum to Fortune by a Castle employee. It indicated Fortune would be given full credit for the goods. It was within the regular responsibilities of Castle's employees to send such credit memorandums; they had sent similar memorandums before on other occasions. Although on this occasion the employees were specifically instructed by management not to send the memorandum, a mistake occurred and it was sent anyway.

In court, Fortune contended it was entitled to rely on the memorandum and that it would not have returned the fabric if it had known it would be given $20,000 less than full credit. It claimed the employees that sent the memorandum were agents of Castle and thus Castle was chargeable with any mistake they made. Castle claimed it was not chargeable with the actions of its employees because they disobeyed specific instructions not to send the memorandum. How should the court resolve this issue? Why? ● *Castle Fabrics, Inc. v. Fortune Furniture Mfrs.*, 459 F.Supp. 409 (N.D. Miss. 1978)

8. The Bradleys were black prospective home buyers in Sumter, South Carolina. They called the John M. Brabham Agency, Inc., a real estate agency. They talked to Pate, a salesperson for the Brabham Agency and asked for an appointment to see a house at 2377 Tall Oak Road. The Bradleys had driven by the address and noticed a "for sale" sign of the Brabham Agency in the front yard. Pate refused to show the Bradleys the home, stating he was not interested in selling it to blacks and would rather lose the sale than show it to them. Pate had a relationship with the Brabham Agency in which the fee he received was divided between himself and the agency. In return he received office space, telephone and secretarial support, advertising, business cards, and use of the firm's broker's license.

The Fair Housing Act made it illegal for Pate to refuse to show the house to the Bradleys for racial reasons. The Bradleys brought suit for damages under the act against the John M. Brabham Agency, Inc. The agency responded that Pate was acting as an independent contractor and that therefore the agency was not responsible for his actions. How would the court hold in respect to the argument of the Brabham Agency? Explain why. ● *Bradley v. John M. Brabham Agcy., Inc.*, 463 F.Supp. 27 (D.S.C. 1978)

Chapter 29

Operation and Termination of Agency

Agency law is concerned with acts that are within and without the course and scope of an agent's actual or apparent authority while contracting with third parties on behalf of a purported principal. Such actions generally involve the liabilities of the principal, the authority of the agent, and the rights of third parties. And in the course of creating contracts, noncontractual wrongs (i.e., torts) are often the cause of agency litigation. The authority of an agent ceases to exist when the agency is terminated.

29-1. Principal, Agent, and Third-Party Relationship

The relationship between the agent and the principal establishes certain rights and obligations. They may be expressed in the contract or implied.

A. Obligations and Liabilities of Agent to Principal

In addition to the responsibilities stipulated in a written or oral contract, an agent owes other obligations to a principal. Violations in these obligations may allow the principal to begin a suit against the agent for appropriate recovery of any losses or damages or for tortious (wrongful) conduct.

1. Fiduciary. The agent has an implied *fiduciary* duty to act in the best interests of the principal at all times. This requires loyalty, trust, and confidence, in addition to the subordination of an agent's own interests to those of the principal. As such, an agent cannot compete with the principal, act on behalf of anyone whose interests conflict with those of the principal, or act on behalf of the third party against the principal.

● With his own personal funds, Yeager, manager of Compudata's service department, purchased 10,000 jumper wires (used for wiring panels) from Page Wire Products at a special discounted price. Each time Compudata replenished its inventory of jumper wires, Yeager accounted for the jumpers from his personal supply at the regular price. He would record the transaction as if the jumper wires were purchased from an acceptable supplier and pocket the difference. This practice represents a breach of the fiduciary relationship since agents employed to buy may not buy from themselves. This breach of duty would permit Compudata to sue to recover the profits made by Yeager.

2. Skill, Judgment, and Propriety. The agent who is paid by the principal must carry out the purpose of the agency so as not to bring disrepute upon the principal or business. Without prior approval, the agent should not take any action that subjects the principal to risk of expense or that reasonably appears unlikely to accomplish the objectives of the agency. An agent must conform to a standard of care that reflects public expectations. This requires the exercise of reasonable skill in performing duties for which the agent was employed; when the agent was hired as an expert, special skills must be exercised. The agent may be liable to the principal for losses resulting from personal neglect or incompetence.

● Thermotec sent a fractional-horsepower motor to Delco Motors for repair. When the motor was returned and installed on a plastic fabricating machine, it was discovered that the motor's speed had been reduced from 3,000 to 1,500 revolutions per minute. A number of acrylic sheets were damaged before the error was discovered. The shop supervisor for Delco Motors had miscalculated and could be held responsible to Delco Motors for failure to use ordinary prudence, skill, care, and diligence in performing the necessary repair to the motor.

3. Accounting. The agent must keep a true account of money or property belonging to the principal. The agent must give the principal an account within a reasonable period of time after money or property is received or disbursed. Funds held by the agent in trust for the principal must be held separate from funds belonging to the agent. Failure to keep several individual funds separate is known as confusion or *commingling*, and the agent may be held liable for any resulting losses.

● Moffat made c.o.d. deliveries for Taylor Rental Service. Each time a cash collection was made, Moffat would mix the money with his own. Should he fail to keep an accurate record of customers' c.o.d. payments or be unable to account for all money collected during the working day, Taylor Rental Service would have a right to demand all Moffat's commingled money.

4. Information. The agent has a duty to give the principal information obtained in the course of the agency which the agent knows the principal expects and desires. This duty of full disclosure of known facts bars agents from using secret information for their own benefit.

● Ludder, in her capacity of real estate broker for Seymour, learned that the principal's property was to be rezoned from single-family residential to commercial. Ludder did not share this information, which would increase the value of the property, with Seymour. Instead, she arranged the sale of the property to a friend at the asked-for price, with the understanding that she would share in the profits when the property was subsequently sold for commercial use. Ludder would be liable to Seymour in a suit for such profits made at the principal's expense.

5. Obedience to Instructions. The agent must obey all reasonable and legal instructions of the principal with respect to the matters entrusted to the agent. The principal who suffers loss as a result of the agent's failure to obey may sue the agent for contract breach or for tortious conduct.

Even a gratuitous agent must follow instructions or become responsible for any loss resulting from failure to do so.

B. Duties of Principal to Agent

The principal's duties to the agent may be expressed or implied by the terms of the contract or in tort law. Even when the agency contract is silent, there are obligations which a principal owes to an agent.

1. Compensation. The principal is under duty to pay an agent an agreed amount or the fair value of services that the agent is requested or permitted to perform. If the amount of compensation has not been expressly stated, the agent is entitled to a customary or reasonable sum of money. The principal's duty to compensate the agent exists whether the services rendered were authorized by agency contract or were ratified by the principal. The agent may not, however, recover compensation for illegal services, even though they were rendered at the request of the principal. A person who acts as agent for two or more parties to a contract with their knowledge is entitled to receive compensation from each. Contracts of dual agency are voidable, however, when the agent's representation of both is not known to each party.

● Fidelity Trust Company agreed to act as an agent for Fabrizio with the aim of procuring a loan. Without the knowledge or consent of Fabrizio, Fidelity Trust entered into an agreement with AMICA whereby AMICA would pay Fidelity Trust a finder's fee and a servicing fee in the event the loan was made. Fabrizio refused to pay the agreed fee for obtaining the loan commitment, claiming an unauthorized duality of agency. Judgment would be entered for Fabrizio.

2. Reimbursement. The principal has a duty to reimburse the agent for any money which the principal has expressly or impliedly authorized the agent to lay out on the principal's behalf. The agent cannot recover, however, for expenses due to the agent's own negligence. Recovery is also barred when expenses incurred by an agent are not necessary in the discharge of the agency for the benefit of the principal.

● Starrett, while in Houston on business for Bicor Machinery, Inc., decided to attend a professional football game. Although his attendance at the game was made possible by the business trip, the expense was of a personal nature and would not be considered reimbursable.

3. Indemnification. A principal is under a duty to *indemnify* an agent (i.e., secure against loss or damage) in accordance with the terms of the employment agreement. In the absence of terms to the contrary, the principal has a duty to indemnify the agent for payments authorized or made necessary in carrying out the principal's affairs. The duty of indemnity also holds when the agent suffers a loss which, because of the agency relation, the principal should in fairness bear.

Unless otherwise agreed, the principal does not have a duty to indemnify an agent for monetary loss or other harms, not of benefit to the principal, arising from unauthorized acts or from the agent's negligence. The duty to indemnify is avoidable if the loss results from an action which the agent knew to be illegal.

Although a private employer generally has a common-law right of indemnity against an employee whose negligent actions have made the employer liable,

Part 7:
Agency
and
Employ-
ment

374

this is not the case when the federal government is the principal. The U.S. Supreme Court has ruled that it could find no intention on the part of Congress to allow such a suit by the federal government against one of its employees.

Public policy also requires employers to indemnify employees for personal injury in the course of and arising out of employment, except for self-inflicted injury and intoxication. State workers' compensation laws hold that the cost of paying for such injury should be a part of the operating expense of the business.

4. Not to Interfere With Agent's Work. A principal who has contracted to give an agent an opportunity to work has a duty to refrain from unreasonably interfering with that work. The duty exists both where the agent's compensation is proportionate with the work done and where a fixed sum is paid for the agent's time. In either case, if the interference constitutes a material breach of contract, the agent may terminate the relation and has the right to receive the amount of any net losses caused and gains prevented by the principal's breach.

● Yarus appointed Silver to act for her as an attorney in partition proceedings, contracting to compensate him if, but only if, the proceedings were successful. Yarus prevented the success of the proceedings. In a jurisdiction in which it is a breach of contract for a client to discharge an attorney without cause, Yarus has committed a breach of contract and would be liable to Silver for the gains prevented by the breach.

C. Contract Liability

The agency relationship has a significant impact on contract law.

1. Agent as Party to Contract. To avoid contract liability to a third party, the agent must disclose the agency relationship to that party. The agent must also have authorization to act on the principal's behalf. And when a written contract with a third party is signed by the agent, the agent's capacity in the transaction must be disclosed. Failure to do so would bar the agent from giving oral evidence (under the parol-evidence rule) that would indicate the third party knew the agent was acting on behalf of the principal. For example, the agent who signed a negotiable instrument to a third party as maker or drawer would be held liable unless the principal's name appears somewhere on the instrument. The principal's name followed by the agent's signature and title would be sufficient protection.

2. Agent's Warranty. When acting in a representative capacity for a principal with a third party, the agent makes an *implied warranty* that he or she has authority to so act. The agent who does not have authority or exceeds the scope of authority becomes liable to the third party for damages.

The agent does not make an implied warranty to the third party that the principal is capable of being contractually bound. The fact that a third party is willing to contract with a principal acting through an agent indicates that the third party has some knowledge of the principal. Thus, an agent representing a principal who is insane or a minor does not impliedly warrant the contractual capacity of the principal. And the agent is not liable for nonperformance by the principal.

The contractual authority of public officials is part of the public record. They generally assume no personal contractual liability when acting as agents of the government.

3. Principal's Contract Liability. The third party's knowledge of a principal's identity determines whether the principal is disclosed or undisclosed. A *disclosed principal* is a person who is known or who should be known by a third party to be a principal of the agent. A contract made with a third party on behalf of a disclosed principal is between the principal and the third party. The principal, not the agent, is liable for its nonperformance.

When the identity of the principal is reasonably not known to the third party or it appears an agent is acting on his or her own behalf, the principal is known as an *undisclosed principal*. The agent and the third party are each directly liable to the other in respect to the terms of any resulting contract. If and when the principal becomes known to the third party, the principal is liable. The third party may then elect to hold either the principal or the agent responsible, but not both. The liability stems from the principal's authorization of the agent to act in behalf of the principal. Hence, each of the three parties to the contract —agent, principal, and third party—is liable as a contracting party.

● Broderick contracted, on a commission arrangement, for the services of Computer Sciences Corporation. He was acting for an undisclosed principal, Die-Craft Tool Company. Computer Sciences refused to carry out the terms of the contract. It called for the remote application of computers to improve payroll, accounts receivable, and accounts payable for Die-Craft. Broderick should be permitted to sue as though he were the principal. In the event Broderick should breach the contract, Computer Sciences can elect to hold either Broderick (agent) or Die-Craft Tool Company (principal) liable, not both.

D. Tort and Criminal Liability

The three parties to an agency contract are each liable for wrongful acts that injure the person or property of one of the others. In addition to the liabilities which contract law imposes upon a principal or employer for the acts of an authorized agent or employee to third parties, there are liabilities for torts and related business crimes.

Ordinarily, the principal or employer is *vicariously liable* (substitutively liable) to a third party for wrongful acts of the agent or employee while in the principal's employ and during the ordinary course of business. The agent who does a wrongful act, however, is not relieved from liability even though acting at the command of the principal or on account of the principal. The wrongful act may be one of negligence, intentional tort, fraud or misrepresentation, or violation of government regulations. When the act is a threat to private interest or offends it, a civil lawsuit for damages may result. Criminal prosecution may be instigated when the act violates a public law.

1. Liability for Torts. Where a principal authorized an agent to commit a tortious act, the principal is liable to the damaged third party. If the agent acted without the principal's authorization, the principal is still generally held liable if the act was committed within the scope of the agent's authority. A wrongful act committed by an agent while not under contract to the principal or not on the job does not impose third-party liability on the principal.

Part 7:
Agency
and
Employ-
ment

376

The legal justification for imposing liability is found in the doctrine of *respondeat superior* ("let the superior respond"). It is founded on the logic that the principal/employer has the right to control or exercise control over the physical conduct of employees who are acting in the scope of their employment. In making this determination, the courts generally hold that the tortious harm to third parties and property is a hazard of doing business, the cost of which the principal's or employer's business should bear.

● Donoughue, a passenger in a taxicab owned by LaPenna Company, brought a suit for damages suffered when the taxi driver assaulted her. Donoughue argued that a common carrier is liable to a passenger who is assaulted by one of its employees before the transportation has been completed, under the doctrine of *respondeat superior*. The court should hold for Donoughue. The taxi driver's willful and intentional misconduct was directly related and incidental to the performance of duties for which the driver was employed. LaPenna Company would have the right to seek recovery against the driver for any losses it sustains as a result of the wrongful act.

Whether the principal or employer is liable to a third party for the torts committed by an agent or employee does not affect the agent's or employee's liability. The *tortfeasor*, the person who actually commits the tort, is always liable to the victim. The liability of employees or agents to third parties for misdoings (i.e., *misfeasance*) includes all acts a person might lawfully perform. In the absence of a legal obligation to act, however, neither agent or employee is liable for not doing anything (i.e., *nonfeasance*). Having no duty to third parties, an agent or employee is not liable for total neglect of duty or for failure to do what ought to be done.

In addition to the liability imposed by the doctrine of *respondeat superior*, the principal or employer may be held for damages to third parties due to personal negligence in conducting business by means of employees or agents. Such negligence or recklessness may stem from giving improper or ambiguous orders or from failing to make proper regulations. The principal or employer is also liable for damages to third parties for the employment of improper persons in work involving risk of harm to others and in the supervision of the activity.

2. Liability for Crimes. A principal or employer may be subject to penalties under the rules of criminal law for acts done by an employee or other agent. In some of the minor crimes, many regulatory statutes do not require intent to violate them. Principals or employers are generally held liable for the conduct of employees and agents acting on their behalf or conducting transactions of the kind for which they are employed. Thus, at common law a person authorizing another to do or to say something which constitutes a criminal libel or a public nuisance may be subject to a fine.

In statutory crimes, the same result follows. Illustrations of such statutes are those which penalize the sale of impure food or alcoholic beverages. A principal or employer is normally penalized for the violation of such statutes by employees or agents acting in the scope of employment, even though they acted disobediently.

Apart from statute, an employer or principal is not subject to a penalty for an unauthorized crime committed by an ordinary employee in the scope of employment, if the basis for liability is a specific criminal intent. However, an employer may be penalized for the acts of advisory or managerial persons acting in the scope of employment, unless they act in disobedience of instructions and not for the purpose of serving the employer.

3. Federal Tort Claims Act. The federal government is liable under the Federal Tort Claims Act whenever a federal employee harms a third party or private property while driving a motor vehicle in the course of employment. Under this legislation, the federal employee is exempted from all resulting liability.

29-2. Termination of Agency

The agency agreement may be terminated by contract limitations and acts of the parties or by operation of law.

A. Termination by Acts of the Parties

Both principal and agent may terminate an agency agreement by their acts.

1. Mutual Agreement. Created by common accord, the agency relationship may be terminated by mutual agreement of principal and agent.

2. Fulfillment of Purpose. The agency may terminate at the end of a specified period of time. Agencies created for a particular purpose also terminate automatically upon accomplishment of the purpose. Thus, if several real estate agents have been authorized to sell a house and one succeeds in that task, the authority of the other agents is automatically terminated.

3. Revocation or Renunciation. The principal or the agent usually has the power (not necessarily the right) at any time to terminate the agency relationship. Acting with or without cause, the principal may terminate by simply recalling the agent's authority to act (i.e., *revocation*). Even though the principal's act of revocation may be a violation of contract, the agent's authority is terminated. Agents may terminate by simply giving notice to principals that they are quitting (i.e., *renunciation*). Unless the terms of the agency agreement permit termination "at will," agents and principals who end their relationship may be liable for damages resulting from the violation of the contractual promise.

B. Termination by Operation of the Law

The termination of the agency agreement by operation of law results when events make the continuance of the agency impossible or impractical. Termination by operation of the law occurs in the following ways.

1. Death. The death of the principal or agent terminates the agency, even without notice. Thus, any agreement made between the agent and third party is ineffective upon the death of the principal. Although the agent may be liable to third parties for breach of the implied warranty, third parties cannot recover from the estate of the principal because the contract was not binding.

2. Insanity. Insanity of either a principal or an agent usually terminates the authority of the agent. A few states have held that the agent has authority to bind the principal who becomes insane, if the third party has no knowledge of the insanity.

Part 7:
Agency
and
Employ-
ment

378

3. Bankruptcy. The bankruptcy of either party ends the agency. In case of the bankruptcy of the principal, the agency is ended because title to the principal's estate is vested in a trustee for the benefit of creditors. An exception would be a doctor or attorney who has been acting for a principal prior to bankruptcy, or an artist who has completed 75 percent of a painting for the principal.

4. Destruction of Subject Matter. The destruction or loss of the subject matter of the agency automatically ends the agency. Destruction of a house by fire ends the real estate broker's agency to sell the property. Imprisonment of the agent makes performance impossible and terminates the agency. In such cases, the agent is not relieved of an action on the agency agreement for damages to the principal. In addition, the statute of limitations against such actions will not be in force while the agent is confined to prison.

5. War. The agent's authority to act on behalf of the principal ends if an outbreak of war makes the parties alien enemies or makes the agent's authorized actions hazardous.

6. Changed Circumstances. The authority of the agent is terminated by notice or knowledge of a change in business conditions or values that substantially affect the agent's exercise of authority. An agent's loss of a license required to conduct the principal's business ends the authority of the agent. A change in the law which causes authorized acts to be illegal also terminates the agent's authority.

C. Agency Coupled With an Interest

An agency agreement in which the agent is given an interest in the substance of the agency in addition to the amount of compensation for services is said to be an *agency coupled with an interest*. A principal lacks power to revoke agencies of this kind without the consent of the agent. Such agencies, sometimes called *irrevocable agencies*, arise in situations where a principal allows an agent to sell property or collect rent as a means of liquidating a debt to the agent. The agent deducts a commission and applies the proceeds to the credit of a debt that is owed by the principal.

● Wong contracted with Economy Sales Company, on a 30 percent commission arrangement, for an exclusive five-year agency in a designated area for the sale of vacuum cleaners. A $1,000 check was deposited with Economy Sales as evidence of Wong's good faith. The money was to be returned to Wong from the proceeds of sales of the vacuum cleaners. Economy Sales attempted to revoke the agency, claiming dissatisfaction with the sales effort made by Wong. Since Wong, in addition to his interest as agent, had an interest in getting back the $1,000 advance from the proceeds of the sales, Economy Sales could not revoke the agency.

D. Notice of Termination to Third Parties

The principal should give prompt notice of the termination of an agency by acts of the parties to all parties who may be aware of the agency. Failure to do so may leave the agent with apparent authority which binds the principal contractually to third parties. Those parties with whom the agent has been dealing must be informed individually by oral or written communication that the agency is terminated. A public notice in a newspaper of general circulation is sufficient notice to all others.

When the termination of an agency results from the operation of law, notice need not be given to third parties. The courts generally hold that agency terminations due to death, insanity, or bankruptcy receive adequate publicity through newspapers and public records. No additional notice need be given by the principal.

E. Rights and Duties After Termination

Unless otherwise agreed, after the termination of the agency, agents may compete with the principal. Terminated agents have a duty to the principal not to use, for their own benefit in competition with the principal, trade secrets or confidential matters given to them only for the principal's use. However, agents are entitled to use general information concerning the method of business of the principal and the names of customers retained in memory, if not acquired in violation of their duty. In most states, contracts by agents not to compete with their principal during such time as may reasonably be necessary for the protection of the principal are valid. Such a contract must not, however, impose an undue hardship on the agent.

● Fowler employed Ross as a sales representative in a mercantile business for five years. As part of the contract of employment, Ross promised never to compete with Fowler within that state. In most jurisdictions, an agreement which imposes such unreasonable restraint upon an agent can be reformed to operate within reasonable limits.

Understanding Legal Terms

Define, identify, or explain the following terms.

accounting	fiduciary	*respondeat superior*	tortfeasor
agency coupled with	indemnify	revocation	undisclosed
an interest	nonfeasance	scope of	principal
commingling	reimbursement	employment	vicariously liable
disclosed principal	renunciation		

Questions for Review and Discussion

1. Explain the fiduciary duty that arises out of the agency relationship.

2. What duties other than fiduciary are imposed upon the agent in compliance with the agency contract relationship?

3. Describe the principal's primary obligations to an agent who is acting within the scope of actual or apparent authority.

4. What is the agent's implied warranty to third parties when acting in a representative capacity for a principal?

5. Discuss the contract liability of a disclosed principal and that of an undisclosed principal.

6. Explain the tort liability of the three parties to an agency agreement when the wrongful act of one injures the person or property of one of the others.

7. Explain the extent of liability imposed on a master, employer, or principal by the doctrine of *respondeat superior*.

8. In what ways may the agency relationship be terminated?

9. What is meant by an agency coupled with an interest and how does its existence affect the ability of the principal to revoke an agency?

10. Discuss the notice required when the termination of an agency results from acts of the parties.

Analyzing Cases

1. Mularchuk was employed as a part-time reserve officer for the Borough of Keansburg, New Jersey. In this capacity, Mularchuk wore a regular police uniform with badge and carried a nightstick and a revolver in a holster. He was generally assigned less difficult tasks than the regular police officers. He was never given any training, nor was he required to submit to any training with respect to the revolver he carried. In addition to the part-time job as a reserve officer, Mularchuk was employed as produce manager of a local supermarket.

Late one night, McAndrew, a seventeen-year-old New Jersey resident, had car trouble and called a tow truck to assist him. Although the tow truck completed its task, the amount of money the driver demanded was considered exhorbitant by McAndrew. The amount was also more than either he or his friends had available. A quarrel followed. Officer Mularchuk proceeded to arrest some of the participants. In the course of events, Mularchuk shot and seriously injured McAndrew. In court, Mularchuk's testimony as to the exact circumstances under which McAndrew was shot differed from a statement he had given to the prosecutor. The jury did not regard Mularchuk's defense as very substantial and found the shooting and serious injury of McAndrew to be unjustified. A judgment was issued against Mularchuk, which he was unable to satisfy. McAndrew's attempt to sue the Borough of Keansburg was rejected by the trial court, which held that Keansburg, as a municipal corporation, was immune from suit. How would the New Jersey supreme court rule on the questions of whether Mularchuk was an agent or servant of the municipality and whether it should be held liable under the doctrine of *respondeat superior*? Why? ● *McAndrew v. Mularchuk*, 162 A.2d 820 (N.J. 1960)

2. Granahan, representing himself as Advance Masonry Company, contacted Delaware Valley Equipment Co., Inc., seeking to purchase a forklift truck. Granahan explained that he needed the forklift immediately on a job site where he was a masonry subcontractor. It was arranged that the forklift would be delivered and that the $28,832 sale price would be invoiced to Advance Masonry. When Delaware Valley Equipment failed to receive payment and inquired, Granahan said that financing for the transaction had been turned down by his bank. The forklift subsequently was repossessed. But when Delaware Valley Equipment was unable to sell it, the company sued Granahan for damages resulting from the breach of contract. Granahan defended by arguing that the contract of sale was between Delaware Valley Equipment and Advance Masonry, Inc., a Pennsylvania corporation, which was not a party to this suit. Granahan contended that he was not personally liable on the contract, but only an agent of Advance Masonry, Inc. Delaware Valley Equipment argued that it was never informed that Granahan was acting as agent for Advance Masonry, Inc., and that it had every reason to believe the transaction was with Granahan personally. Delaware Valley Equipment emphasized that it had no notice of the existence or identity of Advance Masonry, Inc. It pointed out that its

invoice was addressed to "Advance Masonry" and not to "Advance Masonry, Inc." How should the court dispose of Granahan's defense? Why? ● *Delaware Val. Equipment Co., Inc. v. Granahan*, 409 F.Supp. 1011 (E.D. Pa. 1976)

3. Gooding, a farmer, possessed a policy of automobile liability insurance issued by Southern Farm Bureau. The policy contained some ambiguous and contradictory language concerning the exact circumstances under which the insurance would be in force. Gooding was involved in an accident and was sued by the injured party for personal injuries. Southern Farm Bureau contended that it was not liable for the accident as the precise conditions described in the insurance contract were not met. Gooding sued both Southern Farm Bureau and Rodman, the issuing agent, claiming the company and its agent were liable if the injured victim prevailed against him. Southern Farm Bureau and Rodman in turn sued each other, insisting that the other was liable for any possible recovery.

The supreme court of Arkansas ultimately found that Gooding was negligent in causing the victim's injuries, that the injury was properly covered by the issued policy, and that Southern Farm Bureau as the insurance company was liable for the indemnification of Gooding. The court held that Rodman as the issuing agent had no liability to Gooding in either tort or contract. Rodman therefore was an innocent victim drawn into the litigation by the conduct of Southern Farm Bureau in drafting an ambiguous policy. How should the Arkansas supreme court rule in respect to Rodman's reimbursement from Southern Farm Bureau (his principal) for attorney fees in successfully defending the Gooding claim against him? Why? ● *Southern Farm Bur. Cas. Ins. Co. v. Gooding*, 565 S.W.2d 421 (Ark. 1978)

4. The *S.S. Unicoi* was a ship owned by the United States Maritime Commission, an agency of the United States government. It was operated under contract for the commission by the Roosevelt Steamship Co., a private corporation. Brady, a United States customs inspector, was fatally injured when a ladder he was climbing broke while the vessel was docked at a pier in New York City. Brady's widow sued the operator of the vessel to recover damages for the benefit of herself and the children. The suit, brought in the New York supreme court, was removed to the federal district court and ultimately reached the U.S. Supreme Court. How should the Supreme Court rule on the question of whether Brady's widow can sue the operator of the *S.S. Unicoi*, the agent, or the United States Maritime Commission, the principal? If the operator of the vessel should be held liable on a theory of negligence, must the United States Maritime Commission as principal indemnify the operator as agent? Why? ● *Brady v. Roosevelt Steamship Co.*, 317 U.S. 575 (1943)

5. Gilman, an employee of the United States, driving a government automobile while in the course of employment, collided with the car of Darnell. Darnell sued the United States, alleging negligence of its employee Gilman and liability of the United States under the doctrine of *respondeat superior*. Darnell collected a judgment of $5,500. The United States sued its employee Gilman, arguing he must indemnify the United States since it was Gilman's negligence which caused the loss to the principal. (Gilman was also an agent of the United States, since all employees are usually considered agents of the government.) On request for review, should the U.S. Supreme Court allow the United States to collect indemnification from Gilman for the loss? Why? ● *United States v. Gilman*, 347 U.S. 507 (1954)

6. Davis, an attorney, closed a loan for the purchase of a residence from Miller Builders & Developers. Davis disbursed the proceeds of the sale to several parties by check. One check was made payable to the Louisiana

Bank & Trust Company to pay off and cancel a mortgage on the property sold.

Davis's employee wrote a deposit slip to deposit the Miller check in Miller's account in the Commercial National Bank. Through negligence, both the check made payable to Miller and the check payable to Louisiana Bank & Trust were placed on the same deposit slip. On the back of both checks, Davis's employee wrote "for deposit to the account of Miller." The check made payable to Louisiana Bank & Trust was never properly indorsed. Commercial National Bank, nevertheless, credited the money to the account of Miller.

When Louisiana Bank & Trust foreclosed its mortgage, Davis sued both Miller and Commercial National Bank. The bank argued that it had acted as Davis's agent to collect the check. The trial court found against Davis. The court held that by preparing and submitting the deposit slip, Davis made Commercial National Bank his agent. On appeal, how should the court of appeal of Louisiana dispose of Davis's claim against Commercial National Bank? Why? ● *Davis v. Miller Builders & Developers, Inc.*, 340 So.2d 409 (La. 1976)

7. Holiday Food Co., Inc., is a Connecticut corporation which sells and delivers frozen food and associated products. Its customers are solicited by telephone, referrals, and television and newspaper advertising. The names and addresses of several hundred customer prospects were compiled into a customer list. The list was kept on the desk of the owner-president's secretary and was accessible to Holiday Food's employees.

Munroe was employed as a Holiday Food sales representative. He never used or even examined Holiday Food's customer list, although he knew of its availability to him. He customarily was given various names of potential customers from the list. Munroe compiled these names in a personal notebook in which he kept records of sales, commissions, and customer reorder dates. Holiday Food's owner-president knew of this customer notebook and never objected to its existence or use by Munroe.

During Munroe's term of employment by Holiday Food, he had refused to sign a restrictive covenant not to compete in the event he terminated his employment. After resigning his employment, Munroe retained his customer notebook and subsequently organized his own frozen food delivery service in direct competition with Holiday Food. Some of the customers listed in the notebook had become Munroe's personal friends during his employment with Holiday Food. Munroe contacted these people, seeking their business and referrals for his newly formed company. Holiday Food objected and brought suit against Munroe. The company argued that the customer list was a trade secret. It also argued that any customer with whom an employee has contact while employed by a principal can never become a customer of a terminated employee who becomes a competitor. At the time of the lawsuit, Munroe had successfully sold his services to eight or nine customers with whom he had first made contact while still employed by Holiday Food. How should this case be disposed of? Why? ● *Holiday Food Co. v. Munroe*, 426 A.2d 814 (Conn. 1981)

8. Marchant was a passenger in an automobile that collided with a gravel truck owned by Columbia County, Oregon. Marchant alleged negligence and brought action for personal injuries against Clark, the driver of the truck. The complaint of Marchant was that Clark was operating the truck on the left side of the road. Clark defended by stating he had been ordered to so operate the truck by his employer.

At the close of the trial, the judge instructed the jury that Clark was an employee of Columbia County and, as an employee, was not in charge of the road improvement in which he was engaged. The judge reminded the jury that the defendant had operated the truck on the left side of the road, following the instructions of the employer which were conveyed by the road supervisor. The judge instructed the jury that if it should conclude that Clark was instructed by the employer to operate the truck as he did, even if such action was negligent, Clark as an employee would not be responsible for the negligence. Rather, the responsible parties would be Clark's employer and the supervisor who conveyed the instructions.

The jury returned a verdict in favor of Clark. Marchant moved for a new trial, contending that the instructions to the jury were not a correct statement of the law. The jury therefore may have decided the case employing improper legal standards. The case ultimately reached the Oregon supreme court. How should the court dispose of the case? Why? ● *Marchant v. Clark*, 273 P.2d 541 (Or.S. 1960)

9. Upton purchased two tracts of farmland near Effingham, Illinois, subject to a written lease with Suckow, who was to continue as a tenant. Shortly after acquiring the farm, Upton met with Suckow and discussed the necessity of constructing a low water bridge between the two tracts. The possibility of removing a hedgerow on the property in order to provide sufficient work for a bulldozer contractor was also discussed. Suckow subsequently contacted Johnston, who reluctantly agreed to accept the job after Suckow guaranteed that there would be a sufficient amount of work to make the job economically feasible. Upton was present at the farm on the day Johnston began bulldozing. A few weeks later, Upton paid for concrete that he had earlier instructed Suckow to purchase for use in the construction of the bridge.

A few weeks later, Johnston presented a bill to Suckow for $760 for the bridge construction and the removal of the hedgerow. He was told by Suckow that the bill would be forwarded to Upton. Thereafter, a long series of telephone conversations took place between Johnston, Suckow, and Upton. According to the testimony of Suckow and Johnston, Upton promised to pay the bill after financial troubles that he was facing were cleared up. Johnston eventually received only $300 from Upton. Johnston sued Suckow for the remaining $460 and was awarded a favorable judgment. Suckow then, in turn, sued Upton for indemnification (reimbursement) of the $460 and for recovery of investigation expenses and attorney fees incurred in defending the complaint brought by Johnston. Suckow recovered a judgment against Upton for $782.50. Upton contested his liability for reimbursement to Suckow. How should the appellate court dispose of this case? Why? ● *Johnston v. Suckow*, 370 N.E.2d 650 (Ill. Spp. 3d 1977)

Chapter 30   Law of Employment

To a great extent, the law of employment is determined by federal and state statutes. The laws that regulate wages and hours, equal employment opportunity, safe working conditions, indemnification, social security, and retirement are discussed in this chapter.

30-1. Wages and Hours

Early efforts to regulate employees' wages and hours of work were held by the courts to violate the employer's right to make contracts free of limitations. Gradually, the idea that employment contracts were subject to reasonable restrictions gained judicial support.

A shift in thinking came when the U.S. Supreme Court upheld the right of state governments to set minimum conditions of employment for women and children. In *West Coast Hotel v. Parrish,* the Court ruled in part that "freedom of contract is a qualified, not an absolute right." This reinterpretation of the due process clause of the Constitution's Fourteenth Amendment recognized reasonable regulation in the interests of health, safety, morals, and welfare of the people as due process. In short, state governments may interfere with freedom of contract in order to set minimum standards of employment needed to protect the worker's health or safety and to avoid harm to the public welfare.

The path was thus cleared for Congress to begin to regulate hours and wages for workers in firms which produce goods sold across state borders. One significant result is that today about 70 percent of the states have minimum wage laws or wage boards which fix wage rates on an industry-wide basis. An equal number of states have laws regulating daily or weekly hours to a maximum of eight hours per day, forty-eight or less hours per week, or both.

The principal federal laws affecting wages are (*a*) the Fair Labor Standards Act, as frequently amended; (*b*) the Walsh-Healey Act, which applies to government contracts; (*c*) the Davis-Bacon and Service Contract Acts; and (*d*) the Portal to Portal Act, which defines when compensable time starts and stops.

A. Fair Labor Standards Act

Congress passed the Fair Labor Standards Act (FLSA) in 1938. Commonly referred to as the Wage and Hour Act, the FLSA established standards for a minimum wage, overtime pay, and child labor. Its purpose was to bar from interstate and foreign commerce goods produced under conditions harmful to minimum standards of living, health, and general well-being.

1. Minimum Wages. The current minimum wage requirements of the FLSA for general industry are fairly clear. Beginning January 1, 1981, employers engaged in commerce or in the production of goods must pay employees not less than $3.35 an hour in any workweek. Because the act is amended periodically, the Wage and Hour Division of the U.S. Department of Labor should be consulted regarding the most up-to-date minimum wage rate provisions.

2. Overtime. The FLSA requires overtime to be paid for hours worked in excess of forty hours per week, or eight hours per day in the case of a government contract worker. The general rule is that the employer must pay nonexempt employees not less than $1\frac{1}{2}$ times their regular rate of pay for overtime. And the rate from which the overtime rate is determined must include any incentive payments or bonuses that are received during the period. When time off the job is given in return for overtime work, it must be granted at $1\frac{1}{2}$ times the number of hours worked as overtime. The FLSA does not require overtime pay for work performed on Saturdays, Sundays, holidays, or for the sixth or seventh days in a week, unless such work caused the total work performed to exceed forty hours in a workweek.

3. Exemptions. The FLSA provided for exemptions from coverage. One of the most common exemptions stems from the overtime provision relating to *exempt* and *nonexempt* employees. Only the nonexempt group (nonmanagement personnel) must be paid overtime. Exempt employees (managerial, administrative, and professional personnel) are not covered by the minimum wage and overtime provisions of the FLSA. A key test for exempting this group of employees is a weekly salary of at least $250. Exempt workers are further identified as those who manage and direct the work of two or more other employees. At least 50 percent of their primary duties must be in the performance of office or nonmanual work relating to the operations of the company or in the performance of work requiring scientific or specialized study. Legal problems arise when disgruntled exempt employees decide to sue for back pay. In such actions, an analysis of the employee's duties is required to determine whether the person was truly exempt or nonexempt and entitled to a recovery of overtime pay. The determination usually hinges on the percent of the employee's time spent on work not directly related to the activity that placed the employee in the exempt category, and on certain presumptions about the compensation.

● Stockman was employed as a plant supervisor. He spent 20 percent of his time directing the work of three subordinates and 80 percent of his time operating plant equipment. He was paid a salary of $260 a week. Since Stockman's salary was more than $250 a week, he would qualify as an exempt employee. This would probably be the ruling even though less than 50 percent of Stockman's time was spent performing nonexempt work.

Nearly a third of the labor force is excluded from FLSA coverage. In this category are state, local, and federal employees; self-employed persons; and members of the armed forces. Other excluded groups of personnel include outside salespeople, many retail and service workers, domestic service workers, and workers in agriculture. Handicapped workers, messengers, students, and apprentices are not covered by FLSA provisions. These workers may be paid less than minimum wages, provided the employer obtains a certificate of approval from the Wage and Hour Division of the Department of Labor.

Part 7:
Agency
and
Employ-
ment

386

4. Child Labor. Sixteen is the minimum age for employment in nonhazardous work. Minors between the ages of fourteen and sixteen, in accordance with various regulations, may be employed in a few occupations such as office and clerical work, cashiering, selling, and dispensing gasoline. Minors between fourteen and sixteen, however, cannot be employed in occupations involving the operation of machines or work in rooms where processing and manufacturing take place. Minors under fourteen years of age may be employed on farms and by parents, outside school hours, provided the work is nonhazardous. Minors may sometimes work for less than the minimum wage to gain experience where opportunities are limited and a savings to the employer results.

● Ansley, a fifteen-year-old, was employed as a roofer helper. He carried bundles of roofing shingles and supplies up and down extension ladders to workers engaged in waterproofing roofs. He worked four hours a day, six days a week, outside of school hours, and was paid $80.40. A school official charged the work was hazardous and thus violated the provisions of the FLSA which regulate child labor. The attorney general would rule the work to be hazardous. In a willful violation of the provisions of the FLSA, the employer would be subject to a criminal prosecution and a fine of up to $10,000.

The regulations governing child labor are long and detailed. Employers can protect themselves from unintentional violations by getting a certificate (as prescribed in the regulations) that the youthful person is above the minimum age allowed for the job.

B. Other Federal Laws Affecting Wages and Hours

The Walsh-Healey Act, which applies to government contracts, requires overtime pay for hours worked in excess of eight per day. The Davis-Bacon Act covers minimum wages paid to workers engaged in public works contracts worth more than $2,000. The Portal to Portal Act defines exactly when compensable time starts and stops; it provides that employees need not be paid for transportation from their home to their job or for time spent after leaving a work station.

30-2. Equal Employment Opportunity

A variety of federal and state statutes, executive orders, and federal guidelines, as well as court decisions and rulings, prohibit discrimination in employment. While some confusion on several key issues awaits final court clarification, the greater part of the equal employment opportunity area is quite clear.

A. Civil Rights and Equal Employment Acts

The Civil Rights Act of 1964, as amended by the Equal Employment Act of 1972, was enacted to assure equality of employment opportunity. Title VII of the Civil Rights Act makes it unlawful for anyone acting in interstate commerce who employs fifteen or more regular employees to practice discrimination in hiring or employment practices. Employers, unions, and employment agencies may not refuse to hire, discharge, or restrict the employment status of any person because of race, color, religion, sex, or national origin.

Chapter
30:
Law of
Employ-
ment

387

● Martha Graber was a cashier for National Bank. She had been rated superior and given a raise in salary. Shortly thereafter, her manager promised her a promotion if she would be sexually "cooperative" and got her fired when she refused. The court would find that where sex harassment is the act of an employer's agent who is authorized to hire, fire, discipline, or promote, or recommend such actions, the employer is responsible and subject to Civil Rights Act remedies.

B. Equal Employment Opportunity Commission

Title VII of the Civil Rights Act provides an alternative procedure to civil suit and criminal action for dealing with employment discrimination cases. It created the Equal Employment Opportunity Commission (EEOC), with power to eliminate any improper practice by informal and formal means. That is, the EEOC can stop unfair employment practices by persuasion, seek a court injunction restraining discriminatory actions, and/or sue in court for damages. The EEOC has broad authority to subpoena and require testimony of witnesses under oath. It can also compel employers to keep necessary records and to make them available upon demand.

1. EEOC Proceedings. Complaints of employment discrimination may be filed with the EEOC by any person, organization, or agency. However, the complaint must be filed within 180 days of the alleged discriminatory practice.

In the event the alleged practice violates state or local statutes, the complaint is referred to the state or local agency with jurisdiction. If no state or local action is taken after sixty days, investigative responsibility returns to the EEOC. The findings of the investigation of the complaint are evaluated and attempts to negotiate an informal compromise are made. When reconciliation fails, a formal investigation, using the administrative powers of the EEOC begins. Following the hearing and a determination that the complaint is worthy of litigation, charges are filed against the respondent in a federal district court. If the decision of the commission is against litigation, the claimant is informed and issued a right-to-sue notice. The claimant may then file a civil suit, but the EEOC will not provide further assistance.

2. Expanded EEOC Authority. The 1972 Equal Employment Act amendments transferred discrimination cases from the Justice Department to the EEOC and authorized the establishment of a general counsel. The EEOC was given authority to initiate civil cases against wide-ranging patterns of discrimination. The responsibility to prosecute cases involving discrimination by a state or local government remained with the Justice Department. In addition, the amendments placed all federal employees under the protection of Title VII and extended coverage to state and local government employees and to private and public education personnel.

In 1979 the EEOC became the centerpiece of equal employment opportunity programs and enforcement. It assumed responsibility from the Labor Department for equal pay and age discrimination statutes, including the Age Discrimination in Employment Act, the Equal Pay Act, and the Rehabilitation Act.

C. Uniform Guidelines on Employee Selection Procedures

The EEOC adopted uniform guidelines covering the use of tests and other employment selection procedures used in employment decisions. Included are pro-

Part 7:
Agency
and
Employ-
ment

388

cedures applying to hiring, promotion, demotion, and labor organization membership.

1. Adverse Impact. The fundamental principle underlying the guidelines is that employer practices which have an adverse impact on employment opportunities of any race, sex, or ethnic group are illegal. The guidelines adopt a rule of thumb for detecting the existence of adverse impact. The rule, known as the "80 percent rule," is not a legal definition of discrimination. It is a practical device to focus attention on serious discrepancies in hiring or promotion rates. By the rule, an adverse impact on employment opportunity may exist when the selection rate for any protected group is less than 80 percent of the rate of the highest selection group. For example, when 60 percent of white applicants are selected, at least 48 percent of minority applicants (i.e., 80 percent of 60 percent) should be selected.

Once it is established that there is adverse impact, the employer can modify or eliminate the procedure which produces it. Failing to do this, the employer must justify the use of the procedure on grounds of *business necessity*. This means showing a clear relation between performance on the selection procedure and performance on the job.

2. Reverse Discrimination. An unresolved issue, *reverse discrimination* generally refers to the practice of favoring minorities over whites or women over men for affirmative action purposes. The U.S. Supreme Court has held that it is just as illegal to favor minorities because of race or sex as it is to discriminate against them for the same reason. The law itself says no employer is required to grant preferential treatment to correct racial imbalance. But in *United Steelworkers of America V. Weber* (1979) the court permitted an employer to do so, under some circumstances. These circumstances were as follows:

○ Purpose was to break down old patterns of racial segregation.
○ Purpose was to open up to minorities employment opportunities that have been historically closed to them.
○ Action did not necessarily infringe upon the rights of white employees.
○ Action did not require the firing of white employees to create openings for black workers.
○ Action did not create an impassable obstacle to the advancement opportunities of white workers.
○ Action was not intended to run indefinitely.
○ Purpose was to eliminate a manifest racial imbalance.

In any event, if white employees can show that they were discriminated against, a cause of action is justified.

● Two white and one black employees were caught stealing company supplies. The two white employees were fired and the black employee was placed on probation, but not fired. The white employees sued, charging discrimination. The company argued it took the action in an effort to satisfy its affirmative action commitment. The court would hold that the white employees who were fired had a cause of action for discrimination against the employer because the black employee who was guilty of the same offense was not disciplined the same way.

3. Affirmative Action Plan. To correct past discrimination, the EEOC can require a company to take some affirmative action. Government, through its power of purchasing, can also require companies with government contracts to prepare an *affirmative action plan,* even when they have not engaged in any discriminatory practice in the past. This is a written document which analyzes the company's work force and which sets forth goals and timetables to remedy any situation where minorities and women are not adequately represented.

4. Remedial Affirmative Action. When there is a finding of discrimination through investigation or through employer self-audit, remedies and requirements are outlined by the federal courts. Courts have ordered quotas for hiring and promotion when these are necessary to correct the effects of past discrimination. It is important, therefore, to know what the courts have identified as discrimination prohibited by law and what remedies have been ordered.

○ Where *classwide discrimination* is found to exist, action to eliminate it must apply to all members of the affected class.
○ The *consequences* of employment practices, *not the intent,* determine whether discrimination exists and requires remedial action, subject to validity of the practice or bona fide business necessity.
○ Any employment practice or policy which has an unequal effect on members of a protected class—those groups specified in the law—or which continues the effect of prior discriminatory practices amounts to unlawful discrimination. To justify any such practice or policy, an employer must prove that the policy is required by business necessity. Courts interpret business necessity very narrowly, requiring convincing evidence that a discriminatory practice is essential to safe and efficient operation of the business and/or a demonstration of extreme adverse financial results.

5. Employment Testing. The guidelines adopted by the EEOC counsel employers on the effect of preemployment tests on equal employment opportunity. The Supreme Court has ruled that any tests used which result in discrimination against minority group members must be related to the requirements of the jobs involved. To be acceptable legally, tests or other performance standards must be fair measures of qualities needed to handle specific jobs.

● Duke Power Co. required applicants for jobs in any but the lowest-paid department to have a high school education and satisfactory scores on two professionally prepared general aptitude tests. The record showed that whites fared far better than black applicants under these requirements. The Court ruled that this consequence appeared to be directly traceable to race and inferior education. The Court subsequently ruled that neither of the aptitude tests used was directed or intended to measure the ability to learn or perform a particular job or category of jobs.

6. Application Forms and Employment Interviews. The EEOC views with disfavor questions on application forms or in interviews that directly or indirectly relate to a job applicant's race, color, religion, sex, age, or national origin. Although not expressly prohibited under federal laws, the EEOC recognizes that many such questions tend to discriminate against minorities and females. They are often questions not related to qualifications deemed necessary to the safe and efficient operation of the business.

Part 7:
Agency
and
Employ-
ment

390

7. Equal Employment Opportunity Exemptions. State and local elected officials and their personal assistants and advisers are exempted from equal employment protection. And it is not unlawful employment practice to discriminate if a *bona fide occupational qualification* (BFOQ) exists. This is a good-faith requirement for employment that does not deceptively prevent certain groups of persons from qualifying for employment. For example, discrimination exemptions are given religious orders that require employment of persons of a particular religion. Thus, it would be permissible for a Presbyterian church to hire only Presbyterian ministers and refuse employment to individuals of other denominations. National security also justifies employment discrimination, as does membership in the Communist Party, and laws give preferential status to veterans and Indians.

D. Age Discrimination in Employment Act

Enacted in 1967 and amended in 1978, the Age Discrimination in Employment Act outlaws employment discrimination against workers who are involved in a business affecting interstate commerce. Also covered are persons employed in federal, state, and local governments, public and private educational institutions, public and private employment agencies, and labor unions. Training and apprenticeship programs are exempted under the act, since they are offered to help youth enter the work force.

1. Exclusions. There are subtleties in the age discrimination law which moderate the full effect of its broad goal of prohibiting discrimination of any kind against older employees. Employers may discriminate where age is a BFOQ. For example, FAA regulations bar pilots from carrier operations as pilots after they reach the age of sixty. Employers may also observe the terms of any bona fide seniority system or employee retirement, pension, or insurance plan. However, no such system or plan can be used as the reason for not hiring any individual or for requiring or permitting the involuntary retirement of any employee because of the age of such person. Thus, if the normal retirement age is sixty-five, employees between the ages of sixty-five and seventy do not have to retire.

2. Discriminatory Employment Practices. Under the terms of the Age Discrimination in Employment Act, an employer may not:

○ Advertise for job applicants in such a way as to indicate or suggest a preference, specification, or limitation on age.
○ Discriminate in any way, including refusing to hire and discharging an employee or applicant because of age. This provision prohibits discrimination in matters of pay, working conditions, and privileges of employment.
○ Put limits on older employees so as to deprive them of employment opportunities equal to those of younger employees.

Employment agencies are subject to the Age Act in most of their functions. Want ads that express age preference are outlawed. Phrases, such as "prefer recent graduate," "25 to 35," "young girl," or "young boy," that imply an age preference are forbidden. Stress on age in interviews with clients and failure or refusal to refer older persons for jobs may expose an employment agency to challenge.

E. Equal Pay Act

The Equal Pay Act of 1963 and its 1972 amendments deal with sex-based wage discrimination. The act authorizes governmental intervention to eliminate wage differentials when men's and women's jobs are identical or nearly so and hence of equal weight. Specifically, the act provides that no employer subject to FLSA provisions shall discriminate against employees on the basis of sex by paying wages to employees at a rate less than the rate at which wages are paid to employees of the opposite sex for equal work on jobs requiring equal skill, effort, and responsibility and performed under similar working conditions. Henceforth, men and women must be treated equally for purposes of base pay, opportunity for overtime, raises, bonuses, commissions, and fringe benefits such as health and life insurance, pensions, profit-sharing and bonus plans, and credit union benefits.

● A review of the salary structure in a state university was ordered to determine whether inequities existed. Average salaries paid to male employees were compared with those paid to female employees for comparable jobs, using a formula based on levels of education, specialization, experience, and merit. It was found that thirty female faculty members were being underpaid, so the university raised the minimum pay of the females to the formula level. Approximately ninety male faculty members also discovered that they were receiving salaries below the average. The men claimed that the university's attempt to equalize male and female pay discriminated unlawfully against the lower-paid males. The U.S. Eighth Circuit Court of Appeals found the university in violation of the Equal Pay Act and ruled that the same formula must be applied to raise the minimum pay of the lower-paid males to the formula level.

The Equal Pay Act is also concerned with the more subtle kinds of unequal wage problems, such as the existence of different base rates for equal jobs where women are predominantly in the lower-paid job category.

● Anaconda Aluminum Company was ordered to pay $190,000 in back wages and court costs to 276 women who charged that the company had sex-segregated job categories. Jobs classified "female" and "male" had been reclassified as "light" and "heavy," but women were prevented from transferring to heavy jobs. After layoffs, the company hired new male employees for heavy jobs rather than recalling females with seniority in light jobs. The company was ordered to assure opportunity for all jobs to anyone who could qualify.

The Equal Pay Act mandates that the sexes must be treated equally, but it does not provide that they be treated "the same." There are exceptions for a bona fide seniority system, a merit system, a system measuring earnings by quantity or quality of production, or a differential based on any factor other than sex.

Payment of different wage rates to permanent employees and temporary employees does not violate the Equal Pay Act. Another provision is that state or other laws regarding hours of work, jobs requiring physical strength, rest periods, and the like do not make work "unequal."

The U.S. Supreme Court, in a 1981 decision likely to encourage a new round of sex discrimination suits, ruled that women who are paid less than men are

Part 7:
Agency
and
Employ-
ment

392

entitled to sue their employers, whether or not the jobs performed by the two sexes are identical. Thus, the Supreme Court held that the Civil Rights Act of 1964, which prohibits discrimination in employment on the basis of sex as well as race, is not limited to claims of "equal pay for equal work," the standard adopted by Congress in the Equal Pay Act of 1963.

F. Rehabilitation Act

The Rehabilitation Act of 1973, as amended in 1975, requires government contractors to take affirmative action to employ and promote qualified handicapped workers. The term *handicapped* was defined as referring to any person with a physical or mental impairment which limits one or more of the person's major life functions. A separate affirmative action plan for the handicapped is required from all government contractors with plans for minorities.

30-3. Employee Indemnification and Safety Laws

Laws that compensate covered and eligible workers or their dependents for injury, disease, or death in the course of employment are known as *workers' compensation laws*. The federal Occupational Safety and Health Act protects employees from dangerous working conditions.

A. Workers' Compensation Laws

Workers' compensation statutes are in effect in all states. Although the provisions differ in each state, there are common areas of coverage. Workers are paid for occupational diseases and temporary disabilities caused as a result of employment. Compensation for an injury or disease that results in permanent impairment is recognized. Death benefits are paid to survivors.

1. Employer Defenses. Payments are made for all accidental injuries arising out of and in the course of employment, regardless of the fault or negligence of the worker. Thus, employees recover money at specified rates even though they were careless, knowingly worked in a dangerous area, or were injured owing to co-worker negligence.

The compensation statutes provide employers with defenses. Employees who intentionally injure themselves are denied compensation benefits. Those who suffer injury or death due to drugs or alcohol are denied benefits. Temporary workers and independent contractors are not covered by most workers' compensation statutes.

Injured employees must be acting in the scope of their employment in order to be awarded benefits under state statutes. If employees are engaged in activity for the benefit of the employer, the workers' compensation board would rule that they are acting in the scope of employment. Of course, the facts of each situation must be examined carefully.

● DeRosa, an employee of High Ridge Oil Co., was on his way to work when he noticed and hailed a passing High Ridge Oil truck. The driver recognized DeRosa, having transported him several times before. During the ride, DeRosa fell from the truck and was killed. DeRosa's widow claimed workers' compensation benefits for this transportation-related injury, and the workers' compensation board awarded them to her. The employer appealed, arguing that such accidents are compensable only where the employer is obligated by contract to furnish transportation to the employee. The board found that High Ridge Oil drivers frequently and regularly carried employees to and from work. There was no rule against this practice. The oil company in effect had acquiesced in such conduct. It was advantageous to the company, since employees were more likely to get to work on time. The court found there was no meaningful distinction between transportation furnished by custom and that provided by contract. It ruled that DeRosa's fatal accident did arise out of and in the course of his employment.

2. Administering Workers' Compensation. Employees must notify their employers of an accident within a specified period of time. The state statute will state when, how much, and for how long benefit payments are to be made. The actual amount depends on the extent of disability and the injured employee's average weekly earnings.

Most states use a form such as the Universal Standard Workers' Compensation and Employers' Liability Policy to determine a company's liability. The premium paid by the employer is based on the size of the company's payroll and the kind of work performed. A commission usually administers the provisions of the statute. It has authority to direct payments of claims and to hear appeals.

An appeal to the courts may be made if the commission's ruling seems unfair. Courts have become liberal in upholding awards questioned on the grounds that an injury did not arise in the course of the employee's work.

In many states, an employee who brings suit for injuries is required by law to accept the court's decision and may not thereafter decide to accept the grant provided under workers' compensation. In similar fashion, if a compensation award is accepted a worker is usually barred from later court action for further damages.

Most state statutes which establish rights related to employment forbid retaliation against an employee who tries to use such rights. Even when a statute does not specifically say so, any attempt to block the broad corrective purpose of such a law usually gives the employee a cause of action for damages.

3. Federal Employers' Liability Act. At the national level, the Federal Employers' Liability Act (FELA) covers certain kinds of employees, such as railroad workers, for injuries disease, and death arising out of the course of employment. The FELA, unlike state workers' compensation laws, requires proof of employer negligence, but it does not limit the amount of recovery. By eliminating the defenses the employer would have at common law, however, the act greatly increases the chances of a worker's winning a lawsuit.

B. **Occupational Safety and Health Act**
The Occupational Safety and Health Act (OSHA) of 1970 assures all workers a safe and healthful place of employment. Under the act's provisions, every employer engaged in a business affecting interstate commerce is required to eliminate recognized work environment hazards, comply with the occupational safety and health standards issued under the act, and submit to inspections by government health and safety inspectors. Employers must also comply with certain record-keeping and reporting requirements.

Part 7:
Agency
and
Employ-
ment

394

1. Recognized Hazards. Employers must eliminate any work environment hazard that can be detected on the basis of the human senses. Such a hazard is considered to be one generally recognized in the particular industry in which it occurs and/or detectable by means of sight, smell, touch, and hearing. Recognized hazards also apply where there are generally known and accepted tests for their existence which should make their presence known to the employer.

● A construction crane manned by an operator and an oiler went out of control, causing a fatal injury to another worker. The oiler had put the crane through a test run by raising and lowering the boom. It was revealed, however, that the boom brake bands were covered with grease and the backup brake system was not operating because of a missing part. OSHA regulations require the employer to designate a competent person to inspect cranes both before and during use. Neither the operator nor the oiler knew he had been designated to carry out such inspections. The court of appeals would rule that *designate* means that an employee must be informed of the existence and nature of his or her inspection duties. In short, that means formal selection and notification.

2. Standards. The core of OSHA is the specific standards proclaimed under the act. The standards range all the way from commonsense provisions to elaborate provisions such as those dealing with toxic substances. Hearings on objections to standards proposed by the Secretary of Labor are authorized. Standards may be revised or revoked within sixty days after a hearing has been completed. Exemptions from OSHA standards are permitted any employer who applies for an exemption and meets certain standards.

3. Inspections. The OSHA's provisions authorize periodic federal inspections of all working conditions. The Supreme Court has ruled that OSHA inspectors are not authorized to enter a plant unannounced to conduct an inspection without a search warrant. Probable cause that there was a violation need not be shown, however, in order to get a search warrant. The employer and employee representatives are permitted to accompany the federal official during the inspection. Employees are permitted to request an inspection if they believe that a safety or health violation exists.

When a violation of a standard is observed, the federal inspector issues a citation. A posting of the citation near the violation site is required. If an employer contests the citation, a hearing is conducted by the commission. The basic function of the commission is to review the facts involved in the violation, recommend changes, or, if it is appropriate to do so, void the citation or penalty entirely. If the employer does not give notice that the citation is being contested, the citation and penalty are considered final and not subject to review by the commission. Persons affected by a commission order can obtain review in a U.S. court of appeals within sixty days after receiving the order.

The Secretary of Labor is also required to petition a U.S. district court to issue an order restraining any practices in a plant that pose an "imminent danger" to employees. In each case, the inspector must notify the affected employees and employer of the danger. In effect, an OSHA inspector has the power to close a plant when violation of a standard threatens lives.

4. Penalties. Along with a violation citation, OSHA may assess a penalty of up

Chapter
30:
Law of
Employ-
ment

395

to $1,000 for nonserious violations. If the violation is not corrected, additional penalties of up to $1,000 a day may be assessed. Willful or repeated violations may result in penalties of up to $10,000 for each violation. A criminal penalty of not more than $10,000 or six months' imprisonment or both may be assessed if a willful violation causes the death of an employee. If that violation is repeated, the punishment level increases to $20,000 or one year's imprisonment or both.

30-4. Social Security

The Social Security Act of 1935 and subsequent amendments protect those covered by it against loss of income due to retirement, disability, death, hospitalization, and unemployment. Both the federal and state governments participate in these programs of insurance that provide a safety net of basic sustenance for people who have no other means of support.

A. Retirement and Disability Benefits

Loss-of-income benefits are provided under the Federal Insurance Contribution Act for those who retire at age sixty-five and to those who elect to retire earlier, at a reduced benefit. Financial benefits are also available on death of a covered worker and to those under sixty-five years of age who are physically disabled.

1. Retirement Benefits. Employers are required to withhold employee contributions from employees' paychecks and to add an equal amount. The combined funds for each worker are sent to the Internal Revenue Service and credited to the appropriate social security accounts. Self-employed persons participate in the insurance coverage by means of an annual self-employment tax which is due with their individual federal income tax returns.

The maximum amount of an employee's annual earnings that are subject to the tax is referred to as the *annual wage base*. The tax rate that is applied to the annual wage base is set by statute. Both the base and the rate have been rising steadily in order to meet increasing benefit demands on the fund.

The law sets limits on how much a person can earn while receiving retirement benefits. At seventy years of age, a full monthly benefit is received no matter how much the retired worker earns. Only earnings from a job or self-employment are considered when figuring allowable income, not pension benefits, interest, annuities, or dividends.

2. Disability and Survivor's Insurance. The Federal Insurance Contributions Act provides survivor benefits on death of a covered worker. This form of life insurance benefit is payable to a spouse and children, dependent parents, divorced spouse with dependent children under eighteen years of age and unmarried, or college students under twenty-two years of age.

Income benefits are also assured when workers under sixty-five years of age become unable to work because of an illness or other physical disability. Covered workers are considered disabled when a physical or mental condition prevents the performance of any substantial, gainful work and is expected to last (or has lasted) at least twelve months, or is expected to result in death. The key consideration is the extent to which the condition interferes with the individual's ability to work. A person who can engage in productive work performed for money, even when the extent of the activity is part time, is not disabled in the eyes of the law. Disability benefits are figured as if the person had retired at sixty-five years of age in the year the disability began. Regular retirement benefits are substituted in the event the disability persists until sixty-five years of age.

B. Medicare

Medicare is a health insurance program for persons sixty-five years of age and older and for certain persons under sixty-five who are disabled.

Hospital insurance is provided without cost to persons sixty-five years of age and older who have adequate credits for work under social security. Those who fail to qualify under the work credit provision can obtain this protection by paying a monthly premium.

Anyone with hospital insurance is eligible for federal medical insurance. Monthly premiums, paid quarterly, which are subject to increases as medical costs rise, are required. Patients must pay an initial specified percentage of covered medical expenses in each calendar year. The hospital insurance pays 80 percent of the reasonable charge for any additional covered expenses incurred during the year.

C. Unemployment Insurance

The Federal Unemployment Tax Act provides temporary compensation to persons unemployed through no fault of their own, who have accumulated credits from prior employment. The act requires employers engaged in interstate commerce and industry, who are not exempt, to pay a quarterly tax to the federal government. In addition, each state taxes covered employers who are in turn entitled to a federal tax credit (offset). Employers submit the tax to the state, which then deposits the revenue in a federal trust fund with a separate account for each state.

1. **Benefit Structure.** Each state is responsible for administering its own unemployment program for determining benefit coverage, tax rates, and eligibility. A portion of the state tax is retained by the federal government to finance administration of the program at the federal and state levels. Retained funds are also used to offset the federal share of extended and emergency benefits paid during periods of high unemployment. States may also borrow from the retained funds when their state benefit fund account is exhausted.

2. **Eligibility Determination.** Formerly employed persons must file a claim for benefits and register for employment at the state employment office in order to qualify for unemployment compensation payments. In addition to meeting state requirements regarding length of time employed and amount of wages, former employees must be ready, able, and willing to take a suitable full-time job that becomes available.

● Wilkins, a machinist, was furloughed from his job with Hughes Helicopters because of economic conditions. He registered with the state employment agency and requested unemployment compensation. The interviewing official told him about a job opening for a machinist with United Technologies. Wilkins refused it on the grounds that he needed a rest before accepting another job. Wilkins would be ineligible for compensation for any week in which his unemployment resulted from failure to accept suitable work offered to him by the employment office or by any employer.

3. Rights to Unemployment Benefits. Formerly employed persons generally are partly or completely denied unemployment benefits when they quit work voluntarily or are discharged for proper cause, misconduct, or theft.

Workers out of work while participating actively in a labor dispute or strike generally do not qualify for unemployment benefits. The courts have held, however, that workers on *layoff* (period of employment inactivity or idleness) at the time a strike is called are still on layoff and qualify for unemployment benefits, unless notified to return to work during the strike period. Disregarding a recall notice while on layoff would disqualify a worker from receiving unemployment benefits.

● Madrone Excavating, Inc., began a layoff of its employees during the coldest winter months, when construction work was halted. During the layoff, the labor contract with the operating engineers expired. When the bargaining deadlocked, the union declared a strike to be in effect. Madrone Excavating filed protests against granting unemployment benefits to any of the employees during the strike period. The unions argued that none should be disqualified by the strike. The appeal court held that the workers on layoff at strike time who were not notified to return to work during the strike period were still on layoff and thus qualified for unemployment benefits.

Floaters—that is, persons who linger on a job just long enough to qualify for unemployment pay and then plot for dismissal—may risk forfeiting their unemployment benefits.

● Rimland performed well for five months and then suddenly made mistakes in her work, arrived late, was often absent, developed a sullen attitude, and became sloppy in appearance. She boasted to a coworker that this behavior would result in dismissal and unemployment compensation. Most state unemployment agencies would rule such behavior as misconduct connected with Rimland's job and would bar her benefits to which she might otherwise have been entitled.

30-5. Pension Regulation

Federal law regulates the pension plans many employers have established to benefit employees after they retire. Other retirement plans are authorized for small businesses that do not have regular pension plans.

The Employee Retirement Income Security Act of 1974 (ERISA) calls for basic changes in laws relating to private pension plans. ERISA differentiates between *defined benefit plans* and *money purchase plans*. Defined benefit plans promise a certain dollar amount of benefits to employees upon retirement. Money purchase plans, for example, a profit-sharing plan, merely deposit funds into a plan and provide that employees will receive what is in the account when they retire. Each company with a covered plan is required to file reports with the government and communicate the provisions of the pension plan to the participating employees.

ERISA provides for *funding,* that is, the amounts of money placed in the plan to satisfy the obligations of the pension plan. New plans must use a thirty-year period to fund *past service liability* (i.e., obligations attributable to all current employees). Existing pension plans that were funded on the basis of forty years were allowed to continue. Under this funding requirement, the entire past service liability is determined and an amount equal to one-fortieth of that is contributed.

ERISA established the Pension Benefit Guaranty Corporation, which is a federal insurance company which insures benefits from private pension plans. Up to certain limitations, the pensions which have been promised participating employees will be paid, regardless of the available assets in the fund to pay them.

Understanding Legal Terms

Define, identify, or explain the following terms:

adverse impact	child labor	exempt employee	reverse
affirmative action	defined benefit plan	funding	discrimination
annual wage base	discrimination	medicare	workers'
BFOQ	employment	nonexempt	compensation
business necessity	contract	employee	

Questions for Review and Discussion

1. Describe the standards for a minimum wage, overtime pay, and child labor as provided in the Fair Labor Standards Act.

2. Explain in what manner the Supreme Court's reinterpretation of the due process clause of the Constitution affected the meaning of "freedom to contract."

3. What does Title VII of the Civil Rights Act identify as the principal kinds of discrimination that cause inequality of employment opportunity?

4. What are the significant factors that determine whether an employer is subject to the job discrimination provisions of Title VII of the Civil Rights Act?

5. Explain the scope of a voluntary affirmative action plan.

6. Two applicants, one aged forty-nine and the other sixty-one, applied for the same job. The senior applicant had more experience and a better test score, but the younger applicant was hired. The older applicant sued, but the company argued that the Age Discrimination in Employment Act did not apply because both men were over forty. Who has the better case? Explain.

7. Describe the scope of coverage afforded workers covered by the provisions of state workers' compensation laws and name the primary employer defenses.

8. In what manner does the Federal Employers' Liability Act differ from the protection offered by the state workers' compensation statutes?

9. Outline the financing obligations imposed on employees and employers by the provisions of the Social Security Act.

10. How does ERISA differentiate between a defined benefit plan and a money purchase plan?

Analyzing Cases

1. Peter Bennerson was employed by the Checker Garage Service Corp. as an auto mechanic. His duties included both assisting mechanics in the garage and making road calls to service vehicles owned and operated by his employer. During his lunch hour, Bennerson used one of his employer's taxicabs to drive to a restaurant. En route to the restaurant, he was seriously injured when the taxicab struck a pole. Bennerson filed a claim before the workers' compensation board for compensation, which was granted. Checker Garage appealed, claiming among other things that the taxicab Bennerson drove did not "go out of control" but that Bennerson "lost control." How should the appeals court dispose of this argument? What other legal arguments are relevant? ● *Bennerson v. Checker Garage Serv. Corp.*, 388 N.Y.S.2d 374 (1976)

2. Sarah Ziskin was disabled by polio at the age of two. Notwithstanding her illness, she succeeded in earning a college degree and obtained employment as a teacher. The job, however, was obtained through "political pressure" and the skilled services of a lawyer working on her behalf, rather than on the basis of her merit and ability as a teacher. While she was academically qualified to teach, because of her physical condition she performed woefully inadequately. She often fell down because as a polio victim she had trouble standing. There was a concerted effort on the part of school administrators to "ease her out of the school system." When her illness forced her to discontinue work, Ziskin filed a claim for child disability benefits under the Social Security Act. Although similar to regular disability benefits, child disability benefits are based on (a) dependence on a now dead parent's earnings instead of on one's own earning record and (b) disability starting on or before one reaches eighteen years of age.

The Secretary of Health, Education, and Welfare denied the claim. He reasoned that since Ziskin was able to graduate from college and hold a job for a while subsequent to her reaching age eighteen, she could not have been disabled at age eighteen. On appeal, how should the court rule? Why? ● *Ziskin v. Weinberger*, 379 F. Supp. 124 (S.D. Ohio 1973)

3. Nancy Barillaro and Nancy Fotia were employed in the inspection and trimming departments at Elwood Knitting Mills for approximately sixteen years. Barillaro was laid off in September and Fotia in November. Both were offered the option of returning to work in March of the following year as knitting machine operators, but at an 18 percent reduction in pay. Neither accepted the offer. They argued (a) that the offered work would have involved a loss of seniority and a substantial reduction in pay, (b) that their ability to perform the work was questionable (Fotia claimed lack of familiarity with the machine, and Barillaro claimed she was "too short" to operate the machine), and (c) that, the union contract made them eligible for unemployment compensation even if they turned down work offers. The Pennsylvania Unemployment Compensation Board decided that the claimants were ineligible to receive benefits because they refused offers of suitable work without good cause. On appeal to the court, who should win? Why? ● *Barillaro v. Unemployment Compensation Bd. of Review*, 387 A.2d 1324 (Pa. 1978)

4. The Security Bank and Trust Company employed a number of men and women as tellers and cashiers. The male workers were paid higher salaries than their female counterparts. The Secretary of Labor brought action to enjoin the bank from violating the equal pay provisions of the Equal Pay Act.

The Secretary took the position that female tellers in general, and female supervisors in certain instances, were paid less than male tellers and supervisors performing substantially the same work. It was the bank's position that any disparity in pay between female and male employees was based on factors other than sex. The bank claimed that the male employees performed extra and difficult duties which rendered the jobs unequal. The bank also argued that the male employees were not regarded as permanent tellers, but were being trained in all aspects of the banking business for future placement in managerial positions as officers at the bank.

The trial court concluded the bank did not maintain a bona fide training program, but that the male employees who received higher wages than their female counterparts were thought of as potential bank executives. That is, the only "training program" that existed was the fact that management thought the males were more qualified and thus more likely eventually to be promoted. The trial court found for the Security Bank and Trust Company. On appeal, how should the case be resolved? Why? ● *Marshall v. Security Bank & Trust Co.*, 572 F.2d 276 (10th Cir. 1978)

5. Aetna Insurance Company employed Nellie Barratt as a commercial casualty underwriter and paid her a salary of $11,900 a year. She had been employed by the company for a number of years and had received a number of raises. Aetna hired Christopher Archer, who had eight years of underwriting experience, to perform the same duties and assume the same responsibilities as Barratt, at a rate of $14,700 a year.

The Secretary of Labor, on behalf of Barratt, brought suit based upon sex discrimination in violation of the Equal Pay Act, contending Barratt had been paid less for the same work. Aetna, on the other hand, attributed the differential to a dual merit system and the superior qualifications and greater potential for promotion of Archer. With respect to the merit system of incoming employees, the company assessed the merit of prospective employees by evaluating their job application information and their re-

sponses to a number of interviews by supervisory personnel. The merit system for persons already employed at the company was in writing and made periodic salary adjustments for employees who had accumulated service with the company according to past performance and the company's goals and objectives. It was not uncommon in the company for long-term employees to be compensated less than newly hired persons because the raises did not necessarily keep up with inflation.

How should the U.S. court of appeals resolve the issue? Is the finding of this appeals court in respect to the issue of "potential for promotion" different from that held by the court in the preceding case? ● *Equal Employment Etc. v. Aetna Ins. Co.*, 616 F.2d 719 (4th Cir. 1980)

6. Loretta Rice, a black, for lack of a college degree was denied consideration for employment by the city of St. Louis as a public health program representative. Rice took the position that the city's requirement of a formal college degree as a condition precedent to consideration for employment as a program representative was not rationally job-related and was racially discriminatory. She filed a complaint with the Equal Employment Opportunity Commission. After exhausting her remedies before the agency without obtaining relief, she brought suit in the U.S. district court.

While Rice had thirty hours of college credit, it was not known that those credits could be applied toward a degree. Rice also had some experience in public health and social work in the black community of St. Louis. Blacks were only approximately 55 percent as likely as whites in the St. Louis area to have a college degree. Emphasizing this, Rice took the position that the degree requirement for employment more heavily burdened blacks than whites. Thus she argued the requirement had an "adverse impact" upon blacks and was invalid under Title VII of the Civil Rights Act. Testimony introduced showed that program representatives in St. Louis were called upon to engage in difficult and taxing tasks. The performance of those tasks in a satisfactory manner required maturity, persistence, and tact; also required were the ability to communicate with others, frequently in a sophisticated atmosphere, and the ability to speak and write intelligibly. There was also some risk to the public health and safety in the employment of unqualified representatives. Rice was denied relief by the U.S. district court. How should the court of appeals rule? Why? ●*Rice v. City of St. Louis*, 607 F.2d 791 (8th Cir. 1979)

7. Virginia, which had a long history of racial and sex discrimination in its state police hiring practices, required all applicants for state troopers to be between twenty-one and twenty-nine years of age, be at least 5 feet 9 inches tall, and weigh at least 156 pounds. The height and weight requirements eliminated 98 percent of female applicants. The basic employment requirements also required that all employment applicants, including applicants for civilian dispatcher positions, complete and pass written mental ability tests. Blacks were more likely than whites to fail the tests. The tests for dispatcher positions were not valid predictors of job performance. Tests for trooper positions were not shown to be predictors of job performance, but were valid predictors of training school performance. The United States brought suit charging that Virginia engaged in a "pattern and practice" of discrimination against black applicants for civilian positions with the state police and against both black and women applicants for trooper positions. In light of these Title VII charges, how should the appeals court hold? Why? ● *United States v. Com. of Va.*, 620 F.2d 1018 (4th Cir. 1980)

8. L. Mets Lerwill and Charles Perry, covered by a collective bargaining agreement, brought suit against their employer, Inflight Motion Pictures, Inc., for themselves and on behalf of all employees to recover overtime pay as provided in the agreement and required by the Fair Labor Standards Act. During the relevant period, the technicians who put projectors in place, threaded the film, and serviced other equipment used to show movies to passenger audiences were not paid by Inflight for hours worked in excess of forty hours per week. Inflight argued that the union and a number of employees agreed to waive overtime pay in order to obtain a larger salary through an extended workweek. What would be the court's determination? Why? ●*Lerwill v. Inflight Motion Pictures, Inc.*, 582 F.2d 507 (9th Cir. 1978)

Chapter 31   Labor Relations

Labor relations law is chiefly made up of statutory law dealing with employment, working conditions, and rights of employees, unions, and employers to participate in various activities. Although local and state laws apply to many labor problems (such as picketing and the right to work), this chapter deals primarily with federal laws. Highlighted in the following paragraphs are the federal laws that govern unfair labor practices, union organization, and collective bargaining.

31-1. Evolution of Labor Relations Law

The first federal statute relating to labor was the Clayton Act in 1914. It attempted to prohibit federal courts from forbidding activities such as picketing and strikes in disputes over terms or conditions of employment. *Picketing* involves the placement of persons at the place of employment to inform the public of the existence of a labor dispute by word or carried sign. A *strike* is a concerted stoppage of work by employees as a means of enforcing a demand made on their employers. The Clayton Act also stated that the antitrust laws did not apply to labor unions or their members in carrying out their lawful objectives.

In 1926 Congress passed the Railway Labor Act, which provided procedures for dealing with labor disputes in the railroad industry. It encouraged *collective bargaining,* that is, a good-faith meeting between representatives of employees and employer to discuss the terms and conditions of employment. Its provisions were later extended to the airline industry.

The Norris-LaGuardia Act was passed by Congress in 1932. Often referred to as the "anti-injunction statute," the law limits the authority of federal courts to issue injunctions sought by private parties in labor disputes. In general, the statute provides that strikes, picketing, and boycotts may not be prohibited by a federal court where they arise out of a labor dispute. A *boycott* is a concerted refusal to have dealings to force acceptance of certain conditions. The statute did nothing, however, to impose any duty on employers to deal with or even recognize unions.

The passage of the National Labor Relations Act (Wagner Act) in 1935 opened the door for the rapid growth on the union movement. It is probably the most significant labor relations statute in that it expressly sets forth the unfair labor practices of both employers and unions. The National Labor Relations Act was amended by the Labor-Management Relations Act of 1947, which was in turn amended by the Labor-Management Reporting and Disclosure Act of 1959.

31-2. National Labor Relations Act

The National Labor Relations Act established the legal rights and obligations (*substantive law*) governing the conduct of unions and employers. It sought to assure American workers the right to organize to counterbalance the collective activities of employers. The statute also established procedures for representative elections and for determining the bargaining unit. It created the National Labor Relations Board (NLRB), an independent administrative agency, to hear and adjudicate charges that unfair labor practices have been committed by either employers or unions.

A. Unfair Labor Practices of Employers

Section 8 of the National Labor Relations Act as amended provides the basic laws relating to unfair labor practices and for representative elections. Various activities are prohibited as *unfair labor practices* of employers.

1. Interference With Employees' Rights to Organize. It is an unfair labor practice for an employer to interfere with, restrain, or coerce employees in the exercise of the rights of employees to self-organization and to bargain collectively. Employees have the right to form, join, or assist labor organizations and to bargain collectively through representatives of their own choosing. They also have the right to engage in mutually agreed-upon activities for the purpose of collective bargaining or other mutual aid or protection. Threats to eliminate certain benefits or privileges, to close down the business, or to discharge employees for union activity are prohibited.

● Knickerbocker Aviation, Inc., learned that its employees were planning to organize into a labor union. The management felt it had been fair in its treatment of the workers and resented the move to have a union certified. Notices were placed in each employee's pay envelope stating that anyone joining the proposed union would be fired. The organizers filed a complaint with the NLRB, and the company action was ruled an unfair practice. A cease and desist order was issued to Knickerbocker Aviation.

Similarly, an employer's award of increased benefits during an organization attempt can be challenged. For example, the employer cannot award increased benefits after a union organization drive begins. However, if a benefit was planned previously, it may be put into effect even if it happens after the organization drive begins.

2. Domination and Assistance to Unions. It is an unfair labor practice for an employer to dominate or interfere with the formation of a union or to contribute financial or other support to it. The object of this provision is to prohibit company-formed unions that are simply the dupes of management, where there is no real collective bargaining in any meaningful sense. Unlawful domination can result when a member of management takes part in meetings or activities of the union or when the union has no meetings, constitution, or assets.

Unlawful assistance can result if an employer coerces employees into a favored union or assists the favored union in seeking membership or any direct financial support. Where two rival unions are attempting to organize a company's employees, the company may not grant the use of its facilities unless it does so on a uniform basis to both unions.

3. Discrimination Based on Employee's Union Activity. It is an unfair labor practice for an employer to discourage or encourage union membership by discrimination in regard to any term or condition of employment. For example, employers are prohibited from discharging an employee discovered to be engaging in union activities which are disapproved, even though minor work rules have been broken. Of course, employers may uniformly enforce valid company rules provided the enforcement of reasonable rules is not carried out to thwart a union organization attempt. Another example of union activity discrimination is the *yellow-dog contract*. This is any agreement in which the employee must promise the employer not to join any labor union and to renounce existing union memberships and refrain from union membership if employed. All such conditions of employment are expressly prohibited by the National Labor Relations Act.

Discrimination may also involve assigning an employee to less desirable work or denying an employee the opportunity to participate in overtime work. Also viewed as discrimination is *constructive discharge*, where an employee is demoted to a position of lesser pay or authority or poorer working conditions or is subject to supervisory harassment. Meaningful economic reasons are generally necessary in order to offset the inference present when an employee active in union affairs is so treated.

● Draper was selected by the union members to serve as their representative in collective-bargaining meetings with Detroit White Line Company. After his selection, Draper was harassed by the production manager and the general manager for trivial matters concerning work schedules and productivity. Draper has the right to file a complaint with the NLRB charging employer harassment due to his union activities.

4. Discharge for Filing Charges or Giving Testimony. It is an unfair labor practice for an employer to discharge or otherwise discriminate against employees because they file charges or give testimony under the National Labor Relations Act. The courts interpret discrimination under this provision to include discharge, layoff, failure to rehire or recall, and transfer of covered employees.

5. Refusal to Bargain Collectively. It is an unfair labor practice for an employer to refuse to bargain collectively with the representatives of employees who have been selected by the majority of the employees in the bargaining unit. The method generally employed by a union to organize a company is to solicit the employees to sign a union *authorization card*. This is a signed statement by employees either authorizing an election or designating a union as the representative of the employees or both. The results of the election determine whether the employer is required to bargain collectively with the union. Problems may arise, however, where the employer has reason to believe that coercion was used in obtaining the authorization cards. In such cases, an employer is entitled to insist upon a NLRB certification ruling before bargaining with the union.

● The union obtained authorization cards from a majority of Caterpillar Diesel, Inc., workers and demanded that it be recognized as the collective-bargaining representative. Caterpillar Diesel doubted the majority that was claimed and insisted that the union petition the NLRB for a secret-ballot election. The union struck for recognition as the bargaining representative and filed a charge of unfair labor practice against Caterpillar Diesel based on its refusal to bargain. The NLRB held that unless Caterpillar Diesel interfered with the union's organizational campaign efforts, the union had the burden of taking the next step in obtaining an NLRB election, even though it held authorization cards supposedly representing a majority of the workers. The law did not intend to place the burden of getting a secret election on the employer.

In the event the employer commits an unfair labor practice that disrupts election conditions, the National Labor Relations Board may withhold the election or set it aside. An order for the employer to bargain would then be issued as a remedy for the violation.

B. Unfair Labor Practices of Unions

The Section 8(b) amendment to the National Labor Relations Act defines the types of activities that are recognized to be unfair labor practices of unions.

1. Employee Restraint or Coercion. It is an unfair labor practice for a labor union or its agents to restrain or coerce employees in the exercise of the rights to organize and bargain collectively. This provision does not impair the right of a labor union to designate its own rules with respect to the acquisition or retention of membership.

The union has a duty to represent all its members on an equal basis. However, it may fine its members for activities that are contrary to the interest of the union so long as prior notice to that effect has been given the member. Fines may not be levied merely to punish a union member for an activity it does not like.

● The union levied a $200 fine on Coker and McKeown because of their strike-breaking activities after they had resigned from the union. In the hearing before the NLRB, the union argued that their constitution expressly prohibited members from strike-breaking. The NLRB found that the union restrained both Coker and McKeown in this exercise of their right to bargain collectively by seeking to enforce the fines.

2. Cause Employer to Discriminate Against Employee. It is an unfair labor practice for a union to attempt to force an employer to discriminate against employees in an arbitrary way. Uniformly enforced rules, such as the payment of dues and initiation fees as a requirement for joining a union, must apply to everyone.

● Colton was a member of the union representing Dalmar Ken Films, Inc. She learned that another union member was stealing blank tape and reels from the company warehouse. She warned the person that the theft would be reported. When informed of the warning, the union representative revoked Colton's membership and asked the company personnel officer to have her fired. Colton filed a complaint with the NLRB, charging the union with illegal restraint in the exercise of her legal

Part 7:
Agency
and
Employ-
ment

406

rights. The NLRB ruled that Colton's union membership could not be withdrawn and ordered the union to restore her membership.

Generally, a *closed shop* provision, which prohibits employers from hiring anyone except union members, is an unfair labor practice. However, it is usually lawful to have a *union shop* contract provision, which requires new employees to become union members after a specified period of employment. In approximately twenty states with right-to-work laws, however, agreements requiring membership in a labor organization as a condition of continued employment are prohibited.

An *agency shop* practice, whereby everyone in the bargaining unit must pay dues to the union but is not required to become a member, is lawful.

3. Refusal to Bargain Collectively With Employer. It is an unfair labor practice for a union to refuse to bargain collectively with an employer or the employer's authorized representative. Under this provision, a union must give notice to the employer of an intention to strike prior to the termination date of the contract. Failure to give notice and to indicate willingness to meet and bargain over contract terms before the contract expires prevents the union from legally striking.

4. Secondary Boycotts and Hot Cargo. It is an unfair labor practice for a union to engage in a *secondary boycott*. This is any union action against a company which does not have a labor dispute with the employees represented by the union. For example, it would be illegal to picket a company which purchased goods from or supplied goods to another company that was subject to a legal economic strike.

● Steel Specialists, Inc., sold strip steel to Thomas Spring Company. The steel is transported by Roadway Express, Inc., whose employees are nonunion. The union representing Steel Specialists instructed its members to refuse to load Roadway Express trucks with steel in order to force Steel Specialists to stop using Roadway Express. This form of secondary boycott is an unfair labor practice.

Similarly, the *hot cargo* provision of the National Labor Relations Act makes it illegal for the union and an employer to agree that union members will not handle, use, sell, or transport goods which are not made by union members.

5. Discriminatory Fees and Featherbedding. It is an unfair labor practice for a labor union to require the payment of excessive or discriminatory fees of employees covered by an agreement as a condition to becoming a union member. In making such a determination, the National Labor Relations Board considers union practices and customs as well as the wages paid to affected employees. It is also illegal for a union to request an employer to pay for services which are not performed (*featherbedding*). It is not featherbedding for a union to demand payment for members to "stand by" at the employer's place of business, ready, willing, and able to provide services if requested, even if they do not perform any work.

6. Picketing. It is an unfair labor practice for a labor union to picket an employer in order to cause the employer to recognize the union when the action frustrates the purpose of collective bargaining. Hence, picketing is not lawful when another union has been certified as the bargaining agent or where a union certification election has been held within the past twelve months. Similarly, picketing is illegal where there has not been negotiation and discussion of the issues and a filing of notice to the National Labor Relations Board. *Informational picketing* (to let customers and others know the nature of a dispute with the employer) is constitutionally protected as a First Amendment right and thus not an unfair labor practice.

31-3. Collective Bargaining Process

The Labor-Management Relations Act of 1947 (Taft-Hartley Act) amended the National Labor Relations Act. It added to the previously presented list of unfair labor activities which unions as well as employers are forbidden to practice. The right of unions to insist on a union shop was also restricted. In addition, however, the act established a process for helping management and labor settle their disputes without endangering the national health and safety. Central to this collective bargaining process is the National Labor Relations Board and the procedure it follows in settling labor and management disputes.

A. National Labor Relations Board

The NLRB has exclusive jurisdiction to act on cases brought before it that involve employers' operations or labor disputes affecting interstate commerce. Excluded from NLRB jurisdiction and provisions of the labor relations statutes are the employers and employees of the federal and state governments and their political subdivisions, nonprofit hospitals, persons subject to the Railway Labor Act, independent contractors, and persons employed as agricultural laborers and domestic servants. Also excluded from NLRB jurisdiction are schools operated by religious bodies, which are protected by the Constitution's First Amendment religious liberty provisions. The NLRB may perform its duties only upon the filing of a *petition* (request for a representative election) or *charge* (complaint of unfair labor practice). It is administered by a general counsel and a five-member board appointed by the President with the advice and consent of the Senate. The general counsel supervises regional office staff who investigate and prosecute unfair labor charges. The counsel also conducts elections to determine whom employees wish to represent them. The board acts as the judicatory arm of the NLRB. It decides cases involving unfair labor practices and determines union election questions referred to it from the regional offices.

B. Union Certification

Either employees or a labor union, by ballot or orally, can present themselves as a unit for bargaining purposes. The unit so formed must have common bargaining interests. The unit formed may not be a mix of nonprofessional and professional employees or guards and other workers. Collective bargaining may begin unless the employer, any workers, or any labor organization objects to the unit's appropriateness. When an objection is raised, a petition to the NLRB may be filed. A petition on behalf of workers must show that at least 30 percent of them desire an election and that their employer refuses to acknowledge their repre-

Part 7:
Agency
and
Employ-
ment

408

sentation. A petition filed by an employer must allege that one or more individuals or organizations have made a claim for recognition as the exclusive representative of the same unit of employees.

Once a petition is filed, the NLRB regional director must investigate it, hold a hearing if necessary, and direct an election. The election may be held by agreement between the employer and the labor organization. In such a case, the parties state the time and place agreed upon, the choices to be included on the ballot, and who is eligible to vote, and they authorize the NLRB regional director to conduct the election. If the parties are unable to reach an agreement, the NLRB decides that a question of representation exists and orders a secret ballot election. To be certified as the bargaining representative, the labor organization must receive a majority of the votes cast. *Certification* represents the NLRB's assent that a union has fulfilled the legal requirements to qualify as bargaining agent for the employees at a particular work place for at least a twelve-month period.

Any party who believes that the NLRB's election standards were not met may file an objection with the regional director who supervised the election. A ruling on the objection may be appealed to the NLRB for a decision. An election will be set aside if the NLRB determines that one of the parties acted in such a way as to inhibit or interfere with the employees' free expression of choice.

C. Unfair Labor Practice

Employee representatives or employers may file an unfair labor practice charge. The appropriate NLRB regional director then investigates the charge to determine its validity. If it is found that an unfair labor practice was or is occurring, a complaint is issued notifying the offending party that a hearing is to be held. Every effort is made to resolve the dispute before the hearing date. If the *arbitration* efforts (i.e., the substitution of the decision of selected persons for that of the NLRB) do not lead to an acceptable agreement, the NLRB resumes jurisdiction.

Unfair labor practice cases are conducted before an NLRB administrative law judge in accordance with procedures that apply in federal district courts. The judge's findings and recommendations to the NLRB are based upon testimony taken at the hearing. The parties involved in the hearing may appeal the judge's decision to the NLRB. If the board concurs with the judge's finding, it is authorized to issue a cease and desist order requiring the offending party to take required *affirmative action*. This is the process by which the federal government encourages parties to remedy discriminatory or unfair labor practices. Anyone not complying with an NLRB order can be punished for contempt by the courts. NLRB decisions may be appealed to the appropriate circuit court of appeals. Either party may then appeal proceedings to the U.S. Supreme Court.

D. Mediation and Injunction Authority

Congress has authorized the formation of the Federal Mediation and Conciliation Service to assist in negotiating settlements of labor and management disputes. This body can act on its own initiative or on request of either party to a labor dispute. Its *mediation* role is to offer nonbinding settlement recommendations, require the parties to negotiate, and obtain a vote on employer offers.

The labor relations laws give the President special powers to deal with actual or threatened strikes that would affect interstate commerce or endanger the national health or safety. A board of inquiry can be appointed to determine the strike issues, which are then reported to the President. On the basis of these findings, the President can order the Attorney General to petition a federal district court to issue an injunction (a restraining order) stopping the strike for sixty days. At the end of that period, the board of inquiry will report the most recent settlement offer, which the union members must vote on within fifteen days. The results of the vote are sent to the Attorney General within five days after the balloting. At the end of this eighty-day period, the injunction ends and the employees may strike. Only collective bargaining or congressional action can then resolve the labor dispute.

E. Strike Rights

As defined by the National Labor Relations Act, a *legal economic strike* is one called solely to enforce demands for improved wages, hours, and other terms and conditions of employment. Generally, the employer may not discriminate against legal economic strikers. For example, the employer may not refuse to reinstate the strike leaders when the strike is over and may not discharge strikers before permanent replacements have been hired and trained. Employers are also prohibited from adopting procedures which benefit employees who stayed at work differently from those who went on strike.

A *legal unfair labor practice strike* is one in which workers are objecting to some unfair labor practice of the employer. The employer must reinstate all the strikers who engage in such a strike, even if it involves discharging other workers hired to replace the strikers.

Strikes that do not qualify as a legal economic strike or a legal unfair labor practice strike generally permit the employer to discharge striking workers. For example, the employer may discharge the strikers when the strike is in violation of a no-strike agreement. Strikers may also forfeit their rights to reinstatement when they destroy company property or subject employees, customers, or visitors to violence. Employees who become unemployed due to active participation in a labor dispute are ordinarily disqualified from receiving unemployment compensation benefits.

31-4. Union Reform Legislation

The Labor-Management Reporting and Disclosure Act of 1959 (Landrum-Griffin Act) provides that the courts of any state can deal with labor disputes which the NLRB will not hear. The main thrust of the statute, however, is the correction of corruption in labor unions—embezzlement of union funds, conversion of union resources to union officials, and violence at union meetings.

A. Equal Rights of Union Members

Title I of the Labor-Management Reporting and Disclosure Act is a bill of rights for members of labor unions. Subject to reasonable rules and regulations, all members have an equal right to nominate candidates, vote in elections, receive notice of all meetings, and attend and participate at such meetings. They

Part 7:
Agency
and
Employ-
ment

410

have the right to vote on dues, initiation fees, and assessments by secret ballot and cannot be subjected to an arbitrary increase in dues or fees by union leaders as a punishment. Members have the right to meet freely with other union members and to express their views. They also have the right to begin an action in court against union leaders when a dispute is not resolved following union procedures. Members are also safeguarded against disciplinary action (except for nonpayment of dues) without adequate notice of the violation and sufficient time to prepare a defense, and they are entitled to a fair hearing. In addition, all union members have the right to receive on request a copy of each collective bargaining agreement made by the labor organization with the employer.

B. Union Report and Requirements

Every labor union must adopt a constitution and bylaws for its operation and conduct of business and file them with the Secretary of Labor. Unions are also required to file an annual financial audit which discloses the union's financial condition and operations for the preceding fiscal year. Conducted by a certified public accountant, the audit report must certify all receipts and expenditures made by the union, salaries and other payments to union leaders, and loans made by the union.

Union officers are required to file yearly reports with the Secretary of Labor. Among other things, they must report any financial interest in the company that employs the union's members or its suppliers.

31-5. Labor-Management Relations in the Public Sector

Certain public employment groups are exempted from NLRB jurisdiction and the provisions of the National Labor Relations Act as amended. These include the employees of the federal and state governments, political state subdivisions, and persons subject to the Railway Labor Act. Thus, strikes by police, firefighters, refuse collectors, air traffic controllers, and other public employees performing vital services are generally illegal unless specifically authorized by state statutes.

The Taft-Hartley Act, while protecting the rights of employees of businesses affecting commerce to bargain collectively, join a union, strike, and petition the NLRB to determine union representation, forbids strikes by government employees. Executive Order No. 11491 established standards of conduct for federal employee unions and authorized the Labor Management Services Administration to decide complaints of alleged unfair labor practices.

Understanding Legal Terms

Define, identify, or explain the following terms:

agency shop	collective	hot cargo	strike
authorization card	bargaining	mediation	unfair labor practice
boycott	constructive	picketing	union shop
certification	discharge		
closed shop	featherbedding		

Questions for Review and Discussion

1. Discuss the substantive and administrative provisions of the National Labor Relations Act.

2. What are the practices by employers declared unfair to labor by the National Labor Relations Act?

3. What are the practices by unions declared unfair to labor by federal labor relation laws?

4. Discuss the jurisdiction and responsibilities of the National Labor Relations Board.

5. What is the procedure either employees or a union must follow in order to be certified by the NLRB as bargaining agent for all employees in a labor unit?

6. What is the procedure followed after employee representatives or employers file an unfair labor practice charge with the NLRB regional director?

7. Discuss the scope of the President's powers to deal with actual or threatened strikes that would affect interstate commerce or endanger the national health or safety.

8. Discuss the central purpose of the Labor-Management Relations Act and the scope of its major provisions.

9. State the primary thrust of the Labor-Management Reporting and Disclosure Act and the specific rights it gives to union members.

10. What reports must unions and their officers file with the Secretary of Labor?

Analyzing Cases

1. The Beaver Valley Lodge No. 200 charged that Jones & Laughlin Steel Corporation had violated the National Labor Relations Act by engaging in unfair labor practices affecting commerce. The alleged practices were that Jones & Laughlin was discriminating against members of the union with regard to hire and tenure of employment and was coercing and intimidating its employees in order to interfere with their self-organization. The discriminatory and coercive action was the discharge of certain employees.

The NLRB held hearings and sustained the union's charge. Jones & Laughlin was ordered to cease and desist, to reinstate the named employees, and to make good their losses in pay. Failing in its petition to the court of appeals to enforce its order, the NLRB petitioned to the U.S. Supreme Court.

Jones & Laughlin contended that the National Labor Relations Act was unconstitutional. The corporation argued that the Tenth Amendment reserves to the states all powers not delegated to the federal government. The corporation pointed out that the only delegation of congressional power to enact the statute could be the power granted to Congress to "regulate commerce . . . among the several States." It was further argued that the discharged employees were engaged in manufacturing only; that the power to regulate commerce does not extend to the power to regulate manufacturing, because "commerce succeeds to manufacturing and is not a part of it." How should the Supreme Court rule on the question of constitutionality of the National Labor Relations Act? Why? ● *NLRB v. Jones & Laughlin Steel Corp.*, 301 U.S. 1 (1937)

2. The NLRB certified a union as bargaining agent for lay teachers in schools operated by the Diocese of Fort Wayne–South Bend, Inc. Its five parochial high schools provided a traditional secular education but were oriented to the beliefs of the Roman Catholic faith. The diocese refused to recognize or bargain with the union, which represented only the lay teachers and nonteaching employees, not religious faculty. The diocese

argued that the NLRB had no jurisdiction over religious schools both on statutory grounds and by the religion clauses of the First Amendment. The NLRB issued cease and desist orders, holding that its exercise of jurisdiction was in line with its policy of declining jurisdiction only when schools are "completely religious," not just "religiously associated," as was the case here. The diocese challenged the NLRB order, and the court of appeals denied enforcement. Accepting a petition for review, how would the U.S. Supreme Court hold on the jurisdiction challenge? Why? ● *NLRB v. Catholic Bishop of Chicago,* 440 U.S. 490 (1979)

3. Republic Aviation Corporation adopted a rule against soliciting in its factory or offices, well before any union activity occurred at its Suffolk County, New York, plant. After being warned by management, an employee persisted in soliciting union membership by passing out application cards to employees. The cards were passed out on the employee's own time during lunch periods in nonworking portions of the plant. For violation of Republic's no-solicitation rule, the employee was discharged. The NLRB found that the discharge was without discrimination on the part of the employer toward union activity per se. That is, the no-solicitation rule would have been enforced not merely against union solicitation but against any solicitation. However, the NLRB found that the enforcement of the rule in these circumstances constituted an unfair labor practice. The NLRB emphasized that although the solicitation took place upon company property it also took place during the employee's lunch hour, when he was on his own time. The court of appeals affirmed, and the U.S. Supreme Court agreed to review the decision. How should the Supreme Court hold? Why? ● *Republic Aviation Corp. v. NLRB,* 324 U.S. 793 (1945)

4. Ninety percent of the Babcock and Wilcox Company employees lived within a thirty-mile radius of the plant and drove to work in automobiles which they parked in a company lot. Because of the traffic conditions, it was practically impossible for union organizers to distribute leaflets safely to employees in their cars as they entered or departed the lot. Union representatives had successfully communicated with a number of the company's employees through the mails, over the telephone, by driving to the home of employees, and by encountering them on the streets of the local community.

Babcock and Wilcox refused to allow union organizers who were not employees to distribute literature promoting union organization on the company-owned parking lot and on the walkway from it to the gatehouse where employees punched in for work. The NLRB found that it was unreasonably difficult for the union organizers to reach the employees off company property. Thus, in refusing the union's access to the parking lot and walkway, the employer had unreasonably impeded their employees' right to self-organization. Babcock and Wilcox challenged the NLRB's order that it rescind its policy of no distribution of union literature in its parking lot and walkway. The court of appeals granted enforcement of the NLRB's order, and Babcock and Wilcox petitioned the U.S. Supreme Court for review. How should the Supreme Court hold? Explain why. ● *NLRB v. Babcock and Wilcox Co.,* 351 U.S. 105 (1956)

5. Exchange Parts Company of Fort Worth, Texas, was advised by the International Brotherhood of Boilermakers that it was conducting an organizational campaign at the plant. The union petitioned the NLRB for an election to determine whether it would indeed be certified as the bargaining agent of the employees. The NLRB held a hearing, granted the union's petition, and set a date for the election.

During the organizational campaign, while the election was pending, the company announced additional benefits for the employees, such as an additional holiday and a new system for computing vacation pay. The new system would have the effect of increasing the amount of pay received by employees while on vacation. Three additional benefits were granted, two of which were announced only a few days before the election. At the election, the employees voted against being represented by a union. The union then filed a complaint with the NLRB charging that Exchange Parts was guilty of an unfair labor practice. The union argued that the granting of benefits while the campaign was taking place and the election pending interfered with the freedom of choice of the employees to determine whether they wished to be represented by the union. The NLRB found the company's announcement of the new benefits to be an unfair labor practice and issued an appropriate order. On the NLRB's petition for enforcement of the order, the court of appeals rejected the board's finding. Having accepted a petition for review, how would the U.S. Supreme Court hold? Why? ● *NLRB v. Exchange Parts Co.*, 375 U.S. 405 (1964)

6. Darlington Manufacturing Company, a South Carolina corporation operating one textile mill, was controlled by the Milliken family, which controlled twenty-seven other mills. The Textile Workers Union initiated an organizational campaign which the company resisted vigorously. After the union won the election, Darlington's board of directors voted to liquidate the corporation, and the decision was approved by the stockholders. All company operations ceased, and the plant machinery and equipment were auctioned off piecemeal.

The employees filed charges of unfair labor practices with the NLRB. The NLRB found that the different mills controlled by the Milliken family represented an integrated enterprise and that the closing of the Darlington mill was due to the antiunion hostility of Deering Milliken, its majority stockholder. Thus, the NLRB found the

closing of the mill to constitute an unfair labor practice. It ordered Deering Milliken to provide back pay to the workers until they obtained similar work or were put on preferential hiring lists at the other Milliken family mills. The court of appeals denied enforcement of the NLRB order. The court held that an independent employer has an absolute right to close a business regardless of motive. On review by the U.S. Supreme Court, how should the Court rule? Explain why. ● *Textile Workers Union v. Darlington Mfg. Co.*, 380 U.S. 263 (1965)

7. The National Labor Relations Board conducted a secret ballot election among production and maintenance employees of Savair Manufacturing Company to determine whether the union would represent the employees. During the election, "recognition slips" were circulated. Employees were told by the union that if they signed the slips before the election they would not have to pay an initiation fee if the union won. The employees were further told that if they failed to sign the slips or signed after the election they would be required to pay the fee if the union won. At least thirty-five employees signed the slips before the election, which the union won by a vote of 22–20. Savair Manufacturing contended the union, by offering possible benefits to employees for signing the recognition slips, was guilty of an unfair labor practice. The company refused to bargain with the union. After a complaint by the union to the NLRB, the board ordered Savair Manufacturing to bargain. The court of appeals denied enforcement of the bargaining order. Should the U.S. Supreme Court hold the court of appeals correct in its denial of the NLRB's order? Why? ● *NLRB v. Savair Mfg. Co.*, 414 U.S. 270 (1973)

8. The General Drivers Allied Automotive and Petroleum Local Union was the certified bargaining agent for employees of Cardinal

Manufacturing Company, Inc. The union concluded a contract with the corporation which contained an agency shop provision. Higgins and two other nonunion employees of Cardinal Manufacturing refused to pay any money to the union. When the union demanded that Cardinal Manufacturing discharge these employees pursuant to its labor contract with the corporation, the employees brought suit in the state courts of Kansas. They requested an injunction prohibiting their discharge, citing the Kansas constitutional amendment commonly known as the "right-to-work amendment." It prohibited compulsory membership in a union. How should the supreme court of Kansas resolve the question of whether an agency shop provision in a labor contract is prohibited by the right-to-work law of Kansas? Why? ● *Higgins v. Cardinal Mfg. Co.*, 360 P.2d 456 (Kan. 1961)

Part 7

Case Briefs

**Audit Services, Inc. v. Elmo Road Corp.,
575 P.2d 77 (Mont. 1978)**
Union representatives requested that Elmo Road Corporation become a participant to certain union trust funds. Winslow, the general manager of Elmo, duly executed collective bargaining compliance agreements with the union representatives. Elmo paid the required contributions to the trust funds for seven months. It then stopped contributing and failed to honor delinquency notices. The trusts then turned the accounts over to a collection agency, which brought suit. The trial court found for Elmo, but the collection agency appealed to the supreme court of Montana.

Petitioner's Position: The general manager, because of his position in the corporation, had both implied and apparent authority. The conduct of the employer, in making payments for a period of time, constituted ratification of the general manager's actions.

Respondent's Position: The authority of the general manager was expressly limited in the bylaws and regulations of the corporation, which did not give Winslow power to make decisions concerning such "major questions of policy."

Legal Issues: (1) Did the general manager have authority, whether actual, implied, or apparent, to sign the contract? (2) Did the corporation, in making contributions for a period of time, ratify the general manager's actions?

Court Decision: The general manager had both implied and apparent authority to sign the contract. The partial payment of an unauthorized contract is strong evidence of ratification.

Court Reasoning: The supreme court agreed with the trial court that Winslow had no actual authority to bind the corporation. However, the general manager was held to have had implied authority when he acted. It was one of the manager's responsibilities to procure the work for the corporation. In order to procure the work, Winslow had to sign the agreements. Thus, the general manager's signature was proper, usual, and necessary in the transaction of his regular responsibilities. Winslow was also held to have had apparent authority to sign the agreement. It was not the responsibility of the union to examine the bylaws and regulations of the corporation. General managers usually sign such agreements on behalf of their corporation. Winslow's position as general manager made him appear to have authority to sign. The court further explained that when a principal, with knowledge of all the material facts, voluntarily makes partial payment on an unauthorized contract, the making of the payment is strong evidence of ratification. The supreme court emphasized that the Taft-Hartley Act had been interpreted to protect the jurisdiction of state courts to enforce the provisions of contracts between labor and management.

**Jurek v. Thompson,
241 N.W.2d 788 (Minn. 1976)**
Jurek, a farmer, trucker, and harvester in grain, entered into an oral contract by telephone for the sale of 19,000 bushels of Thompson's corn to be delivered five months hence. Thompson was to receive $1.50 per bushel and was to pay Jurek 11 cents per bushel for hauling the corn. Jurek contended that a similar second contract was later made concerning the sale of 15,000 bushels at

$1.46 per bushel on the same hauling terms as the first contract. Performance was only partially completed on the first contract, for reasons Thompson thought justifiable, and was never completed on the second contract, which Thompson denied making. After trial, a jury returned a verdict finding that Jurek was Thompson's agent for the sale of the corn and that Jurek sustained damages of $18,563 as a result of nondelivery of the corn. On appeal, the agency issue and the UCC Statute of Frauds were considered relevant. That is, in a transaction characterized as a sale between buyer and seller, the UCC Statute of Frauds is applicable (i.e., a contract for the sale of goods for $500 or more is not enforceable unless there is some writing). However, a contract or agreement between principal and agent is not a sale, and the UCC Statute of Frauds is not applicable.

Plaintiff's Position: Jurek contended he was the agent of the defendant, Thompson, for purposes of reselling the corn. This position was adopted to avoid the application of the UCC Statute of Frauds.

Defendant's Position: Thompson denied that there was an agency relationship between him and the plaintiff, Jurek. The UCC Statute of Frauds was alleged as a defense to the second contract as there was no writing.

Legal Issues: (1) Was the plaintiff the agent of the defendant? (2) What was the effect of the UCC Statute of Frauds?

Court Decision: The court of appeals found there was no agency relationship, only an agreement by Thompson to sell corn to Jurek to conduct hauling as a nonagent independent contractor. The court further found that the second contract was not enforceable be-cause of the UCC Statute of Frauds. Since Thompson admitted making the first contract, the UCC Statute of Frauds was held no bar to enforcement. Other reasons, however, not relevant to agency law were found to bar recovery by Jurek.

Court Reasoning: The court of appeals quoted from the *Restatement (Second) of Agency*, which defines agency as "the fiduciary relation which results from the manifestation of consent by one person to another that the other shall act on his behalf and subject to his control, and consent by the other so to act." The court found the necessary elements for an agency relationship to exist to be lacking. First, there was not found to be any manifestation of consent on the part of Thompson that the plaintiff be his agent in the resale of the corn. There was at most a manifestation of consent that Jurek pick up his corn and pay Thompson an agreed price. Also, the court found the critical element of the right of the alleged principal to control the alleged agent's actions to be totally lacking. Thompson had no control over any phase of Jurek's actions. Thompson merely surrendered the corn and was paid.

Eastex, Inc. v. NLRB,
437 U.S. 556 (1978)
Employees of Eastex, Inc., sought to distribute a union newspaper in nonworking areas of the plant during nonworking time. Portions of the newsletter urged the employees to support the union. Other portions advocated political goals not within the power of the management of Eastex, Inc., to grant or deny. These portions included criticism of a presidential veto of a bill raising the minimum wage and opposition to a proposed in-

corporation of the state's right-to-work statute into a revised state constitution. Eastex denied permission to distribute the literature. Upon complaint of the union, the NLRB found the employer guilty of an unfair labor practice, and the court of appeals enforced the board's order. The U.S. Supreme Court granted *certiorari*.

Petitioner's Position: The NLRB's rules associated with *Republic Aviation Corp. v. NLRB* (see Chapter 31, case 3), that employees may solicit other employees to join a union on the employer's property during nonworking time, should not apply because the newsletter advocated political goals beyond the control of the management of Eastex. The employer's property interest should be interpreted to allow it to bar distribution of such literature on company property.

Respondent's Position: Distribution of the contents of the newsletter was protected by provision of the National Labor Relations Act which protects concerted activity for the "mutual aid or protection" of employees. The matters dealt with by the newsletter were of sufficient concern to the employees as employees that distribution was protected by the act.

Legal Issue: Should *Republic Aviation Corp. v. NLRB* rules be interpreted to require management to permit union distribution of literature (by employees during nonworking hours in nonworking portions of the plant) when the literature addresses political matters?

Court Decision: The employer was required to permit distribution of the literature.

Court Reasoning: The National Labor Relation's Act was interpreted to protect distribution of political, not merely organizational, literature. The political activity was of interest to workers generally. To permit management to bar distribution of the literature would frustrate the policy of the act to protect the right of workers to act together to better their working conditions. It cannot be said, therefore, that the NLRB erred in applying the Republic Aviation rule to the facts of this case.

Part 8   Business Organization

Chapter 32

Creation of Partnership and Special Ventures

There are various forms of business organization. The *sole proprietorship,* a one-person operation, is the simplest and most common form. The net income from the sole proprietorship is added to the proprietor's income from all other sources and taxed like salary. Any operating losses from the business can be directly passed through to the owner, reducing the amount of individual income that is subject to tax. One virtue of a sole proprietorship is its simplicity. No legal forms or agreements need to be drawn up, and the business can be closed down at the owner's discretion.

The *partnership* is another form of business organization. It is an association of two or more persons to carry on as co-owners a business for profit. A partnership does not have an existence separate and apart from the partners. As such, it does not have a legal entity. Thus, a lawsuit cannot be brought against or by a partnership, but only against or by the individual partners. The partners share the income or losses from their business. The partnership serves as a conduit and does not itself pay any taxes. The partners pick up their share of the income or losses on their individual tax returns. Every partnership, however, must file a U.S. Partnership Return annually with the Internal Revenue Service to report the income, deductions, credits, gains, and losses from the operation of a partnership. The law governing partnerships, as discussed in this chapter, is essentially the state statutory law of the Uniform Partnership Act (UPA), adopted by all states except Georgia and Louisiana.

32-1. General Partnership Characteristics

General partnerships may be classified as trading or nontrading. A *trading partnership* is one that buys and sells property or combines the selling of goods with the providing of service. A *nontrading partnership* is one that provides only service, generally on a fee basis, such as a legal, medical, or accounting practice. Trading partners have substantially broader apparent and implied authority to bind the partnership with third parties than do partners in a nontrading partnership.

A. Kinds of Partners

As Table 32-1 shows, partners are classified according to their involvement in the business operations and their obligations to the partnership. They may be general, limited (or special), secret, silent, dormant, or nominal (also known as ostensible partners or partners by implication).

An actual partner who in law and in fact is a co-owner of a business for profit in association with one or more other persons is known as a *general partner*. General partners have unlimited liability for partnership debts, and they publicly and actively engage in the transaction of the business.

A *limited partner* (or *special partner*) is one who does not share in the management of the partnership business. The contribution of a limited partner may be in cash or other property, but not in service. A limited partnership is made up of one or more general partners and one or more limited partners. Limited partnerships may be formed only when permitted by statute, and the liability of the limited partners for debts is limited to the extent of the capital they contributed.

An actual partner who takes an active part in the management of the partnership business but is not known outside the partnership is a *secret partner*. An actual partner who has no voice or active part in the management of the business is a *silent partner*.

Dormant partners do not take an active part in the management or operation of the business, and are unknown publicly as partners. They are nonetheless actual partners and are subject to liability for all partnership obligations.

Occasionally a person appears to be a partner but is only a *nominal partner* (or ostensible partner) by estoppel—that is, one who is not an actual partner but by whose actions can be reasonably believed to be a partner. A nominal partner is as liable as an actual partner to anyone who extends credit in good faith on the assumption that the person is an actual partner both in law and in fact.

B. Partnership Name

The name adopted for a partnership may consist of the names of the general partners or of one partner's name followed by such words as "and sons" (e.g., Melvin Henderson and Sons). Although a partnership name may be adopted or coined, such as The Fashion Conspiracy or Cove Pizza, it may not be decep-

Table 32-1. Kinds of Partners

Type	Business Participation	Relationship to Public	Liability
General	Active	Known	Unlimited
Limited (or special)	Not active	Known	Limited
Secret	Active	Unknown	Unlimited
Silent	Not active	May not be known	Unlimited
Dormant	Not active	Unknown	Unlimited
Nominal (or ostensible)	Not active	Misrepresented	Unlimited

tively similar to that of an existing business. Most states have statutes that require a partnership doing business under a fictitious name to file a business certificate designating the names and addresses of the partners and where the partnership maintains its principal office. Some states prohibit the use of "and company" or "company" unless there is some indication that the business is a partnership.

32-2. Partnership Formation

A partnership agreement may be oral or written. A partnership formation may even result from an informal arrangement in which the terms are not definitely expressed. In the interest of better understanding of the rights and liabilities of partners, however, it is desirable to express the terms of the partnership in writing. The statute of frauds requires that a contract that cannot be carried out within one year must be evidenced by a written agreement if it is to be enforceable.

A. Articles of Partnership

The written agreement that establishes a partnership is called the partnership agreement or *articles of partnership*. In addition to the date of formation, the identity of the partners, and the purpose of the partnership, the agreement generally includes the following information:

○ Name and duration of the partnership
○ Amount of *capital* (net assets) each partner contributed to the partnership
○ Amount of *reserve funds* (retained earnings) from profits to be accumulated
○ Location and withdrawal procedure for all partnership funds
○ Duties of partners
○ Location and accessibility of a full and accurate account of partnership transactions
○ The times and amounts each partner is entitled to withdraw from partnership earnings
○ Provision for the preparation of an annual inventory of assets, liabilities, and income; and the distribution of net profits or net losses between partners
○ Limitations on partners
○ Termination notice procedure

B. Determining Partnership Existence

Courts look for facts that prove the intention of the parties when it is not clear whether a partnership relationship exists. Where the parties have entered into a written agreement, such intentions are chiefly determined from the terms of the writing and from the surrounding circumstances.

Another indication of co-ownership is mutual agency and control of the operations of the business. The sharing of profits and losses of a business is *prima facie* evidence that a partnership relationship exists. This is not the case, however, when the profits shared are received in payment of a debt, wages, annuity, or interest or as consideration for the sale of a business's *goodwill* (i.e., the expected continuance of public patronage). Neither does a joint tenancy or a tenancy in common of itself establish a partnership, even though such co-owners have profits. In like manner, *tenancy by the entirety,* which permits a joint holding of property by a husband and wife with survivorship rights, does not establish a partnership. The profits received in these ways are from property ownership and not from the operation of a trade, occupation, or business. The manner in which a business is described in a tax return or an application for a license may also be helpful in determining whether a partnership actually exists.

32-3. Partnership Property

All property originally brought into the partnership by the partners or acquired by purchase with partnership funds is partnership property. Included in this account are the *capital contributions* of the partners. These are the sums contributed by the co-owners as permanent investments and which they are entitled to have returned to them upon partnership dissolution. Loans that individual partners make to the partnership and accumulated but undivided profits are considered individual property, not partnership capital. Goodwill, including the partnership name, trademarks, and trade names, are also considered to be partnership property.

A. Property Acquisition

Both personal and real partnership property may be acquired in the name of the partnership or in the name of an individual partner as a member of the partnership. It may also be acquired in the name of a third party as *trustee* (person entrusted with the management and control of another's property). The UPA provides that "any estate in real property may be acquired in the partnership name." Also, under common law, legal title to partnership real property can be held in the name of one or more partners or other legal entity. Thus, partnership members may agree that real property owned by one or more partners is in fact partnership property.

1. Ownership Determination. The determination of whether a partner retained ownership of property used in a partnership or turned it over to the partnership may be difficult, unless the intent is expressed in a written agreement. In the absence of a clearly expressed agreement, the courts will make the determination. In doing so, the courts rely on such facts as the intended use of the property turned over, whose funds were used to purchase the property, and who pays for the upkeep of the property and claims depreciation for tax purposes.

● When Wisecarver and Woodcock formed the Wisecarver and Woodcock Electronics partnership, they located their shop in a garage owned by Woodcock. Although the electric, oil, and water services used in the business were billed to the partnership and paid with partnership funds, the taxes and insurance on the property were paid by Woodcock. If the partnership were dissolved, ownership of the garage would remain with Woodcock and would not be considered a part of Woodcock's capital contribution to the partnership.

2. Conveyance. Partnership property can be subsequently *conveyed* (i.e., transferred) only by and in the name of the partnership. The partnership may recover transferred property if the partner who transferred it had no authority to act for the partnership. In order to recover, however, the person with whom the partner dealt must have had knowledge of the fact that the partner lacked such authority. Title to partnership property, in the name of one or more but not all the partners, may be transferred by a partner in the partnership name or in the partner's own name. However, the partner must be authorized to so act.

B. Property Rights of a Partner

The UPA distinguishes between partner rights in specific partnership property and partner interest in the partnership.

1. Tenancy in Partnership. Each partner has a property interest in partnership property and is a co-owner in such property. This form of ownership is known as *tenancy in partnership* and has characteristics that distinguish it from a joint tenancy or a tenancy in common. The characteristics of a tenancy in partnership are such that:

○ A partner, subject to any agreement to the contrary between the partners, has an equal right with partners to possess and use specific partnership property for partnership purposes. Such property cannot be possessed for any other purpose without the consent of the partners.

○ A partner's interest in partnership property may not be *assigned* (i.e., transferred by sale, mortgage, pledge, or otherwise) to a nonpartner, except in connection with the transfer of rights of all the partners in the same property.

○ A partner's right in partnership property is not subject to *attachment* (taken to furnish security for debts or costs), except on a claim against the partnership.

○ Under the doctrine of *equitable conversion,* a deceased partner's interest in real property held by the partnership passes to the surviving partners.

○ A partner's right in specific partnership property is not subject to any allowances or rights to widows, heirs, or next of kin. Only the partners' rights to their share of the partnership's profits can pass to their heirs at law.

2. Partner Interest in the Partnership. Partners' interests in the partnership are their share of the profits and *surplus.* The latter is any funds of a dissolved partnership that remain after the payment of all partnership debts and other prior obligations.

3. Assignment of Partner Interest. Partners may voluntarily assign their interests in the partnership without dissolving the partnership. The assignee in such an action is not entitled to take part in the management or administration of the partnership business or affairs. There is no entitlement to receive information or account of partnership transactions or to inspect partnership records. The assignee is entitled to receive, in keeping with the assignment contract, the profits to which the assigning partner would otherwise receive.

32-4. Partner Rights, Duties, and Liabilities

Every partner is an agent of the partnership. Hence, the act of every partner, for the purpose of its business, binds and thus obligates the partnership. Any unauthorized act of a partner in a particular matter, where the person with whom the partner is dealing has knowledge that the partner has no such authority, does not bind the partnership. Subject to any agreement between partners, their rights and duties in relation to the partnership are determined by UPA provisions.

A. Right to Participate in Management

All partners have equal rights in the management and conduct of the partnership business. Participation rights are not limited by the value or kind of contribution each partner makes to the partnership. Any differences arising as to ordinary matters connected with the partnership business may be decided by a majority of the partners (or by unanimous decision, if there are only two partners). Acts that might obstruct any agreement between partners or affect the successful operation of the business, however, may not be done rightfully without the consent of all the partners. In addition, no person can become a member of a partnership without the consent of all the partners.

● Guarino and Barnes, law partners of Pettengill, were convinced that the firm would benefit if the partnership was enlarged. They proposed to Pettengill that a new partner be brought in to handle the increased case load. Pettengill disagreed and threatened to go to court, if necessary, to dissolve the partnership. Pettengill is acting within her rights. The court could issue a decree recognizing that the action of Pettengill's partners had dissolved the partnership.

B. Right to Profits, Contributions, and Compensation

Each partner has a right to share in the profits that result from the operation of the partnership business, but not to receive a salary. If the ratio in which the partners are to share profits is not spelled out in the articles of partnership, partners share the profits in equal proportions. Whether in writing or not, the ratio in which partners share profits is not necessarily dependent on the ratio of each partner's capital contribution to the partnership. Partners must also contribute toward the losses, whether of capital or otherwise, sustained by the partnership in the same proportion in which they share in the profits.

● Illness required McDougal to be hospitalized for six weeks. Her partner in McDougal & Rockwell Antiques had to work long hours to keep the business operating. In spite of her extra effort, Rockwell is not entitled to a greater share of the profits than that established in the articles of partnership. In the event a loss results from McDougal's inability to participate in partnership operations, each partner's liability remains proportionately equal.

All partners have a right to receive the balance of their capital contribution upon liquidation of the partnership, after all creditors have been satisfied. There is no right to receive interest on capital contributions, unless there is a delay in transferring money back to the contributor. Advances of money to the partnership, beyond the capital contribution, are considered loans. The partner making the loan becomes a creditor of the partnership and has a right to recover the loan with interest. Moreover, a partner is entitled to *indemnity* (the right to compensation) from the other partners for any losses suffered while discharging the partnership business or in preserving its property.

● Ling, Lawson, and Filgate operated a partnership and accumulated a substantial debt with Pilgrim Freight Carriers which they were unable to pay. The carrier brought suit against Ling alone and secured a judgment. Ling would be successful in a suit against his partners for proportionate reimbursement. A partner is entitled to indemnity, which would require Lawson and Filgate to contribute their share of the debt to Ling.

A partner is not entitled to *remuneration* (payment for personal service, loss, or expense) for acting in behalf of the partnership business unless the articles of partnership between the partners authorize it. It is proper, however, to charge a partner the cost of hiring someone, even another partner, to do the work not performed that is called for in the partnership agreement.

C. Right to Partnership Books and Accounting

Partnership books must be kept at the principal place of business of the partnership. Every partner has access rights to the books at all times as well as the right to inspect and copy any of them. This right may be exercised by a partner's lawyer, accountant, or other agent.

● After an extended business trip, Sykes returned to her office and discovered that the firm's records of receipts and expenses kept by her partner had been removed from the office. Sykes's partner had taken them home, explaining that it was more convenient to record an accumulation of transactions in the privacy of his home. This unauthorized removal of the firm's records and accounts could be considered a breach of the partnership agreement.

Any partner has the right to a formal accounting of partnership affairs whenever a dissolution of the partnership is decreed by the court. The Uniform Partnership Act also gives partners the right to a formal accounting whenever they have been wrongfully excluded from the partnership business or from possession of partnership property by copartners.

D. Fiduciary Duties

Each partner has a fiduciary duty to act primarily for the other's benefit in all matters connected with partnership affairs in the highest good faith, fairness, and trust. Partners must account to the partnership for any benefit and hold as trustee for it any profits gained from any partnership transaction. A partner may not use partnership funds or property secretly for personal benefit or payment of personal debts. In addition, a partner may not compete with the partnership business.

● O'Keefe discovered that her partner Mays was servicing several clients and pocketing the fees collected. O'Keefe demanded a full accounting of these transactions and requested that all such fees be deposited in the partnership account. If Mays failed to do so, she would be giving further evidence of bad faith, which constitutes a breach of the partnership agreement.

A partner is not generally required to account, however, for profits acquired from business transactions beyond the scope of the partnership business.

E. Liability of Partners

The liability for torts committed by a partner or an employee of the partnership in the course of partnership business is joint and several. This means that each partner is liable and may be sued in a separate action or a joint action. A judgment may be against one or more partners but not others, and the release of one partner in one action does not of necessity release the others. Partners who participate in a criminal act are separately liable.

Partners are jointly liable on all contractual obligations of the partnership. This means that in a suit brought jointly against all partners, each partner is a defendant. A judgment must be against all or none of the partners, and a release of one partner releases all of them.

● Johnson disagreed with Ernst on the need for a new chain hoist used in lifting engines that the partnership was servicing. Without Johnson's agreement, Ernst placed an order for the hoist in the partnership name. Since Ernst acted within his apparent authority as an agent of the partnership in carrying on the business of the partnership, the partners would be jointly liable for the contractual debt.

Business and investment needs have given rise to new forms of business organizations. Each of these minor organizational forms seeks to obtain a beneficial objective such as increased financial gain, reduced personal liability, or a tax advantage.

32-5. Limited Partnership

Limited partnerships are governed by the 1916 Uniform Limited Partnership Act and by 1976 revisions in a few states. The limited partnership is a popular form of noncorporate business organization for investors who desire limited liability and the right to deduct expenses and losses of the business from other income. A limited partnership is formed by filing a certificate with the designated public official (often the office of the secretary of state) where the partnership is doing business. Each limited partnership must have at least one general partner and one or more limited partners. The limited partner is a nonparticipating investor. That is, limited partners do not take part in the management or control of the business and are not bound by partnership obligations. Limited partners' personal liability for partnership debts is limited to their capital contribution to the business. Although the contribution is generally in the form of cash or property, the 1976 revisions of the act allow contributions of services.

Limited partners may be employed by the partnership and paid for services rendered like any other employee or agent. Limited partners share profits earned by the partnership as specified in the partnership certificate, but not losses in excess of their capital contribution. The death of a general partner may dissolve the limited partnership unless it is continued by the remaining general partners. Each limited partner has priority over general partners in the distribution of net assets upon liquidation. Deceased limited partners pass their limited partnership interests on to their estate, and the partnership continues.

32-6. Special Business Ventures

Various minor forms of business organization have evolved through modification of old forms of organization.

A. Franchise

In franchising arrangements the *franchisor* (party granting the franchise) generally authorizes the use of a trademark or trade name and imposes some rules as to identification. In the Holiday Inn type of arrangement, the franchisor provides a *franchisee* (person to whom a franchise is given) with a complete ready-to-operate business. The relationship between franchisor and franchisee is similar to that between two separate and technically independent contractors. That is, their rights are determined by the contract between them.

Controls are generally the most significant characteristic of a franchise, since effectiveness and profitability depend upon the public's receiving the same product and/or service at all franchisor's locations. Although such controls as the uniforms of employees or the color of the building do not present antitrust problems, those that affect the franchisee's income often do. For example, the franchisor cannot dictate to an independent franchisee the ultimate resale price of the product or service involved. Tying arrangements in any form are illegal per se. Thus, if a patented process, machine, or product is involved, it is illegal to tie it to the use, sale, or purchase of unpatented articles. Territorial allocations are generally illegal. Franchisees are free to sell the franchisor's product or service wherever and to whomever they wish. Other restrictions are not illegal per se. These include granting exclusive distribution rights, establishing sales quotas, and placing restrictions on the handling of competitive products.

There is no such thing as a typical franchise period. The term of the agreement can range from one year to ten years. Often the agreements allow a franchisor to terminate the arrangement upon thirty days' notice or less. However, courts may refuse to allow the franchisor a sudden termination on the ground that it is unconscionable, particularly when a franchise has failed to earn back its initial investment. Some states have passed laws protecting the franchisee or dealer or both from a sudden termination except for *good cause*. The courts generally determine good cause to be the failure to comply substantially with franchisee obligations under lease and dealer agreements.

B. Joint Venture

A *joint venture* is, in effect, a temporary creation of a new business in which two or more individuals, partners, or corporations combine part of their assets for the purpose of accomplishing a particular result or project. For example, joint venturers may organize a business to produce a specific product. Although joint ventures differ from partnerships in respect to their more temporary tenure and limited objective, the courts generally hold them subject to partnership law. A joint venture also differs from a merger, where two or more companies combine all their assets to create a new business and the merged company becomes a part of the acquiring company.

The management and operation of a joint venture are shared equally by all joint venturers. Usually, each joint venturer has joint and several liability for all joint venture obligations, including injury to third persons due to the negligence of members. Joint venturers also have a fiduciary duty to account for profits which are taxable when earned, even though not distributed to members.

C. Business Trust

A *business trust* is essentially a voluntary agreement whereby owners of property transfer legal title to one or more persons (trustees) so that the property can be managed for the benefit of the original owners. An early form known as a Massachusetts trust was established to avoid a former prohibition that denied corporations the authority to own and deal in real estate.

Certain key features distinguish the business trust. Grantors, by the terms of the agreement, are entitled to a trust certificate showing their ownership of a stated interest in the trust. The grantor's interest can be sold or otherwise transferred. Trustees have the sole right to manage and control the business free of the control of the grantors. Shares in a business trust may be transferred. The trust agreement usually sets forth the property being transferred, the life of the trust, and the duties of the trustees in respect to the management of the property. It may also state the persons to whom the income of the trust is to be paid, the share to be received by each grantor, the method of winding up the trust, and the number of shares to be left in the trust property when it is terminated.

The trustees are personally liable for the debts of the business, since they are its legal owners. To escape liability on contracts of the business, trustees must obtain agreement with the grantors that all such obligations rest with the assets of the trust. All personal responsibility for trustee torts or torts of their agents and employees cannot be avoided, although it can be offset by insurance.

D. Joint Stock Company

A *joint stock company* or association is a form of business organization with some characteristics of both a partnership and a corporation. Its capital is represented by certificate shares which may be transferred. Management is generally in the hands of a board of trustees or delegated to designated officers who have sole authority to bind members who are not agents. A member's death or the transfer of a member's shares does not dissolve the joint stock company. Unlike members of a corporation, members of a joint stock company have unlimited liability for the debts and obligations of the company, as well as liability for tort claims.

Understanding Legal Terms

Define, identify, or explain the following terms:

articles of partnership	general partner	nominal partner	secret partner
business trust	goodwill	nontrading partnership	silent partner
capital contribution	joint stock company	partnership	tenancy in partnership
dormant partner	joint venture	reserve funds	trustee
franchisee	limited partner		

Questions for Review and Discussion

1. How is a general partner defined in the Uniform Partnership Act?

2. Compare a dormant partner and a secret partner in respect to management and involvement in partnership business.

3. Explain how the existence of a partnership is determined by law, if there are no articles of partnership.

4. Discuss the limitation placed on a partner in the conveyance of personal or real

property acquired only in the partnership name or in the name of one or more but not all the partners.

5. Differentiate between the partner's rights in specific property and the partner's interest in the partnership.

6. What are the rights of partners with respect to one another?

7. Discuss the fiduciary duty in the conduct of partnership affairs.

8. What is a partner's liability for (*a*) contracts entered into by copartners and (*b*) torts committed by copartners while acting within the actual or apparent scope of partnership business?

9. Define a franchise, and explain why this arrangement is a desirable method of controlling business operations.

10. Contrast a joint venture relationship with that of a partnership in respect to duration and liability to third persons.

Analyzing Cases

1. Annette and Enos White owned farm property in Vermont, where they conducted business. The property was held as a tenancy by the entirety. This is a form of joint tenancy of husband and wife that can be terminated only by joint action of both during their lives and in which after death of one the survivor takes the whole. They devoted their full time and all their financial resources to their family business. Receipts and proceeds from the business transactions were deposited into a joint bank account (account used by both). Disbursements for operating the business were made by checks drawn on the account. The vehicles used in operating the business were registered in the name of Annette. They were taken by Enos to the garage of Raymond S. Roberts, Inc., for servicing and repairs and billed to Enos. Certain payments for repairs were not made, and a suit was brought against both Enos and Annette White for breach of contract. While other grounds for not making payment were also raised, Annette argued that the bill was Enos's responsibility and that she was not liable for payment. She contended that no partnership between herself and her husband existed and that it had never been the parties' intention to form a partnership. Since the court found no valid defenses existed, Enos clearly was liable to the garage for the repair services provided. On these facts, is Annette liable as well? Why? ● *Raymond S. Roberts, Inc. v. White*, 97 A.2d 245 (Vt. 1953)

2. Summers and Dooley formed a partnership for the purpose of operating a trash collection business. The business was operated by the two men, and when either was unable to work, the nonworking partner provided a replacement at his own expense.

Summers approached Dooley and requested that they hire a third worker. Dooley refused. Notwithstanding Dooley's refusal, Summers, on his own initiative, hired a worker. Summers paid the employee out of his own pocket. Dooley, upon discovery that a third person had been hired, objected. He stated that the additional labor was not necessary and refused to allow partnership funds to be used to pay the new employee. After paying out more than $11,000 in wages without any reimbursement from either partnership funds or his partner, Summers brought suit in the Idaho state courts. The trial court held that Summers was not entitled to reimbursement for the wages he had paid the employee. On appeal to the supreme court of Idaho, how should that court decide the case? Why? ● *Summers v. Dooley*, 418 P.2d 318 (Idaho 1971)

3. Investment Exchange Corporation established Auburn West Associates as a limited partnership. Although Investment Exchange Corporation was to be the sole general partner, a number of other partners invested in the business as limited partners. The latter purchased their shares after being supplied with a prospectus (printed statement that describes a business) required by the Securities and Exchange Commission. The purpose of the partnership was to acquire for investment purposes and to improve and resell real property. The articles of partnership of Auburn West specifically and expressly stated that the real estate would be purchased for the partnership from the general partner which controlled the business. The general partner was given broad discretion by the partnership articles to manage the partnership affairs. The articles left to the "sole determination" of the general partner the responsibility for deciding which tracts of land to acquire. The articles also specifically gave the general partner the right to have an interest in another business which would deal with the partnership.

The general partner carried out the business by selling property Investment Exchange Corporation had originally purchased to the partnership at prices higher than it had paid. On property known as the Murakami property, the general partner marked up the price to the partnership by $167,500. Certain limited partners brought suit in the Washington state courts to recover the $167,500 profit the general partner had realized. The trial court found that in issuing the prospectus and financial statements to the investors, the general partner made no false or fraudulent statements.

The court found that an understanding had existed that the general partner would acquire property and would sell it to the partnership at a fair price and would realize a profit on the transaction. Moreover, the court did not find that any formula was agreed upon to determine how much profit could be realized by each transaction. On appeal of the trial court's ruling in favor of the general partner, how should the supreme court of Washington resolve the case? Why? ● *Bassan v. Investment Exchange Corporation*, 524 P.2d 233 (Wash. 1974)

4. St. John and three others entered into an agreement to purchase about 6½ acres of land in Connecticut for investment purposes. They agreed to share equally in the cost of the property, the maintenance expense, and the profits or losses upon its resale. Their agreement was silent on the question as to whether or not they were partners. The property was purchased for $33,000. The sum of $8,000 was paid in cash, and the remaining $25,000 was financed through two mortages.

When it became necessary to refinance one of the mortgages, St. John was the only one of the four able to obtain credit. He used his personal credit to obtain a $25,000 mortgage, which he used to refinance both of the previous mortgages. The three others with whom St. John conducted business paid their share of the maintenance expenses for only a short time, then defaulted. For a period of three years, St. John made repeated requests for payment of the maintenance expenses. Finally, St. John sent notices to the others that the enterprise was terminated and offered to return their original investment if in the near future the property was sold for a profit. Shortly thereafter St. John sold the property for $100,000. The three others brought suit against St. John. They contended that a partnership agreement existed between themselves and St. John and that an accounting of profits was in order. How should the contentions of the plaintiffs be resolved? Why? ● *Travis v. St. John*, 404 A.2d 85 (Conn. 1978)

5. Brew was driving a car on a state highway in California when he collided with another vehicle. All occupants of both cars were killed. The wife and mother of the occupants of the other car commenced a wrongful death action, naming as defendants Brew's estate and a number of other parties. One of the defendants named was United Plumbing & Heating Co., Inc., which was asserted to have been one of Brew's employers.

The facts showed that Brew was employed by Taylor, a Los Angeles contractor. Taylor was presented with the opportunity of doing jobs in Las Vegas on a basis of cost plus 15 percent. Not licenced to act as a contractor in

Las Vegas, Taylor enlisted the aid of United Plumbing, which was licenced to do work there. It was agreed between Taylor and United Plumbing that United Plumbing would "take over" the jobs by obtaining the necessary permits, hiring and paying the workers, and furnishing such material as Taylor requested. Taylor was to draw the plans, direct the men on the job, and furnish the part of the material which was not supplied by United Plumbing. United Plumbing was to receive its costs plus 10 percent; Taylor was to receive the balance of the 15 percent profit from the jobs. United Plumbing was paid directly by the contractor on some occasions, through Taylor on others.

Brew had come to Las Vegas from Los Angeles to work on the jobs in question. He was transferred from Taylor's payroll to that of United Plumbing. When the accident occurred, Brew was driving Taylor's car and was to be reimbursed by Taylor for gas and oil. United Plumbing argued that it did nothing more than sell labor and material to Taylor and that the money it received was in the nature of compensation. Was United Plumbing responsible for the negligence of Brew? Why? ● *Holtz v. United Plumbing and Heating Co.*, 319 P.2d 617 (Cal. 1957)

6. Irving and Hyman Zemelman were partners and did business under the name Art Seating Company. Their partnership place of business was damaged by fire, and claims were filed with several fire insurance companies with which the partnership had insurance. In filing certain of the claims, Irving made false statements. Irving was convicted after a jury trial on the charge of filing false insurance claims. The various policies contained clauses, each policy stating that the "entire policy shall be void if . . . the insured has wilfully concealed or misrepresented any material fact or circumstance. . . ." Hyman argued that the misrepresentation by Irving should not be imputed to him, that he was innocent, and that he should be allowed to collect his one-half of the proceeds from the insurance companies which had been defrauded even if Irving could not collect. Was Hyman's contention correct? Why? ● *Zemelman v. Boston Ins. Co.*, 84 Cal. Rptr. 206 (1970)

7. Steitz and Hamrick were partners in the operation of a restaurant in Fresno, California, known as the Desert Inn. The partnership had been in existence for many years. Hamrick lived in Fresno and acted as manager for the business. Steitz resided in another city. Hamrick made and executed for the partnership a promissory note in writing for the sum of $6,700 with interest. When the note was not paid, suit was brought for collection. Steitz was one of the parties named as a defendant. He argued, among other defenses, that he was not liable because the formalities of the UCC were not properly complied with.

The UCC, as adopted in California, states in part that no person shall be liable on an instrument unless that person's signature appears on the instrument. Steitz's signature did not in fact appear on the note. Hamrick had affixed his own name (with "Desert Inn' underneath) to the note. Should Steitz's argument be accepted by the court? Why? ● *McCollum v. Steitz*, 67 Cal. Rptr. 703 (1968)

8. George Chapman and his brother William were agents for Western Life Insurance Company. They operated an insurance agency under the joint trade name of Western Life Agency in the state of Illinois. Western Life Agency's checking accounts were joint accounts in the name of George and William Chapman. George and William filed partnership tax returns which indicated their income was divided equally. They were responsible for the collection and forwarding of insurance premiums to Western Life Insurance Company. These premiums were required to be kept in segregated accounts and not used for any business or personal purpose of the Chapmans. The agency became delinquent in forwarding payments. This delinquency was partly due to the fact that cer-

tain payments of premiums to the agency were never reported to Western Life Insurance Company. Also contributing to the delinquency was George's withdrawal of $12,630.41 from a trust account used for the purpose of handling the premiums, causing checks written for purposes of paying the premiums to Western Life Insurance Company to bounce.

Western Life Insurance Company commenced a suit to recover the delinquent amounts. George did not defend the action for collection. William, however, defended himself. He argued that the business was owned by his brother as a sole proprietorship, that he was merely an employee of the business, and that any wrongdoing by his brother could not be imputed to him. Judgment for whom, and why? ● *Western Life Ins. Co. of America v. Chapman,* 334 N.E.2d 806 (Ill. 1975), *cert. denied* 424 U.S. 927 (1976)

9. Pedersen and two others were employed on a barge and crane anchored in the Hudson River. The three were injured when part of a crane on the barge broke, causing them to be thrown into the river. Pedersen was killed, and the two others survived but suffered injuries. Their employer, Snare-Dravo, was a joint venture. Frederick Snare Corporation and the Dravo Corporation were participants. In the Jones Act, Congress had provided that seamen who suffer injury in the course of employment could sue their employer for damages. Suit was brought in the state courts of New York against Frederick Snare Corporation and the Dravo Corporation. These parties raised several defenses, one of which was their contention that they were not proper party defendants. They argued that an action based upon the Jones Act was required to be brought against the employer, and the plaintiffs were not their employees but employees of Snare-Dravo. The case reached the court of appeals of New York (that state's highest court). How should the court of appeals of New York dispose of this case? Is it relevant that Snare-Dravo was a joint venture and not a partnership? ● *Pedersen v. Manitowac Co.,* 255 N.E.2d 146 (N.Y. 1969)

Chapter 33

Termination of Partnership

Events may interrupt the operation of a partnership and bring about its dissolution and a subsequent winding up and termination of its business affairs. Each of these formal steps in ending a partnership—dissolution, winding up, and termination—alters the legal capacity of the partnership and of its partners.

33-1. Dissolution of Partnership

The UPA defines *dissolution of partnership* as a change in the relation of the partners caused by any partner ceasing to be associated in the carrying on of the business. Dissolution is automatically caused by the death of a partner, by the admission of a new partner, or by the retirement of an existing partner. Dissolution is to be distinguished from the winding up and termination of the partnership, which effectively put it out of business. Dissolution may be caused without violation of the partnership agreement by the expiration of the term of partnership, the accomplishment of its objectives, or the death or bankruptcy of a partner. It may also occur at the will of a partner or by mutual agreement of the partners, where no third-party interests are involved. In a few special instances, a court will decree the dissolution.

A. Dissolution by Acts of the Partners

A partnership may be dissolved without partner liability by the passage of a specified period of time, the occurrence of an agreed-upon event, or the completion of a purpose called for in the agreement. For example, a partnership formed to buy and develop a particular tract of land is dissolved when the land is subdivided and the houses or other structures are built and sold. In the event no definite term or particular undertaking is designated in a partnership agreement, a *partnership at will* exists. Any partner may dissolve a partnership at will at any time. A partnership at will also exists if the partners dissolve the partnership but at their pleasure continue to do partnership business without a new agreement. Generally, a partner who dissolves a partnership at will is not liable for any damages to other partners.

By the mutual consent of all the partners, a partnership may be dissolved without violating the partnership agreement. This right by unanimous action is retained by the remaining partners even when a nonpartner is assigned all or part of a partner's interest in the partnership, for instance, as security for a loan.

Dissolution is also brought about when a partner is expelled by the other partners for cause, when such a power is conferred by the agreement between the partners. For example, the agreement may specify such causes for expulsion as misconduct or failure to perform duties or when the action is in the best interest of the partnership. The expelled partner is entitled to a cash payment of the expelled partner's share of the net worth of the partnership and goodwill, less any debts or obligations owed by the expelled partner to the partnership. When a partner is expelled, and the remaining partners continue the business without liquidation of the partnership affairs, creditors of the dissolved partnership are the creditors of those partners or the partnership continuing the business.

● The partnership of Gregory, Belovsky, and West suffered serious losses because of West's damaging conduct, which violated their partnership agreement. Gregory and Belovsky served notice expelling West, explaining why the expulsion was in the best interest of the partnership. West would receive in cash the net amount due her from the partnership and would be discharged from all partnership liabilities. The partnership assets need not be liquidated. Gregory and Belovsky may form a new partnership and continue the business either alone or with other partners.

B. **Dissolution by Operation of Law**

Dissolution of the partnership is caused automatically by the death of a partner. In this form of dissolution by operation of law, the deceased partner's estate has the right either to have the partnership wound up within a reasonable time or to be paid the value of the deceased partner's share in cash.

Bankruptcy of the partnership or of one of the partners also causes a dissolution by operation of law. However, *insolvency* (i.e., inability or failure to pay debts as they fall due) of the partnership or one or more partners alone does not cause a dissolution. Being insolvent is insufficient cause for dissolution until action required by law is taken that entitles creditors to have partnership or partner assets administered for their benefit.

Events may also operate to dissolve a partnership by operation of law. For example, the disbarment of a law partner would prevent the excluded attorney from practicing law, thereby dissolving the partnership.

C. **Dissolution by Court Decree**

When partners cannot work out their differences by agreement, one or more of them may petition a court for a decree ordering a dissolution or recognizing that one has taken place. A partner may apply to the court for a dissolution because of insanity or incapacity of a partner to perform part of the partnership agreement. Decrees are also granted when a partner acts in a way which is harmful to the partnership or willfully or persistently breaches the partnership agreement. Where the partnership can be carried on only at a loss or where other circumstances such as fraudulent conduct or irreconcilable dissensions render a dissolution just and fair, a court will decree a dissolution. Trifling causes such as temporary illness, differences in opinion, and errors in judgment are not sufficient grounds for a dissolution decree. A *judgment creditor* (i.e., one who has obtained a determination against a debtor, in this case against a partner) is also entitled to have the partnership dissolved by court decree.

D. **Dissolution in Contravention of Partnership Agreement**

A partner at any time has the power to dissolve the partnership. Withdrawing partners will be liable for damages to the remaining partners, however, if their withdrawal constitutes a breach of the partnership agreement. Wrongfully withdrawing partners nevertheless are entitled to the value of their interest in the partnership, excluding the worth of the partnership goodwill.

E. Notice of Dissolution

Until they are given notice or have knowledge that a partnership has been dissolved, third persons who deal with a partnership are justified in continuing to deal with it in their usual manner. *Actual notice* of a dissolution rather than an implied one must be given directly to persons who have extended credit to the partnership. Persons who know of a partnership's existence, but have not extended credit, may be given *constructive notice*. It may be in the form of an advertisement placed in a newspaper of general circulation in the area in which the partnership business was carried on.

Notice must be given to the other partners when the partnership is dissolved by the acts of a partner. Failure to do so binds the withdrawing partner in respect to third parties by the contracts created for the partnership.

● The partnership of Dalton, Kimberling, and Bucur made contracts with B & C Graphics for product design services on a number of occasions. During one of these transactions, the partnership became a corporation. When the services were not paid in full, B & C Graphics sued the partnership as individuals. Since no notice of the incorporation of the business had been given B & C Graphics, the individual partners were jointly and severally liable. It would be of no importance to the court that the business was in fact a corporation in regard to the contractual obligation.

Notice to third persons is not necessary when partnership dissolution is caused by operation of law. Neither is notice between partners necessary when dissolution results from a partner's death or from bankruptcy.

33-2. Winding Up of Partnership Affairs

In the event of a *partnership termination* (that is, an ending of the partnership's life), there must be a *winding up* of the partnership business following dissolution. This action involves the orderly *liquidation* of the partnership's assets, the payment of partnership creditors from cash on hand and from assets, and the distribution, if any, of the remaining surplus to the partners according to their profit-sharing ratios. Until this action is accomplished, the partnership continues. The partners continue to owe a fiduciary duty to each other, but they have only limited authority to bind the partnership through acts which are reasonably necessary to carry out the winding up.

A. Right to Wind Up

The right to wind up the partnership is generally granted to the partners who have not wrongfully dissolved the business, except where they cannot agree. Where the partners cannot agree, a court-appointed receiver may carry out the winding up.

B. Process of Winding Up

The partner or person charged with the winding up has the power to do all acts reasonably necessary to wind up partnership affairs or complete transactions unfinished at dissolution. Debts and other liabilities of the partnership must be satisfied. Real and personal property of the partnership may be sold in order to discharge them. Debts due the partnership must be collected, and court action may be taken, if necessary, to collect them. Executory contracts must be carried out. These are contracts which have not been performed by all the parties to them.

● The partnership of Rossetti, DiCorcia, and Mileto was awarded a contract by the city of New Britain, Connecticut, to build a new courthouse. After 30 percent of the blueprints were completed, the partnership was dissolved. Upon receiving notice of the dissolution, New Britain terminated the services of the partnership by hiring new architects for the project. Rossetti brought suit against New Britain for breach of contract for architectural services. The court held that when New Britain hired other architects to do the work, the agreement was unjustly terminated. The court noted that it is a principle of partnership law that, on dissolution, the partnership remains in existence for the purpose of performing existing executory contracts.

The person charged with the winding up may make new purchases and even borrow money in the name of the partnership in order to preserve the value of partnership assets. Partnership members are liable for any debts or for torts committed in the course of winding up.

After the winding up, all partners have the right to be paid their capital contribution together with a respective share of any surplus funds. In the event a debt is owed one or more of the partners, partnership property may be transferred to satisfy that debt. The assets remaining after the debt is paid may then be distributed equitably among the partners.

Partners are entitled to a true and full account of the assets and liabilities of the partnership as of the date of dissolution and after winding up. This final *accounting* is a statement detailing the financial transactions of the partnership and the status of its assets. It includes a listing of original contributions and current assets and liabilities. Canceled checks, bills, vouchers, and other appropriate documents are provided to support the statement.

C. Settling Accounts After Dissolution

In settling accounts between the partners after dissolution, unless otherwise agreed, the assets of the partnership are its property and the contributions of the partners necessary for the payment of its liabilities. The liabilities of the partnership are ranked in the following order:

○ Those owing to creditors other than partners
○ Those owing to partners for loans or advances made to the partnership
○ Those owing to partners as repayment for their capital contributions
○ Those owing to partners for their share of profits, if any

● In a partnership formed by Siebert, Bottom, and Khandpur, Siebert made a capital contribution of $15,000; Bottom, $10,000 plus services; and Khandpur, experience and goodwill. They agreed to share equally in partnership profits. On dissolution and winding up, it was found that the partnership had no assets to meet a creditor's bill of $12,000 or to pay off $5,000 that Siebert had loaned the firm. In settling the partnership accounts, the court determined the following obligations:

$12,000 (creditor's bill)
 5,000 (Siebert's loan)
15,000 (Siebert's capital contribution)
10,000 (Bottom's capital contribution)
$42,000 total obligations

Inasmuch as the partners agreed to share equally in the partnership's profits, the court held that they must cover losses equally. Hence, each partner's share of the obligation was $14,000. In determining the partners' required contributions, it was found that Siebert's $15,000 capital contribution exceeded his $14,000 obligation. The balance due him was $1,000. Bottom's contribution was $4,000, the difference between his capital contribution of $10,000 and his $14,000 share of the obligation. Khandpur must contribute a full $14,000 share of the obligation, since she had not made a money contribution to the firm. Thus, the total required contribution was $18,000.

In the settlement of accounts, the $18,000 would be distributed as follows: $12,000 to the creditor for debt repayment, $5,000 to Siebert for loan repayment, and $1,000 to Siebert for partial return of capital contribution.

Thus, in keeping with Section 18(a) of the Uniform Partnership Act, each partner contributed toward the losses, whether of capital or otherwise, in accordance with their profit-sharing ratios.

1. **Insolvency.** If the partnership becomes insolvent, each individual partner must personally contribute sufficient money to satisfy outstanding partnership debts which exceed total partnership capital. If any of the partners are personally insolvent as well, the solvent partners contribute funds in the same ratio that they share losses in the normal course of partnership business.

2. **Marshaling of Assets.** Where the individual partners as well as the partnership are insolvent, the doctrine of *marshaling of assets* is applied. In doing so, the court segregates the property of the partnership from the property of the individual partners. Partnership creditors are given first claim over nonpartnership creditors in the partnership assets. If these are insufficient to satisfy all the outstanding debts, partnership creditors may then make claim against the assets of the individual partners. Nonpartnership creditors, however, are given priority over partnership creditors in the individual assets of the partners and an inferior claim in partnership assets. Thus, each class of creditor is not permitted to make demands on the asset entitlements of another class until the claims of that other class of creditors have been satisfied.

3. **Partnership Continuance.** Partnerships often continue without a winding up following a dissolution at will, the completion of the partnership term, or the expulsion or wrongful withdrawal of a partner. Although a change in the membership of the partnership technically dissolves the old partnership, the dissolved partnership's business may be carried on without interruption. The continuing partnership becomes a new partnership. The law assumes that the continuing entity is carried on by the remaining partners, whether or not additional partners are brought into the business. In any event, the creditors of the first or dissolved partnership are also creditors of the partnership continuing the business.

Partners who retire or rightfully withdraw from a partnership are entitled to the fair value of their interest in the business as of the date of the partnership dissolution. Outgoing partners remain personally liable for partnership debts incurred before but not after dissolution, assuming they have given appropriate notice to third parties. If appropriate notice is not given by withdrawing partners, they remain personally liable on debts with third parties which were incurred before or after the dissolution. The estate of a deceased or bankrupt partner is not liable for the debts of the partners who continue the business, but it remains liable to any partnership creditor whose claim arose before the partner's death. The value of the deceased partner's interest in the partnership is determined as of the date of the partner's death. This value may be an amount equal to the deceased partner's share of the assets with interest or a proportion of the profits of the continuing business for the use of the deceased partner's share. Where partners sell their partnership interests to third parties, the withdrawing partners continue to be liable to the partnership's creditors, unless there is a *novation*. In the context of partnership law, this is a consent by the creditors to release the withdrawing partner of liability and to substitute the new partner who has agreed to pay the old debts. If there is no novation, the incoming partner is responsible only for obligations incurred after becoming a member of the partnership.

● Mason sells her interest in a partnership to another party. She notifies the creditors of the partnership of her withdrawal. In the exchange of correspondence, there is a mutual agreement that the new partner will assume all Mason's partnership obligations. The result is a novation, whereupon the new partner by substitution takes over Mason's debt obligations incurred prior to her withdrawal from the partnership and the creditors agree to release her.

Understanding Legal Terms

Define, identify, or explain the following terms:

accounting	insolvency	marshalling of	partnership
actual notice	goodwill	assets	termination
constructive notice	judgment creditor	partnership at will	winding up
dissolution by court	liquidation		
decree			

Questions for Review and Discussion

1. Indicate what is meant by dissolution of a partnership.

2. What are the circumstances under which a partner or a third party may petition a court to dissolve a partnership?

3. How may a partnership be dissolved by acts of the partners?

4. Explain the liability of partners if the partnership or a partner becomes insolvent.

5. What are the rights of partners when a partnership dissolution is caused by something other than a breach of the partnership agreement? What are their rights when the dissolution is caused by breach of the agreement?

6. Identify the three ways the dissolution of a partnership is automatically caused.

7. Explain what the remaining partners and

a withdrawing or retiring partner can do to protect themselves from incurring creditor and general public liability after dissolution.

8. Discuss the extent of an incoming partner's liability for the debts of an existing partnership before admission to the business and from the day of admission on.

9. Indicate the order of claims on a partnership's assets if the partnership or an individual partner is bankrupt and assets must be liquidated to pay partnership or individual debts.

10. Explain when liquidation takes place and the manner in which it is accomplished.

Analyzing Cases

1. George Fisher, his brother Carlos, and his three sons operated an insurance business under ten-year-term partnership agreements. All of the agreements required each partner to contribute 15 percent of all fees and commissions received to the partnership. Carlos's partners discovered that he had been receiving moneys for which he failed to account properly to the partnership. They suspended Carlos from the partnership and divided his interest in the partnership among themselves.

Carlos wrote a letter protesting the action taken and claiming his right as a partner. He was then given notice that he was permanently suspended from the partnership because of his failure to account to it. Carlos then brought an action for a partnership accounting. How should the court rule on the legality of Carlos's exclusion from the partnership and in regard to his suit for a partnership accounting? Why? ● *Fisher v. Fisher*, 227 N.E.2d 334 (Mass. 1967)

2. Anna Reid and three others had entered into a written partnership agreement for the purpose of leasing for profit certain real property located in Pennsylvania. The partnership agreement contained no provision for any specific term of duration of the partnership.

Subsequently, by letter to her partners, Reid notified them that she was dissolving the partnership. She requested that the partnership assets be liquidated as soon as possible. Meetings between the partners following receipt of this letter failed to produce agreement for a plan for liquidation. Reid then brought suit in the state courts of Pennsylvania. During the course of the proceedings Reid died

and the executors of her estate were substituted for her in the litigation.

The issue before the court was whether Reid's letter or her death dissolved the partnership. How should that court resolve the issue? Why? ● *Girard Bank v. Haley*, 332 A.2d 443 (Pa. 1975)

3. The partnership of Ernest and Sylvia Timmermann and their two sons, Stanley and Lynne, was organized for the purpose of farming grain and peas. The partnership agreement provided that the parents were to keep the books of the partnership and provide management advice. The sons were to provide the labor in connection with the farming. The agreement provided that the assets of the partnership were to be divided equally upon dissolution.

The partnership agreement was to run for five years but was extended by agreement for another five years. The partnership agreement remained the same except for the added provision that any partner could terminate the agreement upon the giving of written notice. Although this extension expired, the partners continued their farming activities without a written agreement. Sylvia Timmermann died and left her partnership interest to her husband and sons. Lynne then gave notice of his intent to withdraw and stopped contributing labor to the partnership. Settlement of the partnership affairs proved difficult, and Lynne finally gave notice of termination of the partnership and filed suit for accounting, winding up, and termination of the farming partnership.

How should the court resolve the issues of (*a*) when the dissolution of the partnership had occurred, and (b) how to divide up the assets of the partnership, including the profits earned after Lynne stopped contributing labor? Why? • *Timmermann v. Timmermann*, 538 P.2d 1254 (Ore. 1975)

4. Kurtz, Adrian and Richard Fisher, and Lonning entered into a written partnership agreement concerning the development of a mobile home park. The agreement contained a clause permitting the expulsion of a partner by a vote of the remaining partners for any reason they might deem appropriate. Financial difficulties and dissension among the partners developed. Lonning wrote to the partners stating he would accept a certain sum, plus certain equipment and materials, in settlement of his interest. If the offer was unacceptable, Lonning stated, the letter was to be considered notice to sell his interest in the partnership. The partners met to discuss the matter but were unable to reach an agreement. Thereafter, Lonning did not associate himself with the partnership. The remaining partners arranged financing and continued to develop the property as a partnership without the involvement of Lonning.

Six months later, Lonning sued for an accounting and appraisal of the partnership assets along with an interest in the assets proportionate with his investment.

How should the appeals court hold in regard to the issues of (a) whether the partnership was dissolved by the expulsion of Lonning—in effect through the acts of the other partners and Lonning himself, if not by an actual vote; and (b) whether Lonning was entitled to the value of his interest in the partnership property? Why? • *Lonning v. Kurtz*, 291 N.W.2d 438 (N.D. 1980)

5. Feldman and DeMaria operated the Youngstown Aluminum Products Co. as partners. Prior to the formation of the partnership, Feldman had done business alone, employing the same company name. His business had purchased merchandise from Kaydee Sales Corp. The merchandise had

been purchased on a c.o.d. basis. After the partnership with DeMaria was formed, it was arranged that merchandise would be purchased by the partnership from Kaydee Sales Corp. on credit. Kaydee Sales relied upon the financial responsibility of DeMaria in extending the credit. The Kaydee Sales ledger sheets indicated that goods continued to be delivered on a credit basis for four months. After that, delivery of merchandise was again made only on a c.o.d. basis or its equivalent. When payment was not received for merchandise delivered on credit, Kaydee Sales brought action against Feldman and DeMaria.

The defendants claimed that their partnership had been dissolved prior to Kaydee Sales resumption of c.o.d. deliveries. The trial court was to find that Kaydee Sales received no notice of DeMaria's withdrawal from the partnership until after c.o.d. deliveries were resumed. Can Kaydee Sales hold DeMaria liable for any of the partnership debts? Why? • *Kaydee Sales Corp. v. Feldman*, 183 N.Y.S.2d 151 (1958)

6. Mrs. Marley and her son-in-law Patch were engaged in the grocery and produce business in Arizona and were joined in the work of the business by Mr. Marley. They operated the business for approximately four years and then executed articles of partnership. These articles provided the Marleys with a one-half interest and Patch with a one-half interest in the firm of Patch and Marley. Within a year, the three partners entered into an option agreement whereby the Marleys granted Patch an option to purchase their one-half interest, with some of the purchase price to be paid in installments. The option was exercised, but the final $3,000 payment was never made.

At the time the option agreement was executed, the partnership was in financial difficulty and owed money to several creditors. Olds Brothers Lumber Co. was one such creditor. Patch executed a promissory note to Olds Brothers for $3,000, which represented debts that had accrued to that company. The note was secured by a mortgage on the realty. When the note was given, Olds Brothers had no notice that the partnership had been dissolved by Patch's purchase. Olds Brothers subsequently filed suit in the state courts of Arizona against Patch to collect on its $3,000 note. The Marleys claimed that the final $3,000 owed to them had to be paid before Olds Brothers could collect on its note.

The main question was whether Marley or Olds Brothers had the superior lien. How should the case be disposed of? Why? ● *Olds Bros. Lumber Co. v. Marley,* 236 P.2d 464 (Ariz. 1951)

7. A partnership known as Lebanon Trotting Association was created for the purpose of conducting the business of harness racing in the state of Ohio. A new agreement was subsequently executed with some change in membership and interests of the partners. The main asset of the partnership was a lease with the Warren County Argicultural Society of a racetrack known as the Warren County Fairgrounds. The partnership agreement provided that the partnership should continue for a term of twenty years.

At the time the partnership was dissolved, its lease of the Warren County Fairgrounds was unexpired. In litigation commenced in Ohio, the court held that the partnership could not continue to operate the lease after it had been dissolved. Should the appellate court find that the partnership must necessarily immediately sell or dispose of the leasehold interest (the main asset of the partnership)? Why? ● *Lebanon Trotting Ass'n v. Battista,* 306 N.E.2d 769 (Ohio 1972)

8. Leonard Fielder formed a partnership with Lowman to construct and operate a house trailer camp. In the course of business, a note was issued to the First and Peoples Bank of Russell, Kentucky, for $6,000. Fielder died, and it developed that the assets of the partnership were insufficient to meet the claims of all creditors of the partnership. Neither were Fielder's individual assets sufficient to meet the claims of his personal creditors and the claim of the bank.

The suit to settle Fielder's estate joined all interested parties, including the First and Peoples Bank, which had asserted a claim against Fielder's estate for a balance of $3,400 due on the note which bore the signatures of Fielder and Lowman. Litigation resulted in the state courts of Kentucky between the Fielder estate and the bank. Under the doctrine of marshaling of assets, from what funds should the debt to the bank be paid? Why? ● *First and Peoples Bank v. Fielder,* 323 S.W.2d 855 (Ky. 1959)

Chapter 34   Corporate Formation, Finance, and Regulation

The corporate form of business organization has become a key institution in the American free enterprise system. It provides, among others, three basic advantages: limited liability, perpetual existence, and transferability of ownership shares.

The *corporation* is a legal entity, created by state or federal statute which authorizes persons to carry on an enterprise. It exists separate and apart from its owners and is taxed directly on the income it earns. *Limited liability* is usually extended to the corporation's owners. This means that the personal assets of the corporation's owners generally cannot be attached if the corporation defaults on its obligations or commits a tort or crime. As a legal entity, the corporation can own property, bring suit, and have a suit brought against it in its own name.

34-1. The Corporation's Status as a Legal Person

Under provisions of the U.S. Constitution, a corporation is considered an artificially created legal person. Within the meaning of the Fourteenth Amendment, therefore, a corporation—like any natural person—may not be deprived of life, liberty, or property without due process of law. Nor may a corporation be denied equal protection of the laws within the jurisdiction of a state.

For purposes of jurisdiction, the corporation is also considered a citizen of the state in which it is incorporated and where it has its principal place of business. By virtue of the due process clause of the Fourteenth Amendment, a state court may also exercise jurisdiction over a nonresident corporate defendant. However, there must exist minimum contacts between the defendant corporation and parties within the state of jurisdiction, such as minimal business ties, relations, and contracts.

34-2. State Regulatory Authority

In exercise of their police powers, state governments can create and regulate corporations. It is for this reason that corporations are said to be essentially the creatures of state governments. (Congress, however, has an implied right to create corporations at the federal level pursuant to the powers granted it by the U.S. Constitution.)

Each state has a general corporation statute that establishes incorporation requirements, financial guidelines, directors' and shareholders' rights and duties, and dissolution procedures. While state general corporation statutes differ, thirty-two states have adopted substantial portions of the *Model Business Corporation Act* (MBCA), as proposed by the American Bar Association. The MBCA, most recently revised in 1979, serves as a model by which states may revise their corporation statutes to meet the changing needs of the free enterprise system.

34-3. Kinds of Corporations

Corporations may be classified in various ways in order to emphasize a purpose or characteristic. For clarity, however, this chapter is limited mainly to a discussion of the major kinds of corporations that are created by statute and authorized by state-granted charters to incorporate.

A. Business Corporations

Ordinary business corporations are formed by private persons for the purpose of making a profit, which may be distributed to shareholders as declared dividends. The *shareholders* or stockholders are the persons who own units of interest (shares of stock) in a corporation as evidence of their ownership. *Dividends* represent the distribution from corporate assets, made on a pro rata basis to shareholders as authorized by the corporation's directors.

1. Close Corporations. A business corporation may be designated as a *close corporation* when the outstanding shares of stock and managerial control are closely held by fewer than fifty shareholders (often members of the same family) or by one person. State business corporation statutes generally accommodate closely held corporations by allowing them to have a few directors or a sole director and president with no voting shares in the hands of the public.

Subchapter S and Section 1244 of the Internal Revenue Code give closely held small business corporations special tax advantages. If the corporation was begun with ten or fewer shareholders and derives its income from the sale of goods and services, it may avoid corporate taxes on net income. Shareholders in such *Subchapter S corporations* may elect to be directly taxed as individuals on their shares of the corporation's profits (or losses). In this way they avoid double taxation. A proportionate share of ordinary losses up to a maximum of $25,000 per shareholder per year may also be passed through to the shareholders.

2. Special Service Corporations. State legislatures have enacted statutes for the incorporation of such *special service corporations* as insurance companies, banks, savings and loan associations, and railroads. Both state and federal administrative agencies regulate in detail the manner in which these special-function entities conduct their business.

3. Quasi-Public Corporations. Corporations which are privately organized for profit, but provide a service upon which the public is dependent, are generally referred to as *quasi-public corporations*. In most instances, they are public utilities which provide the public with such essentials as water, gas, and electricity. Although formed under general business corporation statutes, their articles of incorporation must be approved by the appropriate regulatory agency before they are recognized by the state of incorporation.

● An incorporated town lacked sufficient funds for creating an adequate water supply by means of a watershed. It granted a special franchise to a group of area residents who agreed to form a corporation for the purpose of supplying water to homes, industry, and commerce and for fire protection. Customers would pay according to an approved rate schedule. The new corporation would be a quasi-public corporation whose ultimate purpose was supplying a required service for a profit.

B. Public Corporations

Public corporations are created for governmental purposes by the state or federal government or by a local municipal government. Incorporated cities and sanitation districts are examples of public corporations. Separate incorporated bodies such as parking and housing authorities are also organized by governments to provide public services.

C. Professional Service Corporations

All states have enacted statutes allowing professionals such as doctors, lawyers, and accountants to incorporate their practices in order to obtain the benefits of tax-sheltered (shielded from taxation) pension and profit-sharing plans not otherwise available to them as employers or partners. Contributions to the profit-sharing plans are tax deductible by the professional service corporation. The income invested remains tax exempt until it is distributed to the employees at retirement.

D. Foreign Corporations

A corporation is a *domestic corporation* in the state which grants its charter. It is a *foreign corporation* in all other states. The right to do business in other states (subject to reasonable regulation) is granted by the commerce clause of the U.S. Constitution. In order to qualify to do business in another state, a foreign corporation must obtain a *certificate of authority* by providing information similar to that of a domestic corporation applying for a charter. A registered office and agent must be maintained within the state upon whom service of process (notice of proceedings in a suit) upon the corporation may be made. Courts also recognize as doing business that which subjects the foreign corporation to a suit in the state courts and that which subjects the foreign corporation to taxation by the state.

● Precision Tool, Inc., incorporated in Ohio, brought suit against National Bank of Pennsylvania, charging that the bank wrongfully dishonored certain of its checks. The bank brought a motion for dismissal of the suit on the ground that Precision Tool was a foreign corporation doing business in Pennsylvania without having filed a certificate of authority with the secretary of state. Precision Tool maintained that its activities in Pennsylvania were insufficient to require a filing. The state court should hold for the bank and dismiss the complaint if it can be shown that the scope of Percision Tool's intrastate activities required that the corporation comply with the Pennsylvania statute requiring foreign corporations to file a certificate stating the name and address of its registered agent in Pennsylvania.

A foreign corporation does not have to qualify to do business in a state if its only business in that state is the transaction of business in interstate commerce, such as carrying goods by carrier across a host state. The MBCA also provides that a foreign corporation shall not be considered to be transacting business in a host state when it maintains bank accounts, generates sales through independent contractors, or holds meetings of its directors or shareholders.

E. Nonprofit Corporations

Most states have statutes that allow the formation of nonprofit corporations such as hospitals. Sometimes referred to as membership or nonstock corporations, nonprofit corporations determine their membership by agreement rather than by the acquisition of stock. Most nonprofit corporations are formed to provide the public with charitable, educational, social, or recreational services.

Cooperative associations are often certified in conformance to nonprofit corporation statutes. For example, a cooperative apartment is a form of cooperative association. Tenants purchase shares of stock which represent the capital required to complete the construction. Holders of sufficient shares receive a long-term lease which entitles them to the right of possession of an apartment.

34-4. Corporate Formation

A corporation may be incorporated in any state that has a general incorporation statute. Thus, the choice of the state of incorporation is usually made according to the statutory provisions which are most beneficial to those proposing a corporation. In addition to the state's general incorporation statute, corporations are generally governed to some extent by provisions of a state's constitution and by court decisions. Federal agencies also regulate corporate activity. The regulation of securities by the Securities and Exchange Commission is an example of such federal regulation.

A. Procedure for Forming a Corporation

Incorporation is accomplished and a corporation comes into existence as a result of the actions of promoters, incorporators, and subscribers and the satisfaction of procedural requirements.

1. Promoters. One or more independent organizers, called *promoters,* begin the incorporation process. They plan the incorporation, attend to its organization, and try to interest the public in subscribing to the stock of the proposed corporation.

Acting in a fiduciary role, promoters have a duty to disclose all relevant information to prospective stock subscribers and to act in the best interest of the proposed corporation and its owners. They also have a duty to account for all moneys taken in and paid out for the benefit of the corporation and its shareholders. Promoters may make a profit in completing incorporation transactions as long as they are open and fair with persons purchasing stock and with creditors. Although promoters may enter into contracts for the benefit of the proposed corporation, the corporation can be bound by such contracts only if it expressly or impliedly ratifies them after it becomes legally incorporated.

Hirsh, a promoter, entered into a $40,000 contract for equipment on behalf of a yet-to-be-formed corporation, believing she was acting as an agent for the corporation. After the incorporation was completed, Hirsh was primarily liable for the amount of the contract. Signing her name or that of the proposed corporation bound only Hirsh, not the yet-to-be-incorporated corporation, which had no legal existence at that time.

2. Stock Subscribers. *Stock subscribers* are persons who agree to purchase shares of a corporation's new stock issue. They become shareholders and must pay the entire purchase price due once their offer to purchase stock has been accepted. Subscribers enjoy all the rights and owe all the duties of a shareholder.

3. Articles of Incorporation. The *articles of incorporation* are the written application to the state for permission to incorporate. This written application is prepared by the corporation's *incorporators*. They are the persons who sign the articles of incorporation and submit them to the appropriate state official. The articles together with the applicable statutes of the state of incorporation represent the legal boundaries within which a corporation must conduct its business. The articles of incorporation require basic information such as the corporation's name and address, the names and addresses of the incorporators, and the purpose for which the corporation is being organized. The corporate name chosen cannot be the same as or too similar to that used by another corporation. Any determination made by the secretary of state that the names of two corporations are not deceptively similar is generally binding on the court. The articles must also specify the number of shares and the classes of stock which the corporation is authorized to issue and the rights associated with each class. Most states require the names and addresses of the provisional directors and officers of the corporation who hold office until they are confirmed or new directors elected at an organizational shareholders' meeting.

4. Commencing Business. After the articles of incorporation are approved by the state and upon filing of the articles and the payment of a filing fee, a *certificate of incorporation* or charter is issued by the secretary of state. The corporation then becomes a fully and legally incorporated entity. The work of the promoters and incorporators ends, unless they become directors or officers of the corporation, and the subscribers then become shareholders.

5. Organizational Meeting and Bylaws. Most corporation statutes provide that the first order of business upon incorporation be the holding of the first directors' meeting. It is called by the provisional directors, and its participants usually elect the corporation's directors and begin to carry on the business of the corporation, including the sale of stock.

The corporation's *bylaws* are also adopted at the organizational meeting. These are the rules and regulations which guide the corporation's day-to-day internal affairs. They are subsequently ratified by the shareholders, as are any modifications. Bylaw provisions usually stipulate the time and place of shareholders' and directors' meetings, manner of meeting notice required, quorum requirements, qualifications and duties of directors and officers, and procedure for filling board vacancies.

B. Defective Incorporations

For various liability reasons, the courts may be called upon to decide whether a business entity is a de jure corporation, a de facto corporation, no corporation, or a corporation by estoppel.

1. De Jure Corporations. A corporation whose existence is the result of the incorporators' having fully or substantially complied with the relevant incorporation statutes is a *de jure corporation*. Its status as a corporation cannot be challenged by private citizens or the state.

2. De Facto Corporations. A *de facto corporation* exists when corporate business is carried on in the belief that the incorporation statute has been fully complied with, when in fact the incorporators have not done so in some respect. Its existence can be challenged by the state alone, not by private citizens. De facto corporations have the same rights and duties as de jure corporations, provided a good-faith attempt to comply with statutory requirements can be proved.

● Incorporators met for the purpose of organizing Ace Excavating Company as a corporation. They signed and filed a copy of the proposed articles of incorporation with the secretary of state and appointed a secretary and agent of the company. Prior to the issuance of an official certificate of incorporation by the state, the secretary and agent of Ace Excavating posted notice in the name of the corporation to begin construction of a ditch intended to divert water from a creek. Should the legality of the company's corporate existence and ability to transact business be challenged, the court would rule that there had been a good-faith attempt to organize a corporation and make actual use of its corporate powers. Thus, a de facto corporation would have existed, even though the organization of the corporation was defective in that a formal certificate of incorporation had not been issued. Only the state could challenge Ace's legal existence as a corporation if its operations adversely affected the public interest.

3. No Corporation. The courts may decide that a business is not a corporation and hold those who are actively involved in the management of the enterprise personally liable for its debts. A noncorporation may result when the organizers of a business association do not intend or attempt in good faith to comply with the mandatory provisions of the state's incorporation statute.

● Mohawk Motors Company was equally owned by four persons who each held 2,500 shares of stock. The owners never filed incorporation papers, but were actively conducting business as though the company were a corporation. The owners borrowed $20,000, secured by a supposed corporate note signed by one of them as president and all four as sureties (persons directly and immediately liable for the debt) on the note. Mohawk Motors was not a de jure corporation. And even though the owners intended to create a corporation eventually, they would be unable to assert the doctrine of de facto corporation successfully in defending suits by the company's creditors against them personally.

4. Corporation by Estoppel. Third parties who deal with a defectively formed corporation cannot avoid liability for contracts by relying on a defense that the corporation does not legally exist. The third party would be estopped (barred) from raising such a defense. Neither can a business entity that holds itself to be a corporation escape liability by denying its corporate existence. The *doctrine of corporation by estoppel* prevents a later denial of corporate existence to avoid contractual liability in specific transactions, but it does not create a corporation.

34-5. Corporate Finance and Shareholder Liability

The original assets of a business corporation come from the promoters and investors. Once the corporation is operating, however, additional assets and funds may be obtained from earnings, loans, and the issuance of additional shares of stock. The issuing and selling of shares of stock in order to raise capital is known as *equity financing,* and the equity securities give their holders an interest in the assets, earnings, and control of the corporation. Borrowing money from banks or individuals, on the other hand, is known as *debt financing.* The sale of bonds, for example, is one form of borrowing which gives the holder the status of being a creditor of the corporation as opposed to an owner of it. Such debt securities are often secured by liens on part or all of the corporate assets.

A. Equity Securities

The number of shares and classes of stock which a corporation is authorized to issue are established in its charter. Where more than one class of stock is issued, the rights of the corporation's common stock with regard to profits, assets, and voting are inferior to those of preferred stock. A shareholder who purchases corporate stock invests money, property, or service in the corporation and receives a *stock certificate* (written evidence of ownership of a unit of interest in the corporation).

1. Common Stock. Ordinary stock that has no preferences over any other class of stock is known as *common stock.* The shareholder is usually entitled to one vote for each share of stock held. The holders of common stock are paid *dividends* (i.e., net profits or surplus set aside for distribution to shareholders) when the corporation elects to make such a distribution. Holders of common stock risk whatever they invest. There is no guarantee that the corporation will operate profitably, and the common stock purchased may become less valuable or even lose its value entirely. Shareholders of common stock participate in the distribution of capital upon dissolution of the corporation, if capital is available, only after preferred shareholders' and creditors' claims have been satisfied.

2. Preferred Stock. Those classes of stock which have rights or preferences over other classes of stock are known as *preferred stock.* These preferences are generally as to dividends and/or assets on liquidation or dissolution of the corporation. Preferred stock may be either cumulative or noncumulative. Dividends on *cumulative preferred stock,* if not paid in one year, are payable in subsequent years if funds become available for the payment of dividends. Dividends on *noncumulative preferred stock,* on the other hand, which are not paid in one year are not payable in a later year. Shareholders of *participating preferred stock* have a priority on a certain stated amount or percentage of dividends. After a prescribed dividend is paid to common stock shareholders, both participating preferred and common stock shareholders share in any additional dividends paid. The holders of *nonparticipating preferred stock* are not entitled to any distribution of surplus dividends along with common stock shareholders. It should be noted, however, that the rights which preferred shareholders enjoy in regard to dividends do not include the inherent right to receive them. They are merely superior rights to dividends over common stock shareholders, when and if dividends are declared by the corporation's board of directors.

3. **Stock Valuation.** Stock can be issued with or without a par value (face value printed on the stock certificate). *Par value stock*, or par stock, is issued for a stated certain price, and the amount of the corporation's capital stock or stated capital is the total par value of all issued stock. Corporate stock which is issued without any stated price is known as *no-par stock*. The cash and/or fair market value of the property, services, or goodwill paid for acquired stock must equal at least its par value. Although the practice of placing a par value on a share of stock has been criticized as irrelevant, it does have some practical impact. Many states limit the ability of a corporation to pay dividends out of paid-in capital, which is defined as the total of the par value for all shares of stock issued. Hence, with too high a par value, dividend flexibility may be limited. Taxation is a factor in those states that tax corporations on the par value of their stock. Other states use the market value of the stock in taxing a corporation if no par value is stated. This generally results in a very high rate of taxation.

4. **Treasury Stock.** Publicly traded stock may be repurchased by the corporation itself. A corporation's own stock repurchased from shareholders ready and willing to sell is known as *treasury stock;* it cannot be reissued and must be canceled. The effect is a reduction in the corporation's net assets, which include the value of the total number of stock shares issued multiplied by their selling or market price. The reduction also reduces the stated *capital account* (total par value of the corporate stock shares issued), which in turn reduces the corporation's ability to pay dividends. Generally, a corporation is not permitted to repurchase its own shares as treasury stock unless it does so out of its earned surplus or unearned capital surplus. To do otherwise would reduce the value of corporate assets, impairing the rights of the corporation's creditors should the business become insolvent.

B. **Debt Financing**

The debt securities of a corporation are generally in the form of bonds, debentures, or notes. *Bonds* are long-term loan obligations which are secured by a lien on some or all of the corporation's assets. The amount of the loan is payable at a designated maturity date, and the interest is payable at a fixed rate at regular intervals or payable out of profits. Short-term indebtedness may be incurred by a *note* (a two-party instrument in which the borrower promises to pay money to a payee) or a longer-term unsecured bond known as a *debenture,* which is backed by the reputation of the issuing corporation rather than its specific pledge of assets. Bondholders and holders of other debt securities generally have preference over all classes of shareholders in respect to claims to a corporation's assets, if the corporation becomes bankrupt.

C. State and Federal Securities Regulation

Both state and federal regulatory acts protect the investor in corporation security transactions.

1. Blue-Sky Laws. Security statutes, known as *blue-sky laws,* have been enacted in nearly every state to protect the public from security issues of fraudulent intrastate companies. Although blue-sky laws differ in detail, in general they contain fraud-penalty provisions, requirements for registration of brokers or dealers in securities, and registration requirements with state authorities. In connection with the offer, sale, or purchase of any security, directly or indirectly, for example, it is unlawful to engage in any act, practice, or course of business which operates or would operate as a fraud or deceit upon any person. Failure to satisfy such state statute requirements subjects the violator to fines, criminal sanctions, and rescission of stock sale claims.

2. Federal Securities Legislation. Two pieces of federal legislation which affect *securities* (i.e., stock certificates, bonds, or other evidence of a secured indebtedness or a right or interest in a profit-making business) are the Securities Act of 1933 and the Securities Exchange Act of 1934. In addition to such documents as notes, stocks, and bonds, securities include *investment contracts,* which are any contracts or schemes for the placing of capital or laying out of money in a way intended to secure income or profit from its employment.

● The Securities and Exchange Commission took action to restrain W. J. Howey Co. from using the mails and interstate commerce in the offer and sale of unregistered and nonexempt securities. The nonresident purchasers of land strips and service contracts, who lacked the knowledge, skill, and equipment necessary for the care and cultivation of citrus trees, were offered an opportunity to contribute money and to share in the profits of a citrus fruit enterprise managed and partly owned by W. J. Howey Co. The company argued it merely sold land and service contracts. The court held that all the elements of a profit-seeking business were present. The investors provided the capital and shared in the earnings and profits. The promoters managed, controlled, and operated the citrus groves. Thus, the land sales contracts and the service contracts constituted an investment contract within the meaning of the Securities Act of 1933.

The 1933 Securities Act regulates the issuance of new securities by corporations and partnerships. Offers of securities by mail or through interstate or foreign commerce must be registered with the SEC. A *registration statement* and a prospectus must be filed with the SEC. These documents contain prescribed information about the corporation, including data about its management and control, capitalization, and financial condition.

The 1934 Securities Exchange Act deals with the subsequent trading in securities. It requires periodic reports of financial information concerning registered securities and prohibits manipulative and deceptive actions in the sale and purchase of securities. The act prohibits insiders, including officers and directors, from realizing profit from any purchase and sale of securities within any period of less than six months. For example, the courts have held that insiders are not permitted to trade on information until that information has been made available to the public.

D. Foreign Corrupt Practices Act

The Foreign Corrupt Practices Act was passed by Congress in 1977. The act imposes new accounting standards on *multinational corporations* (businesses with plants and offices in different countries) and prohibits improper payments to foreign officials by United States nationals.

1. Accounting Standards. The act requires that corporations, subject to SEC jurisdiction, "keep books, records, and accounts which in reasonable detail, accurately and fairly reflect the transactions and disposition of corporate assets." Corporations are also required "to devise and maintain a system of internal accounting controls. . . ." In furtherance of this provision, transactions must be executed in accordance with management's authorization. Transactions must be recorded in conformity with generally accepted accounting principles and appropriately to maintain accountability for assets. Access to assets is permitted only in accordance with management's authorization. Recorded accountability for assets must be compared with the existing assets at reasonable intervals and appropriate action taken with respect to any differences.

2. Prohibitions. The act makes it unlawful for any officer, director, employee/agent, or shareholder of a corporation to make use of the mails or any means of interstate commerce corruptly to offer, promise to give, or give anything of value to any foreign official for the purpose of influencing any act, inaction, or decision in order to obtain or retain business.

3. Penalties. The act imposes fines of up to $1 million for the corporation and up to $10,000 or imprisonment of up to five years for persons who violate the prohibitions provisions.

E. Shareholder Liability

Shareholders ordinarily are not personally responsible for the contract and tort liabilities of the corporation. Their potential loss is limited to their capital investment. The limited liability of shareholders is a central characteristic of the corporate form of business organization. There are occasions, however, when liability can be imposed on shareholders. The court can ignore the corporate entity under certain circumstances, and the corporation can be so defectively organized as to be considered nonexistent.

1. True-Value Liability. The original holders of watered stock are liable to corporate creditors for differences between the par value and the consideration (money, services, property, goodwill) actually paid for the stock. *Watered stock* results when the consideration given for stock shares is overvalued and worth less than the par value of the share.

Watered stock also results when payment of an unlawful dividend and distribution is made without a transfer of the surplus to the corporation's capital account, a gratuitous stock issue is made, or a stock bonus is paid.

● A director of Steel Specialists, Inc., suggested that the officers of the business be given a bonus of five hundred shares of the corporation's common stock for the loyalty shown during the first year of operations. A bonus such as this, unless rightfully earned and owed to the officers, would be considered watered stock.

In any such action, the shareholders as well as the corporation are liable for deceiving corporate creditors who have relied on the misrepresented fact that outstanding par value stock has been paid in full.

2. Piercing the Corporate Veil. Courts can refuse to recognize a legally formed corporation in order to impose personal liability on anyone who uses it to commit fraud or crime or activities which go against public policies. When justice demands it, the courts hold wrongdoers (usually controlling shareholders) personally liable for the illegal acts in the corporation's name. Most often, the courts will go behind the legal status of a corporate entity to *pierce the corporate veil* of closely held corporations, where the interests of the corporation and its controlling shareholder(s) are unacceptably united.

● Woodward formed a corporation for the purpose of operating a cosmetics business. The corporation issued 200 shares of stock, 196 to Woodward, 2 to a son, and 2 to Syphers. The corporation proceeded to purchase certain real property which it proposed to resell. Woodward's wife brought suit charging that the property was purchased in the name of the corporation solely for the purpose of denying her of rights in and to that real estate. The facts showed that Woodward held all the stock, notwithstanding the four shares in the name of two others. A shareholder's meeting was never held, and bylaws were not adopted. Corporate funds had been intermingled with Woodward's funds and used to pay his personal debts. The court concluded that the corporate creation was a mere hoax in order to conceal the truth and, therefore, fraudulent. Thus, the court could exercise the right to pierce the corporate veil in order to defeat the use of the corporate form of organization to promote fraud.

Understanding Legal Terms

Define, identify, or explain the following terms:

articles of incorporation	corporation	foreign corporation	promoters
bylaws	debt financing	incorporator	securities
common stock	de facto corporation	par value	shareholders
	equity financing	preferred stock	watered stock

Questions for Review and Discussion

1. What are the three basic advantages of the corporate form of business organization?

2. Explain to what extent a corporation is treated as a person within the meaning of the Fourteenth Amendment of the Constitution.

3. Discuss the actions required to create a corporation.

4. Distinguish a de jure corporation from a de facto corporation.

5. Describe equity securities and debt securities and the legal status of their holders.

6. What are the two common preferences that holders of preferred stock have over holders of other classes of stock?

7. Discuss the purpose of state blue-sky laws.

8. Discuss the intent and the scope of the Foreign Corrupt Practices Act.

9. Explain what is meant by a shareholder's limited liability.

10. When will the courts pierce the corporate veil in order to hold controlling shareholders personally liable for illegal acts carried out in the corporation's name?

Analyzing Cases

1. Harry and Kay Robinson of New York purchased a new Audi automobile from a retailer in New York. They brought a product liability action against the retailer and its wholesale distributor in the district court in Oklahoma. They claimed that injuries which they suffered in an accident involving their automobile in Oklahoma were caused by the defective design and placement of their automobile's gas tank and fuel system. The retailer and wholesale distributor, who were incorporated in New York and did business there, contended that Oklahoma's exercise of jurisdiction over them would offend the limitations on state jurisdiction imposed by the due process clause of the Fourteenth Amendment. They further contended that they performed no services and closed no sales in Oklahoma. In addition, they solicited no business in Oklahoma either through salespersons or through advertising, nor did they indirectly through others serve or seek to serve the Oklahoma market.

How should the U.S. Supreme Court rule on the question of Oklahoma's trial court jurisdiction over a nonresident corporation? Why? • *World-Wide Volkswagen Corp. v. Woodson,* 444 U.S. 286 (1980)

2. KTEN, an Oklahoma television broadcasting company, was organized as a corporation by the Morrises and Hoover. The articles of incorporation authorized issuance of both voting and nonvoting stock. The incorporators were elected directors of the corporation, with Hoover as president. The incorporators each purchased with cash two shares of the voting stock. They received much of the remaining voting stock; however, the consideration for it was not money, but rather their time, talent, and goodwill.

From the beginning, the incorporators contributed their time and services to the new business. They pledged their personal assets toward its success and two of the incorporators, including Hoover, even borrowed money on their personal credit to keep the station in operation. The contributed goodwill included Hoover's many years of broadcasting experience, expertise, and favorable broadcasting record with the Federal Communications Commission, a record which proved valuable in the acquisition of the licensing permits needed to operate the station and the allocation of a television channel to the geographic area in which KTEN was located.

A shareholder of KTEN brought suit challenging the validity of Hoover's ownership of most of the corporation's voting stock, contending that the corporation did not receive adequate compensation for the shares. For whom should the court enter judgment—KTEN or the shareholder? Why? • *Eastern Okla. Television Co. v. Ameco, Inc.,* 437 F.2d 138 (10th Cir. 1971)

3. Lewis owned Class A stock of Investors Funding Corporation (IFC) of New York. Jerome, Norman, and Raphael Dansker (the Danskers) were the principal officers and directors, owning 90 percent of IFC's Class B shares. The shareholders of IFC, at a special meeting, approved a plan submitted by the directors by which 15,000 shares of Class A shares would be sold by the corporation to the Danskers. The corporation was to receive as consideration non-interest-bearing notes for $15 per share, payable over a five-year period. Lewis brought suit in district court against the Danskers.

Lewis charged that the Danskers obtained shareholder approval of the sale by means of a materially false and misleading proxy statement which failed to disclose the market price of IFC stock ($31 per share) at the latest practicable date preceding the shareholders' solicitation. In addition, Lewis contended that the issuance and sale of 15,000 IFC shares to the Danskers for their promissory notes (promises to pay money in the future) violated the New York Business Corporation Law. One pertinent part of the statute states, "Neither obligations of the subscriber for future payments nor future services shall constitute payment or part payment for shares of a corporation.

How should the court rule on Lewis's motion for summary judgment requiring the cancellation of all the options granted under the plans proposed in the proxy statement? Why? ● *Lewis v. Dansker,* 357 F. Supp. 636 (S.D.N.Y.), as modified 68 F.R.D. 184 (S.D.N.Y. 1975)

4. Kane, a broker and dealer in securities, sold two units of a limited partnership in a project known as Walker Springs to Graham. The primary purpose of Graham's purchase was to obtain tax shelter, that is to reduce the amount of taxes he would have to pay. The Walker Springs project was not registered with the Arkansas Securities Commission. An exemption from registration was never issued or requested. Kane had consulted with the Arkansas Securities Commission prior to making the sale to Graham. An attorney for the Arkansas Securities Commission had informed him unofficially that the shares of the partnership were not considered securities and thus not subject to the registration requirements of the Arkansas Securities Act. When Graham purchased the units he was furnished with written material which clearly stated that the units were not registered.

Three years after the purchase, Graham became dissatisfied with the performance of the investment. He offered to return the two units to Kane and demanded that Kane return the full purchase price of some $37,000. When Kane refused, Graham brought suit. By the time of trial, Graham had realized tax savings of around $25,000.

How should the supreme court of Arkansas rule on the issue of Graham's demand that Kane return the purchase price he paid for the two units of the limited partnership? Why? ● *Graham v. Kane,* 576 S.W.2d 711 (Ark. 1979)

5. Naftalin was the president of a registered broker-dealer firm and a professional investor. He engaged in a "short selling" scheme. That is, he selected stocks that, in his judgment, had peaked in price and were entering into a period of market decline. He then placed orders with five brokers to sell shares of these stocks, although he did not own the shares he said he was selling. Before he was required to deliver them to the selling brokers, Naftalin planned to make offsetting purchases through other brokers at lower prices.

Naftalin was aware, however, that had the brokers who handled his sell orders known that he did not own the shares, they either would not have accepted the orders or would have required a margin deposit (i.e., cash deposited with the brokers to secure them from loss). Naftalin therefore falsely represented that he owned the shares he directed the brokers to sell. Unfortunately for Naftalin, the market prices of the shares he "sold" did not fall prior to the delivery date, but instead rose sharply. He was unable to make covering purchases, and never delivered the shares.

Naftalin was charged with employing a scheme to defraud in the offer or sale of stock in violation of provisions of the Securities Act of 1933 and convicted in a district court and sentenced. The court of appeals found the evidence sufficient to establish that Naftalin had committed fraud, but vacated his conviction with the explanation that the purpose of the Securities Act was to protect investors from fraudulent practices and not brokers. Accepting a petition to review the matter, how should the U.S. Supreme Court dispose of this case? Why? ● *United States v. Naftalin,* 441 U.S. 768 (1979)

6. Overstreet was injured in a railroad crossing accident in Forrest County, Mississippi, by a locomotive operated by the New Orleans & Northeastern Railroad Company. Six years after the accident, Overstreet brought an action against the Southern Railway Company for damages. The defendant railroad moved for summary judgment, arguing that Overstreet had brought action against the wrong company. The evidence showed that Southern Railway Company owned 100 percent of the stock of New Orleans & Northeastern Railroad Company. The locomotive involved in the accident had the word "Southern" painted on it, although it was actually owned by a company called the Alabama Great Southern Railroad Company and leased to the New Orleans & Northeastern. Although the members of the Southern Railway Company system were separate legal businesses (entities), these members constituted a family. Overstreet argued it was proper to sue Southern Railway Company because of the the facts of the case, including Southern's 100 percent ownership of New Orleans & Northeastern. The trial court granted the defendant's request for summary judgment, and Overstreet appealed. How should the court of appeals dispose of the case? Why? ● *Overstreet v. Southern Ry.*, 371 F.2d 411 (1967), *cert. denied* 387 U.S. 912

7. Haversack Wine Company was incorporated in Texas. Alban, president of Alban Group, Inc., was contacted by Joyner to design a label or corporate image for Haversack Wine. An action was subsequently brought by Alban Group, Inc., against Joyner and Haversack Wine Company when an invoice for $12,720 went unpaid. Alban testified that when he first started doing the design and artwork he assumed that he was dealing only with Joyner as an individual proprietor. He also stated that he never made any inquiry to determine whether the Haversack Wine Company was incorporated. There was, however, no doubt that Alban knew he was performing work for a business entity known as Haversack Wine Company. Joyner defended on the ground that he was not personally liable and that only Haversack Wine Company was liable. The trial court rendered judgment against both defendants. On appeal, how should the appellate court dispose of the case? Why? ● *Joyner v. Alban Group, Inc.*, 541 S.W.2d 292 (Tex. 1976)

8. Neustadt acquired land known as Candlewood Lake Estates in the town of Sherman, Connecticut and commenced a rustic development in the area. He used a standard form of contract and deed in selling homes in his development. The deeds provided that the purchasers of the property were to pay the sum of $25 annually, to be set aside in a road fund and applied to the maintenance and construction of the roads. Neustadt, who had personally signed the deeds, subsequently transferred ownership of all roads, beaches, and open areas in the development to a corporation known as Candlewood Lake Estates Service Corporation (CLESCO). Neustadt was the president and sole shareholder of CLESCO. No records were kept of annual meetings of its directors, and no records of annual elections of directors existed. Neustadt alone directed CLESCO's affairs, only he could deal with CLESCO's funds, and CLESCO had never filed a corporate income tax return.

The landowners were not satisfied with the condition in which the roads were maintained, and they sought damages and equitable relief through a class action.

Assuming the landowners' funds were misapplied, could a court hold Neustadt personally liable for the misspending of the fund money by CLESCO? Why? ● *Saphir v. Neustadt*, 413 A.2d 843 (Conn. 1979)

Chapter 35

Corporate Management and Dissolution

A corporation's powers are derived from the applicable statutes of the state of incorporation, the purpose clause of its articles of incorporation, and court decisions. The duties and management are vested in the board of directors, with the shareholders holding the ultimate control over corporate affairs. These powers and management functions as well as termination, merger, and consolidation of corporations are discussed in this chapter.

35-1. Corporate Powers, Limitations, and Liability

The *corporate powers* of a corporation pertain to its legal capacity to carry out its business purpose. The source of this legal capacity is the state constitution and applicable statutes which establish the limits within which a corporation must operate.

A. Scope of Corporate Powers

In addition to the powers permitted by state statute, a corporation has the *express powers* stated in its articles of incorporation to carry out its business purpose. A corporation can also perform unspecified acts that are consistent with its express powers. Such *implied powers* are said to exist "by implication" and are sufficiently established by the purpose clause of the articles of incorporation.

1. Statutory Powers. Section 4 of the Model Business Corporation Act lists seventeen powers that are generally given each corporation by state corporation statutes. Among others, a corporation has the power to have perpetual existence, unless limited by its articles of incorporation, and to sue and be sued in its corporate name. A corporation may acquire real or personal property and dispose of all or any part of its property and assets. It may lend money to assist its employees, and it may acquire interests in other domestic or foreign corporations. A corporation has the power to make contracts and incur liabilities, borrow money, issue notes and bonds, and secure any of its obligations. It can conduct its business within or without the state of incorporation, and it can elect or appoint officers and agents of the corporation and define their duties and fix their compensation. In addition, a corporation generally has the power to make and alter bylaws, pay pensions and establish pension plans, and have and exercise all powers necessary or convenient to effect its business purpose.

2. *Ultra Vires* Activities. The articles of incorporation may restrict the statutory powers granted to a corporation. In the event a corporation engages in any action in excess of corporate authority, the act is unauthorized and *ultra vires,* that is, beyond the corporation's powers. For example, if a corporation engages in manufacturing when its charter forbids it to do so, the activity will be *ultra vires,* but not necessarily contrary to statute or public policy. Section 7 of the Model Business Corporation Act abolishes the defense of *ultra vires* in a suit for breach of contract for or against a corporation. However, shareholders may restrain a corporation's *ultra vires* acts. The corporation itself may bring suit to enjoin the unauthorized acts by directors or officers or to recover damages for such acts already committed.

B. Tort and Criminal Liability

The agency rules discussed in Chapter 29 apply to the officers and employees of a corporation who are acting as its agents. Under the doctrine of *respondeat superior* an injured party may hold the corporation liable for the torts of employees committed during the course and scope of employment, even though the act was not authorized. Both unintentional negligence and intentional torts such as fraud or conversion committed by officers and employees are credited to the corporation as a matter of law.

Corporations may also be held liable for the commission of crimes, even though the crime requires intent (wherein the party knows and desires the consequences of an act). Such intent is found from the acts of directors, officers, and agents of the corporation who commit crimes during the performance of authorized duties. A quasi-criminal violation occurs when a corporation fails to comply with a state reporting requirement, such as failing to file an annual report. Federal statutes such as the Social Security Act, the Securities Act of 1933, and the Sherman Act also impose criminal liability on both the corporation and its agents. A corporation found criminally liable is generally subject to a fine (not imprisonment) of its officers and directors.

35-2. Shareholder Rights

A contractual relationship exists between shareholders and the corporation. The corporation's bylaws, the state corporation statute, and the stock certificate are parts of the contract, and they establish the rights of shareholders in regard to the corporation.

A. Right to Stock Certificate

A *stock certificate* is evidence of the contractual relationship that exists between shareholders and the corporation. Section 23 of the MBCA provides that no certificate shall be issued for any share until such share is fully paid. In addition, each certificate representing shares under the laws of the incorporation state must state the following on its face:

○ That the corporation is organized under the laws of the state
○ The name of the person to whom the certificate is issued
○ The number and class of shares it represents
○ The par value of each share represented by the certificate, or a statement that the shares are without par value

Shareholders have the right to transfer their stock. They can sell their shares, give them as a gift, or pledge them as security for a loan. This is done by delivery of the certificate(s) and indorsement to the purchaser. The person to whom shares are transferred has the right to have the stock transfer entered on the corporate books. The transferee then becomes a shareholder of record and is entitled to enjoy all shareholder rights. The corporation may properly refuse to recognize a transferee when the corporation is given notice or has knowledge that a certificate is lost or stolen. If the corporation registers a certificate transfer wrongfully, it generally must issue a replacement certificate to the original owner.

Court decisions recognize that corporate control by ownership of a majority of shares may be misused. Thus, in any transaction where the control of the corporation is material, the controlling majority shareholder(s) must exercise good faith and fairness. This includes the controlling shareholder's duty to conduct a reasonable and adequate investigation of one who might buy his or her shares. The object of such an investigation is to prevent such a potential buyer from later looting the corporation's assets to cover the cost of the purchased shares.

B. Right to Vote at Shareholders' Meetings

Most corporation statutes provide for an annual meeting of the shareholders to be held at a time designated in the bylaws. Special shareholders' meetings are also authorized when extraordinary matters require prompt action. Notice of meetings must be given to all shareholders of record, that is, shareholders listed on the corporation's stock transfer books as of a certain day and who are entitled to vote at the meetings. A *quorum*, usually of at least one-third of the shares entitled to vote, must be represented in person or by *proxy* (appointed agent who votes for shareholder) at the shareholders' meeting. The corporation is not entitled to vote stock it has not yet issued or treasury stock it has reacquired.

Shareholders have the right to one vote for each vacancy on the board of directors and on other matters at annual and special shareholders' meetings. *Nonvoting shareholders* are holders of any class of stock who are denied the right to vote in the articles of incorporation. Some state statutes allow shareholders the option of *cumulative voting*. This system allows shareholders to multiply the number of their voting shares by the number of directors to be elected. All these votes may be cast for one candidate or distributed among several candidates. The procedure allows minority shareholders an opportunity to be represented on the board of directors.

Most states permit *voting trusts*, whereby many shareholders agree to accumulate their shares of corporate stock in a single person or several persons, in order to control the business of the company. The voting trust permits owners of stock with voting rights to divorce the voting rights from ownership. Thus, stock ownership is retained but voting rights are transferred to trustees, in whom voting rights of all the shareholders in the trust are pooled.

C. Right to Receive a Dividend

Shareholders have the right to expect to share in the earnings of the corporation through dividends. Unless a dividend is declared by the board of directors, however, the shareholders have no right to receive one. Dividends may be paid so long as there is earned surplus shown on the corporation's balance sheet. Dividends are also allowed out of current net profits even though the earned surplus account is depleted. The MBCA prohibits dividends which would render the corporation insolvent.

By state statute and MBCA provision, there are tests to determine whether, in the event of sufficient current or accumulated profits, a refusal by the directors to declare dividends is for arbitrary, personal, or non-business-related reasons. To justify court intervention to compel declarations of dividends, it must be shown that the decision not to declare dividends amounted to fraud, bad faith, or abuse of discretion by those authorized to declare the dividends.

● Uhle, the controlling shareholder of Lund Corporation, declared that she would never pay a dividend as long as she lived. In a suit brought by minority shareholders against the directors of the corporation, the court should grant an injunction and require the board to declare a dividend, provided there is an earned surplus. Uhle and the other board members appear to have other than proper business reasons for retaining all the earnings of Lund Corporation.

If the directors give reasonable business reasons supporting their decision not to declare dividends, the court will not interfere with the corporate board's right to make that determination.

D. Right to Inspect the Corporate Books

Shareholders have the right under common law to inspect all the books, papers, records, federal reports, and other data of the corporation as to its assets, liabilities, contracts, operations, and practices. This right extends to any correspondence between the controlling officers relating to the internal affairs of the corporation. Refusal of a request to inspect is proper, however, if the request is made in bad faith or if the shareholder is making improper use of the information obtained. Any corporate officer or agent who refuses to allow a shareholder to examine and make copies from corporate books, records of account, minutes, and records of shareholders, for any proper purpose, is obligated in law to the shareholder. A penalty of 10 percent of the value of the shares owned by the shareholder may be levied by the court, in addition to any other damages or remedies afforded the shareholder by law.

Section 52 of the MBCA says nothing directly about the scope of the corporate records intended to be made subject to statutory damages. Generally, state statute and court interpretation extends the right to inspect to all instruments from which any information can be derived that will better protect the shareholder's interests.

● Burke, a shareholder of voting stock in Tucson Power & Light Company, requested permission to examine the corporation's voting list. Burke's purpose was to determine whether a certain company officer was a holder of stock in the company. The request should be granted, provided Burke's purpose is not to make improper use of the information. The request could be enforced by an injunction compelling the corporation to make this information available to Burke or to an authorized agent. A penalty in the form of damages could be assessed on corporate officers who might improperly interfere with Burke's rights.

E. Preemptive Rights

All states except New Hampshire recognize the *preemptive rights* of shareholders, but permit the articles of incorporation to limit or deny such rights. These are the rights of shareholders to preserve their proportionate stock interest by purchasing shares of a new issue ahead of others.

● Mills owns 400 shares ot stock of PPG Industries, Inc., which has 1,200 shares outstanding. The corporation decides to increase its capital stock to 2,400 shares. Mills has the right to protect his proportionate interest in PPG Industries. He and every other shareholder must be offered one share of the newly issued stock for every share they own. If Mills accepts the offer and buys, he will have 800 shares out of the total 2,400 outstanding. Thus his relative interest in the corporation will remain unchanged.

Even when corporations are allowed to avoid preemptive rights, the courts normally grant relief to shareholders where majority shareholders or officers issue new shares to themselves in order to gain an advantage over other shareholders.

F. Right to Sue on Behalf of the Corporation

Normally, the directors of the corporation begin lawsuits in the corporate name when a third party harms the corporation. Recovery of damages increases the value of corporation shares and the shareholders benefit. If the directors, deliberately or otherwise, fail to act in such situations, one or more shareholders may begin a *derivative action* on behalf of the corporation. This is a suit based upon a primary right of a corporation, but asserted on its behalf by the shareholder(s) because of the corporation's failure to act. In order to take a derivative action, the shareholder(s) must own shares of the corporation at the time of the wrongdoing and show that the directors refused a demand that they take court action on behalf of the corporation.

35-3. Functions of Directors and Officers

Although shareholders own the corporation and have ultimate control over corporate affairs, the duties of management are normally in the hands of the board of directors. Generally, the shareholders' direct managerial power is limited to the approval or disapproval of extraordinary transactions. These include such questions as reductions in stated capital, disposal of substantial corporate assets, loans to directors, stock option plans for directors and officers, voluntary dissolution, mergers, and consolidations. Shareholders also have direct power to amend the articles of incorporation and to adopt, amend, and repeal the bylaws of the corporation.

A. Board of Directors

Initial directors are usually named in the articles of incorporation and serve until the first annual shareholders' meeting, when their successors are elected by the shareholders.

1. Management Functions. Although elected by shareholders and removable by them for cause, directors are not the agents of shareholders. As persons in control of corporate affairs and of property belonging to others, directors are fiduciaries with power derived from state statute. Generally, directors of corporations are not entitled to recover any compensation for performing their ordinary duties unless such compensation is authorized. Thus, a director cannot retain an undisclosed profit while engaged in transactions for a corporation. And in the exercise of their duties of management, the directors, when duly convened as a board, are required to use their best judgment and independent discretion. They are responsible for the determination and execution of corporate policy. This includes policy decisions with respect to products, services, prices, wages, and labor relations. Directors also determine dividends and financing. They select, supervise, and remove officers and other executive personnel as well as fix executive compensation and pension and retirement plans. Directors delegate day-to-day management decisions to the officers and employees of the corporation.

2. Number and Qualifications. Nearly all state statutes previously required that there be at least three directors, but many now permit one or two directors in closely held corporations. The number is usually stated in the articles of incorporation or bylaws of the corporation.

Some state statutes expressly require that directors be at least twenty-one years of age, but do not prescribe a maximum age. Other qualifications for directors, such as residence, citizenship, and that directors be shareholders, may be prescribed in the corporation's articles or bylaws, but are becoming rare. Some boards are composed of *insiders* (i.e., directors who are also officers of the corporation) and other boards consist of *outsiders* (i.e., nonofficers), but most boards are mixed.

3. Tenure and Removal. Directors are elected at an annual shareholders' meeting and hold office until the next meeting or until their term expires and successors are elected. Vacancies in the board are generally filled by persons who are shareholders who serve for the unexpired term.

Directors are removable for cause (misconduct or action contrary to the interest of the corporation) by shareholders, even if such power is also conferred on the board of directors.

4. Directors' Meetings. Although directors traditionally exercised their management functions only when duly convened as a board, a number of states allow directors to act without a meeting if they unanimously consent in writing. They always vote *per capita* (i.e., one vote for each director) and may not vote by proxy. The vesting of authority in the board rather than in the directors individually is justified on the grounds of the value of consultation, deliberation, and collective judgment.

Boards of directors may meet at regular or special meetings which usually may be held within or without the state of incorporation. Notice requirements often differ, depending on state statutes, bylaws, and corporation practice. A quorum for board meetings is usually a majority of the whole number of directors.

5. Liabilities. Directors are not liable for errors in business judgment or honest mistakes. Under most state statutes, before becoming liable for losses, directors must have participated in illegal, fraudulent, and wrongful acts, or must have been charged with negligently permitting violations of law resulting in losses. And under applicable common law, directors can be held liable only for their failure to exercise ordinary care and diligence in conducting affairs of the corporation. Directors are not usually personally liable for breach of corporate contracts unless they are personally bound as party, surety, or guarantor. However, directors are liable to the corporation for any injury caused the corporation by their negligence, such as failure to keep informed on corporate affairs.

An increasing number of state and federal statutes impose civil punishments on directors who fail to comply with consideration requirements for shares or who cause improper dividends or distributions, improper purchase of the corporation's own shares, improper loans, or preferential transfer of corporate assets to creditors. Directors are also liable under other state statutes such as criminal codes or blue-sky laws. Liabilities, in addition, are imposed by federal statutes such as the Internal Revenue Code, antitrust and trade regulation statutes, and federal securities legislation.

B. Officers of the Corporation

Generally, officers of the corporation are selected and are removable by the board of directors. The board delegates to them authority to execute and administer the policies determined by the board of directors. Unlike directors, officers are agents of the corporation and, as such, are subject to the principles of agency law, including the fiduciary duties of agents, within the scope of their delegated management functions.

Statutes often prescribe that a corporation must or may have certain officers. Bylaws often designate a president, one or more vice presidents, a treasurer, and a secretary and define their authority. The chief executive officer is usually the president of the corporation or the chairman of the board of directors. Officers have the express authority given them by the board or by the bylaws, but may also bind the corporation on the basis of apparent authority, even though acting beyond their actual authority. Nonofficer employees may also be designated to act as agents.

35-4. Consolidations and Mergers

Corporations sometimes combine in order to invest accumulated income or to reduce economic risks through diversification of interests. This is generally accomplished by consolidation or merger, provided the effect does not reduce competition in interstate commerce and thus violate federal antitrust statutes.

A. Consolidation

Two or more independent corporations may effect a *consolidation* by combining their total assets to form a new corporation. The corporate parties to the consolidation transfer their separately owned assets to a new corporation and then dissolve. The liabilities of each of the consolidating corporations are valid against the new consolidated corporation. The board of directors and the majority of voting-right shareholders of each corporation must agree to the plan. Dissenting shareholders may demand the fair market value of their preconsolidation stock from the new corporation.

B. Merger

A *merger* involves the combining of the assets of two or more corporations, but one retains its legal form while the other(s) are absorbed and dissolved. The surviving corporation holds title to all combined assets and assumes all the debts and liabilities of the acquired corporation(s). The same approvals and rights of dissenting shareholders that apply in a consolidation are applicable in a merger.

35-5. Liquidation, Dissolution, and Reorganization

Most corporations are formed for theoretically perpetual duration. Without a statutory provision for some duration other than perpetual existence, a corporation continues until dissolution or annulment of its charter. Statutes usually provide for dissolution without judicial proceedings, known as *nonjudicial dissolution* and for dissolution by judicial procedure, known as *judicial dissolution.*

A. Nonbankruptcy Liquidation

Corporate liquidation is the process of collecting assets, paying the expenses involved, satisfying creditors' claims, and distributing the net assets, first to preferred shareholders and then pro rata among the remaining shareholders. Liquidation is closely related to dissolution. Liquidation may or may not be under court supervision. Partial liquidation is also possible, in which case the corporation would continue rather than be dissolved.

B. Dissolution Methods

The Bankruptcy Reform Act of 1978 mandated new substantive law for bankruptcy. It also initiated a new and functionally independent bankruptcy court with the power to reject executory contracts of the debtor, including collective bargaining agreements. A federal bankruptcy court is to be designated in each judicial district in 1984 as an adjunct to the existing district court.

A corporation may be dissolved either voluntarily by the incorporators or shareholders or involuntarily by the state, shareholders, or creditors.

1. Voluntary Dissolution.

A corporation which has not commenced business and has not issued any shares may be voluntarily dissolved by its incorporators. A majority of the incorporators must execute, for delivery to the secretary of state, articles of dissolution which justify that intention. The voluntary dissolution of a corporation may be achieved by the written consent of all its shareholders. The board of directors may also adopt a resolution recommending that the corporation be dissolved. The question must be submitted to a vote of the shareholders at either an annual or a special meeting. Such a resolution is generally adopted upon receiving the affirmative vote of the holders of a majority of the shares of the corporation entitled to vote.

It should be noted, however, that under a voluntary liquidation and dissolution plan, majority shareholders are considered trustees for minority shareholders and owe legal duties to them. Any plan of liquidation that would misapply the corporation's assets to the benefit of the majority shareholders at the expense of minority shareholders would be held oppressive by the courts and require equitable relief.

2. **Involuntary Dissolution.** A commercial corporation may be dissolved involuntarily by court decree in an action filed by the state's attorney general and by proclamation by the secretary of state. Grounds for such action include incorporation by fraud, corporate abuse of the authority conferred upon it by law, failure to file its annual report within the time required by statute, and delinquency in the payment of taxes due the state. A corporation dissolved by court proclamation for tax delinquency cannot use the judicial process to collect debts for services rendered after dissolution unless the rights or liabilities of the obligated party are not affected in any material way by the dissolution.

Courts have full power to liquidate the assets and business of a corporation when an action is brought by a shareholder or a creditor or when a corporation makes application by filing a statement of intent to dissolve. The MBCA sets out four conditions required by most states for involuntary dissolution at the request of a shareholder:

○ A deadlock of directors that the shareholders cannot break and that threatens irreparable harm
○ Evidence of illegal or oppressive or fraudulent acts
○ A deadlock of shareholders that has prevented the election of directors for at least two consecutive years
○ A misapplication or waste of corporate assets

● Minority shareholders of United Credit, Inc., brought suit to force dissolution of the corporation on the grounds that the directors were deadlocked, that the shareholders could not end the impasse, and that irreparable injury to the corporation was being suffered. The shareholders charged that LeGros, who controlled the affairs of the business, was taking salary and bonuses in such amounts as to leave insufficient net profit for needed capital improvements. Having been given notice of the shareholders' concern that corporate affairs were being manipulated, the directors were unwilling to act. Gross sales had declined from $20 million to $500,000 in four years. The court should find for the minority shareholders and compel dissolution. LeGros's conduct of the business was defeating the end for which the corporation was formed.

Some state statutes permit involuntary dissolution of a corporation where liquidation is reasonably necessary for the protection of the rights or interests of any substantial number of shareholders, but not dissolution at will. The minority must persuade the court that fairness requires drastic relief.

Under the Bankruptcy Code, farmers are exempt from involuntary bankruptcy proceedings. Farming operations include farming; tillage of the soil; dairy farming; ranching; and production or raising of crops, poultry, or livestock. Churches, schools, and charitable institutions and foundations are also exempt from involuntary bankruptcy proceedings.

3. **Chapter 7 Liquidation.** Any person (i.e., corporation, individual, or partnership) who lives or carries on business in the United States may file for relief under Chapter 7 of the Bankruptcy Reform Act of 1978. Excluded from these liquidation provisions are municipalities, railroads, and domestic banks or insurance companies. Special subchapters of Chapter 7 deal with the liquidation of stockbrokers and commodity brokers. In liquidation proceedings, the court

has the power to issue injunctions and to appoint a receiver(s) to preserve the company assets and carry on the business until a full hearing is conducted.

Chapter 7 petitions may be either voluntary or involuntary. An *order for relief* is entered automatically by the court upon the commencement of a voluntary case and after default or proof of insolvency in involuntary cases. Once a petition is filed, the debtor has an obligation to file a list of creditors, a schedule of assets and liabilities, and a statement of the debtor's financial affairs. After a hearing, an *interim trustee* may be appointed by the court until the creditors elect a *liquidating trustee*. The duties of the liquidating trustee, among others, are to collect and reduce the debtor's assets to money and to investigate the financial affairs of the debtor. The trustee examines proofs of claims and objects to the allowance of any improper claims. The trustee also makes a final report and files a final statement of the liquidated estate with the court. The court may authorize the trustee to operate the debtor's business for a limited period, if this is consistent with the orderly liquidation of the estate.

The proceeds resulting from the sale, conveyance, and disposal of the debtor's assets are applied to the expenses of the liquidation and the payment of liabilities and obligations. Any remaining assets or proceeds are distributed among principals or shareholders according to their respective rights or interests. The court then enters a decree dissolving the business, whereupon its existence ceases. Statutes may continue corporate or partnership existence after dissolution, however, for various purposes, including suing and being sued.

C. Chapter 11 Reorganization

Significant changes mandated by the Bankruptcy Reform Act affect the treatment of business organizations. Chapter 11 provisions of the new Bankruptcy Code are important to financially troubled businesses at a time when effective reorganization is still possible. The purpose of Chapter 11 provisions is to restructure a business's finances so that it may continue to operate, pay its creditors, provide employment, and produce a return for its shareholders. Central to a Chapter 11 reorganization is the formulation and confirmation of a *reorganization plan*. The plan outlines how much creditors are to be paid and in what form the business is to continue. A successful plan produces a newly organized company. Any person who may proceed under the liquidation provisions of Chapter 7 may be a debtor under Chapter 11. Chapter 7 liquidation is discussed above.

1. Automatic Stay. A principal benefit of Chapter 11 is the *automatic stay* provision, which maintains the status quo of certain activities. Its purpose is to allow the debtor time to work out reorganization. The filing of the bankruptcy petition operates as a stay of any act to obtain possession of the property of the debtor's estate and any act to create, perfect, or enforce any lien against property of the estate. Regardless of who has possession, even a secured party cannot proceed to dispose of the debtor's property without bankruptcy court approval. Excluded from the scope of the automatic stay is the commencement or continuation of a criminal action or proceeding against the debtor. The stay remains in effect as long as the debtor has an interest in the property or until a reorganization plan is confirmed or the case is dismissed by the court.

A secured party may seek relief from the stay by applying to the court. Generally, a party requesting a stay must provide cause, such as lack of adequate protection of the interest of the secured party under the stay. Another cause for relief is a showing that the termination of the stay would not interfere with the effective reorganization of the business.

2. Trustee. Chapter 11 provisions allow the debtor to remain in possession of the business and to operate it, unless a request is made for the appointment of a trustee. In such debtor-in-possession cases, the court may appoint an examiner to investigate the affairs of the debtor. After a reorganization petition is filed, on request and after notice and a hearing, the court will appoint a trustee if certain grounds are shown. These grounds include fraud, dishonesty, incompetence, or gross mismanagement of the affairs of the debtor. A trustee also would be appointed if the appointment was in the interests of creditors. The *trustee* is a disinterested and bonded person who is found competent by the court to perform the required reorganization duties. A Chapter 11 trustee is accountable for all property received. Other duties include the filing of the list of creditors, the schedule of assets and liabilities, and a statement of the debtor's financial affairs. The trustee must file the reorganization plan, report why a plan will not be filed, recommend transfer of the case to one under Chapter 7 provisions, or recommend dismissal of the case. In addition, the trustee has the duty to employ professional persons to represent or assist the trustee in carrying out these responsibilities.

3. Creditors' Committee. Within a reasonable time after the court issues an order for relief, the Bankruptcy Code requires a meeting of creditors. Although the court may not be present, the debtor must appear and submit to examination under oath. The scope of the examination conducted at this meeting is broad. Among other relevant matters, inquiry is made into the liabilities and financial condition of the debtor, the operation of the debtor's business, and the desirability of its continuance.

The court also appoints a committee of general *unsecured creditors,* generally made up of creditors who hold the largest claims against the debtor. Its members investigate all matters relevant to the bankruptcy and participate in the formulation of a Chapter 11 reorganization plan for the debtor. This plan determines how much and in what form creditors will be paid and in what form the business will continue. On the request of a party of interest, the court may order the appointment of additional committees of creditors, such as secured debt holders, if necessary, to assure their adequate representation.

4. Reorganization Plan. The debtor has 120 days to file the plan for the reorganization of the business and an additional 60 days to obtain acceptances. The appointment of a trustee deprives the debtor of the right to file the plan. In the event the debtor fails to file the plan before 120 days after the date of the court's order for relief, or the plan is not accepted before the 180 days, then any party of interest, including the trustee and the creditors, may propose a plan.

The proposed plan must designate the classes of claims and the means for its execution. It must specify any class that is not impaired under the plan as well as the treatment of claims that are impaired under the plan. The plan must provide the same treatment for each claim or interest of a particular class, unless the holder of a particular claim agrees to a less favorable treatment. Provisions of a plan may allow it to be a liquidation plan under which the debtor's exempt property is protected.

The plan must be accepted by two-thirds of the creditors in dollar amounts and more than one-half in number of the allowed claims that vote on the plan. Equity and security holders are not held to this requirement. Their acceptance is recognized when holders of at least two-thirds of the amount of outstanding secured debt actually vote to support the plan. An acceptance vote of all classes of creditors or equity interest is not required for approval of a plan. A class of claims that is not impaired under the plan is deemed to have accepted it. If an impaired class of claims fails to accept the plan, it may still be confirmed if it meets certain standards of fairness to dissenting creditors or equity security holders. The key test is that the plan be fair and equitable with respect to each impaired class that has not accepted the plan.

5. Confirmation and Discharge. The court, after notice, holds a hearing on the confirmation of the reorganization plan. The confirmation of the plan vests all the property of the estate in the debtor or in the court order confirming the plan. After confirmation, all property dealt with by the plan is free and clear of all claims of creditors and equity security holders. The debtor is discharged from any debts that arose before the date of confirmation. Even nondischargeable debts such as taxes are discharged for a corporation or partnership.

Understanding Legal Terms

Define, identify, or explain the following terms:

automatic stay	derivative action	preemptive rights	*ultra vires*
board of directors	dividend	proxy	unsecured creditor
consolidation	liquidating trustee	reorganization plan	voting trust
cumulative voting	merger	stock certificate	

Questions for Review and Discussion

1. What is meant by the corporate powers of a corporation and from what sources are they derived?

2. Identify the rights of shareholders in regard to the corporation.

3. Discuss the function of directors of a corporation when duly convened as a board.

4. To what extent are directors personally liable for losses to the corporation due to their conduct of corporate affairs?

5. What is the source of authority that officers of the corporation have, and what is the extent of their liability for torts committed during the course and scope of employment?

6. What is meant by corporate liquidation?

7. On what grounds may a corporation be dissolved involuntarily by a decree of the court?

8. Under what conditions are the courts inclined to appoint a receiver in proceedings to liquidate the assets and business of a corporation?

9. Discuss the purpose of Chapter 11 provisions of the Bankruptcy Reform Act of 1978.

10. Distinguish between a corporate consolidation and a corporate merger.

Analyzing Cases

1. Gay's Super Markets, Inc., was a closely held corporation. A controlling interest of the common stock was owned by Hannaford Bros. Co. Lawrence E. Gay and his brother owned the remaining common stock.

Hannaford was a food wholesaler and retailer. It conducted part of its retailing business through Gay's Super Markets, Inc. Lawrence Gay was the manager of the Gay's Super Market in Machias, Maine, until he was dismissed from his employment. In the year of Lawrence Gay's dismissal, the directors did not declare a dividend.

Lawrence Gay brought suit against the corporation, claiming that by refusing to declare a dividend the corporation was not acting in good faith. He contended that the corporation was using this action as a means of forcing him to release his interest in the business. He sought an injunction ordering that a reasonable dividend be declared and distributed.

At trial, Lawrence Gay failed to present specific evidence that the failure of the corporation to pay dividends was due to improper motives. Testimony, however, showed that the failure to declare a dividend was due to the capital needs of the business. Specifically, it was shown that the capital was needed for start-up expenses in opening a new market in another city. Judgment for whom? Why? ● *Gay v. Gay's Super Markets, Inc.*, 343 A.2d 577 (Me. 1975)

2. Meyer and others were shareholders of Ford Industries, Inc. They requested the right to inspect certain business records of the corporation. The records they requested were not merely accounting records, but rather were more general business records of the firm. For example, they requested the right to inspect agreements between Ford Industries and any former employee including, but not limited to, one Herbert L. Brown. They also requested any written documents relating to an offer to purchase, merge with, or underwrite any portion of Ford Industries. The company refused to allow inspection of the requested records. The plaintiffs sued for statutory damages. The company argued the plaintiffs had the right to inspect only regularly maintained accounting records. The company also argued that even if the plaintiffs were found to have the right to inspect the requested records, statutory damages were not proper. The trial court found in favor of Ford Industries, Inc. On appeal to the supreme court of Oregon, how should that court dispose of the case? Why? ● *Meyer v. Ford Industries, Inc.*, 538 P.2d 353 (Ore. 1975)

3. Pablo was president and a director of Hawaiian International Finances, Inc. He had been traveling to California at his own expense in connection with his private real estate business. Upon his return from one such trip, Pablo advised Hawaiian International Finances of attractive real estate investment opportunities in California. The corporation's board of directors appointed a subcommittee of four persons, including Pablo, to represent the corporation and go to California to investigate these investments. While in California, agreements were entered into by Pablo on behalf of the corporation to purchase two parcels of land. The sellers were represented by California real estate brokers. These brokers eventually split their commissions (which were paid by the sellers) with Pablo. At the time, the corporation did not know of Pablo's receipt of a portion of the commissions. After learning of the commissions, the corporation brought suit against Pablo. It requested the trial court to order Pablo to turn the money he secretly received over to the corporation. The trial court ruled in Pablo's favor. On appeal to the supreme court of Hawaii, how should this case be resolved? Why? ● *Hawaiian Int'l Fins., Inc. v. Pablo*, 488 P.2d 1172 (Hawaii 1971)

4. The Bank of Commerce was declared in-

solvent by Oklahoma authorities just a few days after its president and key director, Boone, had died. The insolvency was due in large part to a long series of secret and dishonest acts by Boone to defraud the bank by forging notes and having bank loans made against them. Boone was able to successfully cover up and hide these acts from the other bank directors.

The Federal Deposit Insurance Corporation (FDIC) covered the losses to bank depositors and liquidated the bank's remaining assets. The FDIC then filed suit against the estate of Boone and also the other directors of the bank to recover its losses—over $230,000—caused by Boone's fradulent activities. Boone's estate, of course, was held liable.

At trial, however, the following facts were established concerning the FDIC's claim against the other bank directors: (a) the books of the bank were regularly examined by the FDIC, Oklahoma banking authorities, and certified public accountants, and none of these examining authorities had detected the schemes of Boone; (b) it was not the practice or responsibility of the bank directors to examine documents and checks for forged signatures; and (c) the other bank directors had no knowledge of the fraud, nor did they profit from it. The bank directors contended that they had exercised the ordinary care required in such situations and should not be held liable. In view of these circumstances, how should the court rule? Why? ● *FDIC v. Boone,* 361 F. Supp. 133 (D. Okla. 1972)

5. Voigt and Harbison owned a controlling interest in the stock of Lafayette Realty Corporation. Certain other shareholders owned a minority interest of approximately 20 percent. Voigt served as president, and Harbison as secretary. For all practical purposes, Voigt and Harbison ran and controlled the business. Minority shareholders began to question Voigt's and Harbison's actions. For example, Voigt and Harbison caused Lafayette Realty to enter into a contract with General Asbestos and Supply Company, which was a corporation they owned. Under the terms of the contract, 6 percent of the gross receipts of Lafayette Realty was to be paid to General Asbestos in return for management services. There was evidence to support the proposition that the price that General Asbestos was to receive was exhorbitant. The minority shareholders contended that Voigt and Harbison were fraudently "milking" Lafayette Realty.

The minority shareholders brought action seeking damages, an accounting, and appointment of a receiver. The trial court held a preliminary hearing and ordered a receiver appointed immediately, while the trial was progressing. The management appealed this ruling to the Indiana supreme court. Should the supreme court of Indiana uphold the appointment of the receiver, which would probably result in liquidation of the corporation? Why or why not? ● *Lafayette Realty Corp. v. Moller,* 215 N.E.2d 859 (Ind. 1966)

6. C. S. Stumpf & Sons, Inc., was formed to conduct a masonry and general contracting business. The corporation was owned in equal shares by Stumpf and his two sons, who had previously operated the same business as partners. Hostility between the two sons grew so extreme that one, Donald, ended contact with his family and was allowed no say in the operation of the business. The corporation had never paid dividends. Instead, profits had been invested in land held by the corporation for rental purposes. After Donald's withdrawal from the business, he received no salary, dividends, or other revenue from the company. He brought suit seeking involuntary dissolution of the corporation.

How should the court of appeals of California rule on the trial court's order that an involuntary dissolution of the corporation was necessary? Why? ● *Stumpf v. C. S. Stumpf & Sons, Inc.,* 120 Cal. Rptr. 671 (1975)

7. Expomotion, Ltd., was duly incorporated

in New York. After operating for a period of time, the corporation became delinquent in its payment of taxes due the state and was dissolved by proclamation by the secretary of state. Despite the dissolution and forfeiture of its charter, Expomotion, Ltd., continued to carry on its affairs as usual, exercising its corporate powers, entering into leases, maintaining its bank account, filing federal tax returns, withholding taxes from employees, and filing subsequent state tax returns. One such conduct of corporate business with Heidepriem-Santandrea, Inc., resulted in charges to that business in excess of $32,000. Heidepriem-Santandrea paid approximately 80 percent of the charge but refused to pay the remainder. Expomotion instituted suit for payment of the balance. In defending the suit, Heidepriem-Santandrea argued that since Expomotion had been dissolved, Expomotion could not avail itself of the benefits of the judicial process to collect debts based on services rendered after its dissolution. Heidepriem-Santandrea pointed out that New York statute provides that a dissolved corporation "shall carry on no business except for the purpose of winding up its affairs. How should the court resolve the case? Why?
● *Expomotion, Ltd. v. Heidepriem-Santandrea, Inc.*, 421 N.Y.S.2d 520 (1979)

8. Kevin Steel Products, Inc., filed a petition for relief under Chapter 11 of the Bankruptcy Reform Act. The bankruptcy court authorized Kevin Steel to continue operating its New York fabrication business as a debtor in possession, under the court's control. Thereafter, Kevin Steel petitioned the court for permission to reject, as an overly burdensome executory contract, its collective bargaining agreement with the Shopmen's Local Union No. 455, which was granted. The union appealed in district court, which reversed the decision of the bankruptcy court. Kevin Steel appealed to the court of appeals.

Kevin Steel relied upon the Bankruptcy Act, which specifically provides that the bankruptcy court may "permit the rejection of executory contracts of the debtor." The union argued that this language should not be interpreted to apply to collective bargaining agreements because of what, in its words, was "the enormous difference between a labor agreement and an ordinary commerical contract." The union contended that to allow Kevin Steel to terminate its labor agreement would frustrate the purpose of the National Labor Relations Act. It also argued that to allow a bankrupt company to reject a labor contract would encourage the use of bankruptcy as a refuge for businesses that would prefer to operate free of union contracts. How should the court of appeals dispose of this case? Explain the reasons for your answer. ● *Shopmen's Local 455 v. Kevin Steel Prod., Inc.*, 519 F.2d 698 (2d Cir. 1975)

Part 8

Case Briefs

Ramirez v. Goldberg,
439 N.Y.S.2d 959 (1981)
Goldberg, president and sole shareholder of International Affiliates Co., Inc., entered into a business arrangement with Ramirez. Goldberg agreed to pay Ramirez 50 percent of the profits of the business and appointed him vice president of International Affiliates Co., Inc. Ramirez and Goldberg referred to each other as partners. However, in a letter Ramirez noted that, due to the fact that Goldberg was providing the initial capital for the business, he (Ramirez) agreed that Goldberg alone would temporarily sign the checks for all transactions and would take charge of the shipping of goods and the collecting of payments from customers. Ramirez stated in his letter that when the volume of sales increased so that profits were sufficient, a new company would be formed with each partner signing all checks related to the business. When conducting business, Ramirez referred to himself as vice president of International Affiliates Co., Inc. He did not hold himself out as a partner.

After a period of six years, Goldberg terminated his business association with Ramirez. Ramirez brought suit for an accounting. He claimed he was a partner and/or joint venturer and had the rights that would be accorded such a party. The trial court agreed. Goldberg appealed.

Petitioner's Position: Ramirez was not a partner or joint venturer with Goldberg. The share of the net profits he was to receive was merely compensation for services rendered. It was only agreed to give Ramirez a proprietary interest in the business if he put up capital, either from his share of the profits or from other sources.

Respondent's Position: The relationship between Ramirez and Goldberg was one of partners and/or joint venturers. Thus, Ramirez had the rights of a partner or joint venturer, including the right to an accounting.

Legal Issues: What was Ramirez's status in the business? Was he a partner or joint venturer with Goldberg?

Court Decision: Evidence established that Ramirez, who performed services and who was entitled to share profits, was not a partner or joint venturer.

Court Reasoning: In determining Ramirez's status, the factors to be considered are (1) the intent of the parties (express or implied), (2) whether there was joint control and management of the business, (3) whether there was a sharing of the profits as well as a sharing of the losses, and (4) whether there was a combination of property, skill, or knowledge. The court explained that an individual who offers services for a share of the net profits from several transactions risks losing the value of those services. Therefore the person is subject to losses. However, the fact that an individual is to receive a share of the profits is not alone sufficient to make the determination, since all the elements of the relationship must be considered. Here, Ramirez received a share of the profits for his services. However, the fact that he had no capital invested and never held himself out as a partner or participant in a joint venture is significant. Ramirez had acknowledged in his letter that Goldberg was the principal giving the initial capital to start, with sole authority to sign checks, and with control over the operations of the business. Furthermore, since the enterprise was conducted in the corporate

471

name, Ramirez was not personally liable for any of the obligations of the enterprise.

Auer v. Frank,
38 Cal. Rptr. 684 (1964)

Auer and Loomis were partners and did business as Century Homes, a licensed general contractor. Frank and Sumner were shareholders and officers of a California corporation called Castro Valley Sales and Investment Company. Auer and Loomis entered into an agreement whereby Century Homes agreed to provide labor, services, and materials for the completion of five homes owned by the corporation. Auer and Loomis were to be paid a sum equal to their costs plus 10 percent. Frank and Sumner entered into the contract on behalf of the corporation. Auer and Loomis knew at the time that the agreement was made with a corporation and that Frank and Sumner were acting in a representative capacity on behalf of the corporation. For a period of four months, Century Homes performed services and provided materials as called for by the contract. When the corporation failed to make payments that were due, Auer and Loomis filed an action against both the corporation and Frank and Sumner. The corporation filed a petition for bankruptcy relief and was adjudicated a bankrupt.

The trial court that heard Auer and Loomis's complaint held that they were to have judgment against the corporation but not against Frank and Sumner. Auer and Loomis appealed.

Petitioner's Position: The trial court should have pierced the corporate veil and found Frank and Sumner individually liable. The corporation had never issued any stock. Injustice would result if immunity from liability for the corporation's obligations were permitted Frank and Sumner as individuals. In fact, the corporation was merely an alter ego of Frank and Sumner. That is, they were the corporation's other self—the moving force behind the corporate entity—and should be held to account for its obligations and wrongful acts.

Respondent's Position: Frank and Sumner are not personally liable for the corporation's debt. The trial court properly found that the corporation was not an alter ego of the individual defendants and that this was not an appropriate case for piercing the corporate veil.

Legal Issue: Should the individual defendants be held personally liable for the debt of the bankrupt corporation?

Court Decision: The appellate court refused to hold Frank and Sumner personally liable for the corporation's debt. The ruling of the trial court was affirmed.

Court Reasoning: In making its determination, the appellate court considered two basic requirements for applying the alter ego doctrine: (1) that there be such unity of interest and ownership that separate personalities of the corporation and the individual(s) no longer exist and (2) that an inequitable result would follow from treating the acts as those of the corporation alone. Both of these requirements must be found to exist before the corporate existence will be disregarded by the court.

The appellate court recognized that the failure to issue any stock or to apply for permission to do so was a factor to be considered in determining whether the corporate veil should be pierced and the individuals held liable. However, the court held this inaction as not conclusive since California law permits the transaction of business by a corporation prior to the issuance of its stock. In determining whether the corporate veil should be pierced, the court gave weight to additional factors. Since eight other persons whose financial interest in it was equal to that of Frank and Sumner participated in the formation of the corporation, there was adequate capitalization of the corporation. The corporation had also obtained loans from a lending institution upon applications signed by Frank and Sumner as officers of the corporation. Also recognized were the facts that Frank and Sumner had informed Century Homes that it was dealing with the corporation and not with them as individuals and that the directors of the corporation had held meetings and kept minutes. Accordingly, the appellate court concluded that Frank and Sumner acted in a representative capacity, that materials and services were furnished by Century Homes to the corporation at its request, and that the sum owed was due from the corporation and not from Frank and Sumner as individuals. Thus, the corporation was not the alter ego of its officers.

DeBaun v. First West. B. & T. Co., 120 Cal. Rptr. 354 (1975)

Alfred S. Johnson Incorporated was incorporated by Alfred Johnson. Johnson later sold twenty of the one hundred outstanding shares of the corporation to DeBaun and ten shares to Stephens. When Johnson became seriously ill, the managerial control of the corporation was assumed by DeBaun and Stephens. When Johnson died, his will named First Western Bank and Trust Company as executor. The will also named the bank as trustee of a trust created by the will. Johnson's seventy shares of the corporation passed to the trust which the will created. The bank allowed DeBaun and Stephens to continue the management of the corporation. It did, however, vote its seventy shares at shareholders' meetings and also sent a representative to attend virtually all directors' meetings. Under the direction of DeBaun and Stephens, the net profit after tax of the corporation increased dramatically. After a period of twenty-two months the bank decided to sell the seventy shares and received repeated offers from Mattison to purchase them. At the time these offers were being received, a vice president of the bank had knowledge that the Los Angeles superior court had entered a judgment against Mattison as a result of his fraudulent misrepresentations and a fraudulent financial statement in obtaining a loan. In fact, at that time, the public records of Los Angeles revealed thirty-eight unsatisfied judgments against Mattison or businesses he controlled and fifty-four additional pending actions. However, the bank did not investigate these public records. Mattison entered into an arrangement with the bank whereby he was to pay $250,000 for the seventy shares. Mattison was to make a $50,000 down payment and pay the balance over a five-year period. The bank was to retain a security interest in the stock.

Upon acquiring control of the corporation, Mattison diverted $73,144 in corporation cash to himself. He also caused the corporation to assign all its assets to himself in exchange for an agreement for management services. He diverted all corporate mail, opened it, and extracted all incoming checks. He ceased paying trade creditors promptly, and did not pay some at all. Mattison also removed the corporation's books and records. The corporation, which had a net worth of some $220,000 before Mattison took over, became insolvent, and owed $218,426 to creditors. DeBaun and Stephens filed a shareholders' derivative action against the bank. The trial court found in their favor and awarded a large judgment for damages. The bank appealed.

Petitioner's Position: A majority shareholder owes no duty to the corporation in the sale of its majority interest, if it is not seeking to gain an advantage over the minority shareholders or the corporation. A majority shareholder is free to sell its shares to whomever it chooses and on such terms as it wishes. A majority shareholder does not become a fiduciary for other shareholders merely because of ownership of the corporation's stock.

Respondent's Position: A majority shareholder has a fiduciary responsibility to the corporation in the sale or transfer of corporate control. The rule of good faith and inherent fairness to the minority in any transaction where control of the corporation is material, under California law, requires inherent fairness from the viewpoint of the corporation and those interested therein. The rule applies to controlling shareholders in the exercise of powers that are theirs by virtue of their position. The bank, by its conduct in going forward with the sale, breached its fiduciary duty.

Legal Issues: Is a majority shareholder free to sell its stock to whomever it chooses, regardless of the circumstances? Is the freedom to transfer one's shares absolute? Did the bank have a duty not to sell its shares to someone whom it should have expected would loot the corporation of its assets, to the detriment of the minority shareholders?

Court Decision: The appellate court affirmed the holding of the trial court in favor of DeBaun and Stephens.

Court Reasoning: The appellate court explained that in California controlling shareholders owed no duty to minority shareholders in the sale of their stock. The court explained that the law has, however, more recently recognized the reality that corporate control may be misused. Thus, in California, the rule of law is that in any transaction in which the control of the corporation is material, the controlling majority shareholders must exercise good faith and fairness in selling their stock.

In this case the bank, which was the controlling majority shareholder of the corporation, became aware of facts that would have alerted a prudent person that Mattison was likely to loot the corporation. The bank knew that the only source of funds available to Mattison to pay for the shares he purchased lay in the assets of the corporation. Thus, it should have been evident that the corporation could not have been expected to earn enough profits and to declare and distribute dividends sufficient to enable Mattison to pay the balance due on the seventy shares over a five-year period.

Part 9
Real Property and Inheritance

Chapter 36 — Nature, Acquisition, and Sale of Real Property

The largest investment most families make is the buying of real property such as a house. This often involves financial obligations over a period of twenty-five or thirty years and can entail many complicated legal issues. This chapter deals with the nature of real property, estates in real property, co-ownership of real property, methods of acquiring title to real property, and other legal matters related to the ownership of realty.

36-1. The Nature of Real Property

Real property includes not only the soil or earth, but also things of a permanent nature that are attached to the soil or found within it. It also comprises the air-space above the land and includes minerals, water, shrubbery, grass, trees, fences, buildings, and fixtures attached to buildings.

A. Trees and Vegetation

Trees, shrubs, vineyards, and field crops which are harvested each year without replanting (perennials) are included in real property. These plants have been planted and cultivated with the intention that they remain as a part of the realty. Once planted and growing, such improvements to the land are defined as the *fruit of nature*.

● The graduating class of 1983 planted a grove of copper beech trees on the campus of Oldman College. Members of the class, in a fit of pique, dug up and removed three of the trees. If they had been stealing personal property, they would have been subject to arrest on a charge of larceny. But the trees, being the fruit of nature, were real property. Thus a more proper charge would be one of criminal trespass or malicious destruction of real property.

Crops or garden plantings that produce flowers, vegetables, or other harvest only for the year in which they are planted are defined as the *fruit of industry*. The fruit of industry constitutes personal, not real, property.

● When the Woodring farm was sold early in the spring, the new owner was deeded "all the real property consisting of what is known as the Woodring Farm." A 25-acre section of winter wheat had been planted the fall prior to the sale. Woodring, in July, demanded the right to come into the farm and harvest the wheat. The wheat crop is the fruit of industry, that is, personal property. The buyer did not receive title to personal property on the farm, so Woodring would be permitted the right to enter the farm and remove the wheat.

B. Air Rights

One who owns land owns the airspace above that land. Common law interpreted this right to include all the air above the land. Commercial aviation interests asked for interpretation of this right in a case decided by the Supreme Court in the early 1920s. The court confined ownership to a point above the land over which the owner might be said to have reasonable control. This decision removed the possibility of charging pilots with trespassing when flying even at great heights. Present interpretation allows the owner of land to claim property rights in an area defined as being a reasonable height over the highest structure on the land.

Federal agencies require the owners of structures that are over a prescribed height and are within the flight pattern of aircraft to install lights for the purpose of warning pilots of their presence. Other laws prohibit construction of signs or buildings above a certain height when adjacent to public airports. State and federal laws regulating aircraft and altitudes at which they may fly have little bearing on the rights of property owners over whose lands aircraft may operate.

Air rights are often valuable and may be sold to interested buyers, particularly in land-depleted metropolitan areas. Developers purchased air rights over a railroad terminal in New York City, using the space for construction of the new Madison Square Garden. Other developers bought air rights over the access to the George Washington Bridge and constructed multistory buildings. Use of air rights becomes important when land is no longer available for new buildings.

C. Subterranean Rights

The owner of land has exclusive title to material below the surface of the land. The right extends to a point determined to be the exact center of the earth. These *subterranean rights* are at times sold to corporations exploring for coal, oil, or other mineral deposits. Taking out oil or minerals from below the surface would constitute trespass if such rights were not obtained from their owners.

● McGee's house and lot were adjacent to land on which a small industrial plant had been built. McGee discovered that the plant owners had driven drainage pipes underground from the plant into her land. She may charge the plant with trespass. She can also sell this right to the plant or demand that the practice be stopped and the pipes removed.

Part 9:
Real
Property
and
Inheri-
tance

476

A landowner must not dig a cellar or other excavation so close to the boundary of a neighbor as to cause the neighbor's land to cave in or the neighbor's building to be damaged. A person excavating who fails to shore up the adjoining land is liable in damages for negligence.

● Downie Community Club owned an unimproved lot adjacent to the Darlington Apartments. Excavations were started on the Downie lot in preparation for building a clubhouse. No effort was made to shore up the side of the excavation bordering on the Darlington Apartment site. The Darlington property suffered serious damage. Downie Community Club or the independent contractor doing the work would be responsible for money damages and the repair of the Darlington Apartments.

D. Water Rights

The rights that a landowner has in a flowing stream are known as *riparian rights*. The owner of lands through which flows a stream, creek, or other body of water owns the soil beneath the water. The landowner does not own water in the stream, but may draw from it whatever might be needed for domestic purposes, watering of animals, bathing, and other ordinary uses. The owner also has the right to construct and use a dock out to a navigable point in the stream. A landowner may not use the watercourse in any way that would damage the rights of others further downstream. Water may not be drawn for sale or use on another property if this might injure the riparian rights of others. Interestingly, riparian rights give owners title to ice in the stream, but not to the waters therein.

Percolating waters are the waters running below ground in springs, underground streams, and other bodies. They serve property owners when brought to the surface through the convenience of dug or artesian wells. Common law gave property owners absolute right to percolating waters below the titled land. Under modern statutes, property owners may draw only the water that is reasonably required to satisfy their needs. Other property owners damaged by unreasonable and excess use may seek an injunction against such use by petitioning a court of equity.

● Valleybrook Swim Club drilled a deep well from which water was pumped to fill an Olympic-size pool. The pool water was changed periodically. Adjacent property owners complained that their wells ran dry during the periods when Valleybrook's pumps were running round the clock. The club was enjoined from this excessive pumping to the damage of others who depended on the same water source.

Suburban water companies supply thousands of families with water pumped from artesian wells. Persons depending on water from the same underground streams are at times deprived of their supply because of excessive pumping by the water companies. The latter have been ordered to reduce pumping in favor of those whose supplies have been depleted.

Runoff water resulting from rain and drainage may not be diverted by a property owner to the damage of a neighbor. Such water must be left to its natural watercourse.

Chapter 36:
Nature,
Acquisition, and
Sale of
Real
Property

477

E. Fixtures

In Chapter 17 it was pointed out that a fixture is something that was once chattel (tangible, movable personal property), but which becomes real property by attachment to the soil or to a structure that is part of the soil. The removal of the fixture would damage the property, so it is considered part of the realty. Whether property is a fixture can be difficult to determine. In the absence of any prior agreement by the parties, questions often arise over whether a particular item is chattel belonging to the tenant or real property subject to the landlord's demand of ownership. In deciding the issue, the courts apply a threefold test of installation, attachment, and intention. In general, the courts will hold that a particular item is a fixture if, in light of all the circumstances, a reasonable person would assume that it was the intent of the *annexor* (the person attaching the item) that it become permanently installed and attached to the realty.

36-2. Easements

An *easement* is the right of one person to make legal and beneficial use of the real property of another. It is a right that "runs with the land"; it is not a personal right conferred upon an individual or a family as such. The property to which the right or privilege of easement attaches is known as the *dominant tenement*. By contrast, the property through which the easement is created or extends is known as the *servient tenement*.

● By warranty deed in 1907, Jesse Horney conveyed the northern portion of his real estate to Wayne County Lumber Company. That deed included the following provision: "Said Jesse Horney hereby conveys to Wayne County Lumber Company the right of ingress and egress for teams and wagons in conducting their business through an open driveway along the South line to South Main Street." The property was conveyed to another lumber company in 1930 and to a third lumber company in 1943. Later, in a dispute over the easement, the court held that the easement ran with the land. In this case, Horney's property was the servient tenement. The lumber company's property was the dominant tenement.

Easements may consist of a right-of-way over another's land; the right to take water from another's well; use of a party wall, a driveway, a stairway, or almost anything related to another's land. Easements may arise through contract and may be recorded in the deeds of both the dominant and servient lands. They may also be created through adverse use, that is by passing over another's property openly and continuously for a period of time set by state statute. This is called an *easement by prescription* and is similar to adverse possession, discussed later in this chapter.

Easements, however created, may not be disregarded by subsequent purchasers of the servient property at the expense of the one being served. They may be terminated only by mutual agreement or by abandonment of use by the owners of a dominant tenement. A decree in equity may also terminate an easement.

● Donaldson, Inc., developed a residential area, laying out streets, building houses, and providing deeds to buyers. Each deed provided for a common driveway between any two homes. One half of each driveway was constructed on each adjoining prop-

Part 9:
Real
Property
and
Inheri-
tance

478

erty. The deed contained easement rights covering this situation. Thus each property was both a dominant and a servient tenement. The owners would be barred from denying a neighbor the use of their portion of the common driveway.

Easements in deeds may make provision for wires, cables, water lines, and other necessary items that go under or above ground. Utilities may enforce this right even though subsequent owners demand the removal of unsightly wires and cables from their property.

Utilities, pipeline companies, and the like purchase easement rights for the construction of underground pipelines through private property. These easement rights are written into the deeds of property owners and become an obligation for all subsequent owners of the servient properties.

Profits à prendre are a special type of easement with the added privilege of removing something of value from the servient property. For example, the right to enter another's property and remove sand, gravel, soil, or the like is a profit *à prendre*. A profit *à prendre* may be created by deed, will, or adverse use.

● The Bates Company and Sawyer executed an agreement which provided that Bates could enter upon Sawyer's land and remove sand, gravel, and stone. Bates agreed to pay Sawyer a set rate per cubic yard or short ton for all the sand it removed. The agreement stated, "Sawyer will not grant to anyone else the privilege of removing sand and stone from said parcel during the period hereof . . . but Sawyer reserves to herself, her successors and assigns, the right during said period . . . to go on and use said tract of land for any purpose they may desire, but without unreasonable interference with the rights of said Bates." The court held that Bates possessed a profit *à prendre* under the agreement.

36-3. Estates in Real Property

An *estate* is the interest or right that a person has in land. Estates in land are of two kinds: freehold estates and leasehold estates.

A. Less Than Freehold Estates

A *freehold estate* is an estate in which the holder owns the land for life or forever. A person having a freehold estate may transfer that interest to another by sale, by gift, by will, or by dying without a will. Freehold estates are either estates in fee simple, life estates, or determinable or conditional estates.

1. Estates in Fee Simple. A person who owns real property outright—that is, forever—is said to have an *estate in fee simple*. This is the kind of estate that descends, on the death of the owner, to the heirs if the owner has left no will. The holder of an estate in fee simple has *absolute ownership* in the real estate, with the right to use it or to dispose of it as desired, so long as the use of it does not interfere with the rights of others. This is the most common form of ownership of real property.

● When the Gerlachs bought the land on which to build their house, they received an estate in fee simple from the former owners. They thus received full rights to the property. They may sell it, give it away, or use it as they wish. The only restrictions are those contained in the deed or required of them by law.

2. Life Estates.

A person who owns real property for life or for the life of another owns an interest in real property called a *life estate*. Such an estate may be created by deed, by will, or by law. When the terms of a deed or a will state that the land is to pass, upon the termination of a life to someone other than the grantor or the grantor's heirs, the future interest is a *remainder estate*.

● Rosengard deeded her farm to Kinkaid for life. She stated in the deed that upon Kinkaid's death, the property was to pass to Arakelian in fee simple. Kinkaid owns a life estate in the farm. Arakelian owns a remainder estate.

The owner of a life estate may convey that interest to another. Thus, in the above example, if Kinkaid conveys his interest to Jenkins, Jenkins will own a life estate for the duration of Kinkaid's life, after which the property will belong to Arakelian. When the terms of a deed or a will state that land is to return to the grantor or to the grantor's heirs at the expiration of a life estate, the future interest is a *reversion estate*.

Legal life estates are sometimes created by the operation of law, such as the right of dower, curtesy, and homestead. By common law, the *dower* right of a wife in her husband's property amounted to a one-third interest and extended during the wife's lifetime. A number of states still respect this right. Statutes in these states vary regarding the property interest given the wife, some allowing a surviving wife a one-third interest, others allowing one-half. In states which recognize the common-law dower right, a husband cannot convey by sale or gift any real property owned by him without the wife's written permission. This is true even though the wife's name does not appear on the deed along with her husband's name. In the event of her death, the dower right is lost, and the heirs of the husband then have final and complete ownership of what had been the wife's interest.

● Jarvis owned three parcels of real property at the time of marriage. During their married years, his wife's name never appeared on the three deeds. Jarvis's will left the properties to a son by a previous marriage. The surviving widow has a superior claim and may exert her dower right during her own lifetime.

Under the common law, *curtesy* is a life interest that the husband acquires in all the inheritable realty of his wife provided children have been born alive to them, even though they may have died before the mother. In most states, the wife has the right to defeat the right of curtesy by selling the land during her lifetime or by willing it away at her death.

● Before her marriage, Clark received title to an old house through a will left by her grandfather. While her husband had no rights in this property at the time of their marriage, such rights arose at the birth of their first child. Her husband thereafter had the right of curtesy should Clark die while she was still married to him.

A husband or a wife sometimes leaves a will in which a bequest is made to the survivor *in lieu of dower*. This means that if the will is accepted, the surviving spouse will give up the common-law right in the other's real property. The husband or the wife may elect to accept the bequest named in the will or to claim dower or curtesy rights.

Part 9:
Real
Property
and
Inheri-
tance

480

Legislation in many states has removed the common-law rights of dower and curtesy, replacing them with rights that seem to be fairer. The new statutes give the surviving spouse an estate in fee simple rather than a life interest in a fractional part of the other's real and personal property. Both husband and wife are treated alike under most of these new laws. Some states have passed *community property laws*. Community property assures both the wife and the husband a one-half interest in the property of the other both during their lifetimes and at the death of one of them. Of course, a husband or a wife may provide more in a will for the surviving spouse than is guaranteed by law.

A *homestead estate* is a statutory life estate in the realty of the deceased spouse granted to the surviving spouse or to the children during their minority. It is the right to enjoy, free from liability for debts and exempt from tax levy, a fixed amount of the real property that is being occupied as a residence. The amount of land exempted under the right of homestead varies in the different states: in some, the amount is fixed by area; in others, by value; and in still others, by both area and value.

3. Determinable and Conditional Estates. A *determinable fee* is an estate which continues until the happening of a certain event and then comes to an end. The event may happen at any time or it may never happen. Because it may last forever, it is called a fee, but since it may end upon the happening of the event, it is called a determinable fee.

● W. E. and Jennie Hutton executed a deed in which they conveyed certain land, to be known as the Hutton School grounds, to the trustees of School District No. 1. The deed specified: "This land to be used for school purpose only; otherwise to revert to Grantors herein." The court held that the language in the deed created a determinable fee in the trustees followed by a possibility of a reversion estate in the Huttons and their heirs.

When the duration of an estate is dependent upon a condition in a will or a deed, the estate is a *conditional estate*. The condition determines the right of the one named to continue as owner of the property. This condition may be a condition precedent or a condition subsequent. A property that is leased for ten years with a condition that the tenant is to have absolute ownership upon payment of $120,000 is an estate on condition precedent. Property granted to a young girl provided she earns a college degree before reaching the age of twenty-eight is an estate on condition subsequent. If the condition were not filled in these examples, the estate could be terminated.

B. Leasehold Estates
An estate which does not bestow the right of ownership to real property is less than a freehold estate. Estates of this kind are also called *leaseholds*. The holder of such an estate has the right of enjoyment only for a fixed or determined period, but not for a lifetime. Leaseholds are discussed in Chapter 37.

36-4. Co-Ownership of Real Property
Real property may be owned individually or by two or more persons known as *cotenants*. The most common cotenant relationships are tenants in common, joint tenants, tenants by the entirety, and tenants in partnership.

A. Tenancy in Common

When two or more persons own real property as *tenants in common*, each person owns an undivided share and upon one cotenant's death, that person's share passes to the heirs or devisees of that cotenant. A *devisee* is a person to whom real property is given by will. Each cotenant is entitled to possession of the entire premises. This is known as *unity of possession*. Tenants in common have the right to sell or deed away as a gift their share in the property without permission of the other cotenants. When this occurs, any new owner becomes a tenant in common with the remaining cotenants. One cotenant's interest is not necessarily the same as another cotenant's interest.

● Ingalls and Carpenter owned a parcel of real property as tenants in common. When Ingalls died, his three children inherited his estate. The children became tenants in common (each owning a one-sixth interest) with Carpenter, who owned a one-half interest in the property.

Tenants in common may separate their interests in the property by petitioning the court for a *partition* of the property. If the court allows the petition, either it will divide the property into separate parcels so that each cotenant will own a particular part outright or it will order the property sold and divide the proceeds of the sale among the cotenants. Creditors may reach the interest of a tenant in common by bringing a lawsuit against a cotenant and, if successful, having the cotenant's interest sold to pay the debt.

By statute in most states, co-ownership of property by two or more persons is considered to be a tenancy in common unless the relationship is expressly indicated as a joint tenancy or a tenancy by the entirety.

B. Joint Tenancy

When two or more persons own real property as *joint tenants*, the estate created is a single estate with multiple ownership. Each tenant owns the entire estate, subject to the equal rights of the other joint tenants. All joint tenants' interests in the property are equal, and all have the right to possession of the entire estate. Upon the death of one joint tenant, the entire ownership remains in the other joint tenants and does not pass to the heirs or devisees of the deceased cotenant. For this reason, joint tenants are often identified as *joint tenants with the right of survivorship*.

● If Ingalls and Carpenter, in the previous example, had owned the parcel of real property as joint tenants instead of as tenants in common, Carpenter would have owned the entire property outright when Ingalls died. Ingall's three children would not have been entitled to any interest in the real property whatsoever.

Joint tenants may deed away their interest to new owners without permission of the other joint tenants. The new owner, in such a case, becomes a tenant in common with the remaining joint tenants. As in the case of a tenant in common, a joint tenant may petition the court for a partition of the estate, which would end the joint tenancy. Creditors may levy upon the interests of a joint tenant on execution and take over the joint tenant's interest as a tenant in com-

Part 9:
Real
Property
and
Inheri-
tance

482

mon with the remaining joint tenants. To *levy on execution* means to collect a sum of money by putting into effect the judgment of a court.

C. Tenancy by the Entirety

A *tenancy by the entirety* may be held only by a husband and wife and is based upon the common-law doctrine known as *unity of person.* Under this doctrine, a husband and wife are regarded, in law, as one. In theory, each spouse owns the entire estate, which neither can destroy by any separate act. The husband, however, has the entire control over the estate, including the exclusive right to possession and the right to all rents and profits. Upon the death of either spouse, the surviving spouse owns the entire estate outright. Advantages of this type of tenancy are that both parties must agree to any sale or conveyance of the property, and an execution by a judgment-creditor resulting from an action against a husband or wife alone may not be placed against the property.

● The DeVoes owned their home together as a tenancy by the entirety. While driving a car titled in her name alone, Mrs. DeVoe caused an accident. A judgment far exceeded insurance covering the owner's liability. The house owned jointly by the DeVoes would not be subject to sale to cover the judgment.

Another important aspect of a tenancy by the entirety is that no administration of the estate is necessary upon the death of one of the parties. This eliminates the costly and time-consuming details of making a settlement of the property, as required in the probate of a will.

In the event that husband and wife are separated by a divorce, the tenancy by the entirety no longer exists and they then become tenants in common, with separate and equal rights in the property.

Some states have done away with the tenancy by entirety by statute. Still other states have enacted statutes giving equal rights to husbands and wives who own property as tenants by the entirety.

D. Tenancy in Partnership

Ownership of real property by partners is called a tenancy in partnership and is governed by the Uniform Partnership Act in those states which have adopted it. This type of co-ownership of real property is discussed in detail in Chapter 32.

36-5. Methods of Acquiring Title to Real Property

Title to real property may be acquired by sale or gift, will or descent, or occupancy.

A. Title by Sale or Gift

Ownership and title to real property are most frequently transferred from one owner to another by sale or by gift. This is done by transferring a written instrument called a *deed.* The person transferring the title to the realty in the deed is the *grantor.* The person to whom the title is transferred is the *grantee.* A deed becomes effective when it is delivered to the grantee or an agent of the grantee. A deed to real property may be bestowed as a gift from the owner or through a sale. In the case of a gift, consideration is not given by the grantee for the conveyance.

B. Title by Will or Descent

Owners of real property are permitted by law to designate in a will the person or persons who are to share in the distribution of their property at death. A surviving spouse, however, may always enforce those rights guaranteed by law rather than accept the will's provisions.

When an owner of real property dies without leaving a will (intestate), the property is distributed according to statute. The property will descend to the heirs, with certain rights providing for the surviving spouse.

C. Title by Occupancy

Title by occupancy includes ownership secured through conquest, discovery, and other means in which no consideration is given to the rights of former owners.

● A Coast Guard vessel discovered an uncharted island that had erupted in the wastes of the Arctic Ocean. After a study of the island's location and description and a radio consultation with the State Department in Washington, a landing party claimed the island as a U.S. possession. The island now is the property of the United States, as recognized by international law.

Title to real property may be obtained by taking actual possession of the property openly, notoriously, exclusively, under a claim of right, and continuously for a period of time set by state statute. This method of obtaining title to real property is called *adverse possession*. To establish such ownership rights, claimants must prove that they have had continuous use of the property for twenty-one years or a period set by state statute. They must also prove that this use has been without interruption by the owner, without the owner's permission, and with the owner's knowledge. Proof of these facts in court will give a person superior rights over the one in whose name a deed is recorded. A court of equity has the power to declare the one claiming under adverse possession to be the new owner.

● Wilhelm and Kupersmith were next-door neighbors. Not realizing where the true property line was, Wilhelm built a garage and driveway 2 feet onto Kupersmith's land. He used the garage and driveway continuously, with Kupersmith's knowledge, for the next twenty-two years. The error was discovered when Kupersmith sold her property to a new owner who had it surveyed. Wilhelm, through court action, will be able to obtain title to the land on which the garage and driveway are located, by adverse possession.

36-6. Purchase of Real Property

Part 9:
Real
Property
and
Inheritance

484

The purchase of real property is usually the most significant purchase ever made by most families. It is important that proper legal steps be taken to protect such a purchase.

A. Purchase and Sale Agreement

The purchase and sale agreement is probably the most important document in a real property sales transaction. A poorly drawn agreement may lead to disagreement between the parties involved, open controversy, failure to perform, and expensive court action. The purchase and sale agreement (often referred to as an offer to purchase or a binder contract) must include all the essentials of a contract to be valid. A purchase and sale agreement must be in writing, as required by the statute of fraud.

B. Property Survey

To assure the purchaser that the property itself conforms to the dimensions and acreage defined in the contract or in the seller's deed, a survey of the land should be made by a competent surveyor or civil engineer. Differences between the surveyor's findings and the description in the deed should be settled before proceeding further with the purchase.

● The seller's deed stated that the land totaled 22 acres, designating in feet and inches the measurements of its perimeter and the angles at the corners. However, Rezk's surveyor reported that the tract contained only 21.5 acres. The seller would be expected to make an adjustment in the contract price in order to compensate for the 0.5-acre difference.

C. Protection of Title

The buyer of real property may obtain an abstract of title as a result of a title search, a policy of title insurance, or a Torrens system registration to guard against the claims of others to the land.

1. Title Search. Careful and prudent buyers of real estate insist upon a *title search,* an investigation of the legal history of the property and the seller's rights and interest in the property. A title search requires the professional scrutiny of a lawyer who understands the importance of details which might have little meaning to the average buyer. Conditions looked for in the search include unpaid taxes and other liens against the property, assessments, easements and restrictions placed on the property by previous owners or by adverse use, cases pending in the courts against the seller or members of the seller's family, unpaid judgments against the owner or the owner's family, the seller's marital status, the rights of the present owner as defined by former deeds or wills, and numerous other matters disclosed only through the careful inspection of records in the county courthouse and other state and federal offices.

2. Title Insurance. Insurance policies, called *title insurance,* guaranteeing that one's title to real estate is good are available through companies specializing in this type of insurance. Should the purchaser of a title policy ever be called upon to answer for any liabilities created through another's ownership, the insurance company will indemnify the insured against all damages suffered because of errors in the public records, incompetency of grantors, or lack of delivery in the chain of title over the years.

In many states, corporations have been chartered to make title searches and sell title policies. The advantage of this type of service by such corporations is

Chapter 36:
Nature,
Acquisition, and
Sale of
Real
Property

485

the continuing liability of the corporation for any damages that the insured may suffer due to a defective title. If a buyer discovers in later years that the search was not competently made and suffers a financial loss as a result, the buyer could seek damages from the corporation that searched the title.

3. Torrens System. The *Torrens system* is a system of land registration which establishes clear title to land. It was first adopted in Australia and is used in England and many states in the United States. To register land under the Torrens system, a petition for registration is filed with the court together with a deed and a plan of the land. The court will have the title searched, and notice of the petition will be published in the newspaper. In addition, notice of the petition will be posted on the land and sent to all interested parties. If anyone raises an objection to the land being registered, a hearing will be held to settle the issues that are raised. If the court finds that the petitioner has proper title for registration, a decree will be issued registering the land and confirming that title is absolutely clear except for anything noted on the certificate. From that point on, each owner of the property will receive a certificate of title rather than a deed to the property. Any *encumbrances* (liens or claims against the property) are noted on the certificate.

D. Types of Deeds

Four types of deeds are in general use: general warranty deeds, special warranty deeds, bargain and sale deeds, and quitclaim deeds.

1. General Warranty Deed. A *general warranty deed,* sometimes called a *full covenant and warranty deed,* contains express warranties under which the grantor guarantees the property to be free of encumbrances created by the grantor or by others who had title previously. It is the most desirable form of deed from the point of view of the grantee because it warrants (gives assurances) that title is good. The typical general warranty deed contains the following three promises or guarantees (called covenants) made by the grantor:

○ *Covenant of seisin.* The grantor guarantees to be the owner of the property in fee simple with the right to convey title.
○ *Covenant against encumbrances.* The grantor guarantees that there are no liens, mortgages, or other encumbrances against the property other than those stated in the deed.
○ *Covenant for quiet enjoyment.* The grantor guarantees present and succeeding grantees that they will not be evicted and that their quiet legal enjoyment will never be disturbed by third parties who may prove a better title or claim.

2. Special Warranty Deed. A *special warranty deed* contains express warranties under which the grantor guarantees that no defects arose in the title during the time that the grantor owned the property. No warranties are made as to defects which arose before the grantor owned the property. The warranties do not extend beyond the seller, and they do not guarantee the title against claims arising from situations existing prior to the seller's title interest.

● Harkness sold a vacant lot to Grahm. The lot had been left to Harkness through the will of a distant relative. Harkness had never had the title searched, but she could guarantee Grahm that no liens or claims against the property had been created

Part 9:
Real
Property
and
Inheri-
tance

486

since the execution of the will. Harkness would be safe in granting title under this special warranty deed. Likewise, the buyer would be protected, but only by making a title search that would disclose claims not covered by the seller's warranty.

3. Bargain-and-Sale Deed. A *bargain-and-sale deed* is one which transfers title to property but contains no warranties. The form of the deed is the same as a warranty deed's except that the covenants are omitted. Since a bargain and sale necessarily involves the idea of a valuable consideration, this type of deed is not valid without consideration. It could not be used to convey a gift of real property.

4. Quitclaim Deed. A *quitclaim deed* (also called a *deed without covenants*) is one that transfers to the buyer only the interest that the seller may have in a property. This type of deed merely releases a party's rights to the property. It contains no warranties. It is used when one gives up some right in property, such as an easement or dower and curtesy, or to cure a defect in the chain of title.

E. Statutory Requirements of a Deed

The execution and transfer of title must follow the requirements set forth in the laws of the state in which the property is located. Although the grantor and grantee may live in other states, laws of those states are not applicable to the transfer of ownership. Generally, all states require the following procedures.

- ○ Deeds must be in writing and must be signed by owners who transfer title. Many states require both the signature and seal of the grantors.
- ○ Deeds must contain words that show the grantor's intention to transfer title.
- ○ A deed must contain sufficient description of the realty to identify it unmistakably.
- ○ The signatures on the deed must be witnessed in some states.
- ○ The deed must be *acknowledged* before being recorded in the books of the registrar or other public office recording deeds to real estate. A deed is acknowledged by being signed in the presence of a notary public or other authorized official whose signature and seal are then affixed to the deed.
- ○ The deed must be delivered to and accepted by the grantee. In the event of the buyer's absence at settlement, an attorney may act as the buyer's agent.

F. Tender and Performance

On the date of final settlement specified in the sales contract, the grantor must show readiness to deliver a proper deed to the buyer, and the buyer must make tender of the purchase price named in the contract. If it is impossible or inconvenient for them to be present at the settlement, they may be represented by agents who have power of attorney. Failure of either party to perform results in a breach, permitting the injured party to sue for damages, to rescind the contract, or to require specific performance of the contract.

G. Escrow

While delivery of a deed, in most states, is made to the buyer or one appointed by the buyer, some states require delivery in *escrow*. This is accomplished by delivery of the deed to a disinterested third party who has been accepted as the

Chapter 36:
Nature,
Acquisition, and
Sale of
Real
Property

487

escrow agent by both parties. Delivery is made with a condition that the deed will be given to the grantee only on payment of the purchase price (or other conditions). The escrow agent may not return the deed to the grantor, except after a stated period of time during which the buyer has agreed to comply with the condition of payment. Delivery in escrow eliminates the possibility of the new deed's being delivered and recorded in the new owner's name before the buyer has made full performance.

H. Recording the Deed

It is the obligation of the grantee and the grantee's attorney to have the new deed recorded in a county office maintained for that purpose. Recording the deed is public notice to all that the property has been transferred to a new owner. Records are available for inspection by attorneys and others who, in good faith, have reason to inspect them. One whose name appears on the deed is known as the *owner of record*. All mortgages, liens of any kind, and unsatisfied judgments are likewise recorded in the same office.

Failure to record the deed of a new owner may result in another's superior claim of ownership. A second sale by the owner of record before the first sale has been recorded may defeat the original buyer's claim of title. A search of the deed by the second buyer will fail to show that there has been a previous deed issued if it has not been recorded, and the second buyer will receive *title by estoppel*.

I. Real Estate Mortgage

In purchasing a dwelling or other real estate, the buyer may use the property as security for a loan. When this is done, the property owner gives the lender a document, known as a real estate *mortgage*, as evidence of such security. The person who signs and gives the mortgage is the *mortgagor*, or debtor. The one to whom the mortgage is given is the *mortgagee*, or creditor.

Accompanying a mortgage is a bond, or note, executed by the mortgagor to the lender, making the debtor personally liable for the debt. A mortgage on real estate creates a lien on the property and gives the lender the right to have the property sold if the debt is not paid. Mortgages are discussed in more detail in Chapter 41.

36-7. Restrictions on Private Property Ownership

State and local laws provide restrictions against particular uses of real property. Zoning laws are commonly found in most cities and towns. In addition, federal, state, and local governments have the right to take private property for the public good.

A. Zoning Laws

Zoning laws are laws which regulate the uses that may be made of properties within specified geographic areas or districts. Residential zoning prohibits properties from being used for commercial purposes within a given area. Multifamily zoning permits construction of apartment buildings. Limited-commercial zoning allows the construction of small stores but restricts the building of large department stores and commercial centers. Industrial zoning allows the

Part 9:
Real
Property
and
Inheritance

488

building of factories and industries within a particular area. Zoning laws tend to protect property values and permit property owners to make improvements with some certainty that the comforts and value enjoyed as a result will not be threatened by construction of undesirable buildings or by offensive use being made of existing properties.

Newly passed zoning laws do not apply to existing uses of the land. Such uses are called *nonconforming uses*. They may continue in existence but may not be enlarged or expanded.

By appeal to the local zoning board, variances may be given to individuals or businesses when justified and reasonable. A *variance* is an exemption or an exception permitting a use that differs from those permitted under the existing ordinance. Variances are granted in special circumstances to protect citizens who might otherwise suffer a hardship if zoning laws were applied and enforced arbitrarily.

Decisions of a local zoning commission may be appealed to county commissioners, a county court, and to the highest court in the state.

B. Eminent Domain

All ownership of private property is subject to the government's superior rights if property is needed for purposes of the public good. *Eminent domain* is the right of federal, state, and local governments, or other public bodies, to take private lands, with compensation to their owners, for public use. The right is exercised for such purposes as new highway construction, public parks, state hospitals, and other facilities.

The right of eminent domain is not available to persons or businesses when taken for private profit. In such situations, property may be acquired only through mutual agreement and for consideration acceptable to the owner. Eminent domain is at times extended to public utilities when it can be shown that denial of a right-of-way for electric, telephone, gas, or other lines may interrupt construction of installations providing needed services to an entire community.

When private property is taken by eminent domain proceedings, the owner is compensated for the fair value of what has been taken. The owner is not required to accept an amount offered by those assessing the value of the property. But if an offer is refused, the owner must then defend a demand for greater compensation through action in the state or federal courts.

● Interstate 95 was designed to cut a swath through a residential section of Chester. Hundreds of homes, businesses, and churches lay in the path of the new highway. Kovach refused to accept the $9,500 offered by assessors for his property. An appeal was made through the county court, with Kovach claiming a fair value of $15,000; this amount would provide the family with a similar home in a comparable neighborhood of the same city. The court might accept the assessors' figure as final; might increase the amount offered; or, in some instances, might reduce the $9,500 if it was considered excessive when reviewed.

36-8. Other Forms of Ownership

Less than one hundred years ago there appeared in this country a system of cooperative ownership of apartment residences. The demand for cooperatives waned during the 1930s, but in recent years they have again become popular in certain metropolitan areas where apartments represent a sizable part of all available residential housing. Condominiums and mobile homes are now very popular.

A. Condominium Ownership

A *condominium* is a legal invention which gives the purchaser of an apartment or household unit an estate in fee simple in the unit that is purchased. The buyer's property becomes separate and distinct from the corporation or business enterprise that developed the project. After all apartment or household units have been sold, the original corporation or entity that developed the project is dissolved, and ownership is vested entirely with those who have deeds to the units sold.

A condominium, in effect, grants to its owner two deeds: an estate in fee simple in the apartment or household itself and co-ownership with all other owners in those parts of the grounds and structure that are not under the supervision or care of one individual.

B. Cooperative Ownership

The cooperative begins with the formation of a corporation which builds an apartment building containing a number of living units. The corporation usually places a mortgage on the land for the purpose of constructing the building. Prospective tenants purchase shares of stock in the cooperative to bring in the necessary capital to complete the apartment building. The purchase of a specified number of shares gives a prospective tenant the right to a *proprietary lease,* which is a long-term lease issued by the corporation. Such a lease gives the tenant all the usual rights of ownership. The tenant has the right of possession of an apartment, for which regular payments are made to the corporation for the tenant's share of operating expenses, mortgage debt and reduction, and taxes. The amount levied against each tenant is determined by the number of shares of stock held. The larger apartments are held by those owning a greater number of shares. Tenants provide their own electrical appliances, floor coverings, and interior maintenance.

The disadvantage of cooperatives is the possibility of a mortgage foreclosure, in which case the tenants may lose their rights. In such a case, a receiver would be appointed for the operation of the apartment project for the benefit of the mortgagee, and each tenant would then be required to pay either a proportionate share of the mortgage or full rental for the tenant's apartment as a means of liquidating the mortgage.

C. Mobile-Home Ownership

Mobile homes, sometimes called trailers, are becoming increasingly popular and represent a sizable segment of dwellings in this country. They offer certain advantages which have made them desirable in many areas and to many people. Among the advantages of a mobile home are freedom from assessments and real-property taxes, efficiency living, and mobility, making possible a change of location.

○ Mobile homes, unless placed on permanent foundations and given other special treatment, are said to be personal property and therefore do not come

Part 9:
Real
Property
and
Inheri-
tance

490

within the jurisdiction of real estate tax boards. However, most states have passed legislation requiring special fees to be paid by trailer residents. These fees, in addition to the usual highway license, provide income from the mobile-home owners for use in providing schools and other services enjoyed by all citizens.*

○ Because of the efficient construction and utilization of space, owners of mobile homes find that less time is needed in maintenance and care than is required of the ordinary dwelling. This is a saving in both cost and time.

○ At a minimum of cost, mobile homes may be moved from place to place either by the owner or through the services of trailer-moving specialists. Persons engaged in work that requires frequent changes of residence find that the convenience and saving offered by a mobile home are great.

Owners of mobile homes are required to observe many statutes adopted in most states for the regulation of mobile homes, both as dwellings and as moving vehicles. The states are gradually adding more restrictions and obligations each year for the regulation of mobile homes.

Understanding Legal Terms

Define, identify, or explain the following terms:

adverse possession	easement	joint tenants	riparian rights
bargain-and-sale deed	estate in fee simple	life estate	special warranty deed
conditional estate	general warranty deed	quitclaim deed	tenancy by the entirety
condominium	grantee	real property	
determinable fee	grantor	remainder estate	tenants in common
		reversion estate	

Questions for Review and Discussion

1. In what ways may one develop an easement in another's property? Explain the terms *servient tenement* and *dominant tenement*.

2. Explain each of the following: (a) dower right, (b) curtesy right, and (c) community property.

3. In each of the following tenancies, who succeeds to the deceased's title interest? (a) Tenancy in common, (b) joint tenancy , and (c) tenancy by the entirety.

4. What special qualification distinguishes a tenancy by the entirety from a joint tenancy?

5. What must claimants prove to establish ownership of real property by adverse possession?

6. Give several reasons why it is recommended that an attorney make a title search before one accepts the deed to a property.

7. For what reasons would a buyer of real property purchase title insurance on the new property?

8. Name the three covenants, or warranties, included in a general warranty deed.

9. Explain eminent domain. When and by whom may it be applied?

10. Discuss the principal advantage of condominium ownership over having a proprietary lease in a cooperative.

---

* In most cases, the fees levied on mobile homes are not proportionate to those levied on real property or in consideration of the benefits received. This condition creates dissension and hostility at times between homeowners and those who occupy mobile homes.

Analyzing Cases

1. In her will, Alma Rand left a parcel of real property to John F. Rand "in fee simple with the proviso that he shall never deny access or occupation to the several heirs hereinafter named during their lifetime." The will then named five children and stepchildren as heirs. Upon Alma's death did John inherit an estate in fee simple in the real property? Explain. ● *Babb v. Rand*, 345 A.2d 496 (Me. 1975)

2. Lillian Bellows delivered a bargain-and-sale deed conveying two lots of land to John Caton. Later, Caton conveyed the two lots by a general warranty deed to Somerset County. Sometime thereafter, another person claimed ownership to part of one lot and an easement over the other lot. The county claims that Caton is liable to it for its loss. Caton claims that Bellows is liable to him for breach of the warranties given in her bargain-and-sale deed. Is the county correct? Is Caton correct? Why or why not? ● *County of Somerset v. Durling*, 415 A.2d 371 (N.J. 1980)

3. The Eisenmanns purchased a 90-acre tract of land on which they drilled a 179-foot-deep irrigation well. When the well was completed, they began pumping water at the rate of 650 gallons per minute. Two of the surrounding landowners, the Prathers (whose well was 121 feet 10 inches deep) and the Furleys, lost the use of their wells the next day. A third neighbor, the Zessins, lost the use of their well three days later. The surrounding landowners seek money damages for the loss of the use of their wells from the Eisenmanns. Will they recover? If so, how much? Explain. ● *Prather v. Eisenmann*, 261 N.W.2d 766 (Neb. 1978)

4. Two years after Jean Russell was divorced from Billy Russell, Jean signed a deed conveying her interest in their jointly owned real property to Billy. Later, she tried to have the deed set aside on the ground that Billy gave her no consideration. Will she be successful? Why or why not? ● *Russell v. Russell*, 361 So.2d 1053 (Ala. 1978)

5. In the early 1930s, Mary and Fred Squiers built a hunting camp on a small section of their land. In 1947, they sold the entire land to Sarah Vedder. At that time, Mary moved into the hunting camp and lived there openly and continuously for twenty-two years, first with her husband, Fred, and after his death with her second husband, Willard Best. In 1967, Vedder conveyed the entire property to Darling. In 1969, Mary Best (formerly Mary Squiers) and Willard Best conveyed the hunting camp section of the same property to Ennis. Darling brought an action to eject Ennis from the hunting camp. Will he succeed? Explain. ● *Darling v. Ennis*, 415 A.2d 228 (Vt. 1980)

6. Walter and Emma Barrett jointly executed a warranty deed conveying three lots of land to Chandler and Jean Clements as joint tenants with the right of survivorship. Six years later, Jean Clements conveyed her one-half undivided interest in the property to Wheeler. Chandler claims that Jean could not sell her interest to another person without his approval. Is he correct? ● *Clements v. Wheeler*, 314 So.2d 64 (Ala. 1975)

7. Richard and Olive Misner began to develop a campground on land that they owned on Olive Lake. The zoning law in existence at the time allowed campgrounds to be built in that area. A year later, however, the county rezoned the area to "agricultural and lake resort" use, which did not permit campgrounds. At the time the new law went into effect, the Misners had constructed ten campsites with facilities and three primitive campsites on their property. When they continued to use and expand the campground after the new zoning law was passed, neighbors complained that they were violating the law. Can the Misner's continue to use and

expand the property as a campground? Explain. ● *Misner v. Presdorf*, 421 N.E.2d 684 (Ind. 1981)

8. Fannie P. Hood, who was in her mid-eighties, entered a hospital for surgery from which she believed she might not recover. While in the hospital, she asked an attorney to draw a deed conveying her farm to her son, Kenneth. The deed was executed by Mrs. Hood at the hospital and recorded at the registry of deeds. Kenneth had no knowledge of the transaction until sometime later when he visited his mother in the hospital. When she told him what she had done, Kenneth said that he wanted no part of the property. He requested his mother to "take it right back." Mrs. Hood tried to contact the attorney who had drawn the deed but was unsuccessful because he was on vacation. Kenneth died two months later. His heirs claimed title to the farm. Mrs. Hood claimed that she still owned the farm. Do you agree with Mrs. Hood? Give a reason for your answer. ● *Hood v. Hood*, 384 A.2d 706 (Me. 1978)

9. Rebecca Thomas deeded a parcel of real property to Luvonia Childers. The deed described the property as "32 acres, more or less, in the Southeast of Lot No. 105 in the 13th District and 2nd section of said County." When Thomas died, it was claimed that the deed did not convey title because the description was too indefinite. How would you decide? ● See also *Mathews v. Logan*, 247 S.E.2d 865 (Ga. 1978)

10. Soon after Walter and Elsie Wienke were married, Walter conveyed property on Ridgewood Drive that was owned by him to himself and Elsie as tenants by the entirety. At the same time, Elsie conveyed property on Harlan Street that was owned by her to herself and Walter as tenants by the entirety. Twelve years later, Elsie conveyed the Harlan Street property by warranty deed to Colonial Discount Corporation. Walter objected to this sale and did not sign the deed. Colonial Discount Corporation sold the property to Danny and Glenda Lynch. Walter Wienke contends that a conveyance by one tenant by the entirety is inoperative. Do you agree with Walter? Why or why not? ● *Wienke v. Lynch*, 407 N.E.2d 280 (Ind. 1980)

Chapter 37 Landlord and Tenant

Does home ownership always serve the best interests of a family? Why do so many people find it more desirable to live in rented houses or apartments? Are the legal rights and obligations of these people more favorable than those enjoyed by the homeowner? This chapter explains the landlord-tenant relationship issue and reviews the law as it applies to the leasing of real property.

37-1. The Landlord-Tenant Relationship

The landlord-tenant relationship is a contractural arrangement whereby the owner of real property allows another to have temporary possession and control of the premises in exchange for consideration. The agreement which gives rise to the landlord-tenant relationship is called a *lease*. The property owner who gives the lease is the *lessor* or landlord, and the person to whom the lease is given is the *lessee* or *tenant*. There are five elements necessary for the creation of the landlord-tenant relationship:

○ Consent of the landlord to the occupancy by the tenant.
○ Transfer of possession and control of the property to the tenant in an inferior position (in *subordination*) to the rights of the landlord.
○ The right by the landlord to the return of the property, called the right of *reversion*.
○ The creation of an estate in the tenant known as a *leasehold estate*.
○ Either an express or implied contract between the parties which satisfies all the essentials of a valid contract (mutual assent, competent parties, consideration, lawful purpose).

Although rent is usually paid by the tenant to the landlord for the arrangement, it is not essential to the creation of the landlord-tenant relationship.

37-2. Leasing Versus Other Relationships

Other relationships that may be compared with the landlord-tenant relationship are licensing and lodging.

A. Leasing Compared With Licensing

A lease differs from a license in that a lease conveys an interest in real property and transfers possession, whereas a *license* conveys no property right or interest to the land but merely allows the licensee to do certain acts which would otherwise be a trespass.

● The city of Topeka was given a gift of 80 acres of land for use as a public park by the heirs of Guilford G. Gage. The deed that was signed by the heirs contained a

494

condition that the property would revert back to them if the property were ever deeded or leased to a third party. After the park was established, the city granted the exclusive right to McCall to construct and operate, for a period of five years, a miniature train on the premises. Under the agreement, McCall was subject in virtually all respects to the control of the city, and either party could end the arrangement by giving thirty days' notice. The heirs of Gage claimed that the transaction was a lease and that the property should be returned to them. In holding that McCall had a license rather than a lease, the court said that all McCall had was "the exclusive right to operate as the City may dictate."

Since a license confers a personal privilege to act, and not a present possessory estate, it does not run with the land and is usually not assignable. It may be made orally or in writing and may be given without consideration. In addition, a license need not delineate the specific space to be occupied.

In contrast, a lease gives the tenant exclusive possession of the premises as against all the world, including the owner. It describes the exact property leased and states the term of the tenancy and the rent to be paid. In addition, in some states, a lease must be in writing.

● Union Travel Associates operated a gift shop in the lobby of the International Inn. Under the terms of the agreement, Union was permitted "for the convenience of the guests of the hotel" to sell gifts, tobacco, packaged food, reading materials, and artwork, and to give out tour and travel information. Union was required to promote actively guest business for the hotel and to provide the hotel with a key to each entrance to the gift shop. The hotel had the right "to use space in and through the premises for pipes, wires and conduits, to approve the selection of the gift shop employees, and to regulate the appearance of all gift shop signs, merchandise, and fixtures." In addition, the hotel retained the right to substitute at any time in its discretion any equivalent part of the hotel for its gift shop. The court held the arrangement to be a license rather than a lease, saying that the agreement did not grant an estate in real property. Rather, it conferred the limited privilege to occupy a portion of the hotel lobby to conduct services as a nonleasehold concession.

Permission to sell Christmas trees at a gas station, to hold dance parties in a hall, and to place a sign on the outside of a building have all been held to be licenses rather than leases.

B. Leasing Compared With Lodging

A *lodger* is one who has the use of property without actual or exclusive possession of it. A lodger is a type of licensee, with a mere right to use the property. The landlord retains control of the premises and is responsible for its care and upkeep. Unlike a tenant, a lodger has no right to bring suit for trespass or to eject an intruder from the premises. One who lives in a spare room of a house, for example, whose owner retains direct control and supervision of the entire house is a lodger.

37-3. Types of Leasehold Interests

The interest conveyed by a lease is called a *leasehold estate* or a *tenancy*. There are four kinds of tenancies: tenancy at will, tenancy for years, periodic tenancy, and tenancy at sufferance.

A. Tenancy at Will

When no specific term of lease is agreed upon, the relationship is called a *tenancy at will*. It continues indefinitely until terminated. In some states notice is not required to terminate a tenancy at will. Other states, however, require thirty days' notice in writing from the landlord before a tenant can be forced to give up a leasehold under a tenancy at will.

● Kenton had a permanent residence in Smithville, but his company assigned him for an indefinite period to its plant in Jonesboro, 80 miles away. Rather than commute, Kenton rented an apartment in Atlantic Arms Apartments under an agreement of a tenancy at will. He paid rent on a weekly basis and could terminate the lease at any time by giving the proper notice.

The rule generally followed in this country is that a tenancy at will is terminated by a conveyance of the premises by the landlord to a third party.

B. Tenancy for Years

A *tenancy for years* is an estate for a definite or fixed period of time, no matter how long or how short. It may be for one week, six months, one year, five years, ninety-nine years, or any period of time so long as it is ascertained. Such a tenancy automatically terminates on the expiration of the stated term. A tenant who remains in possession of the premises at the expiration of the term with permission of the landlord but without a new lease is a tenant at will in some states. In others, such a tenant is known as a periodic tenant, described below.

In most states, a tenancy for years must be evidenced by a writing to satisfy the statute of frauds. If the writing fails to state a definite term, only a tenancy at will may be created.

C. Periodic Tenancy

A *periodic tenancy,* which is also known as a *tenancy from year to year* (or month to month, or week to week), is a tenancy which continues for successive periods until one of the parties terminates it by giving notice to the other party.

Unless the landlord or the tenant gives advance notice of an intention to terminate the lease, it will be automatically renewed at the end of each period for the same term. Advance notice varies from state to state, but it generally is defined as a period of three months for periodic tenancies of one year or longer and "one period" for periodic terms of less than a year.

● Orsini's year-to-year lease expires on December 21. On November 1 she gave her landlord notice of her intention to terminate the lease. In her state, three months' notice is necessary to terminate a year-to-year tenancy. Orsini's landlord can hold her to an additional year.

The death of a tenant who holds a periodic tenancy does not terminate the tenancy. Rather, the interest of the tenant passes to the personal representative of the deceased's estate.

● Clay Wilson was in possession of rental property originally leased to his father on a month-to-month basis. After the father's death, the landlord notified Wilson to va-

Part 9:
Real
Property
and
Inheri-
tance

496

cate the premises on the ground that the tenancy had ceased automatically. When Wilson refused to leave, criminal trespass charges were filed against him. He was found not guilty. The court held that his father's interest in the premises passed to him and that he was entitled to proper notice to end the month-to-month tenancy.

A periodic tenancy may be created impliedly by a landlord accepting rent from a tenant for years whose lease has expired or who is wrongfully in possession. Some states which do not recognize a tenancy from year to year treat the latter situation as a tenancy at sufferance.

D. Tenancy at Sufferance

A *tenancy at sufferance* arises when tenants wrongfully remain in possession of the premises after their tenancy has expired. It often comes about at the expiration of the term of a tenancy for years or when a tenancy at will has been properly terminated and the tenant remains in possession. Such a tenant is a wrongdoer, having no estate or other interest in the property. A tenant at sufferance is not entitled to notice to vacate and is liable to pay rent for the period of occupancy. A periodic tenancy or a tenancy at will may come about, however, instead of a tenancy at sufferance if a landlord accepts rent from a tenant whose tenancy has expired.

● Kimberly Sutherland, an attorney, rented a suite of rooms in the Metropolitan Building in Chicago which she used for law offices. When her two-year lease expired, she negotiated with the owner of the building for a new lease. The negotiations extended over a period of several months, and the parties could not reach agreement. The landlord accepted rent each month from Sutherland during the period of negotiations. Sutherland was not a tenant at sufferance during the negotiation period because the landlord accepted rent from her during that time. A month-to-month tenancy was created. The landlord was required to give Sutherland a month's notice to end the tenancy.

37-4. The Lease Agreement

The agreement between a lessor and a lessee, called a lease, creates the landlord-tenant relationship. It provides the tenant with exclusive possession and control of the real property of the landlord. Since the lease is a contract, the general rules of contract law apply to it.

● Piccarelli, a representative of Mister Donut, expressed interest in leasing Tull's property. He sent a letter to Tull describing the "rudiments of our deal" and concluding with an expression of hope "that in the very near future preliminaries will be completed." This was followed by a form of lease sent by Piccarelli to Tull for the latter's approval. Tull signed the lease, after changing it materially, and returned it to Mister Donut for a countersignature. Nothing further was done, and the transaction never materialized. Tull's building was vandalized and burned after his tenants were evicted in anticipation of leasing the property to Mister Donut. When Tull sued Mister Donut, the court held that no contract and, thus, no lease came about. The initial letter was no more than an agenda for further discussion. The first draft of the lease sent by Piccarelli to Tull was an offer, and the revised document a counteroffer, never accepted by Mister Donut.

The essential requirements of a lease are: (*a*) a definite agreement as to the extent and bounds of the leased property, (*b*) a definite and agreed term, and (*c*) a definite and agreed price of rental and manner of payment.

● Henry D. Schumacher leased a retail store to Joseph Martin, Jr., Delicatessen, Inc., for a five-year term. The renewal clause stated that "the Tenant may renew this lease for an additional period of five years at annual rentals *to be agreed upon;* Tenant shall give Landlord thirty (30) days written notice, to be mailed certified mail, return receipt requested, of the intention to exercise such right." The tenant gave timely notice to renew the lease, but the parties could not agree on the rent for the new term. The court held that the agreement to renew the lease was unenforceable because the amount of rent was uncertain. A mere agreement to agree, in which a material term is left for future negotiations, is unenforceable.

A. Parties to a Lease

A lease contract must be entered into by the property's owner or agent and the tenant who will actually occupy the leased premises. Often the property owner delegates the authority to execute leases to a rental or management agent. Typically, the management company collects all rents and performs all building services for the property owner. It collects a percentage of the gross rents (usually 5 to 8 percent) for its efforts.

An agent may execute the lease for the lessee, but must disclose who the actual tenant will be. That is because the landlord will usually ask for references, that is, a list of the prospective tenant's business contacts or former landlords. The purpose is to help in deciding whether the prospective lessee would be a responsible tenant.

Since a lease is a contract, it may be disaffirmed by a party who did not have the capacity to execute the contract when it was entered into (see Chapter 10). Similarly, if a person adjudged to be incompetent has entered into a lease, that lease may be disaffirmed by someone who has the authority to govern the affairs of the incompetent. A minor may also disaffirm a lease, unless it is shown to be a necessity. Minors who are married are *emancipated* from this right, in some states, however, and may be held responsible by the lessor for all unpaid rents and any damages inflicted upon the rented premises.

B. Oral and Written Leases

In some states, a lease may be oral if the term is shorter than one year. Other states require all leases for a definite term to be in writing. Because of misunderstanding and possible troubles between landlord and tenant, it is advisable that even a short-term lease be put in writing, to spell out all the conditions of the lease in regard to the tenant and the landlord.

● Chapman rented an apartment for six months under an oral lease. At the end of the leasehold, the landlord demanded $150 for repairs that Chapman claimed were not discussed when the lease was entered into. (In general, written leases indicate who will bear the costs of certain repairs.) A magistrate or small-claims court might have to determine Chapman's rights and obligations in the oral lease.

C. Interpretation of Leases

If a landlord and tenant disagree over the interpretation of their lease, they may find themselves arguing over their differences in court. The usual rules for in-

Part 9:
Real
Property
and
Inheri-
tance

498

terpretation of contracts would come into play. As a result, one very important rule might favor a tenant. That rule says that, in an adhesion contract, any ambiguities or doubts as to interpretation are resolved in favor of the party who did not prepare the contract. An adhesion contract, you may recall, is an agreement drawn entirely by one party and presented to the other party for agreement or rejection. Typically, prospective residential tenants are presented with a proposed lease which they can either sign or reject; they are not given an opportunity to modify the landlord's terms. Business tenants, on the other hand, usually play an active part in negotiating lease terms with a landlord. Any vagueness in a tenant's adhesion lease, then, will usually be interpreted in the tenant's favor.

D. Security Deposit

Traditionally, leases have required security deposits to protect landlords against damages to their apartments as well as nonpayment of rent. In recent years, consumer groups have brought to public attention landlord abuses in improperly holding onto a security deposit when a tenancy ends. Some landlords deducted charges for ordinary wear and tear, rather than for actual damages to their premises. Others charged amounts for unnecessary cleaning expenses. Still others gave no accounting at all.

While tenants have always had the right to take a landlord to court to get back an improperly withheld security deposit, most state legislatures have now passed statutes governing security deposits for residential tenants. Such laws spell out tenant rights and make it easier for tenants to prevail in court. While these laws differ from state to state, certain characteristics are commonly found.

○ Most states limit security deposits to 1, $1\frac{1}{2}$, 2, or $2\frac{1}{2}$ months' rent.
○ Most states require that security deposits be placed in interest-bearing accounts. The interest is either paid to tenants on an annual basis or accrued in their favor.
○ The landlord is given a specific period, usually thirty days after the lease ends, to account for the security deposit and return the balance due to a tenant.
○ Many states have now "put teeth" into the law by providing for double damages, court costs, and attorney's fees for tenants whose security deposits were wrongfully withheld.

● Santos rented a $450-per-month apartment from Hollis for a term of two years. When Santos's tenancy ended, Hollis refused to return any of the $450 security deposit to Santos, claiming that the damages to the apartment fully offset the amount of the deposit. Santos hired a lawyer, who brought suit against Hollis. The landlord was able to demonstrate only $70 in damages to Santos's apartment. The court found that Hollis had wrongfully withheld $380 of Santos's security deposit. The court awarded Santos a judgment for double damages of $760 plus attorney's fees of $200. With court costs, the landlord was forced to pay over $1,000.

Landlords of commercial property may also require security deposits, but the statutes do not usually cover commercial leases. Some landlords do not require security deposits at all. Instead, they favor collecting the first month's rent and the last month's rent in advance.

E. Option to Renew

Many leases contain a provision allowing the lessee to have the option to renew the lease for one or more additional terms. An *option to renew* gives the lessee the right, at the end of the lease, to a new lease for an additional period. The new lease is on the same terms as the old one with the possible exception of an increase in the rent. To exercise the option, the lessee must notify the lessor on or before the date set forth in the lease to do so. If there is more than one lessee to a lease agreement, an option-to-renew provision in the lease must be exercised by the lessees jointly to be effective.

F. Option to Purchase

A lessee may, if the lease so provides, be given an *option to purchase* the property. This is an agreement by the lessor to sell the property to the lessee for a stated price. To exercise the option, the lessee must notify the lessor, within the time period stated in the lease, of the desire to purchase the property.

● Hazel Larson purchased a parcel of real property for $19,140 and leased it to the Panhandle Rehabilitation Center. The lease was for ten years and contained an option to buy for $19,000. After leasing the premises for five years and spending $5,000 to improve it, Panhandle notified Larson of its intention to exercise its option. By this time, the property was worth $38,000. Larson refused to sell the property to Panhandle. The court ordered her to do so.

37-5. Rights and Duties of Landlords and Tenants

A good lease agreement will carefully spell out the respective rights and duties of landlord and tenant. However, appropriate laws may restrict or expand upon what is set forth in the lease.

● The standard lease at Helmsly Arms provides that residential tenants may renew automatically after expiration of their standard two-year leases at a new rental rate 12 percent higher than the previous rental. A local "rent-leveling" ordinance limits rent increases in such circumstances to 8 percent. When the ordinance was first passed, a group of landlords brought suit to attack its constitutionality. The matter went all the way to the highest court in the state, where the ordinance was upheld. Helmsly cannot impose its terms despite the clear language of the lease.

A. Landlord's Duty to Lease Property

A landlord may not discriminate in selecting tenants on the grounds of race, creed, color, or sex. In most states a landlord may restrict rentals to persons without children, but may not restrict a married couple's freedom to bear children during the leasehold.

● The Stimsons, a married couple, rented a luxury apartment from Chester Realty Associates. A condition inserted in the lease read, "The lessee agrees that if a child or children are born to the tenants during the period of the lease, the lease will be automatically terminated without the necessity of notice from the landlord." This condition is not enforceable against the Stimsons. Persons may not be denied the freedom of bearing children through contracts made with a landlord or others.

Part 9:
Real
Property
and
Inheri-
tance

500

B. Warranty of Habitability

When real property is rented for single- or multiple-family dwelling purposes, there is an implied warranty in most states that the premises are fit for human habitation. This means that the landlord warrants that there are no defects vital to the use of the premises for residential purposes.

● Burke and Maltbie, students at Indiana University, rented an apartment in an older home for a term of one year from Breezewood Management Company for $235 a month. Upon moving in, they discovered numerous defects: rotting porch floor boards, broken and loose windows, an inoperable front door lock, leaks in the plumbing, a back door that would not close, a missing bathroom door, inadequate water pressure, falling plaster, exposed wiring over the bathtub, and a malfunctioning toilet. Later, they discovered a leaking roof, cockroach infestation, the absence of heat and hot water, more leaks in the plumbing, and pigeons in the attic. The conditions remained largely uncorrected, even after notice to the landlord from the tenants and from the city's code enforcement officers. Burke developed pneumonia and was hospitalized owing to the inadequate heating of the apartment, and Maltbie moved out after occupying the premises for nine months. The court held that Breezewood breached the implied warranty of habitability.

In ordinary circumstances, the measure of a tenant's damages for the landlord's breach of the implied warranty of habitability is the difference between the value of the apartment as originally warranted and the rental value of the apartment in its defective condition. In the above case, Burke and Maltbie were required to pay only the reasonable rental value of the property during the time they lived there. This was found to be $50 a month during the cold weather and $75 a month during warmer weather.

C. Landlord's Rights Under Lease

Under most leases, a landlord has the following rights.

1. Right to Rent. The landlord has the right to collect rent from the tenant.

2. Right to Possession. The landlord has the right to recover possession of the rental premises, in good condition, at the expiration of the lease. The tenant must keep the property in good repair, unless the landlord has accepted that obligation.

● O'Neal Music Center rented a store under a lease in which nothing was said about obligations of either landlord or tenant in the matter of repairs. A plate glass window was destroyed by high winds and required immediate replacement. The music center would be responsible for the replacement.

3. Right to Evict. The landlord has the right to evict a tenant for nonpayment of rent, disorderliness, or illegal or unpermitted use of the premises.

● Harrison had been a tenant of Driscoll for thirteen years, and rent control laws prevented his eviction without good cause. One morning Harrison was late for work. As he was going to his car, which was in the parking lot of the building, he saw that a truck was blocking the exit from the lot. Frank Driscoll, the landlord's son, had arrived in the truck a short time earlier to collect rubbish. Harrison asked Frank Driscoll to move his truck, and Frank Driscoll asked Harrison why he had failed to report a leak in his apartment which had caused water to seep into the unit below his. Harrison denied knowledge of the leak, and a shouting match ensued. It quickly escalated into a physical altercation with both individuals touching the other with their finger in a light pushing fashion. The light pushing as well as the shouting ended when Harrison took a 4-foot closet pole from the trunk of his car and hit Frank Driscoll in the shoulder with it. The court allowed the landlord to evict the tenant for striking his son, saying that the tenant "used excessive force and committed a serious act of violence."

A tenant does have the duty to observe the restrictions contained in the lease. Leases may impose duties of all kinds as long as they are legal and do not deny a tenant's constitutional rights. Failure to abide by the restrictions agreed to at the time of the signing of the lease gives the landlord the right to seek eviction of the tenant.

● Boggs's lease states that he cannot paint any exterior woodwork or walls without first getting written permission from the landlord. Painting these surfaces, even though doing so improves the property, gives the landlord the right to terminate Boggs's lease.

4. **Right to Retain Permanent Improvements.** The landlord has the right to keep fixtures that have been made a permanent part of the real property by the tenant during the leasehold.

● Dr. Hembly installed partitions in the rented house, dividing the living room for consultation offices. New lighting fixtures were installed, as well as a built-in air-conditioning system. Hembly would be barred from removing the additions at the expiration of her lease or upon her eviction, as they had become real property.

D. **Tenant's Rights Under Lease**

Under most leases, a tenant has the following rights.

1. **Right of Quiet Enjoyment.** The tenant is entitled to the peaceful possession and *quiet enjoyment* of the rental premises. This includes both the physical and legal rights of possession. The landlord may not interfere with the tenant's rights of possession as long as the tenant abides by the conditions of the lease and those imposed by law.

● Smith Grocery & Variety, Inc., leased one store in a two-store mall from Northern Terminals, Inc. The lease entitled Smith to the use of the parking areas (between fourteen and twenty spaces) abutting the leased premises. Five months after Smith opened for business, Northern Terminals added an additional store to the mall without increasing the mall's parking facilities. Smith's business declined due to the severe parking shortage caused by the opening of a Triple-S Blue Stamp Redemption Center in the new addition. The court held that Northern Terminals, Inc., breached the covenant of quiet enjoyment. There was a substantial interference with the lessee's use of the premises, which was caused by the lessor's taking away of the parking spaces.

Part 9:
Real
Property
and
Inheri-
tance

502

The right to exclusive possession by the tenant makes the landlord a trespasser should there be any unauthorized entry by the landlord into the rented premises.

● Benson & Childs rented a skylight suite for their architecture offices. The lease gave the owner permission to enter only when request had been made or in the event of extreme emergency. The landlord entered the offices late one evening for what he termed his regular safety and fire inspection. Benson & Childs may treat the landlord's trespass as a breach of their right to sole possession, giving them the right to terminate the lease or charge the landlord in either a civil or a criminal complaint.

2. Right to Terminate Lease When Wrongly Evicted. A tenant who is wrongfully evicted is not required to return and may consider the lease as ended. An *eviction* is an act of the landlord which deprives the tenant of the enjoyment of the premises. It is called an *actual eviction* when the tenant is physically deprived of the leasehold. When the tenant is deprived of something of a substantial nature that was called for under the lease, it is termed a *constructive eviction*. The tenant is justified in abandoning the premises without paying rent when a wrongful eviction occurs. The tenant must mitigate (lessen) any damages, however, if possible.

● Sound City, U.S.A., was interested in renting space in a shopping center. An inspection of the premises disclosed portions of the ceiling tile missing or hanging loose, water marks on the ceiling, and bare fluorescent light fixtures. As a result, Sound City included in its one-year lease an addendum (addition) whereby the landlord agreed to repair and paint the ceiling tile, cover the light bulb fixtures, panel the south wall, and erect a partition. Sound City moved into the shopping center, but after three months and many complaints the repairs were never completed. It then moved out. The landlord brought suit for the remaining nine months' rent. The court held against the landlord, saying that there had been a constructive eviction. The physical appearance of the store was an important factor in the successful operation of Sound City's business. The failure to repair the premises properly in accordance with the lease rendered the premises unsuitable for the purpose for which they were rented.

3. Assignment and Subletting. An *assignment* of a lease occurs when the interest in the leased premises is transferred by the lessee to another person for the balance of the term of the lease. The new party, called the *assignee*, steps into the shoes of the tenant, or *assignor*, and is liable for all the old tenant's obligations and entitled to all the old tenant's rights under the lease. It is called a *sublease* or *underlease* if the transfer is for a part of the term but not for the remainder of it. Virtually all leases require landlord approval for an assignment or a sublease. However, in some states the landlord cannot withhold such approval unreasonably. An assignment or sublease will be held valid if the landlord accepts rent over a period of time from either an assignee or a subtenant.

E. Responsibility for Repairs

The obligation for repairs to rental property has been the subject of much legislation over the past decade. What was formerly regulated by common-law practices and court decisions is now under the supervision of public housing authorities in many states and municipalities.

1. Obligations of Tenant. At common law, a tenant was obligated to return premises to the owner in the same condition as when delivered to the tenant. Normal wear and tear and depreciation are not included in this definition. Some states have in the past interpreted this duty in the strictest way, requiring tenants to rebuild structures that have been destroyed for whatever reason during the leasehold. Other states have taken a milder view of the tenant's obligations through judicial interpretation or the passing of laws that limit the tenant's obligations. A lease may be written to contain a more thorough description of the tenant's obligations in the matter of repairs, rather than leaving decisions to judicial decision and statute. In any case, tenants will be held responsible for all repairs resulting from their negligence, illegal use, or uses not described and permitted by the lease.

● Turner rented a house in Westminster. The lease contained the usual statements covering repairs by tenant and landlord. When Turner negligently plugged in an electric space heater with a defective thermostat and left the house, a serious fire resulted. Turner is responsible for all repairs necessary because of his negligent act.

2. Obligations of Landlord. Traditionally, a landlord needed to make only those repairs detailed in the terms of the lease contract. But certain parts of a structure have also been considered the landlord's responsibility. Outside walls, foundations, and structural parts of a building are examples. Most leases for apartments or office suites require the landlord to make all repairs to stairways, halls, outside walls, roof, heating and air-conditioning systems, plumbing, and the like. The tenant's obligations would be confined to the areas assigned to the tenant under the lease.

● Daniels and Cohen, attorneys, rented a suite of offices in the Farmers Bank Building. Excellent management kept the offices clean, well decorated, and comfortable. But leaking water from the roof was reported to the bank management, which made no effort to remedy the situation. A heavy storm resulted in serious water damage to the office, ruining $4,000 worth of valuable law books. The landlord, not the tenant, is responsible for this loss.

Many municipalities have adopted ordinances to protect tenants from unsafe or unhealthy conditions created by a landlord's refusal to make necessary repairs. Building inspectors, health authorities, and other public officials are empowered to make inspections and demand improvements when they are contacted by dissatisfied tenants. In many cases, ordinances permit the tenant to cease payment of rent for the period during which the landlord fails to make the repairs or improvements ordered.

F. Tort Liability

When a person is injured on leased property, the one who is in control of that part of the premises where the injury occurs is generally responsible if the injury was caused by that person's negligence. The landlord, for example, is often

Part 9:
Real
Property
and
Inheri-
tance

504

responsible for injury to others caused by a defect in the common areas, such as hallways and stairways.

● On the morning of January 7, Mrs. Wilson emerged from the front entrance of her duplex apartment in New Orleans with a small pot of soup she intended to take to a neighbor. She stepped onto the top riser of four cement steps which abutted the sidewalk and placed the soup down in order to close the door to the apartment. When she turned to descend before picking up the pot of soup, the step on which she was standing tilted, throwing her off balance and causing her to fall on the sidewalk. Mrs. Wilson sustained serious injuries. The landlord was held liable for Mrs. Wilson's injuries because he was negligent in failing to keep the steps in a reasonably safe condition.

Similarly, tenants are often responsible for injuries to persons caused by defects in the portion of the premises over which they have control.

● Thrash, a tenant in an apartment house, notified the rental agent that the ceiling was "in need of urgent repairs." He was told that the ceiling would be repaired in the immediate future. A week later, Thrash was struck and injured by falling debris from the ceiling. The court held that the landlord was not liable for Thrash's injuries because he had no control over the area where the injuries occurred.

The majority of states hold that a landlord has a duty to clear common entryways of natural accumulations of snow and ice. Some states nevertheless still follow the older rule that the landlord owes no duty to tenants to clean common entryways of ice and snow unless there is an agreement on the part of the landlord to do so.

37-6. Dispossess Actions

Three principal methods are available to landlords to regain possession of premises when tenants fail to leave at the end of a tenancy: peaceable entry of the premises by the landlord, ejectment, and unlawful detainer.

Most states today do not allow landlords to use force to evict tenants. Instead, they must make use of statutory remedies that are available to them. Some states do, however, recognize the right of landlords to enter wrongfully held premises and take over possession if it can be done peacefully.

Ejectment is the common-law name given to the lawsuit brought by the landlord to have the tenant evicted from the premises. This older remedy is still available in many states; however, it is time-consuming, expensive, and subject to long delays.

The most commonly used method to evict tenants in modern times is a statutory remedy known in some states as *unlawful detainer*. Other states refer to the remedy as *summary process, summary ejectment, forcible entry and detainer,* and *dispossessory warrant proceedings.* The remedy provides landlords with a quick method of regaining possession of their property and protects tenants from being ousted by force and violence. Strict notice requirements must be followed by the landlord, after which both parties are given their day in court. If a forcible eviction becomes necessary, it is done by the sheriff under the supervision of the court.

● Several months after Koonce fell behind in her rent payments, her landlord brought summary process proceedings against her. The court issued an execution (an order to carry out its judgment) giving the landlord possession, rent arrearages, and costs. Armed with the execution, a sheriff went to the premises and removed three fans, a stereo system, a record collection, a digital clock radio, a double-bed quilt, an iron, and a portable tape recorder. He also left a note saying that execution would be carried out if the rent were not paid up. The court held that this was an improper procedure. It was the duty of the sheriff, once the execution was placed in his hands, to remove all Koonce's possessions, sell such of them as were necessary to satisfy the execution, and make the rest of her possessions available to her. Piecemeal exercise of an execution is not permissible.

Understanding Legal Terms

Define, identify, or explain the following terms:

constructive
  eviction
ejectment
landlord
lease
leasehold estate

lessee
lessor
license
lodger
option to purchase
periodic tenancy

quiet enjoyment
sublease
tenancy
tenancy at
  sufferance
tenancy at will

tenancy for years
tenant
unlawful detainer
warranty of
  habitability

Questions for Review and Discussion

1. Name the five elements that are necessary for the creation of the landlord-tenant relationship.

2. How does a lease compare with a license and with lodging?

3. In what ways do the following tenancies differ: (a) tenancy for years, (b) periodic tenancy, (c) tenancy at will, (d) tenancy at sufferance?

4. What are the three essential requirements of a lease?

5. Is a lease signed by a minor enforceable? Explain.

6. When and by whom is the implied warranty of habitability made?

7. What rights do landlords have under a lease?

8. What rights do tenants have under a lease?

9. Discuss the obligations of the tenant and the landlord in the matter of repairs to rented premises.

10. Describe the three principal methods available to landlords to regain possession of premises when tenants fail to leave at the end of a tenancy.

Analyzing Cases

1. Gale Zurcher, who owned and operated the Grandview Trailer Court, entered into a contract with the American Coin-Meter Company. The contract leased to Coin-Meter for six years "all laundry space in the trailer court for the purpose of installing, maintaining and servicing a special washing, drying, and laundry equipment system." The contract provided that Coin-Meter would be allowed access to the installation "during reasonable hours of the day for the purpose of further installations, servicing, or removal of coins from the installation." When Zurcher sold the trailer court to the Pooles, the Pooles removed Coin-Meter's machines and installed their own. Coin-Meter asserts that the contract is a lease and that the Pooles are bound by its terms. Do you agree with Coin-

Meter? Explain. • *American Coin-Meter, Inc. v. Poole*, 503 P.2d 626 (Colo. 1972)

2. Sarah H. Brown and Sandy F. Soverow agreed to rent separate apartments from Osborn, the owner of an apartment complex called Nob Hill Apartments, which was being constructed. Since their single apartments were not yet completed, Brown and Soverow agreed to rent one larger apartment in the complex and live in that until their separate apartments were finished. A fire occurred in the apartment shortly after Brown had put some leftover livers and gizzards for her dogs on the electric stove and had left the apartment. In the lawsuit that followed, the contention was made that Brown and Soverow were lodgers rather than tenants. Do you agree with the contention? Explain. • *Osborn v. Brown*, 361 So.2d 82 (Ala. 1978)

3. Alabama Outdoor Advertising Co., Inc., leased part of a lot from All State Linen Service Co. to erect a commercial advertising sign. The term of the lease was for "indefinite years, beginning 1st day of January, 1973 and ending year to year thereafter." When All State sold the lot, it was contended that Alabama's lease was a tenancy at will and, therefore, came to an end when the lot was sold. Do you agree with this contention? Why or why not? • *Industrial Mach., Inc. v. Creative Displays, Inc.*, 344 So.2d 743 (Ala. 1977)

4. Graff rented office space in a building and placed a sign on the front consisting of 1-foot-high plastic letters spelling out, "Sol K. Graff & Sons, Real Estate Consultants." Seven years later with the sign still in place, the building was sold to Leopold, who entered into a one-year lease with Graff. The lease was a printed form and contained the provision "Lessee shall not place any signs on the leased premises . . . without Lessor's prior written consent." After the execution of the lease, Leopold asked Graff to remove the plastic letters from the building.

When Graff refused, Leopold had them removed and in their place installed large aluminum numerals indicating the street number of the building, 3425. Graff claims that there was an implied covenant between the parties allowing them to continue to display the sign and that Leopold breached that covenant. Do you agree with Graff? Give a reason for your answer. • *Sol K. Graff & Sons v. Leopold*, 416 N.E.2d 275 (Ill. 1980)

5. Friedman's tenancy came to an end on June 30, 1978. His landlord did not return or account for any portion of Friedman's security deposit until September 1, 1978. A statute in that state requires landlords to either return or account for security deposits within thirty days after the termination of a tenancy. Failure to do so entitles the tenant to an award of damages equal to three times the amount of the security deposit plus 5 percent interest from the date when the payment became due, together with court costs and reasonable attorney's fees. Is Friedman entitled to recover from the landlord? • *Friedman v. Costello*, 412 N.E.2d 1285 (Mass. 1980)

6. Elmer and Bonnie Cummings, as lessors, entered into a lease with Leo and Glen Ward for the rental of a building from March 16, 1966, to July 31, 1974. The lease provided that there could be no assignment without the written consent of the lessors. In October 1966, the Wards assigned the lease to Robert and Alice Smith with no written consent from the Cummings. The Cummings accepted rent from the Smiths for five years without objection. Was the assignment valid? Why or why not? • *Smith v. Hegg*, 214 N.W.2d 789 (S.D. 1974)

7. Sorrells rented a single-family dwelling house from Pole Realty Company. When eviction proceedings were brought against her for nonpayment of rent, Sorrells claimed that there had been a breach of the implied warranty of habitability. Pole Realty Company argued that the warranty of habitability does not apply to the rental of single-family

residences. Do you agree? Explain. ● *Pole Realty Co. v. Sorrells*, 417 N.E.2d 1297 (Ill. 1981)

8. The Kings leased a residential dwelling from a partnership called JA-SIN. The lease agreement provided that the tenants were to "take good care of the house" and "make, at their own expense, the necessary repairs caused by their own neglect or misuse." A guest of the Kings, Sharon Ford, tripped on a loose tread on one step while descending an outside stairway and sustained personal injuries. Who was responsible, the landlord or the tenant? Give the reason for your answer. ● *Ford v. JA-SIN*, 420 A.2d, 184 (Del. 1980)

9. Rossow owned a house which had been converted into a three-apartment dwelling. All apartments exited through a single outside door onto a porch. Three concrete steps lead from the porch to the sidewalk. Jones, a tenant who occupied one of the apartments, slipped and fell on the steps as he was attempting to leave the house and was injured. At the time, the steps were covered with a natural accumulation of ice and snow. There had been a hand rail along the steps from the porch to the walk, but the landlord had removed it sometime earlier. In addition, snow shovels and a box of salt had been available for cleaning the entryway, but these had been locked away by the landlord, and Jones could not use them. Moreover, on two or three occasions prior to Jones's injury, Rossow had shoveled the snow from the walkway. However, prior to Jones's fall, the ice and snow had been accumulating for a week. During this time, the steps were not shoveled. Did Rossow breach a duty owed to Jones? Explain. ● *Rossow v. Jones*, 404 N.E.2d 12 (Ind. 1980)

10. Sempek leased a parcel of land from Minarik on a year-to-year basis for $200 a year. The land was on a river and was used by Sempek for family recreation purposes. Sempek built a modern two-bedroom cabin on the site at a cost of $4,000. Soon afterward, he was informed by Minarik that the latter was going to sell the property but that his interests would be protected. Six months later, without giving the notice required by the law of that state to end a year-to-year tenancy, the new owners of the property physically prevented Sempek from entering the premises. Did the landlord breach the covenant of quiet enjoyment? ● *Sempek v. Minarik*, 264 N.W.2d 426 (Neb. 1978)

Chapter 38

Wills, Intestacy, and Trusts

After years of study, hard work, and careful investment, a great many people die *intestate*—without making any provision for the distribution of their property. Untold millions of dollars in real and personal property are at this moment unclaimed in our courts because people neglected to make wills. Endless litigation and family argument often follow the death of a person who has not made a will. In some cases, an entire estate dwindles to nothing because of such litigation. Often the estate *escheats* to (becomes the property of) the state when property remains unclaimed for a number of years (specified by statute). By means of a document known as a will, one can often avoid these problems and may also determine the distribution of one's property after death.

38-1. The Will and Its Advantages

A *will* is a legal document which takes effect upon the death of the will's maker, who is known as the *testator* (male) or *testatrix* (female).* After death, the will's maker is often called the *decedent*. It directs an *executor* (male) or *executrix* (female) as to the manner in which the decedent's property is to be distributed. A will may be changed or canceled at any time during the maker's life.

Personal property that is left by will is a *bequest*, or legacy; real property, a *devise*. Those who receive the property by will are referred to as *beneficiaries* or *heirs* (when related by blood or marriage). They are also known as *legatees* if they receive personal property and *devisees* if they receive real property.

In addition to providing for the disposition of one's property at death, a will has other advantages. It designates the executor and often provides for an alternate in case the executor named in the will is deceased or unable to perform the task. A will may make provisions for the guardian of the person and property of minor children. It may also contain trust provisions (discussed later in this chapter). A will often has tax-saving provisions and gives special powers to executors and trustees which they otherwise would not have.

38-2. Who May Make a Will

Anyone may make a will, but not all persons have what is called *testamentary capacity*. Testamentary capacity relates to a person's age, mental ability to comprehend the meaning of what is written in the instrument, and intent, as expressed by the testator. If the maker lacks capacity, the instrument is void.

* The masculine forms of terms like *testator* are used for purposes of discussion. They refer to people of either sex.

A. Testamentary Capacity

Persons of legal age and sound mind generally may make a valid will. There is no real conformity among the states as to the age requirements, although the age of majority in most states today is eighteen. Statutes often permit younger persons to make bequests of personal property, while restricting them from devising any interest in real property. Physical incapacity at the time of drawing an instrument will not invalidate a will if such physical debility has not had an effect upon the testator's mental competence.

Persons need not possess superior or even average intelligence as long as they are capable of understanding the nature and extent of the property they own, the persons who would be the most natural recipients of their estate, and the disposition being made of the property. They must also have the intelligence and understanding to relate each of the foregoing with one another, resulting in the ability to come to an orderly understanding of how they intend to leave the property.

● At the time of the execution of his will, Zdanowicz was suffering from deterioration brought on by a serious disease and from loss of memory. His son, who had worked for his father for forty-one years, observed his father's failing health and mental illness over a period of time. He once observed his father's failure to recognize his own wife. Zdanowicz's daughter also observed her father's degeneration, including his failure once to recognize her and another relative, both of whom he saw frequently. The court disallowed the will, saying, "The testator did not have mind and memory sound enough to know and understand the businesses upon which he was engaged at the time of execution."

B. Undue Influence

A will may be attacked and held invalid if a probate court finds that the testator made the will under circumstances of undue influence. When persons come under the influence of another to the degree that they are unable to express their real intentions in a will, the will may be declared invalid. The court must distinguish between undue influence and the kindnesses, attention, advice, guidance, and friendliness shown toward the testator by the one named in the will.

● Smolak executed a will prepared by a lawyer whom he had selected and with whom he had conferred several times before the date on which the will was signed. His niece, Sandra, was the major beneficiary under that will. A week later, he executed another will under which his nephew Michael and Michael's brother were named principal beneficiaries. This was done at the same time that he executed a deed conveying his farm to Michael and Michael's brother (which conveyance he promptly sought to rescind, claiming that it was procured by fraud). The second will was executed at the office of a lawyer employed by Michael. Michael had made arrangements for a conference between his lawyer and Smolak. Michael attended that conference and also attended the execution of the resulting will. Smolak never conferred privately with Michael's lawyer concerning the second will and therefore never had an opportunity to express his true intentions out of earshot of his nephew. The court held that the second will was procured through undue influence and was, therefore, void.

Part 9:
Real
Property
and
Inheri-
tance

510

38-3. The Execution of Wills

Since they are a product of state statute, the laws governing the making and signing of wills are not uniform throughout the United States. Nevertheless, a will that is properly executed according to the laws of one state will be given full faith and credit in another state. The laws are highly technical and require strict adherence to detailed formalities. Many lawsuits have occurred over the years because people have attempted to make their own wills without consulting a lawyer. Often, in such cases, a technicality causes the will to be disallowed by the court, and the true wishes of the deceased are not carried out.

A. Formal Requirements

With a few exceptions, wills must be in writing, signed by the testator, and attested in the testator's presence by a prescribed number of witnesses. Each of the particular statutory requirements of the state where the will is made must be met for a will to be valid.

Dugan's will contained the following clause: "All United States Savings Bonds in safety deposit box #559 Farmers Bank 10th and Market Sts. Wilmington Del. to be given to the people and places as marked." When Dugan died, a number of U.S. Savings Bonds were found in his safe-deposit box. There was also a handwritten list of the names of various individuals and organizations, and beside each name were serial numbers, dates, and face amounts corresponding to specific bonds. Further specific notations were written on small slips of paper and attached to each bond with a rubber band. The court held that there was no effective testamentary transfer of the bonds. Neither the list, the envelopes, nor the small slips of paper satisfied the statutory requirements for executing a will. They were not properly signed and witnessed. Dugan's wishes as stated in the will were never carried out.

1. Written Instrument. A will may be typewritten, handwritten, or consist of a filled-in form. It need not be under seal. The will offered for probate must be the original copy, not a carbon, unless the carbon is fully executed with the same formalities as the original. In a case in which a testator executed both an original and a carbon copy of a will and then later canceled only the carbon, the court held that it could be presumed that the testator also intended to cancel the original. Problems of this nature can be avoided by executing only the original copy of a will.

2. Signature of the Testator. A will must be signed by the testator. The place of the signature on the will and the requirement as to who must be present at the signing vary from state to state. In some states a will must be signed at the end of the instrument, but in others the signature may be placed anywhere on the paper. Similarly, some states require a will to be signed in the presence of the witnesses, whereas others allow a will to be signed privately if the testator acknowledges to the witnesses when they sign that it is his or her signature. Testators who are not able to write may make a mark, such as an X, attested to by the required number of witnesses. If the testator's condition makes movement impossible, as in paralysis, another may sign for the testator. This must be done in the testator's presence and in the presence of the witnesses.

P 1682—Will

JULIUS BLUMBERG, INC., LAW BLANK PUBLISHERS
80 EXCHANGE PL. AT BROADWAY, N. Y. C. 10004

Last Will and Testament

I, William E. Paxton *of the* Town *of* River Forest *in the County of* Cook *and State of* Illinois *being of sound mind and memory, do make, publish and declare this my last* **Will and Testament,** *in manner following that is to say:*

First. *I direct that all of my debts and funeral expenses be paid as soon after my death as may be practicable.*

Second, after my lawful debts are paid, I give to my wife Anne M. Paxton, all my real property, to have and to hold as she sees fit, and in addition, Forty-five Thousand Dollars ($45,000) in cash.

Third, to my son Patrick, Fifteen Thousand Dollars ($15,000) in cash.

Fourth, to the Hospital for the Blind, the balance of my estate remaining after the above bequests have been distributed.

Lastly *I hereby appoint* Robert Anderson, 406 Franklin Street, River Forest, Illinois *executor of this, my last Will and Testament, with full power and authority to sell and convey, lease or mortgage real estate, hereby revoking all former wills by me made.*

In Witness Whereof *I have hereunto subscribed my name the* fourth *day of* February *in the year Ninteen Hundred and* --.

William E. Paxton (L. S.)

We, whose names are hereunto subscribed, **Do Certify** *that on* February 4, *19*--

the testator above named, subscribed his *name to this instrument in our presence and in the presence of each of us, and at the same time, in our presence and hearing, declared the same to be* his *last* **Will and Testament,** *and requested us, and each of us, to sign our names thereto as witnesses to the execution thereof, which we hereby do in the presence of the testator and of each other, on the day of the date of the said Will, and write opposite our names our respective place of residence.*

Myra Evans *residing at* 121 Lake Street, River Forest, Illinois

Andrew Youngman *residing at* 231 Chicago Avenue, River Forest, Illinois

Figure 38-1. A formal will.

3. Witnesses. The number of witnesses varies according to local statutes. Usually two or three are required. Witnesses must sign in the presence of the testator and, in some states, in each others' presence. Since the witnesses may be called upon to attest to the genuineness of the testator's signature and soundness of mind, it is advisable that witnesses be young persons. In most states, minors may witness a will as long as they are of sufficient understanding and competent to testify in court as to the facts relating to the execution of the will. The law usually states that persons and their spouses named as beneficiaries in a will may not be witnesses. The failure to observe this provision may result in their being disinherited.

- Elliott executed a will leaving all his property to his three daughters, Jane, Noreen, and Frances. Jane's husband was one of the subscribing witnesses to the will.

When Elliott died, Jane received nothing from her father's estate. A statute in that state makes void any testamentary gift to a subscribing witness or spouse of such a witness.

4. Accuracy and Precision. Certain words often used in wills may have a legal interpretation that is different from their everyday meaning. Care should be taken to describe each bequest and devise in a manner that will satisfy the legal definition. For instance, a testator may use the word *heirs* when really meaning *children*. The difference in the meaning of the two words could result in much dispute and expensive litigation. It is also important to avoid ambiguous language.

● In his will, Sparacio left his property to his daughter and her friend, "as in their mutual agreement they decide." The court held that the will could not be implemented judicially because it was impossible to determine how much to give each person.

Property is sometimes willed to one person with a polite "request," "wish," or "desire" that that person distribute the property to others. These words are known as *precatory words,* and such requests are not required to be carried out. In such cases, the person to whom the property is given to distribute to others receives it outright and has the option of distributing it or keeping it.

a. Omitting Names of Children From the Will. Some states have passed laws to protect children whose names have been unintentionally left out of a will. By these laws, forgotten children will receive the same share that they would have received had the parent died intestate.

These laws do not imply that a parent may not disinherit a child. A parent is not obliged to leave children anything at all. A testator who intends to disinherit a child should mention the child's name, leaving the child $1, or stating that the child is to receive nothing.

b. Subsequent Children. State laws have generally protected children born after a will has been drawn in the same way that forgotten children are protected. Exceptions to this rule would be cases in which the testator expressly excluded unborn children from any distribution of the estate.

c. Adopted Children. The common law gave no rights of inheritance to adopted children. In recent years, however, there has been a dramatic shift in public policy, causing many state legislatures to enact laws giving adopted children the same rights as natural children. Only children who have been legally adopted by the testator can share in the estate if not mentioned in the will. Children who have been taken into the family for one reason or another, but never legally adopted, are not protected by the provisions described in the previous two situations. This rule extends to children of a wife by previous marriage in cases where they have not been formally adopted by the second husband.

● The Hartleys took into their home three preschool children whose parents had been killed in an accident. The couple developed a strong love for one of the children, adopting her through proper legal proceedings. Only the adopted child would have any rights equal to those of the Hartleys' own children.

d. Surviving Spouses. Surviving spouses are assured a share of the spouse's estate in every state. The right may be a dower right, a right under community property, or some other special right declared by a state legislature.

5. Alterations and Codicils. Alterations, write-overs, erasures, and the like serve to invalidate otherwise valid provisions of a will. Alterations, additions, or changes may be made, however, but only through a *codicil,* or supplement. Adding a codicil requires the same formalities as the creation of the will itself. The codicil must be written, signed, and witnessed. The document should refer to the will in such a way as to leave no doubt that it is a part of the will.

● Rabel's will provided that her entire estate would pass to her husband at the time of her death. Rabel later enjoyed unusual financial success and felt inclined to leave $100,000 toward a new church building under construction in her parish. Rabel's attorney prepared a codicil which, when signed and witnessed, was attached to the original will. The bequests contained in the codicil became an integral part of the will itself.

A properly executed codicil has the effect of *republishing* a will. This means that the codicil will reestablish a will that had been formerly revoked or improperly executed.

6. Revoking and Rewriting Wills. Because of changes in economic conditions, family responsibility, and many other reasons, testators often rewrite wills. Divorce, remarriage, birth of children, death of persons named as beneficiaries— all may lead to changes in wills.

Under the law of many states, a will may be revoked by burning, tearing, canceling, or obliterating the will; executing a new will; subsequent marriage of the maker; and the maker's divorce or annulment of marriage, which serves to revoke all gifts made under a will to a former spouse.

● Clark's company prospered, and he became a very wealthy man. He felt that the will he had once prepared was outdated. His attorney prepared a new will, which Clark signed and witnessed, at the same time destroying the old will by burning it. The new will contained the customary phrase "my last will and testament, all others having been revoked." By these acts Clark now replaced the older will with the new will.

B. Informal Wills

A *holographic will* is one written entirely in the handwriting of the testator. In the states that recognize it, no formalities are followed, and even witnesses are not necessary. It is important that the testator be of legal age and of sound mind when the will is made and that the document be proved to be that of the testator.

● Sedmak resided in Pennsylvania. The following handwritten document was found among his papers when he died:

Part 9:
Real
Property
and
Inheri-
tance

514

My Brother Mil   Oct 6–72

Please see that Zella Portenar receives $5000 from my Savings account—it is in the Western Saving Bank.

George A. Sedmak
or Alexander Sedmak

The court held the document to be a valid holographic will.

Oral wills made by persons in their last illness or by soldiers and sailors in actual combat are *nuncupative wills*. Nuncupative wills are not valid in all states, and usually they are restricted to the bequest of personal property only. Testators must make statements to indicate their bequests. Testators must also state that those hearing the statements are to be considered witnesses to the oral will. A nuncupative will is difficult to prove, is subject to deception, and is not desirable in the distribution of a testator's property.

38-4. Intestacy

Intestacy is a term given to the estate of one who dies without having prepared a valid will. The deceased's property will be distributed according to the laws of intestate succession of the state where the deceased was domiciled (resided) at the time of death. These laws vary slightly from state to state, although they all have their origin in a statute that was passed in England in 1670. Under that early statute, real property passed directly to the heirs upon the death of the owner, whereas personal property passed to the executor or administrator to be distributed to the heirs. This practice is still followed in the United States today.

A. Rights of the Surviving Spouse

Under a typical statute, if a person dies intestate, the rights of the surviving spouse are as follows:

○ If the deceased is survived by one or more descendants (also called *issue*), the surviving spouse is entitled to one-half of the estate.

○ If the deceased is survived by no descendants but by blood relatives, the surviving spouse is entitled to $50,000 plus one-half of the remainder of the estate.

○ If the deceased is survived by no descendants and no blood relatives, the surviving spouse is entitled to the entire estate.

B. Rights of Other Heirs

Under the same typical statute, if a person dies intestate, the property will pass, subject to the rights of the surviving spouse mentioned above, as follows:

○ If the deceased is survived by descendants, the property passes in equal shares to the deceased's children, with the descendants of any deceased child taking that child's share.

○ If the deceased is survived by no descendants, the property passes in equal shares to the deceased's father and mother or the survivor of them.

○ If the deceased is survived by no descendants and no father or mother, the property passes to the deceased's brothers and sisters, with the descendants of any deceased brother or sister taking that brother's or sister's share.

○ If the deceased is survived by no descendants and no father, mother, brother, sister, or descendants of any deceased brother or sister, the property passes to the deceased's *next of kin* (those who are most nearly related by blood).

○ If the deceased is survived by no blood relatives and no surviving spouse, the estate *escheats* to (becomes the property of) the state.

● Henrietta Johnson died intestate. She was survived by her husband, Arnold, a daughter, Bertha, and two grandchildren, Candice and Daniel, who were the children of her deceased son. Under the laws of intestate succession, Arnold will inherit 50 percent of the estate, Bertha will inherit 25 percent, and Candice and Daniel will each inherit $12\frac{1}{2}$ percent.

38-5. Probate of the Will or Administration of the Estate

The rules controlling the management of a decedent's estate are statutory and vary from state to state. In all states, however, the estate is managed and finally disposed of under the supervision of a court. The procedure is known as *probate.* The court which supervises the procedure is usually called a *probate court,* but in some states it is known as a surrogate court, or an orphan's court. The system of administration under the influential Uniform Probate Code (UPC) is highly flexible.*

A. Executor and Administrator

The first step after death of the testator is to determine whether the deceased left a will. The testator's personal attorney may have the will on file. Sometimes a careful search of the safe-deposit box and personal papers of the deceased is necessary.

If a valid will exists, it ordinarily names the executor (usually the spouse, a friend, or a trust company). If there is no will, or if the executor named in the will fails to perform, the court will upon petition appoint an *administrator* (male) or *administratrix* (female) to take charge of the estate in accordance with statues.

To ensure faithful performance, the executor or administrator is required to post a bond. A *bond* is a promise by the executor or administrator (and the sureties, if any) to pay the amount of the bond to the probate court if the duties of the position are not faithfully performed. *Sureties* are persons or insurance companies that stand behind executors or administrators and become responsible for their wrongdoing. In some states, a bond is not required if the will indicates that the executor or administrator need not post bond. In other states, a bond is always necessary, but sureties are not required if the will so indicates.

Part 9:
Real
Property
and
Inheri-
tance

516

* At the time of this writing, the Uniform Probate Code had been adopted by fourteen states: Alaska, Arizona, Colorado, Florida, Idaho, Maine, Minnesota, Montana, Nebraska, New Jersey, New Mexico, North Dakota, Pennsylvania, and Utah.

B. Steps in Probate

A will must be proved before the court by those who witnessed the signing. The witnesses must also testify to the mental condition of the testator at the time the will was executed. Testimony is not necessary when all heirs and next of kin assent to the allowance of the will and no one contests it. When satisfied that the will is proved, the court enters a formal decree admitting the will to probate and issues a certificate to the executor called *letters testamentary*. In the case of an administrator, the certificate is known as *letters of administration*. The executor or administrator is then authorized to proceed. The executor or administrator must file an inventory of the estate. A bank account is opened in the name of the estate, and the executor or administrator begins the process of collecting assets, paying outstanding debts and taxes first, and disbursing the remaining assets in accordance with the will.

C. Assets

Securities and items of personal use are part of the estate of the deceased. The executor or administrator exercises the same powers in the handling of such property as the deceased exercised while alive. Insurance on the life of the deceased passes directly to the named beneficiary. Taxes are imposed by both the federal and state governments. It is the responsibility of the executor or administrator to pay these taxes. An income tax return must be filed on income received during the partial year preceding the death of the testator or intestate and also on income received during the administration of the estate.

1. Federal Estate Tax. A tax is levied upon the total value of the deceased's estate by the federal government through the Internal Revenue Service. In recent years, however, Congress has gradually increased the amount of money that is excluded from the federal estate tax. By 1987, $600,000 will be exempted from taxation. Also permitted as deductions are the debts of the deceased, funeral expenses, administration expenses, charitable gifts, and gifts to a surviving spouse. This latter exclusion from the estate tax is known as the *marital deduction*.

2. State Inheritance Tax. The state imposes an inheritance tax upon the beneficiaries or heirs of a bequest or legacy and not upon the estate. The exemption and the tax rate are graduated according to the relationship of the recipients to the decedent. Thus, a member of the deceased's family pays less tax than a stranger who might be a beneficiary of the will.

38-6. Letters of Last Instruction

The testator often prepares an informal, nonlegal instrument known as a *letter of last instruction*. Such a letter gives much valuable information to the executor, such as the exact location of the will, burial instructions, location of safe-deposit boxes and keys, names of insurance companies and insurance brokers, names of lodges and other organizations to which the testator belonged, and other information of value in carrying out the duties of the executor. The letters, however, have no legal value whatsoever, and they need not be followed by an individual's survivors; their value is purely informational.

38-7. Trusts

A *trust* is a right of ownership to property held by one person for the benefit of another. When a trust is established, the legal title to the trust property (also known as the *corpus* or *trust fund*) is separated from the equitable or beneficial title in the same property. The person, bank, attorney, or fiduciary organization to which legal title of the property is given is called the *trustee*. The person or persons for whom the trust is created and who own equitable or beneficial title are the *beneficiaries*. The person who establishes the trust is called the *settlor*. A trust is useful for many reasons. The owner of property may wish to create a trust as a means of protecting an estate from the anticipated habits of those who may squander a hard-earned fortune, whether large or small; to assure a continued income to those who survive; to provide dividend or interest income for the education of younger children; or for any other purpose. It may also be to the advantage of the survivors in consideration of taxes that might be saved through the use of a trust. Many trusts are made for the protection of family members until they have reached the age of caution and maturity. At a predetermined age, such as twenty-one or twenty-five, the money or property that is held in trust will be distributed to them.

There must be an intent, with exceptions, to have the trust terminated at some time in the foreseeable future. Otherwise the trust violates what is known as the *rule against perpetuities*. This rule requires trust property to become owned by the beneficiary outright not later than twenty-one years after the death of some person alive at the creation of the trust. If it is violated, the trust may be declared unenforceable.

A. Types of Trusts

The two principal types of trusts are testamentary trusts and living trusts. A *testamentary trust* is a trust that is created by will. It comes into existence only upon the death of the testator. The terms of the trust together with the names of the trustee and beneficiaries are set out in the body of the will itself.

● Urie died, leaving four grown sons and daughters. His children had never demonstrated any real ambition and had depended heavily on prospects of receiving large legacies from the estate. Urie feared that his heirs would quickly spend their inheritances and have nothing to support them in the years ahead. He therefore provided for this possibility in his will by placing all assets in trust. The assets would remain intact, safely invested, and a small income would be paid from the trust income to the children. Urie's purpose was realized in that the estate would be preserved and the surviving children would not squander their inheritance.

In a trust such as the one illustrated, provision must be made for final distribution of the trust assets when the purpose of the trust has been served. For example, Urie could have the trust property go to a church, college, or some other worthy nonprofit organization on the death of the last surviving child. He also could have designated a grandchild or grandchildren as the ultimate beneficiaries.

A *living trust,* also called an *inter vivos trust,* is created while the settlor is alive and is established by either a conveyance in trust or a declaration of trust.

Part 9:
Real
Property
and
Inheritance

518

In a *conveyance in trust,* the settlor conveys away the legal title to a trustee to hold for the benefit of either the settlor or another as beneficiary. In a *declaration of trust,* the settlor holds the legal title to the property as trustee for the benefit of some other person (the beneficiary) to whom the settlor now conveys the equitable title. A living trust may be either irrevocable or revocable. If is is *irrevocable,* the settlor loses complete control over the trust and cannot change it. The advantage of an irrevocable trust is that the income from the trust is not taxable to the settlor, and estate and inheritance taxes are avoided. The disadvantage of such a trust is that it can never be rescinded. The settlor can never get back that which has been put in an irrevocable trust regardless of the circumstances. A *revocable* living trust may be taken back or changed at any time during the settlor's lifetime. It has neither estate tax nor income tax advantages; however, it can serve the purpose of relieving the cares of management of money or property as well as other purposes.

A *spendthrift* is one who spends money profusely and improvidently. A *spendthrift trust* is designed to provide a fund for the maintenance of a beneficiary and, at the same time, to secure the fund against that person's improvidence or incapacity. In some states, all trusts are considered to be of this type. In others, a clause must be placed in the trust instrument to the effect that the beneficiary cannot assign either the income or the principal of the trust, and neither the income nor the principal can be reached by the beneficiary's creditors. Spendthrift trusts are not permitted in some states.

A *charitable* or *public trust* is one established for charitable purposes, such as the advancement of education; relief to the aged, ill, or poor; and the promotion of religion. To be valid, the person to be benefited must be uncertain. The rule against perpetuities does not apply to a charitable trust.

A *sprinkling* or *spray trust* allows the trustee to decide how much will be given to each beneficiary rather than having the settlor make the decision. The advantage is that the trustee can compare the tax brackets of the beneficiaries, long after the settlor is dead, and cause a smaller tax liability to occur by giving more money to those beneficiaries in the lowest tax brackets. It also has built-in spendthrift provisions. The chief objection to this type of trust is that it gives the trustee too much control.

B. Obligations of the Trustee

The trustee is obligated by law to use reasonable care and prudence in the investment of funds allocated to the trust. If real property is held in trust, it is the trustee's obligation to supervise and care for the property. When economic and other reasons indicate the need to shift trust assets to safer areas of investment, it becomes the duty of the trustee to make such changes. If investments selected by the trustee fail, the trustee is held liable unless a court rules that the action was taken with reasonable prudence and caution.

The trustee relationship is one of great and continuing responsibility. Appointment as a trustee should not be accepted by those without the knowledge and background that would afford prudent and good management. Banks, trust companies, and other kinds of fiduciary corporations offer professional services in the administration of trusts. They provide professional investment services and generally give maximum security and benefit for the fees charged.

Understanding Legal Terms

Define, identify, or explain the following terms:

administrator/
  administratrix
beneficiaries
bequest
devise
executor/
  executrix

holographic will
inter vivos trust
intestate
issue
letters of
  administration
letters testamentary

next of kin
nuncupative will
settlor
testamentary trust

testator/
  testatrix
trustee

Questions for Review and Discussion

1. Explain some of the advantages of preparing a will rather than accepting the risk of dying intestate.

2. Who may make a valid will? What must a person be capable of understanding to have testamentary capacity?

3. Differentiate between holographic and nuncupative wills, describe their characteristics, and compare them with the formal requirements of executing most wills.

4. Discuss procedures and requirements to be observed in signing and witnessing a will.

5. In what ways may a will be revoked under the laws of many states?

6. Who will inherit, and in what amount, from the estate of a person who dies intestate survived by (*a*) a spouse and two children ($30,000 estate), (*b*) a spouse and a father and mother ($75,000 estate), (*c*) a spouse and no blood relatives ($90,000 estate), (*d*) three children ($90,000 estate), (*e*) a brother and two children of a deceased sister ($90,000 estate), (*f*) no blood relatives and no surviving spouse ($90,000 estate), and (*g*) a spouse and a ninety-year-old aunt ($200,000 estate).

7. How does an administrator differ from an executor in duties to be performed?

8. Discuss the steps required in the probate of a will.

9. How important are the letters of last instruction? Is a letter of last instruction a legal document requiring survivors to follow its commands?

10. Summarize the duties and obligations of a trustee. What type of person or agency is best fitted for this responsibility?

Analyzing Cases

1. Bechtold was adjudicated a mental incompetent in proceedings instituted by his sister, Alice Williams. At the hearing, a physician testified, "In my opinion, he is totally and permanently disabled mentally, and the prognosis is poor because of his mental deterioration, which is progressive." Alice was appointed his guardian. Nine months later, Bechtold executed a last will and testament leaving his entire estate to Alice. When he died, some other relatives of Bechtold claimed that the will should be set aside. They argued that he did not have testamentary capacity to make a will. Do you agree with Bechtold's relatives? Why or why not? ● *Matter of Estate of Bechtold*, 383 A.2d 742 (N.J. 1978)

2. D. W. Elmer, a hospital patient, was seriously ill and unable to write his name. He executed his will, however, by making a belabored "X" on the paper in the presence of witnesses. Can a signature on a will made by an "X" be valid? Explain. ● *In Re Estate of Elmer*, 210 N.W.2d 815 (N.D. 1973)

3. Julia Dejmal executed her will while a patient in St. Joseph's hospital. The will was witnessed by Lucille and Catherine Pechacek. Catherine was nineteen years old and was employed as an assistant x-ray technician at the hospital. The age of majority at the time in that state was twenty-one. It was contended that the will was not valid because one of the witnesses to it was a minor. Do you agree with the contention? Why or why not? ● *Matter of Estate of Dejmal,* 289 N.W.2d 813 (Wis. 1980)

4. The seventh clause of Jennie Wielert's will provided that if any of her children died before her, leaving "issue of their body" surviving, the issue would take the child's share. (The word *issue* is synonymous with the word descendant, and the phrase *heirs of the body* has commonly referred to heirs borne by the person referred to.) Jennie's son, Clarence, died before her, survived by an adopted daughter, Jan. Will Jan take Clarence's share under the will? Why or why not? ● *Wielert v. Larson,* 404 N.E.2d 1111 (Ill. 1980)

5. The fifth clause of Chisby's will read, "All the rest, residue and remainder of my estate I give, devise and bequeath to my cousin, Anna Sklepinska. It is my wish and desire that my said cousin, Anna Sklepinska, mails parcels containing food, clothing, jewellery etc. to the following persons, to-wit: To my brother MYKOLA IWAN-OWIYCH CICKYJ, to my nephew EWHEN CICKYJ, to my nephew IWAN CICKYJ, to my niece OLGA STADARSKY, to my nephew IWAN DENYS, to my niece SOPHIA MACALAP and to my niece ANNA KRAJDUBA—all residing in the village of Novosilka, County of Pidhajci and Distr. of Tarnopil, U.S.S.R." Is Sklepinska required, under the terms of the will, to mail the parcels to the relatives in Russia? Explain. ● *Mykola v. Skeltinska,* 417 N.E.2d 699 (Ill. 1981)*

* The defendant's surname was incorrectly spelled in the actual citation, but the surname was correctly spelled "Sklepinska" in the will and the probate proceedings.

6. An original and a carbon copy of Tong's will were presented to the court for probate. Both papers were signed by the decedent, witnessed by the same two witnesses, and verified by the same notary public on the same day. The following words were written in Tong's handwriting on the carbon copy, "This Last Will & Testament is now null, and void. . . ." The carbon also contained numerous obliterations. The original, which was not in the decedent's possession at his death, contained no similar language or obliterations. Was the will revoked? Why or why not? ● *Matter of Estate of Tong,* 619 P.2d 91 (Colo. 1980)

7. Evidence was introduced in court to show that, at the time she executed her will, Blanch Robinson suffered from schizophrenia. She had delusions as to having had a love affair with Nelson Eddy and was suspicious, mistrustful, and perhaps deluded about her friends and acquaintances. Dixon, who had been left out of her will, contended that she lacked the mental capacity to make a will. Do you agree with Dixon? Explain. ● *Dixon v. Fillmore Cemetery,* 608 S.W.2d 84 (Mo. 1980)

8. Howard R. Hughes, Jr., domiciled in Nevada, died on April 5, 1976. No will executed by him was found. There was evidence that he may have executed a will in 1925, leaving most of his estate to the Howard Hughes Medical Institute, although only an unexecuted draft of that will was found. There are also indications that other wills were drafted in 1930, 1938, and sometime during the 1940s. The Howard Hughes Medical Institute sought to prove the 1925 will by the deposition (written statement under oath) of John Pettit, who allegedly read a will signed by Hughes which left all his estate to the institute. A Nevada statute requires the testimony of at least two witnesses to prove the provisions of a lost or destroyed will. Should the will be allowed? Explain. ● *Howard Hughes Medical Inst. v. Gavin,* 621 P.2d 489 (Nev. 1980)

9. A 6- by 9-inch notebook with a blue cover was found among Betty Sue Jessup's belongings when she died. The writing in it was in her own handwriting. The first page of the notebook was neither numbered nor lettered, but on it was printed the word "Will." The back of the first page was completely blank except in the top left-hand corner was written "Page 1(a)." The next three pages were torn and removed from the book and never found. The writing began on page 4 with the words "Special Instructions To Executors" and contained seven more pages, giving instructions to the executors and making relatively minor gifts to former employees and friends. Above her signature on the last page were the words, "I haven't time to write more now—Will resume later." Was the will revoked because of the missing pages? Why or why not? ● *Jessup v. Jessup,* 267 S.E.2d 115 (Va. 1980)

10. Walsh, as settlor, executed a declaration of trust, naming himself as trustee and giving him the income from the trust during his lifetime. After his death, the income was to be paid to his second wife for her life, and upon her death to his two children, Edward and Margot. Upon their deaths, the income was to be paid to their children, after which it terminated. The trust expressly provided that the settlor had not made any provision for his third child, Patricia, because "previous provision had been made in her behalf." After executing the instrument, Walsh transferred to the trust the family residence, three farms, and a checking account. Patricia argued that the trust was testamentary and therefore invalid because it failed to comply with the statute of wills. Was this a testamentary or an *inter vivos* trust? Explain. ● *First Nat'l Bank v. Hampson,* 410 N.E.2d 1109 (Ill. 1980)

Part 9

Case Briefs

Board of Comm'rs v. Joeckel,
407 N.E.2d 274 (Ind. 1980)
The Board of Commissioners of Vanderburgh County built a bridge which required the purchase of two easements from Anna Joeckel. An agent for the board had negotiated with Joeckel, and she was paid $2,260 for the easements. No mention was made either in the negotiations or in the easement itself of the disposition of the marketable timber existing on the site of one of the easements. The subcontractor who cleared the area had bid for the job on the basis that he would receive the timber. He subsequently sold the timber, consisting of forty-five pecan trees, for $4,252.91.

Plaintiff's Position: Joeckel claimed that the grant of the easement to the board did not include a property interest in the trees. She contended that even though the board had the right to clear and otherwise use the land in the enjoyment of its easement, she retained the property right in the severed trees.

Defendant's Position: The board of commissioners contended that the property interest in the trees passed to it upon the grant of the easement. The board argued that Joeckel could escape the binding effect of her grant of easement only by showing some ground for rescission, such as fraud, failure of consideration, mistake, misrepresentation, or duress.

Legal Issue: When a public body acquires an easement for a right-of-way and no mention is made of the disposition of trees thereon, does the owner of the fee simple title retain the property right in the trees or is that property right included in the grant of the easement?

Court Decision: An easement for highway purposes does not include the property interest and ownership in the trees growing thereon. The trees remain the property of the owner of the fee simple. Joeckel was awarded $14,000 in damages by the jury hearing the case.

Court Reasoning: In the absence of an agreement to the contrary, the owner of the servient estate may use the property in any manner and for any purpose consistent with the enjoyment of the easement by the owner of the easement. All rights necessarily incident to the enjoyment of the easement are possessed by the owner of the easement, and the owner of the servient estate may not interfere with such enjoyment. The laying out of a roadway gives the public a mere right of passage, and the owner of the soil is not thereby divested of title to the land. An abutting property owner owns the fee in land upon which a highway is located and is the owner of the soil and of the trees growing thereon so far as that ownership is not inconsistent with the public use.

Perry v. Evanston YMCA,
416 N.E.2d 340 (Ill. 1981)
The YMCA is an organization which leases rooms to over 160 residents at stipulated weekly rates. The plaintiffs, Perry and Amoss, are former residents. Perry occupied Room 536 from December 12, 1976, to April 10, 1977. Amoss occupied Room 427 from September 12, 1976, until May 5, 1977. Each signed a separate residence hall agreement under which they agreed (1) to pay a stipulated rental charge in advance, (2) to observe "quiet hours" between 11 p.m. and 7:30 a.m., (3) that one day's notice by either party can-

cels the contract, and (4) that the YMCA may require the immediate vacating of rooms for violation of rules, failure to make room rent and membership payments in advance, unseemly conduct, immorality, or any other good cause.

On April 5, 1977, Holtz, the Executive Director of the YMCA, wrote a note to Perry informing him that he was playing his radio too loud and that, if he continued, he would be evicted. On April 7, 1977, Holtz informed Perry by letter that because of his violation of quiet hours, he would be evicted at 2 p.m. on April 10, 1977. On the same day, Perry wrote a letter advising the YMCA that the noise emanated from another room. On April 8, Holtz acknowledged receipt of Perry's letter but again stated he would be evicted at 2 p.m. on April 10. Perry and Holtz had had a previous confrontation regarding the use of the YMCA's gym equipment. As a result, Holtz had "plugged" Perry's door by placing an object in the lock, making it impossible for him to enter his room. Because of this prior encounter, Perry maintained that he had good reason to believe that Holtz, although not threatening such action, would "plug" the door to his room to effect an eviction at this time. Perry vacated the premises at 1 p.m. on April 10, 1977.

On April 20, 1977, Holtz informed Amoss that there was too much noise coming from his room. On May 4, 1977, Holtz left a note in Amoss's mailbox stating he would be evicted the following day at 2 p.m. On May 5, at about 3 p.m., Holtz confronted Amoss and said that if Amoss did not leave the premises Holtz would place a "plug" in the lock of his door so that he could not gain access to his room. Amoss vacated the room a half hour later.

Perry and Amoss brought this action alleging that Holtz and other YMCA employees forcibly entered each of their rooms in violation of the forcible entry and detainer statute of Illinois. This statute provides that "no person shall make an entry into lands or tenements except in cases where entry is allowed by law, and in such cases he shall not enter with force, but in a peaceable manner."

Plaintiffs' Position: Perry and Amoss contended that actual force is not necessary to constitute a forcible entry within the meaning of the forcible entry and detainer statute. They argued that because of implied force, they were compelled against their will, and without having an opportunity to contest the grounds of their eviction, to vacate the rooms. They also claimed that the threatened lockouts constitute forcible entries in contravention of the statute.

Defendant's Position: The YMCA contended that it did not violate the forcible entry and detainer statute because both Perry and Amoss voluntarily gave up possession of their rooms. It argued that no YMCA personnel entered either room until both plaintiff's had left and that no one used or threatened to use force upon the plaintiffs in order to gain entry.

Legal Issue: Does a threat to "plug" a tenant's door without any overt act in furtherance of that threat constitute a forcible entry?

Court Decision: No. Where an entry is made by one having a paramount title and a right to immediate possession in a peaceable and orderly manner, no offense is committed under the statute.

Court Reasoning: The general rule is that

an action under a forcible entry and detainer statute may not be maintained where an individual's possession is terminated prior to the alleged wrongful entry by (1) lawful surrender, (2) voluntary abandonment, or (3) eviction which has ripened into a peaceful possession on the part of the intruder. An invasion of an individual's actual possession of the premises at the time of the alleged entry is a prerequisite to recovery. Perry was given written notice on April 7 that he would be evicted because of quiet-hour violations. This notice was in accordance with the rental agreement and terminated Perry's right to possession of his lease. Perry did not allege that this notice was insufficient to terminate his right to possession nor does he claim any right to continued possession. He merely asserted that due to a previous confrontation with Holtz in which his door was actually "plugged," he had good reason to believe that he would do so again. No matter how well-founded this belief may have been, the fact remains that no actual or implied force, threat of force, or intimidation was used to gain entry to Perry's room. Perry's departure was consistent with the termination of his right to possession. He did no more than that required by any tenant on the expiration of his lease. Neither Holtz nor any YMCA personnel entered Perry's room until after he vacated the premises. Since Perry was no longer in possession of the room at the time of the alleged entry, the defendant did not enter against Perry's will. Consequently, defendant's actions did not constitute a forcible entry.

Like Perry, Amoss did not allege that the YMCA's notice was insufficient to terminate his right to possession of his room. Neither did he claim a continued right to possession. Rather, Amoss argued that Holtz's statement to leave or have the lock on his door "plugged" constituted a forcible entry. Actually, Amoss was attempting to argue that Holtz's statement amounted to a constructive eviction which was accompanied by implied force, since it was against his will, and therefore constituted a forcible entry under the statute.

For an act to constitute a constructive eviction, it must disturb the tenant's possession or amount to a clear indication on the part of the landlord to deprive the tenant of the enjoyment of the premises. Mere notice to the tenant to vacate the premises is insufficient to constitute an eviction. Where the landlord tells the tenant to leave, and the tenant replies that it is all right and removes his possessions, there is no eviction. The fact that Amoss remained in possession for another half hour supports this conclusion and belies any argument that these words were of a sufficiently grave and permanent nature to constitute a constructive eviction. Pursuant to the written notice, Amoss's right to possession of his room terminated at 2 p.m. on May 5. He was under a duty to surrender the premises to the defendant. The defendant at no time prior to his departure used force, actual or implied, to remove Amoss. It undertook no overt act in furtherance of its statement. Neither Holtz nor any other YMCA personnel entered Amoss's room until after he vacated the premises. In light of the fact that Amoss did not have a continued right to possession and was no longer in possession of his room at the time of the alleged entry, defendant's entry cannot be said to be against his will.

Part 10

Insurance and Secured Transactions

Chapter 39

The Nature of the Insurance Contract

Every moment of our lives, we are subject to different kinds of risks or uncertainties. We never know when we will be injured in an automobile accident, have our car stolen, or have our property damaged or destroyed. It is impossible to escape the risks of life. The known hazards—such as accidents, fires, illness, and the like—pose a continual threat to our personal and business lives. With some exceptions, all foreseeable losses or risks may be insured against. Thus, the principal way of protecting ourselves against losses from such hazards is insurance. *Insurance* may be defined as a device for the transfer to an insurer of certain risks of economic loss which would otherwise be borne by the insured. In effect, insurance spreads one person's risks among many others, who may or may not experience losses.

39-1. The Insurance Contract

Insurance policies are like other contracts in that they require mutual assent, capable parties, consideration, and valid subject matter. To have mutual assent, the minds of the parties must have met; they must have reached agreement on the terms of the contract. As with other contracts, an insurance agreement is voidable if made by a party who does not have the capacity to contract. Thus, in most instances, insurance contracts are made with persons who have reached the age of majority. State statutes sometimes make exception to this, allowing minors sixteen years of age or older to contract for automobile insurance. Consideration in an insurance contract arises from the premiums paid by the insured and the promise of the insurer to pay money to the beneficiary upon the happening of a certain event. The subject matter must not be tainted with illegality. A life insurance contract written for someone whom the beneficiary intends to kill would never be honored if that person were killed. A fire insurance policy written on a building where the owners permitted the illegal manufacture of fireworks would be void in the event of fire.

The parties to an insurance contract are the insurer, or underwriter; the insured; and the beneficiary. The *insurer* accepts the risk of loss in return for a *premium* (the consideration paid for a policy) and agrees to indemnify the insured against the loss specified in the contract. The *insured* is the party (or parties) protected by the insurance contract. The contract of insurance is called the *policy*. The period of time during which the insurer assumes the risk of loss is known as the *life of the policy*. A third party, to whom payment of compensation is sometimes provided by the contract, is called the *beneficiary*.

39-2. Insurable Interest

A person or business applying for insurance must have an insurable interest in the subject matter of the policy, whether it is a person or property. *Insurable interest* is the financial interest that an insurance policyholder has in the person or property that is insured. The qualifications of an insurable interest are different in the case of life insurance and property insurance.

A. Life Insurance

The person who insures the life of another must have an interest in the person insured such that a financial loss will occur if that person dies. Thus, a person has an insurable interest in the life of another if the first person is dependent on the other person for education, support, aid in business (partners), collection of debt (interest of creditor in debtor's life), and the like.

● The Security Loan Company introduced the practice of insuring all persons to whom it granted loans on notes not secured by collateral (property of the debtor). The cost of the insurance was added to the debtor's loan charges. The loan company was, of course, made beneficiary of each policy, whose face value equaled the amount of the loan. In this way, the company was assured that the loan would be repaid, even if the debtor died.

A life insurance policy will remain valid and enforceable even if the insurable interest terminates. It is necessary only that the insurable interest exist at the time the policy was issued. Thus, if a debtor whose life was insured by a creditor subsequently pays the debt, the life insurance policy continues in force provided the former creditor pays the premiums.

B. Property Insurance

Property insurance covers a variety of items including real property, automobiles, and many other types of goods. Fire insurance is a major kind of insurance covering real property. To enforce a claim through fire insurance, the insured must have had an insurable interest in the covered property at the time of securing the policy, and at the time of a reported loss. Any attempt to assign a fire insurance policy to a new owner is void. By agreement with the insurer a novation may be made—that is, the new owner takes over the policy. Later, the insurer issues a new policy in the new owner's name to replace the old policy.

In the case of goods, both the buyer and the seller can have an insurable interest in them at the same time. A buyer obtains an insurable interest in goods when they are identified to the contract. This occurs when specific goods have been selected as the subject matter of the transaction. This insurable interest arises even though the goods are nonconforming and the buyer has an option to return or reject them [2-501(1)]. At the same time, the seller retains an insurable interest in the goods until title passes to the buyer or for as long as the seller has a security interest in the goods [2-501(2)]. Security interests are discussed in Chapter 41.

●McCabe selected a used car in Wade's Used Car Lot. Agreement was made for the car's delivery the next day, at which time McCabe would pay the $2,800 promised. McCabe called an insurance agent immediately and covered the car with a fire and theft policy. The car was stolen from Wade's lot that night. Both McCabe and Wade's Used Car Lot had an insurable interest in the car at the time it was stolen.

39-3. Form of the Insurance Contract

In most states, contracts of insurance come in a prescribed form. These standard forms are carefully drafted by an insurance commissioner with help from the state's legal advisers (for example, the attorney general or state's attorney). In this way the consumer-buyer is protected from deception or fraud. Approval of a standard contract is a public trust. Most people buying insurance do not read, and probably would not understand, all the provisions of such a complicated written document. As an additional protection to consumers, some states now require that, to the greatest extent possible, insurance contracts must be written in clear, understandable language and printed in a readable typeface. Courts also give protection to the insured by broadly interpreting the terms of an insurance contract in favor of the one who was not responsible for its writing, especially when the terms of the contract come into dispute or are ambiguous. In other words, the courts tend to rule against the insurer whenever there are "gray areas" involving the contract's interpretation. Matters of dispute and questions arising from the ambiguity of the contract terms are most likely to result from the addition of *riders* (indorsements) to the contract of insurance. These are special provisions not contained in the basic policy contract but added to it.

In the absence of a statutory provision to the contrary, an oral contract of insurance is valid. Its essential elements can be established by implication if they are not stated explicitly. So long as the parties manifest a common understanding of the policy's provisions, a meeting of the minds will be presumed, and the contract is considered complete upon the insured's agreement to pay the premium.

●Mato spoke to an agent by telephone and requested the same coverage for his new car that he had on his former auto through the agent's company. He was orally assured by the agent that he would have such coverage. Later, after an accident, the insurance company denied coverage. The court, holding in favor of Mato, said that there is no doubt that the parties agreed upon the essential elements of a contract of insurance. It is sufficient to form an insurance contract if the elements are understood or can be ascertained.

The price of the policy is an essential element of a contract to insure. However, even if the amount of the premium is not fixed, the contract is enforceable if the insured simply agrees to pay the amount to be charged by the insurer.

Part 10:
Insurance
and
Secured
Trans-
actions

528

A. Application for Insurance

The first step in obtaining an insurance policy is the filling out of an application. This is not a contract; rather, it is an offer or proposal made by the applicant to the insurance company for a contract of insurance. Before any contractual relationship comes about between the parties, the application must be accepted by the insurance company, which the company may or may not do. As with other offers, the application may be withdrawn at any time before it has been accepted by the insurance company. This is true even if the applicant paid premiums with the application.

● Hiatt filled out an application for insurance and gave it to her insurance agent with a check for the first quarterly premium. Before the application had been accepted by the company, Hiatt learned of another insurance company that provided the same protection for a smaller premium. She notified the insurance agent that she was withdrawing her application. She would be entitled to the return of the money she had given to the insurance agent.

B. Binders

Between the time an individual's application for insurance is received and either approved or rejected, an insurer or an insurance agent may issue a *binder*, or *binding slip*. These are brief legal memorandums providing temporary insurance coverage until a policy can be written. In life insurance, this memorandum is referred to as a *conditional receipt*.

● The owners of Brittingham's department store signed an application for a fire insurance policy covering both building and contents. The agent accepted the application and issued a binder for the insurance. Before the policy was issued, the insured property burned to the ground. The insurance company is fully liable on the contract and must reimburse Brittingham's for the loss up to the face value of the policy.

C. Premiums

An insurance contract differs from most other contracts in that it requires the payment of premiums. This, you will recall, is the consideration or payment an insured gives the insurer for its acceptance of risk. The amount of the premium is determined by the nature and character of the risk involved, and by its likelihood of occurring. The premium increases as the chance of loss increases. Thus, an insurance premium on a fireproof building in a city with an efficient fire department will be much lower than the premium on a barn located where fire-fighting equipment is not available. Similarly, a life insurance premium for a young person is lower than the premium for an older person owing to the increased risk of death as one grows older.

Since the amount of a premium is greatly affected by the likelihood that a particular risk will occur, the role of *actuaries* is very important. They are professional experts who apply mathematical principles to determine as accurately as possible the amount of losses that might occur from a given category of risk. Based on their calculations, premium rates for any given amount of insurance coverage can be determined.

Chapter
39:
The
Nature of
the
Insurance
Contract

529

D. Lapse of Policy and Grace Period

When the insured stops paying premiums, an insurance contract is said to *lapse*. This does not mean, however, that the contract will terminate automatically on the date that the last premium is paid. Nor will it lapse automatically if the insured makes a delayed payment. Most contracts allow for a *grace period* of thirty or thirty-one days in which the insured may make payments so the policy can remain in force. Beyond this period, however, the insurance contract will lapse and the policy terminate.

39-4. Open and Valued Policies

There are two general types of personal and property insurance policies—open policies and valued policies.

A. Open Policy

A contract of insurance in which the amount recoverable is determined by the amount of the loss is an *open policy*. Although the amount recoverable for any loss is left "open," the maximum amount that can be recovered for that loss is stated in the face of the contract.

● Nugent insured a power boat for $2,500. The insurer issued an open policy that would reimburse Nugent for losses resulting from fire, explosion, or damage from storms and submerged and uncharted navigation hazards. The boat sank during a storm and was completely ruined. A claims agent confirmed that the boat could be replaced for $1,500. That is the amount the insurer is bound to pay Nugent.

B. Valued Policy

A *valued policy* is one in which the insurer puts a definite value on the subject matter of the insurance. The figure is conclusive in the event of loss.

● Suppose in the previous example that Nugent had requested a valued policy for the power boat. On proof that the boat was completely ruined, the insurer would have paid Nugent the value of the policy, or $2,500.

Valued policies are issued in life insurance and in health and accident liability. In fire insurance, such policies are illegal in most states. Some states, however, have so-called valued-policy laws requiring that fire insurance policies on buildings be treated as valued policies in the event of total loss by certain perils. In most cases, nonetheless, property insurance is written as an open policy.

39-5. Cancellation of Insurance Policies

Under certain conditions the insurer is given a legal right to forfeit, or cancel, an insurance policy. Proof of forfeiture permits cancellation either before a loss or at the time the claim is made on a policy. Among grounds permitting forfeiture are a lack of contract essentials in the insurance agreement, a policy that is improper in form, a breach of warranty, or a concealment of some material fact by the insured. Neither the insured nor the insurer may deny statements or acts previously made or committed that might affect the validity of the policy.

Part 10:
Insurance
and
Secured
Trans-
actions

530

A. Warranties

In insurance, a *warranty* is an insured's guaranty of facts, statements, or promises contained in an application. It may also be an insured's promise to abide by restrictions especially written into a policy. An insured's warranty must be literally true; otherwise it gives the insurer in some jurisdictions the right to void the policy. By statute in many states, an insurance company has the burden of proof in establishing that a warranty was fraudulently made. If this is proved, the insurer may refuse payment of loss to the insured or to a beneficiary.

● Sexton applied for life insurance after having had two serious accidents while mountain climbing. The insurer was aware of Sexton's climbing experiences. On instructions from the insurer, Sexton promised to do no more climbing while the policy remained in force. Sexton was killed during an especially difficult expedition in the Andes Mountains. The insurer may rescind any obligation to pay Sexton's beneficiary.

B. Concealment

Fraudulent concealment is any intentional withholding of a fact that would be of material importance in the insurer's decision to issue a policy. The applicant need only give answers to questions asked. However, by act or statement the insured may not conceal facts that would be material in acceptance of a risk.

● Evans applied for car insurance with a company that did not accept drivers who were habitual drinkers. When questioned about drinking, he answered, "I never take a drop." The policy was issued. Evans was later charged in a civil action for damages resulting from a serious accident which he had caused. The insurer learned that Evans was a heavy drinker and was intoxicated at the time of the accident.

The insurer would be permitted to forfeit Evan's policy. The insured intentionally withheld information about his drinking habits, knowing that if the truth were told the application would be rejected. Any judgment levied against Evans in this action would be paid out of Evan's own assets, with no assistance from the insurance company.

C. Misrepresentation

If an insured gives false answers (misrepresentations) to questions in an insurance application which materially affect the risk undertaken by the insurer, the contract is voidable. The insurer may void the contract. A representation is material if the facts represented influence the insurer's decision to issue the policy or the rate of premium to charge.

● Brezhinski applied to Guaranty Insurance Company for a liability policy on a new car. When asked how many miles she drove each year, Brezhinski answered 5,000. In fact, as field auditor for a large corporation, she drove approximately 20,000 miles each year. Thus, Brezhinski managed to get a smaller premium charge in recognition of a risk 75 percent less than it actually was. Brezhinski's policy may be voided. If her misrepresentation had resulted in proven damage to the insurer, the latter could have sued her for these damages.

If a claim is made on a life policy on whose application the insured misstated the age of the person whose life is covered, the insurance company need pay only the amount of insurance that could have been purchased by the premium paid, based on the decedent's true age.

● Larkins applied for a $25,000 life insurance policy. She had been raised by a relative and was never sure about her correct age. At age twenty-one, by her reckoning, she purchased the policy. Prior to death, the insured discovered that she was actually twenty-three when she had applied for the policy. Her beneficiary will not be paid $25,000, but a lesser amount equal to what the premiums actually paid would have purchased if her correct age had been utilized.

D. Estoppel

An insurer may not deny acts, statements, or promises that are relevant and material to the validity of an insurance policy. This bar to denial is called an *estoppel*. The insurer is said to be *estopped* from denying its liability under a policy. A *waiver* is one type of estoppel. For example, when the insurer agrees to rescind one of its customary rights for the benefit of the insured, it may not later deny its waiver; it will be estopped from using that waived right to its advantage.

● Farmers Insurance Company insured Snaveley's house and barn against fire, water, and windstorm damage. All of Farmers' policies contained a condition that insured properties must be within 300 feet of a fire plug, with water tested at 50 pounds of pressure. The house and barn were a mile from a water main, but less than 300 feet from the property was a farm pond containing approximately 100,000 gallons of water. Farmers waived the fire-plug requirement in view of the water available in the event of fire. Farmers would be estopped from denying that the waiver had been made in the event of a reported fire loss by the insured.

In most states, however, insurers simply may not waive certain rights. For instance, an insurer cannot waive the necessity of having an insurable interest. The reason is that most legislatures strongly believe that lack of an insurable interest would promote fraud and crime by persons buying a policy. When a waiver refers to a rule or regulation of the insurance company itself, the courts will usually hold the insurer liable for a loss. Acceptance of an insured's application, with knowledge that its information would ordinarily reject the application, makes the insurer liable.

● Apex Insurance Company sold fire and burglary insurance to the owners of the Baumann Building even though it was located in an area designated "high risk." The home office had issued instructions that no buildings in that area would be issued fire and burglary coverage. Once it was issued, however, Apex would be liable on the Baumann policy. The insurer would be estopped from denying liability because its agents and employees violated company policy and rules in issuing the policy.

39-6. Subrogation

Part 10:
Insurance
and
Secured
Trans-
actions

Subrogation is the right of an insurer to claim damages from third parties through whose fault, negligence, or intentional wrongdoing the insurer has been required to pay a claim. The insurer may subpoena all evidence and may summon all witnesses to its case who might have been available to the insured. Persons responsible for damage are not, therefore, released from responsibility merely because benefits have been paid by the insurance company to the injured party.

Understanding Legal Terms

Define, identify, or explain the following terms:

actuaries	grace period	insurer	riders
binder	indorsements	lapse	subrogation
estoppel	insurable interest	open policy	valued policy
fraudulent concealment	insurance	policy	waiver
	insured	premium	

Questions for Review and Discussion

1. How do open policies differ from valued policies?

2. In what ways do the requirements of insurable interest differ in property insurance and life insurance.?

3. What is a binder, or binding slip, in property insurance? What is the term used in life insurance that means the same thing?

4. Explain the term *warranty,* as applied to insurance.

5. How does subrogation work to the disadvantage of third parties who have been responsible for damages caused insured persons or their property?

6. List the grounds whereby an insurer may forfeit an insured's insurance policy.

7. How does misrepresentation of the insured's age affect a life insurance policy?

8. Describe the legal significance of an application for insurance and explain when it may be withdrawn.

9. Describe the legal effect when an insured stops paying premiums on an insurance policy.

10. Explain how both the buyer and the seller can have an insurable interest in goods under the Uniform Commercial Code.

Analyzing Cases

1. Devers telephoned her insurance company's office to obtain insurance on a new automobile. She told the agent she wanted the same coverage she had had on an earlier vehicle, although she could not recall any specific provisions. The agent asked her several questions about her new car, including its serial number. She did not have the number with her and asked if she could call back later in the day. She also asked whether she was covered. The agent replied that she was. About an hour later, she called back and gave the agent the serial number of the car, and they discussed the price of the policy. She gave him her billing address, and the agent told her he would mail the policy and statement to her. Later that day, Devers and her car were involved in an accident. The insurance company refused to pay, claiming that the insurance was not yet in effect. Do you agree with the insurance company? Explain. ● *Devers v. Prudential Prop. & Cas. Ins. Co.,* 408 N.E.2d 462 (Ill. 1980)

2. Nelson rented his house to Green for $40 a month until it was destroyed by fire. Prior to the fire, Nelson had sold the land on which the house was located to Durant. It was agreed, however, that the sale of the land did not include the house and that Nelson

would move the house in the indefinite future onto other land he owned. The house was covered by a $5,000 fire insurance policy. The insurance company denied the claim on the ground that Nelson had lost his insurable interest in the property when he sold it to Durant. Does Nelson have an insurable interest in the property? Why or why not? ● *Nelson v. United Fire Ins. Co.*, 267 S.E.2d 604 (S.C. 1980)

3. On an application for life insurance filled out in 1973, Brooks answered in the negative when asked whether he had been a patient in a hospital; whether he had been given an electrocardiogram other than one in 1953; whether he had been told he had or had been treated for high blood pressure; and whether he had dieted or taken any treatment for diabetes, heart trouble, or blood pressure. In fact, he had been hospitalized in 1967, was treated for diabetes, heart trouble, and high blood pressure in 1966 and 1967, and was given an electrocardiogram in 1966 and 1967. When Brooks died in 1974, the insurance company denied the beneficiary's claim for the proceeds of the policy on the ground of misrepresentation. Can Brooks's beneficiary recover under the policy? Explain. ● *Ratliff v. Coastal Plain Life Ins. Co.*, 242 S.E.2d 424 (S.C. 1978)

4. Adams, an insurance agent, sold Schweigert an insurance policy covering his pickup truck and landscaping business. After the policy had been issued, Schweigert asked Adams if his homemade trailer was covered, and Adams responded that it was. Thereafter, Schweigert was involved in an accident when his trailer became unattached from his truck and crossed the center line and collided with an oncoming vehicle. The insurance policy issued to Schweigert did not, in fact, cover trailers. Must the insurance company pay the claim against Schweigert? Why or why not? ● *Country Mut. Ins. Co. v. Adams*, 407 N.E.2d 103 (Ill. 1980)

5. Wendy Schmitt was injured in a single-car accident while riding in a car driven by Kopeika. She was Kopeika's sister-in-law (his wife's sister) and resided with Kopeika and his wife. A provision in Kopeika's insurance policy read: "This insurance does not apply to bodily injury to any member of the family of the insured residing in the same household as the insured." The insurance company denied coverage, claiming that Kopeika's sister-in-law was a member of the family. Schmitt, however, argued that the meaning of the words *member of the family* was left ambiguous when the insurance company wrote the policy for Kopeika. She contended that she was entitled to coverage. With whom do you agree? Why? ● *State Farm Mut. Auto. Ins. Co. v. Schmitt*, 419 N.E.2d 601 (Ill. 1981)

6. When Lynch was appointed a firefighter for the city of Des Moines, he chose his wife, Pauline, to receive his death benefits. On the designation form, Lynch wrote in Pauline's name, and he wrote in the word *wife* so that the form read, "Said nominated beneficiary has an insurable interest in my life by reason of being my wife." This beneficiary designation was never changed even though Lynch and Pauline were divorced five years later. After the divorce, Lynch paid child support for his three children while they were minors and alimony to Pauline until he died. After a second marriage and divorce, Lynch married Marcene, with whom he had two children. Marcene was his wife at the time of his death. The state statute regarding death benefits for firefighters read: "Upon the receipt of proper proofs of the death of a member in service, there shall be paid to such person having an insurable interest in his life as he shall have nominated by written designation duly executed and filed with the respective board of trustees . . . his accumulated contributions. If there be no such nomination of beneficiary, the benefits shall be paid to his estate." Who is entitled to Lynch's death benefits, Pauline or Marcene? Why? ● *Lynch v. Bogenrief*, 237 N.W.2d 793 (Iowa 1976)

Chapter 40

Major Types of Insurance

It is possible to obtain insurance against almost any risk if one is willing to pay the price. The premium charged will depend on the risk involved. Property insurance is available to cover the risk of loss or damage to realty or personal property. Life insurance and personal insurance are obtainable to provide indemnity for losses suffered by reason of death, accident, or ill health.

In this chapter, life insurance and annuities; health, accident, and sickness insurance; fire insurance; ocean and inland marine insurance; and automobile insurance are discussed. Workers' compensation and social security are covered in Chapter 30.

40-1. Life Insurance and Annuity Contracts

A *life insurance* contract provides funds to a beneficiary on the death of the person insured. An *annuity* contract provides the *annuitant* (the person entitled to the annuity) with an income as long as that person lives.

A. Exemptions From Risk

Many life insurance policies contain clauses which exempt the insurance company from liability in certain cases. Often, for example, policies do not cover the insured while riding in an airplane, while engaged in military service, or while working in certain dangerous occupations. Many policies exclude coverage when the insured is killed while violating the law. Some policies are void when death is caused by an intentional act of another or by the use of intoxicating liquors or narcotics.

1. **Legal Execution of Insured.** A number of courts have held that there can be no recovery on a life insurance policy when the death of the insured is caused by legal execution. These courts base their reasoning on the theory that it would be against public policy for beneficiaries to receive insurance proceeds in such cases. They also note that death by legal execution is not one of the risks assumed by the insurance company. In contrast, other courts do allow recovery of life insurance proceeds in such cases on the ground that denial of recovery would not be a deterrent to crime.

2. **Causing Death of Insured.** In most cases, the courts allow recovery on a life insurance contract where the insured is murdered. Exceptions are when the insurance policy excludes such recovery and when the murderer is also the beneficiary. A beneficiary who murders or feloniously causes the death of the insured forfeits all rights under a life insurance policy. Similarly, the children or

others claiming through the beneficiary who killed the insured cannot collect the proceeds of the policy. Usually, in such a case, the money will be paid to the insured's estate.

3. Suicide of Insured. Most courts allow a beneficiary to recover the proceeds of a life insurance policy when the insured commits suicide. The beneficiary must be someone other than the insured's family members or the insured's estate; for example, a creditor of the insured. On the other hand, when life insurance is taken out in contemplation of suicide, the courts hold the policy to be void on the ground that it is a fraud on the insurer.

Policies frequently provide that the insurance company is not liable for death by suicide, whether the insured was sane or insane, within two years of the issuance of the policy. Under these policies, if death by suicide occurs after the two-year period lapses the company must pay.

4. War Activities. Life insurance policies usually include an exemption of liability in time of war. The exemption states that the insurer will not be liable on the policy if the insured is killed (*a*) while a member of the armed forces, generally outside the continental United States, and (*b*) from service-connected causes.

B. Kinds of Life Insurance Policies

The most common types of life insurance policies are straight life, limited-payment, endowment, and term insurance. Annuity contracts are also offered by life insurance companies.

1. Straight Life Policy. An *ordinary, whole,* or *straight life insurance* policy is one for which the insured pays premiums at fixed dates until the policy is terminated by death or discontinuance. The face value of the policy is to be paid to the beneficiary or to the estate of the insured on the death of the insured. Premiums normally stay level throughout the life of the policy. The exact level of the premium is determined by the age of the insured at the time of purchase. The younger the insured, the lower the premium, because the company expects to collect many years' worth of premiums. The older the insured, the higher the premium.

Straight life insurance contains an investment feature known as the *cash surrender value,* which is something like a savings account. The cash surrender value usually builds up slowly at first, but in later years it approaches the face amount of the policy. At some stated point (usually at the age of ninety-five or a hundred) it equals the face value of the policy. An insured can cancel a straight life policy at any time and receive its cash surrender value.

At age twenty-two, LaFarge purchased a straight life insurance policy with a face value of $10,000. The premiums were quite modest. At some later time he could trade in the policy for its cash surrender value. Or, LaFarge could continue premium payments until death or age one hundred.

An insured may borrow against the cash surrender value of the policy, usually at a relatively favorable rate of interest. During inflationary times, when

Part 10:
Insurance
and
Secured
Trans-
actions

536

bank interest rates are high, insurance policies are often excellent sources for loans at low interest rates.

● Dugan took out a $10,000 ordinary life insurance policy ten years ago and paid premiums regularly. A family emergency required $1,500 immediate cash. Dugan was able to borrow the money on her policy at a low rate of interest, as the policy had an immediate cash value of more than $1,700. Borrowing on the policy would keep it in force, and her beneficiary would receive the face amount of $10,000 less the amount of the loan should Dugan die before repaying the loan.

2. Limited-Payment Policy. A *limited-payment life insurance policy* is one for which the insured makes a specified number of periodic payments. When these payments have been made, the insurance is fully paid for, and on the death of the insured the amount of the policy will be paid to the beneficiary. Thus, a twenty-payment life policy is one for which twenty equal annual payments must be made. Because of the limited number of payments made by the insured on this type of policy, the premiums are proportionately higher than those for straight life.

3. Term Insurance. *Term insurance* is similar to a straight life policy, but it is written to expire after only one, two, five, ten, or more years. Premiums are smaller than with any other type of life insurance. This is because term policies have no cash (or loan) value, as others do. Term insurance offers protection alone, in contrast to straight life, which combines protection with a savings plan. Premiums for term insurance, unlike those for straight life, commonly go up at the end of each term. It costs a twenty-five-year-old relatively little to buy term insurance. By the age of sixty, however, the insured must pay much higher premiums for this same coverage. But by that time, ordinarily, the insured's overall financial responsibility to others has lessened and thus less coverage may be needed.

A term policy is *renewable* if the coverage can be continued at the end of each period simply by paying the increased premium, without need for a new medical examination. Term policies are commonly renewable until the insured reaches the age of sixty-five or seventy; then all coverage stops. A term policy is *convertible* if the insured can convert it into a straight life policy without taking a new medical examination. Many term policies are both renewable and convertible and thus allow protection throughout the insured's lifetime.

A modified form of term insurance is *decreasing term insurance.* The premium stays constant from year to year, but the amount of protection (death benefit) decreases over the years. This type of policy is widely used to cover the outstanding balance of a home mortgage.

4. Endowment Policy. An *endowment policy* assures the insured a cash payment of the face amount of the policy at the expiration of a prescribed number of years. Like straight life insurance, endowments build up cash value in a kind of savings account. But in an endowment the cash value builds up faster, so that it equals the entire face amount of the policy within a specified time (often twenty years) or at a specified age (often sixty-five). At that time, the insured receives the entire face amount. Should the insured die before the end of that period, a beneficiary is paid the full amount of the policy. Because this type of policy builds up a cash value more rapidly than other policies, the premium is higher.

● Sutton, aged twenty-one, purchased a $10,000 face value, twenty-year endowment policy. His beneficiary will get $10,000 if he dies before age forty-one. If he survives, he gets a check for $10,000 at age forty-one.

5. Annuity Contract. An *annuity contract* provides the insured with a monthly, quarterly, or annual income upon reaching a specified age written into the policy. For example, an annual premium of $100, on a policy purchased at age twenty-one, might pay the insured an income of $32 a month for life, with payments beginning at age sixty. Multiples of the $100 annual premium could assure the person of a specific income to be added to social security or pension benefits.

A *joint and last-survivor annuity contract* provides a husband or wife with fixed monthly benefits commencing at the death of the spouse and lasting until the survivor's death. Premium payments for such a policy are based on the ages of both husband and wife.

C. Optional Provisions

Life insurance policies have many optional provisions that may be purchased by the insured. Three popular options are double indemnity, waiver of premium, and guaranteed insurability.

1. Double Indemnity. For a small, extra premium the insured may purchase an additional benefit known as *double indemnity* or an accidental death benefit. This provides that if the insured dies from accidental causes, the insurer will pay double the amount of the policy to the beneficiary. Death must occur within ninety days of the accident, however, for this benefit to apply.

2. Waiver of Premium. The *waiver-of-premium* option excuses the insured who becomes disabled from paying premiums. Some insurance policies automatically include the waiver in their provisions; others offer it as an extra-cost option.

3. Guaranteed Insurability. A *guaranteed-insurability* option allows the insured to pay an extra premium initially in exchange for a guaranteed option to buy more insurance at certain specified times later on. The additional insurance can be purchased with no questions asked; thus no new medical examination is required even if the insured develops a serious illness before exercising the option.

40-2. Health, Accident, and Sickness Insurance

Health, accident, and sickness insurance provides compensation to the insured for losses due to accidental injury or disease. Losses include accidental loss of life, loss of members (such as hands or feet), loss of sight, medical expenses, and loss of time. Loss of time refers to total or partial inability to work. *Total disability* is defined as complete inability to engage in one's regular occupation. *Partial disability* is the ability to perform one or more but not all of the duties of one's occupation.

Part 10:
Insurance
and
Secured
Trans-
actions

538

Table 40-1.   Payments of a Typical Accident Insurance Policy

For Accidental Loss Of:	A Typical Policy Pays:
Life	$10,000
Both hands or both feet	10,000
Sight of both eyes	10,000
One hand and one foot	10,000
One hand or one foot and sight of one eye	10,000
One hand or one foot	5,000
Sight of one eye	3,500
Thumb and index finger of either hand	2,500

A. Accident Insurance

Accident insurance pays monthly (or weekly) income to people who are disabled by accident. An *accident* is an unexpected, unforseen, or unintentional incident resulting in personal injury. Some accident insurance policies pay particular sums for particular injuries. Table 40-1 shows payments of a typical policy.

Most accident insurance policies provide for coverage for accidental bodily injury. Other policies, however, provide coverage for bodily injuries effected solely through accidental means. The former coverage is broader than the latter; it includes any injury that is unexpected or fortuitous. The latter, on the other hand, covers injuries the *cause of which* was unexpected or fortuitous.

● While lifting weights with a newly acquired barbell set, Brotchie strained his back. He was out of work for several weeks. Although he received an accidental bodily injury, it did not result from accidental means. The weight lifting was done intentionally. Thus, his accident, under some court decisions, would not be covered if the policy contained the phrase, *bodily injuries effected solely through accidental means.* However, it would be covered under a policy which used the phrase *accidental bodily injury.*

B. Health or Sickness Insurance

Health insurance provides coverage for loss of income and expenses due to sickness or disease. *Sickness* is a condition interfering with one's usual activities, whereas *disease* may exist without such result. Generally, however, they are considered by most courts to have the same meaning. Neither alcoholism nor drug addiction is considered to be a disease as such term is used in insurance policies.

The most widely purchased forms of medical care insurance are hospitalization, medical care, and surgical care policies, such as Blue Cross and Blue Shield. Most medical plans have maximum limits of coverage. *Major medical expense insurance* is designed to absorb the shock of major medical care that could cause catastrophic economic hardship to an individual or family. Most policies contain a deductible which the insured must absorb before major medical insurance applies. *Comprehensive major medical insurance* combines benefits for minor medical costs with the coverage for major medical expenses.

● Bancroft was stricken with a serious heart ailment which resulted in a lengthy stay in a hospital and costly medical bills. Fortunately, she was covered by major medical expense insurance through the group insurance plan where she worked. Bancroft was required to pay $50 of the medical bill, the amount of the annual deductible. The insurance company paid the balance. Before the calendar year ended, she was readmitted to the hospital for a different problem. This time the insurance company paid the entire medical bill, her deductible for that year having already been paid. Had her second hospitalization occurred in another calendar year, Bancroft would have had to pay another $50 to cover the deductible for that calendar year.

C. Uniform Policy Provisions Law

The Uniform Individual Accident and Sickness Policy Provisions Law has been adopted, either in whole or in part, by all the states. The purpose of this law is to make sure that accident and health insurance policies have provisions which are fair to the insured and, at the same time, give protection to the insurer. The law is also designed to reduce uncertainty as to the terms of the insurance policy by promoting clarity and uniformity. Much of the language found in accident and health insurance policies is dictated by this law. Such things as grace periods, reinstatement provisions, times for filing and paying claims, proof of loss, physical examinations, and provisions for change of beneficiaries are spelled out in this uniform act.

40-3. Fire Insurance

A *fire insurance policy* is a contract whereby the insurer promises, for a stipulated premium, to pay the insured a sum not exceeding the face amount of the policy if a particular piece of real or personal property is damaged or destroyed by fire.

A fire insurance policy or a binder is effective as soon as it is unconditionally delivered to the insured, even though the premium has not yet been paid. Even an oral binder is valid and will make fire insurance effective.

A. Losses

The insurer's liability under a fire policy usually covers losses other than those directly attributed to fire. Under most policies, claims may also be made for losses from (1) water used to fight the fire; (2) scorching; (3) smoke damage to goods; (4) deliberate destruction of property as a means of controlling a spreading fire; (5) lightning, even if there is no resultant fire; (6) riot or explosion, if a fire does result; and (7) losses through theft or exposure of goods removed from a burning building.

B. Kinds of Fire Insurance Policies

The most common fire policies are the ordinary policy, the policy containing a coinsurance clause, and the homeowner's policy.

1. Ordinary Policy. Under the *ordinary fire insurance* policy, the insurance company will compensate the insured for any fire losses up to the amount of insurance carried, but never more than the actual loss suffered by the insured nor more than the amount of insurance carried.

Part 10:
Insurance
and
Secured
Trans-
actions

540

● Watson insured his $60,000 house for only $30,000. A fire broke out, causing damages amounting to $25,000. Under an ordinary fire insurance policy, Watson would recover the entire loss of $25,000. However, if the house had been insured for $20,000, that would be the limit of any recovery.

2. Coinsurance Clause Policy. A *coinsurance clause* in an insurance policy is based on the premise that the insured is a coinsurer with the insurance company if the property is insured for less than its actual value. The difference between the value of the property and the amount of insurance is assumed to be the personal risk of the insured. Under an *80 percent coinsurance clause* policy, which is the most common type of coinsurance, the insurance company will pay that part of a loss that the insurance carried bears to 80 percent of the value of the property. Thus, if a house valued at $50,000 is insured for $30,000, only

$$\frac{\$30,000}{80\% \text{ of } \$50,000} \text{ or } \frac{\$30,000}{\$40,000} \text{ or } \frac{3}{4}$$

of the loss can be recovered by the insured, since only three-fourths of the 80 percent value was insured. If, on the other hand, $40,000 of insurance had been carried, the full loss up to $40,000 could have been collected from the insurance company, since this amount is 80 percent of the value of the property.

● Watson insured her $50,000 summer home for $30,000 under an 80 percent coinsurance clause policy. A fire loss was determined to be $20,000 by an insurance adjuster. Under the formula shown above, Watson would recover three-fourths of her claim, or $15,000.

The 80 percent clause in a policy does not mean that 80 percent of the value of the property is the maximum amount collectible. If the property is insured for its full value, the full amount would be collected in case of a total loss.

3. Homeowner's Policy. Many of the leading insurance companies offer a new combination policy known as the *homeowner's policy*. This gives protection for all types of losses and liabilities related to home ownership. Among the items covered are losses from fire, windstorm, and related damage; burglary; vandalism; and injuries suffered by other persons while on the property. These policies usually contain deductible clauses for some of the protection given. The rates are much lower than if each protection offered were covered by a separate policy.

All homeowner's policies are based on the 80 percent coinsurance clause, although more or less than 80 percent can, of course, be purchased.

● Andrews insured her house under a homeowner's policy. One evening, two children went into Andrews' yard and were injured when they fell into a hole being excavated for a swimming pool. Under the doctrine of *attractive nuisance*, their parents were permitted to sue for all costs relating to the injuries. (Attractive nuisance is a doctrine in tort law that holds that one who maintains a dangerous instrumentality on his or her premises which is likely to attract children is under a duty to reasonably protect those children against the dangers of that attraction.) The homeowner's policy covered Andrews' liability for injuries to persons on the property.

C. Policy Provisions

Fire insurance policies have many standard provisions. Three of the most important ones are discussed here.

1. Vacancy Clause. Fire insurance may be voided by the insurer when insured property is left vacant or unoccupied for more than sixty days. An insurer may accept the risk through agreement with the insured and the paying of an added premium. A building is vacant when it is empty. If goods or furniture are left in a building, it is not said to be vacant, even though it is not occupied by the owner or others by permission. If an owner or tenant is absent but has every intention of returning, the insurance company cannot claim that insured premises are vacant or unoccupied.

2. Double Insurance. Double insurance occurs when two or more policies provide protection or coverage for the same risk. In the event of a reported loss, each company would pay the insured only a proportional amount of the claim. The insured is barred from making two complete recoveries through a single loss.

● Hampden owned a house which was insured against fire by Mutual of New Holland. As a double assurance of protection, Hampden took out another policy with Fire Writers of America. Each policy was written with a face value of $25,000. Hampden's house was completely destroyed by fire. Instead of receiving $25,000 from each insurer, he would receive only half of the claim from each.

3. Extended-Coverage Indorsement. The original intent of a fire policy, historically, was to cover losses directly traceable to fire or lightning. Other policies were available for risks such as windstorm, explosion, riot, or water damage. Issuance of five or more separate policies covering the same property resulted in confusion and misunderstanding between insurer and insured. *Indorsements* to the fire policy have now been developed. These cover all such related risks and are obtained by payment of a relatively small additional premium.

● Pell owned a large home in Allentown. It was covered by a policy written with indorsements for extended coverage. A fire was discovered in his home, and because of its stubborn nature, thousands of gallons of water were used to keep it from spreading. While some loss was attributed to fire, greater losses resulted from water damage to plastered walls, lighting fixtures, woodwork, and tiled floors. A claim for all damages would be enforceable because of the extended-coverage indorsement in Pell's policy.

40-4. Ocean and Inland Marine Insurance

Marine insurance is one of the oldest types of insurance coverage. It dates back to the Lombard and Venetian traders who sailed the Mediterranean. Marine insurance is of two types, ocean marine and inland marine.

A. Ocean Marine Insurance

Ocean marine insurance, as its name implies, covers ships at sea. Special terminology, unique to this field, is used to describe different types of marine insurance coverage. *Hull insurance* covers the ship itself, *cargo insurance* covers the

Part 10:
Insurance
and
Secured
Trans-
actions

542

goods that the ship is carrying, and *freight insurance* covers the income that the shipowner expects to receive for carrying the cargo. *Perils-of-the-sea* coverage has been traditionally held to insure only against extraordinary perils such as shipwreck, foundering, stranding, collision, and damage resulting from violent wind and waves that constitute a peril of the sea. It does not cover ordinary perils which every vessel regularly and ordinarily encounters, such as depreciation, wear and tear, rot, worms, and similar perils. Ocean marine insurance policies very often contain old-fashioned, unwieldy language that was put into standard use by Lloyds of London in 1779. Since every word and comma in the standard policy has been interpreted by the courts over the years and their meaning established, insurers today are reluctant to make changes in the old-fashioned language. For this reason, marine insurance policies are sometimes difficult to read and understand by the average person.

B. Inland Marine Insurance

Inland marine insurance first developed to meet the need of carriers and shippers to place insurance on goods moved by rail, truck, and air transportation. At that time, most insurance companies insured only property at a fixed location. They were not used to insuring property that was moved about. Since ocean marine insurance companies had a good deal of experience in insuring property that moved on the ocean, it was only natural for them to enter the field of insuring property that moved on land. Similarly, they were used to writing insurance on new and unusual items, which was not true with other insurance companies. Thus, inland marine insurance underwriters often insure unusual items, such as bridges and tunnels, as well as property that does not stay in a fixed location.

In addition to insuring shippers and carriers against loss of their property, inland marine policies are often written to cover such items as jewelry, fine arts, musical instruments, and wedding presents. Also covered are customers' goods in the possession of bailees, such as fur storage houses and dry cleaners. Some inland marine policies cover against named perils (specific items listed in the policy), while others cover all risks with certain stated exceptions.

● Kimball owned a valuable stamp collection which she inherited from her grandfather. To protect the collection, her insurance broker obtained a stamp-collection floater policy from an inland marine underwriter. The policy insured her stamp collection but excluded "fading, creasing, denting, scratching, tearing, thinning, transfer of colors, wear, tear, inherent defect, dampness, extremes of temperature, moths, vermin, gradual depreciation or deterioration or damage sustained from handling or while being worked upon and resulting therefrom."

A *floater policy* is one which insures property that cannot be covered by specific insurance because the property is constantly changing in either value or location. A *personal property floater* covers all kinds of personal property, not just certain stated items, as would be covered by a camera floater or a fur floater.

40-5. Automobile Insurance

Among other coverage, automobile insurance provides for indemnity against losses resulting from fire, theft, or collision of motor vehicles and damages arising out of injury by motor vehicles to the person or the property of another.

A. Kinds of Automobile Insurance

The most common types of automobile insurance are:

○ Bodily injury liability insurance
○ Property damage liability insurance
○ Collision insurance
○ Comprehensive coverage
○ Medical payments insurance
○ Uninsured motorist insurance
○ No-fault insurance

1. Bodily Injury Liability Insurance. *Bodily injury liability insurance* covers the risk of bodily injury or death to the insured's passengers, to pedestrians, or to the occupants of other cars arising from the negligent operation of the insured's motor vehicle. Under liability insurance the insurer is liable for damages up to the limit of the insurance purchased. The insurance company also must provide attorneys for the insured's defense in any civil court action. Obviously, the company hopes to introduce a good defense for the insured, since it will have to pay any final judgment handed down by the jury or judge.

2. Property Damage Liability Insurance. *Property damage liability insurance* provides protection when other people bring claims or lawsuits against the insured for damaging property of theirs, such as a car, a fence, or a tree. The person bringing the claim or suit must prove that the driver of the motor vehicle was at fault.

● In parking her car on a hill in the center of Duluth, Hortin failed to engage the emergency brake. The car rolled down the hill, hitting a passing car, wrecking both cars, and injuring the occupants of the other car. Hortin's bodily injury liability insurance would cover claims made by the injured persons, and her property damage liability insurance would cover damages to the other car. Hortin's own car is not covered by the liability policy.

3. Collision Insurance. *Collision insurance* provides against any loss arising from damage to the insured's automobile caused by accidental collision with another object or with any part of the roadbed, or by an upset, such as a turning on its side. Liability under collision insurance is limited to the insured's car.

Unless there is a provision in the policy to the contrary, the company is still liable even when the collision that caused the loss occurred while the insured was violating the law, for example, driving recklessly, driving inattentively, or speeding. Although the insured may be found guilty of such charges, this will not necessarily relieve the insurer of liability for damages claimed.

In determining the amount of an insurance company's liability for damage to an automobile, the maximum liability is the cash value of the car before the collision. Quite often, to obtain lower-premium insurance, the owner of the car will buy *deductible collision insurance.* Under this policy, the insured person typically pays the first $50 or $100 of the loss, and the insurer is liable only for the remainder up to the amount specified in the policy. Some policies include *coinsurance clauses,* whereby the insured person bears a certain proportion of each loss, such as 20 or 25 percent, and the insurer pays the difference up to the maximum liability indicated in the policy.

Part 10:
Insurance
and
Secured
Trans-
actions

544

4. Comprehensive Coverage. *Comprehensive coverage* provides protection against loss when the insured's car is lost or damaged because of fire, lightning, flood, hail, windstorm, riot, vandalism, and theft. The insurance company's liability is limited to the actual cash value of the vehicle at the time of the loss.

5. Medical Payments Insurance. *Medical payments insurance* pays for medical (and sometimes funeral) expenses resulting from bodily injuries to anyone occupying the policyholder's car at the time of an accident. In some states it pays for the medical bills of all family members who are struck by a car or who are riding in someone else's car when it is involved in an accident.

6. Uninsured-Motorist Insurance. *Uninsured-motorist insurance* provides protection against the risk of being injured by an uninsured motorist. The coverage applies when the person who caused the accident was at fault and had no bodily injury liability insurance to cover the loss. It protects the insured, the insured's spouse, relatives in the same household, and any other person occupying an insured automobile. It also protects people who are injured by hit-and-run drivers. No coverage is provided, however, to persons injured in an automobile used without the permission of the insured or the insured's spouse. In addition, uninsured-motorist insurance provides no reimbursement for damages to the insured's property.

7. No-Fault Insurance. *Under no-fault insurance,* drivers collect damages and medical expenses from their own insurance carriers regardless of who is at fault in an accident. This helps to cut down on fraudulent and excessively high claims. It also eliminates costly litigation needed to determine the negligence or lack of negligence of people involved in automobile accidents. Instead, it requires the insurer to pay all claims, within certain limits, without regard to negligence or fault. Injured parties, under this system, lose their right to bring suit against people whom they believe have been negligent toward them. Their only recourse is against their own insurance company for an amount of money determined according to guidelines set by state statute.

● Porter collided with a car driven by Reed, causing a great deal of damage to both cars and physical injuries to Reed. It was very difficult to determine who was at fault in this accident. Under no-fault insurance, both Porter and Reed would recover damages from their own insurers. In states without this legislation, no recovery would be allowed either driver until responsibility was determined by court action or out-of-court agreement.

No-fault insurance laws vary from state to state. Some cover both bodily injury and property damage. Others limit coverage to bodily injury. In general, they all do the following:

○ Provide for an amount to be paid for medical expenses, or in the case of death, funeral expenses.
○ Provide for an amount to be paid for lost income to an injured wage earner.
○ Provide for an amount to be paid to a person to perform essential services that an injured non-income producer (homemaker) is unable to perform.
○ Establish a threshold for suit, that is, set conditions under which injured parties may bring suit against alleged *tortfeasors* (people who commit torts). The

conditions usually include death, permanent injury or disfigurement, or a specified amount of medical expenses.

B. Financial Responsibility Laws

Some states have enacted laws that either require all automobiles to be covered by bodily injury liability and property damage liability insurance or provide penalties for drivers who are not financially responsible. These laws are made necessary by the great increase in accidents involving motor vehicles, often caused not only by negligent drivers but also by financially irresponsible ones.

Understanding Legal Terms

Define, identify, or explain the following terms:

annuity contract
bodily injury
   liability insurance
cash surrender value
coinsurance clause
comprehensive
   insurance
   coverage

convertibility clause
double indemnity
endowment policy
floater policy
inland marine
   insurance
limited-payment life
   insurance

major medical
   expense insurance
no-fault insurance
ocean marine
   insurance
partial disability
property damage
   liability insurance

straight life
   insurance
term insurance
total disability
uninsured-motorist
   insurance

Questions for Review and Discussion

1. Name the five most common types of life insurance policies, and briefly describe each type.

2. Discuss the advantages of term insurance over other kinds of life insurance.

3. Why are the waiver-of-premium option and the guaranteed-insurability options popular optional provisions of life insurance policies?

4. Distinguish between accidental bodily injury and bodily injuries effected solely through accidental means.

5. What other losses, in addition to those directly attributed to fire, are covered by most fire insurance policies?

6. Distinguish between an ordinary fire insurance policy and a homeowner's policy.

7. Describe how inland marine insurance first developed, and discuss the kinds of risks that this insurance covers.

8. Name seven kinds of automobile insurance, and discuss the risks covered by each of these policies.

9. How does a collision policy differ from a liability policy in automobile insurance? Give an example.

10. Distinguish between hull insurance, cargo insurance, and freight insurance.

Analyzing Cases

1. Moore named his wife, Mary, as the beneficiary of his life insurance policy. He was murdered, and his wife was convicted of the murder. After her conviction, while in prison, Mary claimed the proceeds of the insurance policy. Is she entitled to the money?

Why or why not? ● *Moore v. Moore*, 186 S.E.2d 531 (Ga. 1971)

2. Pauline M. Davis, who was named as the beneficiary of her son's life insurance policy, sought to recover the face value of the policy

plus double indemnity for death caused by accidental means. Her son was shot and killed by a police officer while he was committing two serious felonies, assault by means of a dangerous weapon (a gun) and attempted murder. A clause in the policy limited the amount payable to premiums paid "if the insured dies by his own hand or act, whether sane or insane," within two years of the date of issue of the policy. The policy had been in effect for over three years. A double indemnity benefit provision in the policy was excluded when death "is caused by accidental means if such death results, directly or indirectly, or wholly or partially from suicide, or attempt thereat, while sane or insane, from committing an assault or a felony or from participating in a riot or insurrection." The insurance company refused to pay anything on the policy except the amount of premiums that had been paid by the insured. Is Mrs. Davis entitled to the face value of the policy? Is she entitled to double indemnity? Explain. ● *Davis v. Boston Mutual Life Ins. Co.*, 351 N.E.2d 207 (Mass. 1976)

3. Edwards advertised his car for sale. Davis responded to the ad and, after some negotiations on price, agreed to buy it. Edwards signed the title and gave it to Davis along with the possession of the car. Davis gave Edwards a check for $3,400. This check was returned by Edwards's bank marked "insufficient funds." Neither Davis nor the car could be found. Will Edwards's comprehensive insurance (which included "theft," without defining the term) cover the loss? Explain. ● *Edwards v. State Farm Mut. Auto. Ins. Co.*, 296 N.W.2d 804 (Iowa 1980)

4. Bayer took his car to Whitaker's auto repair shop for repairs. Whitaker took the car for a test drive, with Bayer seated in the passenger seat. During the test drive, a car operated by another person drove on the wrong side of the road and collided with Bayer's vehicle, injuring Bayer. Neither the Bayer vehicle nor the vehicle owned by the wrongdoer was insured. Whitaker carried insurance on his own vehicles, including uninsured-motorist insurance. Can Bayer recover from Whitaker's insurance company under the uninsured-motorist provision of the policy? Why or why not? ● *Bayer v. Travelers Indemnity Co.*, 267 S.E.2d 91 (Va. 1980)

5. Howard, a member of the U.S. Air Force at the time of his death, was in the crew of a four-engine radar patrol aircraft which because of mechanical difficulty was forced to ditch into the ocean. Howard and three other crew members survived the crash uninjured. They were wearing life jackets and Air Force exposure suits. They stayed in the ocean throughout the night, a period of eight to ten hours. Eventually, water seeped through Howard's exposure suit, and by the time the men were rescued by a West German destroyer, Howard had died. His death, according to the medical examiner's certificate, resulted from "asphyxia due to drowning; overexposure." The beneficiary of his life insurance policy sought to recover under an accidental death benefit. The policy stated, "No accidental death benefit will be payable if death resulted from travel or flight in, or descent from, any aircraft of which the Insured was a pilot, officer, or member of the crew of the military, naval, or air forces of any country." The beneficiary claims that death was caused by the malfunction of the exposure suit rather than the ditching of the airplane. Why is the court's finding as to the legal cause of death critical to the outcome of this case? Do you think the court would allow Howard's beneficiary to recover under the claim of accidental death? Why or why not? ● *Howard v. Equitable Life Assurance Soc'y of U.S.*, 274 N.E.2d 819 (Mass. 1971)

6. Larson acquired a Bantam C-450 hydraulic backhoe, which he loaded onto a lowboy trailer (a low-slung trailer used to transport construction equipment). As he drove his tractor towing the trailer along a major highway, the backhoe collided with a bridge abutment, sustaining damage to the extent of $18,300. Neither the lowboy nor the tractor

pulling it collided with the bridge. The backhoe was insured under a floater policy which read in part: "This policy insures against direct loss or damage by (h) Collision, Derailment or Overturning of land conveyances while the insured property is being transported thereon." The insurance company refused to pay for the loss, claiming that there was no collision, derailment, or overturning of a land conveyance (the tractor or lowboy trailer) transporting the insured property. Should Larson recover from the insurance company? Why or why not? • *Larson v. Travelers Indemnity Co.,* 294 So.2d 702 (Fla. 1974)

7. Vining's boat, the *Connelly-Kay,* sank in the Atchafalaya River at Berwick, Louisiana, while moored at a 90 degree angle to the bank. The night before, at about 9:30 p.m., the boat was inspected by a crew member, and its engine compartment was dry. The next morning, at 4:30 a.m., it was found sunk in about 10 feet of water. The sinking occurred during a period of high water when considerable logs and debris floated down the river. There was also heavy boat traffic on the river which caused heavy wave washes. The vessel sank because a jam nut, which secures the stuffing box or packing gland (through which the shaft penetrates the hull), came loose allowing water to enter through the stuffing box. Vining believes that the perils-of-the-sea clause in his marine hull insurance policy covers this loss. The insurance company disagrees. How would you decide? Explain. • *Vining v. Security Ins. Co.,* 252 So.2d 754 (La. 1971)

8. Lynas entered into an agreement to sell his house to Smith. Under the agreement, Lynas was permitted to remain in the house for sixty days after the closing date, and Smith was to obtain insurance coverage on the property. During the sixty-day period, Lynas moved into an apartment, leaving many of his household items and personal possessions in his former house. He notified the oil company that the house had been sold, and asked it to discontinue service. Soon thereafter, he fell in his apartment and had to be hospitalized. While he was in the hospital, the oil supply to the house ran dry, causing the heat to go off in the dwelling. The water pipes froze and burst, causing extensive damage. Smith's insurance policy on the dwelling excluded losses "caused by and resulting from freezing while the building covered is vacant or unoccupied." The insurance company refused to pay, claiming that the dwelling was unoccupied. Do you agree with the insurance company? Why or why not? • *Smith v. Lumbermen's Mut. Ins. Co.,* 300 N.W.2d 457 (Mich. 1981)

Chapter 41   Security Devices

Very few people have enough money in cash to pay the full purchase price at the time they buy a house. This is also true in the case of other expensive consumer needs such as automobiles, household furnishings, and the like. Similarly, businesses often do not have cash on hand to pay outright for many of their needs such as inventory, equipment, and supplies. Farmers likewise are often short of available cash prior to the harvest and sale of their animals or crops. They all must borrow the money from such places as banks, credit unions, mortgage companies, and insurance companies, or from private parties. In addition, sellers of goods must often sell their goods on credit, hoping to receive the money at a later date from their buyers.

Lenders of money and people who extend credit need to have security—some way of getting their money back in case the borrower or debtor does not pay. Mortgages and security interests are used for this purpose. A *secured loan* is one in which creditors have something of value from which they can be paid if the debtor does not pay. An *unsecured loan* does not have this important feature.

41-1. Real Property as Security

A *mortgage* is a transfer of an interest in property for the purpose of creating a security for a debt. The one who borrows the money (the *mortgagor*) conveys his or her interest in the property to the lender (the *mortgagee*) while at the same time retaining possession of the property. If the mortgagor does not pay the money back according to the terms of the agreement, the mortgagee can have the property sold to satisfy the obligation. Prior to the adoption of the UCC, when personal property (in contrast to real property) was used as security for the loan, a *chattel mortgage* was created. This is now called a security interest, which is discussed below. Real property mortgages are discussed here.

A mortgage on real estate creates a lien on the property and gives the lender the right to have the property sold if the debt is not paid. It creates a secured interest in real estate, but it does not constitute any security in other assets of the debtor. The mortgage usually provides that, in the event of default in the payment of any installment of principal or interest, the entire amount of the debt shall become immediately due and payable. It also usually provides for payment by the mortgagor of taxes, assessments, insurance, and other expenses.

Accompanying a mortgage is a bond, or note, executed by the mortgagor to the lender, making the mortgagor personally liable for the debt.

● Morea bought a house in Pendleton Acres. Purchase price was $55,000, toward which Morea used his savings of $20,000. Home Savings and Loan Association loaned the buyer $35,000 on a note secured by a mortgage on the house. Morea defaulted on the mortgage, and the house was sold to cover the loan. The house actually brought $4,850 less than Morea owed. Morea will be held personally liable for the $4,850, with interest, until the debt is cleared.

A. Types of Mortgages

There are different types of real property mortgages. Some of the most common types are discussed here.

1. Conventional Mortgage. A *conventional mortgage* is one which has no government backing by way of either insurance or guarantee. The loan which such a mortgage secures is made by private lenders, and the risks of loss are borne exclusively by them. In the past, conventional mortgages had fixed interest rates which stayed the same during the life of the mortgage regardless of fluctuations in the economy. Rapid inflation in recent years, however, has resulted in the creation of variations to the fixed-interest-rate mortgage.

2. Variable-Rate Mortgage. A *variable-rate mortgage* has a rate of interest which changes according to fluctuations in the index to which it is tied. The index rate may be the bank's prime rate, or the Federal Reserve Board discount rate. As the index rate goes up and down, so does the rate of interest charged on the loan. This rate may be more or less than in the index, but varies with it.

3. Graduated-Payment Mortgage. A *graduated-payment mortgage* has a fixed interest rate during the life of the mortgage; however, the monthly payments made by the mortgagor increase over the term of the loan. In the first years of the mortgage, the payments are low. The payments gradually increase over time, usually reaching a plateau at which the payments remain fixed. This type of mortgage is advantageous for young people, whose income may be expected to increase as their mortgage payments increase.

4. Balloon-Payment Mortgage. A *balloon-payment mortgage* is one which has relatively low fixed payments during the life of the mortgage followed by one large final (balloon) payment. The mortgage has a fixed interest rate but is written for a short time period, such as five years. At the end of the time period, the mortgagor usually must find new financing, either with the same or with a different lender, at the then current interest rate.

5. FHA and VA Mortgages. Some mortgages, although given by private lenders, are backed by federal agencies. The Federal Housing Administration (FHA) and the Veterans Administration (VA) are responsible to the lending institution in the event of a mortgagor's default and foreclosure on an FHA or VA mortgage. The U.S. government, through these agencies, reimburses the mortgagee for any loss and takes over the property. Such properties are then offered for sale to interested buyers to recover the loss that had been sustained by the government.

6. Deed of Trust. In some states, a deed of trust is used instead of a mortgage. Under a *deed of trust,* the secured property is conveyed to a disinterested third party, known as the trustee, who holds the property for the benefit of a creditor or creditors. In the event of default, it is the duty of the trustee to foreclose upon the property. The provisions of many deeds of trust allow the trustee to sell the property at a foreclosure sale without the requirement of judicial process.

Part 10:
Insurance
and
Secured
Trans-
actions

550

B. Recording the Mortgage

Like a deed, the mortgage must be in writing; must be under seal; and must be executed, acknowledged, and recorded. Recording a mortgage has the effect of serving notice on any third parties who may be interested in purchasing the property or in lending money to the owner that the mortgagee has an interest in the realty covered by the mortgage.

If the mortgage is not recorded and a subsequent mortgage is given on the same property, the new mortgage would be superior to the first one, provided the second mortgagee paid value, had no knowledge of the first mortgage, and recorded the mortgage first.

● Lacey borrowed $5,000 from First Savings and Loan. She gave a first mortgage as security. First Savings neglected to have the mortgage recorded in the county recorder's office. Lacey later sold the house to Samuels, whose attorney found no mortgage recorded against the property. Samuels will take the property, free of the mortgage. First Savings, of course, may collect the $5,000, with interest, by enforcing Lacey's note.

Sometimes an owner of realty may execute a second mortgage and subsequent mortgages on the property. If all the mortgages are recorded, the holders of second and subsequent mortgages may exercise their rights against the property only after the first or prior mortgages have been satisfied. Thus, if the first mortgagee causes the property to be sold and is paid off in full, the second and subsequent mortgagees take such rights in the proceeds of the sale as remain.

● Holden borrowed $10,000 from Central Savings Bank, giving a first mortgage on a business property as security. Five years later, he needed additional cash for alterations and improvements to the building. Marshallton Building and Loan took a second mortgage on the property and loaned Holden another $2,500. In the event of default and sale, Central Savings Bank will be paid any balance owed on the $10,000 mortgage. Any money remaining will be available for satisfying the $2,500 second mortgage.

C. Rights and Duties of the Mortgagor

By law and by agreement, the mortgagor has the following rights and duties in conjunction with a mortgage.

○ The right to the possession of the mortgaged property. The mortgagor continues to be the owner of the property, with right of possession.
○ The right to sell, lease, or assign the mortgaged property.

● Bankers Trust Company held a mortgage on a house owned by Hanscomb. Hanscomb rented the house to a tenant of whom the mortgagee disapproved. There were no restrictions in the mortgage or deed that restricted Hanscomb's right to rent the house to a tenant of her own choice.

○ The right to use the same property as security for second or third mortgages.
○ The duty to insure the premises for the benefit of the mortgagee, to the amount of the mortgaged debt.
○ The duty to preserve and maintain the mortgaged property for the benefit of the mortgagee's interest and security.

○ The duty to pay interest and payments on the principal according to the conditions of the bond or note.

○ The duty to make repairs and pay all taxes and assessments that may be levied against the property.

Mortgage terms usually prohibit the owner of the property from assigning or transferring the mortgage to a third party without the consent of the creditor. A creditor has the right to select the risks accepted in the repayment of money loaned to anyone.

1. Mortgage Insurance. The mortgagor often protects his or her spouse and children by taking out what is known as *mortgage insurance*. This is a term insurance policy which will pay off any of the remaining mortgage debt in the event of the mortgagor's death. Such policies are recommended not only as a benefit to the mortgagor's estate but as security to the mortgagee as well.

● The Padgetts lived in a house on which they had a $20,000 mortgage. The monthly payments to a home savings and loan society reduced the amount of the debt monthly. The couple purchased a term insurance policy that was written to pay the savings and loan association any remaining balance owed on the mortgage in the event of the insured's death.

2. Equity of Redemption. By statute law in many states, a mortgagor who has defaulted on payments to the mortgagee is given a certain period in which to redeem property by paying the amount due with interest. This right to redeem is known as the mortgagor's *equity of redemption*.

If the property is sold as a result of foreclosure, the statute provides that a deed is not to be executed to the purchaser immediately after the sale. It also provides that the mortgagor may recover the property within a certain period by paying the total debt plus the costs of sale. If the mortgagor fails to redeem the property within the allotted time, it becomes the absolute property of the purchaser.

● After defaulting on the mortgage, Benson lost his house through foreclosure and sale by the bank that held the mortgage and bond. The property brought $18,000 at public auction. Benson's fortunes changed during the ensuing eight months. Before the end of the year, Benson succeeded in having the house returned by paying the purchaser $18,000 plus the interest accrued over the eight-month period.

D. Rights and Duties of the Mortgagee

Both state and federal legislation prohibits lenders from discriminating against borrowers because of race, creed, color, sex, or ethnic background. Thus, a lender may not refuse a mortgage to a woman making application for a loan under a real estate mortgage. While the loan may be refused for reasons other than sex, basing rejection on sex alone subjects the lending institution to a heavy fine.

The mortgagee has the unrestricted right to sell, assign, or transfer the bond and mortgage to a third party. Whatever rights the mortgagee had in the mortgage are then the rights of the assignee. The only way the mortgagor may bar such an assignment would be to make full payment of the mortgage debt.

Part 10:
Insurance
and
Secured
Trans-
actions

552

1. Foreclosure. If the mortgagor fails to pay the debt when due or fails to perform other covenants or conditions in the mortgage, such as a condition to pay a tax escrow, the mortgagee has the right to apply to a court to have the property sold. This is known as the *right of foreclosure.* A mortgage is foreclosed when the mortgagee proves the amount of the unpaid debt (including interest and other charges), and the property is sold by and under the direction of a court of equity. The proceeds realized from the sale are then applied to the payment of the debt. Any money remaining after the claims of the mortgagee have been satisfied goes to the mortgagor or to the second and subsequent mortgagees.

Frequently, a mortgage contains a provision giving the mortgagee a power of sale without requiring that an action of foreclosure be brought.

If the amount realized at the sale is less than the amount due on the foreclosed mortgage, a *deficiency decree* or a *deficiency judgment* is entered against the mortgagor for the remainder. If the mortgagor does not or cannot pay the judgment, the court may garnishee the borrower's salary; that is, it may order an amount to be taken regularly from salary or wages until the amount of the judgment is fully paid.

2. Real Estate Settlement Procedures Act. The Real Estate Settlement Procedures Act, known as RESPA, was enacted to minimize "the unnecessary costs and difficulties of purchasing housing." It is designed to give greater protection to consumers. The act applies to all federally related mortgage loans which are secured by a first mortgage on residential real property including condominiums and cooperatives. The property must be designed principally for the occupancy of from one to four families. The Real Estate Settlement Procedures Act sets forth the following provisions:

○ The lender must provide the borrower with a booklet prepared by the U.S. Department of Housing and Urban Development (HUD). The booklet is designed to help borrowers understand the nature and costs of real estate settlement services.
○ The lender must provide the borrower with a good faith estimate of the amount or range of charges for specific settlement services. The estimate must be given to the borrower when the lender receives or prepares a written application for a loan.
○ The lender must fill out a form, known as the Uniform Settlement Statement, which spells out the settlement costs of the real property purchase. It must be made available to the borrower, if requested, on the day before the date of settlement.
○ Sellers may not require that, as a condition of sale, the buyer purchase title insurance from a company specified by the seller.
○ The lender may not collect from the buyer and hold in escrow more than one month's advance payment on taxes and property insurance.
○ Anyone connected with the settlement may be fined up to $10,000 if found guilty of participating in a scheme to kick back fees collected in the settlement process. This sometimes occurred when the seller required the buyer to purchase title insurance from a title company which the seller specified, a practice now banned.
○ Lenders must comply with state consumer protection laws whenever these are more stringent than the Real Estate Settlement Procedures Act.

3. Satisfaction. A mortgage becomes satisfied on payment of the entire debt or on performance of the obligation. When the debt is paid, the mortgagee, on demand of the mortgagor, must execute and deliver a certificate that the mortgage has been discharged or satisfied and may be so recorded.

E. Purchase by Mortgage Takeover

By consent of both the mortgagee and the purchaser of mortgaged property, existing mortgages are often permitted to remain on properties being sold. In such takeovers, the transfer of title to a new buyer is subject to the buyer's payment of the seller's mortgage at the existing rate of interest.

In purchasing a property already mortgaged, the buyer will either *assume the mortgage* or take the property *subject to the mortgage*. When buyers decide to assume the mortgage, they agree to pay it. When they take the property subject to a mortgage, the seller agrees to continue paying the debt.

41-2. Personal Property as Security

In the past various devices were used to give people security when they sold goods on credit. One commonly used security device was a *conditional sale,* in which goods were sold with the understanding that title remained with the seller until the purchase price was paid. Another method was a chattel mortgage, mentioned above, in which the buyer took title to the goods but gave a mortgage back to the seller. A third security device was a *bailment lease,* under which the buyer rented the goods from the seller. When the amount of the rental paid equaled the purchase price, the buyer could take title to the property by paying a token amount, usually $1. There was much confusion because each of the many different security devices was governed by a different set of rules which varied from state to state.

Article 9 of the UCC brings all the different security devices, or security interests, together under one law. A *security interest* means an interest in personal property or fixtures which secures payment or performance of an obligation [1-201(37)]. The property that is subject to the security interest is called *collateral.* A security interest is created by a written agreement, called a *security agreement,* which identifies the goods and is signed by the debtor. The lender or seller who holds the security interest is known as the *secured party.* A security interest is said to *attach* when the goods have become subject to the security interest. It is said to be *perfected* when the secured party has done everything that the law requires to give the secured party greater rights to the goods than others have.

A. Security Agreement

A security agreement is an agreement which creates or provides for a security interest [9-105(1)]. It must be in writing, signed by the debtor, and contain a description of the collateral that is used for security. When the security interest covers crops or timber, the security agreement must describe the land concerned [9-203(a)].

● Canna borrowed money from the First County National Bank & Trust Co. to buy a car. He signed a promissory note, and his title certificate contained a notation that

Part 10:
Insurance
and
Secured
Trans-
actions

554

the bank was a secured party. Later, when Canna defaulted on the note, the court held that the bank did not have a security interest in the automobile because no security agreement had been signed by the debtor. A promissory note signed by the debtor which does not contain language that grants or creates a security interest in the collateral is not a security agreement under the UCC. Similarly, a notation on the title certificate of an automobile that a person is a secured party does not create a security interest in that person's favor.

B. Attachment of a Security Interest

To be effective, a security interest must attach. This occurs when all the following conditions are met (9-203):

○ Either the collateral comes into the possession of the secured party by agreement or the debtor signs a security agreement as described above.

● Pell loaned Maddox $2,500 for one year at an agreed rate of interest. To secure the debt, Maddox gave Pell two diamond rings that she had inherited from her grandmother. It was agreed that the rings would be returned to Maddox upon payment of the debt on the maturity date of the loan. Pell's security interest in the rings attached when she took possession of them.

○ The secured party gives value.

● Watson TV & Appliance, Inc., sold Kendrick a 21-inch color television set on credit. To protect its interest, Watson took a security interest in the set by having Kendrick sign a security agreement. Value was given by Watson when it delivered the television set to Kendrick.

○ The debtor has rights in the collateral.

● In the cases above, Maddox had ownership rights in the diamond rings and Kendrick had similar rights in the television set.

Creditors may obtain security interests in after-acquired property of the debtor (9-204). This is done by placing a provision in the security agreement that the security interest of the creditor also applies to goods that the debtor acquires at a later date. This is particularly important to creditors who take security interests in inventory and other items that are sold and replaced within short periods of time. Security interests attach to after-acquired property as soon as the debtor has rights in the property.

C. Perfection of a Security Interest

A security interest is effective only between the debtor and creditor when it attaches. To be effective as to others who might claim the collateral, such as other creditors or people who buy the collateral from the debtor, another step must be taken. The security interest must be perfected. This is an extremely important step for secured parties to take to protect their interests in the collateral. There are three ways to perfect a security interest:

○ By attachment only
○ By possession of the collateral
○ By filing a financing statement in a public office

Sometimes the secured party has a choice as to which of the three methods to use. At other times there is no choice; one of the three methods is required. The method used depends on the type of collateral that is used as security.

1. Perfection by Attachment Alone. In limited situations, a security interest is perfected the moment it attaches, that is, as soon as the security interest comes into existence. One situation in which this occurs is when someone lends money or extends credit to a consumer and then takes a security interest in the goods that the consumer buys [9-302(1)(d)]. This is called a *purchase money security interest* and applies only to consumer goods. Goods are *consumer goods* if they are used or bought for use primarily for personal, family, or household purposes [9-109(1)]. Motor vehicles are excepted from this rule. Purchase money security interests in motor vehicles are not perfected by attachment alone.

● Dumas bought a late model Volvo from Allbright Motors. To pay for the vehicle, he borrowed $4,000 from his local bank. The bank took a security interest in the vehicle by entering into a security agreement with Dumas. Because the collateral for the security interest was a motor vehicle, the security interest did not become perfected the moment it attached. Instead, it was necessary for the bank to file a financing statement with a public office. This is discussed in detail below.

Similarly, purchase money security interests in fixtures are not perfected by attachment alone. Goods are *fixtures* when they become so related to particular real estate that an interest in them arises under real estate law [9-313(1)(a)].

2. Perfection by Possession. A security interest may be perfected when the secured party (or a bailee on behalf of the secured party) takes possession of the collateral (9-305). This is called a *pledge*. The borrower, or debtor, who gives up the property, is the *pledgor*. The lender, or creditor, is the *pledgee*.

● Bloomberg needed $75 to buy new textbooks for college. Rogers agreed to lend her the money if he could have her typewriter as security for the repayment of the $75. Rogers's security interest in the typewriter became perfected when he took possession of it.

A secured party who has possession of the collateral must take reasonable care of the property. Ordinary expenses incurred in its custody and preservation, including taxes and insurance, are chargeable to the debtor. The debtor assumes the risk of accidental loss beyond any insurance coverage (9-207).

3. Perfection by Filing. Security interests in most kinds of personal property are perfected by filing a financing statement in a public office. The office may be a central one (secretary of state's office) or a local one (county or city clerk's office) where the debtor resides or has a place of business. The proper office for filing depends on the type of collateral and varies from state to state. As a general rule, financing statements dealing with consumer goods and farming are filed locally; others are filed centrally. Table 41-1 defines the different kinds of collateral and indicates the method of perfecting security interests for each kind.

A financing statement must give the names of the debtor and the secured party. It must be signed by the debtor and give the address of the secured party from which information concerning the security interest may be obtained. It

Part 10:
Insurance
and
Secured
Trans-
actions

556

Table 41-1. Methods of Perfecting Security Interests

Type of Collateral	Definition	Method of Perfection
Goods	All things which are movable at the time the security interest attaches or which are fixtures	Filing or possession
Consumer goods	Goods used or bought primarily for personal, family, or household purposes	Attachment only for purchase money security interest; filing for motor vehicles
Farm products	Crops, farm livestock, and the products of a farmer	Filing
Inventory	Goods held for sale or lease or materials consumed in business	Filing, usually
Equipment	Goods used or bought for use primarily in a business (including farming or a profession)	Filing, usually
Accounts receivable	Money due on open accounts from debtors	Filing
Chattel paper	A writing evidencing both a debt and a security interest, such as a promissory note and a security agreement	Either filing or possession
Documents of title	Bills of lading, warehouse receipts	Either filing or possession for negotiable documents
Instruments	Negotiable instruments, securities, and any other writing which evidences a debt	Possession only
General intangibles	Patents, copyrights, etc.	Filing only

must also give a mailing address of the debtor and contain a statement indicating the types, or describing the items, of collateral. When the financing statement covers such things as crops, timber, minerals, oil, and gas, the statement must also contain a description of the real estate concerned (9-402).

4. Priorities and Claims. Frequently two or more parties claim a security interest in the same collateral. At other times, unsecured parties claim that they have better rights than secured parties. The UCC contains provisions to help resolve these conflicts (9-312). Some of the more important provisions, stating who prevails over whom in particular situations, are described below.

○ A perfected security interest prevails over an unperfected security interest.
○ When two or more parties have perfected security interests, the first to perfect prevails over the other parties.
○ When two or more parties have unperfected security interests in the same collateral, the first to attach prevails over the other parties.
○ Perfected security interests, lien creditors, trustees in bankruptcy, and buyers in the ordinary course of business prevail over unperfected security interests.
○ Buyers of goods in the ordinary course of business prevail over security interests in the seller's inventory.
○ A purchaser of second-hand consumer goods without knowledge of a security interest prevails over a security interest of a seller who perfected without filing.

D. The Floating-Lien Concept

Security agreements sometimes state that after-acquired property is covered by the agreement. This is called the *floating-lien concept.* It allows security interests to transfer from old property that is sold to new property that is bought later on (9-204).

● Surefire Sales Co. borrowed $5,000 from State Bank & Trust. As security for the loan, State Bank & Trust took a security interest in Surefire Sale's inventory. The security agreement contained an after-acquired property provision. Each time Surefire Sales Co. sold goods, State Bank & Trust lost its security interest in those goods. However, the bank automatically acquired a security interest in the new goods that Surefire Sales Co. bought to replace those that it had sold.

An important part of the floating-lien concept allows secured parties to retain a ten-day security interest in the proceeds of collateral that has been sold. *Proceeds* are whatever the debtor receives for the goods that are sold, such as cash or accounts receivable (agreements to pay later). In the above case, State Bank & Trust would have a security interest in the proceeds of each sale by Surefire Sales Co. for a period of ten days after each sale was made (9-306).

E. Protection of Certain Buyers

Sometimes the perfection of a security interest does not protect secured parties against claims of others. For example, when goods are bought from a person who is in the business of selling such goods, the buyer takes the goods free of all security interests. This is true even though the security interests are perfected [9-307(1)]. This type of buyer is called a *buyer in the ordinary course of business.* The exception is designed to protect people who buy goods from merchants. Customers can be assured that the goods they buy will not be taken from them to satifsy the merchant's obligations to other parties.

Even a buyer who does not buy in the ordinary course of business is given

Part 10:
Insurance
and
Secured
Trans-
actions

558

priority over secured creditors on certain occasions. In the case of consumer goods, buyers take them free of a security interest even though that interest is perfected (other than by filing) if they buy without knowledge of the security interest. Buyers must give value for the goods, and the goods must be for their own personal, family, or household purposes [9-307(2)].

● Clearview Appliance Inc. sold a color television set to Garza on credit, taking a purchase money security interest in the set as collateral. Since the TV set was a consumer good, Clearview's security interest was perfected without filing. Shortly thereafter, Garza sold the set to his neighbor, Rueda, for her own personal use. She had no knowledge of Clearview's security interest in the set. Rueda took the TV set free of Clearview's security interest. Although Clearview was not required to file a financing statement in a public office, had it done so, its security interest would have prevailed over Rueda's interest in the set.

F. Default of the Debtor

If a debtor defaults by failing to make payments when due, the secured party may satisfy the debt by taking possession of the collateral. Because of the difficulties of doing this, the perfection of a security interest by possession, as in a pledge, has an advantage over other types of perfection. Collateral may be repossessed without judicial process if it can be done without breaching the peace. Otherwise legal process must be used.

● Faircloth bought a new car with money she borrowed from Baybank. She signed a security agreement with the bank, which took a security interest in the automobile. The security interest was perfected by filing with the secretary of state's office. Within six months of taking out the loan, Faircloth stopped making payments. The bank telephoned her several times and wrote her a letter in an attempt to work out arrangements for payment but received no response. The bank's agent took the vehicle from its parking place near Faircloth's place of employment and drove it to the bank's storage area, where it was placed under lock and key. The repossession was within the law because there was no breach of the peace.

After obtaining the goods, the secured party may keep them (with some exceptions) or sell them. If the secured party decides to keep the goods, the debtor and any other secured creditors must be notified of this fact. If any of them object within twenty-one days, the secured party must sell the collateral and apply the proceeds of the sale to satisfy the debt. The secured party must account to the debtor (and any other secured creditors who demand it) for any surplus. The debtor, unless otherwise agreed, is liable for any deficiency. If there is a sale, it may be public (an auction) or private as long as the terms of the sale are reasonable. If the goods are consumer goods and the debtor has paid 60 percent of the cash price or more, the secured party cannot keep the goods. They must be sold. The debtor is entitled to receive any surplus of a sale after expenses have been paid, the debt has been satisfied, and any other security interests have been paid off. The debtor is entitled to be notified of any such sale, and in most cases, has the right to purchase the goods back (9-504).

Understanding Legal Terms

Define, identify, or explain the following terms:

balloon payment mortgage
buyer in the ordinary course of business
chattel mortgage
collateral
conditional sale
equity of redemption
mortgage
mortgagee
mortgagor
perfected
pledge
pledgee
pledgor
purchase money security interest
right of foreclosure
secured party
security agreement
security interest
variable-rate mortgage

Questions for Review and Discussion

1. In what principal way does a conventional mortgage differ from an FHA or VA mortgage?

2. What is the difference between a variable-rate mortgage and a graduated-payment mortgage?

3. Discuss the importance of recording a mortgage in a public office in the county where a property is located.

4. How does equity of redemption provide relief to a mortgagor whose property is sold through foreclosure of the mortgage?

5. Discuss the mortgagor's obligations when, in a foreclosure sale, the property is sold for less than the existing debt.

6. In the purchase of real property, what is the difference between assuming the mortgage and buying the property subject to the mortgage?

7. Name three security devices that were used in the past, and explain what the UCC did with these devices.

8. What conditions must be met for a security interest to attach?

9. Explain the reason for perfecting a security interest and describe the different ways that this may be done.

10. What right does a secured party have if a debtor defaults by failing to make payments when due?

Analyzing Cases

1. Putignano gave a second mortgage on his real estate to Petti. The mortgage required monthly payments to be made by the fourteenth day of each month and contained a thirty-day grace period. Putignano made payments according to the following schedule:

Due Date	Expiration of Grace Period	Payment Date
Nov. 14, 1976	Dec. 14, 1976	Dec. 6, 1976
Dec. 14, 1976	Jan. 13, 1977	Jan. 31, 1977
Jan. 14, 1977	Feb. 13, 1977	Feb. 28, 1977
Feb. 14, 1977	Mar. 16, 1977	Apr. 9, 1977
Mar. 14, 1977	Apr. 13, 1977	May 1, 1977

Putignano's April payment, due no later than May 14, 1977, was not made until May 31, 1977. Petti brought foreclosure proceedings on May 19, 1977. Putignano made further payments so that his payments were current by the time of the trial date. He claims that the mortgage cannot be foreclosed because his payments are currently up to date. Is Putignano correct? Explain. ● *Petti v. Putignano*, 393 N.E.2d 935 (Mass. 1979)

2. Bloom executed a real estate mortgage in favor of Lakeshore Commercial Finance Corporation on September 16, 1974. On October 4, 1974, Bloom executed another mortgage on the same described real estate in favor of Northridge Bank. Northridge, with-

out notice of the mortgage to Lakeshore, recorded its mortgage at 9:28 a.m. on October 25, 1974. On that same date, at 3:07 p.m., the prior mortgage executed in favor of Lakeshore was recorded. Bloom defaulted on the mortgages. The value of the real estate was insufficient to fully satisfy both mortgagees. Which party has a superior interest, Lakeshore or Northridge? Why? ● *Northridge Bank v. Lakeshore Com. Fin. Corp.*, 365 N.E.2d 382 (Ill. 1977)

3. Virginia Cramer's mortgage contained a provision requiring her to pay monthly tax and insurance escrow payments to the bank in addition to principal and interest. Cramer paid the principal and interest regularly but refused to pay the tax and insurance escrow payments. The bank brought foreclosure proceedings. Did it have the right to foreclose on Cramer's mortgage? Explain. ● *Cramer v. Metro. Sav. & Loan Ass'n*, 258 N.W.2d 20 (Mich. 1977)

4. Adams sold a business and some real estate to Lincoln for $33,000. She received $10,000 in cash and took a second mortgage on the real estate for the balance. A first mortgage on the property was held by Henrietta Silverstein and Libby Baumholtz. When Lincoln defaulted on the first mortgage, Silverstein and Baumholtz foreclosed. Lincoln's real property was sold at a sheriff's sale. The proceeds of the sale were not sufficient to pay the full amount owed to the first mortgagees, Silverstein and Baumholtz. Lincoln was still indebted to them for $5,700.

They claim that they have a perfected security interest for this amount in the rest of Lincoln's assets. Do you agree? Why or why not? ● *Adams v. Lierka Corp.*, 345 A.2d 632 (Pa. 1975)

5. In exchange for certain performance bonds (assurances that a job will be done), Maple Contractors, Inc., gave Reliance Insurance Company a security interest in its equipment. The insurance company filed a financing statement with the secretary of state's office. The financing statement was signed by the insurance company, but it was not signed by Maple Contractors, Inc. Was the security interest perfected? Explain. ● *Matter of Maple Contractors, Inc.*, 411 A.2d 1186 (N.J. 1979)

6. U.S. Electronics, a Missouri corporation with a place of business in DeKalb County, Georgia, borrowed money from a Missouri bank. The corporation gave the bank a security interest in all its machinery and equipment. The bank filed a financing statement in Fulton County rather than DeKalb County as required by law. U.S. Electronics defaulted on the loan and fell behind on its rent. The corporation's landlord obtained a judgment against it for past due rent, becoming a lien creditor. The landlord claims priority over the bank to the proceeds of a sheriff's sale of the machinery and equipment, arguing that the bank's security interest was not perfected. Do you agree? Why or why not? ● *United States v. Waterford No. 2 Office Center*, 271 S.E.2d 790 (Ga. 1980)

Part 10

Case Briefs

**Edison v. Reliable Life Ins. Co.,
495 F.Supp. 484 (W.D. Wash. 1980)**
Edison lost his life when his sport parachute failed to open while he was engaging in a sport parachuting event. His life insurance policy limited aviation coverage to riding as a passenger (and not as a pilot or member of the crew) in a civil aircraft having a valid airworthiness certificate. The policy specifically excluded injury sustained while riding as a passenger or otherwise in any other vehicle or "device for aerial navigation." The insurance company refused to pay Edison's beneficiary, Gaylene Edison, the proceeds of the policy.

Plaintiff's Position: Gaylene Edison contended that a sport parachute is not a device for aerial navigation and that, therefore, injuries resulting from riding therein are not excluded from the policy. In support of this position, she pointed out that sport parachutes are not mentioned specifically and that the language of the exclusion is ambiguous and should be interpreted most favorably for the insured.

Defendant's Position: The insurance company contended that at the time of his death the insured was engaged in aviation and that he was not riding as a passenger in a civil aircraft having a valid airworthiness certificate.

Legal Issue: Was the insured, at the time of his death, engaged in aviation while riding as a passenger in a civil aircraft having a valid airworthiness certificate, and was the parachute a device for aerial navigation and thus excluded from coverage?

Court Decision: The insured, at the time of his death, was engaged in aviation, but he was not riding as a passenger in a civil aircraft having a valid airworthiness certificate. His death, therefore, was not the result of any risk against which the policy insured him. Furthermore, the insured's parachute was a device for aerial navigation and thus excluded from coverage.

Court Reasoning: Webster defines *aircraft* as a "weight-carrying structure for navigation of the air that is supported either by its own buoyancy or by the dynamic action of the air against its surfaces." It seems clear, therefore, that at the time of the accident, the insured was engaged in an activity the attendant insurable risks related to which fell within "aviation coverage" as used in the policy.

In the court's view, any parachute is a device for aerial navigation. Webster defines *navigation* as "the act or practice of navigating." *Navigate* is defined as "to travel by ship." *Aerial navigation* therefore means "to travel by air."

If persons riding as passengers in certified aircraft are forced to use a parachute to save themselves from disaster because of some crisis which affects them as passengers, they might well be covered by the policy until they safely reach the ground. But people riding as passengers in certified aircraft lose their status as such when they voluntarily leave the plane, choosing an alternate means of returning to earth. In the former illustration, if the parachute fails to open, the insured dies as a consequence of having been riding as a passenger in a certified aircraft. In the latter illustration, if the parachute fails to open, the insured dies as a consequence of riding in a device for aerial navigation which has been specifically excluded from the policy.

Pilotte v. Aetna Cas. & Sur. Co.
427 N.E.2d 746 (Mass. 1981)
Pilotte was seated in an unregistered and un-insured vehicle stored on private property. A motor vehicle owned and operated by Harrison left the roadway, went onto the private property, and struck the stored vehicle with such impact that Pilotte was killed. Pilotte's widow and administratrix, Kathleen, claimed entitlement to the personal injury protection benefits relating to pedestrians provided by Harrison's insurance policy. The policy defined a pedestrian as "a person who is walking or who is operating a bicycle, tricycle or similar vehicle, or a person on horseback or in a vehicle drawn by an animal." The term *pedestrian* as defined by that state's no-fault statute also included "persons operating bicycles, tricycles, and similar vehicles and persons upon horseback or in vehicles drawn by horses or other draft animals." The insurance company refused to pay the claim.

Plaintiff's Position: Pilotte's widow claimed that, at the time of his death, Pilotte was a pedestrian within the meaning of the insurance policy and that she was, therefore, entitled to insurance benefits.

Defendant's Position: The insurance company claimed that Pilotte was not a pedestrian, at the time of his death, within the meaning of the insurance policy.

Legal Issue: Is a person who is seated in an unregistered and uninsured vehicle stored on private property a pedestrian within the purview of an insurance policy and thus entitled to insurance benefits?

Court Decision: No. Pilotte was not a pedestrian when the insured's vehicle struck him, and therefore his estate is not entitled to insurance benefits.

Court Reasoning: A person seated inside a motor vehicle cannot be a pedestrian. The term *pedestrian,* from the Latin word *pedester,* means one who travels on foot. If the legislature intended to include, within the definition of *pedestrian,* those people inside parked motor vehicles, it could have expressed such an intent. The court said that it could not extend the plain meaning of the terms of the statute to accomplish a result not expressed.

United States Fire Ins. Co.
v. Schnackenberg,
411 N.E.2d 1057 (Ill. 1980)
Maria Strehlow was struck and injured by a bicycle ridden by Mark Schnackenberg. The accident occurred approximately $2\frac{1}{2}$ blocks from Mark's house, which was owned by his mother, Barbara Schnackenberg. The insurance policy on Schnackenberg's house covered injuries "arising out of the ownership, maintenance or use of the insured premises and all operations necessary or incidental thereto." *Insured premises* was defined in an endorsement on the policy as "the premises described below or designated in the policy as subject to this endorsement, including the ways immediately adjoining and including garages and stables incidental thereto, gardens incidental thereto on land now owned by the named insured, and individual or family cemetery plots or burial vaults." Strehlow brought a personal injury action against Mark Schnackenberg, and the insurance company denied coverage.

Plaintiff's Position: The insurance company contended that because the accident did not occur on the insured premises as defined in the insurance policy, no coverage was afforded for the cause of action asserted by Strehlow.

Defendant's Position: Schnackenberg argued that instead of focusing on the definition of *insured premises*, the court should examine the scope of coverage under the policy and determine whether the use of a bicycle for pleasure by a child of the insured to travel to and from home is incidental to the ownership, maintenance, or use of the insured premises, a family residence.

Legal Issue: Is the scope of coverage in the insurance policy limited by the definition of *insured premises?*

Court Decision: No. The scope of coverage is not limited by the definition of *insured premises.* There is coverage under the policy. The insurance company is obligated to defend Mark in Strehlow's personal injury action against him.

Court Reasoning: The policy does not define what is incidental to the use of the insured premises. The phrase is ambiguous. The insured could reasonably conclude that her child's recreational use of a bicycle to travel to and from home is incidental to the use of her residence. When an ambiguity exists in an insurance policy, that ambiguity must be resolved in favor of the insured. The reason for this rule is that the insurer drafted the policy and should be held responsible for any ambiguity which results from the words it selects.

Pearson v. First Nat. Bank,
408 N.E.2d 166 (Ind. 1980)
Pearson purchased a restaurant building. As part of the purchase transaction, Pearson agreed to assume two mortgages in favor of First National Bank of Martinsville and the Small Business Administration which had unpaid principal balances of $144,143.51 and $41,406.15. Pearson also agreed to insure the premises for the duration of the loan "with a loss payable in favor of the bank and the Small Business Administration as their interests may appear." Six months later, the restaurant was heavily damaged by a fire. Pearson arranged to have it rebuilt from the proceeds of the insurance policy at a cost of $85,773.48. The bank, however, refused to put the insurance proceeds into the building. Instead, it retained the proceeds and applied them to the outstanding mortgage debt. Bank officials told Pearson that they would work with him on a new construction loan at a higher interest rate if he so desired.

Plaintiff's Position: Pearson claimed that the bank breached its contract when it refused to make the fire insurance proceeds available for reconstruction of the restaurant and, instead, chose to apply the proceeds to reduce the outstanding mortgage debt on the property. He categorized the bank's offer to negotiate a new construction loan at a higher rate of interest as "tortious misconduct."

Defendant's Position: The bank argued that there was no evidence to show anything but full compliance with the terms and conditions of its contract with Pearson.

Legal Issue: Did Pearson have a contractual right to have the insurance proceeds applied to reconstruction of the restaurant?

Court Decision: No. The mortgagee is entitled to the proceeds of the policy to the extent of its interest in the mortgage debt. It may apply the proceeds to the outstanding mortgage debt as it falls due.

Court Reasoning: Generally speaking, a mortgage agreement is a contract. As such, the mortgagor and mortgagee are free to enter into an agreement concerning the application of insurance proceeds in the event of a loss. The well-established rule is that where insurance is made payable to the mortgagee "as his interest may appear," the mortgagee is entitled to the proceeds of the policy to the extent of the mortgage debt. The mortgagee must hold the surplus, if any, for the benefit of the mortgagor. The words *as their interest may appear* refer to debts owing the insured. They mean that the insurer will pay the mortgagee to the extent of its lien at the time of loss. The terms refer, therefore, not to an interest in the property insured, but to payment of the loss. Properly viewed, an open mortgage loss payable clause signifies that the insurance proceeds will be applied to the mortgage debt. Several prior cases have also held that a mortgagee named in a loss payable clause will prevail over a mortgagor who desires to use the money to repair.

Glossary

A

abandonment The voluntary relinquishment of personal or real property with intention of terminating ownership; in contract performance, discontinuing performance once started with apparent or expressed intention of vacating further performance in the future.

absolute defense A defense that is good against everyone, even a holder in due course of a negotiable instrument. Also called *real defense* or *universal defense.*

acceleration clause A provision in a contract or other document giving the creditor the right to hasten payment of the entire debt upon the debtor's default. Such clauses are usually found in installment contracts.

acceptance A promise or act on the part of an offeree indicating a willingness to be bound by the terms and conditions contained in an offer. In commercial paper, the acknowledgment of a drawee that binds the drawee to the terms of a draft.

acceptor A drawee of a draft who has promised to honor the draft as presented by signing it on its face.

accessions Additions to or modification of presently owned goods, for example, a button that is sewed onto a person's coat.

accident insurance A kind of insurance that provides benefits to people who are disabled or injured by accident. An accident is defined as an unexpected, unforeseen, or unintentional incident resulting in personal injury.

accommodation party A person who signs an instrument as a maker, acceptor, or indorser without receiving value therefor and lends his or her name to another person as a means of guaranteeing payment on the due date.

accord and satisfaction An agreement (accord) whereby one party makes payment of money, or some other consideration, of usually less than the amount owed, in return for the extinguishment of a debt or some other claim.

accounting A statement showing the total asseta and debts of a business entity at the date of dissolution and at termination.

acknowledgment The affixing of a notary public's signature and seal in witness of the signing and execution of a document.

act of God An unpredictable event that occurs as an act of nature, beyond human control, intervention, or responsibility; for example, tornadoes, hurricanes, floods, lightning, and the like.

actual damages An amount of money awarded for damages directly attributable to another party's breach of contract or tort; for example, physicians' fees and hospital charges when one party wrongly injures another, and financial losses resulting from failure to deliver goods already contracted for.

adhesion contract A printed or previously prepared agreement submitted by one party for acceptance by the other without right of negotiation; at times unenforceable on grounds of unconscionability and the absence of fair and equal rights of the parties.

adjective law That law which specifies the formal steps to be followed in enforcing or asserting rights, duties, privileges, or immunities. Also called *procedural law.*

administrative agency An officer, board, bureau, or commission—other than legislatures and courts—having power to determine private rights and obligations by making rules and rendering decisions.

administrative law The law concerning the powers and procedures of administrative agencies, including the law governing judicial review of administrative action.

administrator A person appointed by the court to settle the estate of someone who died intestate, that is, without a will.

adverse impact A selection rate for any protected racial, ethnic, or sex group of less than 80 percent of the selection rate of the majority group.

adverse possession Title to real property obtained by taking actual possession of the property openly, notoriously, exclusively, under a claim of right, and continuously for a period of time set by state statute.

advisory opinion The formal opinion of an administrative agency or court which has no binding force as law.

affirmance A statement or act in the present that serves to confirm a promise made in the past; an express or implied confirmation of a contract made by a minor after reaching majority. See also **ratification.**

affirmative action Positive steps to remove any existing discrimination in hiring and promotion practices which must be taken by employers that have any business dealings with the government, including contracts, and employ over fifty employees.

agency Legal agreement between two persons, whereby one is designated the agent of the other.

agency coupled with an interest An agency agreement in which the agent is given an interest in the substance of the agency in addition to compensation for services rendered.

agent A person authorized to act on behalf of another and subject to the other's control in dealings with third parties.

agreement A meeting of the minds. See also **mutual assent.**

agreement in restraint of marriage An agreement whereby one party promises not to enter into marriage with anyone, in consideration of money or other benefit promised by the other party. Such agreements are universally void because they are in opposition to public policy.

agreement in restraint of trade A monopoly, combination, contract, or other type of agreement that interferes with free trade and competition.

allonge A strip of paper attached to a negotiable instrument for the writing of additional indorsements.

annual percentage rate The effective or actual true cost of credit to the consumer.

annuity A guaranteed retirement income which a person secures either by paying a lump-sum premium or by periodically paying a set amount to an insurer.

anticipatory breach Repudiation of contract obligations by one of the parties at a time prior to the time when performance was to commence. Also called *constructive breach.*

appellant The party who appeals a decision by bringing the proceeding to a reviewing court.

appellate court A court with jurisdiction to review the law as applied to a prior determination of the same case. It is not a forum in which to develop a new case.

appellee The party against whom an appeal is brought. See also **appellant.**

apportionment The practice of dividing and distributing the tax burden of an interstate business among states entitled to tax it.

arbitration Settlement of a dispute by one or more persons selected by the disputing parties, or by an established tribunal of justice, by whose decision the parties agree to be bound.

arson The willful and malicious act of causing or procuring the burning of property.

articles of incorporation The instrument which creates a private corporation, pursuant to the general corporation laws of the state.

articles of partnership A written contract that establishes a partnership association.

assault An attempt, with unlawful force, to inflict bodily injury upon another, accompanied by the apparent ability to carry out the attempt if not prevented.

assignee See **assignment.**

assignment The transfer by a contracting party (assignor) to a third party (assignee) of a contract right or of the whole of any real or personal property.

assignor See **assignment.**

auction with reserve An auction at which the auctioneer has the right to withdraw goods and not sell them if acceptable bids are not made.

auction without reserve An auction at which the auctioneer must sell the goods to the highest bidder.

automatic stay A court-ordered halt in a judicial proceeding whereby no further judicial action will occur until some event has taken place.

B

bailee The person to whom personal property is delivered under a contract of bailment.

bailment Possession of the personal property of another without ownership and for a special purpose, under the express or implied contract that it will be redelivered to the bailor.

bailor The owner of personal property which has been temporarily transferred to a bailee under a contract of bailment.

bait-and-switch scheme An illegal promotional practice in which a seller attracts the consumer by promoting a product (bait) which he or she does not intend to sell, then switches the consumer's attention to a higher-priced product.

balloon-payment mortgage A mortgage which has relatively low fixed payments during the life of the mortgage, with one large final (balloon) payment.

bank draft An order drawn by one bank directing itself or another bank in which it has funds on deposit to pay a specified sum of money to a named person.

bankruptcy An inability of a debtor to pay debts as they become due. A legal process under the Federal Bankruptcy Act by which the assets of the debtor are liquidated to pay off creditors and to free the bankrupt to start anew.

bankruptcy liquidation The conversion of the debtor's nonexempt assets into cash, its distribution in accordance with the provisions of the Bankruptcy Code, and the discharge of the debtor from most of the remaining debts.

barren promise A promise to do that which one is already bound to do either by law or contract.

battery The unlawful application of force to the person of another; the least touching of another person willfully or in anger.

bearer A person who is in possession of a negotiable instrument that is payable to "bearer" or "cash" or that has been indorsed in blank.

bearer paper An instrument that may be negotiated by delivery only. Also called *bearer instrument.*

beneficiary The person named in an insurance policy to receive benefits paid by the insurer in event of a claim; also, a person for whom a trust is created and who owns equitable or beneficial title to the trust property.

bilateral contract An agreement consisting of mutual promises of rights and obligations. See also **unilateral contract.**

bilateral mistake A mistake of relevant, material facts by both parties to a contract; sufficient in an action to cancel a contract. See also **unilateral mistake.**

bill of exchange See **draft.**

bill of lading A document evidencing the receipt of goods for shipment and issued by a person engaged in the business of transporting or forwarding goods.

binder A verbal or written memorandum of an agreement for insurance, intended to give temporary protection pending investigation of the risk and issuance of a formal policy.

blank indorsement An indorsement in which the holder or payee does no more than sign his or her name on the instrument. See also **bearer.**

blue laws State laws adopted during the nineteenth century that restricted commercial and social activities on Sundays. Such laws have been rescinded in many states because of public demand.

bona fide occupational qualification A quality or skill required in good faith that does not intentionally prevent certain groups of people from qualifying for employment. Abbreviated as BFOQ.

bond A certificate of indebtedness that obligates a government or corporation to pay the bondholder a fixed rate of interest on the principal at regular intervals, and to pay the principal on a stated maturity date; a written instrument with sureties, guaranteeing faithful performance or acts contemplated.

boycott A concerted refusal to have dealings with a business or product in order to force acceptance of certain conditions. See also **group boycott.**

breach of contract Failure to carry out the terms of a contract.

bribery The act of giving something of value in order to influence the actions of an official.

bulk transfer "Any transfer in bulk and not in the ordinary course of the transferor's business of a major part of the materials, supplies, merchandise, or other inventory of an enterprise." [UCC 6-102(1)]

burglary At common law, act of breaking into and entering in the night the building of another for the purpose of carrying out a felony. Modern statutes have expanded this definition to include any breaking and entering into another's building with the intent to commit a felony or to steal property of value.

bylaws The rules and regulations which guide the corporation's day-to-day internal affairs.

C

cancellation The revocation and abrogation of contract obligations.

capital contribution The sum invested to receive an interest in a business, either as the purchase of stock in a corporation or the amount contributed by each member of a partnership.

capital surplus The excess over par when capital stock is issued at a price higher than its par value.

case law The aggregate of adjudged cases or court decisions, as opposed to statutes and other sources of law.

cash surrender value The amount that a policyholder will receive in the event an insurance policy is canceled.

cashier's check A check drawn by a bank upon its own funds.

caveat emptor "Let the buyer beware." By common law, a buyer's implied obligation to inspect goods at the time of purchase, when inspection is permitted; a defense against buyers' complaints of defective merchandise when reasonable inspection would have disclosed complained-of defects.

caveat venditor "Let the seller beware." The rule of law that applies to most sales transactions today.

cease and desist order The command from an administrative agency or court telling a party to stop a forbidden practice.

certificate of incorporation A document that grants an organization permission to do business as a corporation; a charter.

certification Legal assent by the National Labor Relations Board that a union has qualified as the bargaining agent for a particular group of employees.

certified check A check that has been marked, or certified, by the bank on which it was drawn, guaranteeing payment to the holder.

certiorari A writ issued by a superior court to an inferior jurisdiction commanding the record in a particular case so that a determination can be made as to whether there are any irregularities.

check A draft drawn on a bank and payable on demand.

class action A court action in which one or several persons sue on behalf of themselves and all other similarly affected persons.

clean hands The concept in equity that claimants who seek relief must not themselves have indulged in any impropriety in relation to the transaction upon which relief is sought.

close corporation A business corporation whose outstanding shares of stock and managerial control are closely held by fewer than fifty shareholders.

closed shop An establishment in which the employer by agreement hires only union members in good standing.

codicil An addition to or change in an existing will.

coinsurance A kind of fire insurance in which the insured must keep his or her coverage at an agreed percentage of the value of the property; if the insured does not do so and suffers a loss, the company will pay less than the actual loss.

collateral Property such as bank accounts, contract rights, and chattel papers used as security; a value that is additional to the personal obligation of the borrower.

collective bargaining A good-faith meeting between representatives of employees and employer for purposes of discussing the terms and conditions of employment.

comaker A person who signs a promissory note on its face with another and becomes primarily liable for its payment if the other defaults.

commerce Trade, traffic, transportation, or communication among the several states or between any foreign country and any state or territory.

commingle To put together property and money in one mass. See also **confusion of goods.**

common carrier A company that transports goods or persons for compensation and offers its facilities to the general public without discrimination. Compare **private carrier.**

common law The system of law which is based on judicial precedent and principles of justice, reason, and common sense rather than legislative enactments. Compare **statutes.**

community property A statutory right giving each spouse joint title to all personal and real property acquired after marriage.

comparative negligence The proportional sharing between plaintiff and defendant of compensation for injuries, based on the relative negligence of the two.

compensatory damages An award of an amount of money that compensates a complainant for actual damages resulting from breach of contract or a tort.

complaint The initial pleading in which the plaintiff alleges the facts constituting a cause of action and requests the desired legal relief; i.e., a formal accusation.

complete performance Full and satisfactory execution of all terms and conditions of a party's contracted promises.

composition of creditors A bargained-for agreement between a distressed debtor and the creditors, whereby the creditors each agree to accept a lesser amount than owed in full settlement of the debtor's obligations.

concealment The intentional withholding of information or covering up of defects, knowledge of which would affect one's decision in negotiating a contract.

concurrent condition A promise or act that must be performed or tendered at the same time performance is tendered by the other contracting party.

condition precedent A condition that requires performance of certain promises or acts before the other contracting party is obligated to pay money or tender other agreed-to consideration.

condition subsequent A condition that terminates the rights and duties of the parties under an existing contract.

conditional indorsement An indorsement which is subject to certain events or conditions such as the age of the indorsee.

conflict of laws The body of law used to resolve the question of which state law a court will apply when there is a legal action or contest involving two or more states.

conforming goods Goods which are in accordance with the obligations under the contract.

confusion of goods The blending or intermingling of property belonging to different owners, making it impossible to determine what each one owns. See also **commingle.**

consent decree An agreement by all parties involved in a court settlement to be bound by certain stipulated facts.

consideration The exchange of benefits and sacrifices by contracting parties that serves to create a binding agreement.

consignee The party to whom goods are shipped under a bill of lading.

consignor The party shipping goods under a bill of lading.

consolidation The process by which two or more corporations are joined to create a new corporation.

constructive breach See **anticipatory breach.**

constructive discharge Harassment or demotion to a position of lesser pay or authority or poorer working conditions.

contract An agreement between two or more competent parties binding them to legally enforceable obligations.

contract of record A contract that has been adjudicated and confirmed by a court, with an accompanying judgment rendered in favor of one of the parties.

contract to sell An agreement to pass title to goods from the seller to the buyer for a price at a future time.

contributory negligence The failure of the plaintiff to use sufficient due care to insure his or her own safety.

conventional mortgage A mortgage which has no government backing, either by way of insurance or guarantee.

conversion The unauthorized and unlawful assumption of ownership of goods or ideas known to belong to another.

conveyance The transfer of title in personal or real property.

cooling-off period The span of time within which the purchase of merchandise made in the customer's home may be rescinded by the customer without need of customary defenses against a valid agreement. In labor relations law, a procedure designed to avoid strikes by requiring a period of delay before a strike may begin, during which time negotiations must continue.

copyright Exclusive right of ownership of literary, musical, or artistic creations, granted by the government for a limited period of time.

corporation A legal entity created by state statute authorizing an association of persons to carry on an enterprise.

cost-plus contract A contract in which the consideration to be paid for performance is to be determined by all costs of labor and materials, to which is added an agreed-to percentage for profit.

counteroffer A response to an offer in which the terms and conditions of the original offer are changed. A counteroffer acts, in most cases, as a rejection of the original offer.

crime A wrong which the government determines is injurious to the public good.

curtesy Under common law, the estate to which a husband is entitled on the death of his wife, provided they have had children born alive who might have been capable of inheriting the estate. Compare **dower.**

custom of the marketplace "Any practice or method of dealing having such regularity of observance in a place, vocation or trade as to justify an expectation that it will be observed with respect to the transaction in question." [UCC 1-205(2)]

D

deceit A tort action requiring the proof of the same elements required in seeking a contract rescission based on fraud. See **fraud.**

de facto corporation A business entity which has inadvertently failed to comply with the provisions of the laws relating to the creation of a corporation, but has made a good-faith effort to do so and has in good faith exercised the franchise of a corporation.

de jure corporation A corporation that has all the legal characteristics of a corporation and whose incorporators have substantially complied with the provisions of the laws of the state of incorporation relating to the creation of a corporation.

decree A decision by a court of equity.

deed A written instrument signed, sealed, and delivered in a special form, that is used to pass legal title of real property from one person to another; a conveyance.

defamation Any false statement communicated to others that harms a person's good name or reputation.

default Failure to discharge a duty according to the terms of an agreement.

default judgment A judgment entered upon the failure of a party to appear or to plead in court at the appointed time.

defendant The person against whom a suit has been brought.

del credere agent A factor who guarantees the credit of a third party, the solvency of the purchaser, and performance of the contract.

delivery Voluntary transfer of possession of instruments, documents of title, chattel papers, securities, or personal property.

demurrage charge A fee charged by a carrier for the storage of goods still remaining in its possession beyond the time allowed for unloading by the consignee.

depositary bank The bank to which a commercial paper is transferred for collection; the depositary bank may also be the payor bank.

deposition A written statement made under oath by a witness or party to an action in response to questions from the opposing lawyer.

derivative action A lawsuit filed in the corporate name by one or more shareholders to enforce a corporate cause of action.

destination contract A contract under which the seller is required to deliver goods to a place of destination; title passes to the buyer when the seller delivers the goods.

disaffirmance An act or statement in the present that serves to repudiate and rescind a voidable contract made in the past, such as a minor's repudiation of a contract before or immediately after reaching his or her majority.

discharge A general word covering methods by which a legal duty is extinguished; to release, annul, or dismiss the obligations of contract or debt.

disclaimer Denial of an interest or a right.

disclosed principal The person known or who should be known by a third party to be the principal of an agent.

dishonor To refuse to accept or pay a negotiable instrument when it is presented.

disputed amount A claim for money owed when no exact amount had been agreed on by the contracting parties; usually settled by an accord and satisfaction.

dissolution The termination of a corporation by legislative act, judicial decree, voluntary action of the shareholders, or expiration of the period of time for which the corporation was formed; the change in the relation of partners when any party ceases to be associated with the business.

dividends Distribution from corporate assets (usually earned surplus) made on a pro rata basis to shareholders of a designated class of stock, as authorized by the corporation's board of directors.

divisible contract A contract consisting of two or more parts, either of which may be performed or breached without affecting the validity and enforceability of the other parts.

document of title A paper which serves as evidence that the person holding the paper has title to the goods mentioned in the document.

dormant partner Person who is not active in the partnership business and is not known to the public as a partner. Compare **secret partner.**

double indemnity A clause found in some insurance policies which provides that in the event of the accidental death of the insured, the beneficiary receives double the amount of the face value of the policy.

dower By common law, the vested rights of the wife to a one-third lifetime interest in the real property owned by her spouse; a life estate to which a wife is entitled upon the death of her husband. Compare **curtesy.**

draft A written order drawn upon one person by another, ordering payment of money to a designated third party. Also called a *bill of exchange.*

drawee The party named in a draft who is ordered to pay money to the payee.

drawer The party who draws a draft, that is, the party who orders that the money be paid.

due process of law A course of legal proceedings carried out according to the established rules of jurisprudence for the enforcement and protection of the individual rights of life, liberty, and property.

duress Use or threat of force against a person, property, or family to coerce another in an unwilling acceptance of an agreement. See also **extortion.**

E

earned surplus The portion of the surplus of a corporation equal to the balance of its net profits, income, gains and losses from the date of incorporation.

earnest money Something of value given by a buyer as a down payment to a seller to bind a bargain.

easement The right to make use of land belonging to another.

easement by prescription An easement right created by passing over another's property, or using another's property openly and continuously for a period of time set by state statute.

ejectment The common-law name given to the lawsuit brought by a landlord to have a tenant evicted from the premises.

emancipation The removal of restrictions imposed on minors when it is proved that the relationship between a minor and his or her parents has been irrevocably severed.

embezzlement The wrongful taking of the property of another for one's own use, in breach of the owner's trust.

eminent domain The right of federal, state, and local governments or other public bodies to take private lands for public use, with compensation to their owners.

employee One who works for an employer for salary or wages. The term *servant* is synonymous.

employer One who employs others in exchange for wages or salaries. The term *master* is synonymous.

endowment insurance A kind of insurance which provides protection for a stated time, generally twenty to thirty years. The face value of the policy is paid to the insured at the end of the agreed period, or if the insured dies during that period, the face value is paid to the beneficiary.

enemy alien One residing in the United States who is not a U.S. citizen but holds citizenship in another nation with which the United States is at war.

entire contract A contract comprising two or more parts, each of which is closely interrelated, requiring satisfactory performance of all parts to be enforceable. Compare **divisible contract.**

equal-dignities rule A rule that requires a principal to follow the same formalities in the appointment of an agent as the formalities required in any negotiations the third party may make for the principal.

equity A branch of law granting relief when there is no adequate relief otherwise available. The body of law which seeks to adjust conflicting claims on the basis of fairness and natural justice.

escheat The right of the state to title to property when no legal owner may be found.

escrow A deed, bond, or deposit which one party places in the keeping of a second party who is obligated to deliver it to a third party upon fulfillment of some condition.

estate All that a person owns, whether real or personal property.

estate in fee simple An estate in which the present owner owns the land for life (i.e., freehold), with the right to use it or dispose of it as he or she pleases, so long as the use of it does not interfere with the rights of others.

estoppel A legal bar to alleging or denying a fact because of one's own previous actions or words to the contrary, or because of one's silence, which induced another person to believe something that was not true.

exculpatory clause A clause or condition that tends to excuse a party of any liability, fault, or guilt emanating from that party's negligence or failure to perform in what is called a skillful manner.

executed contract A contract whose terms and conditions have been fully and satisfactorily carried out by both contracting parties.

executor The party named in a will to carry out the terms of the will.

executory contract A contract all of whose terms and conditions have not yet been carried out by both parties.

exemplary damages See **punitive damages.**

express authority The authority of an agent to perform the duties that are specifically stated in the contract of agency.

express warranty See **warranty.**

extortion The taking of another's property with consent, influenced by a threat to injure the victim's person, property, or reputation. See also **duress.**

extradition The surrender by one state to another of an individual accused or convicted of an offense outside its own territory and within the jurisdiction of the other.

F

factor A special agent employed to buy or sell consigned goods in his or her own name on another's behalf.

failure of consideration A personal defense that may be used by a maker or drawer of a negotiable instrument when the party with whom he or she dealt breaches the contract by not furnishing the agreed consideration. A holder in due course is not subject to this defense.

false imprisonment An intentional tort involving the unjustified detention of a person. The restraint must be total so that it amounts to imprisonment and not merely obstruction, stopping, or locking someone out of a room. Also known as *false arrest* if done with purported legal authority.

fault An error or defect of judgment or conduct, such as neglect of duty, care, or performance resulting from inattention, negligence, or perversity.

featherbedding Causing an employer to pay money for services which are not or will not be performed at all.

felony A crime punishable by death or imprisonment in a federal or state prison for a term exceeding one year.

fiduciary A person having a duty, created by his or her undertaking, to act primarily for the benefit of another in matters connected with the undertaking; in the nature of a position of trust or holding of confidence, such as the fiduciary relationship an attorney has with a client.

finance charge The sum of all charges which the consumer must pay in order to obtain credit.

fixture An article of personal property physically attached to real property and considered part of the real property.

foreclosure The right given a mortgagee to take and sell the property of a mortgagor who has defaulted in payments on a secured note or bond.

foreign corporation A corporation that is doing business in a state other than the state of incorporation.

formal contract A written contract bearing the signatures and, in some states, the seals of the parties involved, or otherwise following formalities specifically required by law.

franchise An arrangement in which the owner of a trademark, trade name, or copyright licenses others to use the device in purveying goods or services; also a special right given public-service corporations to operate free of competition. See also **private-investment franchise** and **public-service franchise.**

fraud The intentional false statement or concealment of facts that, if known, would have been relevant to another party's decision in either accepting or rejecting an otherwise valid offer.

freehold estate An estate in which the holder owns the land for life or forever.

frustration of purpose A doctrine in contract law that releases a party of the obligation of performance when performance is possible but would be thoroughly impractical and without reason as a result of the occurrence of a contingency, the nonoccurrence of which was a basic assumption of the contract.

full-covenant-and-warranty deed A deed containing express warranties under which the grantor guarantees the property to be free of all encumbrances. Also called *general-warranty deed.*

full faith and credit The obligation of each state to recognize the public acts and proceedings of other states.

full indorsement An indorsement made by first writing on the back of a negotiable instrument an order to pay to a specified person and then signing the instrument. Also called *special indorsement.*

full warranty Under the Magnuson-Moss Warranty Act, a defective product will be fixed or replaced free within a reasonable time after a complaint has been made about the product.

fungible goods Goods of which any unit is, by nature or usage of trade, the equivalent of any like unit; wheat, flour, sugar, and liquids of various kinds are examples.

future goods Goods that are not yet in existence or under the control of people; they include fish in the sea, minerals in the ground, and goods not yet manufactured.

G

garnishment A court order authorizing the attachment (taking) of property, usually wages, in order to satisfy an unpaid claim.

general release An agreement in writing and signed by a creditor releasing a debtor of all or part of a debt owed by another party. In certain states such a release must usually be under seal.

general-warranty deed See **full-covenant-and-warranty deed.**

gift _in causa mortis_ A gift given during one's lifetime in contemplation of death from a known cause.

good faith "Honesty in fact and the observance of reasonable commercial standards of fair dealings in the trade." [UCC 2-103(1)]

goods All things (including specially manufactured goods) which are movable at the time of identification to the contract for sale, other than money in which the price is to be paid, investment securities, and intangible items. Goods include growing crops and the unborn young of animals.

goodwill The advantage or benefit that has been acquired by a business with the name under which it is managed.

grantee A person to whom real property is transferred.

grantor A person who transfers real property to another, who is called the grantee.

gratuitous agent One not legally obligated to fulfill a performance promise.

gratuitous bailment A bailment for the sole benefit of either the bailor or the bailee, in which the other party receives no consideration for benefits bestowed.

group boycott A group of manufacturers, distributors, retailers, or others, acting in concert to deprive a particular individual or business entity of access to goods or access to the market in which goods are sold. See also **boycott.**

H

habeas corpus The procedure for obtaining a judicial determination of the legality of holding an individual in custody.

hold-harmless clause A contract condition that tends to relieve contracting parties of performance obligations by reason of eventualities over which they have no control, for example, an act-of-God clause.

holder A person who is in possession of a negotiable instrument which is issued or indorsed to his or her order or to bearer.

holder in due course A party who has taken a negotiable instrument in good faith and for value without any knowledge that there is anything irregular about the instrument. Such a holder is treated as favored and is given immunity from certain defenses.

holographic will An informal will written entirely in the handwriting of the testator.

homestead estate A statutory life estate in the real property of a deceased spouse guaranteed to a surviving spouse or to the children during their minority.

homicide The killing of one human being by another.

horizontal restraint Price fixing engaged in by those in competition with each other at the same level.

hot cargo An agreement between the union and the employer that union members will not handle, sell, or transport goods which are not union-made.

I

illusory promise A veiled promise by a contracting party that does not actually bind the party to any specific obligation; insufficient in any claim of consideration thereby.

implied authority The authority of an agent to perform acts which are necessary or customary in the carrying out of expressly authorized duties.

implied contract A contract whose rights and obligations are created by acts or gestures of the parties or imposed by law. See also **quasi-contract.**

implied warranty See **warranty**

in pari delicto In equal fault. A contract relationship where both parties are equally wrong in the intention of carrying out an agreement, which is deemed void because it is illegal or against public policy, or for any other reason. See also **clean hands.**

incapacity The lack of legal, physical, or mental power, as in the case of a minor's lack of legal power to create a binding contract; in workers' compensation law, incapacity is the inability to perform the usual tasks of a worker as a result of injury.

incidental beneficiary An outside third party who would benefit from contract performance but for whose benefit a contract is not created.

incidental damages Reasonable expenses that indirectly result from a breach of contract. They include such expenses as those incurred in stopping delivery of goods, transporting goods, and caring for goods that have been rightfully rejected by a buyer.

incorporator The person who organizes a corporation by signing and filing the articles of incorporation with the designated officer of the state.

indemnity Absolute obligation to pay for another's loss.

independent contractor A person who contracts to do work for another according to his or her own judgment and method.

indorsee A person to whom a draft, note, or other negotiable instrument is transferred by indorsement.

indorsement A signature placed on the back of an instrument, the effect of which is to transfer the instrument and to establish a new contract by which the indorser becomes party to the instrument and liable under certain conditions for its payment.

indorser A person who indorses a negotiable instrument.

injunction A judicial remedy awarded for the purpose of requiring a party to do or to refrain from doing a particular act. See also **mandatory injunction.**

insolvent Inability of a business entity to pay its debts as they become due in the usual course of business.

insurable interest Evidence that shows an insured person would lose some financial benefit through the death of another, through destruction of property, or through some other insured risk.

insurance A contract whereby, one party pays premiums to another party, who undertakes to pay compensation for losses resulting from risks or perils specified in the contract.

insured A person whose risks are covered by an insurance policy.

insurer A party that issues an insurance policy protecting the insured against specified risks.

intangible property Property consisting of rights rather than goods and chattels; property not perceptible to the senses; evidenced by documents in some cases. Compare **tangible property.**

intended beneficiary A party or parties not in privity on a contract but for whose benefit the contract performance is to be made, such as a creditor, donee, or insurance beneficiary.

interest A right to the advantage accruing from anything; a right to a share.

interrogatory A pretrial discovery tool in which adversaries must reply to questions under oath.

interstate commerce Commerce or the transportation of persons or property from one state to another state.

intervening cause An event which comes into active operation in producing the result, following the negligence of the defendant.

intestate Having died without leaving a valid will. Compare **testate.**

intoxication As a defense to contract performance, a party's claim of having been so affected by alcohol at the time of contracting that said party did not comprehend the obligations imposed by the agreement.

intrastate commerce Commerce or the transportation of persons or property between points located in the same state.

invitation to trade A public announcement made to two or more persons, intended not to be an offer but to serve as an inducement to generate offers from among those who have read, seen, or heard the announcement; usually evidenced by advertisements, form letters, and the like.

involuntary bailment A gratuitous bailment implied by law; a bailment arising from the leaving of personal property in the possession of a bailee through an act of God, accident, or other uncontrolled phenomenon.

involuntary manslaughter An unintended killing of another person that results from an absence of proper caution. See also **manslaughter** and **voluntary manslaughter.**

J

joint and several An obligation binding two or more persons individually as well as jointly. The obligation can be enforced either by joint action against all the persons or by separate actions against one or more.

joint liability A liability which arises when two or more persons act as one in accepting a contract obligation. Persons involved in a joint liability are usually sued together; they may be sued individually by some state laws.

joint tenancy Ownership of property by two or more persons wherein the right of any deceased owner is automatically transferred to other surviving owners.

joint venture An association of two or more entities to carry out a single business enterprise for profit, for which purpose they combine their property, money, skill, and knowledge.

judgment The determination of a court of competent jurisdiction upon matters submitted to it.

jurisdiction The power of a court to hear and determine a case.

L

lack of consideration A personal defense that may be used by a maker or drawer of a negotiable instrument

when no consideration existed in the underlying contract for which the instrument was issued. A holder in due course is not subject to this defense.

landlord A person who owns real property and who rents or leases it to someone else; a lessor.

last clear chance The doctrine in some jurisdictions that a party who has the last clear chance to avoid damage or injury to another is liable.

lease A contract granting the use of certain real property to another for a specified period in return for the payment of rent.

legacy In a will, a bequest of money or personal property.

legal monopolies Monopolies protected by law when within the restrictions of public policy and when operated for the public good; usually restricted to public utilities, patents, copyrights, trademarks, and the like.

legal tender Coin and currency issued by a government and declared valid for payment of all debts, both public and private.

legatee One who receives a gift of personal property given under the terms of a will.

lessee A tenant under a lease of real property.

lessor See **landlord.**

liability without fault Strict liability without evidence of fault or negligence, even if the utmost care is used.

libel A false statement that harms another person's good name or reputation, made in a permanent form such as writing.

license A grant of permission to do a particular thing, to exercise a certain privilege, to carry on a particular business, or to pursue a certain occupation; a personal privilege or permission with respect to some use of land, revocable at the will of the landowner; a privilege granted by a state or city upon payment of a fee, which is not a contract and may be revoked for cause, conferring authority to perform a designated task, such as operating a motor vehicle.

licensee A person to whom a license is given; a social guest; a person entering or using premises by permission or by operation of the law but without express or implied invitation; a person entering premises by permission only; a person on another's premises solely in pursuit or furtherance of his or her own business, pleasure, or convenience.

life estate An estate in which the owner owns real property for his or her life or for the life of another.

limited defense In negotiable-instruments law, a defense that can be used against a holder but not against a holder in due course of a negotiable instrument. Also called *personal defense.*

limited liability Status which restricts shareholder liability for corporate wrongs to his or her capital investment.

limited partnership An entity in which one or more persons, with unlimited liability, called *general partners,* manage the partnership, while one or more other persons, called *limited partners,* only contribute capital and have no right to take part in the management or control of the business and assume no liability beyond their capital contribution.

limited warranty Under the Magnuson-Moss Warranty Act, a warranty that is not a full warranty.

liquidated amount An exact amount that a contracting party is obligated to pay as contained in an agreement for purchase of goods or services; a fixed or determined amount that is not in dispute.

liquidated damages An amount of anticipated damages, agreed to by both parties and contained in a contract, to be the basis of any award in the event of a breach of the contract.

liquidation The assembling and mobilizing of the assets of a business, settling with the creditors and debtors, and apportioning the remaining assets, if any, among the owners or shareholders. See also **bankruptcy liquidation.**

litigation The legal contest in a court of law through which legal rights are sought to be determined and enforced.

locus sigilli "The place of the seal." The abbreviation LS is often used in place of the seal itself on formal written contracts.

lodger Any person staying at a hotel, motel, or rooming house for a definite period of time.

long-arm statutes Laws which allow local courts to obtain jurisdiction over nonresident defendants when the cause of action is local and affects local plaintiffs.

M

majority The status of one who has reached the age of competency required to be obligated under contracts or to perform other acts covered by special state statutes, common law, or constitutions; the status of one who is no longer a minor.

maker A person obligated as the payor on a promissory note. See also **comaker.**

malice aforethought An endangering state of mind for which no justification, excuse or mitigating circumstances exist.

malpractice A breach of contract or a tort based in negligence resulting from the failure of a professional to exercise such skill and care as to maintain standards of performance set or followed by a given professional calling.

mandatory injunction A decree awarded by a court of equity demanding that a party either do or undo a certain act which is deemed harmful or offensive to another party or to the public at large.

manslaughter The unlawful killing of another person without malice aforethought. See also **involuntary manslaughter** and **voluntary manslaughter.**

marshaling of assets To arrange funds under court administration so that all parties having equities therein may receive their due proportion.

master A principal who controls or has the right to control the physical conduct of a servant or employee. See also **employer.**

material alteration Changing the terms of a written agreement in an important way without the consent of both contracting parties; grounds for discharge of the contract.

maxims Truths or rules that need no proof or argument and that are based on moral rights and natural justice.

mediation A procedure for settling disputes between parties by bringing the case before a qualified person or body that makes nonbinding recommendations.

memorandum A word used to describe a written document that satisfies the requirements of the UCC Statute of Frauds.

merchant A person who deals in goods of the kind sold in the ordinary course of business, or who otherwise claims to have knowledge or skills peculiar to those goods.

merger The absorption of one corporation by another corporation.

midnight deadline In banking, midnight on the banking day following the day on which the bank receives a relevant item.

minority The status of one who has not yet reached the age of competency to be obligated under contracts or to perform other acts covered by special state statutes, common law, or constitutions; the status of one who has not yet reached a majority in age.

misdemeanor A less serious crime that is generally punishable by a jail sentence of not more than one year.

misfeasance The doing of an act in a wrongful or injurious manner; the improper performance of an act which might have been lawfully done. See also **nonfeasance.**

misrepresentation An untrue statement of fact; one of the elements of fraud.

mitigation of damages A doctrine that requires an injured party in either contract or tort to do everything reasonably possible to minimize the amount of damage resulting from the other's wrong.

monopoly Any combination or organization so extensive, exclusive, and unified as to prevent competition, usurping the power to control prices and supply and demand, and causing harm to the public good.

moral consideration Acts or deeds of kindness and appreciation motivated by pangs of conscience that are not accepted as valid consideration in the creation of a contract.

mortgage A transfer of an interest in property for the purpose of creating a security for a debt.

mortgagee A party who lends money and takes back a mortgage as security for the loan.

mortgagor A party who borrows money and gives a mortgage to the lender or mortgagee as security for the loan.

mutual assent An agreement between contracting parties created by an offeree's acceptance of a valid offer; a meeting of the minds.

mutual-benefit bailment A bailment in which both the bailor and the bailee receive some benefit.

N

necessaries Goods and services deemed to be reasonably essential to one's health, welfare, and safety.

negligence Failure to exercise a degree of care which a reasonable person would exercise under the same circumstances.

negotiable instrument A written document signed by the maker or drawer, containing an unconditional promise or order to pay a certain sum of money on demand or at a definite time, to the bearer or to order.

negotiation The transfer of a negotiable instrument in such form that the transferee becomes a holder.

nexus A logical linkage with the taxing state.

nominal damages Damages awarded by a court when a successful plaintiff has proven a legal injury but no actual resulting damage; 6 cents by common law, usually $1 today.

nonconforming uses Uses of land permitted to continue in existence even though newly enacted zoning laws no longer permit similar uses.

nonfeasance Nonperformance or failure to perform an act that one is duty-bound to perform.

nonperformance Less than complete or substantial performance; equivalent to a breach of contract.

novation The substitution of another party for one of the original parties to a contract with the consent of the remaining party; the old contract is extinguished, and a new contract, with the same content but with at least one different party, is created.

nuncupative will An oral will declared in the presence of witnesses by the testator; made by a person in a final illness or by soldiers and sailors in actual combat.

O

obligee A party to whom an obligation of performance is owed by an obligor, originating from an exchange of promises, or a promise for an act.

obligor One who is bound by contract to perform an obligation to another known as the obligee.

offeree One to whom an offer is made in anticipation of its being accepted.

offeror One who proposes an offer, or proposition, in anticipation of its acceptance and the formation of a binding contract.

opinion (puffing) Statements, obviously not factual, that tend to persuade an offeree's decision in accepting or rejecting an offer; not considered fraudulent in an action on a contract. See also **professional opinion.**

option A contracted right, supported by consideration, giving a party the right to choose; for example, paying consideration to have an offer kept open for an agreed-to number of days.

order bill of lading A negotiable bill of lading, containing words of negotiability.

order paper An instrument that may be negotiated by indorsement followed by delivery. Also called *order instrument.*

output contract An agreement under which a seller agrees to sell "all the goods he or she manufactures" or "all the crops he or she produces" to a particular buyer. See also **requirements contract.**

P

palpable mistake An obvious, unilateral, and glaring error known and recognized by an offeree or one who has been invited to trade.

par value The face value of a stock or like instrument and not its actual value on the open market.

parol-evidence rule A rule that restricts a party from introducing oral evidence that tends to change, add to, or delete from the terms and conditions of a written document or contract.

partial disability The ability to perform some but not all of the duties of an insured's occupation.

partial performance Performance of a contract which is abandoned at some time after commencement, with the indication that any intention to complete performance has been abandoned; equal to nonperformance.

partnership A contract in which two or more persons invest their money, efforts, and skills in a lawful business and divide the profits and bear the loss in certain proportions; co-owners of a business for profit.

partnership at will A partnership that is designed to continue only during the pleasure of the parties, and that may be dissolved by any partner without previous notice.

past consideration A promise of reward in return for uncontracted-for acts performed in the past, such as a promise to pay for voluntary services at some time after the services have been performed.

patent An exclusive property right in an invention, granted to the inventor by the government, to make, use, and sell an invention for a term of years.

pawn The act of giving up personal property as security for performance of a promise or future payment of a debt, usually associated with a loan made by a pawnbroker; a pledge.

payee The party named in commercial paper, to whom payment is to be made.

per se In or by itself; not requiring extraneous evidence to establish its existence.

percolating waters Water flowing below the surface in underground streams and rivers and in surfacing springs.

perfected A security interest in which the secured party has done everything that the law requires to give the secured party greater rights to the goods than others have.

performance The execution or carrying out of promises, terms, and conditions of a contract.

periodic tenancy See **tenancy from year to year.**

personal defense See **limited defense.**

personal property All property and property rights, both tangible and intangible, not included within the definition of real property.

picketing The posting of persons at the place of employment to inform the public, by word or carried sign, of the existence of a labor dispute.

pierce the corporate veil The process of disregarding the corporate entity and imposing liability for corporate activity on a person or entity other than the offending corporation itself.

plaintiff The one who initially brings suit in court to seek remedy for an injury to or a withholding of rights.

pleadings The written statements by parties to a court action in regard to the cause of action and the grounds of defense.

pledge The giving up of personal property as security for performance of an act or repayment of a debt.

pledgee A person to whom property is given as security for a loan.

plenary Complete authority or power.

police power The state and local governmental authority to regulate where needed, to promote, and to maintain the health, safety, morals, and general welfare of the public.

postdate To date an instrument for negotiation at a later time.

power of attorney A written authority by a principal to an agent.

preemptive right The right of a shareholder to preserve his or her proportionate stock interest by purchasing shares of new issues ahead of others.

preference The paying or securing by an insolvent debtor to one or more of his or her creditors the whole or a part of their claims, to the exclusion or detriment of other creditors.

preferred stock A class of stock that has superior rights to dividends and, upon dissolution of the corporation, to corporate assets.

premiums In insurance, the consideration paid by the insured for protection afforded by an insurer.

presentment A demand for acceptance or payment of a negotiable instrument made upon the maker, acceptor, or drawee by or on behalf of the holder of the instrument.

prima facie evidence Evidence sufficient to support but not to compel a certain conclusion by the trier of the facts.

primary liability Absolute liability to pay a negotiable instrument.

principal A person who authorizes an agent to act on his or her behalf and subject to his or her control.

private carrier A company that transports goods or persons under individual contract with those seeking its services; a private carrier is not required to serve all who apply, unlike a common carrier.

private-investment franchise The special right given to a private person or corporation to market another's product within a certain area.

private nuisance The interference with a person's use or enjoyment of land.

privity of contract The relationship that exists between two or more contracting parties.

probate The proving of a will to the satisfaction of public authorities and the carrying out of the terms of such a will by the executor or administrator.

procedural law See **adjective law.**

product-liability laws Laws which make manufacturers and sellers responsible for injuries to consumers caused by defective, unhealthy, or unsafe products.

professional opinion The opinion of one accepted as an expert in any specific area, such as the opinion of an engineer, physician, attorney, or the like; in contract actions it is deemed to be equal to a statement of fact.

profit à prendre An easement that gives its owner the right to remove something of value from another's property, as the right to enter lands of another for the purpose of cutting hay, harvesting wheat, and the like.

promissory note A negotiable instrument wherein the maker or promissor agrees to pay a certain sum at a definite time to the promissee.

promoter The person who plans the organization of a corporation.

protest A formal certification by a notary public (or other authorized party) that an instrument has been refused payment at maturity.

protest waiver The act of dispensing with formal protest, as well as demand and notice of nonpayment, which ordinarily precede a protest.

proximate cause In tort law, the cause which sets in motion the train of events that results in damage or injury.

proxy One authorized to vote or speak in place of a shareholder of a corporation.

public corporation A corporation established for the administration of public affairs which acts under the authority granted by the state.

public nuisance An unreasonable interference with a right common to the general public, such as the health, safety, peace, or comfort of the general community.

public offer A valid offer made through the public media but intended for only one person, whose identity or address is unknown to the offeror, as an advertisement in a lost-and-found column of a newspaper. Not to be confused with an invitation to trade.

public policy The concept of law under which the freedom to act is limited for the good of the community.

public-service franchise A special privilege granted by local, state, or federal governments awarding a license to operate a proprietary business without the threat of competition; usually restricted to public utilities, such as electric and telephone companies, toll roads and bridges, and the like.

punitive damages Damages in excess of losses suffered by the plaintiff awarded to the plaintiff as a measure of punishment for the defendant's wrongful acts. Also called *exemplary damages.*

purchase-money security interest A security interest which occurs when someone lends money or extends credit to a consumer and then takes a security interest in the goods that the consumer buys.

Q

qualified indorsement An indorsement in which words such as "without recourse" have been added to the signature that limit or qualify the liability of the indorser to answer for the default of the maker.

quasi-contract An implied contract not created by mutual agreement but imposed upon the parties by law, thereby preventing an unjust benefit to one party at the innocent expense of the other. See also **implied contract.**

quitclaim deed A deed to real property in which the grantor transfers only what rights he or she may have and gives no warranties of quiet enjoyment or other such benefits.

R

ratification The principal's approval of an otherwise voidable act or contract performed by an agent; an express or implied confirmation of a contract made by a minor after reaching majority. See also **affirmance.**

real defense See **absolute defense.**

real property The ground and anything permanently attached to it including land, buildings, growing trees and shrubs; the airspace above the land is also included.

reasonable care That degree of care which a reasonably prudent person would have used under the same circumstances and conditions.

recording The process of registering a deed, contract, lien, or other claim in a public office as a protection to a party from later claims made by outside parties; recording also serves as a protection to outside parties against possible fraud in resale of goods or denial of an established debt.

rejection An offeree's expressed or implied intention, through word or deed, of not accepting an offer. See also **counteroffer**.

reorganization plan A plan negotiated by both debtor and creditor for the adjustment and discharge of debts which permits a financially troubled company to stay in business while it undergoes a process of financial rehabilitation.

replevin A common-law action by which a party seeks the recovery of personal property wrongfully held by another.

requirements contract An agreement under which one party agrees to purchase all his or her requirements of a particular product from another (UCC 2-306). See also **output contract**.

rescission The nullification of contract obligations by mutual consent or court decision.

respondeat superior If an employer is acting through the facility of an employee, and a tort liability is incurred because of some fault of the employee, then the employer must accept the responsibility.

restatements The attempt by the American Law Institute to present an orderly statement of the general common law of the United States.

restraining injunction A decree from a court of equity that restrains or prevents a party from carrying out some particular act that would be unfair or unjust to others.

restrictive indorsement An indorsement in which words have been added to the signature of the indorser that specify the purpose of the indorsement or the use to be made of the commercial paper, such as "for deposit only."

reverse discrimination The practice of favoring minorities over white or women over men for affirmative-action purposes.

revocation Withdrawal of an existing offer through communication to the offeree, by the passage of time, by the terms of the offer, or by operation of law; the recall of a power or authority conferred.

rider In insurance, an attached writing which modifies or supplements the printed policy.

right-to-work-law A state law prohibiting agreements requiring membership in a union as a condition of employment.

riparian rights Rights of an owner to access to a stream of water flowing either through or along the border of the owner's land.

robbery The act of taking personal property in the possession of another person against that person's will and under threat of great bodily harm or damage.

S

sale The passing of title to goods from the seller to the buyer for a price.

sale on approval A conditional sale which becomes absolute only if the buyer approves or is satisfied with the article being sold.

sale or return A sale that allows goods to be returned even though they conform to the contract.

satisfactory performance Performance determined to be satisfactory to either the demands of the promisee, the custom of the marketplace, or a third-party referee.

scope of employment Furtherance of the principal's or employer's business which has apparently or by implication been delegated to an agent.

seal A mark or an impression placed on a written contract indicating that the instrument was executed and accepted in a formal manner. In modern usuage usually indicated by addition of the word *seal* or the letters *LS* (*locus sigilli*) following a party's signature.

secondary liability Liability to pay a negotiable instrument only after certain conditions are met.

secondary boycott Any union action against a company which does not have a labor dispute with the employees it is representing.

secret partner A person who takes an active part in partnership management but is not known to the public as a partner. Compare **dormant partner**.

secured party A lender or seller who holds a security interest on goods belonging to a debtor.

secured transaction A transaction which creates an interest in personal property which secures payment or performance of an obligation.

security An investment in a profit-making business, evidenced by a stock or bond certificate, in which the investor usually profits solely from the efforts of others; protection or assurance (usually in the form of a pledge, mortgage, deposit, or lien) given by a debtor to a creditor to make sure the debt is paid.

security agreement A written agreement which creates or provides for a security interest. It must identify the goods and be signed by the debtor.

security interest An interest in personal property or fixtures which secures payment or performance of an obligation.

serious intent Requisite of a valid offer; requirement that offers must be made seriously, not under emotional stress or distress or in the spirit of frolic, jest, or fun.

servant A person employed to perform services in the affairs of another and who with respect to the physical conduct in the performance of the service is subject to the other's control or right to control. See also **employee**.

servient tenement In an easement, the property over which a dominant property has an easement right.

several "Separate and apart from." In a judgment against more than one defendant, each may be liable for the entire amount, thereby permitting the successful plaintiff to recover the entire amount of the judgment from any defendant against whom he or she chooses to institute a suit. See also **joint and several** and **joint liability**.

shareholder The person who owns and is a holder of record of shares in a corporation. Also called a *stockholder*.

shipment contract A contract under which the seller is required to send or ship goods (such as by carrier) to the buyer but has no obligation to deliver them directly to the place of destination. Under this type of contract, title passes to the buyer at the time and place of shipment.

sight draft A draft that is payable as soon as it is presented to the drawee for payment.

slander A false statement that harms another person's good name or reputation, made in a temporary form such as speech. Compare **libel.**

special indorsement See **full indorsement.**

special-warranty deed A deed containing express warranties under which the grantor guarantees that no defects arose in the title during the time that he or she owned the property.

specific performance A decree from a court of equity (or chancery) demanding that a contracting party carry out the promises made in a contract; available only in those cases where money would not be a satisfactory solution to a wrong.

speculative damages Damages not founded on fact but on the expectations that a party may have hoped for from a contract that has been breached; insufficient in any claim for money damages.

stale check A check which is presented for payment more than six months after its date.

stare decisis The principle by which a court relies upon the rules of law applied in previous decisions when deciding a similar case before it.

stated capital The sum of the par value of all corporate shares having a par value that have been issued and the consideration received by the corporation for all corporate shares without par value that have been issued, except such part that may have been allocated to capital surplus.

statute of frauds An act of the English Parliament dating from 1676 and designating, among other things, those contracts that must be in writing to be enforceable; adopted in the United States by state governments after the Declaration of Independence, July 4, 1776.

statutes The laws enacted by legislatures to prescribe conduct, define crimes, appropriate public monies, and promote the public good and welfare. Compare **common law.**

statutes of limitations Statutes that determine the time limits in which legal actions may be taken for the enforcement of contract rights, damage suits in tort actions, and arrest and conviction in certain crimes.

stockholder See **shareholder.**

stop-payment order An order by the drawer of a check to the drawee bank not to pay the check when it is presented.

straight bill of lading A bill of lading that does not contain words of negotiability; may not be negotiated but may be assigned.

straight life insurance A kind of insurance which requires the payment of premiums throughout the life of the insured and which pays the beneficiary the face value of the policy upon the insured's death. Also called *ordinary life insurance.*

strict liability A legal theory which imposes liability on manufacturers or suppliers for selling goods which are unreasonably dangerous, without regard to fault or negligence.

sublease A lease given by a lessee to a third person conveying the same interest for a shorter term than the period for which the lessee holds it.

subrogation The right of one party to substitute itself for another party.

subscriber One who pays for a certain amount of the authorized capital stock in a corporation whether before or after incorporation.

subsequent illegality Illegality legislated and imposed at some time after a contract has been created but before complete performance has been made; serves to void an existing contract.

substantial evidence Evidence that a reasonable mind might accept as sufficient to support a determination.

substantial performance Performance of all contracted obligations with exception of minor and unimportant items that do not detract from the fundamental intent of a contract.

substantive law That part of the law which creates, defines, and regulates the rights and duties of parties to a court action.

subterranean rights Rights that an owner of real property has to the ground below the earth's surface.

summary judgment The device designed to effect a prompt disposition of a controversy, owing to the absence of a genuine issue as to any material fact, without resort to a lengthy trial.

summons The mandate requiring the appearance or response of a named defendant in a named action.

Sunday agreements Agreements made on Sunday ruled as void by blue laws except when proven to be necessary to the health, safety, or welfare of one of the parties; extinct today in many states.

surety One who is directly and immediately liable for a debt.

T

tangible property Property which may be seen or touched and which may be given an actual physical description. Compare **intangible property.**

tenancy at sufferance A leasehold estate, or tenancy, which arises when a tenant wrongfully remains in possession of the premises after his or her tenancy has expired. Such a tenant is a wrongdoer, having no estate or other interest in the property.

tenancy at will A leasehold estate, or tenancy, that continues for as long as both parties desire.

tenancy by the entirety Ownership by husband and wife, considered by law as one, with full ownership surviving to the living spouse on the death of the other. The husband has the entire control over the estate, including the exclusive right to possession and the right to all rents and profits.

tenancy for years A leasehold estate, or tenancy, for a fixed period of time.

tenancy from year to year A leasehold estate, or tenancy, which continues for successive periods until one of the parties terminates it by giving notice to the other party. Also called a *periodic tenancy.*

tenancy in common Ownership of an undivided interest in property by two or more persons, with each owner's rights going to his or her heirs upon death rather than to the surviving coowners.

tenancy in partnership Ownership in which each person has an interest in partnership property and is coowner in such property.

tenant A person who has temporary possession of and interest in the land of another.

tender An offer or performance by one party to a contract which, if unjustifiably refused, places the other party in default and permits the party making the tender to exercise remedies for breach of contract.

tender years In tort and criminal law, the years between birth and age seven.

termination The agreed-to discharge of existing contract obligations either through satisfactory performance or by mutual assent prior to complete performance.

testamentary capacity In wills, the proof of sufficient age and mental capacity required of a testator to a will.

testate Having made a valid will. Compare **intestate.**

testator A person who makes a will.

time draft A draft that is not payable until the lapse of a particular time period stated on the draft.

time is of the essence An expressed condition of performance that demands full performance of contracted promises on or before a time stated in the contract.

title search An investigation of title rights to real property, usually conducted by a lawyer who scrutinizes all recorded evidence of ownership, encumbrances, and other legal and equitable claims against a parcel of real estate.

torrens system A system of land registration which seeks to establish clear title to land.

tort A private or civil wrong or injury independent of contract, which results from a breach of a legal duty.

tortfeasor Person who actually commits a tort and who is always liable to the victim.

tortious bailee Any party unlawfully in possession of another's personal property.

total disability Complete inability of an insured person to engage in his or her regular occupation. Compare **partial disability.**

trade acceptance A draft used by a seller of goods to receive payment and also to extend credit. It is often used in combination with a bill of lading.

trade fixtures Items of personal property brought upon the land by a tenant which are necessary to carry on the trade or business to which the land will be devoted. Contrary to the general rule, trade fixtures remain the personal property of the tenant and are removable at the expiration of the term of occupancy.

trade name A name used in trade to designate a particular business or class of goods in order to secure the advantages of a good reputation or goodwill.

trade secret A plan or process or device used in one's business known only to its owner and those employees who need to know.

trademark Any word, name, symbol, or device adopted and used by a manufacturer or merchant to identify goods and distinguish them from those manufactured or sold by others.

transfer The act by which the owner of a negotiable instrument delivers it to another with the intention of passing rights in it to the other.

transient A hotel guest; a person who accepts the services of a hotel or other public accommodation without obligation to remain a specified length of time.

traveler's check A draft purchased from a bank or express company and signed by the purchaser at the time of the purchase and again at the time of cashing as a precaution against forgery.

treason A crime defined by the U.S. Constitution as the levying of war against the United States or giving aid and comfort to the nation's enemies.

treasury stock A corporation's own stock repurchased from ready and willing-to-sell shareholders.

trespass to personal property Unlawful interference with the control and possession of any portable property of the owner.

trespass to real property The entry upon private property without the owner's consent.

trust A right of ownership to property held by one person for the benefit of another.

trustee The person, bank, attorney, or fiduciary organization to which legal title to trust property is given.

trustee in bankruptcy A person appointed by the court or elected by creditors who takes legal title to the property and/or money of the bankrupt and holds it in trust for equitable distribution among creditors.

tying agreement An agreement between a seller and purchaser or lessor and lessee that the sale or lease of a product is contingent upon the purchase or lease of another product of the seller or lessor.

U

ultra vires That which is beyond the power authorized by law for a corporation.

unconscionable Contract terms and conditions deemed to be oppressive, overreaching, or shocking to the conscience; under the UCC, grounds for rescission of a contract or parts thereof.

undisclosed principal One who is not reasonably known by a third party to be a principal for an agent.

undue influence Use of one's ability to influence another with whom one has a confidential relationship such as exists between married partners or between doctor and patient, financial adviser and client, etc.

unfair labor practice Improper employment practices of either employer or union which are prohibited by federal law.

Uniform Commercial Code A uniform law relating to certain commercial transactions, including the sale of goods, commercial paper, bank deposits and collections, letters of credit, bulk transfers, warehouse receipts, bills of lading, and secured transactions.

Uniform-Gift-to-Minors Act A uniform law designed to make it easier to make gifts to minors and to satisfy the provisions of the Internal Revenue Code, allowing income from such gifts to be taxable to the minor rather than the donor.

unilateral contract A contract consisting of a promise by one party in exchange for a requested act to be performed by the other. See also **bilateral contract.**

unilateral mistake A mistake of relevant, material fact by only one of two contracting parties; it is insufficient as grounds of contract cancellation. See also **bilateral mistake.**

union shop A workplace where an employee is required to join a union after a specified period of time in order to obtain or keep a job.

universal defense See **absolute defense.**

unlicensed transactions Agreements ruled unenforceable owing to the failure of one of the parties to have secured a license for the carrying on of a business or professional practice.

usury Interest charged for the use of money borrowed in excess of the amount permitted by law; varies from state to state and for different commercial transactions.

V

valued policy An insurance policy in which the insurer is obligated to pay the face value of the policy in the event of a total loss.

variable-rate mortgage A mortgage with a rate of interest that changes according to fluctuations in the index to which it is tied.

variance An exception allowed by public authorities in the enforcement of zoning regulations when deemed unfair and unreasonable in a singular situation.

verdict The official finding of fact by the jury; the jury's decision.

vertical restraint Price fixing engaged in by members of different levels of production, such as manufacturer and retailer.

void Lacking in qualities and requirements that are necessary to create a binding obligation.

voidable An imperfect obligation that may be either enforced, corrected, or annulled at the option of only one of the contracting parties.

voluntary manslaughter A killing that results when a person acts in a state of extreme fright, anger, or rage that destroys reason. See also **involuntary manslaughter** and **manslaughter.**

voting trust The accumulation in a single hand, or a few hands, of shares of corporate stock belonging to many owners in order thereby to control the business of the company.

W

wagering agreements A promise by one party to pay another a stated amount of money dependent on the uncertain outcome of some future event. Also called a *bet* or *gambling agreement.*

warehouse receipt A receipt issued by a person engaged in the business of storing goods for hire.

warehouser A person engaged in the business of storing goods for hire.

warehouser's lien The right of a warehouser to retain possession of goods stored in the warehouse until the amount of money owed for storage charges, transportation charges, insurance, and preservation expenses is paid.

warranty A statement, promise, or other representation that a thing has certain qualities; also, an obligation imposed by law that a thing will have certain qualities. Warranties made by means of a statement or other affirmation of fact are called *express warranties;* those imposed by law are *implied warranties.*

warranty of fitness for a particular purpose An implied warranty that goods will be fit for a particular purpose. This warranty is given by the seller to the buyer of goods whenever the seller has reason to know of any particular purpose for which the goods are needed and the buyer relies on the seller's skill and judgment to select the goods.

warranty of merchantability An implied warranty that goods are fit for the ordinary purpose for which such goods are used. Unless excluded, this warranty is always given by a merchant who sells goods in the ordinary course of business.

warranty of title A warranty given by a seller to a buyer of goods that the title being conveyed is good and that the transfer is rightful.

watered stock The shares of stock that are overvalued and worth less than the par value of the shares.

will A legal document, not valid until the testator's death, expressing his or her intent in distribution of all real and personal property.

winding up The liquidation of the partnership business and the settling of its affairs.

workers' compensation Payments to injured or diseased workers in the course of their employment, without consideration of the negligence of any party.

writ of execution A court order by which the court attempts to enforce the judgment that has been granted a plaintiff by authorizing a sheriff to levy on the property belonging to the judgment debtor.

Y

yellow-dog contract An agreement whereby an employer requires as a condition of employment that an employee promise not to join a union.

Z

zoning law A local regulation or ordinance which restricts certain areas to specific uses; for example, areas zoned for residential, commercial, agricultural, industrial, or other uses.

Index

Mutual rescission, 196
Mutuum transaction, 236

N

National Environmental Policy Act
(1969), 71–73
National Labor Relations Act
(1935), 403–411
National Labor Relations Board, 6,
404–411
Necessaries, contracts for, 137–138
Necessity, agency by, 366–367
Negligence
bailee, 242
of the parties, termination of
agreements and, 202
product liability and, 293
professional, 17
torts and, 14–15
Negligence defenses, torts and,
16–17
Negotiable instruments, 312–314
(*see also* Commercial paper)
Negotiable Instruments Act, 10
Negotiable warehouse receipts, 256
Negotiation, commercial paper (*see*
Commercial paper, issue,
transfer, and negotiation of)
Nexus in state and local taxing, 63
No-fault insurance, 545–546
No-par value stock, 449
Nominal damages, 211
Nominal partners, 420
Nonbankruptcy liquidation of cor-
porations, 463
Nonconforming uses, 489
Noncorporation, 447
Noncumulative preferred stock, 448
Nondelivery, 304–305
Nonexempt employees, 386
Nonfeasance, 377
Nonjudicial alternatives to litiga-
tion, 36–37
Nonjudicial dissolution, 463
Nonparticipating preferred stock,
449
Nonperformance, 184
Nonprofit corporations, 445
Nontrading partnership, 419
Nonvoting shareholders, 458
Norris-LaGuardia Act (1932), 403
Notes, 314, 449

Notice
of agency termination to third
parties, 379–380
of assignment, 189–190
of dishonor, and secondary liability of parties, 339–340
holders in due course without,
332–333
of partnership dissolution, 435
printed, 112–113
to seller of defective product, as
duty, 292
of termination of contract, 196
Novation
all rights and obligations transferred by, 192
discharge by agreement and, 197
in executory agreement, 192–193
partnership continuance and, 438
Nuclear Regulatory Commission,
71
Nuisance, public, 21
Nuncupative wills, 515

O

Obligations (*see also* Rights and
obligations)
abandonment of contract, as
breach, 209
of carriers
for baggage of passengers, 254
to passenger's person, 253–254
general, of parties to a contract
for sale, 297
information, of agent to principal, 373
of landlord for repairs, 504
and liabilities of agent to principal, 372–373
of tenant for repairs, 504
of trustee, 519
Obligator, 97
Obligee, 97
Obligor, 189, 191
Obstruction of justice, agreement
to an, 161
Occupancy, acquiring title to real
property by, 484
Occupational Safety and Health
Act (1970), 394–396
Occupational Safety and Health
Administration, 48, 53, 61

Ocean and inland marine insurance, 542–543
Offeree, 107–112
communication to, 107–108
in contract, 107
direction of offers to specific,
110–112
Offeror, 107
Offers, 107–120
acceptance of, 112–116
definition and requirements of,
107–112
clarity and reasonable definiteness of terms, 108–110
communication to offeree,
107–108
direction of offers to specific
offeree, 110–112
serious intent, 108
firm, 119, 267–268
irrevocable, 119
options on, 119–120
public, 110
rejection of, 118–119
revocation of, 116–118
in special rules pertaining to
sales contracts, 267
Officers
corporate, 460, 462
of the court, 30–31
Official checks, 345
Officials, agreements to pay, for
existing legal duties, 162
Omissions in commercial paper,
319
Open policy, 530
Open-price terms, 268
Opinions
advisory, 67
express warranties and, 287
professional, 124
puffing, 124
Options
concept of local, 158
of leases to purchase properties,
500
on offers, 119–120
to renew leases, 500
in support of promises, 148
Oral agreements, 170
Oral contracts, 98
of sales, 269–271